MORE   PRAISE   FOR

NELSON

L O V E   &   F A M E

"[A] stately . . . literary battleship, bristling with truly terrifying military and biographical detail."—Munro Price, *Sunday Telegraph*

"[A] passionate . . . celebration of Nelson's life and career."—*Economist*

"Vivid and absorbing."—David A. Wilson, *The Globe and Mail* (Toronto)

"Edgar Vincent has written a robust, level-headed account of Nelson's. life, particularly strong in its analysis of Nelson's battles." —Adam Preston, *Financial Times*

"A profusion of detail about Nelson's health and finances, his way with the welfare and discipline of his men and how his battles were fought and usually won. . . . A true portrait of an extraordinary man." —Tom Pocock, *Spectator*

"I can imagine no better life of one of history's greatest captains." —*New Criterion*

NELSON
Love & Fame

Edgar Vincent

Yale University Press
New Haven & London

To Elizabeth, James and Robert
and in Memory of my Mother

Published with the assistance of the Annie Burr Lewis Fund.

Designed by Adam Freudenheim
Set by SNP Best-set Typesetter Ltd., Hong Kong
Printed in the United States of America by Vail Ballou Press, Binghamton, New York

Library of Congress Cataloging-in-Publication Data

Vincent, Edgar.
  Nelson: love & fame / Edgar Vincent.
    p.   cm.
Includes bibliographical references and index.
  ISBN 0-300-09797-2 (hardback)
  ISBN 0-300-10260-7 (paperback)
    1. Nelson, Horatio Nelson, Viscount, 1758–1805. 2. Great Britain – History, Naval – 18th century. 3. Great Britain – History, Naval – 19th century. 4. Great Britain. Royal Navy – Biography. 5. Admirals – Great Britain – Biography. 6. Nelson, Frances, Lady, 1761–1831. 7. Hamilton, Emma, Lady, 1761?–1815. I. Title.
  DA87.1.N4 V55   2003
  940.2'7'092 – dc21   2002014566

A catalogue record for this book is available from the British Library
10 9 8 7 6 5 4 3 2

Frontispiece: *Horatio Nelson*, 1797, by Lemuel Francis Abbott (1760–1803).

Contents

Part I
Early Years

Part II
Unhonoured & Unsung

Part III
The Making of an Icon

Part IV
Finding Love

Part V
Winning & Losing

Part VI
The Road to Trafalgar

Maps & Diagrams

Notes

Map 7 is after Julian Corbett, *The Campaign of Trafalgar* (1910) annotated 'Nelson's track from William Faden's map copied from his Lordship's original MS and special directions published August 12th 1807' and 'Villeneuve's track from Desbrière'.

Diagram 5 is taken from the Plan of Trafalgar attached to the Report of Captain Prigny, Admiral Villeneuve's Chief of Staff (Archive de la Marine BB⁴2321) published in Edouard Desbrière's *Trafalgar, La Campagne Maritime de 1805* (1907) and included in Corbett's *The Campaign of Trafalgar*. While the organization of the British fleet up to the point of battle was later examined by an Admiralty committee (1913) on the basis of an exhaustive analysis of the log of each ship, what happened at the point of contact is frequently obscure even in the ships' logs. What then developed was a general mêlée on which it is impossible to be definitive. Prigny's diagram *may* be open to question in some respects, as are all diagrams of Trafalgar, but it captures well the nature of 'the Nelson touch' and the difference between Nelson's and Collingwood's modes of attack as observed by their enemy.

List of Illustrations

Nature & Nurture

Mentors & Patrons

Political Masters

The Real Nelson?

Nelson's Wife

Acknowledgements

Having written this book direct from primary sources, my major debts are to the British Library and its ninety-two volumes of Nelson papers and documents, its Althorp Papers covering Spencer family correspondence and Lord Spencer's correspondence with admirals during his period as First Lord of Admiralty; to the National Maritime Museum and its collections; Sir Nicholas Harris Nicolas and the seven volumes of his *Dispatches and Letters of Vice-Admiral Lord Viscount Nelson*; Alfred Morrison's collection of letters connected with Nelson and the Hamiltons; George Naish's collection, *Nelson's Letters to his Wife and Other Documents*; the letters of Nelson's contemporaries and colleagues, including Earl Spencer, Earl St Vincent and Lord Keith in the Navy Records Society's editions, and naval documents, letters, reports and minutes held in the Public Record Office at Kew. They have allowed Nelson to unfold in my mind.

Good companions have been the works of Brian Lavery, especially the magisterial detail of his books on Nelson's Navy, and N.A.M. Rodger's seminal work *The Wooden World*, which has led us all to a re-evaluation of life in the Georgian Navy. In the background were memories and impressions culled over forty years from the great biographies of the past, Mahan's *The Life of Nelson*, Carola Oman's *Nelson*, Jack Russell's *Nelson and the Hamiltons*, Tom Pocock's *Horatio Nelson* and Dudley Pope's *The Great Gamble*.

Many individuals have contributed with interest and practical help: the staffs of the British Library, the Public Record Office, the National Maritime Museum especially David Taylor Picture Librarian, the Royal Naval Museum Portsmouth especially Matthew Sheldon Head of

Research Collections, the London Library, the Newbury Central Library, the National Portrait Gallery and Mary Robertson of the Huntington Library, San Marino, California. I thank them for their patience and courtesy.

I am grateful to The Trustees of the Bowood Manuscript Collection, for allowing me to quote from Lord Keith's correspondence, and to the Huntington Library for allowing me to reproduce Nelson's letter to Adelaide Correglia. I thank the Nelson Society for permission to quote from items in the *Nelson Dispatch*, and the 1805 Club for permission to quote from the *Trafalgar Chronicle*, the Miller Papers and reports of the proceedings of conferences on the battles of St Vincent, the Nile and Copenhagen. I am indebted to Martyn Downer and Dr Peter Beale of Sotheby's London for enabling me to read letters in the Alexander Davison Collection before their auction on 21 October 2002.

I am particularly grateful to Stephen Farthing for permission to include his painting *Death of Nelson*, runner-up in the John Moores Prize competition of 1999. His painting is a contemporary symbol of the enduring myth of Nelson as well as mirroring perfectly the concept of my final chapter, 'Dame Fortune's Last Favour'.

I am grateful to former gynaecologist Roger de Vere for helping me to address issues relating to Nelson and Fanny's childlessness, to ophthalmologist Peter Gray for guidance on the problems of Nelson's eyesight, to psychiatrist Andrew Lee for commenting on Nelson's emotional and mental makeup, to anaesthetist James Vincent for observations on Nelson's final hours and on the various symptoms he experienced and frequently described, and to defence academic and former soldier Patrick Mileham for enabling me to realize that Nelson practised the present day military and naval doctrine of Mission Command. In preparing the book for this paperback edition few changes have been made but I should like to thank Colin White of the National Maritime Museum whose encyclopaedic knowledge has enabled me to add or correct detail, in particular enabling me to benefit from his ongoing research among hitherto unpublished Nelson letters and documents.

Needless to say, I alone am responsible for whatever defects of judgement or fact may remain in the finished work.

I owe an immense debt to three people: Sue Wade, Keith Hudson and Anthony Storey. Each read the book's first draft in its entirety and made many illuminating observations. Their understanding and enthusiastic response was very sustaining. Then Rory Muir was wonderfully helpful, making a wide range of suggestions with impressive insight and erudition, and undoubtedly enabled me to improve the book. Matt Holland read my earliest chapters and encouraged me to go on.

My special thanks go to Norman Douglas Hutchinson, the artist who generously produced ideas for a cover, and to Dinah Alan-Smith who produced and arranged my early manuscript in her impeccable way.

I am also grateful to Jean Martin, Anne Boreham, Alain and Maryvonne Olivier, Lady Russell, David Oldland, Louis Hodgkin, Roger Morriss, Andrew Gottschalk, Andrew Whiteley, Dorothy Wilkinson, Anne Pons and Elizabeth Hudson for their kind help in various ways and to John and Jeannie Marcel for guiding us round the Nelson family habitat in Norfolk.

Adam Freudenheim at Yale University Press has been a pleasure to work with. His enthusiasm, empathy and efficiency have made the production of the book as painless and pleasurable as it could be. Beth Humphries was a masterly copy editor. Oxford Designers and Illustrators translated my ideas for maps and diagrams with skill and efficiency. I should also like to thank my agent Jeffrey Simmons, who has given me much wise help and advice, and Douglas Matthews who kindly agreed to undertake the index.

Finally and ubiquitously, my wife Elizabeth, who read the book in its entirety and made many acute suggestions for improving the text. She applied her loving toleration to my continuing mental absence in the eighteenth century, endured disjointed musings with understanding and humour, and contributed shrewd and practical insights into the behaviour and motivation of the men and women who were parading through my mind – in short, a model life support system for an absorbed author.

Introduction

Lavinia Spencer, wife of the First Lord of the Admiralty, spoke of him as 'That dear little creature'. To Vice Admiral Goodall he was, 'My little hero'. He referred to his Nile captains as his 'Band of brothers', and 'My darling children'. He said his reception by the officers of the Trafalgar fleet caused 'the sweetest sensation of my life'. Never has a fighting commander evoked such love and tenderness or exercised such a direct and impelling grasp on our hearts.

Nelson grew to be a man of charisma. In what did this consist? We look for a physical presence across two centuries but cannot find him for certain. Only two portraits out of the two hundred or so catalogued seem to be of the same person, the Rigaud portrait painted in 1771 and the Füger portrait painted in Vienna in 1800. His wife Fanny and his father thought Lemuel Abbott had captured him in the portrait we all know, every inch the Admiral, handsome, kind and resolute. Few of us know that the version we admire has been 'adonized' to convey just such impressions. His mistress Emma Hamilton swore by the Catherine Andras waxwork, remarkable for the portrayal of power in his face. Nelson himself thought a profile sketch by De Koster was the best likeness. Differences between artists underline the fact that the origin of Nelson's charisma was not in his looks. Nor did it derive from physical presence: at five feet six inches he was too small and too slight to be physically dominating. It was when he spoke and acted that he became a person who claimed attention. He was irresistibly positive, filling any vacuum of thought or intention with his mental energy and flow of ideas. Oddly, there seems always to have been a feeling among biographers that Nelson lacked that great lubricant of life, a sense of humour. But he could be droll and jocular, could see the funny side of things, could put people at their ease with a well turned phrase, could pull legs in a caressing sort of way, making his target feel good in being singled out. His personal approach was seductive: the person addressed felt special. Combined with his other gifts, this produced talents for leadership and dominance of an extraordinary kind.

Much of Nelson's behaviour suggests a hidden well of insecurity stemming from his childhood. He was a middle child in a large family. He lost his mother when he was nine. His family life was dislocated by boarding-school. He was totally separated from his family at the age of twelve and a half. Thus his unconscious and unacknowledged motivations were a lifelong search for love and for attention, and a need to prove himself over and over again. At the age of eighteen he invented a conscious purpose for his life which fitted his motivations. He decided to be a hero.

His need for attention became an addiction. While on tour with the Hamiltons in 1802, he discovered that he had a talent for saying what crowds wanted to hear, for evoking an emotional reaction. This was a heady experience, beyond making an impact on the quarterdeck, or being mobbed and lionized as a celebrity in Naples, Vienna or London. When he left Southsea for Trafalgar on a tide of emotion, he thought he had what deep down all charismatics crave: 'I had their Huzzas, now I have their hearts.'

His thirst for love was equally great. He sought with formidable charm and professional brilliance to capture the hearts and minds of his brother officers. With most he succeeded. In 1802 W. C. Macready, then a boy and later a famous actor, met and talked with Nelson at his father's theatre in Birmingham. He noted in his diary, 'the extremely mild and gentle tones of his voice impressed me most sensibly'. A soft-voiced sailor seems a contradiction in terms; a sharp-edged voice seems necessary for command. But this soft voice fits better with Nelson's seductive nature. He very much needed to be liked by others. When he lay dying, 'Kiss me Hardy' was the ultimate softener of a hard man.

With the opposite sex it was different. He was so immature that he seems not to have known how to go about it. Women did not find him attractive. He fell in love with the idea of love but two women rejected him in quick succession and another was unavailable. He precipitately married Frances Nisbet, a widow with a small son living at the time with her uncle on Nevis in the West Indies. It was a mistake. Their personalities were diametrically opposed. There was neither the glue of sex, children, nor mutual interests to hold them together. In 1798 he encountered Emma Hamilton, who became essential to his existence. She met his deep need for unconditional love and admiration, and simultaneously awoke and intoxicated his senses.

Perhaps inseparable from the development of his charismatic power were the paradoxes and contradictions in Nelson's character and behaviour. A fount of kindness and good nature, he exemplified the humane virtues of communication, negotiation and collaboration. But this same man was an eager and committed professional of violence, hyperactively aggressive in carrying the fight to the enemy, eagerly making opportunities to wage an almost personal war against them. Of course, the objective of the business he was in was to kill or be killed and to persuade other men to kill against their better natures; and the killing could be rationalized as in his country's interest, and victory thanks to God. Even so, his seemingly inexhaustible well of aggression strikes us as abnormal. Battle became another addiction. It may have been that he was so taken over by his image of himself as a hero that he felt impelled to seek out danger to prove himself again and again. Certainly one fix led to the need for another.

It is also paradoxical that a man who showed such a fund of common sense should at times have been so unreal and grandiose. He could refer to himself, even to intimates, in the third person. He frequently paraded the Great Me. He said one thing while thinking another, speaking of King, Country, Honour and Glory, when just as uppermost in his mind were Nelson, honours, peerages and pensions. As a young captain in the West Indies he was prissy, sanctimonious and ingenuous, seemingly rather disconnected from the realities of the scene. When he came to assess his personal contribution to the Corsican campaign reality succumbed to fantasy. As with other men and women of charisma, he was given to histrionics, always involving some degree of exaggeration, some leaking away of sincerity and integrity. He had a capacity to coin striking phrases: *England expects that every man will do his duty*. More deeply ambiguous was the matter of Marine Jolly, sentenced to death at Naples in 1799 for striking his superior officer. Nelson ordered the dreadful preparations for his execution to be carried forward but ordered him to be told, at the very last moment, that his life was to be spared.

Was this the ultimate in theatrical mercy, or a way for the parson's son to play God, or more darkly a sadistic impulse?

Always apparent throughout his life was formidable energy being channelled into a frantic pursuit of ambition and self-presentation. Self-belief and self-confidence were his strong points and it was perhaps inevitable that self-knowledge should come a poor second. But while these were such pronounced traits in his personality, there is no recorded instance of his seeking to take credit belonging to another. Quite the reverse, there are myriad examples of his pressing the claims of the deserving, a wonderful characteristic that earned him loyalty and affection from all who served with him. And by the time of his last campaign, when he felt he had full responsibility and accountability for what he did, he commanded like the free spirit he had always struggled to be.

A remarkable emotionalism surfaced after the age of forty, triggered by the stress of the Nile campaign, inner conflicts created by his feelings for his mistress Emma and the deception of his wife Fanny, and later by the insane jealousy of one fearful of loss. Even to an early twenty-first century onlooker his outpourings seem remarkable. Yet his capacity for expressing his emotions was evidently therapeutic; he was never professionally immobilized by them.

In the end his driven mission exacted a terrible price. He left behind the persons he loved the most, to do the thing he drove himself to do. His last thoughts were of Emma and his daughter, the whole business of his fame outweighed by the simple relief of knowing that he had not failed himself or those he had fought with.

The essential contradiction, and how we are variously inclined to react to it, may have been best summed up by two men: the diplomat Lord Minto, Nelson's friend and admirer for more than a decade; and Alexander Scott, Nelson's chaplain, private secretary and interpreter who experienced him at close quarters during his final two years. Minto, visiting Merton to spend the evening with Nelson and Emma before Nelson left for Trafalgar, wrote, 'He is in many points a really great man, in others a baby.' Alexander Scott recognized something of the same dichotomy but expressed it more lovingly: 'That man possessed the wisdom of the serpent with the innocence of the dove.'

Nelson's life was played out on the quarterdeck, or in the great cabin of his ships. From the age of twelve, twenty-eight of his remaining thirty-five years were spent at sea. The Navy fitted Nelson perfectly and he always worked within the bounds of its custom and practice.

Far from being the maverick of tradition, he was a skilled organization man, a frequent player of organization politics, a man who was occasionally economical with the truth, and one whose skill in self-presentation was supreme. As a commander he instinctively understood that a ship could not be managed effectively or survive the sea, or its people fight with spirit, courage and discipline, unless its captain and officers recognized their people's needs for self-respect, for fairness, and for justice. He was instinctively tender, protective and supportive of other men, as indeed were many in these floating communities. Nelson had no doubt where he stood. He told Emma's cousin Charles Connor when he was rated Midshipman in the *Niger*, 'I trust that your future conduct in life will prove you both an officer and a gentleman. Recollect that you must be a seaman to be an officer, and also, you cannot be a good officer without being a gentleman.' Nelson lived the values he espoused.

Yet it is paradoxical that this great fighting commander was on deck for only one hour and a half out of the first eight and a half hour phase of the battle of the Nile, and for only half an hour of the four hours and twenty-five minutes of Trafalgar. What was of immeasurably greater importance was what he did before battles. His unique contribution to the art of warfare was to fasten on the idea of Mission Command, 200 years before it was given a conceptual outline in our own day. Put simply, this is the idea that a commander conveys what he intends, and what he expects of those under him, to the extent that all share in their commander's mind and are empowered to deal with the contingencies of battle without losing their sense of the plot. Nelson was well aware that it was impossible to adopt detailed command and control in a large-scale sea battle and expect a decisive result. His approach worked because his confident trust in the capacity of his officers and men was well founded; their health, seamanship, gunnery and professionalism were factual. The capacities of his people were then infinitely enhanced by his evident belief in them and his undoubted willingness to lead from the front.

This is also the simple explanation for the disasters of his attacks on Tenerife and Boulogne. These were not fleet actions, could not be directed in his visionary terms, and required a level of thinking about contingencies that was simply not in his nature. Nelson fought on a simple prospectus: Death or Glory. He rightly elevated initiative and will to fight above mere numbers. But inevitably there were times when he underestimated his enemy or misread his circumstances.

Deciding to be a hero, deciding to serve King and country, being temperamentally inclined to look for the approval of others, he defined himself as an instrument of others. He did not see himself as one who might supplant Pitt, as a Napoleon would have done, nor as one who might succeed him, as the Duke of Wellington eventually did. He did not have St Vincent's ambition for power and place. All he wanted was recognition. He was not attracted to politics. Had he felt motivated to employ his formidable gifts as a negotiator and wordsmith and to employ his capacity to move easily between truth and fantasy, he might nevertheless have made his mark.

The narrative of Horatio Nelson's life has an operatic flavour, sweeping upwards from an obscure country parsonage to death and incandescent glory at Trafalgar. Not surprisingly there has from the beginning been a remarkable merging of two Nelsons, the person and the icon. Modern biographers have in some senses brought Nelson into sharper focus, but have still left room for a realistic, balanced and interwoven account of the whole of Nelson's emotional and professional experience. In pursuing this objective I allow Nelson's life to unfold chronologically, and allow him to describe his feelings as far as possible in his own words.

After eight years of asking Why did he do that? How did he do that? Did what he said match what he did? I have not ended up with an icon or the Nelson I began with. To do a subject proper biographic justice requires empathy, and a forensic attitude. I hope I have done him justice.

Part I

Early Years

Foundations for Life

The Child is father of the Man

William Wordsworth, 1807

'Jump!' shouted the boatman and on a chilly March morning in 1771 little Horatio Nelson leaped from the boat which had brought him out into the Medway, clutched at the gangway's hanging side ropes, so thick that his childish hands could not close round them, and began an agile and eager assault on the towering side of the *Raisonnable*. Up he scrambled, past the lower deck gun ports and an instant stink of stale humanity and bilge water, past the main deck ports, until at last he hauled himself on to the upper deck which suddenly appeared, smooth and shining white under its great banded masts and filigree rigging, the air heavy with the mingled aromas of wood, rope, tar, paint and metal. At twelve and a half years old he had entered the theatre of his life.

Horatio Nelson is variously reputed to have been born in a coach (not an unlikely possibility, given the state of eighteenth-century roads and the likely obstetrical fluency of a sixth child) or at a neighbouring farm because the family home was under repair, or indeed at Burnham Thorpe Rectory where his father Edmund Nelson was rector.[1] But whether in coach, farm or rectory, he was born on Michaelmas Day, 29 September 1758. His mother Catherine, now thirty-three, was a statuesque, determined woman who had already borne the rector five children. Her first-born Edmund had died soon after he took his first steps. Her next, the first Horatio, died even sooner, a babe in arms. Happily her next three, Maurice, now five, Susannah, now three and William now one and a half, all survived to be Horatio's elder brothers and sister. His own arrival was quickly followed by that of Ann, a second Edmund, then Suckling, then George (who lived for only six months) and then Catherine or 'Kitty', the baby of the family. In eighteen years of marriage Catherine

Nelson had eleven children. Being part of such a family, with motherly attention at a premium, overshadowed by his elders and quickly supplanted by new babies, Horatio had to behave like a puppy in a litter or a chick in a brood. If he wanted or needed more attention than was available he had to compete for it successfully. He went on competing for it, and getting it, for the rest of his life.

But on Boxing Day in 1767 his mother died when he was nine, an event which was to resonate throughout his life. Nothing is recorded of how he coped, whether and how he grieved, with anger and hot tears or childish stoicism; what his own imaginings, fears and desolations were when the candles were put out and he went down to sleep. Whatever may have been the case, it is striking that only twice in his voluminous papers and correspondence did he refer to his mother, and even then only indirectly. He used to say that he had learned his hatred of the French at his mother's knee. In the penultimate year of his life he wrote, 'the thought of former days [at Burnham] brings all my Mother into my heart which shows itself in my eyes'.[2] This deep silence may have been an unconscious rebuke to his mother for so abruptly leaving his life or he may have held himself to be profoundly at fault: in either case a memory suppressed, because too painful to recall. The results of childhood bereavement are now too well understood for there to be doubt about the impact of this traumatic event. Its resonances are found in his life-long search for love and affection, his constant thirst for approval, his periodic bouts of emotional distress,[3] and his acute anxiety that others he loved might, in their turn, desert him. These, to a greater or lesser degree are among the inheritance of all bereaved children. It is pitifully ironic that such childhood loss seems to provide an added and powerful motive force for those who have the capacity and opportunity for great achievement, so that an apparent handicap in life becomes an advantage.[4]

Edmund Nelson was among the kindest, most considerate and most easygoing of men and fathers. It is easy to see where his son's own good nature came from. And so the young Nelson grew up with servants, 'Will indoors' and 'aide de camp' Peter Black,[5] who were treated in a friendly, jocular and whimsical way as unofficial members of the family. He also absorbed the ambiguity of a father who was a man in uniform, a man of the cloth, set apart in authority, in the pulpit or study, a man who combined a kind and considerate nature with a veritable litany of official 'musts', 'shalts', 'must nots' and 'shalt nots' – an interestingly

appropriate model for a future naval officer. More important was the
fact that although like any other paterfamilias Edmund Nelson had his
sticking points – the children had to sit up straight[6] and he was quirky
and arbitrary in forbidding the use of spectacles[7] – there is never a hint
of rigid control, of authoritarianism or of excessive ambition for his
children. Horatio had plenty of room in which to develop his own personality and follow his own star. His father, preoccupied with the weight
of parish duties, might well have been inadequately attentive but no dark
shadows were placed on Horatio's childish psyche by the parental
domination, coldness, over-high expectations or ill treatment which have
produced fatal flaws in so many leaders.[8]

There was however another side to the paternal coin. Edmund Nelson
was to a degree ineffectual, unambitious, something of a hypochondriac,
'easily put in a fuss', 'tremulous over trifles',[9] not a practical person either
about his land and garden or his children's futures. Widowed at the early
age of forty-six he seems not to have had either the energy or the inclination to find himself a new wife, an obviously practical and sensible
step for a widower left with eight children aged between fourteen years
and ten months – although for the same reason it would be a considerable challenge to find another woman to take them on. Whatever his
motivation, he decided 'to take upon the care and affection of double
parent'.[10] His father's unheroic sides did not appeal to the young Nelson
and produced an ambivalent response in him. He would always regard
his father with respect and affection; he would always be generous to
him; but he always treated him protectively, as a person to be sheltered
from reality, not someone to look to for help or advice. Except to the
extent that he might have mimicked certain eccentricities of dress or turns
of phrase, he did not identify with him. There does not seem to have
been closeness between them. His young life, indeed his whole life, was
to be wide open to other influential father figures. Such was this ambivalence that he neither visited his father in the days preceding his death nor
did he attend his funeral.

As Nelson grew up, William, the brother closest to him in age,
inevitably became his playmate and schoolfellow. Supplanted by Horatio,
he had at first tried bullying as a means of expressing his feelings. Horatio
had an instinctive sense of how to deal with bullies. His early biographer Harrison tells how Catherine Nelson said to those who would intervene on Horatio's behalf during one of these ill-matched bouts, 'let them

alone, little Horace will beat him; let Horace alone'.[11] For small boys,
fisticuffs are generally a route to reconciliation. Anyway, when the boys
went off as exiles from home, to board first at the Royal Grammar School
at Norwich and later at the Paston School at North Walsham, they had
to stand shoulder to shoulder against the naturally occurring assaults
and cruelties of other small boys. Horatio seems to have emerged as the
leader and William the follower. Yet it is very noticeable that Horatio
developed a habit of humouring his elder brother. He was never able to
resist the demands which William never ceased making.

Nelson's schooling was chiefly remarkable for making little impression
on him. He was not aroused by learning. His formal education, like his
father's literate example, left few marks on him. Culture, in the wider
sense of books, music, art, architecture, antiquities, seems never to have
had the slightest effect on him. He recalled little, apart from a handful
of half-remembered shadows of quotations from Shakespeare and
surprisingly even fewer biblical allusions. His syntax, punctuation and
spelling were always idiosyncratic, his arithmetic unreliable. He left
school with his native powers of mind and expression intact but with a
potentially limited range of interests. Boarding-school itself was a mixed
blessing. It did for him what it does for all who have the capacity to
survive: it strengthened his resilience, self-reliance, independence and
capacity to mix with others; shipboard life would be less of a shock for
him than for some others, for example his friend and future Admiral,
Cuthbert Collingwood. It also added to the disruption of his early family
life.

Insight into Nelson's childhood is based mainly on deduction from
behaviour in his adult life and from what is known of his family. If anecdotes are by definition untrustworthy, the three most commonly related
are repeated here only because of a characteristic common element. It is
said that as a five- or six-year-old he wandered off with a companion
near his grandmother's home at Hillborough and went missing. When a
search party brought little Horatio home to his grandmother, she scolded
him in her relieved anxiety, 'I wonder that fear did not drive you home'
and he replied, 'Fear Grandmother I never saw Fear, what is it. It never
came near me'.[12] And at the Paston School, where he was lowered from
a dormitory window, to harvest the Headmaster, John Price Jones's pears
in dead of night, he did it, not for the fruit, but 'because every other boy
was afraid'.[13] And then when snowdrifts looked like blocking their way

to the coach which would take them back to school after Christmas and to turn back offered an unexpectedly extended holiday, Horatio urged William on, 'Remember brother it was left to our honour'.[14] It is the voice of these anecdotes that is so interesting. They sound like the first flowering of his capacity for histrionics, his tendency in later life to singularize himself with utterances which surprise, command and always take the moral high ground. A certain grandiosity and priggishness may have been fully fledged in him from the beginning. Conceit, a sense of difference and a certain self-righteousness are supposed to be characteristic of parsons' children, but such attributes are not greatly admired by other small boys so they must have been counterbalanced by some very winning ways, as they were in later life. Alternatively, if we ask what sort of boy would have grown to be a man like Nelson we should think especially of his headlong aggression as a naval officer. Then we can readily imagine how this shrimp of a lad would have flown at his first tormentor and with a tornado of flailing fists, established credibility among his schoolfellows.

Nelson's mother had clearly been a good catch for his father but it is less clear why *she* married him, given her family's position in the county and their grand connections. Catherine's grandmother was Mary Walpole, sister of Sir Robert, 'every man has his price' Walpole, for twenty years Prime Minister of England and as first Earl of Orford founder of an influential dynasty. Catherine's mother, daughter of Mary Walpole and Sir Charles Turner, had married Maurice Suckling, Rector of Barsham in Suffolk, Woodton in Norfolk and Prebendary of Westminster. Catherine's eldest brother, Maurice, a post captain in the Navy, had strengthened the Walpole connection by marrying Mary Walpole, sister of Lord Walpole who was the son of the second Earl of Orford. Maurice lived at Woodton Hall in south Norfolk. Catherine's other brother, William, became a commissioner in the Excise Office and lived in fine style in Kentish Town. Against this, Edmund Nelson came from a family of parsons albeit with a land-owning grandfather. His own father, also an Edmund, had been at Eton and Cambridge and had married Mary Bland, the daughter of a Cambridge baker, a man of considerable fortune and property, including the rectory of Hillborough, where Nelson's father had become incumbent.

When Edmund and Catherine married on 11 May 1749 she was twenty-four. Her portrait suggests she was rather plain. But clearly her

family regarded Edmund as of sufficient substance to be considered an
acceptable match. Then, owing to the Walpole influence, he secured the
Burnham living and the Earl of Orford's younger brother the second Lord
Wolterton became Horatio's godfather and namesake. Socially speaking,
the Nelsons were not invited to Houghton Hall, the great house of the
senior Walpoles the Earls of Orford, but they were from time to time
invited by the Walpoles of Wolterton Hall. As is often the case, the least
well connected partner, in this instance Edmund, took a somewhat excessive pride in these grand connections. And certainly it would seem that
Catherine was in most senses the dominant partner. Decency demanded
that one son be named after his father and so there was an Edmund, but
the rest of the boys, Maurice, William, Suckling, Horatio and two of the
three girls, Anne and Catherine, were given names which exemplified
their Suckling connection. On the Nelson side Horatio had three aunts,
Mary who died a spinster, Alice who married Robert Rolfe the Rector
of Hillborough, and Thomazine who married John Goulty, a Norwich
gentleman. None of these names were perpetuated in their brother's
family and although Nelson spent exeats with the Goultys when at school
in Norwich, these relations were less significant in his life. Otherwise, the
Nelsons mixed with the local gentry, their neighbour Sir Mordaunt
Martin, ex-Marshal of the Vice-Admiralty Court in Jamaica, the Malets
and the Crowes at the Hall and Kitty's godfather Dr Charles Pointz,
parson of North Creake, whose sister became first Countess Spencer.
Socially speaking, Horatio's beginnings were neither humble nor poor
and very characteristic of eighteenth-century naval officers. There were
important connections, some 'interest' and enough money to employ
servants, educate sons, live comfortably, take trips to Bath and identify
with the gentry. On the other hand they were relatively poor relations;
the higher social ladder was there to climb, serious money to be made.

In spite of their Walpole and Suckling ancestors the Nelson–Suckling
alliance brought no striking genetic benefits. With the startling exception
of Horatio, his parents produced a totally undistinguished and untalented
set of children. Maurice was amiable but very modestly endowed.
William made his way almost totally on his brother Horatio's back and
would otherwise have finished his days as a thoroughly boring, unlike-
able and undistinguished rector of Hillborough. Suckling, an amiable
lay-about, was fond of the bottle and sporting pursuits and required a
great deal of financial and moral support to enable him to be curate in

his father's living when the latter retired. Ann went out as an apprentice milliner, possibly became pregnant, and died early, unmarried. Nothing is recorded of Edmund except his declining health and early death. Susannah and Kitty married comfortably but only Kitty in her adult life had the energy and ebullience to suggest kinship with her famous brother. Their mother seems to have brought a weaker strain into the family; she and her two brothers all died relatively young. On the Nelson side, Edmund albeit a 'creaking gate', survived till his seventy-ninth year and his sisters were eighty-two, ninety-three and ninety respectively – obviously very tough stock. This is important. Nelson is usually characterized as physically frail, but the *Narrative* of Dr Beatty, the *Victory*'s surgeon who tended him in the cockpit at Trafalgar, says that those who later examined the dead Admiral, and in effect did a post-mortem, found that, 'all the vital organs were so perfectly healthy in their appearance, and so small, that they resembled more those of a youth than a man who had attained his forty-seventh year; which state of the body, associated with habits of life favourable to health, gives every reason to believe that his Lordship might have lived to a great age'.[15] However, his frequent bouts of emotional distress, the hardships of his naval life and his wounds were to give him a radically different personal view of his health and life expectancy.

Following the death of his sister, Maurice Suckling was instrumental in finding her eldest son, Maurice Nelson, a position as a clerk in the Navy Office. This seemed to be the end of outside help for there is no record of Edmund soliciting his grand relations for any further assistance, or indeed of their offering any. But Maurice Suckling had always been a hero to his sister and through her to her boys. In later years even Susannah recalled in a syntactically confused way that her mother had been 'quite a heroine for the sailors'. They had frequently heard of his exploits in the West Indies during the Seven Years War when his ship the *Dreadnought* aided by two ships of the line put De Kersaint's superior squadron to flight off Cape François in 1759. He doubtless enthralled the children with tales of the battle. Maurice Suckling, a handsome, dashing, successful man of action, was everything Nelson's father was not and, not surprisingly, the catalyst for Nelson's career choice. The critical moment came some three years later in late 1770 when a crisis with Spain over their seizure of the Falklands came to a head. Mr Harris, the British chargé d'affaires, was recalled from Madrid and a naval force

prepared. Home for the Christmas holidays, Horatio and William read
of this in the newspaper. The fact that his uncle was to command a 64-
gun ship leaped to Horatio's eye. He immediately wrote or asked William
to write on his behalf to their father, cosseting himself in Bath, to ask his
uncle to take him to sea. The capacity to make and take his chances was
inborn in Nelson. He pushed himself forward with decision and persuasiveness and his father's customary *laissez-faire* attitude ensured that the
boy's request was forwarded to Captain Suckling. Although tradition has
it that Horatio was his uncle's favourite his reply shows that the request
was unexpected: 'What has poor Horatio done, who is so weak, that he
above all the rest should be sent to rough it out at sea? But let him come;
and the first time we go into action, a cannon ball may knock off his
head and provide for him at once'.[16] The ruthless frankness and rather
ungracious sounding jocularity of these words suggest that Uncle
Maurice felt some impatience with Edmund Nelson's thoughtlessness.
But the request, virtually direct from Horatio himself, was one he could
not refuse. Nelson as ever was in luck. Maurice Suckling was a childless
widower and would lavish on him care and attention equal to the best
of fathers.

And so it was that the Lieutenant of the Watch of His Majesty's Ship
Raisonnable came face to face with young Nelson and hearing his treble-
voiced but not unconfident explanation of who he was, concluded that
he was indeed a new 'squeaker', ordered his chest to be whipped up from
the boat below, gave him totally unintelligible directions to the 'gun
room', 'lower deck and aft' and having many more important things on
his mind, since the ship was getting ready to go downriver to Sheerness,
left him to his own devices.

2

Captain Suckling's Legacy

My boy I leave you to my country.

Nelson, 1786

The *Raisonnable* was moored in the Medway in the final stages of fitting out. She was swarming with life, getting cables on board, rigging the masts, swaying up the yards, bending sails, receiving seamen and marines. Harrison, writing Nelson's biography in 1806, under the direction of Lady Hamilton, adopted her version of the story of his reception, or rather non-reception, which has been repeated and embellished by succeeding generations. 'It would seem however that his uncle could not at this time be on board, or any person whatever who knew of his coming: for he had been repeatedly heard to say, by one of his oldest and most esteemed friends, that he paced the deck after his arrival from Greenwich, the whole remainder of the day, without being in the smallest degree noticed by anyone; till, at length, the second day of his being on board, some person, as he expressed it, 'kindly took compassion on him'. It was then discovered, for the first time, that he was the captain's nephew and appointed to serve on board as a midshipman.'[1]

Thirty years had not expunged the experience of being put on the Chatham coach, left by his father to make the final leg of his journey, alone. His careless father had given him neither information as to where the *Raisonnable* lay, nor instructions for getting to her. These obstacles Nelson had surmounted with characteristic resolution but when he at last climbed on board, there was no friendly uncle waiting to welcome him into his new life. That he chose, thirty years later, to cast himself as a kind of invisible, irrelevant nobody, testifies to the depths of his feelings, and his unquenched thirst for soliciting sympathy, if not to the truth of his situation; the Officer of the Watch must certainly have known he was

on board, must certainly have asked him who he was and directed him
and his belongings to the gun room.

At the time, he coped. Nelson was not the sort of character to play
little boy lost. Other 'squeakers', like the great Collingwood, destined to
become his second-in-command at Trafalgar, might sit and sob for their
distant home but not Nelson.[2] He had an instinctive capacity for self-
possession. And soon, united with his uncle, Nelson had the thrill of
being in a great ship in motion as they went down to Sheerness on the
ebb tide, the leadsman in the chains, calling the depth of the channel in
fathoms, the pilot conning the ship, the anchor cable laid out ready on
the lower deck. He saw the cat-o'-nine-tails brought out of the bag for
the first time and assembled aft with all hands to witness punishment –
John Hollier a dozen lashes for quarrelling and fighting.[3]

His life in the *Raisonnable* was over almost as soon as it began.
Captain Suckling was appointed to the *Triumph* a 74-gun guardship, and
was made senior officer in command of some fourteen ships and vessels,
anchored in the Medway and off the Nore, and bound for nowhere. To
Suckling's active and thoughtful mind this posed a problem. The
majority of the ship's company, not having to work ship, having a relatively idle life, being predominantly young, vigorous and unmarried,
would quickly revert to their natural priorities: drink and fornication.
Given an equal number of 'wives' on board, and an allowance of a gallon
of beer per day per sailor, drunkenness, quarrelling, fighting and a lower
deck seething with sexual activity and petty corruption were guaranteed.
Suckling wisely arranged for his nephew to have real sea time in a West
Indiaman the *Mary Ann* belonging to Hibbert, Palmer and Horton; her
captain, John Rathbone had served under him as a master's mate in the
Dreadnought. This voyage had a profound and formative effect on the
young Nelson. Looking back on it some twenty-eight years later in
his *Sketch of My Life*, written in 1799 for the editors of the *Naval
Chronicle*, he wrote rather dramatically, 'If I did not improve in my education, I returned a practical seaman with a horror of the Royal Navy,
and with a saying then constant with the Seamen, "Aft the most honour,
forward the better man!" – It was many weeks before I got in the least
reconciled to a Man-of-War, so deep was the prejudice rooted; and what
pains were taken to instil this erroneous principle in a young mind'.[4]

For the whole of this first period at sea he lived and worked as a
seaman. There were no concessions to the aspiring naval officer, no edu-

cation in navigation, no writing up his journal. The life of a merchant seaman was a life of hard graft in all weathers; even a thirteen-year-old had to pull his weight. And notwithstanding the snippets of knowledge he had picked up in small boats at Burnham Overy Staithe and more recently in the *Raisonnable*, he had entered a new world of overwhelming strangeness; miles of rope and rigging, objects of incomprehensible purpose, and a way of naming things that might as well have been Greek, sailors having their own arcane vocabulary of several hundred words. He developed growing familiarity with the names and functions of the ropes he was hauling on. Opportunities arose in the ceaseless repair work of a ship at sea to learn how to make 'bends' so as to tie ropes together; to make 'hitches' to attach ropes to objects; to 'splice' by undoing the ends of two pieces of rope and weaving them together; and how to 'worm', 'parcel' and 'serve' ropes, to strengthen the standing rigging. He absorbed the names of the twenty-one or so different sails. He came to grips with the names and functions of 'back stays', 'deadeyes', 'hearts', 'lanyards', 'ratlines', 'carparthins' and 'futtocks'; and with the names of the various yards (the great cross-pieces on the masts bearing the sails) with their 'jeers', 'halyards', 'parrels', 'trusses', 'lifts' and 'braces'; and with the sails and their 'earrings', 'cringles', 'reef points', 'robbands', 'clearlines', 'sheets', 'bowlines', 'buntlines', 'slablines' and 'topping lifts'. And then there were tools like 'fids' and 'marlinspikes'.

As the ship reached the West Indies and sailed in a northerly direction to touch at the major ports of the Windward Islands, then on to the Leeward Islands, and then due west to Jamaica, they were delivering manufactured goods from England, setting down passengers, taking on board sugar, rum and passengers for England. With all the loading and unloading he saw how tackles were rigged from the yards to lift heavy weights and learned by a process of observation and osmosis how a big ship was tacked or wore to change course, how it was hove to, how it dropped and weighed anchor, how it was moored alongside a harbour wall and warped out again – to say nothing of his first experience of an exotic island world of blue seas, burning sun, warm nights, strange birds and fish, dazzling white sands, and jungle greenery. Up in the ship's fo'c'sle we can assume that conversation would be mainly about 'runs ashore', how much they were going to drink and where women were to be found, although Nelson would also have learned that ships' companies could not be stereotyped; they contained their fair share of sober and responsible characters and oddities. The return journey, by the northern route to take advantage of the Gulf Stream and the westerlies, may well have seen him sent aloft for the first time, to work his way along the yards to bend, furl or reef the sails. This is what he meant when he said he came back a 'practical seaman': thoroughly familiarized with the scope of a seaman's work but by no means yet capable of doing it all; that, by general reckoning, required close on two years.

As ever, the unintended consequences of the best intentions were the more significant. Suckling's intention had been to accelerate Nelson's experience. He would not have expected him to return with such a powerful view of the shortcomings of the Navy, or with such disdain for the officer class. It was ironical that popular dread of the press-gang, the power of the Navy to snatch seaman from merchant ships in times of war, horror stories of naval punishments and of arrears in pay, obscured the facts. Sailors in the Navy did not have to work as hard as men in merchant ships; sufficient numbers were needed to form gun crews and so they were generally in a ratio of one man to every two or three tons of ship, whereas the ratio in a West Indiaman such as the one in which Nelson sailed was likely to be one man to every ten tons of ship.[5] Sailors in the Navy were generally better paid, better housed, better fed, lived under better regulated conditions, were looked after better when sick, and were not necessarily more tyrannically managed than their counterparts in the merchant navy. Compared with life ashore in the lower layers of Georgian society theirs was in fact an enviable existence. As for the officer class, Nelson's being 'up forrard,' in shipboard social terms, enabled him to observe at first hand the disdain men could have for those above them. He could experience the reasons for it, seeing that merchant officers were no more admirable in their behaviour than navy officers were held to be. He had absorbed a natural consideration towards others from his father. Now, he understood from practical experience that an officer reaps what he sows. Here were the sources of his determination to make command acceptable; the rest of his service would be a monument to that idea.

Returned to the *Triumph* in July 1772 it was back to writing up his Journal and learning the rudiments of navigation. But the action man in him could not be so easily suppressed. He recalled, again in his *Sketch of My Life*, how he did a deal with his uncle. 'As my ambition was to be a seaman, it was always held out as a reward that if I attended well to my navigation I should go in the cutter and decked long boat, which was attached to the Commanding Officer's ship at Chatham. Thus by degrees I became a good pilot for vessels of that description from Chatham to the Tower of London, down the Swin, and the North Foreland; and confident of myself amongst rocks and sands, which has many times been of great comfort to me'.[6] Later, in the West Indies, in North American waters, among the shoals of Aboukir Bay, among the shallows and deeps off Copenhagen, in his inshore cutting-out work in the Mediterranean and in his service with the inshore squadron blockading Toulon, he would demonstrate consummate skill and confidence in feeling his way through dangerous waters.

By the turn of the year a different point of the compass beckoned. He got wind of a proposed expedition to the North Pole under Captain the Honourable Constantine Phipps. Proposed by the Royal Society and supported by King George III it consisted of two specially equipped and strengthened ships, the *Racehorse* under Captain Phipps and the *Carcass* under Captain Skeffington Lutwidge. Nelson recalls that 'Although no boys were allowed to go in the ships (as of no use) yet nothing could prevent my using every interest to go with Captain Lutwidge in the *Carcass* and, as I fancied I was to fill a man's place I begged I might be his cockswain; which, finding my ardent desire for going with him Captain Lutwidge complied with, and has continued the strictest friendship to this moment.'[7] Obviously Nelson had to have the very necessary personal introductions, but his self-confidence, pushiness and formidable thirst for experience were already propelling him. When the *Racehorse* and the *Carcass* left the Nore on 4 June 1773, Nelson was on board *Carcass* as Captain Lutwidge's coxswain.

Nothing could have been in greater contrast to the *Triumph*. Here there was purpose and preparation. The *Carcass*'s master James Allen noted in his log 'ice saws and axes from London', and how 'Mr Irwin and his men came aboard and finished the operations for distilling salt-water into fresh and provd it and found it to answer to the purpose some of which I tasted and found it to my palate like barley water tho not unpleasant when made into Grog or Mix'd with Wine'.[8] They sailed north, passing Spurn Head, Flamborough Head, Robin Hood's Bay and Whitby. Then came the only punishment in either ship during the whole voyage. On 15 June the log noted: 'Punished Rich[d] Dingle for Theft by making him run the gauntlet'. Punishment for theft from a shipmate was shrewdly shared by the whole ship's company, the prisoner being dragged round the decks on a seat placed on top of a tub: 'The cavalcade starts from the back of the quarterdeck, after the boatswain has given the prisoner a dozen lashes and the ship's crew are ranged round the decks in two rows, so that the prisoner passes between them, and each man is provided with a three yarn knittle; that is, three rope yarns tightly laid together and knotted. With this, each man must cut him or be thought to be implicated in his theft'.[9]

They crossed the Arctic Circle on 20 June and the next day 'saw a whale blow for the first time'. By now the beer had run out and grog was served – half a pint of brandy mixed with a pint of water per day, per man. Then, amid a 'large flock of Sea Parrots, Puffins and Sea Pidgeons', they sighted Spitzbergen about twenty miles ahead. By 5 July they were nine miles off Hakluyt's Head, the north-west tip of Spitzbergen, in fifty fathoms of water. They had arrived and were now above the eightieth parallel in a glittering world of icebergs and floating ice as far as the eye could see. Guided by their ice pilots, they sailed along the edge searching for openings. Frequently they were caught in the ice and had to warp their way westwards by carrying an ice anchor in a boat to the shore, embedding it in the ice and hauling the ship towards it, using the ship's capstan to draw in the rope. At other times they could make progress only by towing the ships. This was grindingly hard and hazardous work, in a dazzling but remorselessly threatening world of sudden fogs, swells, gales and calms. The ice forced the *Carcass* on the *Racehorse* and carried away her bumkin as she drove in on the *Racehorse*'s hawsers. Their helplessness became apparent. The ice was taking them rapidly to the north-east. As fast as they cut to the west, new ice filled the space. As hard as they worked to warp the ship to the west the current set them more rapidly to the east. Phipps decided that he could not risk being trapped in an Arctic winter and prepared to abandon ship and make for the open sea about a mile to the west. Nelson pushed himself forward: 'When the boats were fitting out to quit the two ships blocked up in the ice, I exerted myself to have command of a four-oared cutter raised upon, which was given me with twelve men; and I prided myself in fancying I could navigate her better than any other boat in the ship.' When the second and third lieutenants, two mates and four midshipmen, Nelson included, went off with forty men and the boats, a small gap suddenly appeared in the ice. The remainder of the two ships' companies worked furiously to warp and heave the ships into the opening. They made only half a mile before the ice closed in. Fortunately a wind got up, enabling the ships to set sail and force a way through the ice. Then, with a current setting strongly to the west they were able to recover and hoist in their boats. By dint of further warping, cutting and using the brute force of the ships as battering rams, they escaped into the loose ice. The expedition was over. It was now too late in the year for them to do anything other than return home. This they did through a fearsome North Sea, laconically recorded in the ship's log as 'violent hard gales with great sea'. On 20 September they 'came to at the Nore with Best Bow^r in 7 fm'. The adventure was over, not at all successful from the point of view of finding a passage to the Pacific but wonderfully instructive from young Nelson's point of view. Lutwidge and Phipps had managed their crews with skill, keeping up their activity and morale in the face of the severe psychological and physical challenges produced by the frightening force of nature. In the eight months of the commission only one man had been flogged out of a total of about 200 men. By comparison the previous eight months in *Triumph* had seen men being flogged at a rate of one a week. The lesson that a shared sense of purpose and constant activity reduced indiscipline was not lost on Nelson.

Nelson was now fifteen. He had made a modest mark in the Arctic expedition but more important had gained confidence from the experience. Now, as he passed the boundary of youth to manhood, a new and different experience beckoned. 'A squadron was fitting out for the East Indies; and nothing less than such a distant voyage could in the least satisfy my desire of maritime knowledge. I was placed in the *Seahorse* of 20-guns with Captain Farmer, and watched in the foretop; from whence in time I was placed on the quarter-deck having in the time I was in this ship visited almost every port of the East Indies from Bengal to Bussoraha'.[10]

Captain Suckling made sure he was well received. He asked Mr Bentham of the Navy Office to intervene with Mr Kee, the Master's Agent, telling him that he would be obliged for a letter of introduction to the master of the *Seahorse*, Mr Surridge. As ever, the magic words were 'a recommendation in favour of Horatio Nelson, a young lad, nephew to Captain Suckling, who is going in that ship'. Surridge, who had ambitions to advance himself to Lieutenant, was thus encouraged to keep an eye on the lad.

By the time the *Seahorse* and the *Salisbury*, with Commodore Sir Edward Hughes in command, had crossed the Equator it was becoming

apparent to everybody in Nelson's ship that all was not well between
Captain Farmer and his first lieutenant James Drummond. Drummond
was a difficult man with a penchant for the bottle and Farmer did not
have the strength of character to nip the problem in the bud. They had
a hard time sailing to the Cape. Rigging, masts, sails and yards were in
poor condition and repairs a constant necessity. The Commodore's call
for more sail from the limping *Seahorse* produced a public altercation
between Drummond and the captain. They fell out again in public, over
the loss of a longboat and two marines in the treacherous winds and
waters of Table Bay. By the time they left the Cape their relationship had
broken down completely. Farmer was displaying his weakness for all to
see. After one altercation Farmer appealed pathetically to his assembled
quarterdeck, 'Gentlemen is this to be borne'.[11]

Shortly afterwards, as they changed course to pick up the south-east
trade winds, the mainmast sprung in five places and had to be fished (put
in splints). War broke out again between Farmer and his first lieutenant.
In the words of Mr Surridge:

> Mr Drummond had the watch from 4–6 in the evening . . . he went
> from the Quarter Deck to the Forecastle and took in the Fore top
> gallant sail, when Captain Farmer found the Top gallant sail taken
> in Captain Farmer called for Mr Murray and ordered him to go
> forward and set the top gallant sail. Mr Drummond then made
> answer why not me as it would look more like an officer to order
> me. Captain Farmer then made answer that he would order who he
> pleased to set it. Mr Drummond then desired Mr Murray to wait
> till he ordered him to set it. Captain Farmer called out to set it, which
> I believe was done accordingly.[12]

The weak and ineffectual Farmer had now no option other than to put
an end to this childish power struggle. A laconic note in the master's log
on 26 April reads: 'NB at 8 Captain ordered Mr Drummond 1st Lieut.
under an arrest and suspended him from Duty by Order of the
Commodore Sir Ed^wd Hughes.' The ship was agog, everyone instantly
aware that Drummond's career was at an end and that he had only himself
to blame for not finding a way of managing his relationship with Farmer.

At the court martial in Madras Roads on 30 May 1774, Farmer 'threw
the book' at Drummond, who was 'broke' – finished after being com-

missioned for only three years. But when the thirty-odd pages of cop-
perplate evidence got back to the Admiralty they would not add to
Farmer's reputation either. None of this touched directly on Nelson, but
ships were small closed communities; virtually every word that passed
between Drummond and Farmer would be known to all on board. In his
defence the first lieutenant had called three midshipmen as witnesses.
Nelson was not one of them but he had been an onlooker of this crisis
in command and discipline.

On 19 February 1775 at six in the morning in calm hazy weather,
Nelson first heard drums beat to quarters as the ship was cleared for
action, guns were run out, powder brought up, gun crews assembled.
The ship's log records the incident: 'saw two sail standing towards us
which we imagined to be Bombay Coreizers . . . , they hauld their wind
to the Southward and stood after the *Dodley* and hoisted Hadir Aly's
Colours. We immediately tacked and stood after them, at 8 fired several
shot to bring one of them too, thinking her to be Marratoes [The
Mahratta Confederacy of Hindu princes], at 9 one of the ketches sent
one of her boat on board and told us they belonged to Hadir Aly [of
Mysore] but as her Ketch did not bring too, nor shorten sail and several
other vessels heaving in sight we kept firing round and grapeshot at her.
At half past noon the Ketch Brought too and struck her Colours.'[13]

Although an incident to quicken Nelson's pulses it was hardly an
engagement of consequence: but it was enough to encourage Hidar Ali,
to describe him correctly, to keep his ships out of the way of British merchant traffic. The *Seahorse* continued to Bombay before sailing across
the Arabian Sea on convoy duty, past Muscat, through the Straits of
Hormuz and up the Gulf. Trouble had been building up again. The new
first lieutenant, Thomas Henery, had made an enemy of the gunner,
George Middleton, who was badly piqued by the way Henery had dealt
with him over the business of getting powder up for a salute. When
ordered to get a move on, Mr Middleton's 'God Bless me Sir I make what
haste ever I can,' met with 'God damn me Sir make more haste or else
I'll haste you elsewhere.'[14] Henery had a rough edge to his tongue. The
gunner made a formal complaint in writing, Farmer was unable to knock
their heads together and the upshot was that Henery asked the Commodore for a court-martial to clear his name. He was accused by the
gunner of 'frequent Drunkenness, disobedience to Orders, disrespect of
the Sabbath Day. Tyranny in beating some of the Men and Flogging at

the Gangway in the absence of the Captain and abuse and ill treatment
to the Warrant and Petty officers'. The court found that no part of the
charge was proved and further pronounced the Prosecution to have been
'groundless and litigious'. Perhaps the best indication of Captain Farmer's
unfitness for command came when Lieutenant Henery asked him at his
court martial, 'did you ever disapprove of my punishing the People in
your absence?' Farmer answered, 'I neither approved nor disapproved.'
The gunner had recruited as witnesses some of the midshipmen who had
also been alienated by Henery's unsympathetic behaviour. Midshipman
Keeling's main complaint was, 'I was going on board the *Salisbury* once
to answer a signal and one of the Boats Crew was very insolent to me
and refused to row, on my coming onboard I acquainted the Lieutenant
of it and he told me I certainly must have made too free with the men
or they never would have used you so and told me to go away'. Midshipman Sullivan said the lieutenant, 'often abused me calling me a
Cooley and Puppy and Threatening to flog me from Ship to Ship'. Henery
asked him, 'What were we about when I called you a Cooley?' Keeling
answered, 'I remember one time weighing the anchor the Nippers slipt.
Mr Henery asked me the reason why the nippers were not clipped on
better. I told him the Cable was slippery and he immediately called me
a Puppy and threatened to flog me from ship to ship.'[15] Neither Nelson
nor Thomas Troubridge his fellow midshipman was a complainant.

By now Nelson was sickening with malaria. Hughes had decided to
repatriate invalid officers in the *Dolphin*. Second Lieutenant Evans of
the *Seahorse*'s marines and the Honourable Matthew Fortescue, second
lieutenant of the *Coventry* were mentioned in Hughes's letter to Their
Lordships. Nelson was not mentioned but was also sent home, presumably because of his connection with Captain Suckling. Nelson was later
to say: 'Ill health induced Sr Edward Hughes who had always shewn me
the greatest kindness, to send me to England in the *Dolphin* of 20-guns
with Captain James Pigot whose kindness at that time saved my life.'[16]
After a voyage of six months, three weeks and six days, the *Dolphin*
was paid off at Woolwich on 24 September 1776. Nelson was about to
celebrate his eighteenth birthday.

In a period of five and a half years Nelson had extended his horizons
from rural Norfolk to the Arctic Ocean, the North Atlantic, the
Caribbean, the South Atlantic, the Southern Ocean, the Indian Ocean,
the Arabian Sea and the Persian Gulf. Thousands of miles of deep sea

sailing had initiated him into the profound arts of navigation and the fixed configuration of the great prevailing winds and ocean currents. Endemic problems with the sails, rigging and masts of the *Seahorse* had laid the foundation for a lifelong respect for the skills and ingenuity of boatswains and carpenters. And he had been introduced to naval warfare, albeit of the bloodless variety.

His voyages had provided him with equally formative experience of the dynamics of shipboard life, a nurturing of profound importance for his future behaviour. From his West Indiaman he had his worm's eye view of authority. From the *Carcass* he learned that morale and good discipline flourish where there is purpose and activity. The *Seahorse* had shown him a well-meaning captain who could not exert his authority effectively, nor create a team; a powerful example of how not to behave. The second court martial had surfaced the sensitivity of junior officers to coarse and rough handling by the first lieutenant. From his very first command, Nelson would, as far as he was able, gather round him men, who while not necessarily gentlemen by birth, were gentlemen by nature.

During his voyage home in the *Dolphin* Nelson's self-propelled but powerfully assisted career took on a new dimension as motivation, that element without which talent does not flourish, stirred in him. Life in the Navy was matching his temperament and he had grabbed eagerly at every opportunity for new experience. Now, recovering from a major illness, convalescent and skeletal on board the *Dolphin*, he was suddenly in the depths of despair. Clarke and McArthur, his first biographers and men who knew him, are the only source for what happened: they describe Nelson as having related his experience twenty-seven years later, in 1802:

> I felt impressed with an idea that I should never rise in my pro-fession. My mind was staggered with a view of the difficulties I had to surmount and the little interest I possessed. I could discover no means of reaching the object of my ambition. After a long and gloomy reverie, in which I almost wished myself overboard, a sudden glow of patriotism was kindled within me, and presented my king and country as my patron. My mind exulted in the idea. 'Well then' I exclaimed, 'I will be a hero, and confiding in Providence I will brave every danger.'

They go on, 'The spirit of Nelson revived; and from that hour, in his mind's eye, as he often declared to Captain Hardy, a radiant orb was suspended, which urged him onward to renown.'[17]

In Nelson self-direction was characteristic. Hitherto it had seemed to spring from curiosity, pushiness and confidence. He now went a step further and created a vision of himself and his future: 'I will be a hero, and confiding in Providence I will brave every danger'. It does not matter much how we interpret his experience. It may have been biochemical, a glow of well-being caused by a rush of endorphins releasing him from depression. It may have been his convalescent psyche seizing on models provided by his education or religious upbringing. It may have been that in the absence of an emotional partner and well on the way to becoming institutionalized in an almost totally male setting, he was finding an outlet for his natural urges. It may have been any of those things at the time. On the other hand it may well have been the later Nelson indulging in histrionic myth making and self-glorification, unconsciously diverting attention from the prime importance of his uncle's early patronage. The cause is irrelevant. The indisputable fact is that this is how he lived the rest of his life. He would constantly behave like a hero. He would constantly look for the entitlements of a hero; for this was also a statement of his ambition. The hero, brave, inspiring, truthful, courageous, leading from the front, always honourable, became his internal model. Now that he had a mental map of his future he was fully motivated. His ambition could be focused.

Immediately on his return Nelson's prospects received a huge boost. He heard that his uncle had been appointed Comptroller of the Navy and MP for Portsmouth, both positions commanding much 'interest', that is ability to ask for, and return favours. At that time, the Navy, the most effective and sophisticated professional body in Europe, was directed by the Board of Admiralty. This was composed of civilian and naval members headed by the First Lord and was responsible for the overall allocation of resources, movements of fleets and ships, commissions and promotions. It met daily, including Saturdays and Sundays in wartime, dealt with thousands of detailed matters each month, had two Secretaries and about twenty-eight clerical staff. The Admiralty loomed large in the life of every individual sea officer of whatever rank. As Comptroller,

Captain Suckling was directly accountable to the First Lord of the Admiralty for the performance of the Navy Board, responsible for the design, building and maintenance of ships, and all the contracts and procurement involved; for the operation of the dockyards where the work was carried out; for the supervision of the Victualling Board and the Sick and Hurt Board: in total, for the delivery of a Navy in physical and operational terms (with the exception of powder and guns, the responsibility of the Ordnance Board) and for the appointment of all warrant officers. Thus Captain Suckling was an immensely powerful and influential person in the naval world and in a position to shape Nelson's next steps at will. This he immediately did and Nelson's days as a midshipman came to an end. On the very day *Dolphin* was paid off he was appointed Acting Fourth Lieutenant in the *Worcester* of 64-guns. He joined her to sail on convoy duty to Gibraltar. Convoy duty was infinitely boring but he was now a watch-keeping officer and Nelson says: 'In this ship I was at sea with Convoys till April 2nd 1777 and in very bad weather. But although my age might have been a sufficient cause for not entrusting me with the charge of a Watch, yet Captain Robinson used to say "he felt as easy when I was upon deck as any officer in the ship".'[18]

Captain Robinson's Diary shows him to have been fully aware of the significance of Captain Suckling's nephew and of Captain Suckling's interest as Member of Parliament for Portsmouth. He not only introduced Nelson to Sir James Douglas, Commander-in-Chief at Portsmouth, but also took him with him when they spent evenings onshore with 'my friend Mr P Varlo, Mayor of Portsmouth'.

Coming ashore after the *Worcester* was paid off in April 1771 Nelson went to London to encounter the first and very critical hurdle in his professional career, his examination for Lieutenant. Even though these examinations must have been variable in quality they were a remarkable phenomenon in the eighteenth century. Before individuals could participate in the command of ships they had to be judged competent to do so. The distinction between the competency-based approach of the Navy and that of the Army could not have been more startling; for many more years the Army would allow individuals to purchase the right to command. Nelson entered a room at the Navy Board on 9 April fully prepared and ready to be examined by three assembled captains, John Campbell, Abraham North and his Uncle Maurice Suckling. Nelson's neatly kept journals, his certificates from his commanding officers Lutwidge, Farmer, Pigott, Robinson, and Suckling himself, the breadth of his experience afloat, his ready and enthusiastic attitude, his quick appreciation of the point of questions and his confident and impressive personal chemistry, ensured that he was judged to have the character and ability to be a sea officer. His journals and certificates showed that he had fulfilled the requirements of his sea apprenticeship.

In a period so dominated by interest and patronage it would have been incredible for Campbell and North not to know that their examinee was the Comptroller's nephew. We can be certain that the words brother William put into his mouth for the benefit of his biographers Clarke and McArthur were imaginary. According to William, it was only at the end of the examination that Suckling introduced his nephew. The examining captains expressed their surprise at his not having informed them of this before. 'No', replied the Comptroller. 'I did not wish the younker to be favoured: I felt convinced that he would pass a good examination, and you see gentlemen I have not been disappointed.'[19] The next day, 10 April 1777, Nelson received his commission as Second Lieutenant of the 32-gun frigate *Lowestoffe*, Captain William Locker, then fitting out at Sheerness for Jamaica. Four days later he wrote jocularly and competitively to William: 'I passed my Degree as Master of Arts on the 9th instant [that is, passed the Lieutenant's examination], and received my Commission of the following day, for a fine frigate of 32-guns' adding, 'so now I am left in [the] world to shift for myself, which I hope I shall do, so as to bring credit to myself and friends'.[20] With the Comptroller of the Navy behind him, shifting for himself would be a good deal easier than for many others.

Thus, after six years' actual sea time, Nelson went up the side of one of His Majesty's ships as a commissioned officer. Passing for Lieutenant was one thing; getting an appointment another. Suckling saw to it that he got an immediate appointment. His choice was good, a smaller ship, a frigate, which brought the added possibility of prize money. Nelson's commission, like all commissions, was good only for the duration of the ship's commission. If further employment was not available he faced the possibility of unemployment, 'on the beach', on half pay. Now he would take charge of the ship during his watch and be responsible for his own division of men. He would command a group of guns in action, would eat with the other officers in the wardroom and receive the princely sum of eight guineas a month, roughly half the pay of the captain, the same pay as the master, more than twice that of the most important warrant officers, the carpenter, boatswain and gunner and about seven times more than the ordinary seaman – differentials that would not be greatly out of line with the situation in many walks of life today. Additionally, he could hope for prize money, today's 'incentive bonus', a share of the market value of captured prizes. In the case of major victories there were also expectations of rewards from chartered companies, the City of London and Parliament. His prospects and his Lieutenant's uniform were not all that he carried over the side of the *Lowestoffe*. Captain Suckling had presented his nephew with a six-page memorandum relating to the conduct and professional duties of a naval officer. One section only has survived. It deals with keeping a ship of war 'in very high order', and covers arrangements for sweeping and washing decks, washing clothes, keeping hammocks clean, serving out provisions, security arrangements, hoisting boats in and keeping the ship looking tidy when in harbour. There had also been a section dealing with officer-like conduct which, according to an officer who saw it, had begun on the lines of 'My dear Horatio, Pay every respect to your superior officers, as you shall wish to receive respect yourself.'[21]

A man who is fortunate in his early mentors is blessed beyond price. Nelson was indeed fortunate in Captain William Locker of the *Lowestoffe*. His settled face suggests a man of 'bottom', a man who has 'seen it all'. His portrait exudes an air of worldly wisdom, credibility and authority, the sort of man who was immediately a father figure. Nelson, with his instinctive knack for crossing hierarchic boundaries, quickly won him over and although a mere third lieutenant, soon became a friend of his captain and his family, for life. After only four months' experience of each other, Locker suddenly became unwell and wrote Nelson an encouraging letter from the shore. Both appreciated that death could come swiftly in the West Indian climate. Nelson opened his heart in return. 'My most worthy friend,' he wrote 'I am exceedingly obliged to you for the good opinion you entertain of me and will do my utmost that you may have no occasion to change it. . . . You mention the word "consolation" in your letter – I shall have a very great one, when I think I have served faithfully the best of friends.'[22]

Locker recovered, and Nelson was soon distinguishing himself in his eyes, as an action man. The war with the American colonies was now more than a year old and on 20 October 1777 between Cape Maize and Cape Nicola Mola they had cornered an American letter of marque (armed merchantman) then preying on British shipping. Nelson recalled:

> The first Lieutenant was ordered to board her, which he did not do, owing to the very heavy sea. On his return, the Captain said, 'Have I no Officer in the Ship who can board the Prize?' On which the Master ran to the gangway, to get into the boat: when I stopped him, saying, 'It is my turn now; and if I come back it is yours'. This little incident has often occurred to my mind; and I know it is my disposition, that difficulties and dangers do but increase my desire of attempting them.[23]

Soon he was off on his own again, exhibiting a thirst for independent command and his passion for pilotage. 'Even a Frigate was not sufficiently active for my mind, and I got into a schooner [The *Little Lucy*, named after Captain Locker's daughter], tender to the *Lowestoffe*. In this vessel I made myself a complete pilot for all the passages through the Islands [Keys] situated on the north side of the Hispaniola.'[24] Almost as soon as he was out of sight of the *Lowestoffe* he took a schooner bound from François to Nantucket at four o'clock in the morning, after a chase of eight hours, schooner against schooner.

On 27 May 1778 when the *Little Lucy* and *Lowestoffe* were sailing in company, 'they sighted two strange sail in the Windward Passage between Cuba and Hispaniola. These proved to be an American Schooner escorted by a French frigate the *Inconstant*, commanded by the Chevalier de Cuverville. Determined to board and search the schooner, Nelson stood ahead of Locker and got almost alongside the American, which was lying under the muzzles of the *Inconstant*'s guns. As he was about to board, musket fire crackled from the frigate's upper deck. Locker, watching his protégé's bold approach, at once made the signal for Nelson to haul away and come under his own stern.'[25] *Lowestoffe* herself stood on at action stations, to call the bluff of the French captain and force a search of the schooner. Locker and Nelson were chips off the same block.

Locker then engineered a rather neat piece of patronage. Another bout of sickness meant he would be invalided home. Being an old friend of Sir Peter Parker who had become Commander-in-Chief earlier in the year, he brought Nelson to his attention and so Nelson was transferred to be Third Lieutenant in Parker's flagship the *Bristol*. His quality must have become apparent to Parker during his squadron's offensive sweep past Cape François, the very waters in which Maurice Suckling had distinguished himself twenty years earlier. Nelson had joined the *Bristol* in July as Third Lieutenant. On 4 September he was promoted First Lieutenant.

Then came a shock. In October Nelson received news that his uncle had died in July. Nelson was now in a fever of fear and hope. On 24 October he wrote to his father, 'I am very uneasy as you may suppose having just received the Account of the death of my dear good Uncle whose loss falls very heavy on me. . . . Even in his illness he did not forget me but recommended me in the strongest manner to Sir Peter Parker who has promised me he will make me the first Captain. . . . I shall write again by the Pacquet for my mind is so uneasy at present that I cannot write. . . .'[26]

Two months later, in December 1778, Parker gave Nelson an independent command, promoting him 'Master and Commander' of the *Badger* brig, the natural stepping stone to Post Captain. But the arithmetic of promotion was daunting. There were at least five times as many lieutenants and commanders as there were post-captain appointments. Nelson knew that Sir Peter had taken a liking to him but the death of his uncle had for the first time introduced uncertainty into his advancement. However, Suckling's work had been well and truly done. No father could have done more. In declining health and burdened by an accelerating building programme and organizing shipping for North American troop convoys, 'presiding over the largest trans-Atlantic troop movement known before the twentieth century',[27] he had not forgotten his nephew.

Eight years later, in 1786, Nelson would write to his other Suckling uncle, William, Commissioner in the Excise Office, 'You have been my best friend, and I trust will continue as long so as I shall prove myself, by my actions, worthy of supplying that place in the service of my country, which my dear uncle left for me. I feel myself, to my country his heir; and it shall, I am bold to say, never want the lack of his counsel; I feel he gave it to me as a legacy, and had I been near him when he was removed he would have said, "My boy I leave you to my country: Serve her well, and She'll never desert, but will ultimately reward you".'[28]

That was how he was inclined to look at it when he was twenty-eight and a post captain and what he then said dovetailed perfectly with what he would say sixteen years later in 1802 about his *Dolphin* experience.

Maurice Suckling had provided a naval role for him. He had enabled his nephew's breadth of experience and rapid progression. Nelson himself had developed an inner vision of the character he would play. Would he now be able to live up to it, and would he have the luck and opportunities to succeed?

3

Five Frustrating Years

Life is not worth preserving without Happiness.

Nelson, January 1784

On 11 June 1779, three months before his twenty-first birthday, Nelson was 'made': he received his first appointment as a post captain. The *Hinchinbrook* was a 28-gun frigate, the smallest class of frigate in the Navy. Fully manned, she carried 195 officers and men. Below Nelson were his first and second lieutenants, a lieutenant of marines, four midshipmen, the master, who ranked 'with but after' the commissioned officers, and a further group of warrant officers, gunner, carpenter, boatswain, surgeon, purser, schoolmaster and chaplain.

Hinchinbrook's former captain had been killed in action and the Commander-in-Chief had power to fill the vacancy without permission from the Admiralty. Parker chose Nelson, who thus jumped the most critical hurdle in any sea officer's life. From now on his career would be governed by seniority, his progress to Admiral guaranteed, as long as he survived, and those ahead of him died, retired, or were killed in action. But this is a rather simplified view of his prospects; an ambitious and talented man could hope for more. The Admiralty was not blind to the disadvantages of seniority systems. The inevitable blockages caused by a system of 'dead men's shoes', could be massaged away. Admirals who were not well regarded could be transferred to the 'yellow squadron', placed permanently on half pay and not employed again. If the Admiralty wished to move captains of promise to flag rank, they could promote the captains ahead of them and choose to leave all or some of them on the unemployed list too. If there were individual blockers whose situations called for tender handling because of their political connections, retirement could be lubricated by peerages. Thus, for all its apparent deficiencies this was a system that could be manipulated by a

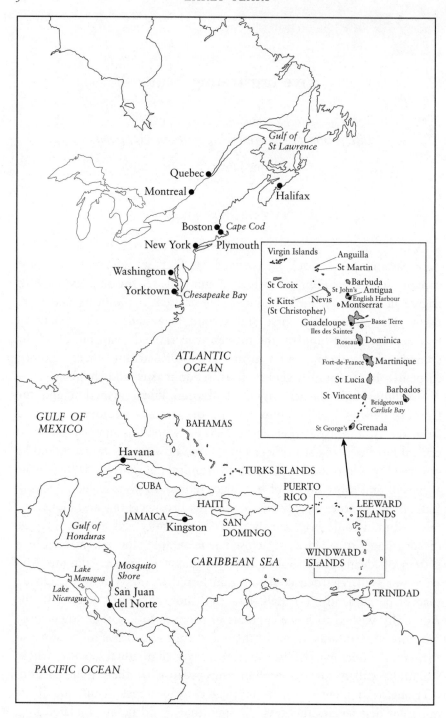

North America, the West Indies and Nicaragua

First Lord who wished to raise the quality of command. In the meantime Nelson could look forward to increases in pay, if and when he graduated to a ship-of-the-line and to a captain's three-eighths share in prize money. He could look for advancement to the temporary rank of Commodore, in command of a squadron of ships assembled for a particular mission, good preparation for the time when he would be promoted to flag rank as a rear-admiral. But, for the moment Nelson simply savoured the glory of becoming a post captain. The date of his promotion was engraved on his memory and would be used to give him the last word in differences with any captain or captains who had been made on a later date; he would be their senior officer.

As master and commander of the brig *Badger* he had been detached, in his own words, 'to protect the Mosquito shore, and the bay of Honduras from the depredations of the American privateers'. Returning to Port Royal and the joyous news of his elevation to Post Captain, he had to kick his heels till his new command returned to harbour. He was not one to miss the opportunity of bringing himself to the notice of the Governor. Forty-eight-year-old Major-General John Dalling had fought under Wolfe at Quebec, was also of East Anglian stock and by temperament and personality just the man to stimulate Nelson's latent love affair with military operations. When the French were tempted to intervene in the war in America and their fleet, at large in the Caribbean, threatened Jamaica, Nelson was given command of the battery covering Kingston harbour, until the French sailed north to support the colonists more directly.

In January 1780 Dalling conceived a grandiose scheme for a strategic intervention in Central America. The aim was to ascend the San Juan river, from its mouth at San Juan del Norte on the coast of Nicaragua, capture the fort of San Juan some thirty miles upriver, take Fort San Carlos at the nearby entrance to Lake Nicaragua, sail a hundred or so miles along its length, take Granada at its far end, press on via Lake Managua and another thirty miles to León, from where it would be only a dozen or so miles to the shores of the Pacific Ocean. At a stroke the Americas would be cut in two, the Spaniards in North America forced to protect their back, and an overland supply route would be created for British ships in the Pacific. Captain Polson of the 60th Foot would be in command of the first wave. Admiral Parker was not enthusiastic about the plan. His major priorities were defence of Jamaica and convoy

protection but he was a man of practical politics. After making sure the
Admiralty appreciated his reservations, he volunteered Nelson's frigate
as the escort he had been asked to provide. Parker seems to have felt a
need to soften the blow of detaching him on a mere escort service, for
he promised him the first 36-gun frigate to become available. Thus
Nelson's comment to Locker was rather casual and muted: 'He has
appointed me to go with an Expedition which is now on foot against the
city of Grenada, upon the Lake of Niguragua. How it will turn out God
knows, I do not expect to return before the middle of June.'[1]

Nelson had not been sent on a combined operation. His orders had
been to accompany the invasion force, cover the landing, and remain as
guard ship off San Juan del Norte. However, when the landing began,
and he witnessed an immediate chaos of colliding, capsizing and over-
loaded boats, he stepped impetuously out of his designated role. Having
a very low threshold for boredom, he offered men, boats and himself. As
Polson later told Dalling, 'Captain Nelson . . . came up with thirty four
seamen, one sergeant and twelve marines; I want words to express the
obligations I owe that gentleman.'[2]

For ten days the advance party of Polson's force blundered slowly and
painfully upriver. Bathed in sweat in the heat of the day, soaked by tropical downpours, wet and chilled by the dank dews and mists of the early
morning they made their way between the green walls of jungle, the line
of boats more and more attenuated by loading and unloading as they
struggled over shallows and rocks. Their constant fears were of poisonous snakes, crocodiles and piranha fish, unaware that the great majority of the men were already incubating the real peril they faced: malaria.
On the tenth day they came across an outpost of Fort San Juan on an
island in the river. They decided to steal past the island by night in light
craft, and in the morning sweep down on its upper end, attacking it from
behind, with flanking fire from the bank. Eager for action, Nelson volunteered to take his two boats to the upstream force. Notwithstanding
their naval skills, they spent most of the night desperately manhandling
their boats over the shoals. With the approach of dawn the cutter was
grounded and Nelson's pinnace was not yet past the outpost. A challenge
and a shot rang out. Without hesitation Nelson ordered his men to pull
for the island. Little more than eighty yards away, they presented the
defenders with a clear target. But, urged on by Nelson, the attackers
rowed furiously and straight at the fourteen defenders, giving them

limited opportunity to gather their wits, serve their four half-pounder swivel guns, fire and reload their muskets. By the time he leaped ashore with sword drawn at the head of his soldiers and sailors only two men had been hit. Unluckily and ingloriously he jumped into deep mud. Fortunately for Nelson, his headlong attack was supported by covering fire from the shore. The defenders turned tail and ran, only to surrender as soon as they encountered firing from ahead.

Soon they had their first view of Fort San Juan itself. It sat on a hill, wooden huts clustered below, cleared ground around it. Its keep was about fifty feet high; its ramparts approximately seventy-five yards by forty-five yards, their walls fourteen feet high and four feet thick with bastions mounting guns at each corner. Its garrison was about seventy-seven. Watering parties signalled its main vulnerability: the absence of a well. Nelson and Lieutenant Despard, the engineer officer advocated an immediate summons to surrender, followed if necessary by immediate attack. Polson viewed things differently. The performance of his people in boats had been less than impressive. Not surprisingly he opted to fight on terra firma. He had no scaling ladders but there were heights to the south and west of the fort from where his guns could batter the fort and then give covering fire for an attack. As yet he did not have sufficient ammunition for either.

Nelson deserved all the compliments subsequently paid to him by Polson. Even at this early stage in his career and out of his element, he could make his presence felt. But the quality of his judgement was immature and said more about his store of courage and dash than it did about his powers of analysis. It is perverse to take the view, which virtually all biographers since have done, that if only Polson had followed Nelson's advice he would have succeeded, in spite of his lack of scaling ladders and paucity of cannon shot.

Although his advice was rejected, Nelson's activity was undiminished: he created batteries and fired guns with great effect while ammunition lasted. According to Polson, 'there was scarcely a gun fired but was pointed by him or Lieutenant Despard'.[3] But in common with many of his men, Nelson had unwisely drunk from a jungle pool and had contracted a violent form of tropical sprue, of which severe dysentery was the first consequence. Luckily for him Lieutenant-Colonel Kemble had

arrived off the mouth of the river on the 20th with 500 fresh troops and
a letter from Admiral Parker, who, true to his word, was ordering Nelson
to return to take command of the 44-gun frigate *Janus*. Cuthbert Collingwood waited offshore, to take over command of the *Hinchinbrook*.
These were orders the sick Nelson could not ignore, and he made his
way downstream to the coast. Polson returned to his campaign and
captured St Juan but did not succeed in pushing on. The operation
dwindled away as sickness and death took their toll.

It says much for Nelson that Polson's opinion changed rapidly from
disparagement: 'a light haired boy . . . of whom I at first made little
account,'[4] to complete confidence: 'in two or three days he displayed
himself and afterwards he directed all the operations'.[5] Polson had no
hesitation in relying on Nelson to report back to Dalling: 'As Captain
Nelson goes to Jamaica he can inform you of every delay and point of
service, as well as I can do, for he knows my very thoughts.'[6] The commendation in his official dispatch was generous: 'I want words to express
the obligations I owe that gentleman. He was the first on every service
whether by night or by day.'[7] Nelson could have suppressed their difference of opinion over St Juan but chose not to hide the fact that he had
himself favoured an immediate attack on the fort. Dalling, impressed by
Nelson's account, wrote to Lord George Germain, the Colonial Secretary, 'humbly entreating that his Majesty would be graciously pleased to
manifest a satisfaction of Captain Nelson's conduct'.[8] To Nelson himself
he wrote, 'Thank you my friend for your kind congratulations [on the
capture of San Juan]. To you, without compliment, do I attribute in great
measure, the cause.'[9] Some twenty years later Nelson briefly touched
again on these events in his *Sketch of My Life*. What he wrote, while not
totally untruthful, was definitely romantic. 'Major Polson who commanded, will tell you of my exertions: how I quitted my Ship, carried
troops in boats an hundred miles up by river, which none but Spaniards
since the time of the buccaneers had ever ascended. It will then be told
how I boarded, if I may be allowed the expression, an out-post of the
Enemy, situated on an Island in the river; that I made batteries and afterwards fought them, and was a principal cause of our success.'[10]

Nelson was an object made for mothering, even by men. When he was
taken ashore in his cot, a sick and emaciated young man, a new friend,

Captain Cornwallis steered him away from the lethal hospital and placed him in the care of his namesake Cuba Cornwallis, a freed slave who nursed him with devotion and herbal remedies. Next it was Lady Parker's turn. Taking him into the Admiral's house she too lavished attention on him as if he were a son. But in spite of such loving care he was forced to make a formal request to return to England. According to three naval surgeons he was suffering from multiple infections of malaria, attended with 'Bilious Vomitings, Nervous Headaches, Visceral Obstructions and many other bodily Infirmities'.[11] They recommended 'an immediate change of climate as the only chance he has for recovery'. But suddenly, as on that journey home from India, the depression of illness lifted and Nelson's natural resilience returned. He scribbled a note to Hercules Ross, the merchant who had fitted out the Nicaraguan expedition and with whom he became firm friends, 'I will ride over tomorrow and have a chat. Now assured I return to England, hope revives within me. I shall recover and my dream of glory be fulfilled. Nelson will yet be an Admiral. It is the climate that has destroyed my health and crushed my spirit. Home and dear friends will restore me.'[12] Admiral Parker was less sanguine and wrote to the Admiralty, 'Captain Nelson is so emaciated and in so bad a state of health that I doubt whether he will live to get home. I wish much for his recovery. His abilities in his profession would be a loss to the Service.'[13]

On 3 September 1780 Nelson left Jamaica with Cornwallis in the *Lion*, probably hoping never to set eyes on the island again. So stormy and difficult was their passage that by the time they anchored at Spithead some three months later, Nelson was as much in need of rest and recuperation as when he set off. Again Cornwallis, and then Locker, took care of him until he was fit enough to travel to Bath to join his father. Some of his more disturbing symptoms lingered. At the end of January 1781 he was telling Locker, 'my inside is a new man,' and by the middle of the next month 'My health, thank God, is very near perfectly restored; and I have the perfect use of all my limbs, except my left arm, which I can hardly tell what is the matter with it. From the shoulder to my fingers' ends are as if half dead.'[14] Some three months later he appears to have had a relapse, for he wrote to brother William, 'I have entirely lost the use of my left arm, and very near of my left leg and thigh . . . When you write to my father do not mention my complaints, for I know it will make him very uneasy, and can do no good; and if you tell it to my sisters, desire

them not to mention it.'[15] Perhaps he was exaggerating a touch; his
incapacities had not been bad enough to prevent his visiting the
Admiralty the previous day for a meeting with the First Lord, now
Lord Sandwich.

We are tempted to imagine that the 'light haired boy' encountered by
Major Polson in 1780 was the young post captain of John Francis
Rigaud's celebrated portrait. The odds are that the officer Polson actually saw before him was more like the figure painted underneath and
recently revealed by X-ray, 'a young man in Lieutenant's uniform, with
a pigtail, a chubby face, and a hat under his arm'.[16] Rigaud had been
commissioned by Captain Locker and had begun the portrait in 1777
when Nelson was still a lieutenant. Now, in early 1781, four years after
the portrait had been started Nelson was enquiring after it. 'As to my
picture, it will not be the least like I am now, that is certain; but you may
tell Mr Rigaud to add beauty to it, and it will be much mended.'[17] Nelson
and Locker met at Rigaud's in May, by which time he was feeling fully
recovered. His uniform had been repainted to reflect his promotion, his
barge and coxwain added for the same reason. Fort San Juan was now
portrayed as a representative achievement. His hat was placed across his
head as he now habitually wore it, his features were thinned out to reflect
his drastic loss of weight. The young man now looking out at us is slender
and fresh faced, his clean jawline set to a pointed chin. Beneath the line
of his hat we encounter a pair of deeply set eyes whose level gaze is aware
and untroubled, calm, but penetrating, an effect simultaneously strengthened by a long and well shaped nose, and softened by his full mouth.
There is not in this face the slightest hint of threat, power or coarseness.
There is no tension or warlike posing, no real or simulated arrogance of
command. His hands rest lightly on the hilt of an upright sword, its exag-
gerated size serving to emphasize his boyishness, the whole enhanced by
a certain stylish carelessness in his dress. It might be hard to imagine this
boy commanding a warship of 200 men. Yet the portrait mirrors an easy
and instinctive habit of command. Combined with his monumental self-
belief, it was enabling him to create a climate in which others believed
that what Nelson thought, mattered, the beginnings of his charisma and
power to magnetize. The very fact that Captain Locker should commission this portrait of a newly appointed second lieutenant was in itself

indicative of the extraordinary impact Nelson had made on him. Locker, it is true, had a predilection for lining his walls with portraits of his young officers who had made good, and this lieutenant's uncle was, after all, Comptroller of the Navy. Even so, at the time this portrait was commissioned, Nelson had achieved nothing.

When Nelson had hobbled out of Lord Sandwich's office, past the porter's desk and through the great portico of the Admiralty into Whitehall it had been with a promise of employment at the first opportunity. Two months later he was appointed to command the *Albemarle*, another 28-gun frigate. Going down to Woolwich to hoist his commissioning pendant he took his eldest brother Maurice with him, and rhapsodized with evident pleasure over his ship's lines. Locker, a vastly more experienced seaman, had also seen her and had been less impressed, to the extent that her new captain was subsequently on the defensive, 'The *Albemarle*, although you abused her at Woolwich, has some good sailing in her.'[18] *Albemarle* was revealing Nelson's characteristically positive approach to life: 'I am perfectly satisfied with her . . . I have an exceedingly good Ship's company. Not a man or Officer in her I would wish to change.' He mentioned to brother William that 'my Quarter-deck is filled, much to my satisfaction, with very genteel young men and seamen'.[19] He was trying to gather round himself men who were not Drummonds or Henerys.

Much less of a pleasure was elder brother William's idea of going to sea as a chaplain. He tried to talk him out of it. Fifty pounds a year as a parson on shore 'is much more than equal to what you can get at sea'. He also knew brother William's habit of thought and behaviour, 'but in that I know you will please yourself'.[20] William continued to nag (Nelson often refers to William's scolding him) and Nelson continued to fend him off. The standing of naval chaplains was low and Nelson probably dreaded such a move, as much for his own sake as for William's. 'I hope you have lost all ideas of going to Sea, for the more I see of Chaplains of Men-of-War, the more I dread seeing my brother in such a disagreeable station of life.'[21] William's one aim in life was preferment and he eventually got a curacy ashore. Nelson responded, 'I wish I could congratulate you upon a Rectory instead of a Vicarage: it is rather awkward wishing the poor man dead, but we all rise by deaths. I got my rank by a shot killing a Post-Captain, and I most sincerely hope I shall, when I go, get out of [the] world the same way; then we go all in the line of our

Profession – a Parson praying, a Captain fighting.'[22] William, the least likeable member of the family, was pre-eminent in Nelson's life. He possessed all his younger brother's ambition but alas none of his charm or talent. The closeness of their schooldays continued, their schoolboy behaviour likewise. William, still seeking to be dominant, used Nelson ruthlessly as a means to his own ends. Nelson continued to keep on the right side of big brother by humouring him.

After a spell of North Sea convoy duty, Nelson was ordered to cross the North Atlantic with a convoy bound for Quebec. Full of foreboding for his health, fearing a cold, damp climate, but feeling it would be wrong and unwise to seek a change in his orders, he had to content himself with cherishing the thought, 'If I can get home in the autumn I hope I shall get a better Ship and a better station.'[23] It took ten days' flog in dirty weather to get as far as Cork. They did not arrive off Halifax until 27 May 1782.

Nelson was now in a war zone, but one which had rapidly cooled down. On land the opposing armies, British and colonists, roughly equal in numbers, were in stalemate. Even before Nelson had left Spithead the Commons had passed a resolution calling for the end of offensive operations. A new government under the Marquis of Rockingham was committed to ending the war and to redeploying part of its North American army to the Caribbean. Some nine months before Nelson arrived in Canada the final events of the war had taken place. September 1781 had seen the indecisive naval engagement at Chesapeake between Admiral Sir Samuel Hood and his eighteen sail-of-the-line and De Grasse with twenty-four sail-of-the-line. Before Nelson had even arrived in the North American theatre Admiral Hood had left it, to join up with Rodney in the West Indies, where their combined fleet of thirty six sail-of-the-line sought, found and defeated De Grasse at the battle of the Saints in April 1782. This battle ended the French threat to the West Indies and won control of the Atlantic for England.

The French were now restricted to harassing convoys and this accounted for the only brush Nelson had with them. Admiral de Vaudreuil had taken a squadron of the defeated French fleet north to Boston, to refit. On 14 August 1782, Nelson was cruising off Boston and Cape Cod when the fog suddenly lifted and he found himself within shot of three French sail-of-the-line and a frigate the *Iris*. Nelson's *Albemarle* was hopelessly outclassed. His only option was to fly before he was trapped.

It soon became evident that Locker's assessment of *Albemarle*'s sailing qualities had been more accurate than Nelson's. By the hour his position became increasingly desperate. He had on board an American, Nathaniel Carver, previously commandeered together with his schooner *Harmony* to act as pilot through the shoals of Boston bay. Carver's local knowledge and Nelson's fearless instinct for inshore work caused him to head for shallow waters, automatically deterring the heavier ships from following. Then, having lured the frigate out of sight of her companions, he backed his sails, put his helm over and presented a broadside to the pursuing frigate. A single ship action against the *Iris* was in principle an attractive proposition but less so at sunset in these waters. Nelson's manoeuvre and bold challenge obliged the French frigate captain to review his options. Rather than risk his ship in a night action in dangerous waters, he broke off the pursuit and steered a course to rejoin his companions. From being within an ace of capture and after spending the best part of a day at bay, Nelson had turned on his enemy, displaying a resilience and mental toughness that must have enormously impressed his officers and men.

What followed a few days later was likewise characteristic. He had been working with Carver for more than a month, and close personal and professional bonds had developed. Some three days after they had given the French ships the slip, his decency and fairmindedness led him to suggest to his officers that they release Carver and his vessel. And so Carver and *Harmony* sailed for home and family, sent on their way with warm expressions of gratitude and, more practically, a certificate of thanks, signed by Nelson, Carver's protection against any future restraint by British ships. Nelson reaped dividends in all directions. Carver knew that *Albemarle* had been without fresh food for some weeks. The next day while they were still off Plymouth, he reappeared, *Harmony* loaded with four sheep, poultry and sacks of fresh vegetables. In these episodes Nelson's behaviour had not only provided his officers with models for their own conduct but had reinforced his power of command and, since reputation spreads by word of mouth, had provided officers and men with vivid anecdotes to recount in other wardrooms and mess decks.

After six weeks' cruising they were obliged to make their way back to Quebec, 'knocked up with scurvey'.[24] Even more disappointing, after six weeks of unfettered freedom to cruise and capture, they had returned to port without a single prize to their credit, no money in the bank for either officers or men. But their return to port brought compensations. Nelson found himself in wonderful form. 'Health that greatest of blessings, is what I never truly enjoyed until I saw Fair Canada. The change it has wrought, I am convinced, is truly wonderful.'[25] The bracing climate, an active and agreeable social life and a lovely Canadian girl all had a part to play. And Nelson's talent for attracting the friendship of powerful and determined characters had led him to make friends with Alexander Davison, a thirty-two-year-old merchant and government contractor, destined to become his future confidant and agent. Quebec was a garrison town; it had an active social whirl and with Davison to smooth his entry he was soon in the thick of it. Nelson was by no means an unsocial animal, even though a certain consciousness of his rank may have caused some to refer to his rather stern aspect.

Not much is known about the girl with whom he fell precipitously in love, except that she was an acknowledged local belle, Mary Simpson, the daughter of Colonel Saunders Simpson, Provost Marshal of the garrison. In Nelson's eyes Simpson had his own claim to fame: like Dalling he had fought with Wolfe. The *Quebec Gazette* rhapsodized about Mary in enthusiastic but McGonagall-like verse, as Diana the Huntress:

> Sure you will listen to my call,
> Since beauty and Quebec's fair nymphs I sing.
> Henceforth Diana is Miss S—ps—n see,
> As noble and majestic is her air.[26]

Nelson set about pursuing Diana the Huntress and may have felt encouraged, in the way men are inclined to feel encouraged, by an open, vivacious and confident young woman. She was a girl of sixteen, she had the world at her feet, the power to pick and choose among the conventionally handsome men who crowded around her. She was not about to fall in love with the diminutive Nelson and his old-fashioned pigtail, however impressive his self-assurance, however intriguing the story of his travels and exploits. Nor could he make himself seem more exotic than he was by flaunting wealth and social position. Nelson's infatuation seemed doomed to come to a natural end when he was torn from this agreeable Quebec society by unexpected orders to escort a convoy to New York. The day after his departure he returned by boat from his anchorage down the St Lawrence, where *Albemarle* lay waiting for a favourable wind. By chance, he encountered Davison, who lived by the quayside. The purpose of his precipitate return, he explained, was to lay himself and his fortune at Mary Simpson's feet. Davison recalled some twenty-five years later that he had replied, 'Your utter ruin, situated as you are at present, must inevitably follow'. Nelson's riposte had been, 'Then let it follow, for I am resolved to do it.' Davison had followed up, 'And I also positively declare that you shall not', as he physically placed himself between Nelson and his intention. The upshot was that Davison prevailed and Nelson returned to his ship.[27] But on what grounds could Davison have concluded that it would be so ruinous for Nelson to propose to Mary? Why did he feel it so urgent to protect Nelson from himself? And why was the head-strong and bold Nelson so easily dissuaded? It is a mystery. Perhaps the clue lies in the absence of any further communication with Mary or mention of her name. Nelson had been rejected. He did not wish to take no for an answer. Davison's advice had been, 'Forget her', and Nelson did.

Nelson sailed off to New York, his search for love unrequited. Peace was imminent, the convoy he was escorting to New York a sign that the evacuation of British troops was beginning. Nelson was not slow to con-sider his career options: to stay with Rear-Admiral the Honourable Robert Digby, Commander-in-Chief of the North American station to whom he was now formally subordinate, or to seek to attach himself to Admiral Hood, one of the victors of the Saints. It was a choice between North Atlantic convoy protection or the possibility of action in the West Indies and maybe command of a ship-of-the-line. A letter home suggests that his mind was made up before he left the St Lawrence, 'Very likely we shall go to the grand theatre of actions, the West Indies.'[28] Fortune favours the prepared mind. As luck would have it, Hood was present when Nelson called on Admiral Digby, who greeted Nelson kindly and with words that would have had great appeal for nine out of ten naval officers, 'You are come on a fine station for making prize money.' Nelson is supposed to have replied, 'Yes sir, but the West Indies is the station for honour.'[29] This does not ring true. Nelson was not the sort of man to offer gratuitous insults to a commander-in-chief. They appear to have been supplied to Clarke and McArthur by Lieutenant Bromwich who had been serving with Nelson in *Albemarle* at the time. As so often, we are probably hearing an echo of how Nelson himself dramatized the encounter for the benefit of others. However, the music of Nelson's response was not lost on Hood, one of the few naval officers of his time who actively despised the prize money mentality. Besides being the nephew of Hood's old friend Captain Suckling, Nelson had by luck or calculation demonstrated himself to be a man after Hood's own heart. From that moment he was noticed and marked out for Hood's patronage.

An invitation to Hood's flagship, the *Barfleur*, quickly followed and as Nelson's gig arrived alongside, the midshipman on watch was seventeen-year-old Prince William Henry, the third son of King George III. His later recollection, also to Clarke and McArthur, of how Nelson appeared to him brings the Rigaud portrait to life and also tells us more about the kind of person Mary Simpson had encountered:

> I was then a Midshipman on board the *Barfleur*, lying in the Narrows off Staten Island, and had the watch on deck, when Captain Nelson of the *Albemarle*, came in his barge alongside, who appeared to be the meerest boy of a captain I ever beheld; and his dress was worthy of attention. He had on a full laced uniform; his lank unpowdered hair was tied in a stiff Hessian tail, of an extra-ordinary length; the old fashioned flaps of his waistcoat added to the general quaintness of his figure, and produced an appearance which particularly attracted my notice; for I had never seen anything like it before, nor could I imagine who he was, nor what he came about. My doubts were however, removed when Lord Hood intro-duced me to him. There was something irresistibly pleasing in his address and conversation; and an enthusiasm when speaking on pro-fessional subjects, that showed he was no common being.[30]

Hood had taken an immediate liking to Nelson, who told Locker, 'I am a candidate with Lord Hood for a Line of Battle Ship: he has hon-oured me highly by a letter, for wishing to go off this Station to a Station of Service, and has promised me his friendship. Prince William is with him . . . money is the great object here, nothing else is attended too.'[31] Nelson had found an exemplar who mirrored his own priorities; what-ever his future yearning for money, he would always remain the least mercenary of sea officers. Hood, judging from Prince William's recollec-tions, also thought highly of Nelson's intense professionalism.

The fleet arrived in Jamaica on 4 February 1783. Nelson very soon had a minor triumph, capturing a ship, belonging to Vaudreuil's squadron which had also sailed from Boston to the West Indies. It was packed with masts, for which the British fleet had a crying need. There was news of the French fleet. Hood sent Nelson to look for it. He was on the crest of the wave: 'My situation in Lord Hood's Fleet must be in the highest degree flattering to any young man. He treats me as if I was his son, and will, I am convinced, give me any thing I can ask of him . . . nor is my situation with Prince William less flattering. Lord Hood was so kind as to tell him (indeed I cannot make use of expressions strong enough to describe what I felt), that if he wished to ask questions relative to Naval Tactics, I could give him as much information as any Officer in the Fleet.' Even allowing for some exaggeration on Nelson's part and the inevitable honeymoon period of a new relationship, Nelson's capacity to make an impact is very evident, as were the first signs of a lifelong tendency to see royalty through rose-tinted spectacles. 'He [Prince William] will be, I am certain, an ornament to our Service. He is a seaman, which you could hardly suppose. Every other qualification you may expect from him. But he will be a disciplinarian, and a strong one.'[32] These latter were unhappily prophetic words.

The next of his West Indian exploits involved a place, unmentioned in *Sketch of My Life*, Turk's Island, and his unsuccessful attempt to recapture it. Those who are so certain he would have succeeded at Fort San Juan should consider what happened here. Nelson's report to Admiral Hood tells how he had learned from the *Resistance* that the French had taken the Turk's Island with 150 regulars and three vessels of war. 'I determined to look what situation the French were in, and if possible retake it. The *Tartar* who joined company a few hours afterwards, I ordered to put herself under my command, which with the *Resistance* and *La Coquette*, a French Ship of War, prize to the *Resistance*, made a tolerable outward show.' He goes on, 'I sent Captain Dixon on shore with a flag of truce to demand a surrender of the Islands. With much confidence of his superior situation, the Commander of the French troops sent an answer that he should defend himself. On Saturday morning at daylight, one hundred and sixty seven Seamen and Marines were landed from the Ships under the command of Captain Charles Dixon, who very much obliged me by offering to command them.' Nelson then sent two brigs, which had just joined him, the *Drake* and the *Admiral Barrington*, 'to go off the Town and batter it'. He continues,

> Upon their getting within shot, I was very much surprised to see a battery of three guns open upon them. . . . The Master of the *Drake* is wounded, and the Boatswain and six men aboard the *Admiral Barrington*. Captain Dixon at this time observed that the guns were fought by Seamen, and that the Troops were waiting to receive him with several field pieces; and that they had a post upon the side of the hill with two pieces of cannon. With such a force, and their strong situation, I did not think anything farther could be attempted.'[33]

James Trevenen, First Lieutenant of the *Resistance* and at the time in command of the captured French 28-gun *La Coquette*, saw things differently. He subsequently sent his mother a scathing report of Nelson's effort: 'But the ridiculous expedition ag[st] Turk's Island, undertaken by a young man merely from the hope of seeing his name in the papers, ill depicted at first, carried on without a plan afterwards, attempted to be carried into execution rashly, because without intelligence, and hastily abandoned at last for the same reason that it ought not to have been undertaken at all, spoilt all.'[34] The tenor of the gossip in other wardrooms during the passage back to Jamaica most likely concentrated on their ill luck at encountering Nelson, and his unsuccessful management of the operation. Of course, when Trevenen wrote these sour comments he was greatly exercised by the fact that having been delayed by Nelson, the sale of his ship's three prizes had been caught by the announcement of peace. They had therefore to be sold to local merchants for a much-reduced sum, Trevenen estimating that his own share had been reduced from £500 to £100. 'This peace is a sad blow to us who were in a fair way of making our fortunes.' While this goes a considerable way towards explaining Trevenen's low opinion of Nelson, whose prime motivation was to attack the enemy, not to make money, there was here further evidence that his early leadership did not include much by way of risk analysis. Aggression, courage and improvisation were being confirmed. But to continue to neglect risk assessment would mean an undue reliance on luck.

Turk's Island underlined Nelson's urge for fighting. Here, in his early years, long before French Revolutionary excesses or the Napoleonic dictatorship, first in the Nicaraguan jungle, then with the French frigate in the shallows off Boston and now at Turk's Island he was showing himself to be proactively aggressive. Having chosen to be a hero he was demonstrating himself psychologically well fitted to be one.

However, there was no immediate future for heroes or moneymakers. On 20 January 1783 Britain, France and Spain made peace at Versailles. On 14 May *Albemarle* parted from the fleet, reaching Spithead on 25 June 1783. Nelson wrote immediately to Locker, still the most important person in his life, 'After all my tossing about into various climates, here at last am I arrived safe and sound.'[35]

Once ashore, he was further encouraged when Hood introduced him to the King at a levee and very flattered by the interest the King showed in his acquaintance with his sailor son. Nelson had gained an entrée. He was also an avid networker, and among the letters he wrote was one to his rich Jamaican friend Hercules Ross, possessor of a London house and currently living near Edinburgh. He introduces the name of a friend, Captain Pringle, who might live near to him. He talks about 'Hanbury, as indefatigable in business as ever, Shaw . . . he has I fancy done pretty well . . . Wallcoff, who was Agent of Transports, I supped with him last night', shares information about Sir Peter and Lady Parker and their new estate in Essex, 'thanks to Jamaica for the money'. He is conscious of 'the innumerable favours I have received from you, be assured I shall never forget; and any opportunity that may offer of making some small return, you may always command'. He goes on rather self-consciously and pointedly, 'I have closed the war without a fortune: but I trust, and, from the attention that has been paid to me, believe that there is not a speck in my character. True honour, I hope, predominates in my mind far above riches.'[36]

There was a counterpoint to his self-absorption in activity on behalf of his officers and men. A captain had to be active on behalf of his officers if he wished to develop a following of men who would look to him for patronage and would in return put their talents at his disposal. He wrote to Lord Keppel, the new First Lord of the Admiralty in support of Bromwich, his acting second lieutenant in *Albemarle* who had passed his examination for Lieutenant but was not confirmed because of an oversight in the recording of his sea time in a previous commission. Although unsuccessful he did not abandon Bromwich, who would go with him in his next ship as a master's mate. And it was not just his officers he was interested in. 'My time, ever since I arrived in Town, has been taken up in attempting to get the wages due to my good fellows, for various ships they have served in the war. The disgust of the Seamen to the Navy is all owing to the infernal plan of turning them over from Ship to Ship, so that men cannot be attached to their Officers, or the Officers care two pence about them.' Because of peace hundreds of seamen were faced with the threat of unemployment but Nelson could still feel justifiably flattered when his 'whole Ship's company offered, if I could get a ship, to enter for her immediately'.[37]

After a month and a half of life with his father at the Rectory, he teamed up with a friend and former messmate, Captain Macnamara, to visit France. His stay lasted for less than three months and was remarkable for how little he accomplished. He neither persevered with learning French, nor engaged in naval intelligence. But he did fall in love again.

Macnamara had advised Nelson that it would be best to stay in St-Omer where there were the English-speaking French necessary for Englishmen wishing to learn French, but Nelson had formed his own view which led them on a fruitless journey sixty miles south to Montreuil, then further south to Abbeville, having in the end to return to St-Omer, a detour of 150 miles. Nelson was quite philosophical, 'I must do Captain Mac the justice to say it was all my doings, and in great measure against his advice; but experience bought is the best; and all mine I have paid pretty dearly for.'[38] Nelson was a chauvinist at heart and although he had praise for the meticulousness of the French agricultural landscape still evident today, little else pleased him. His reaction to French inns, 'O what a transition from happy England',[39] sums up his reaction to difference and his lack of command of the language. Back in St-Omer Nelson was surprised 'that instead of a dirty, nasty Town, which I had always heard it represented, to find a large City, well paved, good streets and well lighted'. There they settled down *chez* Madame La Mourie, his desire to learn French enhanced by the two La Mourie daughters, 'very agreeable young ladies ... who honour us with their company pretty often: one always makes our breakfast, and the other our tea, and play a game of cards in an evening'.[40] Unfortunately the ladies, although easy on the eye, spoke no English and as Nelson put it to Locker, 'The French goes on but slowly; but patience, of which you know I have not much, and perseverance, will, I hope, make me master of it.'[41] That turned out to be a forlorn hope for there were other sail on the horizon in the form of rival attractions in the British expatriate community.

A little more than a week after their arrival Nelson was writing to William, 'Today I dine with an English clergyman, a Mr Andrews, who has two very beautiful young ladies, daughters. I must take care of my heart I assure you.' A fortnight later he made the same observation to Locker. His infatuation with Miss Elizabeth Andrews proceeded like wildfire. Thoughts of a proposal followed and by early December he was confiding in brother William, 'My heart is quite secured against the French beauties: I almost wish I could say as much for an English young lady, the daughter of a clergyman with whom I am just going to dine, and spend the day. She has such accomplishments, that had I a million of money, I am sure I should at this moment make her an offer of them; my income at present is by far too small to think of marriage, and she has no fortune.'[42] Given his train of thought, it was not surprising that his next sentence was an enquiry after the fortunes of their Lottery tickets. By January his feelings for Elizabeth Andrews had reached a climax. As a young officer on half pay he had nothing to offer. He could think of only one way forward: appeal to his surviving Suckling uncle. He did not spare the moral blackmail.

There arrives in general a time in a man's life (who has friends), that either they place him in life in a situation that makes his application for anything farther totally unnecessary, or give him help in a pecuniary way, if they can afford, and he deserves it. The critical moment in my life has now arrived, that either I am to be happy or miserable: – it depends solely on you: . . . There is a lady I have seen of a good family and connexions, but with a small fortune, – 1,000*l*. I understand. The whole of my income does not exceed 130*l*. per annum. Now I must come to the point: – will you, if I should marry, allow me yearly 100*l*. until my income is increased to that sum, either by employment or any other way? A very few years I hope will turn something up, if my friends will but exert themselves. If you will not give me the above sum, will you exert yourself with either Lord North or Mr Jenkinson, to get me a Guard-ship, or some employment in a Public Office where the attendance of the principal is not necessary, and of which they must have such numbers

to dispose of. . . . You must excuse the freedom with which this letter
is dictated; not to have been plain and explicit in my distress had
been cruel to myself. If nothing can be done for me, I know what I
have to trust to. Life is not worth preserving without happiness; and
I care not where I may linger out a miserable existence. I am prepared to hear your refusal, and have fixed my resolution if that
should happen; but in every situation, I shall be a well wisher to you
and your family, and pray they or you may never know the pangs
which at this instant tear my heart.[43]

In the event he did not need his uncle's help. He was soon warning
brother William of a proposed visit to London and hinting at a change
of plan: 'My stay in England will be but very short, without the First
Lord in Admiralty thinks proper to employ me. I shall offer my services.'[44] He was coy with Locker, 'Some little matters in my Accounts
obliged me to come over',[45] and indeed it would have been entirely appropriate for him to tell his uncle that the sought-for subsidy was no longer
required. Then the fact of the collapse of his hopes came out in a letter
to William, 'In about a week or fortnight I think of returning to the
Continent, till autumn, when I shall bring a horse, and stay the winter
at Burnham. I return to many charming women, but no charming woman
will return with me.'[46] Nelson never returned to France, never learned
French, and Elizabeth Andrews like Mary Simpson was forgotten. This
second precipitate infatuation and headlong rush towards matrimony
shows the same tendency, sudden decision, lack of consideration of his
intended as a real person or of their mutual compatibility. Emotionally
immature, he decides he needs a wife and anybody who reasonably fits
the bill is seen through the rosiest of spectacles. Whether or not his
intended is attracted to him is a question that never enters his mind, until
he unexpectedly encounters her refusal. Although Nelson was very susceptible to women, at this stage in his life they seem not to have been
susceptible to him.

Now, for the first time in his life, Nelson became involved in politics.
The period of political chaos and turmoil that had succeeded the loss
of the American colonies was reaching its climax in a struggle between
the Foxite Whigs and the King. Although Nelson noticed in a letter to
William of 3 January 1784 that there had been a change in the administration, he was focusing narrowly on what that change might mean for

William's prospects for patronage rather than on the wider political scene, where George III had completely outmanoeuvred the Fox–North coalition over their bill for reforming the East India Company. This would have transferred a vast area of patronage into the hands of the administration, which for many was synonymous with Fox. The Commons, packed with Fox's supporters, had passed the Bill but it was voted down in the Lords when the King let it be known that he would regard any peer who voted for it as his enemy. He had then dismissed Fox and North, appointing William Pitt as First Lord of the Treasury. Pitt had kept his hands clean of political manoeuvring, had presented himself as a man above faction and with public opinion swinging behind himself and the King, was attempting to take the House of Commons with him. He had brought forward his own India Bill (without alteration in patronage). The point with which Nelson was becoming engaged was whether Pitt would win in the Commons or, if not, seize the moment, seek a dissolution and fight an election. The atmosphere in London was feverish and contagious. On the eve of the vote on the India Bill Nelson was caught up in the excitement, telling Locker, 'Captain Phipps, who was here just now, says, he believes Mr Pitt will have a majority, but he speaks probably as he wishes, not as he thinks.' He went on,

I shall not conclude my letter till late, as perhaps I may hear how matters are likely to go in the House of Commons. Lord Hood's friends [he would be standing in the Westminster Constituency as a Tory or Pitt aligned candidate alongside Fox and Wray for two seats] are canvassing, although not openly, for his interest in case of a dissolution; and it is confidently asserted that Fox will never get Westminster again. I dined on Wednesday with his Lordship, who expressed the greatest friendship for me, that his house was always open to me, and that the oftener I came the happier it would make him.

There may have been talk with Hood of Nelson's own possible candidature. However, whatever feverish speculation was being generated in this heady atmosphere, Nelson told Locker in the same breath of his real plans: 'on Tuesday I am going to Bath for a few days to see my Father, before I return to the Continent, or go to Sea. I have paid my visit to Lord Howe [who had replaced Lord Keppel as First Lord of the

Admiralty] who asked me if I wished to be employed, which I told him I did, therefore it is likely he will give me a ship.'[47]

By the end of the month Nelson's flirtation with the political life came to an end. He wrote to brother William, 'Mr Pitt depend upon it, will stand against all opposition: an honest man must always in time get the better of a villain: but I have done with politics; let who will get in, I shall be left out.'[48] Nelson had been caught up in the excitement of the moment. There are no signs that he had expended energy in attempting to forward his candidature, unlike his friend Captain Kingsmill who had actively sought a seat and was eventually elected member for Tregony. Nevertheless these events serve to position Nelson in the politics of the period, so well described by Amanda Foreman as an 'incohate system of temporary factions'.[49] Although Nelson demonstrated a humane concern for the plight of farm workers in Norfolk and constantly demonstrated in his life as a sea officer that he knew instinctively how to get the best out of his men, he did not resonate to the idea of Fox as the 'man of the people'. Nor did he resonate to the sentiments of lawyer John Dunning, who had expressed the feelings of those who mistrusted the powers of the Crown and were alive to civil liberties, when he declared in 1780, 'The influence of the Crown has increased, is increasing and ought to be diminished.' He showed instead a total mistrust of radical ideas on parliamentary reform. He was innately conservative, a King's man, standing for Church and Country, order and hierarchy, and against faction. He had no political passions, no ambition for political place. The limit of his ambition was to be a hero serving his King and Country.

4

Trying To Get Noticed

I think I have found a woman who will make me happy.

Nelson, March 1786

On 18 March 1784 Nelson was appointed to command the *Boreas*, his third 28-gun frigate. He must have begun to wonder how, in a time of peace, he could ever be promoted to command a ship-of-the-line. He hoped they might be bound for the East India station but their destination was to be in exactly the opposite direction: the West Indies.

It is often said that Nelson showed bouts of irritation only after his head wound at the Nile, but it was a decidedly grumpy officer who went to sea in *Boreas*. To be fair, he was suffering from intermittent ague and fever but he grumbled about his supernumerary cargo in the shape of Lady Hughes, wife of his new Commander-in-Chief, and her daughter Rosy; the inconvenience and expense they entailed. He grumbled that his ship was full of midshipmen, that the Admiralty had not confirmed Bromwich as a lieutenant so he had to be rated Master's mate. He was testy with William when he asked to accompany him. He gave a stuffy rejoinder to William's sniffing-around enquiry, 'by what interest did you get a ship?' 'Having served with credit was my recommendation to Lord Howe, First Lord of the Admiralty Anything in reason that I can ask I am sure of obtaining from his justice.'[1] More likely it was Hood's patronage, which Nelson for some reason did not mention.

His next letter to Locker was a tale of woe, 'The day after I left you, we sailed at daylight, just after high water. The d——d Pilot – it makes me swear to think of it – ran the Ship aground, where she lay with so little water that the people could walk round her till next high water.' A battle with the master of a Dutch East Indiaman, who had Englishmen on board whom Nelson naturally wished to press, had earned him a complaint to the Admiralty which fortunately had supported him. Then he had to admit to a decidedly unheroic episode, involving a female companion of undisclosed character and classification:

> I was riding a blackguard horse that ran away with me at Common, carried me round all the Works into Portsmouth, by the London gates, through the Town out at the gate that leads to Common, where there was a waggon in the road, – which is so very narrow, that a horse could barely pass. To save my legs, and perhaps my life, I was obliged to throw myself from the horse, which I did with great agility: but unluckily upon hard stones, which has hurt my back and my leg, but done no other mischief. It was a thousand to one I had not been killed. To crown all a young girl was riding with me; her horse ran away with mine; but most fortunately a gallant young man seized her horse's bridle a moment before I dismounted, and saved her from the destruction she could not have avoided.[2]

And William was going with him after all. As usual he had pushed and pushed and Nelson, as usual, gave way: 'Bring your canonicals and sermons.' In a wicked aside he promised him 'a fine talkative Lady for you to converse with'.[3]

Swept down to Madeira by a kind sea and favourable wind, Nelson mellowed somewhat, his mind occupied by the business of his ship rather than Elizabeth Andrews. They reached Madeira on 1 June and stayed for a week, long enough to collect a quarter-cask of wine from a friend of Locker's but Nelson, irritated by the British Consul's pretensions, was quickly bored and anxious to push on. Lady Hughes 'wishes to see her husband: and I shall not be sorry to part with them, although they are very pleasant good people: but they are an incredible expence'. Scott of the *Resource* had been to dine, 'a very genteel young man he is: I wish he had been with me'.[4] By now Nelson's gang of young midshipmen, his Children, as he called them, were responding to his talent for empathy. In 1806 Lady Hughes painted for George Matcham's benefit a vivid picture of

> his attention to the young gentlemen who had the happiness of being on his Quarter-Deck . . . the timid he never rebuked, but always wished to show them he desired nothing of them that he would not do instantly himself: and I have known him say – 'Well, Sir, I am going to race to the mast-head, and I beg I may meet you there . . .

but when he met in the top, instantly began speaking in the most cheerful manner, and saying how much a person was to be pitied that could fancy there was any danger, or even anything disagreeable in the attempt. After this excellent example, I have seen the timid youth lead another and rehearse his captain's words . . . he went every day into the School Room, and saw them do their nautical business and at twelve o'clock he was the first upon deck with his quadrant. No one could there be behind hand in their business when their Captain set them so good an example. . . . the day we landed at Barbadoes. We are to dine at the Governor's. Our dear Captain said, 'You must permit me, Lady Hughes, to carry one of my Aid-de-camps with me.' And when he presented him to the Governor, he said, 'Your Excellency must excuse me for bringing one of my Midshipmen, as I make it a rule to introduce them to all the good company I can, as they have few to look up to besides myself during the time they are at Sea.' The kindness and attention made the young people adore him; and even his wishes could they have been known, would have been instantly complied with.[5]

Lady Hughes, for all she might have been a talkative and expensive passenger, had a shrewd sense of what leadership of the young has always been about.

They arrived at Barbados, the southern base of the Leeward Islands squadron on 26 June 1784. A Union Jack flying from the topgallant masthead signalled to Sir Richard that his wife was on board, a 15-gun salute reverberated across the bay and within an hour of *Boreas* coming to anchor, the Admiral's barge was alongside: over the side he came, to be reunited with his wife and daughter, and to welcome his subordinate Nelson. (Both might have recalled their difference five years earlier at the Downs over a replacement anchor Nelson was rather highhandedly demanding and Hughes rather thoughtlessly witholding). Events would show that they were men of a distinctly different calibre. Rear-Admiral Sir Richard Hughes was Commander-in-Chief Leeward Islands, his command stretching more than 300 miles to its northern base in Antigua. Nelson, senior captain on the station, was effectively second-in-command and had under him the sloop *Rattler* whose Master and Commander, Wilfred Collingwood, was the brother of his friend Cuthbert Collingwood, currently on the same station as captain of the *Mediator*. Nelson's orders were to guard the northern group of islands, Montserrat, Nevis,

St Christopher and the Virgin Islands, to protect the commerce of Great
Britain and hinder illicit trade, hardly objectives to make his pulse race.
Here there was no enemy to fight, no beckoning glory, no hope of substantial prizes. Instead there was the prospect of boredom at sea, disease
on shore and, depending on inclination, the consolations afforded by
women, drink and social climbing. His mood of anger and frustration
continued. He had gone back to sea on the rebound from Elizabeth
Andrews. His frame of mind was not helped by being cooped up ashore
during the hurricane season (three months of the West Indies had been
enough for brother William, who left for England in the *Fury* sloop on
30 September on account of fears for his health). One of his midshipmen, George Andrews, younger brother of Elizabeth Andrews, whom he
had magnanimously accepted on board, had been seriously injured in a
duel with another midshipman and looked likely to die. To make matters
worse he was being continually aroused by the tender charms of a thirty-
two-year-old married woman, Mary Moutray. She and her husband, now
installed as resident Naval Commissioner in Antigua, had been passengers on their outward journey with his friend Cuthbert Collingwood.
Thrown much together in English Harbour during the hurricane season,
she captured his heart, 'Were it not for Mrs Moutray, who is very, very
good to me, I should almost hang myself at this infernal hole.'[6]

The hurricane season over and his ship at last offshore, he needed only
targets for his pent-up anger to express itself. A few minor deviants had
the misfortune to cross his bows. He fired on the Barbados fort for not
saluting the departure of a French naval vessel. A few weeks later he fired
on an American schooner for not hoisting her colours. But a bigger issue
was soon on the boil, destined to put such minor infringements of naval
protocol in the shade and himself on a collision course with the Admiral
and with many powerful people in the islands.

Americans were continuing to trade illicitly in the West Indies, as though
America had not gained her independence and thereby become a foreign
country. The islanders were happy for this trade to continue. Indeed from
their point of view it was integral to their prosperity. But under the
provisions of the Navigation Act it was clearly illegal; all trade with
British colonies had to be carried out in British-owned ships, manned
substantially by British seamen. Hughes was inclined to turn a blind eye

but Nelson saw things differently and asked to see him. Caught out by his punctilious little captain, Hughes's only defence was to play the innocent and indulge himself in a little play-acting. He had received no orders, nor had he been sent any Act of Parliament. Nelson persisted, 'I told him it was very odd as every Captain of a Man-of-War was furnished with the Statutes of the Admiralty, in which was the Navigation Act, which Act was directed to Admirals, Captains &c.' Hughes persisted that he had never seen the book. Nelson produced it, read from it and had his Admiral in a corner. It was with heavy irony that Nelson subsequently recounted to Locker that Hughes 'seemed convinced that Men-of-War were sent abroad for some other purpose than to be made show of . . . then gave Orders to all the Squadron to see the Navigation Act carried into execution'.[7]

Nelson had underestimated Hughes's capacity to bend under pressure, and on this occasion to wash his hands of his responsibility. In December he was dismayed to receive an order that he should indeed detain all foreign ships but, 'if the Governor or his Representative should give leave for admitting such vessels, strictly charging me [Nelson] not to hinder them or interfere in their subsequent proceedings'. From the beginning Nelson had been disparaging about his Admiral: 'he bows and scrapes too much for me; his wife has an eternal clack, so that I go near them as little as possible'.[8] 'The Admiral and all about him are great ninnies.'[9] 'The longer I am upon this station the worse I like it. Our Commander has not that opinion of his own sense that he ought to have. He is led by the advice of the islanders to admit the Yankees to a Trade; at least to wink at it. I for one am determined not to suffer the Yankees to come where my ship is.'[10]

They were two very different personalities. The Admiral was inclined to make himself popular, enjoy society, and make advances to local ladies whenever he could escape from Lady Hughes. Nelson, angry, frustrated, too hair-shirted to take a relaxed view of his responsibilities, having too much mental and physical energy to take the easy way out, reached for his Navigation Act, read it again from cover to cover and with cold ruthlessness wrote to his Commander-in-Chief, 'No Governor will I am sure, do such an illegal act . . . at a time when Great Britain is using every endeavour to suppress illicit Trade at Home, it is not wished that the Ships upon this Station should be singular, by being the only spectators of the illegal Trade, which I know is carried on at these Islands.' He did not hesitate to call up his support, 'General Shirley [Governor of the Leeward Islands] told me and Captain Collingwood how much he approved of the methods that were carrying on for suppressing the illegal Trade with America.' He referred to a letter from Lord Sydney Secretary of State saying the Administration, 'were determined that American ships and Vessels should not have any intercourse with our West India Islands.' Nelson then took the awful step and refused point blank to obey Hughes's order. 'Whilst I have the honour to command an English Man-of War, I never shall allow myself to be subservient to the will of any Governor, nor co-operate with him in doing illegal acts. Presidents of Council I feel myself superior to. They shall make proper application to me, for whatever they may want to come by water.' Hughes had said that his order had been based on the Opinion of the King's Attorney-General. To this Nelson gave short shrift: 'How the King's Attorney-General conceives he has a right to give an illegal Opinion, which I assert the above is, he must answer for. I know the Navigation Laws.'[11]

Hughes's hand must have trembled as he put the letter down. He was appalled both by its tone and by Nelson's effrontery in writing it. His first instinct must have been to supersede, court-martial and break this recalcitrant captain. But he quickly realized that court martial was not an option. He also realized where his cosy approach to life had led him and from then on 'stood neuter', as Nelson bore alone the brunt of the islanders' backlash. For Nelson, the point of principle mattered. He was determined to keep on punishing the rebel Americans by invoking the letter of the law. It was not for him to stop and ask what might be best for England in the longer term, or what the value of allowing wounds to heal by a degree of *rapprochement* might be. Politicians in London were as keen on his rigid attitude as he was himself. In this case his aggressively black and white legalistic judgement was very appropriate. It was a quality that would be less appropriate in handling the Neapolitan counter-revolution in fifteen years' time.

Nelson became a hate figure for powerful forces in the islands. As he confided in Locker, 'After what I have said you will believe I am not very popular with the people.' Captain Nelson had made himself *persona non grata*. 'They have never visited me and I have not had a foot in any house since I have been on the station, and all for doing my duty by being true to the interests of Great Britain.' Ever the chauvinist, he had a low opinion of the locals: 'The residents of these Islands are American by connexion and by interest and are inimical to Great Britain. They are as great rebels as ever were in America, had they the power to show it.'[12]

None of this deterred him. Having by now given plenty of notice of his intentions, he in *Boreas* and Wilfred Collingwood in *Rattler* set about systematically challenging and boarding vessels. After ferreting out their duplicate American papers, he would impound any trading vessel he could establish to be of American origin, even though they might be trading under British or Spanish colours.

Soon the islands were in an even greater uproar and on 20 March 1785 this twenty-seven-year-old captain decided to write direct to Lord Sydney, Secretary of State in London, taking care to say that he had been appointed by his Commander-in-Chief 'to protect the Commerce of Great Britain'. It showed considerable boldness to escalate the issue beyond his Admiral, beyond the Admiralty, to the relevant Department of State, an action which demonstrated the high valuation he placed on himself. He intended to singularize himself in the eyes of the powers that be in London, 'My name most probably is unknown to your Lordship; but my character as a man, I trust, will bear the strictest investigation . . . I stand for myself; no great connexion to support me if inclined to fall: therefore my good Name as a Man, an Officer, and an Englishman, I must be very careful of. My greatest pride is to discharge my duty faithfully; my greatest ambition to receive approbation for my conduct.'[13] Although his campaign of seizures was confirmed as justified by decisions of the Vice-Admiralty courts of Nevis and St Christopher in May 1785 and he had been fully supported by the Crown lawyer Adye after some initial doubts, the seizures had, not surprisingly, excited what he called 'a rancorous disposition of some of the inhabitants'. So when four American vessels flying English colours seized in Nevis Roads were pro- secuted and condemned in the Vice-Admiralty Court at Nevis, the enraged island traders conspired with the masters of the vessels to claim damages of £4,000 for assault and imprisonment. So acutely did Nelson feel the pressure that in June he went even further and addressed a Memorial to the King outlining the whole affair and his personal position.

Meanwhile, Hughes stood neutral, merely requiring Nelson to forward relevant documents to the Admiralty; he himself forwarded to the Admiralty a note of what Nelson had done. Here was the first demon- stration of Nelson's capacity to immobilize incompetent superiors and reduce them to the role of spectator.

In late September 1785 Nelson's letter and Memorial bore fruit in the shape of a letter from Lord Sydney, 'signifying his Majesty's approbation of my conduct, and orders for the Crown Lawyers to defend me at his expense from all civil prosecutions, and in case of unfavourable decree, advising me to appeal'.[14] He might have concluded that he had been well and truly noticed. But Admiral Hughes had played his weak hand cleverly, allowing Nelson to shoulder the responsibility, and take the pain. Nelson had shown decency and professional rectitude in casting no aspersions on Hughes in his official correspondence, and because he was by nature a forgiving person his relationship with Hughes also began to mend. So when the storm had died down it was a case of, 'I have dined with him. We are very good friends, nor do I think I should very soon disagree with him.' The fact was, the crafty Hughes had found the key to winning him over – attention, warmth and flattery. 'The Admiral is highly pleased with my conduct here . . . I well know I am not of abilities to deserve what he has said of me, but I take it as they are meant to show his regard for me and his politeness and attention to me is great, nor shall I forget it. I like the Man although not all his acts.'[15]

Worse was to follow. Before he returned home Hughes was formally congratulated by the Admiralty for what was in effect Nelson's work. Nelson exploded to Locker,

The Treasury, by the last Packet, has transmitted thanks to Sir Richard Hughes, and the Officers under him for their activity and zeal in protecting the Commerce of Great Britain. Had they known what I have told you (and if my friends think I may, without impropriety, tell the story myself, I shall do it when I get Home) I don't think they would have bestowed thanks in that quarter and have neglected me. I feel much hurt that after the loss of health and risk of fortune, another should be thanked for what I did against his orders. I either deserved to be sent out of the Service, or at least have had some little notice taken of me. They have thought it worthy of notice and have neglected me; if this is the reward for a faithful discharge of my duty I shall be careful and never stand forward again; but I have done my duty, and have nothing to accuse myself of.[16]

It would be an understatement to say he felt cheated and he set about composing, 'Captain Nelson's Narrative of his proceedings in support of the Navigation Act for the suppression of illicit traffic in the West Indies'[17] to set the record straight. This document was factual but fully exposed Hughes for what he was. According to Clarke and McArthur Nelson sent a copy to Prince William, and we can assume that Locker would have had another. For Nelson this was a crucially formative experience. He realized that achievement counts for nothing if not recognized; for Nelson achievement could never be its own reward. In future he would apply as much mental energy to getting the credit he deserved as he would put into the event itself. From now on he would deal ruthlessly with any real or imagined blockages.

The Nelson of this period was rigid, rule bound and officious. A month after he had first squared up to his Admiral he had again flexed his muscles, this time on the subject of Commissioner Moutray's flag. Admiral Hughes had decided that in his absence from English Harbour, he would order Commissioner Moutray to hoist the broad pendant of a commodore, and require all captains to obey his orders. Moutray was Nelson's friend but that, quite rightly, did not prevent Nelson from refusing to accept his orders. He was in no doubt that he himself was second-in-command of the station and was exercising the functions of such. Unless Moutray could show him his commission as a commodore, he was entitled neither to fly the flag, nor as a half-pay commissioner of the Navy, to give orders to post captains in commission. So, when Nelson arrived in English Harbour to see the *Latona* wearing a broad pendant at her main topgallant masthead, he immediately sent for her captain, a fellow post captain some four years junior to himself. After a brief but fearsomely forensic cross-examination of his authority for wearing the flag, Captain Sandys had to agree that it was wrong. Nelson might have ordered the embarrassed Sandys to haul it down but did not do so, 'as Mr Moutray is an old Officer of high military character; and it might hurt his feelings to be supposed wrong by so young an Officer'. With tact and dignity, he managed to separate the personal from the professional, and to show there were no hard feelings, he then went off to dine with Moutray, twenty-one years his senior and the enviable possessor of the desirable Mary. Moutray himself was not at all fussed by Nelson's stand but Hughes was naturally affronted. Even so he weakly agreed that Nelson should write an explanation of his conduct for the Admiralty. Quite what Nelson thought there was to gain by this is difficult to understand. A little more worldly wisdom would have told him that the outcome was predictable, a ticking-off for not dealing with the matter direct with his Admiral. The Admiralty could never be in the business of encouraging junior captains to think they could teach their admirals lessons of this kind. Pompous, priggish, small minded is how Nelson might appear, but he *was* right. He was the second-in-command and in military organizations above all, it can be fatal for there to be ambiguity about the line of command.

The counterpoint to war with illicit traders was provided by his aching heart. Mary Moutray had become for him a kind of surrogate wife, desirable but unattainable. Collingwood and he spent many happy hours at Windsor, the Moutrays' home overlooking English Harbour. Ironically, though Nelson seems to have made the most fuss, it may have been the reserved and shy Collingwood who most attracted Mary Moutray, for he continued to regard her as a dear friend for the rest of his life, as letters she produced in the 1820s, after his death, amply demonstrate.

When the Moutrays had to return to England because of Commissioner Moutray's ill health, Nelson was like a melancholy Werther, self-consciously posing à la mode on paper: 'My dear sweet friend is going home. I really am an April day.'[18] Throughout March he returned to the subject in his letters to William: 'my sweet amiable friend . . . what a treasure of a woman'. After they had actually gone home in March he wrote again to William in a strain of novelettish sentimentality, 'This Country appears now intolerable, my dear friend being absent. It is barren indeed; not all the Rosys can give a spark of joy to me. English Harbour I hate the sight of, and Windsor I detest. I went once up the Hill to look at the spot where I spent more happy days than in any one spot of the world. E'en the trees drooped their heads, and the tamarind tree died: all was melancholy: the road is covered with thistles; let them grow. I shall never pull one of them up. By this time I hope she is safe in Old England. Heaven's choicest blessing go with her.'[19]

His mind was swarming with thoughts of love. A few days before Mary Moutray's departure he gossiped like a girl to William,

Come I must carry you to our love scenes. Captain Sandys has asked Miss Eliot – refused. Captain Sterling was attentive to Miss Elizabeth E; but never having asked the question, Captain Berkeley is, I hear to be the happy man. Captain Kelly is attached to a lady at Nevis, so he says: I don't much think it. He is not steady enough for that passion to hold long . . . Rosy has had no offers: I fancy she seems hurt at it. Poor girl! You should have offered. I have not gallantry enough. A niece of Governor Parry's has come out. She goes to Nevis in the *Boreas*; they trust any young lady with me, being an old-fashioned fellow.[20]

He writes curiously as an observer rather than a player. Never were Nelson's inhibitions and lack of confidence about women so clearly demonstrated.

Then suddenly he was again caught on the rebound, this time by a young widow, mature and sensible, especially alluring in her resemblance to Mary Moutray, and mother of a five-year-old son Josiah. She was Frances Nisbet. When they first met on 11 May 1785, Nelson was twenty-six and she was about the same age. Later that year Nelson told his uncle that she was twenty-two; but he was frequently inaccurate on detail. She had been widowed for more than four years and had lived on Nevis for the greater part of a life marked by misfortune and insecurity. An only child, her mother had died when she was a toddler and her father William Woolward, Senior Judge of Nevis had died some months before her marriage in June 1779 to Dr Josiah Nisbet, son of the second generation owners of the island's Mount Pleasant estate. Soon after their marriage the couple returned to England, probably for the sake of his health. Josiah was born there in May 1780 but less than a year later the invalid Dr Nisbet had died, leaving Frances with no option other than return to Nevis to live in the house of her mother's widower brother, John Richardson Herbert, President of Nevis. It was here, at his grand house Montpelier, that Nelson first encountered the young widow.

Earlier in the year a friend on the neighbouring island of St Kitts (St Christopher) had described her own encounter with him:

We have at last seen the Captain of the *Boreas* of whom so much has been said. He came up just before dinner, much heated, and was very silent; yet seemed, according to the old adage, to think the more. He declined drinking any wine; but after dinner, when the President, as usual, gave the following toasts, the King, the Queen and Royal Family, and Lord Hood, this strange man regularly filled his glass, and observed that these were always bumper toasts with him; which having drank, he uniformly passed the bottle, and relapsed into his former taciturnity. It was impossible, during this visit, for any of us to make out his real character; there was such a reserve and sternness in his behaviour, with occasional sallies, though very transient, of a superior mind. Being placed by him, I endeavoured to rouse his attention by showing him all the civilities in my power; but I drew out little more than Yes and No. If you, Fanny, had been there, we think you would have made something of him; for you have been in the habit of attending to these odd sort of people.[21]

She might indeed like her friend have perceived him as odd, but this was Nelson preoccupied, sensing enemies in the room, standing on his dignity, intent on avoiding careless words. More recently a very different picture had been conveyed by her uncle, who had described an early morning caller: 'Good God! If I did not find that great little man, of whom everyone is so afraid, playing in the next room, under the dining table with Mrs Nisbet's child.'[22]

Fanny now had an opportunity to make her own assessment. Nelson had come to call on Governor Parry's niece, also a niece of Herbert's, whom he had delivered so chastely to Nevis in *Boreas*. Nelson, a veritable lightning conductor for *coups de foudre*, instantly fell in love. Within six weeks he was confiding to William, 'Entre nous – Do not be surprised to hear I am a Benedict, for if at all, it will be before a month.'[23] Notwithstanding his flurry of action in arresting American schooners and brigs trading under false colours and papers at Nevis and in neighbouring Basseterre Roads, he found time and energy to conduct a whirlwind courtship. Within a space of some twelve weeks the couple had reached an understanding, so that when *Boreas* sailed off to Antigua for a hull examination, all that remained to be done was to seek her uncle's approval. Nelson had responded with characteristic immediacy to this good looking young mother. Her style and manners were strikingly similar to Mary Moutray's, and greatly enhanced by the cool and luxurious elegance of her surroundings. There was the added incentive of an absence of beaux with whom he would have to compete. He catalogued to William, 'her sense, polite manners, and to you I may say, beauty . . . I have not the least doubt but we shall be a happy pair: the fault must be mine if we are not.'[24] She responded increasingly to a man who carried an aura of consequence and responsibility and paradoxically had a delightfully natural gift for entertaining her child, a sure way to a mother's heart.

On the face of it she was a widow, living in relative luxury, secure in the knowledge that her uncle would continue to provide a roof over her head and undertake the upkeep of her child. She had no need to be in a hurry to remarry, especially with a young naval post captain who might be causing a stir locally but by his own confession, had no money and by definition an uncertain future. She did not resist Nelson's headlong courtship, either swept along by its energy, or genuinely in love with him; or maybe her life at Montpelier was not all that it seemed to be. From Herbert, Nelson had gained the impression that he looked upon her in the same light as his daughter, 'if not higher', 'his dear Fanny as he always calls her'. Biographers have invariably taken the line that Fanny was Herbert's hostess or housekeeper, and miss the point that had she been his housekeeper there would have been domestic responsibilities; not to put too fine a point on it, she would have been a poor relation earning her keep. As for being his hostess, it seems inconceivable that a niece should take social precedence over his sister and his daughter, also living with him. So, escape from Montpelier may well have been attractive to her and part of her motivation.

From the moment *Boreas* left Nevis for Antigua on 8 August 1785, until the day of their marriage on 11 March 1787, Nelson and his intended were to spend less than a quarter of their time together. Our impression of their developing relationship has to be based on thirty letters written by Nelson; none of hers have survived. His letters cannot be described as passionate, but they have enough warmth and ardour to convince us that he was a man in love. Certainly his contemporary, Jane Austen would have applauded his balance of sense and sensibility and his attitude to marriage: 'I declare solemnly that did I not conceive I had the full possession of your heart no consideration should make me accept your hand.'[25] 'My heart yearns to you, it is with you, my mind dwells upon naught else but you. Absent from you, I feel no pleasure. It is you my dearest Fanny, who are everything to me . . . it must be real affection that brings us together, not interest or compulsion which make so many unhappy.'[26] The object in his mind seems to have been a companionate marriage with an intelligent, sensible woman, and he was determined to be a good husband. When his brother William was married on 9 November 1786, to Sarah Yonge, daughter of the vicar of Great Torrington, he said as much. 'It is, I have no doubt, the happiest, or otherwise state; and I believe it is most generally the man's fault if he is not happy.'[27] This theme emerged again in January 1787, some three months before they were married: 'You can marry me only from a sincere affection therefore I ought to make you a good husband and I hope it will turn out that I shall. I believe few men before marriage or even after say as much as I do, but I have not a thought that I wish to conceal from you.'[28] The more carnally minded have always doubted his physical hunger for her. His letters reveal none. A mind tending to suggestiveness might catch a hint in, 'A pint of goat's milk every morning and beef tea will make me what I wish to be for your sake, for indeed I am with the most ardent affection, ever yours.'[29] This is as close to the bone as Nelson ever comes in his thirty letters.

During their extended and interrupted courtship there were tiffs and misunderstandings, when each found the other's behaviour less than perfect. After Christmas and the New Year at Nevis he had to do some making up. 'We are none of us perfect and myself probably much less so than you deserve.'[30] In April 1786, something she had written caused him to explode, 'I will not begin by scolding you although you really deserve it for sending me such a letter. . . . You will not send me such another I am certain'.[31] He was in a bad mood. Closeted in courts martial for over a week he was probably being nagged by Fanny about his absence. Four months later he was feeling isolated and beleaguered in Antigua where the locals were ignoring him. Absence and neglect made his heart grow fonder and that same evening he wrote, 'As you begin to know something about sailors, have you not heard that salt water and absence always wash away love? Now I am such a heretic as not to believe that faith: for behold every morning since my arrival, I have had six pails of salt water at day light poured on my head, and instead of finding what the seamen say to be true, I perceive the contrary effect: and if it goes on so contrary to the prescription, you must see me before my fixed time.' He painted a picture of himself, 'alone in the Commanding Officer's house . . . from sunset until bed time I have not a human creature to speak to: you will feel a little for me I think. I did not use to be over fond of sitting alone.' Her reply prompted sweet thoughts. 'What can I say? Nothing if I speak of the pleasure I felt at receiving your kind and affectionate letter. My thoughts are too big for utterance; you must imagine everything that is tender, kind and truly affectionate has possession of my whole frame. Words are not capable of conveying an idea of my feelings.'[32]

Shared intellectual and cultural interests were not an evident facet of their relationship. Nelson joins enthusiastically enough in gossip and tittle-tattle about acquaintances, Captain Kelly, Captain Sandys, 'little Sandys', Miss Whitehead's desertion from her father's house, Captain S, a gentleman well versed in the business of carrying off young ladies. This was an innocent enough way of creating shared experience and common ground, but was not taking them much further forward. By August of the following year he was writing pointedly, 'I would rather have what passes in your mind, than all the news you could tell me, which did not concern you.' On another occasion he refers to her piano in decidedly unmusical terms, 'a man is cracking my head with tuning your pianofort'. The height of his hopes is that the piano will be delivered by his servant Frank Lepee, 'safe and well tuned'.[33] There is no reference to the pleasure of hearing her play, no mention of any piece of music that meant much to them. Nelson was showing himself to be thoughtful but rather narrowly based, and Fanny was a woman unlikely to widen or deepen his outlook.

Nelson always took himself very seriously on paper, and Fanny's evident nagging about his extended absence earned her a broadside of sententiousness: 'Had I taken your advice and not seized any American I should now have been with you but I should have neglected my duty which I think your regard for me is too great for you to have wished me to do.' He continues with wonderful phrases, totally appropriate for inspiring other naval officers (they featured in the *Divisional Officers' Handbook* issued to the author in 1954), but totally inappropriate as an answer to a complaining fiancée: 'Duty is the great business of a sea officer. All private considerations must give way to it however painful it is.'[34] Here, for the first time but by no means the last, we encounter his sharp dichotomy: the hero intent on his fame and posterity, the man in search of love and affection.

From the beginning a constant theme was money. How much was Herbert going to settle on Fanny? Nelson displayed indifference. 'We know that riches do not always ensure happiness, and the world knows I am superior to pecuniary considerations in both my public and private life, as in both instances I might have been rich.'[35] This was probably as much for Herbert's consumption as Fanny's. He could not abide the ambiguity of his situation and wanted desperately to avoid being cast in the role of fortune hunter. But so little progress did he make with Herbert that by November 1785 he felt driven to write again to his uncle, William Suckling.

Anxious to forestall his uncle's likely reaction, he sought to disarm him, putting words into his mouth: 'you will smile . . . and say this Horatio is forever in love'. After cataloguing Fanny's merits in glowing terms he got down to business. 'Herbert is very rich and very proud, – he has an only daughter, and this niece, who he looks upon in the same light, if not higher. I have lived at his house, when at Nevis since June last, and am a great favourite of his. I have told him I am as poor as Job; but he tells me he likes me, and I am descended from a good family, which his pride likes.' Although Nelson was a powerfully motivated and self-directed man, his social uncertainty surfaced when he was faced with such wealth and display. He was outfaced and taken in by Herbert's Olympian self-regard: 'Nelson, I am proud, and I must live like myself, therefore I can't do much in my lifetime: when I die she shall have twenty thousand pounds; and if my daughter dies before me she shall possess the major part of my property. I intend going to England in 1787, and remaining there my life; therefore if you two can live happily together till that event takes place, you have my consent.' In today's money Herbert was talking about leaving Fanny at least a million pounds. This took Nelson's breath away but still left him with the problem of what to live on in the meantime. Swayed by Herbert's grandiloquent temporizing he told his uncle that he intended to adopt a softly softly approach:

> I know the way to get him to give me most, is not to appear to want it: thus circumstanced, who can I apply to but you? The regard you have ever expressed for me leads me to hope you will do something. My future happiness, I give you my honour, is now in your power . . . I think Herbert will be brought to give her two or three hundred a year during his life; and if you will either give me, I will call it – I think you will do it – either one hundred a year, for a few years, or a thousand pounds, how happy you will make a couple who will

pray for you for ever. Don't disappoint me, or my heart will break; trust to my honour to do a good turn for some other person if it is in my power. I can say no more, but trust implicitly to your goodness, and pray let me know of your generous action by the first Packet.[36]

It is an illuminating episode, emphasizing that when Nelson wanted something, he was without pride. On this occasion he was quite possibly responding to pressure from Fanny, for it must have been she who fed him the details of Herbert's financial circumstances, telling him what Herbert had promised her on her first marriage and of his undertakings about Josiah, telling him of the money owed her by Nisbet's brother's estate, which was put at £3,000. In his anxiety to assure her of his intentions Nelson had said, 'No danger shall deter me from pursuing every honourable means of providing for you and yours, and again let me repeat that my dear Josiah shall ever be considered by me as one of my own.'[37] He, or they, were setting his financial sights reasonably high. His current pay as captain of a sixth rate was £201 a year. If he thought Herbert could be prevailed upon to give Fanny £200–300 a year, and he could add £100 from his uncle, their income would be £500–600 a year when he was employed, and £350–£450 on half pay, a very useful income, albeit not as much as his brother William, who had just inherited from his paternal uncle Robert Rolfe the living of Hillborough, worth £700 a year.

Four months went by and at last Nelson received his uncle's reply. It was unenthusiastically helpful. Nelson, strangely insensitive to his own employment of moral blackmail, was over-sensitive to an adverse reaction to it. His uncle had written, 'Your application has in a great degree deprived me of my free agency.' Nelson was pained. 'That sentence would make me suppose that you thought I conceived I had a right to ask pecuniary assistance. Oh my dear uncle! You can't tell what I feel – indeed I can hardly write, or know what I suffer by that sentence – for although it does not make your act less generous, yet it embitters my happiness.'[38] Suckling's position was common sense. It was not his, but Herbert's responsibility to see that Fanny was properly provided for. He pointed out that Nelson's pay was quite enough for him to live independently. Nelson sat down there and then to write to Herbert but even so, two months before his marriage he was still none the wiser. 'I dare say

Mr Herbert will do everything which is handsome upon the occasion. I
hope he will for your [Fanny's] sake for it would make me unhappy to
think I had taken you from a state of affluence to a small pittance. I never
wished for riches but to give them to you and my small share shall be
yours to the extreme.'[39] But although Herbert certainly had substantial
assets – 'many estates in that island are mortgaged to him . . . the stock
of negroes upon his estate and cattle are valued at £60,000 sterling; and
he sends to England (average for seven years) 500 casks of sugar'[40] – he
was a big spender, a man of conspicuous consumption given to grandiose
gesture. Witness Nelson's message to brother William, whom Herbert
had never met: 'Herbert, President of Nevis, says you seem a good fellow;
he will make a cask of remarkably fine rum for you double-proof.'[41]
Witness Herbert's offering to stand bail for Nelson to the tune of
£10,000; it sounds impressive but was a certain bet. Nelson, impressed,
even awed by Herbert's display, treated him as 'a man who must have
his own way'. Uppermost in his mind was not the desire to marry an
heiress but worry that he would not be able to keep Fanny in the manner
to which she was evidently accustomed. A cynical fortune hunter would
have quickly assessed the uncertainty of her expectations and would not
have been so naïve as to be taken in by Herbert. He had promised Fanny
£2,000 when she married Nisbet; it was never paid. He promised Nelson
that he would give Josiah 'one thousand pounds when he grew up; and
that he should bring him up at his expense and put him in the way of
providing for himself'.[42] In the event Fanny would receive £4,000 on her
marriage, which invested in 3 per cents was worth £160 a year.[43] When
Herbert died in 1793 Josiah was not forgotten but was left only half the
amount Herbert had promised, a legacy of £500 not £1,000, to be paid
when he was twenty-one. Fanny was left nothing.

In August 1786 Admiral Hughes returned home and Nelson was left the
senior officer on the station. Some months later, on 2 December 1786,
the Boreas ran into Roseau Bay, Dominica. Nelson's day to day life was
about to be dominated by the captain of the ship lying ahead. On the
two previous occasions they had met, Prince William had been a mere
midshipman. In June 1785 he had been passed for Lieutenant, not by the
usual board of three captains, but by a specially summoned full Board
of Admiralty. Lord Howe, the First Lord of Admiralty, had recommended

that the Prince should spend time in the various grades of Lieutenant. The King unwisely insisted that his son be promoted direct to Post Captain. Now, less than a year after he had passed for Lieutenant, he was a post captain commanding *Pegasus*. But the captain sitting in the stern sheets of the smart looking boat pulling towards the *Boreas* had vast gaps in understanding and experience; his fitness for command had been merely assumed as the heritage of his royal pedigree. He had been neither a junior lieutenant, nor a first lieutenant nor the master and commander of a smaller ship.

Once in the great cabin, Nelson was quick to relax with his old acquaintance. The Prince himself was not slow in asking to see the contents of the Admiralty package he had brought with him. Nelson complied. The Prince pushed even further. His orders from Commodore Sawyer of the North American squadron were, 'to come to the West Indies and to visit such islands in His Majesty's possession as he thought fit and to return to Halifax by the middle of June. He said that Commodore Sawyer considered the *Pegasus* as belonging to his station.' Nelson managed to put the Prince right on that, in a diplomatic way. Then the Prince asked Nelson how he was officered. 'Having told him very well, he said I wish I could say so, for although I think mine know their duty yet . . . they give themselves such airs that he could not bear them. Do you know that they would not go to the ball which Governor Parry gave me at Barbados, which I think a mark of great contempt to me.' Even more alarming was what followed. He referred to his first lieutenant, Schomberg 'and there is your friend Schomberg as he calls himself'. Nelson says, 'I told H.R.H. that I had a great opinion of Mr Schomberg.'

This first conversation had been full of danger signals for Nelson. A week or so later the alarm bells began to ring in earnest. They had sailed north to Antigua on the next stage of the royal progress, *Pegasus* now in company with the rest of Nelson's little squadron, *Boreas*, *Solebay* and *Rattler*. Going on board *Pegasus* for the first time, Nelson was struck by her spick and span air, her precise and well ordered feeling, immaculate sideboys at the gangway ready to assist arriving or departing visitors, the marine guard, a quarterdeck of well dressed officers, all reinforcing the impression he had already formed of Prince William's painted barge and the handsome uniforms of its crew. Although not himself one for prettifying his ship and crew, he was impressed by the ship's disciplined air. Moments later the impression was shattered when the Prince reproved his first lieutenant for not having dressed the crew in their blue jackets, as he had been ordered, for the courtesy call of a French frigate. 'Mr S said he thought that cloth was too warm for this country but that if H.R.H. chose he would order them to be put on directly.' Nelson was instantly alive to the tone of voice in which this exchange took place. The public quarterdeck was not the place for a captain to reprove his first lieutenant nor for the first lieutenant to answer back. In the small society in which they all lived such public behaviour would quickly undermine the morale and discipline of the whole ship. Nelson knew that there must be no doubt about a captain's authority to order and be obeyed. He also knew that a first lieutenant needed space to carry out his function as executive officer of the ship and maintain his standing with his fellow officers. This involved a delicate balance of power and mutual respect for which there was no precise formula. Suffice to say all good captains and first lieutenants developed an effective working relationship, in spite of sometimes marked personality differences. Nelson immediately feared that Prince William and Isaac Schomberg could not work together. The following day there was ample confirmation from Captain Brown of the *Amphion*, who took Nelson aside and offered his own forecast, 'that Schomberg and the Prince would not long be friends, and hoped that I would endeavour to prevent a court martial from happening in the *Pegasus*, that he feared I should have a disagreeable time of it'.[44]

Within ten days of their meeting the Prince had extended his regal patronage to Nelson, who proudly passed it on to Fanny, 'I can tell you a piece of news which is that he is fully determined and has made me promise him that he shall be at my wedding and says he will give you to me. He has never yet been in a private house to visit and is determined never to do it except in this instance.'[45] The little Prince had begun the process of turning his senior officer into a courtier. Even worse, he began to infect Nelson's own leadership. 'On our arrival in English Harbour the *Pegasus* was ordered to the careening wharf. I offered H.R.H. the commanding officer's house and he did me the honour to ask me to stay in it with him, and said he did not wish to ask any officers of the squadron to dine except Captain N., and that his lieutenant could not be spared from the duty of the ship. The lieutenants of the *Pegasus* I saw were displeased with me and the officers of the *Boreas* told me they attributed H.R.H. change of conduct to me.'[46] Nelson had only himself to blame for putting himself into a situation where he was tarred by the Prince's brush. Moreover, close proximity to the Prince and exposure to his views began to have an equally pernicious effect on his thinking, for at the end of December he penned an extraordinarily alien set of sentiments to his brother: 'I begin to be very strict in my Ship, and as I get older, probably shall be more so. Whenever I may set off in another Ship, I shall be indifferent whether I ever speak to an Officer in her, but upon duty.'[47] This was the kind of thing the Prince himself had written to Lord Hood. 'The kinder a Captain behaves to his officers the less he is respected, at least I have found it to be the case.'[48] Could it possibly be that Nelson believed that whatever a prince said was right?

The man whom Nelson regarded as a friend was plump and stumpy, with florid face, fair hair and bulging blue eyes. He made many a good first impression because of his animal vitality and extrovert volubility. When it pleased him, he could be 'one of the boys', merging effortlessly with the loud and coarse, joining wholeheartedly in boisterous horseplay, drinking hard and frequenting brothels. But even in such company his liking for jokes at the expense of others caused many to be wary. In the drawing room he could be genial, amusing, and disarmingly informal. But when the mood passed, or it suited his book, he became very regal. On the quarterdeck he showed that neither nature nor nurture had cut him out to be a captain. His way of command was immature, a matter of orders and rules, crime and punishment. He had no concept of the needs of others for self-respect. All capacity to learn had been stifled by the deference enveloping him since childhood. A pontifical sense of his own infallibility and importance was always at hand. Close to the surface lurked the petulant, thoughtless, and at times brutal behaviour of a spoilt, unloved and rather nasty child.

Coping with this Prince would have required a man of great character. Perhaps a man with the experience, wisdom and toughness of Nelson's old mentor Locker might have been able to achieve more, but Prince William, who had first gone to sea with his tutor to keep an eye on him and had been put successively in the care of Admirals Digby and Hood, was in no mood for yet another nursemaid. Isaac Schomberg was certainly not equal to the challenge. Twelve years older than the Prince he was a seasoned officer of good family. He had been a lieutenant for almost ten years, had served in two flagships, and seen action. It says much for Schomberg that he was well thought of by Lord Hood and by

Nelson. His portrait conveys the sense of a proud man. His rather imperious air, and precise schoolmasterly face, is not that of a man likely
to be too emollient, let alone ingratiating. He was serving under a very
inexperienced but royal captain. William was as determined to hang on
to his divine right as captain, as Schomberg was to try to do what he
thought was his job as first lieutenant. But whatever the Prince's faults,
it was in the nature of things that Schomberg had to give way.

From the beginning of the cruise the Prince had bridled because
Schomberg 'wished to carry on the duty of the ship entirely and, particularly when I found fault, would reason and shew this was not wrong'.[49]
He had already threatened Schomberg with court martial. Then in
English Harbour the Prince began to use the Order Book publicly to
admonish his officers by name. A process more fatal to their co-
operation and commitment could scarcely be imagined. His comments
degenerated into a form of tragicomedy. On 23 January an entry ran,
'From Mr Schomberg's neglecting to inform me yesterday of his sending
a boat on shore and Mr Smollett doing the same, I think it proper to recommend the reading over of these orders with attention to the officers
and gentlemen. As for the future, I shall make them accountable for their
conduct in disobeying my commands or orders I may from time to time
give out.'[50] For Schomberg this public humiliation was the last straw.
He wrote immediately to Nelson demanding a court martial: 'As His
Royal Highness Prince William Henry, Commander of his Majesty's Ship
Pegasus, has thought proper this morning to accuse me with neglect of
duty, in the General Order Book, of which I do not conceive myself guilty,
I must, therefore in vindication of my conduct as an Officer, beg you will
be pleased (whenever an opportunity may offer) to order a Court Martial
on me, to inquire into the charge alleged against me.'[51]

For the moment nothing further could be done as there were not
enough post captains on the station to form a court martial. Nelson
clearly feared that other officers in Prince William's ship might well
follow their first lieutenant's example. Five days later he issued a General
Order to his squadron, an exercise in damage limitation. Anybody who
put in for a court martial 'on a frivolous pretence', and thereby deprived
the squadron of their services (because of their being under arrest) would
be charged by himself under the 14th and 19th Articles of War. So he
put a lid on the Prince's problem and, by implication, condemned
Schomberg's request as frivolous. Prince William, retailing the whole

sorry story to Hood, was in no doubt that 'Captain Nelson approves
entirely of my conduct.' As far as Schomberg and his own officers were
concerned, he had been wild with rage,

> I told him in the presence of the officers, I should try him after his
> Court Martial for Mutiny, that if he was found guilty he should be
> hung or broke . . . that if a Court Martial could not investigate
> the business for the particularity of the case, I should then send the
> business to the Admiralty, who have it in their power to scratch his
> name off the list. . . . I have within these last few days heard many
> things which if they are true are most infamous. Mr Hope the third
> Lieutenant is at the bottom of the whole; if he is, it will come out
> at the Court Martial, in which case I will try him for promoting
> mutiny and sedition. Since these extraordinary rumours have spread
> I have thought proper to order the youngsters to have no commu-
> nication with the officers but upon the King's Service.[52]

The situation in *Pegasus* must have been perfectly obvious, yet the man
who had had personal experience from his *Seahorse* days of disputes
between captains and first lieutenants, and more recently had outfaced
his admiral, found it difficult to intervene positively in this situation.
Why? His problem was that he had placed the Prince on a pedestal. It
had not taken the Prince long to realize that flattery and his characteristic brand of unguarded talk would disarm his senior captain. Nelson
gushed to his brother, 'In every respect both as a Man and a Prince, I
love him. He has honoured me as his confidential friend; in this he shall
not be mistaken.' Nelson's determination to keep in with the Prince in
the expectation of future favours was also obvious. 'I have never lost
sight of his [Maurice's] preferment in the line he is in, but my interest is
but rising. I have already spoken to his Royal Highness about him, but
it must take time to get on; and the Prince has it not in his power to
do all he wishes at present.'[53] The pernicious influence of the Prince's
attitudes and behaviour continued. One wonders what Locker thought
of the following: 'His Royal Highness keeps up strict discipline in his
Ship, and without paying him any compliment, she is one of the first
ordered Frigates I have seen. He has had more plague with his Officers
than enough: his first Lieutenant, will, I have no doubt be broke. I have
put him under Arrest; he having wrote for a Court Martial on himself

to vindicate his conduct, because his Captain thought proper to reprimand him in the Order Book: in short our Service has been so much
relaxed during the War, that it will cost many a Court-Martial to bring
it up again.'[54] The Prince, oblivious that he was the major cause of his
officer problem, continued to publish their misdemeanours in the Order
Book.

Not all aspects of the royal progress through Antigua, Montserrat,
Nevis, the Virgins, Barbados and Grenada were fit for Fanny's eyes.
Women, the younger and the prettier the better, were never far from
the Prince's mind or presence, and many were inclined to bestow their
ultimate favours on him. From Antigua, 'Miss Athill is the belle of the
Island and of course attracted his Royal Highness's attention. I will tell
you much when we meet for you know the danger of putting too much
upon paper.'[55] There had been the 'foolish female' at Barbados, 'ready to
resign herself to His Royal Highness'.[56] At Nevis, 'Mr Forbes etc are far
more convenient companions in certain offices.'[57] One can readily
imagine what those offices were. The Prince himself was more open in
his correspondence. By the end of his visit he had picked up at least one
dose of venereal disease, 'in my pusuit of the Dames des Couleurs', as he
told his elder brother the Prince of Wales.[58]

Nelson, even though he complained to Fanny that he found it all very
wearing, was displaying a kind of fierce protectiveness of his Prince,
alarming in its irrationality and air of desperation, 'I would if possible
or in my power have no man be near the Prince who can have the smallest impeachment as to his character for as an individual I love him, as a
Prince I honour and revere him.'[59] It must have been clear to anybody
with eyes to see that the man the Prince most needed to be saved from
was himself. Nelson's idealization of him was not unlike his idealization
of the various women he had fallen in love with.

From the beginning the Prince had cheerfully involved himself in
Nelson's forthcoming marriage, teasing him unmercifully: 'His Royal
Highness often tells me he believes I am married for he says he never saw
a lover so easy or say so little of the object he has regard for. When I tell
him I certainly am not he says then he is sure I must have a great esteem
for you and that it is not what is (vulgarly) no I won't make use of that
word commonly called love. He is right, my love is founded on esteem
the only foundation that can make love last.'[60] The Prince was puzzled
by Nelson, who was at the opposite end of the spectrum from his own

animal nature. In early March 1787, with the end of his tour in sight, the Prince forced Nelson's hand. Nelson wrote to Fanny,

> I am now feeling most awkward. His Royal Highness has been with me all this morning and has told me that as things have changed if I am not married this time we go to Nevis it is hardly probable that he should see me there again, that I had promised him not to be married unless he was present and that he did it to show esteem for me and should be much mortified if any impediments were thrown in the way to hinder his being present. . . . He told me this morning that since he has been under my command he has been happy, and has given me to understand that there is no doubt whenever he may be placed in a high situation that I will find him sincere in his friendship. By keeping in his esteem there is no doubt but I shall have my right in the Service if nothing more. I hope Mr Herbert can have no objection, especially if he considers how much it is in my interest to be well with the Prince.'[61]

At the time the Prince spoke to him no date had been fixed for his marriage to Fanny, nor had Herbert yet made known what he intended to do for her financially. Nevertheless the Prince got his way and on 11 March Nelson and Fanny were married at Montpelier in the reflected glory of Prince William, who gave her away and made a pretty speech in proposing a toast to the newly weds. The Prince, who had met Fanny once before on his visit to Nevis in February 1787, gave his impressions to Lord Hood: 'Nelson introduced me to his bride. She is a pretty and sensible woman and may have a great deal of money if her uncle Mr Herbert thinks proper. Poor Nelson is over head and ears in love. I frequently laugh at him about it. However seriously my Lord, he is more in need of a nurse than a wife. I do not really think he can live long . . . I had my Lord the honour of giving her away. He is now in for it. I wish him well and happy and that he may not repent the step he has taken.'[62] It seems very evident that Fanny was not Prince William's type, that is not a luscious island belle, not the ripely formed Sally Wynn of Plymouth whom he lusted after, certainly not the well experienced Mayfair *demimondaine*, Polly Finch with whom he briefly lived, and not the spirited and warmly sexual actress Dorothy Jordan, who would live with him and bear him ten children.

The Prince's words throw into sharp relief the fact that so far Nelson's love life had dealt in idealizations. None of his encounters had been highly charged, physically, emotionally or intellectually. He had been in love with love and with the idea of marriage. Whether this would be enough to sustain Nelson and Fanny remained to be seen, but at this stage Nelson displayed all the signs of a happy and contented man. For both there had been shadowy second agendas: money and social advancement for Nelson, security for Fanny, who had taken her second chance when it was offered.

A fellow officer is often quoted as having said on the next day, 'The Navy, sir, yesterday lost one of its greatest ornaments by Nelson's marriage. It is a national loss that such an officer should marry; had it not been for that circumstance, I forsaw Nelson would become the greatest man in the Service.'[63] Wildly mistaken though the forecast was, it nevertheless indicates that even then, some saw Nelson's quality.

Almost as though overwhelmed by the Prince's attentions and the notice he had received in dancing attendance on him, Nelson was now led into exceeding his authority. William Clarke, a seaman of the *Rattler*, had been sentenced to death for desertion. The Prince had interceded for his pardon and Nelson had pardoned and discharged Clarke. The Admiralty would find it difficult to decide whether to be more furious with Nelson for thinking that he, a mere senior captain, had powers to pardon a man (a royal prerogative), or for his accepting that Prince William could exercise that power because he was a royal prince on the spot. Nelson was well and truly under the Prince's thumb and when there were appointments to be made following the death of Wilfred Collingwood, Nelson appointed his own first lieutenant, James Wallis as master and commander of the *Rattler* and his own second lieutenant Digby Dent to replace him. The way in which Nelson then unnecessarily deferred to Prince William was quite extraordinary. 'In appointing Mr Wallis to the command of her, I hope I acted as you wish me. The vacancy as Lieutenant [to replace Dent] I leave to be filled up by your Royal Highness.' Prince William chose his acting lieutenant, George Church to be second lieutenant in *Boreas*.

After a lapse of almost four months Schomberg had still not been brought to court martial. Nelson suggested to the Prince, 'if your health would permit', that he go to America by way of Jamaica, where it would be possible to mount a court martial. Nelson had dodged the issue. He had taken no steps to help Schomberg to understand that his chances of succeeding against the Prince at court martial were nil and that the outcome for him was certain professional ruin. He had taken no steps to counsel the Prince that although he would certainly win the court martial his reputation would suffer immeasurably from what was said there. He had taken no steps to work out the lines of a likely solution, which would have involved Schomberg apologizing yet again, withdrawing his request for a court martial, Nelson in his turn accepting the withdrawal, and undertaking to do his best to secure Schomberg's transfer out of the Prince's ship. None of this would have been easy but overcoming such difficult problems is the measure of a leader's capacity. Nelson did not rise to the challenge. He displayed none of his characteristic bravery, persuasiveness, ingenuity or common sense. He ought to have felt humiliated when the Prince, subconsciously looking for a scapegoat, wrote, 'Gardner [Commodore at Jamaica] being an Officer of experience and judgement will be able to give me good advice how to pursue the best mode through this difficult and disagreeable affair. I wish to God it had never happened, or that Schomberg had seen his error sooner.'[64] Ironically Gardner was the beneficiary of Nelson's inaction. By now both the protagonists had realized what a fix they were in. Gardner went on to achieve exactly the result Nelson ought to have achieved four months earlier.

With the Prince about to depart for Jamaica, Nelson busied himself with fitting the *Boreas* to sail home. But before he could leave English Harbour he was drawn again into the world of commercial intrigue when allegations of fraud were made against the Navy Department. The Prince, having more congenial things to do, delegated all further investigation to Nelson, who quickly realized that he was neither equipped nor empowered to investigate such a matter himself. He also realised that before the administration could be expected to send out investigators from England they would need to be convinced that a prima facie case existed. With typical zeal and energy he threw himself into the hours of examination and discussion necessary to educate himself about the matters in question. By early May he was on top of his subject. Another opportunity to bring himself to the attention of powerful people in London had presented itself and he was determined to take it. So with appropriate references to the involvement of His Royal Highness, he wrote to the top brass, to Sir Charles Middleton, Comptroller of the Navy, to Lord Howe, the First

Lord of Admiralty, to the Duke of Richmond, Master-General of Ordnance, and prepared a draft for the Prime Minister himself.

None of this had been without its anxieties. Delving in the unfamiliar arena of commercial fraud had been worrying enough; a man of action confronted by piles of unintelligible ledgers, endless entries and transactions and the arcane routes of fraud, can hardly avoid feelings of bafflement and frustration. These discomforts and anxieties came hard on the financial and princely pressures surrounding his marriage. The death soon afterwards of his friend Wilfred Collingwood added to them. It was a depressed Nelson who wrote to the Prince on 7 May, 'I have been very unwell since we parted: indeed I attribute it to my frequent excursions to St John's, to investigate this business. Poor Collingwood's death lowered my spirits. I considered our constitutions nearly alike.'[65]

Getting ready to go home was not without its complications either. Having been able satisfactorily to accommodate Lady Hughes and her daughter in *Boreas* on his outward journey, Nelson had quite naturally offered to take Herbert and his daughter Martha with him when they returned to England. It would have been the natural thing for them to travel together and would have saved them all a deal of money. However, Martha had married Andrew Hamilton in May 1787, two months after Fanny's marriage, and that might well have reinforced her preference for the greater privacy and comfort of the West Indiaman *Roehampton*. Many of Nelson's biographers go on to make the bizarre assumption that newly wed Fanny went with them rather than with her husband as though those bonds could have meant more to her. Had she done so it would have been an astonishing reflection on their marriage. The fact is that from early May Nelson was engaged in her transfer to his ship. He told the Prince on 7 May, 'it is impossible to move a female in a few hours – never yet having made *Boreas* her home'.[66] At last their domestic arrangements were completed, the last visits made, the last farewells taken. Josiah watched proudly as his new father ordered the anchor to be weighed and Fanny looked forward hopefully to their life together.

After eight years as a post captain the balance sheet of Nelson's career was not particularly encouraging. He had spent a year in *Hinchinbrook*, four months in *Janus*, two years in *Albemarle*, and now three years in *Boreas*, all, with the exception of *Janus*, small 28-gun frigates. Appointment to a 64-gun ship-of-the-line, or even better a 74, had eluded him. Until he made that step fleet actions and fame would elude him too. It was bitter to reflect that he had spent almost three years under the command of a man who had not only stolen his credit but whose pride he had so injured that he could not expect him to lift a finger on his behalf in future. Moreover he had experienced his first uncongenial encounter with unpopularity, on which he had reflected with a touch of paranoia, 'I fancy the King's servants and the Officers of my little Squadron will not be sorry to part with me. They think I make them do their duty too strictly: and the West Indians will give a Balle Champetre upon my departure.'[67] He could console himself with the thought of his powerful friends, Lord Hood, Admiral Parker and, he hoped, Prince William, and his other good friends, Collingwood, Cornwallis, Davison and Ross, early examples of the men of quality and confidence who would naturally warm to him throughout his life.

But the root cause of why this last commission in the West Indies had been so unsatisfactory was because it was a peacetime commission. He had made a local stir in a certain kind of way, but as yet had had no opportunity to emerge as the hero he wanted to be. He was badly in need of a war.

5

Black Marks and 'On the Beach'

I am sorry that Captain Nelson whom we wished well has been so much wanting in the endeavours which I think could not have failed of success if they had been judiciously exerted.

Lord Howe, First Lord of the Admiralty, 2 July 1787

Just after noon on 4 July, after an Atlantic passage of almost a month, the high land on the Isle of Wight above Dunnose could be seen some eighteen miles to the north-west. Nelson ordered *Boreas* to alter course and for the next six hours she made her way through the approaches, and past the crowded anchorage of Spithead. Turning away from the busy approach to Portsmouth Harbour she came up to the wind near a group of five towering ships-of-the-line. With sails shivering and guns booming a salute to the Port Admiral, her best bower anchor rushed into the sea. Nelson, standing in the evening light on his quarterdeck, must have had mixed feelings. He was home. He had a wife at his side. But his commission would soon be over and already he was having to consider practicalities of where to live and Josiah's schooling. His was now a very uncertain future and, judging by his early exchanges with the Admiralty, a not very glorious past.

Within a week he had sent all the Schomberg papers to Philip Stephens, Secretary to the Admiralty Board, telling him of his rerouting of Prince William's ship via Jamaica in order to achieve the court martial. 'I was not without hope that when a Commander-in-Chief arrived, some mode might be adopted by him to prevent a Court Martial and to get Lieutenant Schomberg removed from the *Pegasus*.'[1] He asked for confirmation of the appointments he had made in the *Rattler* and *Boreas*. 'I sent a blank Commission to his Royal Highness which he filled up. I thought it was the least compliment I could possibly pay him.'[2] He replied to a reprimand from the Admiralty about his having authorized the Prince to disregard a request from the deputy muster master at Antigua for a perfect muster book, which would record the physical counting and naming of his crew. The Admiralty had quoted the 10th and 11th Articles of the *General Printed Instructions* at him. Nelson now quoted other Articles to justify his actions, adding, 'I feel I should be remiss in my duty, did I neglect to acquaint their Lordships that the *Pegasus* is one of the first disciplined Frigates I have seen; and His Royal Highness the most respectful and one of the most attentive obedient officers I know of.'[3]

The Admiralty took what seemed to Nelson to be a bureaucratic and jaundiced view of virtually everything he had done after Admiral Hughes's departure. This was not the kind of notice he had hoped for. He was told he was not authorized to fill the appointments in the *Rattler* and *Boreas* and they could not be confirmed. He was told that the Board was not satisfied with his reasons for diverting the *Pegasus* to Jamaica and if the Crown had been put to needless expense as a result, he would be answerable. He was told in mid-August that he had no authority to discharge the seaman who had been pardoned. Later in the same month he was hauled over the coals for appointing Joseph King, late boatswain of the *Boreas*, as sail-maker's assistant of the yard at Antigua in the face of remonstrances from the officers of the yard and in spite of the fact that the yard, being in the Civil Department, was not strictly within his authority. At this he imprudently adopted a rather high and mighty tone: 'I know of no remonstrance – I never allow inferiors to dictate.'[4]

Whatever Nelson said in his defence, some of it reasonable, some of it sea lawyerish, the Admiralty was not in a frame of mind to give way to the *folie de grandeur* of a senior captain who was not even a commodore and seemed to be setting himself up as a *de facto* commander-in-chief – except when he could not solve the problem of Schomberg and the Prince.

Finding that Commodore Gardner had been able to settle the Schomberg question Nelson wrote in his most oleaginous style to the Prince, 'If to be truly great is to be truly good (as we are taught to believe) it never was stronger verified than in your Royal Highness, in the instance of Mr Schomberg.' He continued naïvely, 'Schomberg was too hasty certainly in writing his letter; but, now you are parted, pardon me my Prince, when I presume to recommend that Schomberg may stand in your Royal Favour, as if he had never sailed with you; and that at some future date you will serve him. There only wants this to place your character in the highest point of view.' Nor was he above soliciting sympathy on his own account: 'I have been reprimanded by the Admiralty for allowing your Royal Highness to proceed to America by way of Jamaica.' More gush followed: 'one more attached and affectionate, is, I am bold to say not easily met with. Princes seldom, very seldom, find a disinterested person to communicate their thoughts to . . . I am interested only that your Royal Highness should be the greatest and best man this country ever produced.' He grovelled. 'When I go to Town, I shall take care to be presented to His Majesty and the Prince of Wales, that I may be in the way of answering any questions they may think proper to ask me. Nothing is wanting to make you the darling of the English Nation, but truth. Sorry I am to say, much to the contrary has been dispersed.'[5]

What Prince William thought of Nelson's awful letter is not recorded but his reply was robustly self-righteous. 'In my opinion Nelson we were both to blame; you in sending the *Pegasus* and *Rattler* down to Jamaica and me in asking and proposing it. . . . Were you in a similar situation again you had better not do it.' As to Schomberg, 'I must confess myself surprised that you should recommend him after what I have so often said and in what we do both agree, namely, the never forgiving an officer for disrespect: rest assured I never shall.'[6] He did not allude to Nelson's sovereign qualities as a friend.

The last word in the Schomberg affair went to Lord Hood, who later in the same year appointed him first Lieutenant in his flagship the *Barfleur*. Hood was a hard judge of men and his action signalled to all the world that he judged Schomberg to have made the best of a bad job. Prince William complained bitterly, 'Your Lordship has given the Service very convincing proof of your approbation of Mr Schomberg's conduct.' He took equal exception to Lord Howe's criticism of his treatment of Lieutenant Hope (who had asked for a transfer to the *Boreas* and been sent on his way by the Prince without the certificate of service he needed to claim his pay). 'There is nothing in this world I feel so sensibly as an attack on my professional character. . . . Much as I love and honour the Navy . . . I shall beyond doubt resign if I have not a satisfactory explanation from both your noble lordships.'[7] This cut no ice with Hood. His reaction was as firm as Nelson's had been weak. He had simply done 'an act of justice to a deserving officer'.[8] The Prince persisted. Hood's reply could not have been in plainer language. 'How was it possible, Sir, as you are pleased to suggest, that I could consult your Royal Highness in the business.'[9]

Of course it would have been risky for Nelson to have been as assertive with Prince William as he had been with Hughes and Moutray, but the betrayal of his professional insight and common sense, his assumption that he would be pleasing the Admiralty in kowtowing to the Prince, revealed a lack of integrity. As it was, Lord Howe wrote to Hood, 'I am sorry that Captain Nelson, whom we wished well, has been so much wanting in the endeavours, which I think could not have failed of success if they had been judiciously exerted, to dissuade the Prince from going so prematurely to Jamaica.'[10] Nelson had backed the wrong horse and as a result his own reputation suffered. He was seemingly blind to the inadequacies of the Prince. Fortunately, Howe and Hood were not blind; Admiralty policy thereafter would be to get and keep the Prince ashore, permanently. Meanwhile Schomberg went on to be made Post Captain in 1790 and eventually rose to be a commissioner of the Navy Board. For Nelson the outcome was all bad. What he hoped for would never happen; the Prince would never do him any professional favours or his family any personal favours. Yet, as Nelson's reputation grew William would pose as his friend and comrade and bask in reflected glory.

From the beginning there had been uncertainty about the future of the *Boreas*. Still at Portsmouth in mid-August and war with France in the air it was clear where Nelson's priorities lay. He told Locker, 'If we are to have a Bustle I do not want to come on shore, I begin to think I am fonder of the sea than ever.'[11] In October he was telling him, 'I have asked Lord Howe for a Ship of the Line but *Boreas* is victualled for three months, and ready for sea, [I am] ordered to hold myself in momentary readiness, the moment my orders come on board. . . . My health thank God, was never better and I am fit for any quarter of the Globe.'[12]

In the event a French threat to the Low Countries was neutralized and in early December 1787 the *Boreas* was paid off and he and Fanny moved to London and took lodgings at 6 Princes Street, Cavendish Square. Towards the end of January they moved on to Bath and Nelson went down to Plymouth to pay his respects to Prince William. 'I fear we must at present give [up] all thoughts of living so near London, for Mrs Nelson's lungs are so much affected by the smoke of London, that I cannot think of placing her in that situation, however desirable.'[13] After that came visits to relations in Bristol, then to Exmouth and finally they headed for Norfolk. Just after Christmas Josiah had gone off to school. Remembering his own exile, Nelson sent his servant Frank Lepee with Josiah, under orders to stay near for three days, 'till the child becomes reconciled'.[14]

Nelson reacted to his treatment by the Admiralty with a blend of self-justification, self-pity and self-delusion. He wrote to his friend Hercules Ross, 'You have given up all the toils and anxieties of business, whilst I must still buffet the waves – in search of what? That thing called Honour, is now alas! thought of no more . . . my fortune, God knows, has grown worse for the Service; so much for serving my Country . . . I have invariably laid down, and followed close, a plan of what ought to be uppermost in the breast of an Officer: that it is much better to serve an ungrateful country, than to give up his own fame. Posterity will do him justice: a uniform conduct of honour and integrity seldom fails of bringing a man to the goal of Fame at last.'[15] Unreal and self-deluding as his reactions were, they sustained the tenacity and power of his motivation during the unfulfilling years that lay ahead.

After Nelson's death Fanny recollected that they had not intended to stay with Nelson's father but to go instead to France. She said they stayed because of her father-in-law. 'This good old man seemed to suffer much at the thought of our leaving him, saying his age and infirmities were increasing and that he could not last long which made us give up entirely our former plan. Then we agreed to live together. A great comfort to Mr N and some convenience to all parties.'[16] Nelson's father, now sixty-five, had been on tenterhooks about receiving them: 'I am in no haste to see and receive a stranger . . . every power of mine is in decay. Insipid, whimsicall and very unfit for society in truth, and not likely to revive by practice.' Nelson made a flying visit, immediately volunteering to return to town to discharge his brother Maurice's debts. His father wrote to his youngest daughter, Catherine Matcham, 'After his return he means to visit you, and that Mr M and you shall conduct Him and His wife to Thorpe, where probably they will cast their Anchor for a time.'[17] Whether the fact that they cast their anchor for a very long time was the wish of Nelson's father or of Fanny is debatable. The view of the Matcham side of the family was that, 'he always spoke warmly of her kindness to him, calling her gentle and considerate yet somehow their mutual arrangements seemed to have generally been an adaptation of his convenience to her wishes'.[18] While Nelson had been on impress

(press-gang) duty during the period of uncertainty about the future of the *Boreas*, and in his own words, 'as much separated from my wife as if I were in the East Indies',[19] his father told Catherine, 'She has been unwell and in poor spirits. Hard she says is the lot of a Sailor's wife.'[20] Very true, but an ominous beginning.

In his *Sketch of My Life* Nelson wasted few words on the period he was unemployed or 'on the beach', for five years and two months. 'The *Boreas* being paid off at Sheerness, on November the 30th, I lived at Burnham Thorpe, county of Norfolk, in the Parsonage House. In 1790, when the Affair with Spain, relative to Nootka Sound, had nearly involved us in a war, I made use of every interest to get a Ship, ay even a boat, to serve my Country, but in vain; there was a prejudice at the Admiralty evidently against me, which I can neither guess at, nor in the least account for.'[21] The fact is he did know what the problem had been but chose not to reveal it. There was nothing unusual in Nelson's being unemployed; there was after all a current recession in warfare. Even so, his attempts to get back to sea began as early as May of the next year, 1788. Having called at the Admiralty and failed on two occasions to see Lord Howe, he left a note expressing his readiness to serve. Three months later, in August 1788, there was a Cabinet reshuffle and Lord Chatham became First Lord. Nelson wrote again asking for employment and went to see Hood. 'He was very civil but harped about PW. I said nothing about him. He agreed with me that a Ship in peaceable times was not desirable: but that should any Hostilities take place, I need not fear having a good Ship.'[22] The incident with Spain over Nootka Sound in 1790 prompted Nelson to reapply: 'I am ready to undertake such employment as their Lordships shall judge most proper.'[23] Hood was still a friend and Nelson had no hesitation in approaching him. This time Hood sheltered behind Chatham and the First Lord's long personal list of powerfully recommended captains seeking employment. At least that was the gist of his official position. But in conversation Nelson gleaned the truth that what really stood against him was his involvement with Prince William and the King's displeasure. The draft of a letter dated 10 December 1792 to Prince William, by then Duke of Clarence, shows that Nelson struck out the words, 'I asked Lord Hood to interest himself with Lord Chatham, that I might be appointed to a ship. His Lordship declined doing it and made a speech never to be effaced from my memory, viz. that the King was impressed with an unfavourable opinion of me.'[24]

He did not try any more. In the minds of those who held his future in their hands, there was the black mark he now knew about, not to mention sundry other question and exclamation marks about his behaviour which he himself had refused to acknowledge. His only hope was war, when every officer would be needed.

The picture coming down to us from that remote corner of Norfolk is of an active Nelson, constantly in touch with his elder brother William and his wife Sarah in the Rectory at Hillborough, his sister Catherine and her husband George Matcham at Barton Hall near Norwich, his sister Susannah and her husband Thomas Bolton in Norwich and his brother Maurice in London. He quickly formed easy and friendly relationships with his sisters' husbands. Thomas Bolton helped him over the purchase of a horse and as a supplier of Christmas turkeys for Locker. George Matcham declared he would present Nelson with a pipe of wine, 'when he should have a ship', and happily collaborated with him in further improvements to the parsonage rose garden, which as 'Capability Matcham' he had initiated. As a family they had plenty to occupy them. Suckling, now twenty-three, was taking over from Maurice in terms of expense and worry and had to be settled with a tutor. The human cycle was moving inexorably on. The William Nelsons' first child Charlotte was born at the same time as they nursed their grandmother Nelson in her final illness, and sheltered schoolboy Josiah. Brother Edmund, twenty-seven, was quietly dying of consumption at the Boltons' house before returning in late 1789 to spend the final weeks of his life at Burnham Thorpe, when the Rector acknowledged, 'Poor Mrs Nelson's tryall in this instance is not a light one.' The first of Catherine Matcham's children was born and would die before Nelson returned to sea. Lord Orford died and the status-conscious Rector observed rather pompously to Catherine, 'We are in mourning the same as that family for a fortnight. You may with great propriety do the same.'[25]

By comparison with the energetic Nelson digging and delving in the Rector's garden and engaged in enthusiastic but ineffective flirtation with rural sports ('shoot I cannot'),[26] Fanny seemed strangely inert and maladaptive, at least in the opinion of Nelson's father. 'I wish his Good Wife had her amusement; a little society and an instrument with which she could pass away an hour. Her musicall powers I fancy are beyond the common sort.' The problem was her lack of motivation, perhaps in this case her unwillingness to ask Nelson to spend money on a piano.

It is not as though there was no society for her to mix with. Besides the extended family there were their grand Suckling relatives at Wolterton, the Pointz (Catherine's godfather) at Creke and, closer to home in Burnham, the Crowes at the Hall and the Mordaunt Martins. As the hard winter of 1778–79 took Norfolk in its iron grip Fanny became even more inert, making even the hypochondriacal Rector feel strong. 'Mrs N takes large doses of the Bed. . . . Myself more accustomed to the climate give no heed to small Inconveniences.' By 1790 he was clearly puzzled by her lack of social ambition: 'Whether solitude and exclusion from all the world can be comfortable to a young woman I know not. She does not openly complain. Her attention to me demands my esteem, and to her Good Husband she is all he can expect.' When members of the Suckling family appeared on the local scene the Rector was immediately over-anxious about a possible visit to Wolterton and suitable clothes for Fanny, but some weeks later he reported to Catherine, 'Mrs N as you may suppose have not been from home, nor didn't seem enclined to.' The Rector may have concluded that her lack of liveliness and the absence of a child after three and a half years of marriage were due to the inhibiting effect of his own presence on the young couple. He took the rather drastic step of leaving home himself. 'I have hired one of the small houses near Ulph church which will lessen the fatigue of Sunday duty . . . leaving Captain and Mrs Nelson in possession of the Parsonage.'[27]

Across the Channel France's internal problems had multiplied since the storming of the Bastille on 14 July 1789. The Revolution had not been immediately perceived as a threat, either to England or to European peace. Many were intoxicated by its promise, 'Bliss was it in that dawn to be alive, but to be young was very heaven,' Wordsworth later wrote. But while Fox's Whigs might see in it a reflection of their own desire for constitutional reform, their idealism was balanced by Edmund Burke's sombre far-sighted realism: 'at the end of every vista you see nothing but the gallows'.[28] Yet there was no mistaking the ferment in the country as clubs and societies sympathetic to the Revolution's ideas sprang up. Even in his remote corner of Norfolk Nelson felt the wind of change, not that he had the least sympathy for radical ideas and was outraged that those who should have known better were entertaining them. He wrote to the Prince, now the Duke of Clarence: 'I have been staying some time with my relation, Lord Walpole near Norwich; at which place, and near it, the Clubs are supported by Members of the Corporation; and they avow that till some of the·Nobles and others in Parliament are served as they were in France, they will not be able to get their rights.'[29] When he complained to a justice of the peace that a well known agitator, Dr Priestly, had not been arrested, he received a frightening reply from a frightened man, 'No Justice would render himself unpopular at this time by being singular; for that his life and property were gone if the mob arose.' He was relieved to find that the Lord-Lieutenant was taking steps to summon all the Norfolk justices to concert a policy of taking away the licences of public houses which allowed societies to meet in them. But while there could be no place in his own thinking for anything that smacked of anarchy his warm heart responded vividly to the plight of the agricultural labourer. 'That the poor labourer should have been seduced by promises and hopes of better times, your Royal Highness will not wonder at, when I assure you they are really in want of everything to make life comfortable.' He included with his letter a detailed account of the income and outgoings of a labourer in Norfolk, assuming a wife and two children, a full year's employment and the recent increase in wages of a shilling a week. After deductions for rent, heating, lighting, clothes and shoes totalling £8 13s. 1od. out of annual earnings of £23 1s. 0d., the labourer was left with £14 7s. 2d. to feed five, not quite twopence each a day, 'and to drink nothing but water, for beer our poor labourers never taste, unless they are tempted, which is too often the case, to go to the Alehouse'.[30] For all his ideological rigidity Nelson was a remarkably sane man. He did not close his eyes to reality and his capacity to empathize was given more than sentimental force by his curiosity for facts.

England did not come to revolution, although by November 1792 French agents were confidently forecasting it.[31] When the politics of revolutionary terror in France amply fulfilled Burke's forecast, British public opinion sobered rapidly. Fox lost support as William Pitt gained it. England's initial stance of non-intervention was tested by aggressive French expansionism in the Low Countries and towards the Rhine. When Nice and Savoy were overrun and France declared war on the Kingdom of Sardinia, steps were taken to put the country on a war footing. One tiny part in this assembling war machine was Nelson's interview with Lord Chatham on 6 January 1793; it brought him the prize he sought most in the world – command of a ship-of-the-line. True she was only a

64, but Lord Chatham had promised him a 74 as soon as one should become available. Seventeen days later the news of the execution of the French King reached London, and in Simon Schama's words, 'It was the Government's sense that it was now dealing with a phenomenon of uncontainable barbarism and irrationality.'[32] Three days later Nelson knew he was to be appointed to the *Agamemnon*. On 1 February 1793 France declared war on England and Holland.

Nelson, now thirty-five, was ecstatic. Making a rare foray into his schoolboy learning he began his letter to Fanny, 'Post nubila Phoebus', but as if doubting Fanny's capacity to understand went on 'Your son will explain the motto', immediately translating it himself, 'After clouds come sunshine.' He needed 600 men as quickly as he could get them and immediately sent a lieutenant and four midshipmen to recruit at every seaport in his home county of Norfolk. His friend Captain Locker, now Commodore Locker, was Commander-in-Chief at the Nore and well placed to help. Naval friends in the North and Yorkshire were asked to be on the lookout. Choosing his officers was his most important personal priority. He built around a core of men who had served with him before. His first lieutenant would be Martin Hinton who had been with him in the *Albemarle*. For boatswain he managed to work the transfer of Joseph King, former boatswain of the *Boreas*, his controversial appointee as sail-maker's assistant of His Majesty's Yard at Antigua, a man he had described to Philip Stephens, the Admiralty Board Secretary, as 'a most excellent gentleman',[33] such an unlikely description for a boatswain that he must have had something very special about him to earn it. His was one of the most important appointments in the ship. Being in charge of sails and rigging he was to a high degree responsible for the safety of the ship and the lives of the men who went aloft in her. In his appointment of a purser, the ship's supply officer, Nelson was likewise very careful. Here was a man who could directly affect the morale of the ship's company, for the better if they came to trust him, for the worse if he got a name for giving short measure or profiteering at the men's expense. The man he appointed, Thomas Fellowes, came with a recommendation from Locker. Even so, Nelson left him in no doubt about what he expected: 'I am very much disposed to like Mr Fellowes, and have told him so, and that every protection of mine he shall certainly have, against a waste of his stores, &c.; but that he must be very careful that no just cause of complaint can be made against him, for I will not suffer any poor fellow to be lessened of his due. He seems perfectly to understand me.'[34] His surgeon, Michael Jefferson, was a stranger but seemed to him a 'very good sort of man'.[35]

The care that Nelson expended in selecting his officers and a flavour of his and their conduct in the early weeks of the commission are vividly reflected in a letter home from Joseph Emmerson, second mate to the surgeon, and new to life in the Navy

Hitherto we have liv'd cheerily and merrily – I have met with nothing to complain of – on the contrary have felt myself comfortable & happy in my new situation hitherto . . . Mr Weatherhead's son, of Brancaster, is a Midshipman in our birth [sic] as is a son of Dixon Hoste's of Godwicke, – neither I nor the 1st mate, who is a genteel man, mess in the Surgeon Mates birth, which is only a canvass one & the 3rd mate is a very dirty disagreeable companion which obliged me to accept an invitation into those of the Master's Mates births, where I enjoy agreeable company & more comfortable accomoda- tion . . . I expect Mr Dallaway on board to dine with us today. – We have a roast leg of Mutton, a plumb-pudding, & beef- steak-pye for dinner – eight of us mess together & are allow'd a pound of meat a day each – we get fresh meat in harbour – Flour and plumbs is likewise allow'd us. . . . Captn Nelson made us a present of seven pounds the other day, because his son in law messes with us. . . . The Captain is a worthy, good man, and much lik'd on board – is much of a gentleman. All the officers behave civilly and respectfully to me. They are all gentlemen like me. I don't think there is a ship in the navy better mann'd throughout. The surgeon is a sensible easy man, & all gentleman. He is very communicative & has much professional merit. I am happy that I can learn something from him. The same advantages are open to me from the 1st mate.[36]

Nelson was a courteous and agreeable man. He was able to listen and explain and by example demonstrate the behaviour he expected to see in his officers. He understood the need that each of his officers had for self-respect and the vexations and tribulations they would auto- matically provide for each other if they could not manage their feelings and behaviour, living together as they did for months on end, cheek by jowl with the minimum privacy. And so Nelson liked to have men about him who knew how to get along with their fellows. In the wider scene of the ship, none of this meant that he avoided any of the hard necessities of command or hesitated to support his officers. In the early weeks of *Agamemnon*'s commission a boy and a seaman were flogged for theft.

Emmerson had no means of knowing, but may have deduced from what he saw and heard of his buoyant captain, that his feelings were fully reciprocated. Nelson was wonderfully pleased with his ship and all in her, 'I not only like the ship, but think I am well appointed in officers, and we are manned exceedingly well.'[37] He was quickly appreciating the joy of *Agamemnon*'s most desirable characteristic: 'We seem to sail very fast.'

Although destined to join Hood at Gibraltar he was first sent to cruise the Channel with Admiral Hotham, commander of Hood's third division of seven ships. Legend has it that Nelson was invariably seasick, but here he was in blowing Channel weather reporting to Fanny that Josiah was a little seasick but saying nothing at all about any difficulties he himself may have been having in recovering his sea legs after the best part of six years on shore. They had a flash of excitement in chasing two French frigates and two armed vessels into La Hogue but he soon concluded that what they were doing was pure public relations, 'We have done nothing or are intended I may venture to say. . . . The King may be told that his fleet is at sea. . . . The Minister may stop the mouths of the opposition by saying the same thing. This is not the first squadron sent out to do nothing, and worse than nothing.'[38]

Ashore, Fanny was taking his absence badly and causing great concern to Nelson's father. For a dependent sort of woman such as Fanny, the fears aroused by such an indeterminate and sudden separation can hardly be overstated. For a second time her family life had disintegrated, and on this occasion she was losing both husband and son. Josiah had gone to sea with Nelson as a midshipman because they had decided they could not afford to finance him in the law. In fairness to Nelson, who might otherwise be accused of some lack of feeling in tearing a son away from his mother, he had left the choice to Fanny. 'My objection to the Navy now he is certain of a small fortune [£500 in Herbert's will] is in some measure done away. You must think of this. Would you like to bring him

up with you? For if he is to go, he must go with me.' Knowing full well
by now her inability to make decisions he ended his letter, 'Think about
Josiah.'[39] *Faute de mieux* she followed Nelson's lead, possibly influenced
by her son's enthusiasm to go with his stepfather. Parting brought a succession of other unwanted decisions and burdens. She had to decide
where and how to spend her time. Knowing how worried and concerned
she always was about money (what Nelson and Fanny were gaining from
the Herbert will, would, in Nelson's opinion, merely offset the loss of
William Suckling's £100 a year) her father-in-law tried to smooth her
decision as much as he could: 'Don't at this time consider the expense.'[40]
Before he put to sea Nelson had encouraged her to visit his uncle, William
Suckling in Kentish Town. He raised the possibility of her visiting his
sister Catherine Matcham in Hampshire, although his messages on that
were unhelpfully mixed; first saying he did not believe a visit would be
'over pleasant',[41] perhaps because he sensed some incompatibility with
the extrovert and energetic Matchams but three days later changing his
tune, 'the Matchams were very kind in their wishes for your going into
Hampshire for a month or two, you would like to go'.[42] She had also
experienced for the first, but not the last time, the difficulties caused
by a husband who tended to treat her as he would a captain's servant:
'You forgot to send my things from Mr Thomas's . . . I have got a keg of
tongues which I suppose you ordered and . . . not very well packed.'[43]
And she was already experiencing the burdens of being a centre for communication as she received reminders from her husband about who she
should write to, or who had not heard from her.

   In Nelson's absence Fanny seems not to have reached out, nor to
have been such an engaging character that others reached out to her.
Allying herself so closely with Nelson's prematurely old and socially timid
father could hardly have helped. Most of all she was lacking that ready-
made centre for independent life, a home of her own with children, or a
baby on the way towards whom she could redirect her love and fears.
Fanny had lost both a husband and a son; she was well and truly on the
beach.

   Nelson's lack of enthusiasm for Fanny was also now apparent. She was
still his wife but the music of his letters to her, although courteous and
controlled, revealed him as devoid of feelings of loss or regret at their
parting, devoid of tenderness and endearment, or even the pretence of
them; he was detached. He had learned that to empathize with her was

merely to release the floodgates of her many worries and fears. To say he had fallen out of love with her would have little meaning but it is clear that he was leaving a woman who had taken second place to his career and was no longer necessary to his physical, mental or professional existence.

Part II

Unhonoured and Unsung

Europe and the Near East in Nelson's time

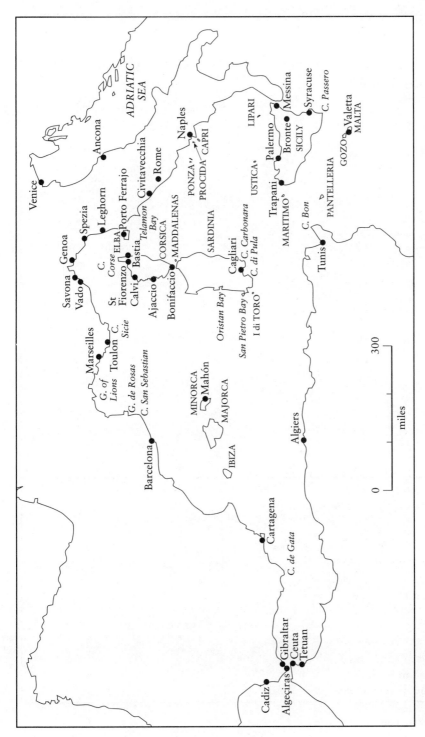

The Western Mediterranean

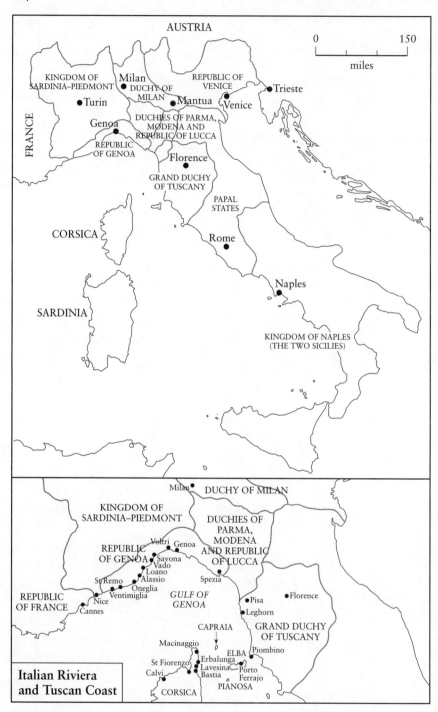

Italian Riviera and Tuscan Coast

Italy in 1794

6

Melpomene, Minerve, La Fortune

Though I know neither the time nor the manner of my death, I am not at all solicitous about it, because I am sure He knows them both and that He will not fail to support and comfort me under them.

Nelson, October 1793

Nelson did not have to endure for long the indignity of cruising fruit-lessly in the Channel. In June they sailed for the Mediterranean to join Hood. After the finest passage and weather possible, they arrived off Cape St Vincent on 14 June, where Nelson made his own emotional *rapprochement* with Hood, 'I paid Lord Hood a visit a few days back and found him very civil. I dare say we shall be good friends again.'[1] Stopping off in Cadiz on their way round to Gibraltar he noted, 'The Spaniards have been very civil to us. More in my opinion than we deserved. For to my surprise Elphinstone (later Lord Keith), our com-modore has amazingly neglected those etiquettes which at all times I should consider necessary in a foreign port, and more particularly so in our new alliance with Spain.' Nelson was always a stickler for form and was not in general forming a good opinion of Elphinstone's sense of pri-orities. 'What our plan of operations is to be in the Mediterranean I can't guess but the Lord is in a hurry. He wrote Captain E to hurry his sailing from Cadiz . . . I think we shall not get into Gibraltar before the morning we are parading when we should be crowding sail.' There had been time for him to run his eye over the Spanish fleet and to make his first visit to a bullfight. He thought the big ships he saw in Cadiz, 'very fine but shockingly manned. If those 21 sail-of-the-line which we are to join in the Mediterranean are not better manned they can't be of much use.' As for the bullfight, he reacted like a true Englishman. 'We felt for the bulls and horses and I own it would not have displeased me to have had some of the Dons tossed by the enraged animal. How women can even sit much more applaud such sights is astonishing. It even turned us sick, and we could hardly sit it out. The dead mangled horses with their entrails tore out, the bulls covered with blood was too much. However we have seen one and agree that nothing shall tempt us to see another.'[2]

Their water supply replenished at Cadiz they made for Gibraltar. In the shadow of the Rock he was one of eleven other post captains anchored there. From *Agamemnon*'s quarterdeck he could see the flags of his commanders fluttering in the breeze, Admiral Lord Hood in the *Victory*, his second-in-command Vice-Admiral Hotham in the *Britannia*, his third-in-command Vice-Admiral Colby in the *Windsor Castle*, and for good measure, Rear-Admiral Goodall in the *Princess Royal*, and Rear-Admiral Gell in the *St George*. The limits on Nelson's capacity to exercise initiative, or contribute to policy formation, were obvious.

They pushed further eastwards up the Mediterranean towards Toulon. Their objectives were to prevent French access to the open Atlantic and take advantage of the fact that Toulon, together with Lyons and Marseilles were defying the government in Paris. On the way they fell in with twenty-one Spanish sail-of-the-line, allies in this early stage of the war. As he watched them trying for several hours to form themselves into a line and not even then succeeding, and learning of their intention to put into Cartagena, 'for they had been sixty days at sea', Nelson was inclined to be cynically chauvinistic. 'The Spaniards...mean to leave us the honour of keeping the French in order. I really expect never to see them out again.' He himself was thirsting for action: 'I hope we shall get off Toulon tomorrow when we may stand a chance to see something like an enemy.'

The political situation ashore was confused. Both Marseilles and Toulon were gripped by the bloody, and fluctuating struggles endemic in counter-revolutions, 'A master of a ship, whom we spoke from Marseilles, says there are now only two descriptions of people in France – the one drunk and mad; the other, with horror painted in their faces, are absolutely starving.'[3] The nominally republican regimes of Marseilles and Toulon had declared themselves against the Jacobin government in Paris and now found themselves caught between a British blockade and advancing government forces. Starvation and fear of retribution drove them into the arms of the British. They negotiated their surrender on Hood's terms: 'If a candid and explicit declaration in favour of the monarchy is made at Toulon and Marseille, and the standard of Royalty hoisted, the ships in the harbour dismantled, and the ports and forts provisionally put at my disposition . . . the people of Provence shall have all the assistance and support His Britannic Majesty's fleet under my command can give.'[4]

Hood was promising more than he could deliver. Nelson had already appreciated the British incapacity to take advantage of French internal divisions in Provence: 'It seems of no use to send a great Fleet here without troops to act with them.'[5] The British generals accompanying Hood also took the view that their 2,000 troops, even augmented by 6,000 Spaniards, were totally inadequate to man the various forts and defend the fifteen-mile perimeter of Toulon whilst Marseilles, in their judgement, was almost totally indefensible. Here lay the origins of Hood's bad relations with the Army which were to remain sour for the rest of his time in the Mediterranean. Hood, characteristically, decided to take his chance but he knew how shaky his ground was. Just as soon as the ink was dry on the surrender he dispatched Nelson and *Agamemnon*, probably the fastest ship-of-the-line in the fleet, to draw on allied resources, first to Oneglia with a requisition for 4,000 Sardinian troops, and then to Naples with a requisition for 6,000. It would be a race against time. In Paris, Robespierre and the Committee of Public Safety knew exactly what was at stake. Toulon, in the words of Frank McLynn, 'was looked upon as a test case; if not recovered it could fan the flames of the Vendée into wholesale civil war'.[6] And so General Carteaux was given 12,000 men plus 5,000 from the Army of Italy to recover Toulon. A day after he sailed Nelson learned from an encounter with the frigate *Tartar* that Carteaux had already taken Marseilles and eliminated those who had surrendered to Hood.

As he sailed past Sardinia towards Naples he penned a jumble of thoughts and emotions to Fanny. He was full of praise for Hood: 'What an event this has been for Lord Hood. Such a one as History cannot produce its equal. That the strongest place in Europe and twenty two sail of the line, should be given up without firing a shot, it is not to be credited.' He was full of what would be done next: 'Nice, Ville Franche, Monaco and Menton which were taken from the King of Sardinia must fall again to him, so soon as our fleet can be liberated from Toulon'; his passion for action and achievement was suppressing his realization of the limitations of the British force. His judgement of Hood's success was superficial and his expectation that it should be recognized instantly,

frankly irrational. He grumbled, 'If Parliament do not grant something
to this fleet our jacks will grumble, for here there is no prize money to
soften our hardships. All we get is honour and salt beef. My poor fellows
have not had a morsel of fresh meat or vegetables for near nineteen weeks
and in that time I have only had my foot twice on shore at Cadiz. We
are absolutely getting sick from fatigue. No fleet I am satisfied ever served
their country with greater zeal than this has done from the Admiral to
the lowest sailor.' He was not usually inclined to complain about the
demands of the service, and although his solicitude for his men was real
enough his Journal shows that he had taken on fresh meat at Oneglia
for the ship's company a week earlier. Perhaps what was really irking
him was the fact that he was having to leave the theatre of action behind.
'Admiral Goodall is Governor of Toulon, Elphinstone commander of the
grand batteries at the harbour's mouth. I may have lost an appointment
by being sent off.'[7]

He arrived at Naples on 10 September as night was falling, Vesuvius
glowing red in the soft purples of dusk. The following day *Agamemnon*
anchored and Nelson was rowed ashore to meet King Ferdinand and
plunge into a whirl of intense diplomatic activity, of which he was the
undisputed centre and from which he emerged four days later with 4,000
troops. Ever a dealer in absolutes, he naturally used superlatives to
describe his own efforts: 'I have acted for my Lord Hood in such a
manner that no one could exceed and am to carry from the King the
handsomest letter in his own handwriting which could be penned.' But
whatever his capacity for blowing his own trumpet there was no mistaking the superb self-assurance with which he managed his Neapolitan
mission. King Ferdinand, Sir William Hamilton the British Ambassador,
and the Prime Minister Sir John Acton all fell under his spell. It helped
that Naples was under treaty obligation to provide support and the Court
was mightily relieved by this early show of British power, but even so,
without command of Italian or French, having to rely on translation,
with only self-projection and body language to convince the King,
Nelson's whole persona declared that he was no mere naval messenger
but a man of consequence. As Nelson shrewdly noticed, 'he wished to
cut a great figure by sending his stipulated force all at the same time and
to that vanity are we now indebted for the 4,000 instead of the 2,000 at
first promised'.[8] Riding at the head of his troops on their way to
embarkation he paraded them before Nelson. 'His Majesty as soon as he

saw us made his troops halt and dressed them before they marched by us.'[9] Ferdinand had gone out of his way to court Nelson, 'I was three times with him out of the four days, and once to dinner, when I was placed at his right hand before our Ambassador and all the Nobles present.' The day the King was due to dine with Nelson the English Quality came on board. 'She was full of ladies and gentlemen – Sir William and Lady Hamilton, the Bishop of Winchester, Mrs North and family, Lord and Lady Plymouth, Earl Grandison and his daughter, besides other Baronets,&c.'[10] In the event the King's visit had to give way to more pressing business. Receiving a report that a French corvette was anchored off Sardinia with an English prize and two Smyrna ships in convoy, and seeing that no Neapolitan or Spanish ship was ordered after them, he immediately sent his guests on shore and got under way. 'I had nothing left for the honour of our Country but to sail, which I did in two hours afterwards. It was necessary to show them what an English Man-of-War would do.'

Nelson had made his mark on Naples. Among those who made a mark on him were the Hamiltons, not only Sir William for whom he developed a considerable respect but also his wife, twenty-eight-year-old Emma Hamilton. She had been married to Sir William for two years, having been his mistress for the previous five. Just as her husband had a European reputation in learned and antiquarian circles she was herself a European celebrity, famed for her beauty, her live representations of characters and situations from antiquity (her 'attitudes'), and her notorious past, all of which constituted a vast provocation to gossip and a universal desire to meet and judge her. Nelson's reaction to her was natural and straightforward. Her good nature, her easy manner, her warm and demonstrative mothering of Josiah, appealed to him. He was nevertheless careful in what he reported to Fanny of this notorious lady. 'Lady Hamilton has been wonderfully kind and good to Josiah. She is a young woman of amiable manners and who does honour to the station to which she is raised.' Even Nelson was wise enough to remain silent about her captivating beauty, lively self-confidence and charm. However, the residual warmth around his heart was underlined by his Journal entry, 'God send us good success. I believe we carry with us the good wishes of Naples and of Sir William Hamilton and Lady Hamilton in particular which I esteem more than all the rest. Farewell Naples. May those who were kind to me be repaid ten fold.' [11]

Arriving back at Toulon on 5 October, exhilarated by the success of his first political and diplomatic mission, he was delighted to tell Fanny, 'the Lord is wonderfully pleased with me',[12] and a few days later, 'The Lord is now quite as he used to be, his dear Nelson etc.' Hood had found the way to handle him. Yet Nelson was feeling out of it: 'Every day at Toulon has hitherto afforded some brilliant action on shore in which the sea officers have cut a very conspicuous figure, Elphinstone in particular who is a good officer and gallant man. I have only been a spectator.'[13] Little did he know that they would soon have to contend with a formidable rising star, as much unknown to them as he was to almost every Frenchman in France, the Corsican Napoleon Bonaparte.

On the evening of 9 October Nelson again set sail, this time under secret orders to join Commodore Linzee who had been sent to attack Corsica. Nine days later there occurred what can properly be called a moment of truth. Although his twenty-three years of sea life had been occasionally punctuated by danger and occasionally by shots fired in anger, he was now in command of a ship, in a serious naval engagement, the first of his career. At two o'clock on the morning of the 21st he fell in with five strange ships. Their rocket signals lit up the sky. They tacked towards *Agamemnon*. By four o'clock the nearest frigate was within hailing distance and Nelson, with no means of knowing whether she was French, Sardinian or Neapolitan, held his fire. Her reply was to make more sail. Nelson ordered a shot across her bows. She did not heave to. He ordered men aloft to crowd on sail for a chase. The accompanying four ships turned to chase Nelson. At daybreak his quarry hoisted the French flag, opened fire with her stern chasers, and thanks to her superior sailing qualities, was able to yaw from time to time and fire broadsides into *Agamemnon*'s bows, killing one man and wounding six. In this running fight there was little Nelson could do, other than occasionally bring his forward guns to bear. Even so both ships were suffering considerably. By seven o'clock the *Agamemnon* and her quarry were leaving the others behind but Nelson believed that one of his pursuers was a ship-of-the-line. Nelson's dispatch to Lord Hood shows how Nelson managed himself and the situation, how he asked his officers to confirm his own opinion that one of their pursuers was a ship-of-the-line; his request for their assessment of the ship's capability to close immediately with their damaged opponent before she could join the others and their unanimous negative; his determination to fight; and his calm handling of preparations for the looming bloody encounter, due in about half an hour – bread and wine for the men at their guns and teams sent aloft to repair rigging and make safe damaged spars. He listened to what his officers had to say but made his own decision. Suddenly *Agamemnon* was all but immobilized by a calm and for the next four or so hours they endured gut-wrenching uncertainty, but the French declined to take her on. It was not until noon that *Agamemnon* was able to haul her wind and proceed.[14]

This had been the outward drama ending in anticlimax but Nelson's Journal reveals an inner drama of greater significance. Like all men in war, Nelson had to find out whether, when the time came, he would be equal to it, whether in the tightest of corners he would feel fear and communicate it to others. Although they had all been mistaken in thinking one of their opponents was a ship-of-the-line the quality of the pack he faced was daunting: three heavy frigates, *Melpomene*, *Minerve* and *La Fortune*, each of 44 guns, a frigate of 24 guns and an armed brig. In his Journal he made the comparison. *Agamemnon*'s complement was 345 men and his 64 guns were capable of hurling 1,200 lbs of metal at the enemy. He calculated that the opposition had in their five ships roughly more than twice the firepower and more than four times the manpower for boarding. The fact that he outfought the frigate he chased could not disguise the fact that when he was at a virtual standstill with his enemy congregating nearby his only options were to surrender, or fight and be battered to a pulp. Nelson himself was clear that his enemy had 'such a superiority they ought to have taken us'.

Hence the heartfelt profundity of his Journal, 'How thankful I ought to be and I hope am for the mercies of Almighty God manifested to me this day. We lost only one man killed and six wounded, although my ship was cut to pieces, being obliged to receive the enemy's fire under every disadvantage believing for a long time one of the enemy to have been of the line.' He went on,

My thanks and offerings to the Almighty have been nearly in the same words and certainly with the same meaning as those so inimitably wrote in the *Spectator*, 'When I lay me down to sleep I recommend myself to the care of Almighty God, when I wake I give myself up to his direction, amidst all the evils that threaten me, I will look up to him for help, and question not but he will either avert them, or turn them to my advantage, though I know neither the time nor manner of my death, I am not at all solicitous about it, because I am sure He knows them both, and that he will not fail to support and comfort me under them.'[15]

For him to enter in his Journal this passage taken from the *Spectator* magazine of 1711, forty-seven years before he was born, suggests the extraordinary significance of this engagement.

This first experience of war was as vital to the physical courage of his leadership as the experience of 1776 had been to his motivation. He was drawing from the deepest well of his Christian belief. He did not choose to remember the secular Shakespeare's Julius Caesar, 'It seems to me most strange that men should fear / Seeing that death, a necessary end, / Will come when it will come.' Nelson was not like Caesar invoking strength from his own strength of mind. The instinct of the motherless boy was to seek love and protection, and with such certainty of it, he would become the epitome of courage and a profound source of strength and inspiration to those around him.

Nelson joined Commodore Linzee at Cagliari on the morning of the 24th. They did not get off on the right foot. He explained to Linzee, 'What has contributed to delay me a little, was four French Frigates and a Brig crossing me. A few shot was exchanged with one of them, who I left in a sinking state. We having lost the use of our main topmast could not haul the wind to them, and they seemed to have got enough: therefore would not come down to me.'[16] Linzee evidently did not take kindly to Nelson's posturing: 'The Commodore did not think it right to give us the least assistance, but sent to me to give my reasons if I could not go to sea with him the next morning totally unfit as my ship was which he knew. I would not say *Agamemnon* was ever unable to go in search of an enemy. We worked all night fishing our masts and yards and stopping holes, mending sails and splicing our rigging.'[17]

After a few days' searching for the French frigates, Linzee's squadron headed for Tunis, their purpose to 'negotiate for or take a French convoy under an eighty gun ship the *Duquesne* and a corvette'. Having already formed such a bad opinion of Linzee Nelson was horrified when he began to engage in fruitless and frustrating negotiation, 'carrying on a dammed palaver', as Nelson called it. 'Whoever yet heard of an Englishman's succeeding in a negotiation against the French. Never, never, never.'[18] The last straw was Linzee's deciding he needed to send to Hood for further orders. Nelson, who possessed a sharp sense of *realpolitik*, would have seized the convoy and negotiated from strength. 'We could I am satisfied have then with ease bribed him to keep the peace, or had he not, have knocked the Goletta and Porto Farino about his ears. He would soon have come to his senses.'[19] Having been asked, there was nothing Hood could do other than direct Linzee to 'expostulate with the Bey, in the strongest and most impressive manner'.[20] To Nelson's great relief Hood's reply also brought an order for him, to leave Linzee's command and take a squadron of frigates away in the direction of Corsica to hunt out the French frigates he had had already encountered, and to reinforce the blockade of Genoa. 'Thank God Lord Hood has taken me from under his command and given me one of my own.'[21]

From Toulon there was ominous news, causing him to write to Locker on 1 December, 'Shot and shell are very plentiful all over the harbour ... General O'Hara, I hope will be able to drive the French from the heights near the Harbour, or we shall be unpleasantly situated; not that I think Toulon is in the smallest danger.'[22] He was wrong: Bonaparte had put himself on the political map and had been appointed to replace the wounded artillery commander at the siege of Toulon. There he further exerted his instinct for intrigue, had himself promoted Major, then with the backing of Saliceti and Robespierre succeeded in having Carteaux removed. He could concentrate on retaking Toulon in his own way. He had his eye on the jugular, L' Eguillette, the fort which commanded both the inner and outer harbours.

Meanwhile Nelson could not have been happier. As a fine wind took *Agamemnon* around Cape Carbonara and he headed north to Cape Corse he told Locker, 'The Lord is very good friends with me: he is certainly the best Officer I ever saw. Everything is so clear it is impossible to misunderstand him.'[23] He told his Uncle William, 'I consider this command as a very high compliment, – there being five older Captains in the Fleet.'[24] Running into St Fiorenzo he was able to see his quarry at anchor close under the batteries, *Melpomene, Minerva, La Fortune* and *Minion*. He could not get at them and they would not come out but he

was exhilarated to learn that *Melpomene*, 'the frigate we fired at October
21st was much shattered in her hull and masts and lost above half
her men'.[25] Off Toulon, Hood was not faring so well. Bonaparte took
L'Eguillette and Toulon rapidly descended into a bloody horror of mass
executions and mob frenzy. On 18 December Hood made his decision to
abandon Toulon and torch the French fleet. News travelled swiftly up the
Mediterranean to Nelson who was now at Leghorn. 'Everything which
domestic wars produce usually are multiplied at Toulon. Fathers are here
without families, families without fathers. In short all is horror we hear.
. . . Each teller makes the scene more horrible.' He was staunch in his
defence of Hood: 'The Lord is the same collected good officer which he
always was.'[26] He must have been relying on hearsay.

In parallel with these pulsating events Fanny was continuing a peripatetic
existence despite an earlier indication that she was to settle in Swaffham
in Norfolk, 'T'is such a sad thing not to know where to direct to you,'[27]
was a minor concern. Nelson had been more disturbed by a letter from
his uncle. 'I cannot but feel uneasy at the accounts you give me of Mrs
Nelson. I wish she was comfortably fixed in a house or good lodgings,
in a place she liked; but I hope and indeed believe she will recover at
Kentish Town.'[28] He wrote to Fanny on the same day, 'I was truly sorry
to hear you were not perfectly well. Why should you fret yourself? I am
well, your son is well and we are as comfortable in every respect as the
nature of our service will admit.'[29] He did not actually receive a letter
from Fanny until hers of 16 September arrived on 1 December. 'It is
impossible my dear Fanny to say the pleasure I felt in receiving your letter
. . . I rejoice to hear you are well. Mr Suckling's letter did not give so
good an account of you as I sincerely wished.' His reply showed what
had been uppermost in her mind, lamentation about his absence and
money: 'I assure you it cannot give you more pleasure than it will me,
for us to be settled again at Burnham and I sincerely hope our father will
not part with the house to anyone so as to prevent our getting into it
again. I am glad you are improving in your music and you must have
a good instrument, we can afford it that I am sure.'[30] Six more of her
back letters arrived after Christmas. She was currently staying with the
Walpoles at Aylsham in Norfolk and was fussing in indecision about
whether or not to go to Bath after Christmas. A certain impatience

appeared in Nelson's attitude: 'As you desire my opinion about Bath etc., I have only to order that you do what you like and give you full power to give my assent to your own wishes, that is settled.' Fanny had brought out a quarterdeck mood in him so it was also a case of, 'Please remember me in the kindest manner to Lady Walpole, Lord Walpole, Mr and Mrs Hussey, and do not omit to every one of the family.'[31] He might have been saying to his first lieutenant, 'Make it so, Mr Hinton.' His father who had been up against the same indecisiveness wrote to Fanny the same month, 'I am indeed vexed your health is so precarious, and your resolution not equal I fear, to the trials you meet with . . . Swaffham, you are not perfectly pleased with; can you fancy any other place? Spending the winter months with me at Bath you have said no word about it.' Not only did she find it difficult to make decisions, she found it difficult to be candid and open about her feelings and preferences. She was so very dependent. Even Nelson's father was driven to a despairing, 'I wish I knew your real inclination.'[32]

7

'Totally Neglected'

Nelson, February 1795

With the fall of Toulon, which ended for the time being any British hopes of supporting insurrection in France, came an urgent need for Hood to decide where to base his fleet. He decided on St Fiorenzo on the north-western side of Corsica. Its wide bay and sheltered port lay some hundred miles from the French Riviera coast. Here he would be strategically well placed to watch French ships-of-the-line in Toulon, guard British commerce, harry enemy shipping, influence neutral states, shield Naples, and by his presence so far up the Mediterranean, provide encouragement and active support to Britain's Austrian allies. There was one significant complication: the French were currently in possession, the island having been ceded to them in 1768 by the Genoese. It was an uneasy and precarious possession. Corsican nationalists, disappointed in their hopes of independence following the French Revolution had, under their leader Pasquale Paoli, risen against them. Paoli, having spent twenty years of exile in London, was pro-British and trusted by the British government. Thus, in early January 1794 Hood concluded a convention with General Paoli whereby the British would help the Corsicans expel the French and Corsica would be ceded to Britain.

Hood gave Nelson the task of liaising with Paoli. He was thrilled at Hood's confidence in him and greatly flattered to be engaged in a mission he believed had initially been intended for his *bête noire*, Linzee; he saw it as 'proof of Lord Hood's confidence in me. . . I shall pledge myself for nothing which will not be acceptable to him.'[1] Hood, according to Nelson's acid letter to Fanny, had decided to give Linzee 'the eclat of taking St Fiorenzo where he was once beat off'. Linzee sent a 74, the *Fortitude*, against the fort. 'She got 56 men killed and wounded and did no good whatever. I am glad Lord Hood did not leave me under his command.'[2]

While Hood opened his attack on St Fiorenzo, Nelson was sent to blockade the fortress city of Bastia which lay almost exactly opposite, on the other side of the island, about seven miles as the crow flies, nearer twelve by the winding road. From St Fiorenzo Nelson had to sail *Agamemnon* north along the northerly neck of Corsica, round Cape Corse and then south to Bastia, some fifty miles. He decided that his arrival off the eastern coast of Corsica would best be announced by active aggression. Off Macinaggio he sent a flag of truce on shore; he had come to deliver them from the republicans and wished to be received as a friend but if a musket was fired, he would burn the place. The French Commandant replied with hauteur, 'We are Republicans; that word alone ought to satisfy you. It is not to Maginaggio, a place without defence, you ought to address yourself. Go to St Fiorenzo, to Bastia, or to Calvi, and they will answer you according to your wishes. As to the troops whom I command, they are ready to show you they are composed of French soldiers.'

Nelson was not impressed. 'I landed and struck the National colours with my own hand on the top of an old castle, and ordered the Tree of Liberty in the centre of the Town to be cut down, not without great displeasure from the inhabitants. The Military Commandant retired to a hill about two miles distant, where he paraded the troops, and kept the National flag flying all day. We destroyed about five hundred tuns of wine ready to be shipped, and ten sail of vessels.'[3]

A few days later he was searching for French privateers around the offshore island of Capraia. He had explicit orders from Hood: 'You must not attempt to take vessels out of Caprera.'[4] The French played into his hands by firing on his barge. 'This was too much for me to suffer. I took the boats, troops and *Fox* cutter, and went to the Cove, where a number of people were posted behind rocks, (where we could not land) who fired on us. It was a point of honour to take her; and after attempting in vain to dislodge the people, I boarded the Boat, and brought her out, I am sorry to say with the loss of six men wounded. She was a French Courier-boat from Bastia to Antibes; an Officer with a National cockade in his hat was killed, with several people'[5] Soon he was back on the coast of Corsica landing sixty troops at Lavesina, marching south with 200 Corsican 'friends' as he called them, to within gunshot of Bastia.[6] He

then embarked his men and sailed thirty miles east to the island of
Pianosa, again to seek out privateers. Then he was back again to Corsica
this time to parley with the Mayor of Erbalunga to find that his aggressive policy had borne fruit: the local people in the countryside surrounding Bastia had declared for him. This hectic action was suiting him.
'I am well, never better, and in active service which I love.'[7] He was a
natural marauder, who could describe the ravages he had wrought on an
enemy flour mill near St Fiorenzo as 'seizing the happy moment'.[8]

Having established his offensive presence it was now time to focus on
Bastia itself. Lying offshore, he could see before him its white Citadel
perched on a rocky outcrop, the tiled roofs of the town and below them
the mole, the port and a forest of masts. Rising immediately behind the
town were hills crowned with forts and strongpoints extending in an arc,
Fort Montserato and Fort de La Croix on the southern flank, Fort San
Gaetano and Fort Straforello directly above and behind Bastia and on
the northern flank Cardo and the redoubt of Camponella.

As *Agamemnon* sailed closer to the shore she was greeted by the boom
of guns from a newly erected battery to the south of the town. Turning
his broadside to the battery Nelson fired his first shots, scattering the
gunners and destroying the battery. Then *Agamemnon* turned and he and
his frigates *Romulus* and *Tartar* pounded the town for the next hour and
a half as they sailed past in a stately and slow-moving line.

Bastia was to mark a new phase in Nelson's experience: working hand
in glove with a flag officer who was not only powerfully decided and tena-
cious in pursuing his objectives but had a similarly active disposition.
Moreover Hood was inclined to take the younger man into his confidence,
which for Nelson was a heady and inspiring experience. He admired the
way Hood worked, 'he is as active as a man of forty [he was actually
seventy] writes all his own orders and correspondences with all the Italian
states. . . His business is enough for three common heads but to him it is
easy.'[9] Fortunate are the ambitious and capable if they work for men from
whom they can learn and who provide an example to emulate.

On 25 February British soldiers appeared on the crest of the hills overlooking Bastia and seemed to spell its doom but when *Victory* appeared
in the offing with five sail-of-the-line Nelson was astounded to learn that
General Dundas had ordered his troops back to St Fiorenzo. 'What the

General could have seen to have made a retreat necessary, I cannot conceive, the enemy's force is 1,000 regulars and 1,000 or 1,500 irregulars.'[10] To the supremely confident and optimistic Nelson the case was open and shut: '*Agamemnon* with only the frigates now here laying against the town for a few hours, with 500 troops ready to land when he had battered down the sea wall would to a certainty carry the place.' So certain was he that he was even beginning to see himself as the prime mover. 'I presumed to propose it to Lord Hood and his Lordship agreed with me, but that he should go to Fiorenza and hear what the General had to say.' His bold aggression had made such an impact on his own people that, according to Nelson, they began to reflect his own attitudes. ' My seamen are now what British seamen ought to be, to you I may say it, almost invincible. They really mind shot no more than peas.' Lord Hood was equally impressed by his firebrand and offered him the *Courageux* 74. 'I declined it, if *Agamemnon* sticks by me I will do the same by her.'[11] Nelson's stock rose to new heights as the grapevine conveyed this news through the ship.

In Nelson's liturgy it was written, 'Beware of dilatoriness. Expedition ought to be the universal word and deed.'[12] Going ashore again at Erbalunga to visit the Corsican camp he fretted at the obvious strengthening of Bastia's defences. He could observe new batteries being constructed in the hills above the town and at a possible landing place just to the north of the mole. 'Bastia will be lost if we are not active.'[13]

A combined operation was called for but the chances of inter-service collaboration were negligible. There were huge clashes of personality between Hood and the senior army officers, fundamental differences in their appreciation of what could be achieved with the resources they had, and no shared view on the necessity to energize the nationalist campaign by British action. General Dundas would not accept Hood's claim to be Supreme Commander of all military and naval forces in the Mediterranean theatre and had turned down flat the idea of attacking Bastia. Hood merely raised the ante: 'I am now ready and willing to undertake the reduction of Bastia at my own risk, with the force at present here, being strongly impressed with the necessity of it.'[14] His wonderfully indiscreet remark to Nelson, 'The General's faculties seem to be palsied – we must therefore do the best we can',[15] was well calculated to heighten Nelson's resolve, especially the intimate and conspiratorial, 'we must do the best we can'. Thirty-two-year-old Lieutenant-Colonel

Moore, who would eventually die a hero's death at Corunna, had a very sharp recollection of Hood's unwillingness to listen to the military point of view at Toulon, and blamed him for the hurried and disorganized withdrawal of British forces and failure to destroy the French fleet. He recorded in his diary, 'We all agreed as to the absurdity of Lord Hood's pretension to command the land forces and agreed to resist any such attempt.'[16] Unable to resolve the situation between himself and Hood, Dundas quit on grounds of ill health.

Hood was no more successful with Dundas's successor, Brigadier-General Abraham D'Aubant although D'Aubant did agree to two of his officers being sent to examine ground that the energetic Nelson had already earmarked for the erection of a mortar battery for bombarding the Citadel and as a place for disembarking guns and stores. Nelson concluded that they 'could readily get guns ashore a mile from where their batteries would be needed; that they could do [so] in twenty four hours'. Hood had been very keen to ascertain with precision the strength of the enemy, since the military, Moore included, were convinced they were outnumbered. Moore's estimate was 1,200–1,300 regulars, and 1,000 armed Corsicans.[17] Nelson's estimate was now 800–1,000 regulars and 1,200 to 1,500 irregulars (i.e. Corsicans). His own advocacy was unblunted, 'for I consider it would be a National disgrace to give it up, without a trial'.[18]

A council of war was held on 20 March. Hood and three flag officers, Admirals Hotham and Goodall and Commodore Linzee, sat opposite Brigadier-General D'Aubant, Lieutenant-Colonels Moore, Villettes, Wauchope, Sir J. St Clair, and Majors Pringle, Brereton and Kochler. Nelson was not involved, for the simple reason that he was not part of the command structure. The outcome was inevitable. The Army against: the Navy for.

Sir Gilbert Elliot, the Viceroy, wanted the attack to go ahead for political reasons but could make no progress in this hotbed of mischief, intrigue and equivocation. Moore's view of D'Aubant was contemptuous: 'It was evident from the beginning that whatever report was made he was determined to do nothing', but he was equally scathing about Hood: 'Lord Hood, he enters little further into the subject than to say, "Take Bastia," just as he would say to a captain, Go to sea. He conceives they are both to be done with equal facility. Having taken upon this idea, no reasoning has the smallest effect upon him.'[19] Moore's private diary shows that though he could see the faults on both sides he did nothing positive to remedy the impasse between Army and Navy. In the event the best Hood could achieve was to take back the regiments acting as marines (which Moore said amounted to half the army force). Nelson's Journal comment was more partisan than accurate. 'The general absolutely refused to attack Bastia but wonderful to tell he refused Lord Hood a single soldier, cannon or stores to assist in the siege.'[20] His own resolve was unshaken: 'I feel for the honour of my Country and had rather be beat than not to make the attack. My reputation depends on the opinion I have given; but I feel an honest consciousness that I have done right.'[21] Even more practical were Nelson's words to Sir William Hamilton, 'When was a place ever yet taken without an attempt?'[22] Almost a month was taken up with these wrangles before it became clear that Hood would have to go it alone and Nelson was soon off Bastia in *Agamemnon*. *Romulus* he sent away to Naples for mortars, shells, field pieces and stores. *Tartar* he anchored four miles to the south of Bastia, *Scout* three miles to the north. His boats he set rowing guard off the mole and his gunboats were positioned to harry the defenders. Bastia was sealed off.

At ten o'clock on the morning of 4 April Lieutenant-Colonel Villettes landed with what seems in retrospect to have been a surprisingly large number of troops, in total 1,183, of whom only 261 were officially classified as marines. Nelson accompanied him with 250 seamen, no more than one-fifth of the total land force, albeit more than three-quarters of those classified as gunners. Landing at Miomo, three miles to the north, their first priority was to advance on Bastia. By noon they were about a mile and three-quarters from the Citadel, mountain peaks to their right, sea to their left, gullies and ridges ahead. Their tasks were then to make roads, battery sites and defences for the batteries, to get guns, mortars, platforms and ammunition up to the battery sites; as Nelson said, 'great labour for so small a number of men'. In the warm but fresh April weather Nelson was in high health and spirits, 'enjoying the confidence of Lord Hood and Colonel Vilettes and the Captains landed with the seamen obeying my orders'. It should be noted that although called captains these officers were not post captains like Nelson; they were masters and commanders, called captains out of courtesy, as was everyone who commanded a ship.

On 11 April a solitary officer was rowed ashore from *Victory* under a flag of truce. He delivered Hood's summons to the Convention's Commissioner La Combe Michel, who rejected it disdainfully: 'I have hot shot

for your Ships, and bayonets for your troops. When two thirds of our
Troops are killed, I will trust to the generosity of the English.' From
his battery Nelson saw a red flag flutter at *Victory*'s main topgallant
masthead and the order was given to open fire on the town, Citadel and
redoubt of Camponella. To the rousing cheers of the British seamen the
British guns and mortars (sixteen in all) opened fire.[23] They had laboured
for eight days to construct battery emplacements and gun platforms and
to secure them from attack with breastworks but it was now obvious to
all concerned that the garrison was not going to surrender. Moore's Diary
recorded, 'Lord Hood's attack has not weakened the place.'[24] Over a
period of more than five weeks during which the British expended a vast
amount of ordnance – 1,058 barrels of powder and 19,297 rounds of
shot and shell (and the defenders probably a similar volume) – casualties were low. The British total was nineteen killed or died of wounds
and thirty-seven wounded, less than 4 per cent of the total British troops
and seamen engaged.[25] Only one ball in about a thousand was a killer.

And so it went on, the British periodically pushing their batteries
forward, engaging in heavy bombardment and counter-bombardment.
On 27 April they had begun to create a battery on a forward ridge only
250 yards from Camponella. Here they lived on the edge of attack. 'The
seamen always slept on the battery with their pikes and cutlasses.'[26]

A fortnight after the guns first opened up Nelson himself was still
optimistic but working himself up into one of his prickly states. He wrote
to Hood that Villettes was treating him perfectly well, 'yet I am considered as not commanding the seamen landed. My wishes may be and are
complied with; my order would possibly be disregarded: therefore if we
move from hence, I would wish your Lordship to settle that point.'[27] A
day later it emerged that Captain Hunt, another of Hood's protégés, was
the problem. Although 'a most exceeding good young man . . . an idea
has entered into the heads of some under him, that Captain Hunt's
command was absolutely distinct from me; and that I had no authority
whatsoever over him, except as a request. It was even doubted whether
I had a right to command the Officers and Seamen landed from the
Agamemnon.' He wanted 'an order to command the Seamen without any
distinction as to any particular services'.[28] Hood very wisely counselled
Nelson that to issue such an order to the other captains would 'imply
dissatisfaction somewhere which you must be aware will do mischief'.[29]
Nelson immediately appreciated the sense of what Hood was saying, and

Hood did not leave things to fester. A few days later when the new battery was being prepared on the ridge close to the Camponella, Hood made use of the opportunity to order Hunt to take orders from Nelson and make it known to the other officers too.[30]

This was a revealing episode. In spite of being so much senior to the other naval officers, none of whom was a post captain, Nelson was not feeling in himself the conviction of command, needing to be bolstered by written authority. Perhaps the military officers were the real problem. Lacking a sufficiently nice sense of naval hierarchy they probably tended to treat the naval officers as interchangeable supporting players. But the episode also reflects on Nelson's limitations. He had already shown in *Agamemnon* that he could select and create a team, that he was an instinctive achiever who defined objectives and drove his men forward to gain them. And just as he could weld his people into a motivated group, he would pay great attention to each as an individual. These were formidable powers, but he was not a team player in the sense that he put the team before himself. He was driven by a need to be first. Whilst there was never any conscious denying of praise due to others, never any tendency to take praise belonging to another, he was most assiduous in seeking his own place in the sun and a jealous man when it came to his own standing, his own contribution and his own credit.

Nelson's personal ownership of the action was by now intense. 'The expedition is almost a child of my own, and I have no fears about the final issue, it will be victory, Bastia will be ours. If so it will be an event which the history of England can hardly boast its equal.'[31] Bastia was indeed on the brink of capitulation. The guns fell silent and six days later Nelson's Journal recorded, 'At daylight this morning the most glorious sight which an Englishman and I believe none but an Englishman could experience was to be seen, four thousand five hundred men laying down their arms to less than 1,000 English soldiers. Our loss of men in taking this town containing upwards of 14,000 inhabitants, and fully inhabited would contain 25,000 was the smallest possible to be conceived.'[32]

Colonel Moore's view was as ever jaundiced. He had believed all along that Bastia would have to be starved into submission and that effectively was what had happened. In his view the whole of Hood's effort was a charade. 'He never advanced one inch. If he had he must have been cut up.'[33] There is a kind of rationality in Moore's judgement but it also speaks volumes against the quality of his own leadership that he so discounted the value of aggression, initiative, and the forcing bid that the land blockade had been. Hood was generous in his thanks to Nelson:

> The Commander in Chief returns his best thanks to Capt Nelson, and desires he will present them to Capt. Hunt, Capt. Serocold and Capt. Bullen, as well as to every officer and Seaman employed in the reduction of Bastia. . . . Notwithstanding the various difficulties, and disadvantages they have had to struggle with, which could not have been surmounted, but by the uncommon spirit & cordial unanimity, that has been so conspicuously displayed, & which must give a stamp of reputation to their characters not to be effaced, & will be remembered with gratitude by the Commander in Chief to the end of his life.[34]

For all the fidget over Hunt, Hood had recognized certain Nelson hallmarks: his capacity to encourage others to collaborate, and his ability to energize and to deliver.

Nelson's hyperbole and self-congratulation began to run riot. To his brother he wrote, 'it was such an event as is hardly on record'.[35] And to Fanny, 'Lord Hood has gained the greatest credit for his perseverance and I dare say he will not forget that it was due to myself in a great measure this glorious expedition was undertaken.'[36] He confided smugly in Fanny, 'Lord Hood's thanks to me both public and private are the handsomest that man can pen. Having ever since our leaving England been in the habit of getting thanks and applauses, I look for them as a matter of course.'[37]

Nelson was at Leghorn when a frigate arrived with news of a French fleet heading towards the west coast of Corsica, in the direction of Calvi, the next British target. Hood weighed immediately to head them off. Completing his reprovisioning at breakneck speed, Nelson hurried after Hood only to be ordered to leave the scene of potential action. He was to return to Bastia, convoy troops to St Fiorenzo, then land them at Calvi some thirty-five miles further south. He sailed from Bastia at noon on 13 July with 1,450 troops in twenty-two transports. Two days later when they came to anchor in Mortella Bay a newly appointed army commander,

General Stuart came on board, anxious to proceed without delay. This chimed totally with Nelson's instincts. Confident that Hood would deal with any French threat, he ordered the expeditionary force to weigh and depart. They cleared Mortella Bay and the Gulf of St Fiorenzo, rounded the Punta di Curza, and kept well offshore until they rounded Cape Revellata which hid Calvi from the west. Here they were in deep water with a rocky sea bed, not at all ideal for anchoring, and offering only one option for landing, a narrow inlet called Porto Agro. It was punctuated with sunken rocks near the shore and prone to a heavy swell which would prevent boats from landing when the sea breeze blew. Tactically, they were reasonably well placed, their landing place some three and a half miles south-west of Calvi.

Lieutenant-General Stuart, recently arrived from England, was a man of entirely different calibre from his predecessors, eager to get moving and ready to collaborate. Although too late to join in the siege of Bastia he was on record as admiring Hood's 'spirited and persevering action'.[38]

Unfortunately this combined operation was getting off to a bad start. Stuart, extremely disenchanted by Hood's absence, doubted his commitment. In fact Hood was very aware that he was letting Stuart down by taking his ships away to look for the French fleet. 'This is a very mortifying circumstance, particularly as it must prevent my giving that attention and support to General Stuart my inclinations strongly lead me to.'[39] To Stuart's great credit his actual reaction was positive. He set about making do with what he had been given, that is Nelson, pushing him hard, badgering him about contingency plans in case of needing to abort the mission, about a hospital tent, and about more seamen for hauling guns ashore. 'Every time I write delay, my dear Sir, I suffer more than I can describe, for it very little suits with my inclination or warmth of disposition.'[40] Nelson did not bridle at Stuart's driving but responded energetically to his confidence, energy and power of command. He was in his active element again. Having landed 1,450 troops and his 250 seamen at the rocky and treacherous inlet of Porto Agro, he had to get the guns out of his ships into the boats, land them and haul them inch by inch up the steep gulley side and then some two and a half miles more across the rugged terrain, making roads where necessary, ferrying powder, shot, shell and gunners' stores behind them. Each gun was about nine feet long and two and a half tons in weight and even for fifty men was a loading of one hundredweight (50 kilos) per man. Moore's diary shows that not all the work was in fact done by Nelson's men: 300 of his soldiers assisted for at least five days.

It was at this point that Nelson learned what Hood's dispatch to the Admiralty had said about his contribution at Bastia. Quite rightly Hood had mentioned first the 'unremitting zeal, exertion, and judicious conduct of Lieutenant Colonel Vilettes'. Then came 'Captain Nelson . . . who had the command and directions of the Seamen in landing guns, mortars and stores. Then came Captain Hunt who commanded at the batteries very ably assisted by Captain Buller and Captain Serocold, and the Lieutenants Gore, Hotham, Stiles, Andrews, and Brisbane.' He ended, 'Captain Hunt, who was on shore in the command of the batteries, from the hour the troops landed to the surrender of the Town, will be the bearer of this Dispatch and can give any further information you may wish to know respecting the siege.'[41] Captain Hunt was being specially noticed, Nelson's role being relegated to that of a workhorse merely involved in the logistics of the operation. Nelson was dumbfounded yet determined to put a brave face on it, for he went on in a more philosophical vein to Fanny, 'But however services may be received, it is not right in any officer to slacken his zeal for his country. I only wish Lord Hood had never mentioned my name. I should have felt more pleasure than in a general way which he has done. . . However the Lord and myself are good friends. I have not seen him since I have the letter.'[42]

He soon found an opportunity, because eight days later, at a critical point in the siege, he told his uncle William Suckling what had transpired, 'Lord Hood and myself were never better friends, – nor, although his letter does, does he wish to put me where I never was – in the rear. Captain Hunt, who lost his Ship, he wanted to push forward for another.' It says a lot for Hood's style, and for Nelson's belief in him, that Hood was able to get away with such an explanation. That having been said, there was an unbridgeable gap between Nelson and Hood's perception of Nelson's role and contribution. Nelson was clear, 'The whole operations of the Siege were carried on through Lord Hood's letters to me. I was the mover of it – I was the cause of its success. Sir Gilbert Elliot will be my evidence, if any is required. I am not a little vexed, but shall not quarrel. We shall be successful here [Calvi]; and a stranger and a landsman [General Stuart] will probably do me that credit which a friend and brother Officer has not given me.'[43]

Nelson was like many men in influential but subordinate roles. They believe themselves responsible for what those above them decide. They forget the distinction between those who have ideas and advocate courses of action and those who take the decisions and are accountable for them. He had told Fanny at the beginning of May, 'The expedition is almost a child of my own.'[44] While it is undoubtedly true that his efforts and commitment were of the highest order and in today's loose parlance might even be described as 'heroic', he was neither responsible nor accountable for the operation. Hood's description of what Nelson had done was closer to reality than Nelson's, although in praising others in the way he did, he diminished Nelson's contribution. Bastia thus provided Nelson with one of the greatest challenges for any ambitious man: to manage his disappointment. Nelson struggled manfully, but it was not in his nature to forget credit he believed due to him.

Rather more serious was Nelson's admission that he had suppressed the truth of what he knew about the force in Bastia. His Journal and letters show that as his commitment to attack increased, the number of likely opponents tended to diminish: from 1,000 regulars and 1,200–1,500 irregulars in a letter to Hood of 18 March, to 800 French in his letters of 26 March and 29 March to William Suckling and Sir William Hamilton, letters in which he poured scorn on the Army's refusal to support an attack. When, after the surrender, 4,500 enemy laid down their arms, he said he had known all along that they were as numerous. Nelson seems to have had no inhibition about massaging figures in order to make his case: here he actually withheld intelligence from Hood. He also had a chauvinistic attitude to enemy numbers which may have clouded his judgement: 'I always was of opinion, have ever acted up to it, and never have had any reason to repent it, that one Englishman was equal to three Frenchmen.'[45]

For the time being however he had to bend his thoughts to the matter in hand as Stuart's strategy began to unfold. Their target stood on a high promontory, the centre point of the angular V-shaped Gulf of Revellata to its left, and the curving Gulf of Calvi to its right. Fort Monteciesco, about 2,200 yards to the town's south-west, guarded the landward approaches and would be directly in Stuart's path. Closer to the town and arranged in a rough semicircular shield were three additional strongpoints: to the west the Mozzello fort, to its north the Fountain battery

and beyond that the San Francesco battery flanking the sea. Stuart's strategy was to establish a battery about a thousand yards to the seaward
side of Fort Monteciesco, then push on a further thousand yards to establish another so that he had Fort Mozzello and the Fountain battery in
his sights. They would then go on to establish batteries even closer to the
Mozzello, which would be bombarded first from 750 yards and then
from 300 yards in preparation for his breakthrough.

On 4 July their first battery opened fire on Fort Monteciesco and
Stuart's infantry made feint attacks. Two days later, as day broke, the
British were caught exposed in their most forward position, guns as yet
unmounted. For four hours they were under fire, unable to reply. Nelson's
companion, Captain Serocold had his head taken off by a grapeshot, a
mate from one of the transports had a leg shot off and a sergeant, two
privates and a seaman from *Agamemnon* were killed. 'It is wonderful
our loss has not been greater.'[46] By ten o'clock they were able to open
fire themselves but it had been a murderous passage. The next day, 'they
kept up a constant heavy fire of shot and shells on our battery. They
destroyed two of our guns and much damaged another and the works.
One shell burst in the centre of our battery amongst the General, myself
and at least a 100 of us, but wonderful not a man was hurt, although it
blew up our battery magazine.' Nelson scribbled a hurried note to Fanny.
'It is possible you may have heard that a Captain of the Navy has fallen.
To assure you it is not me, I write a few lines; for if such a report should
get about, I well know your anxiety of mind . . . I am very busy, yet own
I am in all my glory: except with you, I would not be any where but
where I am, for the world.'[47] General Stuart was up with his troops too,
leading by example. 'He every night sleeps in the advanced battery.'[48]
That day two seamen were killed and three wounded, on the next, one
soldier killed and two wounded, on the next, one artilleryman killed. On
the 12th, enemy fire from the town and the San Francesco battery was
very heavy and 'seldom (very extraordinary) missing our battery'.[49] It
could have been Nelson's turn to die. Moore's diary noted: 'Captain
Nelson was wounded by stones in the face. It is feared he will lose one
of his eyes. My batman was knocked down by my side by rubbish and
a good deal bruised: the ball struck a heap of stones close to us.'[50]

Nelson played down his wound. To Fanny he talked of 'a very slight
scratch towards my right eye which has not been the slightest inconvenience', and to Hood he was equally nonchalant: 'I got a little hurt this

morning, not much as you may judge by my writing.' But Hood knew his Nelson and expressed concern to Elliot: 'he speaks lightly of it, but I wish he may not lose the sight of an eye'.[51] His foreboding was well founded. A blow to Nelson's right eye had ruptured a blood vessel, probably damaged the optic nerve and had caused permanent loss of sight. Surprisingly there was no structural damage to the eyeball, which appeared normal, except for some enlargement of the pupil. And in effect, although Nelson was now monocular it is in the nature of things that the good eye takes over and so he was not operationally handicapped. In later life he would complain much about deterioration and irritation in his good, or left, eye. This deterioration, more noticeable to him because he had no compensating good eye, was probably caused by increasing short sight, and by pterygium, 'an overgrowth of conjunctival tissue over the clear cornea, typical of persons living in hot dry climates and in seafarers', and observable in all his portraits from Lemuel Abbott in 1797 onwards.[52]

News from England of Howe's victory of the First of June did not automatically raise Nelson's spirits: 'our efforts here are at such a distance, and so eclipsed by Lord Howe's great success at home, that I dare say we are not thought of'.[53] His true thirst was for his own recognition.

Nelson, in the thick of it, was as ever alive to the needs of his seamen. 'When I was on the beach, seeing how necessary it was to give encouragement to the Transport's people to exert themselves in getting Stores on shore, I gave them some wine and provisions rather than any delay should be made, but I did not feel myself justified in always continuing it. However the people behaved well, and having worked all day probably, and ordered to work all night, if your Lordship will allow me, I will discretionarily order them a little wine as an encouragement.'[54] Hood's reply illustrates exactly how in some fundamental ways he and Nelson were one of a kind, and how a great commander builds up a relationship with his subordinates: 'I am truly sorry to hear you have received a hurt, and hope you tell the truth in saying it is not much. I shall be glad you will order the Boats' crews of the Transports wine, upon any occasion you judge necessary. I shall send some one in the morning to know how you are, and whether you would not have assistance.'[55]

Nelson, the man in the middle, was finding his position very uncomfortable and his inability to influence events, frustrating. Writing to Hood, he identified Moore as the problem. 'I hope to God the General,

who seems a good Officer and an amiable man, is not led away: but
Colonel Moore is his great friend ... the General took me aside. ...
There seems a little jealousy of my communicating with you daily. ...
Your Lordship will be so good as not to notice any part of this letter to
the General; for you must feel that a more free communication has not
been kept up by the General; but indeed I don't yet say he is to blame.
I wish Moore was 100 leagues off: he will injure him [Stuart] with the
Army I see clearly ... I beg your Lordship to burn this letter.'[56]

This was a critical juncture. Even so, Nelson's words were neither wise
nor mature. He was failing to rise above his situation. It was inevitable
that he, a naval outsider, should be suspected as a source of leaks and
tale telling. It was equally inevitable that he should feel himself an outsider because the military hierarchy was making no attempt to involve
him in its tactical thinking, merely using him as a means for delivering
guns to specified places and supervising their firing. It was an excep-
tionally trying situation to be in, so powerless, so little in control and yet
so accountable to Hood. Yet his reaction was that of a rather ordinary
man. Difficult though it would have been, he was not able to be detached
and analytical, and became overexcited and emotional in his personal
reaction to Moore. His injunction to his Admiral to burn his letter was
absurdly dramatic and indicated the extent to which events were getting
on top of him. Hood felt impelled to counsel him to be careful. Unfortunately he did so in an injudicious and conspiratorial way, calculated to
increase the gap between Nelson and the soldiers, ending, 'but beware
of the Colonel [Moore] you mention'.[57] Hood was not really in the business of collaboration and therefore could not help Nelson to adjust. The
net effect was to mirror his own anti-Army attitudes and encourage the
kind of comment Nelson made on the 19th, 'I can't help thinking sometimes we are too active.'[58]

As at Bastia, the perspective on Nelson's role can be clearly drawn.
General Stuart was making the strategic and tactical decisions about the
conduct of the campaign. There is no indication that Nelson shared in
them, even though Stuart might have shared them with him. Hood was
using Nelson as his executive officer ashore, not as a stand-in for himself.
Nelson was making an invaluable and vital contribution in logistical
management and in organizing and leading his seamen to fight the guns
on shore, but his was essentially a support function. In a sense this is
borne out in Moore's Diary. Other than his mention of the damage to

Nelson's eye there is neither praise nor blame for Nelson's contribution, nor indeed any other mention of him.

The British crept nearer. More guns were landed. They were now on the point of constructing their most forward battery and launching an attack on fort Mozzello. The Fountain battery was taken by Colonel Wemyss without its firing a shot. Moore's men stormed the Mozzello breach and the enemy fled so precipitately that Major Brereton had no time to cut off their escape. But the defenders were far from finished and such was the intensity of fire from the town that six of the Royal Irish were killed and twelve wounded. Stuart paused to send in a flag of truce to know if they had any terms to propose. Their answer was the town motto, 'Civitas Calvi semper fidelis.'

Stuart gathered himself for a final push. He asked for more men and Nelson referred the request to Hood: 'This application I thought was coming, but I do not see there can be any occasion for it; but our exertions must not slacken. Moutray [Mary Moutray's son, a lieutenant in the *Victory*] some days ago said to Colonel Moore something that led Moore to say, "Why don't Lord Hood land 500 men to work? Our soldiers are tired." Here the riddle is fully explained.' Fearing he might have gone too far Nelson hastily added, 'I never write or open my mouth to any one but your Lordship.'[59]

The pressure from the General was for more resources, 'more troops, more seamen to work, and more amunition'. Nelson was powerless to do more than suggest that the General approach Hood direct. Hood combed his ships for more men to move the heavy cannon on the night of the 20th, fifty from each of his frigates and a hundred from the *Victory*. 'Captain Seccombe will command the whole – under your directions,' Nelson found himself being pushed. 'Surely my dear Nelson you can draw more than 77 men from the *Agamemnon* stationary as she lays.'[60] As a result Nelson had 700 men working throughout the night, moving forward eleven guns, mortars and howitzers and 2,000 rounds of shot and shell. On the night of the next day he recorded in his Journal, 'None but seamen and mules at work.' On the 22nd he told Hood, 'We will fag ourselves to death, before any blame shall lie at our doors; and I trust, my dear Lord, it will not be forgotten that twenty five pieces of heavy ordnance have been dragged to the different batteries and mounted and all but three at the Royal Louis battery, have been fought by Seamen, except one Artillery-man to point the guns.'[61] Although not a shot was fired both sides worked frenziedly, the defenders to redeploy their guns and strengthen their battery defences, the British to advance their batteries to within 600–900 yards of the town.

They were all suffering from stress. Nelson told Hood, 'I am far from well; but not so ill as to be confined. My eye is troublesome, and I don't think I shall ever have the perfect sight of it again.' Hood was irritated with him. 'What can you mean by applying to me for empty casks [for filling with soil to strengthen earthworks], when there are a number on shore in the cave where the shot was landed, and the *Nancy* Transport is full of them for God's sake do know what the transports have got.'[62] It seemed to Nelson that General Stuart was not himself. 'What is the matter I cannot tell, but he does not seem satisfied. The General may have his causes to be displeased, but I am confident they cannot be caused by any part of the Naval Department.'[63] Hood kept protesting his willingness to help: 'I can only repeat to you my earnest desire, that you comply with the General's wishes as far as you can and should they be beyond your powers let me know them . . . I am quite unhinged.'[64] Nelson had to be defensive:

> It is morally impossible that the General can be out of humour with your Lordship or with any of us. He has never expressed a wish that has not instantly been complied with, in its fullest extent. I trust he will not forget our services: and when I recollect the mounting of the six gun battery, how he expressed his thanks for our seamen dragging and mounting the guns under a heavy fire of grapeshot, I think he cannot. Sixty Seamen were with the field pieces, and as exposed as any Troops the morning of the Storm, but no notice has been taken of them; but I shall not forget this fact, that every gun is dragged and fought by Seamen.[65]

He was full of pride at his men's performance and behaviour – 'only two have been punished since our first landing'[66] – and full of praise for the lieutenants who had led the gun teams. Nelson was learning that those who are perceived to be ancillary workers rarely have their vital achievement recognized.

On 28 July the Governor of Calvi announced that if no help arrived within twenty-five days they would be prepared to discuss terms for surrender. The British, who had supplies of shot and shell for seven days only and whose ranks were increasingly thinned by sickness, insisted on a thirteen-day deadline.

Much to Nelson's satisfaction hostilities were resumed. 'I own I rejoiced when our fire opened against the Enemy . . . there are times, and I think the present is one of them, when it would be more charitable to our Troops to make the Enemy suffer, than for our brave fellows to die incessantly, four or five a day.'[67]

A day's incessant firing had the desired effect and 'the enemy hung out a flag of truce'. Nelson could not resist displaying his superior judgement to Viceroy Elliot, as he had to General Dalling about San Juan. In the process he cast aspersions indirectly on Hood and Stuart, just as he had on Polson:

I dare say the General and Lord Hood have good reasons for their conduct, nor do I mean in the smallest degree to arraign them; but I hope twenty five years in the service will plead my excuse for giving an opinion, even to you, Sir, who will not let it go further. What are the Enemys' inducements to get this kind of Truce? – their works are not going to ruin, you are getting, they know, every day more and more less able to act against them . . . I have no doubt but we could, after having ruined the defences of this place, have made a breach in the Bastion, – at all events run a mine under it, and blown it into the air in less time than this Truce has lasted; and I own I had rather take a place by our own fire and efforts, than the Enemy being starved and sickly.[68]

His point made, he added a PS in a rather disingenuous attempt to avoid the accusation of disloyalty. 'Perhaps my pen has been too free. Be so good as to burn my letter when read.'

When on 10 August Nelson's second siege came to an end, it turned out that half the French were sick in hospital and so from the beginning had been heavily outnumbered by the British. His rule of thumb that one Englishman was worth three Frenchmen had not turned out to have had much validity in this case. Nelson's chauvinistic underestimate of an enemy would get him into trouble on more than one occasion in the future.

By now the victors were in a bad state. Nelson wrote to the Duke of Clarence, 'we have upwards of one thousand sick out of two thousand,

and the others not much better than so many phantoms. We have lost many men from the season, very few from the Enemy. I am here the reed among the oaks; all the prevailing disorders have attacked me, but I have not strength for them to fasten upon: I bow before the storm, while the sturdy oak is laid low.'[69] Rather uncharacteristically he said nothing to the Duke about what he had contributed in the sieges. He had had enough. As he told Fanny, 'I am not the worse for campaigning, but I cannot say I have any wish to go on with it. This day I have been four months landed (except a few days we were after the French fleet) and I feel almost qualified to pass my examination as a besieging General.'[70]

Everything was now anticlimactic and doubly wearisome: arranging transports for the French garrison, getting his precious guns back on board, keeping his men under control. He told Hood, 'it is as easy to keep a flock of wild geese together as our seamen'.[71] With his guns back on board his aim was Leghorn and a refit; as he told Fanny, 'My Ship's company are all worn out, as is this whole Army, except myself. Nothing hurts me.'[72] He was worried about his invalids. Mary Moutray's son was close to death. 'Poor little Hoste is also so extremely ill that I have great fears about him. Bolton very ill. Suckling that giant knocked up and 150 of my people in their beds.' Disenchantment was creeping over him. 'I left Calvi on the 15th I hope never to be in it again.' As for recognition, he feared the worst: 'But what degree of credit may be given to my services I cannot say. General Stuart and Lord Hood are as far asunder as the other Generals. They hate us sailors, we are too active for them. We accomplish our business sooner than they like.' Most worrying of all was the possible loss of his patron. 'Lord Hood has been very ill and no doubt has applied for leave to go home. I hope he will take me with him.'[73] Young Moutray died of 'Calvi fever' and Nelson reflected to Fanny, 'What a shock it will be to his poor Mother, who was all expectation to hear of his promotion when a very different account will now be told her.'[74] Full of sentiment and remembrance of times past he erected a memorial stone to James Moutray in the church at St Fiorenzo.

By now Stuart had sent off his dispatch. His mentions of Nelson had been brief. Stuart had not lived up to Nelson's hopes and expectations. Hood's dispatch included Nelson's Journal. 'The Journal I herewith transmit from Captain Nelson, who had the command of the Seamen, will show the daily occurrences of the Siege, and whose unremitting zeal and exertion, I cannot sufficiently express, or of that of Captain

Hallowell, who took it by turns to command in the advanced battery twenty-four hours at a time, and I flatter myself they, as well as the other Officers and Seamen, will have full justice done them by the General: it is therefore unnecessary for me to say more on the subject.'[75] In that he was mistaken – and neither Hood nor Stuart had said a word about Nelson's wound.

8

'My Disposition Can't Bear
Tame and Slow Measures'

Nelson, April 1795

It was now known that Hood was to leave the station and Nelson hoped to go with him: 'When Lord Hood quits I should be truly sorry to remain. He is the greatest sea officer I ever knew.' Writing to his Uncle William Suckling from Genoa where he had arrived in thick weather with dispatches for Drake, the Minister, he was clear about his ultimate destination: '*Agamemnon* is still on the wing, and will not rest, most probably, till she gets into Portsmouth, which I hope will be no great length of time, as Lord Hood is inclined to take me home with him, and turn us into a good Seventy-four; for although I have been offered every Seventy-four which has fallen vacant in this Country, yet I could not bring myself to part with a Ship's company, with whom I have gone through such a series of hard service, as has never before, I believe, fallen to the lot of any one ship.'[1] This was no exaggeration. Although his young midshipmen, Suckling, Hoste, Bolton and Weatherhead, were all happily recovered, his people as a whole were in a bad state. Nelson's log for 9 September 1794 read, 'The Physician of the fleet came onboard and surveyed the ship's company, and found them in a very weak state.' Fresh meat, milk, bread and wine were supplied for the sick but several died.[2] As for himself, there were no signs of the weak and sickly Nelson of tradition. 'My constitution is absolutely the wonder of the fleet. Nothing hurts it. I have been 5 nights without sleep (at work) and never felt an inconvenience.'[3]

It was not just the fleet that was in a state of transition. In the summer of 1794 the Portland Whigs coalesced with Pitt; and George, second Earl Spencer, a Whig grandee, became First Lord of the Admiralty at the age of thirty-six. His appointment would soon have immense significance for

Nelson's career. From 1794 to 1801 Spencer would be the pivotal figure in naval appointments.

At the end of September when Nelson was told by Hood to put himself under the command of Admiral Hotham, he felt that *frisson* which always goes with a change of boss: 'with new men, new measures are generally adopted'.[4] He was despondent. 'My ship's company are by no means recovered but we are destined to keep the seas till ship and crew are all rendered unfit for service.'[5] He was naturally worried about losing Lord Hood's patronage but having had reassuring talks with him was able to tell Fanny, 'Lord Hood is very well inclined towards me.' He broke the news of his staying in the Mediterranean sensitively and positively:

> At all events I shall cheat the winter and as I understand I am to have a cruise it may possibly be advantageous. . . Now, how do you intend to spend the winter? Does Norfolk take up any part of it? I hope you will spend it cheerfully. . . . Perhaps if my father goes to Bath you will spend part of it with him. The Wolterton family I am sure will be happy to receive you for as long a time as you please. All I have to beg is that you will not repine at my not coming. I am sure Lord Hood will get *Agamemnon* ordered to England as soon as circumstances will permit of it. When you go to London I beg you will call on Lady Hood and perhaps you will see the Lord. Before Spring I hope we shall have peace when we must look out for some little cottage. I shall return to the plough with redoubled glee. . . I hope you are not sparing in sending to [Marsh and Creed] for money. I have never drawn on them since I have been in the Mediterranean[6]

Unfortunately Hotham did not impress Nelson. He had been sent off to look for the French fleet, 'who had again given Hotham the slip'. There had been a mutiny on board the *Windsor Castle* and Hotham, much to Nelson's disgust, 'had forgiven the ship's company who richly deserved a halter. I am of opinion 'tis mistaken lenity and will be the cause of present innocent people being hanged. I wish Lord Hood was either here or I with him.' As for the enemy, 'should they come out, we shall beat them if our Admiral give us leave, which many doubt'.[7]

Agamemnon was now undergoing a refit in Leghorn and as he surveyed the rather mournful process of dismounting her masts, he was
inclined to muse gloomily, 'What can be expected from a worn out ship
and ship's company? Notwithstanding I am in the best possible health,
yet I don't like any longer to be kicked about. I am tired. Now service
is over I believe for the present, I have more time to think and believe
that no person has been treated so ill as myself.' Tired and increasingly
dispirited, with the fleet under new management, and with no prospect
of action other than watching workmen swarming over his ship, he had
time to romance about the part he had played in the sieges. 'I now think
knowing to be true that I was the humble instrument of Corsica's being
taken, the active instrument for Bastia's being attacked by the English
and without vanity . . . that I was the cause of 4,500 French troops laying
down their arms to 1,000 English marines and seamen.'[8] To make matters
worse he was being made desperate by reports that the French fleet were
at sea while the *Agamemnon* was immobilized, 'It would go nigh to break
my heart, but I will hope the best.' He added, 'the lying in port is misery
to me'.[9]

But it was not all misery. In one of his letters he remarked innocently,
'I have lodgings on shore during the refitment of my ship and a French
master, which with the amusements of the place fully occupy my time.'[10]
The amusements included Adelaide Correglia, an 'opera singer', most
probably introduced to him by the Consul in Leghorn, John Udney who
seems to have had a sideline in introducing naval officers to obliging
ladies. She had no English to speak of and he no Italian, which rules out
the theory that she was one of his intelligence agents (a theory mounted
on the sole basis of Nelson's remark to Elliot,' One old lady tells me all
she hears, which is what we wish'). Certainly Captain Thomas Fremantle, a fellow captain in Hood's fleet, recognized her for what she was. He
mentioned meeting her at Christmas 1794: 'Dined at Nelson's and his
dolly.' She was still around in mid-1795 when Fremantle again noticed,
'Dolly aboard . . . he makes himself ridiculous with that woman.'[11] Fremantle did not trouble to refer to her as Madame, or Signora Correglia,
or La Correglia the opera singer, or simply as his agent. His choice of
the adjective 'ridiculous' suggests a rather comic scene in which he was
struck either by her incongruity as a companion for the slightly built post
captain, or by Nelson's embarrassing personal attentions, most likely the
latter.

Naval officers, like the men they commanded, were not expected to be celibate; a woman in every port was their response to the genetic imperative, but this varied according to the individual, from the naturally celibate or faithful, to the most promiscuously active. Nelson's wooing of Mary Simpson, Elizabeth Andrews, Mary Moutray, and finally Fanny, had suggested that his was not a sexually driven nature. The story of his marriage suggests the same. But this episode in Leghorn, quite possibly his first excursion into sex outside marriage, was enjoyed with a woman who was essentially a courtesan, one who opened his senses to physical pleasure and produced a certain sexual besottedness in his behaviour. His one surviving letter to Adelaide, in fractured French, noteworthy for having been written at all, is infused with a certain warmth and intimacy suggesting some residual tenderness, at least on his part, 'Ma Chere Adelaide, Je suis en ce moment pour la Mere. Une Vaisseau Neopolitan partir avec moi pour Livorne. Croire moi toujours. Votre Chere Amie, Horatio Nelson. Avez Vous bien successe.'[12] Perhaps it was part of the Adelaide effect that he wrote to Fanny, 'My health is extraordinary good and I feel myself 7 years younger than when I left England.'[13]

During his adventures ashore his letters home, not surprisingly, show him anxious to please Fanny. There were regular references to Josiah, affectionate and concerned; he was a good boy doing well, a clever smart young man, though Nelson referred ominously on one occasion to his temper, 'but warm in his disposition which nothing can cool so well as being at sea where nobody [can] have entirely their own way'.[14] Again questions had been raised about Josiah's future and Nelson wrote to Fanny, 'I think if the Lockharts [Fanny's sister-in-law and her husband] will get Josiah a good place he has sense enough to give up the sea, although he is already a good seaman.' A month later he would be more emphatic. 'I wish Mr Lockhart could get Josiah a good place on shore I am sure I don't like his going to sea.' He was beginning to be somewhat equivocal about Josiah and dubious about his future as a naval officer.

Nelson, always exalted by action, did not tell Fanny too much. He kept himself to generalities and expressions of affection. Yet his way of reassuring his wife must at times have had exactly the opposite effect, especially when he tried to make her feel part of his mission and share in it with him: 'I need not I am sure, say that all my joy is placed in you, I have none separated from you, you are present, my imagination be where I will. Every action of my life I know you must feel for, all my joys of victory are two fold to me knowing how you must partake of them, only recollect a brave man dies but once, a coward all his life long. We cannot escape death, and should it happen to me in this place, recollect it is the will of Him in whose hands are issues of life and death.'[15]

When the subject of money came up it usually was prompted by her worries as we have seen. He sent her regular 'spend what you need' messages. There are references to other people's moneymaking. On 27 June, 'I am not sorry to find others get rich it does not make us one bit the poorer. Corsica in the prize way produces nothing but honour, far above the consideration of wealth. Not that I dislike riches, quite the contrary but would not sacrifice a good name to obtain them. The only treasure to you I shall expect to bring back is Josiah and myself.'[16] On 28 June, 'I hope those people who are to get so much money will make a proper use of it, had I attended to the service of my country less than I have I might have made some too. However I trust my name will stand on record when the money makers will be forgot.'[17] We are impelled to conclude that Fanny was a money-minded lady; he preferred to think first of honour and reputation.

It was not until 7 February of the next year, 1795, that Nelson's bitter feelings about Bastia and Calvi really surfaced. He poured it all out to his Uncle William:

and when I reflect that I was the cause of re-attacking Bastia, after our wise Generals gave it over, from not knowing the force, fancying it 2,000 men; that it was I, who, knowing the force in Bastia to be upwards of 4,000, as I have now only ventured to tell Lord Hood, landed with only 1,200 men, and kept the secret till within this week past; – what I must have felt during the whole Siege may be easily conceived. Yet I am scarcely mentioned. I freely forgive but cannot forget. This and much more ought to have been mentioned . . . others, for keeping succours out of Calvi for a few summer months are handsomely mentioned. Such things are . . . every man who had any considerable share in the reduction, has got some place or other – I, only I, am without reward. The taking of Corsica, like the taking of St Juan's, has cost me money. St Juan's cost near £500; Corsica has cost me £300, an eye, and a cut across my back; and my money, I find cannot be repaid me. Nothing but my anxious endeavours to serve my Country makes me bear up against it; but I sometimes am ready to give all up. We are just going to sea, and I hope to God we shall meet the French Fleet, which may give us all gold Chains – who knows.

His PS this time was more understandable. 'Forgive this letter: I have said a great deal too much of myself; but indeed it is all too true.'[18]

Ruminating over the same ground with Fanny on the same day he concluded, 'Totally neglected I must and do feel but I expect no reward. Had I been done justice to in all these points besides other services and skirmishes in which my ship and person have been risked, I believe the King would not have thought any honour too great for me.'[19]

When Nelson left the arms of Adelaide Correglia on 8 March 1795, it was because Admiral Hotham had received an express from Genoa announcing that a French fleet of fifteen sail-of-the-line and three frigates had been sighted off the Isle of Marguerite near Cannes; a signal from the *Mozelle*, just arrived in the offing, confirmed that there was a fleet to the west. Hotham ordered his squadron to prepare to weigh and at 5 a.m. they slipped out to sea on a fine land breeze. On the morning of the 10th the *Mozelle* signalled the presence of twenty-five sail to the north-west. Hotham hoisted the signal for a general chase. On board *Agamemnon* Nelson was preparing himself once more for the possibility of death. Although writing to Fanny he was speaking to himself, going through his own form of cognitive therapy:

Whatever may be my fate, I have no doubt in my own mind but that my conduct will be such as will not bring a blush on the face of my friends. The lives of all are in the hands of Him who knows best whether to preserve it or no, and to His will do I resign myself. My character and good name is in my own keeping. Life with disgrace is dreadful. A glorious death is to be envied, and if anything happens to me, recollect death is a debt we must all pay, and whether now or in a few years hence can be but of little consequence.[20]

As ever, Nelson's speeches to himself lacked all appreciation of how they might resound in Fanny's timid ears.

The next day, 11 March, was one of fickle winds, the enemy nowhere to be seen. It was not until daybreak on the 12th that the becalmed British saw the French fleet taking advantage of a patchy wind to approach from the south. The British were dispersed. The nearest group was that of Admiral Goodall, who signalled his little flock of forward ships, the *Agamemnon* and two 74s, to form ahead and astern of his flagship the 90-gun *Princess Royal*. The French, having found the British squadron so dispersed were well positioned to divide and conquer. The nearest other British ships, a group of three, included the ship Nelson had mentioned in his letter to Adelaide Correglia, the Neapolitan *Tancredi*, commanded by Captain Francesco Caracciolo. Well behind were the rest of the British ships, some with hulls becoming visible over the horizon, others showing only their topsails. In the event the enemy declined to attack. Nelson was not impressed. 'They did not appear to me to act like Officers who knew anything of their profession.'[21] Daybreak on the 13th saw the French about nine to twelve miles away and Hotham, taking the initiative, signalled a General Chase. At about eight o'clock the French 84-gun *Ca Ira* managed to run foul of her companion *La Victoire*, and in the process lost her fore and main topmasts. Fremantle's frigate the *Inconstant* being well ahead of the fleet set about harrying the massive French ship, keeping astern of her and out of sight of her massive broadsides which could have reduced his ship to a battered hulk had he been so foolish as to allow her to become a target. Even so the power of the *Ca Ira*'s stern chasers forced him to break off the action.

About three-quarters of an an hour later Nelson appeared on the scene in his fast-sailing *Agamemnon*, promptly tacked and stood towards the disabled enemy. Two other French ships, the 120-gun *Sans Culotte* and the 74-gun *Jean Bart*, made to aid the *Ca Ira*. The nearest other British ships were still some miles away and Nelson decided to stay astern of the *Ca Ira*, now taken in tow by a French 74, the *Censeur*. Within twenty minutes he was under fire. 'As we drew up with the Enemy, so true did she fire her stern guns, that not a shot missed some part of the Ship, and latterly the masts were struck every shot, which obliged me to open our fire a few minutes sooner than I intended, for it was my intention to have touched his stern before a shot was fired.'[22] His French opponents knew exactly what he intended and were desperate to prevent it. He had positioned himself astern of her and now a hundred yards away he put his helm to starboard, which brought *Agamemnon*'s broadside facing at right angles to the stern of the *Ca Ira*. Nelson knew that when he fired his guns, double shotted for the purpose, there was a killing field ahead, for once they had pierced the relatively unprotected stern they would burst into the open yet confined lower gun decks ahead and make slaughter-houses of them. Once his first broadside was discharged he would swing his ship into pursuit once more and having again closed with his enemy would repeat his manoeuvre with his opposite broadside. For two and a quarter hours he thus raked her with merciless and devastating fire. By one o'clock Nelson was observing 'a perfect wreck, her sails hanging in tatters, mizen topmast, mizen topsail, and cross jack yards shot away'. But he could also see that the ship towing the *Ça Ira* was hauling her round so that her 42-gun broadside could be brought to bear on the *Agamemnon*. The two ships passed within pistol shot and all on deck tensed themselves for the awful broadside to come but the aim of the enemy guns was elevated so that when it came the enemy shot passed through their sails and rigging overhead. At this point, half-past one, the *Sans Culotte* coming nearer, Admiral Hotham signalled for the forward ships to rejoin him, and so Nelson 'instantly bore away, and prepared to set all our sails'.[23]

Agamemnon's sails and rigging had suffered greatly but she had weathered the engagement with only seven men wounded. As day dawned on the 14th there was a fine breeze from the north-west, the British fleet had the advantage of the wind and Hotham saw that the *Ça Ira* and the ship towing her were about three and a half miles downwind and about a mile and a half behind the main French fleet. He immediately ordered two 74s, *Bedford* and *Captain*, to attack. Twenty minutes later a hail from Hotham's flagship *Britannia* ordered Nelson to go to the aid of his two fellow captains. Making all sail he approached the engagement, finding the *Captain* 'lying like a log on the water, all her sails and rigging shot away'.[24] Hotham then saw the French fleet approaching to support the two ships, and ordered his ships to break off the action.

Within another quarter of an hour Nelson was back in the British line. The four British ships were soon sandwiched between the *Ça Ira* and the *Censeur* towing her to leeward, and the French line to windward. *Illustrious*, *Courageux*, *Princess Royal* (Admiral Goodall's flagship) and *Agamemnon* were therefore obliged to fight on both sides of their ship. Fortunately the French fleet did not close with them, although the action with the *Ça Ira* and *Censeur* was so intense that at a quarter to nine the main and mizen masts of the *Illustrious* came crashing down, followed half an hour later by those of the *Courageux*. Less than a quarter of an hour after that the *Ça Ira* lost all her masts and at ten the *Censeur* lost her main mast. As *Agamemnon* came alongside, the two French ships surrendered, and Nelson sent Elizabeth Andrews's brother, now Lieutenant George Andrews, to take possession and convey the French captains to Admiral Goodall's ship. Having made its way slowly past the British line, the French line crowded on all possible sail and stood westwards, presumably running for Toulon.

Nelson's mental and emotional reactions were turbulent and uncertain. He was generous in his praise for his fellow captains, Frederick of the *Illustrious*, Montgomery of the *Courageux* and Reeve of the *Captain*, and Vice-Admiral Goodall. 'These Ships being in the van, had more than their share of the action,'[25] he told the Duke of Clarence. At first he took a realistic view of the action, telling Locker, 'The Enemy would not give us an opportunity of closing with them; if they had, I have no doubt, from the zeal and gallantry endeavoured to be shown by each individual Captain, one excepted, [Caracciolo] but we should have obtained a most glorious conquest.' He was fair to Hotham, who 'has had much to contend with, a Fleet half manned, and in every respect inferior to the Enemy'. He was clear too that it was lack of wind that had prevented the British running down on the French fleet on the 13th when, 'I have no doubt but we should have given a destructive blow to the Enemy's Fleet: however it is very well.' He was as aware as everybody else that if the French did not want to fight a fleet action there was little the opposing side could do to make them. He was pleased with his own part in engaging the *Ça Ira*. 'I am flattered by receiving the approbation of my own fleet, as well as the handsomest testimony by our enemies.'[26] Nelson had killed and wounded 110 in the *Ça Ira* in that two-hour action.

Hotham's dispatch properly described Fremantle's 'attacking, raking and harassing her [the *Ça Ira*] until the coming up of the *Agamemnon*, when he was most ably seconded by Captain Nelson, who did her so much damage as to disable her from putting herself again to rights'. Nelson was not however mentioned in connection with the surrender of the two ships, but nor was any other captain, on the grounds that 'it is difficult to specify particular desert, where emulation was common to all, and zeal for his Majesty's service the general description of the Fleet'.[27]

Ten days later it would seem that Nelson had had more time to reflect and his tune was changing. As they lay at Spezia where they had been forced in by a gale he recounted to his brother how he had been engaged with the *Ça Ira* on the 13th and 14th, and added, 'Had our good Admiral have followed the blow, we should probably have done more, but the risk was thought too great.'[28] This had also come out in a letter he began to Fanny during the action: 'Admiral Hotham seems to have given the business up and thinks we have done enough, whilst Goodall and myself think we have done nothing in comparison to what we might, would the Admiral have pursued our victory, which as it turns out is a very dear bought one, but we want Lord Hood to command us, we should have had a glorious victory . . . these two French ships behaved amazingly well.'[29] On 28 March he returned to his reflections on Lord Hood: 'Had he been with us I am sure we should have done much more but having beat the enemy I don't think we made the most of our victory.' He was forgetting a note he had written to Goodall on the 15th detailing that he had not more than 600 each of 18 pound and 24 pound shot and very few 9 pound shot. He was forgetting the statements he had made about the state of his own ship and its manning, 'having only three hundred and forty four at quarters, myself included'. He had forgotten what a very hard fight *Ça Ira* and *Censeur* had given them for it had taken five British ships to subdue two. Then came a totally unjustifiable mental jump. 'The success of our action chiefly rested on the conduct of the *Agamemnon*, and as all allow it I feel proud on the occasion.'[30] The *Agamemnon* had indeed done well in her single ship action but Fremantle's frigate had bravely preceded him, and the events of the next day had depended essentially on the efforts of the *Captain, Illustrious, Princess Royal* and *Courageux* as well as *Agamemnon*.

By 1 April his feelings had boiled over, ambition corroding his thought:

We make but a bad hand of managing our fleet. I am absolutely at this moment in the horrors, fearing from our idling here, that our active enemy may send out 2 or 3 sail of the line and some frigates to intercept our convoy which is momently expected and which, if taken, would ruin all our affairs in this country but we are idle and lay in port when we ought to be at sea. In short I wish to be an admiral and in the command of the English fleet. I should very soon either do much or be ruined. My disposition can't bear tame and slow measures. Sure I am, had I commanded our fleet on the 14th that either the whole French fleet would have graced my triumph, or I should have been in a confounded scrape.

By now the aggressive, unreasonable Nelson was gaining the upper hand over the earlier more rational commentator, just as his burning conviction had taken him to the Admiral's flagship when the *Ça Ira* and *Censeur* struck, 'to propose to him leaving our two crippled ships, the two prizes, and four frigates to themselves, and to pursue the enemy'.

The British had three badly disabled ships which overall gave the fleeing French an advantage of two ships. British casualties so far had been 75 killed and 280 wounded, most on board the damaged ships to be left behind. The running odds would have justified Nelson's position but Hotham, 'is much cooler than myself and said "We must be contented. We have done very well", but had we taken 10 sail and allowed the 11th to have escaped if possible to have been got at, I could never call it well done. Goodall backed me. I got him to write to the Admiral but it would not do. We should have had such a day as I believe the annals of England never produced but it can't be helped . . . if the Admiral can get hold of them once more . . . we shall do better, and if he does but get us close, we will have the whole fleet. Nothing can stop the courage of English seamen.'

His sense of self-importance was ballooning. 'I have a Mistress given to me, no less a person than the Goddess Bellona; so say the French verses made on me, and in them I am so covered with laurels that you will hardly find my little face. . . However nonsensical these things are, they are better than censure and we are all subject and open to flattery.' That was but a short step in his mind to what was due to him: 'I hope and feel I have now a right to the Marines [colonelcies of Marines were sinecures conferred upon three of the older post captains on the list and subsequently relinquished when they were promoted to Flag rank] and if Lord Spencer does not give it to me he is an unjust man for no man can since Lord Howe's action claim equal to me but I don't expect any favours. I have been infamously treated.'

It was again a short step to thoughts of money and his concern that Hotham would not get the best price for the *Ça Ira*'s 42-pounder guns. 'I much fear I shall not during the whole station get prize money enough to bear my expenses. I have had my share of the fag and no profit.' And to crown it all Hotham was paying no attention to Nelson's officers.

'Hotham has made 5 Post Captains besides Masters and Commanders since he has had the command, but he has offered nothing to *Agamemnon*.'[31] Eleven days later the idea of being made a colonel of marines was still on his mind. 'If the folks will give me the Colonel of Marines I shall be satisfied, but I fear my interest is not equal to get it, although I will never allow that any man whatever has a claim superior to myself.'

Fortunately Viceroy Elliot had been complimentary: 'I need not assure you of the pleasure with which I so constantly see your name foremost in everything that is creditable and serviceable.'[32] Nelson's reaction embraced a preposterous, fanciful and self-serving view of the action: 'All hands agree in giving me these praises . . . what has happened may never happen to anyone again, that only one Ship of the Line out of 14 should get into action with the French fleet, and for so long a time as $2\frac{1}{2}$ hours and with such a ship as the *Ça Ira*, but had I been supported I should certainly have brought the *Sans Culotte* to battle, a most glorious prospect. A brave man runs no more risk than a coward, and *Agamemnon* to a miracle has suffered scarcely anything.'[33]

Now back in England and unknown to Nelson, Hood was making a formal issue of resources in the Mediterranean and was thus under-writing Hotham's caution. By Hood's own public account, a minimum of twenty ships was needed; the British fleet consisted of fifteen ships-of-the-line, was 1,400 seamen short of complement and four of his 64s, including *Agamemnon*, needed to come home. Hood went too far, playing a game in which all the aces were held by Lord Spencer. The new First Lord promptly sacked him. On 8 June when Nelson knew that Hood was not returning he wrote to his brother from near Minorca, 'We have been cruising off here for a long month, every moment in expectation of reinforcements from England. Our hopes are now entirely dwindled away, and I give up all expectation: then comes accounts of Lord Hood's resignation. Oh miserable Board of Admiralty! They have forced the first Officer in our Service away from his command.'[34] His morale was low. His level of frustration was high. At one moment he blamed the Admiralty for their under-resourcing, at another the caution and timorousness of Hotham or the absence of Hood. 'Our Commander is elated at his appointment. It is more than most of his fleet for we have made a sad change. Holloway is to be first Captain of the fleet, both certainly good as men but unfit for such appointments.' None of it really adds up except as an indication of how he was feeling at the time. 'We are tired and fatigued with our laying off here doing nothing, every moment expecting our ships, till even expectation is wore out. I hope I shall be ordered home but at present I see no prospect of it. I am tired of this business, however I hope peace will very soon come and send us all to our cottages again.'[35]

But within a week Rear-Admiral Robert Man appeared on the scene in the *Victory* with a squadron of seven sail-of-the-line. With him came a note for Nelson from Hood enclosing a copy of a letter he had received from Lord Spencer, acknowledging, as he put it to Fanny, 'my pretensions to favour and distinction'.[36] Hood had been doing his best for him. Nelson consoled himself with the thought, 'My services seem pretty well understood.' But there was no escaping the fact that he was uncomfortably poised. A promotion of admirals was due. 'Some say I am to have my flag, some say the Marines, the latter I hope, the former will half ruin me, going home by land and most probably be unemployed, or if not, the war I hope is so near an end that all would be expense and no hope of profit.' His jaundiced and gloomy eye found nothing professional or personal to be pleased about. He had written to Lord Hood about Lieutenant Andrews's future, 'but these great men have neither gratitude nor regards'. He had short shrift for his sister Catherine Matcham who had just given birth to her fifth child: 'She should leave off having any more children.' Fanny and he were still having difficulty over the Herbert bequest. 'Can it be expected we can live on air?'[37] They had just received information that the French fleet of twenty-two sail-of-the-line were at sea, causing him to reflect sharply, 'Sir Sydney Smith did not burn them all – Lord Hood mistook the man: there is an old song, Great talkers do the least we see.'[38] Nelson had marked Sir Sidney Smith's card. On 14 July there was another abortive brush with the French which Hotham discontinued, leaving Nelson with a string of 'if onlys', especially 'Had Lord Hood been there he would never have called us out of action. . . .'[39]

Nelson had anchored great hopes in Hood. He had not only lost the man he had been counting on to take him forward, but he had been deprived of his decisive and understanding leadership.

9

'It Is Active Young Men That Are Wanted, Not Drones'

Nelson, December 1795

The British fleet in the Mediterranean had not yet found an offensive role. Its performance under Hotham had been defensive and ineffective, partly because of its under-resourcing. It could blockade Toulon after a fashion. It could protect convoys, but found it difficult to prevent coastal vessels from supplying the French. It carried insufficient troops to support combined operations.

Politically, the First Coalition against the French, orchestrated and subsidized by Britain, was finding it virtually impossible to act because of conflicting territorial ambitions among its members, especially those between Austria and Sardinia in this region. The port of Genoa was playing the neutral, but effectively under French influence, was supplying its army. The port of Leghorn was an uneasy neutral.

In July 1795 an Austro-Sardinian offensive was opened, albeit reluctantly by Vienna, and the Austrian General de Vins advanced with an Austro-Sardinian army, its objective to drive the French out of the Italian riviera. In mid-July, following Hotham's abortive fleet action, Nelson was given command of a small squadron, *Agamemnon*, the frigates *Meleager* and *Ariadne*, the brig *Tarleton* and the cutter *Resolution*, and sent off on detached duty, 'to cooperate with the Austrian General in driving the French out of the Riviera of Genoa'. As he told Locker a month later, 'As I have been so much in the habit of soldiering this war, the moment that it was known the Austrian Army was coming, it was fixed the Brigadier must go.'[1] Arrived off the Genoa mole he quickly concluded that Hotham's standing orders about how he should deal with the Genoese were 'useless to the common cause and I must run some pecuniary hazard to serve my country'.[2]

It was completely typical of him to define for himself what was needed in the situation he faced rather than act on the assumptions of others, as a lesser man would have done. The Admiral's assumption was that the Genoese could be kept on side only by handling them with kid gloves; hence Nelson was not to institute legal proceedings against any Genoese ships he might detain, without express permission from the Admiralty, to whom he was to send full details of the cargoes being carried. Nelson had exactly identified his Admiral's weakness in such a situation: 'Hotham has no political courage which in an Officer abroad is as highly necessary as battle courage.'[3] Clear in his own mind that 'strong and vigorous measures' were necessary to bring the war to a conclusion, he decided to take the personal risk of stopping all Genoese vessels bound for France, thus effectively halting supplies to French forces on the Riviera. Having persuaded Drake, the British Minister at Genoa of the correctness of his action, he was sufficiently masterful and adept to protect his own back by prompting Drake, their political master, to secure Hotham's agreement. Nelson, faced by a new scenario for action, was as usual positive and bursting with activity, 'almost fancying myself charging at the head of a troop of horse . . . I have no doubt but you will hear by autumn that we are in possession of 60 miles of sea coast, including the towns of Mornarco and Nice'.[4] Writing to Lord Spencer to express his pleasure at his long-awaited appointment as a colonel of marines, he referred to his current assignment and chanced his arm on the subject of De Vins: 'It appears to me that General de Vins is an Officer who perfectly knows his business, and is well disposed to act with vigour on every proper occasion. The Enemy are throwing up strong works near Albinga; but before three days are past, I expect the Army will be to the westward of them.'[5] It was one of Nelson's most endearing and inspiring qualities that he was always so positive. One of life's born optimists he went forward, always confident of the best, never fearing the worst.

Then he was off westward along the coast from Genoa to Vado Bay, in Nelson's opinion more a bend in the land than a bay. He now had eight frigates under his command, including the *Inconstant*, still captained by Fremantle, and the *Lowestoffe* captained by Benjamin Hallowell. Once anchored, he immediately arranged a conference with General de Vins, Trevor, the British Minister at Turin, and Drake. De Vins, confident that he could drive the French out of the Genoese riviera and even take Nice, was happy to talk to Nelson, but not surprisingly wished to have a face to face discussion with the Admiral himself. When the sails of Hotham's fleet were seen in the west on 14 August an opportunity seemed to have arrived for him to throw personal weight behind Nelson's mission and enhance his own grasp of the key issues involved. Amazingly, his mind was totally focused on his fleet's need to reach Leghorn and replenish its wood supply. Displaying a bizarre lack of political acumen, he refused to heave to for a few hours to concert a plan of campaign, even after Nelson had gone on board the flagship to plead its necessity. The General could be forgiven for wondering what British undertakings to collaborate really amounted to if this was the treatment he received from their Commander-in-Chief. Not unnaturally, his first reaction to Hotham's rebuff was a formal request that Nelson find out exactly what help he could expect to obtain from the fleet. He said he wished to land up to 10,000 of his 32,000 men on the coast of Provence and wanted to know whether the Admiral would assist and cover such a landing and protect them in the case of the appearance of a French fleet. Hotham's subsequent reply signalled loud and clear to De Vins that Nelson and his frigates was all the help he was going to get. At a stroke Hotham had ensured that co-operation between Nelson and De Vins would be stillborn.

Now thirty-seven, Nelson had changed. Since his engagement with the *Melpomene* in October 1793 he had been constantly engaged in the profoundly catalytic and testing process of war. Any romantic sense of heroism had been fully tempered by the reality and horror of combat. He had found he could meet its terrible personal challenge, to stand or hide. He could bear the sight of sudden death, sometimes a clean and quiet termination, sometimes a screaming horror, sometimes smearings of brains and guts, detached arms, legs, or shattered mess where once there had been a shipmate or one of his midshipmen. He had discovered that he could armour his spirit and be unafraid in the presence of his own imminent death, so that he was ready, even eager, to seek out the next opportunity to meet the terrible challenge. He knew that in battle he radiated calm, confidence and aggression, could hate the enemy and persuade others to destroy them. He had found he had not miscast himself as a hero and his self-confidence and self-belief, confirmed in battle, were spurring his ambition for a wider stage.

Although not yet flying the broad pendant of a Commodore he thought as much about the deployment of the fleet as he did about *Agamemnon* and his squadron. In his view Hotham was failing in his task. As he said to Locker, 'The Mediterranean command has ever so much business, compared to any other, that a man of business ought to be here. . . . Far be it from me to detract from Admiral Hotham's merits, for a better heart no man possesses, and he is ever kind and attentive to me; but between the abilities of him and Lord Hood can be no comparison . . . we expect Sir John Jervis, who, I understand is a man of business.'[6]

It is a mistake to characterize Nelson's leadership as consisting solely in a kind of generalized care for his men. He was far from being alone in that. There were many other humane, tolerant and effective officers who understood the deep human need for self-respect and fairness. Nelson went well beyond this. He knew how to create an active pride in being 'Agamemnons', encouraging his ship's company to believe there was nothing they could not do. He had a natural instinct to be interested in his officers and men as individuals, and was aware of variations in their individual capacity to contribute, ever ready to guide, encourage and where necessary discipline. His remarks to Locker show that he was also highly focused on a third indispensable element of leadership: setting the agenda, getting the job done, an element that called into play a vastly different set of qualities – driving energy, physical and mental stamina, and capacity to delegate and collaborate. It was these qualities, the qualifications for high command, that Sir Gilbert Elliot recognized when he spoke of 'your present important service, which requires zeal, activity, and a spirit of accommodation and co-operation'.[7]

Hotham was indeed personally kind and attentive to Nelson. When he sent the Admiralty Nelson's dispatch about an action at Alassio where he had captured a French corvette and eight other small vessels and destroyed three, he noted that his 'officer like conduct upon this, and, indeed, upon every occasion where his services are called forth, reflects upon him the highest credit'.[8] This was the first of a number of expeditions against the enemy made by Nelson on intelligence from De Vins. They were not all successful. In an operation to cut out a provisons ship which had arrived at Oneglia, his men were driven off. Three Agamemnons were killed, three mortally wounded and seven wounded. The Southamptons had one killed and three wounded. Nelson, like the hardened warrior he had become, was callously philosophical, even with

Fanny: 'they who play at bowls must expect rubbers and the worse success now, the better, I hope, another time'.[9]

His friend Cuthbert Collingwood, newly arrived in the *Excellent* 74, was warned what he could expect: 'You are so old a Mediterranean man, that I can tell you nothing new about the Country. My command here is so far pleasant as it relieves me from the inactivity of our fleet, which is great indeed as you will soon see.' Collingwood must have been reminded of Admiral Hughes and the Navigation Acts when Nelson continued, 'Our Admiral, entre nous, has no political courage whatever and is alarmed at the mention of any strong measure; but in other respects, he is as good a man as can possibly be.'[10] In writing to tell Elliot of the good outcome of his blockade he took the opportunity for further self-advertisement: 'The Marines have been given to me in the handsomest manner. The answer given to many was, the King knew no officer who had served so much for them as myself.'[11]

By now Nelson had produced his own plan, an offer to convey 4–5,000 men, field pieces and provisions and land them two miles from St Remo, which when taken would provide good anchorage for his squadron and a place for landing supplies. They would be well placed there to harry the French to east or west. Further to the west Nice could be blockaded from the vicinity of St Remo and the British fleet off Toulon, with twenty-three sail-of-the-line, would guard them against attack from that quarter. De Vins's reply was lukewarm and rather devious. Nelson's objective was to do everything in his power to encourage and help De Vins so that blame for the failure of his campaign should not fall on the British.

Meanwhile in England, Sir John Jervis had been appointed to replace Hood as Commander-in-Chief and was now on the way to the Mediterranean. Not only would the man Spencer had selected for this fraught appointment be able to do the business, he would quickly identify Nelson as one of the brightest stars in the Navy's firmament and decisively affect his future career. Jervis, a man of good family, born in 1735, had, at least in his father's eyes, been destined for a career in the law until as a twelve-year-old he was filled by such excitement for the sea and ships that when his parents refused to agree to his entering the Navy, he ran away from school to force their hand. His will prevailed, as it would for the rest of his life, and it was a happy fourteen-year-old who went on board the 50-gun *Gloucester*. After six years in the West Indies, he went on his first combined operation. As master and commander of the sloop *Porcupine* he was entrusted with the challenging task of guiding Wolfe's attacking force to its landing point at Quebec. In 1771 when peace put him on the beach he set out on a quite extraordinary set of continental travels, first to Paris and Lyons where he worked himself hard at mastering French. Then, armed with relevant charts, he took himself off with Captain Barrington, to Cronstadt and St Petersburg, correcting charts, taking notes of dockyards, arsenals, storage facilities, noting slips and ship-building and ships in commission. As they journeyed back through Norway and Denmark he repeated the process, paying particular atten-tion to the harbour and defences of Copenhagen, then on through Germany to Holland and its ports. The following year the pair visited all the major French naval bases and ports, Le Havre, Cherbourg, Brest, Quiberon and its bay, Port Louis, Lorient, Rochefort and Bordeaux. His biographer, Admiral James sums up these journeys: 'It is unlikely that any naval officer, before or since, has, on his own initiative, collected so much valuable intelligence about the naval resources of potential enemies.'[12] This amazing self-directed energy was in stark contrast to the half-hearted efforts Nelson had made to learn French and the use he had made of his own time while on the beach. Nelson had been focused on getting back to sea, to fight and win, gather in glory, and possibly prize money. Jervis had recognized an opportunity to learn and prepare himself.

It was not until 1778, at the age of forty-three, that he experienced his first fleet action as captain of the *Foudroyant*, in Keppel's abortive battle off Ushant, and it was not for another four years that he won his own laurels. It was at the time when the young Nelson was about to leave Cork for Canada that Jervis had an opportunity to make his mark. In a single ship night action off Ushant he outmanoeuvred, boarded and took the *Pégase* 74 without loss. The new and recently appointed First Lord in the Fox–North coalition was Viscount Keppel, who promptly recom-mended him for the Bath. It is a moot point as to whether this was dis-proportionate recognition for such an unbloody single ship action. The knighthood probably reflected Jervis's commandingly succinct support-ing evidence at Keppel's court martial some four years previously. Jervis was also sufficiently worldly wise to understand the beneficial synergies of political and naval careers, especially when the powers that be need votes. Thus the spell of peace which began in 1783 saw Nelson on his way to France with Captain Macnamara, and Jervis entering Parliament, first as MP for Launceston and then, as a result of the 1784 election, for

Great Yarmouth. It was in the run up to this election that Nelson had his first flirtation with politics on the Tory side. Jervis was a Whig, and had important Whig friends, the Marquis of Rockingham, the Earl of Shelburne and the Duke of Richmond, not to mention senior naval officers, Keppel, Saunders and Barrington.

On France's declaration of war in 1793 he resigned his seat, and while Nelson sailed to join Hood in the Mediterranean, Sir John Jervis, now a vice-admiral of the Blue, was busy organizing a combined operation to the West Indies, its objective the capture of Martinique, St Lucia and Guadeloupe. Again, unlike Hood, he demonstrated his considerable capacity for collaboration. The good relations he established with General Grey led Jervis to say, 'Neither of us wrote a letter on service to the other during the whole campaign.'[13] In August 1795, some months after his return he was appointed to command the Mediterranean fleet.

Whereas Nelson was to most people instantly seductive, charming and friendly, Jervis was very different. His measured courtesy, his powerful face and presence, his sharp intelligence and magisterial judgement, exemplified power and command. He did not need his Admiral's uniform to convey the unspoken assumption that he was in charge. On occasions he could be kindly, relaxed, and something of a tease, but everything he did enhanced his power of command and demonstrated commitment to the highest standards of officer- like behaviour. If you were wise you were not tempted to take liberties with him.

Meanwhile there were to be no laurels for Nelson. Neither De Vins nor Vienna was minded to take the offensive in any major way. He reflected grimly on the present operations, 'This Italian campaign has certainly been a most useless and most expensive one. I know of no good it has done. Each ally lays the fault on the other.' Fanny had evidently passed on compliments she had received about him, but he was in a mood to take a dim view of them: 'I am always glad to find that my conduct is approved of by my superiors but very few I assure you work so hard for a few compliments as myself.'[14]

The futile operation was about to reach an unhappy climax but just as the opposing armies seemed to be settling down into a winter stale-mate the French had other ideas. A French frigate, the *Brune* carrying some 700 men, emerged from the supposedly neutral Genoa, took an Austrian strongpoint lying between Voltri and Savona along the coast to the west of Genoa, took possession of a corn store, serendipitously captured £10,000 belonging to the Austrians on its way from Genoa to Savona and were seemingly intent on fomenting insurrection in the Austrians' rear. Although the Austrians regained the post the next day their vulnerability to attack in the rear had been vividly demonstrated. The incident caught Nelson in a cleft stick. He had to decide whether to employ *Agamemnon* behind the Austrians to safeguard their line of retreat; or attack the 100-strong flotilla the French had gathered to take off their troops should their now imminent attack fail. The decision was made for him by Hyde Parker. 'My Admiral, for wise reasons I daresay, did not think it proper to attend to my proposal [to send *Culloden* and *Courageux* to help him deal with the French flotilla, thus reducing the French appetite for attack] and lessened my squadron to the *Flora* frigate and *Speedy* brig.'[15]

The result was that the French attack went ahead with its visible offshore support, and the fleeing Austrians were harassed by fire from offshore gunboats, the exact opposite of the original Austro-British scenario. The Austrians were getting a taste of things to come: 'the French, half naked, were determined to conquer or die'. *Agamemnon*'s purser, who had been ashore with the Austrians at the time, reported how he 'ran with the Austrians 18 miles without stopping, men without arms, officers without soldiers, women without assistance'. Loano, Vado and Savona fell in quick succession. Nelson thought he knew what the real problem had been: 'They [the Austrians] came by the express stipulation of England to the coast and were to take possession of Vado to cooperate with our fleet which has never been near them. However let the blame lay where it will. I do not believe any party will seriously lay it at my door, if they do, I am perfectly easy as to the consequences. I sincerely hope an enquiry may take place. The world will then know how hard I have fagged.'[16]

Though Nelson's Vado operations had ended not with a bang but a whimper, he was nevertheless at great pains to make sure that Francis Drake, John Trevor (the British Minister in Turin) and Sir Gilbert Elliot should have a full appreciation of all that had happened and how and under what conditions he had approached his task. No man who is careless of his own reputation becomes great in the eyes of others. But it was not only Nelson's reputation that was at stake: from Drake he had heard that reports were circulating among the allies of British ships conniving with the enemy to permit coasting vessels to land their cargoes to supply the French Army in the riviera of Genoa. The reports had been brought to Drake's attention by none less than Lord Grenville, Secretary of State for Foreign Affairs. Nelson rose instantly to the defence of his captains and wrote direct to Lord Grenville: 'Officers more alert, and more anxious for the good, and honour, of their King and Country, can scarcely ever fall to the lot of any Commanding Officer.' His defence of himself was equally passionate. He had been 'in more than one hundred and forty Skirmishes and Battles, at sea and on shore; have lost an eye, and otherwise blood, in fighting the Enemies of my King and Country; and God knows, instead of riches, my little fortune has been diminished in the Service . . . and when instead of all my fancied approbation, to receive an accusation of a most traitorous nature – it has been almost too much for me to bear.'[17] This is what subordinates like: bosses who will unequivocally support and stand up for them. Nor was the passionate intensity of his self-defence wasted on Lord Grenville, as the future would show.

Sir John Jervis arrived at St Fiorenzo on 29 November 1795, 'to the great joy of some and sorrow of others'.[18] Most interestingly, news reached Nelson in December of another of the new First Lord's actions: he had dismissed Sir Charles Middleton (later Lord Barham) from the Admiralty Board because he disagreed with Spencer's decision to send a young admiral, Rear-Admiral Christian, to the West Indies. This evoked an approving response from Nelson, 'Everyone knows that Laforey [the current Commander-in-Chief] was unfit for the command. It is active young men that are wanted, not drones.' Although he had not yet met his own new Commander-in-Chief, he knew that Jervis was already making an impact for he told Fanny, 'Sir John seems determined to be active.'[19] With some uncertainty in his mind about how his new Commander-in-Chief would judge him in the light of the Austrians' failure, he decided to strike first. He sent Jervis a full report of his operations with the Austrians and was totally candid about Hotham's nonengagement with the issues he had faced. He was in low and disturbed spirits. *Agamemnon* was 'rotten and must go home'. He was tired: 'it is no wonder that a man that runs a race should be tired'. He grumbled quite properly about Fanny's legacy still not being paid. He was shocked by Fanny's report of gossip that Mary Moutray was bestowing sexual favours in return for assistance in her reduced state.

But his mood suddenly changed when in mid-January 1796 he went up the side of Jervis's flagship to meet his new Commander-in-Chief for the first time. He need not have worried. Won over by the candid account of Nelson's collaboration with the Austrians, Jervis had already written to offer him the 90-gun *St George* or the 74-gun *Zealous*. There were after all only six post captains in the Navy more senior than Nelson, but even so to offer a 90-gun ship had been a shrewd compliment by Jervis, an unsolicited gesture which had already inclined his captain to like him, even though he had decided to stay with *Agamemnon*. Jervis warmed immediately to Nelson's command of the situation, his well expressed criticisms of the previous regime, his description of what he himself had been doing and his obvious enthusiasm and energy. He made an instant decision to keep him. He employed the simple expedient of saying that when Nelson's flag arrived on his promotion to Rear-Admiral, he would like him to stay with him. This was an offer Nelson could not refuse and Jervis built on these concrete expressions of confidence, sharing with him his own 'information opinion and thoughts'. This was irresistible and Nelson was entirely won over, although he had to handle Fanny carefully. 'Thus my dear Fanny, although I wish to get home, yet my fair character makes me stand forward to remain abroad.'[20] The die was cast, his health was 'never better', and his mood transformed.

Within a week Nelson was back off Genoa with Jervis's orders to 'prevent any small number of men making a descent in Italy'. The fact that Nelson was off again on a detached command caused some sour grapes. 'The fleet was not a little surprised at my leaving them so soon, and there is some little envy, I fancy, attached itself to the surprise, for one captain told me, "you did just as you pleased in Lord Hood's time, the same in Admiral Hotham's, and now again with Sir John Jervis. It makes no difference to you who is commander-in-chief." I made a pretty strong answer to this speech.'[21] The exchange was not good humoured and even if the remark had been kindly meant or delivered with teasing irony, Nelson's reaction had clearly been ambivalent; he liked the thought that he had such a reputation, hence he relayed the tale; but he did not like the implication that at least some of his brother officers thought him a mite over-assertive and pushy.

Nelson was now infinitely buoyed up by everything Jervis was doing and the example he was setting: 'Our new Admiral will not land at Leghorn. The late one was so much here that Sir John is determined to act in a contrary way. Reports say the French will have their fleet at sea again. If they do I think they will now lose the whole of them, for we have a man of business at our head.'[22] Hood was well on the way to being replaced especially as the C.-in-C.'s friendliness towards his senior captain became even more pronounced, 'Sir John from his manner I plainly see does not wish me to leave this station. He seems at present to consider me as an assistant more than a subordinate for I am acting without orders. . . . He asked me if I had heard any more of my promotion. I told him no. His answer was, "You must have a larger ship for we cannot spare you either as Admiral or Captain." '[23] After such a declaration any captain, not just Nelson, would have been eating out of his hand and it was no wonder that within two months of meeting Jervis, Nelson was describing him to John Trevor as 'so active and good an Admiral'.[24] All the same he did not lose sight of his own agenda and within a month was pressurizing Jervis: 'I shall feel pleasure in serving under your command; and in case a promotion of Flags should take place, I am confident that your mention of me to Lord Spencer would be sufficient to have my Flag ordered to be hoisted in this Country.' In other words, 'Please write to Lord Spencer.'

He pursued another objective. Vice-Admiral Hyde Parker, who had been in command until Jervis arrived, had, much to Nelson's chagrin, ordered Captain Frederick, next below Nelson on the Captains' list, to command the third Division of the Fleet and to hoist a distinguishing pendant. Nelson drew Jervis's attention to words of support he had had from Francis Drake: 'as I last year represented to Admiral Hotham the propriety of ordering you a Distinguishing Pendant, and also did the same to Lord Grenville, the Admiral will perhaps direct you to hoist it.'[25] He omitted to mention that he had himself written direct to Lord Spencer on 14 November of the previous year asking for a distinguishing pendant and might well by now have received Spencer's negative reply of 15 January 1796: 'As the service on which you have been employed in Vado Bay is of so very temporary a nature and as there are already so many flags employed on the Mediterranean station, I am afraid it will be impossible for me at present to recommend the adoption of the measure.'[26]

Here could be the reason why Nelson seemed to doubt until the last moment that Jervis would be able to make his wishes stick with the Admiralty. Jervis rose to the situation magnificently: 'No words can express the sense I entertain of every part of your conduct and correspondence with Messrs. Trevor and Drake and I shall be most happy to manifest it in the most substantial manner. A distinguishing pendant you shall most certainly wear and I will write to Lord Spencer about you. In short there is nothing within my grasp that I shall not be proud to confer on you.'

Nelson's comment to Fanny sounded an echo of his never satisfied elder brother: 'These blossoms may one day bring forth fruit but I doubt it. My expenses here are too much and it is not the Marines that compensates.' He was seeing his chances of a fortune slipping away. 'Admiral Waldegrave who was sent to Tunis has taken out of that port three frigates belonging to the French, the *Nemesis* one of them. There I lost my fortune by having such a head as Admiral Linzees for our guide.'[27] He was feverish to be recognized and was alas showing signs that whatever was done for him, he was likely to prove insatiable. But for the moment he was temporarily appeased. A broad pendant flying from *Agamemnon's* masthead was there for all the world to see. He would not in fact be appointed an established commodore until 15 August 1796. He would have to wait till then for his extra ten shillings a day allowance, and a flag captain to run his ship.

For some months Nelson had been convinced that the French would descend on Italy in the spring of 1796, and that the friendly ports of Leghorn, Spezia and Naples were under imminent threat of seaborne assault. The actual attack on Italy was ignited in Paris on 9 March 1796 when the twenty-six-year-old, Napoleon Bonaparte, now a General married Josephine Beauharnais. As a reward for taking her off the hands of Citizen Barras, one of the Directors, he was nominated as Commander-in-Chief of the Army of Italy. A fortnight later Bonaparte was in Nice, matching his charisma, brainpower and power of command against his egotistical and battle-hardened generals, Serurier, Augereau and Masséna, to such effect that Augereau allegedly remarked, 'that little bugger really frightened me'.[28] Bonaparte had inherited a command of 37,000 starving, demoralized and unpaid troops, opposed by 52,000 Austrians. The line of his assault and the whirlwind campaign he conducted were not at all what Nelson anticipated, not via the coast road of the Riviera with the French fleet in support, but via the mountain passes of the Ligurian Alps. Within ten days he had fought six battles, and had smashed his way to the edge of the Lombardy plain. Turin lay to the north-west, Milan to the north-east. Vado Bay and Genoa were simply bypassed. Leghorn, Spezia and Naples were as yet unthreatened. Nelson had made the mistake of thinking the French plan of campaign must involve a combined operation and must seek to maximize French naval strength. He could not know that Bonaparte knew nothing about the Navy and cared even less.

But as the Austrians retreated, Nelson advanced in the eyes of his Commander-in-Chief, a situation he had to take pains in getting Fanny to understand:

Sir John Jervis has such an opinion of my conduct that he is using every influence both public and private with Lord Spencer for my continuance on this station. I am sure you will feel how superior is the pleasure of knowing that my integrity and plainness is the cause of my being kept from you, to receiving me as a person whom no Commander-in-Chief would wish to keep under his command. Sir John was a perfect stranger to me, therefore I feel the more flattered and when I reflect that I have had the unbounded confidence of three Commanders-in Chief I cannot but feel a conscious pride and that I have abilities.

But it was now three years since he has sailed from Spithead and although duty might indeed be the great business of a sea officer, temptation could beset wives left at home just as easily as sea officers away from home. So he felt it necessary to read her an hypocritical little homily: 'Rest assured, my dearest Fanny, of my unabated and steady affection which if possible is increasing by that propriety of conduct which I know you are pursuing.' He did not want gossip around the fleet about *his* wife, or reports of domestic difficulties such as those currently afflicting the second-in-command. 'Sir Hyde Parker has left the fleet for England. It seems Lady Parker has behaved infamously ill and almost ruined his future peace of mind as well as his pocket but the newspapers will soon tell all.'[29]

Nelson's cutting-out activities continued but as hopes of an Austrian counter-attack faded Nelson's frustrations increased. The truth was that everything he was now engaged in was small beer; Nelson was not interested in being part of an irrelevant sideshow. He was anxious now to rejoin Jervis, even at the cost of losing his pendant, 'as the service, for

which it was intended to be useful, is nearly, if not quite at an end, I
assure you I shall have no regret in striking it; for it will afford me an
opportunity of serving nearer your Flag, and endeavouring to shew, by
my attention in a subordinate station, that I was not unworthy of commanding.' He was tired too, needed leave and fancied taking the waters
in Pisa. 'If I could, without any impediment to the service, take twenty
days to fit me for another winter, I should not dislike it: and yet, perhaps
I shall do without it. I do not much like what I have written.'[30] A week
later he withdrew his request, even though permission was on its way
from Jervis, who wrote: 'I shall not think it right to remove the Squadron
from the Gulf of Genoa while there is a ray of hope that the Austrians
will rally, but you may take your twenty days in Pisa baths.'[31] Nelson
returned to the subject in June: 'I shall not go to Pisa at present, we may
be useful here; and, to say the truth, when I am actively employed I am
not so bad. My complaint is as if a girth were buckled tight over my
breast, and my endeavour in the night, is to get it loose – which sounds
like a powerful anxiety state.[32]

He needed Jervis to be reassuring, and he was. Nelson would keep his
broad pendant until his flag as a rear-admiral arrived. Mrs Calder (wife
of his Captain of the Fleet) had written to say that a promotion would
take place soon, and when it did Jervis would hope to see Nelson's flag
hoisted. But Nelson remained anxious and was not above showing it. 'I
cannot bear the thoughts of leaving your Command. You have placed an
unbounded confidence in me, and, I own, I feel that no exertion of mine
has been wanting for a moment, to merit so great an honour.'[33] He was
now like a terrier with a bone, for later that day he was at it again: 'I
may have been impertinent in suggesting so many ways by which I might
still remain; but do not, Sir, imagine that I meant anything by my propositions, than what an anxious disposition pointed out.'[34] Whatever Jervis
may have thought of his subordinate's anxiety, he had indeed no wish to
lose him.

On 11 June Nelson left *Agamemnon*, to hoist his broad pendant in the
Captain 74. He took with him Lieutenants Berry, Spicer, Saunders and
Noble. Her captain was the thirty-four-year-old American, Ralph Willett
Miller, 'a most exceeding good officer and a worthy man'.[35] Jervis had
indeed pressed Nelson's claims for flag rank with Spencer, but by mid-
July had to tell him that Spencer had 'a great desire to promote you
to the flag, but confessed he could not face another promotion'.[36]

Fortunately he was able to tell him that Spencer had at least approved his pendant.

Meanwhile, having forced the Austrians back to Mantua but coming under threat from General Wurmser in the north, Bonaparte wheeled south and on 22 June took possession of Leghorn. The Kingdom of the Two Sicilies (Naples) had already signed an armistice on 4 May, and Sardinia made peace on the 28th. French progress in Italy had astonished Nelson, and he told brother William the reason: 'not from the extraordinary valour and good conduct of the French, but from the imbecility and fear of the Italian States'. In return for peace the French were levying huge sums and looting works of art from the Italian States. It now seemed likely that the scale of Bonaparte's success would bring Spain into the war against England, causing Nelson to reflect not on the threat to the British fleet but on his enhanced earnings opportunity: 'If we have a Spanish war, I shall yet hope to make something this war. At present, I believe I am worse than when I set out – I mean in point of riches, for if credit and honour in the service are desirable, I have my full share. Opportunities have frequently been offered me, and I have never lost one of distinguishing myself, not only as a gallant man, but as having a head; for, of the numerous plans I have laid, not one has failed, nor of opinions given, has one been in the event wrong. It is this latter which has perhaps established my character more than the others.'[37] Apart from the truth and balance of that self-assessment he was misleading his brother, perhaps deliberately, in the matter of prize money. Certainly he had not made a fortune, but his accounts show that for the period up to 11 May 1796, from the time he had left Spithead, he had received £2,226 (at today's values about £110,000) as his share of prize money for the capture of some forty-seven vessels. This was nothing like the sums lucky captains could make by capturing rich ships in single actions. In such cases prize money could be of the order of £60,000, say £3 million by today's values, but for any individual captain that was not unlike winning the lottery.

Nelson's current orders were to blockade Leghorn and aid Sir Gilbert Elliot around Corsica, especially in preventing a French landing. By now Elliot had decided that a garrison must be positioned at Porto Ferrajo on the Isle of Elba to prevent its use as a stepping stone for a French invasion of Corsica. This was accomplished on 10 July, swiftly and peaceably as he intended, not least, as Nelson expressed it, because of 'harmony and good understanding between the Army and Navy'.[38]

Although Porto Ferrajo, the blockade of Leghorn, and his diplomatic battles with the still neutral Genoese were employing all his mental and physical vigour, he never allowed himself a narrow focus. He thought of the war in general, the situation in Genoa, in Leghorn, in Spezia, in Corsica, in Rome, in Naples; he tried to see himself in a bigger picture; he worked his lines of communication with the handful of British ministers and consuls; and he sought for advantage by treating the local fishermen out of Leghorn in such a way as to get them on his side. He dealt similarly with foreigners: 'An officer loses nothing but on the contrary gains much for his King and Country in courteous behaviour to foreigners. I do the same strict things but yet the people are contented.'[39] He had letters from the Swedish and Neapolitan ministers to prove it.

His good feelings about himself were not at all helped by a letter from Fanny. Gossip she was passing on inflamed his acute sensitivities about money and recognition. 'I have never been on any secret expeditions except one when I did not command and therefore lost the opportunity of making a fortune.' It would seem that someone had been casting aspersions on him.

As to my letter of some affairs not being gazetted, had all my actions been gazetted not one fortnight would have passed . . . one day or other I will have a large Gazette to myself. I feel that one day or other such an opportunity will be given me. I cannot, if I am in the field of glory be kept out of sight . . . Lord Spencer has wrote to Sir John Jervis how desirous he is of giving me my flag but as circumstances are he does not choose to face a promotion, at the same time fully approving of the pendant. . . . Wherever there is anything to do, there providence is sure to direct my step, and ever credit must be given me in spite of envy.

Fanny had asked yet again when he was coming home. He was straight to the point now: 'I believe when an honourable peace is made or a Spanish war, which may draw our fleet out of the Mediterranean. God knows I shall come to you not a sixpence richer than when I set out . . . I had a letter a few days past from the Duke of Clarence assuring me of his unalterable friendship. Will this ever do good? I will however take care it shall do me no harm.' Then he shifted into another passage of self-congratulation.

> But even the French respect me; their Minister at Genoa on occasion of answering a note of mine returning wearing apparel [Nelson had returned the belongings of a French officer from a ship he had taken] says, 'Your nation, Sir, and mine is made to show all the people of the earth examples of generosity as well as valour.' I shall relate another anecdote, all vanity to myself, but you will partake of it. A person wrote a letter and directed as follows 'Horatio Nelson, Genoa.' On being asked how he could direct in such a manner his answer was, in a large party, 'Sir there is but one H.N. in the world.' The letter certainly came directly. At Genoa, where I have stopped all their trade, I am beloved and respected by both Senate and lower order. If a man is fearful of his vessel being stopped, he comes and asks me; if I give them a paper or say all is right, they are content. I am known in Italy, not a kingdom or state where my name will be forgot. This is my Gazette.

There is something more than faintly ridiculous in this reaction to Fanny's insensitivity and her inability to stroke his ego and recognize his achievement. When Fanny reread the letter there would be little to cheer her other than his good health, 'If I ever feel unwell, it is when I have no active employment, that is but seldom', and the usual one-liner about Josiah, 'Josiah is very well never sick.'[40] To be fair, he did occasionally refer to Josiah's having or not having a cough and on one occasion the height to which he had now grown.

Nelson's ceaseless energy led him to advocate an assault on Leghorn, proposing 1,000 troops under his own command as a colonel of marines with Major Duncan under him, and 'every soldier in my squadron, and a party of seamen to make a show'. His two postscripts were vintage, breathless Nelson: 'It has ever pleased God to prosper all my undertakings, and I feel confident of His blessing on this occasion. I ever consider my motto Fides et Opera,' followed by, 'NB Twenty four hours will do the business. Send an active officer.'[41] He was pulled up short by Elliot who introduced him to the realities of the professional jealousies he, Elliot, was contending with: 'What you mention would blow us all up at once . . . I have reason to think the General [De Burgh commander of the forces in Corsica] himself would command the troops.' He was straight with Nelson: 'If I were writing to most other men I should fear personal feelings in you on this explanation, but I know enough of you to be quite certain that the King's service is the sole object that can either interest your feelings or animate your exertions, and I am therefore afraid of no devilry.' He was not going to side with Nelson against the General. 'You will find General de Burgh one of the most gentlemanlike in the world. He is cool and well skilled in his profession; and his reputation for spirit and courage is established on sure testimony of his former conduct and actions, which have been very distinguished in this war.'[42]

Of course, Elliot had been corresponding with Jervis, who had written approvingly of how he was handling Nelson. 'I am very glad you have a little damped the ardour of Commodore Nelson respecting the republic of Genoa, he is an excellent partisan but does not sufficiently weigh consequences.'[43] As for the Leghorn proposal, 'I agree with you in every part of your reasoning respecting Leghorn, the Commodore is the best and fittest fellow in the world to conduct the naval part yet his zeal does now and then (not often) outrun his discretion. If Marshall Wurmser has fairly beat the enemy in the field . . . the attempt on Leghorn ought to be made.'[44] Between them they were handling Nelson very well, encouraging him, acknowledging his achievement, but remaining in charge, exercising their own authority with skill and judgement. When faced with men of such calibre and skill there was never a hint of insubordination in Nelson, rather a well judged capacity to bow to the wind. Nelson had no quarrel with being told what was what in an acceptable and proper way. In the midst of all this frantic activity he was still cocking his ear for a Spanish decision for war or peace, and Jervis must have smiled to receive his enthusiastic 'Should the Dons come, I shall then hope I may be spared, in my own person, to help to make you at least a Viscount.'[45]

In the event Genoa was the flashpoint. First the Genoese authorities refused to allow bullocks bought for the fleet to pass through the port for fear of offending the French. Then the French formed a battery at St Pierre d'Arena and fired on Nelson's boats. He retaliated by capturing a French tartan, which in turn caused the town batteries to open fire on his ships, which endured a six-hour bombardment without replying – the upshot being that Genoa closed her port to English ships. Nelson's reaction was straightforward: 'I do not think neutrality can be all on one side.'[46]

Some weeks earlier Nelson had told Jervis that in the event of Genoa being closed he intended to advise Elliot. 'instantly to seize Capraja [about nine miles east-northeast of Cape Corse], where he will find all the arms &c. for Corsica and probably French troops'.[47] Elliot was of a like mind. Again Nelson and the army commander collaborated perfectly and the garrison surrendered. Jervis's letter covering Nelson's dispatch significantly drew attention to the lieutenants of the *Captain* who 'have exposed their persons on all occasions with that cool and deliberate courage which forms so prominent a feature in the Commodore's character'. He highlighted Nelson's 'skill, judgement and enterprise'. He underlined 'the good training of those under his command',[48] thereby revealing the emphasis he himself placed on these elements of officer-like conduct.

At such a time it was particularly irritating for Nelson to receive a letter from Fanny complaining about the irregularity of his letter writing, and her health. 'I grieve to hear such a bad account of yourself. Cheer up, I shall return safe and sound. The busy and active scene is my delight.'[49]

Good humoured though he was, he was not prepared to waste more words than that on her. He thought he had told her enough times what being a sailor's wife entailed. Alas, Fanny would never realize how frustrating and alienating it was for a man, far from her side, to receive complaints for which the remedies were entirely outside his control.

Part III

The Making of an Icon

10

Into the Limelight

God knows ambition has no end.

Nelson, November 1796

Politically and strategically the sky had been darkening for some time. Pitt's First Coalition against the French was over. Prussia and Holland had already made peace with France and in July 1796 Spain had allied herself with France and was now only a month away from declaring war on England. Austria, the last of the allies, was reeling in the face of Bonaparte's brilliance in Italy. In May, Naples had agreed an armistice with France, as a prelude to peace. England was vulnerable to uprising in Ireland and invasion across the Channel. It was not difficult for the Cabinet to conclude that the fleet should be withdrawn from the Mediterranean. There was little it could hope to achieve that would justify clinging to Corsica as a base. The nearest friendly territory was Portugal and it was to Lisbon that the fleet should retreat, able from there to blockade Cadiz and command in principle the entry and exit of the Mediterranean.

On 30 September Nelson received a terse and secret order from Jervis: 'All our operations are at an end by the arrival of orders to evacuate Corsica and retreat down the Mediterranean. . . . You must go over to Bastia immediately and co-operate with the Viceroy in retiring the troops from the outposts, keeping Leghorn in blockade to prevent a descent pending this difficult operation.'[1] Nelson had realized that the moment Spain entered the war, retreat down the Mediterranean was inevitable. Now the moment had arrived he felt humiliation at the British retreat. 'I lament in sackcloth and ashes our present orders, so dishonourable to the dignity of England, whose fleets are equal to meet the world in arms, and of all fleets I ever saw I never saw one equal in point of officers and men to our present one, and with a Commander-in-Chief fit to lead them to glory.'[2]

Jervis had himself wished to be at Elliot's elbow but he was blockading Toulon and as he put it, 'I dare not leave this position at present. The moment I know of Admiral Man being on route to join me I will make the best of my way to you, in the mean while Commodore Nelson, whose zeal and activity cannot be exceeded will carry into execution all your plans.'[3] Nelson and Elliot were of the same mind, the Viceroy much distressed by the necessity to withdraw, Nelson worried by the consequences of British withdrawal for the position of Naples. He set about energetically planning the evacuation, well aware of the likely Corsican reaction when British intentions became known. He needed a ship large enough for 1,200 barrels of powder and 300 tons of stores, three ships for 600 Corsican and French émigrés, five ships for 1,500 troops, a hospital ship, and a ship for Elliot's staff and effects, which made eleven ships for Bastia alone, plus another sixteen for Ferrajo, St Fiorenzo, Calvi, Ajaccio and Bonifaccio, a convoy of between twenty-eight and thirty ships, with two ships-of-the-line, eight frigates and three sloops to escort them. When the intention to withdraw was made public the situation in Bastia became chaotic and almost out of control. On 14 October Nelson reported to Jervis:

> At daylight this morning went to General de Burgh, and told him, that from the embarkation of the Vice-Roy, the evacuation and regulation of the Town became entirely military, and of course devolved on us ... I have been to the magazines and have arranged as far as I have the means the embarkation of provisions; and the General says he will have proper guards to keep off the populace. I have recommended to him to send for the Municipality and to tell them that the direction of affairs was in our hands, and that it would be at their peril were they to interfere in the embarcation of any property belonging to us ... it is the terror of the Ships which will keep order here.[4]

Four days later he was writing, 'a number of French have landed near Cape Corse, and have sent to demand of the Municipality what part they mean to take. The Vice-Roy has informed the Municipality, that we wish to quit them amicably, and in the state we promised; but if they permitted the French to enter the Town, or in any way embarrassed our embarcation, that it would end in destruction of the batteries and would be highly detrimental to Bastia. We shall act, I see, with prudence, and retreat in time. The garrison of Capraja is arrived.'[5]

These relatively sober comments to Jervis are in stark contrast with the vividly egotistical account Nelson sent to Fanny on 7 November 'The army,' he said had

> allowed the Corsicans at Bastia to sequester and seize all the English property, to lay a privateer across the Mole and in short by every way to insult them, and had I not arrived, [on the 14th] I am sure they would have taken the Viceroy from them and have submitted to any terms the townspeople demanded and this with a force of 1,800 men in possession of the citadel, but all were panic struck. In one quarter of an hour I settled the whole matter for I sent for the Council of 30 who acted for the Corsicans or French, and told them that if the sequester was not taken off in that time, the armed Corsicans retired and that I was molested in taking off what I thought proper, I would blow the town down. The Corsicans down muskets and run. From this moment all was quiet and I saved £200,000 worth of stores and property. In short it is impossible to say what I did not do. . . . Not a sixpence worth of property belonging to the merchants was left behind. The pleasure of my own mind will be my reward, except having the honour to maintain the Viceroy, Secretary of State and about 40 other persons at an enormous expense, but such things are. . . . Do not flatter yourself I shall be rewarded. I expect nothing therefore shall not be disappointed.[6]

He was not rewarded in a direct sense but here was the foundation of Elliot's lifelong admiration of Nelson. Elliot was by no means lacking in character, courage or decisiveness, but was not a man of action, capable of confronting and dominating. So, from the moment Nelson stepped ashore we can be certain that he was the active element in the scene, outfacing the Corsicans, managing the confused and uncertain situation with transcendent self-belief and, having laid the logistical groundwork for an efficient and effective evacuation, inspiring in his captains such energy that his convoy was able to sail for Porto Ferrajo in Elba at midnight on 19 October. Elliot saw at close hand how the magnetic Nelson created a force field along which others arranged themselves like so many willing iron filings. The after-effects were considerable. Jervis, in reporting to Spencer, had had the benefit of Nelson's personal report and was un-equivocal in pinpointing Nelson's pivotal contribution. 'Happily Commodore Nelson arrived there in the *Diadem* at this most interesting period and by the firm tone he held, soon reduced these gentlemen to order, and quiet submission to the embarcation.'[7]

By midnight on the 19th the embarkation was completed and Nelson's convoy sailed. In the interim the government had changed its mind and a dispatch of 21 October would give Jervis the option of transferring the troops and stores to Porto Ferrajo and so Elliot's final decision fortuitously anticipated the government's fallback position. Nelson was pleased to see the back of Corsica. 'We have now done with Corsica; I have seen the first and last of that Kingdom. Its situation was most desirable for us, but the generality of its inhabitants are so greedy of wealth, and so jealous of each other, that it would require the patience of Job, and the riches of Croesus to satisfy them. They say themselves they are only to be ruled by the Ruling Power shooting all its Enemies and bribing all its Friends.'[8] For Nelson personally, Corsica had been a poor investment.

New threats were looming. The next day a squadron under Don Juan de Langara, twenty-six sail-of-the-line and ten frigates, appeared off Cape Corse. On the other side of the island Jervis was anchored with fourteen sail-of-the-line in Mortella Bay. Langara chose not to seek him out and instead made for Toulon where the combined French and Spanish fleets now added up to thirty-eight sail-of-the-line and about twenty frigates. Jervis, desperate for a sight of Admiral Man and six ships, which he had ordered to Gibraltar to reprovision, sailed down the Mediter-ranean The *Captain* sailed with him but lacking Man's detachment and hampered by a convoy, they had to avoid rather than seek out the enemy. As they made their way down during the course of a month of 'exceed-ing bad weather and foul winds', news reached them that Man had unac-countably and disastrously decided to return to England. During this time Nelson was frequently on board the *Victory*, drawing inspiration from the way Jervis was managing his acute disappointment: 'Sir John Jervis honours me with his confidence and you know me well enough to be assured that in no way will I desert him . . . perseverance is the Admiral's as well as my motto . . . he feels Man's retreat severely, says nothing, not even complains of Man, but laments his rash step. I do not believe any officer ever was left in so delicate a situation and few, very few, would have firmness to bear up against it.'[9] It was not only the confidence of his Commander-in-Chief that was buoying him up. Reports from Jervis and from the Foreign Secretary Lord Grenville were beginning to have an effect at the Admiralty. On 29 November he wrote to his Uncle William, 'This day has brought me from Lord Spencer, the fullest and handsomest approbation of my spirited, dignified and temperate conduct both at Leghorn and Genoa, and my first lieutenant [Hinton] is made a Captain; a share of a galleon and I want no more – but God knows ambition has no end. The Admiralty have confirmed me as an established Commodore: they have done handsomely by me.'[10]

By the time they got to Gibraltar the government had changed its mind yet again and so on the 9th, stretched by his lack of resources, Jervis ordered Nelson to shift his flag from the *Captain* into the frigate *La Minerve*, take another frigate the *Blanche* under his command, and retrace his route up the Mediterranean to evacuate Porto Ferrajo. With the recent experience of Elliot's testimony to Nelson's brilliance in Corsica at the forefront of his mind, Jervis was supremely deft in the tenor of his orders. 'Having experienced the most important effects from your enterprise and ability, upon various missions since . . . I leave entirely to your judgement the time and manner of carrying this critical and arduous service into execution.'[11] Nelson was thrilled. 'I feel honoured in being trusted by Sir John Jervis in the manner I am.'[12] Not surprisingly when a letter arrived from Fanny floating the idea that they buy a cottage he replied expansively; if he had enough money in his account with Marsh & Creed she should do so.

Five days out from Gibraltar, at ten o'clock at night, off Cartagena in 'fresh gales and cloudy weather', they sighted two enemy frigates to leeward. Nelson immediately swooped down on them. At twenty minutes to eleven *La Minerve* passed under the stern of the *Santa Sabina*. As he told his brother, 'When I hailed the Don, and told him, "This is an English Frigate" and demanded his surrender or I would fire into him, his answer was noble, and such as became the illustrious family from which he is descended – "This is a Spanish Frigate, and you may begin as soon as you please."' They fought for an hour and forty minutes. 'I have no idea of a closer or sharper battle: the force to a gun nearly the same, and nearly the same number of men.' After half an hour the *Santa Sabina*'s mizzenmast shattered and fell. 'I asked him several times to surrender during the action, but his answer was – "No Sir; not whilst I have the means of fighting left." When only himself of all the officers were left alive, he hailed, and said he could fight no more, and begged I would stop firing.'[13] The *Santa Sabina* struck her colours at twenty past one in the morning and Lieutenant Culverhouse was rowed over to take possession. Her captain Don Jacobo Stuart was rowed back to *La Minerve* to surrender his sword, which Nelson promptly returned to him; about two-thirds of her crew were dead or wounded. Lieutenant Hardy and a party of twenty-four seamen were rowed over to take command and she was taken in tow by *La Minerve*. About an hour later another frigate approached, which Nelson took to be the *Blanche*. He was mistaken, for soon after the action had begun in darkness the *Blanche* had engaged the second enemy frigate, the *Ceres*. According to her captain, D'Arcy Preston it took only eight or nine broadsides to make her haul down her colours but he could not take possession because three other enemy ships had appeared in the vicinity. When he saw they were not standing towards his adversary, now making sail, he too crowded on sail to chase her. Prize money was wearing more heavily on his mind than supporting Nelson, who realized soon enough that this new frigate coming up on him in the early morning gloom, was not the *Blanche* for she hailed the *Santa Sabina* in Spanish and fired a broadside into her. Nelson immediately cast off his prize and opened fire on their new assailant. After half an hour's firing his quarry suddenly wore ship and passed to his stern where in the morning light those in *La Minerve* could see following them two enemy ships-of-the-line and a frigate. With the *Blanche*, 'far to windward', and *La Minerve* herself caught in light airs they could do little more than concentrate on repairing battle damage. Meanwhile Culverhouse in the *Santa Sabina* had hoisted English colours and tempted away one of the enemy ships-of-the-line which promptly pursued and retook her. At noon Nelson still had three ships chasing him but as darkness fell they gave up their pursuit. After being at quarters for the best part of a night and a day, after close on four hours of actual fighting, the balance sheet was not good. *La Minerve* had lost seven men killed and forty-four wounded and had lost their prize which could well have netted them £14,000–£28,000; nor would there be any share in the capture of the *Ceres* for the *Blanche* had not succeeded in catching her. Two of Nelson's officers and a score of his seamen had been captured

and his ship was badly cut up. The cards had not fallen well for him and
it is no wonder that Nelson summed up the action to Jervis as 'an
unpleasant tale'. But, making the best of a bad job, he was full of praise
for George Cockburn, his captain, and his lieutenants who were all
named. There was special praise for Culverhouse and Hardy, their hoisting of English colours to attract the Spanish, their bravely taking punishment until 'the *Sabina's* main and foremast fell overboard', and they were
retaken. Jervis would have had no difficulty in reading between the lines
of Nelson's comment on the *Blanche*, 'I have not yet received from
Captain Preston an account of his Action; but as I saw the *Blanche* this
morning to windward, with every sail set, I presume she has not suffered
much damage.'[14]

Nelson did not pause to feel sorry for himself. His main objective
was to recover his captured men, all badly needed in his already undermanned ship. He had only one bargaining counter: psychology. He wrote
an elegant and gracious letter to Don Miguel Gaston, Captain-General
of Cartagena:

The fortune of war put *La Sabina* into my possession after she had
been most gallantly defended: the fickle Dame returned her to you
with some of my officers and men in her ... I consent Sir, that
Don Jacobo may be exchanged, and at full liberty to serve his King,
when Lieutenants Culverhouse and Hardy are delivered into the
Garrison at Gibraltar ... I also trust that those men now Prisoners
of War with you will be sent to Gibraltar. It becomes great Nations
to act with generosity to each other, and to soften the horrors of
war.[15]

On that same day he sent Don Jacobo back to Cartagena and with him
a letter, this time to the Spanish Admiral Don Juan Marino giving his
opponent a deserved and glowing reference for his gallant conduct: 'I
have endeavoured to make Don Jacobo's captivity as easy as possible,
and I rely on your generosity for reciprocal treatment towards my brave
officers and men, your prisoners.'[16] To Nelson his men were not numbers.
As he said to Jervis, 'they are all good men. The Gunner of the *Peterel*
is amongst the missing; we hope he is on board the Prize: good men were
wanting and probably he pushed himself forward. My Coxwain, an

invaluable man, is also a prisoner.' And he continued to fight Cockburn's corner. 'If you can, pray Sir, procure some good men for Cockburn; he deserves every praise you are pleased to bestow on him. I take it for granted the Admiralty will promote Lieutenant Culverhouse, and I hope Lieutenant Noble will also be promoted.'[17]

Three days later on 27 December *La Minerve* arrived at Porto Ferrajo. News of Nelson's action had preceded him by the grapevine of the sea so that when he entered General de Burgh's ballroom the General stepped forward to greet him while his band struck up 'See the Conquering Hero Comes' and 'Rule Britannia'. Happy and delighted to receive such public recognition he was nevertheless inclined to discount it. 'What England may think I know not. We are at a distance.'[18] Indeed recognition for his achievements was on his mind for now that the naval campaign in the Mediterranean was drawing to a close it was time to gather testimonials from all those high officials he had been thrown into contact with during the past three years. Elliot was away on a fact-finding mission to the Italian States and Naples and Nelson told him 'I have wrote to Sir WH[amilton], as I have to Mr Drake and Mr Trevor, to ask for a public letter of my conduct as has come under their knowledge . . . and I trust that when you come here, I shall not want for your testimony. I feel a fair right to state my services, such as they are, at the end of the war to our Sovereign, who, I believe is not slow to reward arduous endeavours to serve him.'[19]

In the meantime he was faced with an immediate problem. General de Burgh had received no orders via army channels to withdraw. He was quite aware that since Naples had made peace with France the previous justification for hanging on in the Mediterranean was no longer valid. Nevertheless he felt he needed to wait until such time as orders arrived addressed to himself. Faced by such temporizing Nelson properly stood on the letter of his orders and the government's strategic intentions: 'I shall withdraw nearly all the supplies from this place whether the troops quit it or not, and reduce the naval force here as much as possible. The object of our Fleet in future is the defence of Portugal, and keeping in the Mediterranean the Combined Fleets. To these points my orders go and I have no power of deviating from them.'[20]

Nelson, very sensibly, gave not the slightest impression that there was any scope for negotiation, notwithstanding the flexibility of his own orders. Again he displayed his capacity for diplomacy, mixing firmness and clarity with courtesy and empathy. 'The difficulty of your deciding on the contrary orders of Government, and of guessing what may be their intentions at present, I clearly perceive.' In the event he had found himself facing a hurdle he could not jump, and feeling that he needed to have the reason for the potential failure of his mission to be clearly on the record, he decided to write direct to Spencer. 'The General is without orders, and the Army are not so often called upon to exercise their judgement in political measures as we are; therefore the General feels a certain diffidence. But let me be clearly understood as not intending to convey the slightest criticism on the General's conduct.'[21] He took the apparently extraordinary step of writing again to Spencer on 16 January for the same reason. 'The General will I fancy, be guided in a great measure by Sir Gilbert Elliot, whose arrival is momentarily expected . . . I have stated most fully to the General the Admiral's intention and my instructions. However should the General's determination be to stay . . . I have every Naval store, and all the establishment embarked, and shall take them down the Mediterranean leaving a very small naval force here under Captain Fremantle.'[22] In this he was not simply putting himself in the clear. He was bearing his responsibility as the man on the spot, taking it upon himself to manage the politics of the situation, loyally supporting St Vincent and avoiding any possibility of seeming to leave De Burgh in the lurch.

In the event Elliot had formed his own view from visits to Rome and Naples; the Pope had not yet made peace with the French and in Naples alarm was growing at the potential for French subversion following their peace with them. Elliot judged that the garrison must remain at Elba until the government had fully considered the impact of their leaving on these friendly states. It says much for Elliot's power of argument and firmness of judgement that he was able to prevail in the difficult discussions that must have taken place. Nelson's capacity to take a hard line in an acceptable way was equalled in this case by his capacity to be overruled with good grace; he remained good friends with Elliot. However, in his private afterthoughts he clearly worried about what Jervis would think of him, as his enigmatic words to Fanny written immediately before his departure show: 'Confidence tells me I shall not fail, but as nothing will be left undone by me should I not always succeed my mind will not suffer, nor will the world I trust be willing to attach a blame where my heart tells me none will be due.'[23] He was worrying needlessly. St Vincent would not blame him; the thing he looked for most of all in his sub-ordinates was the strength of character to bear the responsibility of command.

And so, having taken on board all the naval personnel and stores at Porto Ferrajo, having divided his ships into two convoys so as to reduce the risk of encountering the enemy's fleet, having left behind the frigates *Inconstant* and *Blanche*, and some smaller ships to support the military presence, and having prepared fully victualled troop transports for rapid evacuation of the troops should that become a necessity, he set sail on 29 January 1797 for Gibraltar and Lisbon to rendezvous with Jervis.

As he went down the Mediterranean with Sir Gilbert Elliot and some of his personal staff on board – 'I shall be sure of a pleasant party let what will happen'[24] – Nelson's intention was to look into Toulon, Mahon and Cartagena for signs of the Combined Fleet, which at that time would amount to some thirty-eight ships-of-the-line. At Toulon he could see only seven French ships. Rear-Admiral Villeneuve and his squadron were no longer there (they had left at the beginning of December and had subse-quently escaped past Gibraltar and made their way to Brest). He found that Cartagena was empty, the Spanish fleet, twenty-six sail-of-the-line, nowhere to be seen. Arriving at Gibraltar on 9 February he learned that the Spaniards has passed Gibraltar four days previously and had sent in *Le Terrible*, two other sail-of-the-line and a frigate with supplies for their forces currently besieging Gibraltar. When Nelson arrived the Spaniards were still anchored on the Algeciras side of the bay. To his delight Culverhouse and Hardy were among prisoners of war on board *Le Terrible*, could be exchanged for Spaniards and freed to rejoin *Le Minerve*. Nelson, knowing the Spanish fleet was in the Atlantic, was full of anxiety to rejoin Jervis. He paused only a day, to replenish his water and secure his lieutenants, took leave of the Governor, and refused his invitation to dine on the 11th. But there was a mix-up of boats to bring Elliot back to the ship, probably compounded by Elliot's having engaged to dine with the Governor anyway. Whatever his exclamations about lub-berly viceroys in the privacy of his cabin, Nelson kept a perfect public face and his note to Elliot's private secretary was gracious: 'Now the tide is made against us: therefore, I most heartily wish you a good appetite, and only beg you will be on board as early in the evening as possible – say eight o'clock – for I shall sail the first moment after.'[25]

Raising their anchor and getting under way attracted the attention of the watching telescopes aboard *Le Terrible*, which together with its companion ship-of-the-line hoisted sail in pursuit. In any normal circumstances Nelson's frigate would have been able to outsail them but away on the far side of the Bay of Algeciras his enemies had better wind while he was hampered by fitful winds in the lee of the Rock. And so he found himself being chased again and preparing for action.

For what happened next we have to rely on Colonel Drinkwater, a member of Elliot's staff who had transferred to *La Minerve* at Gibraltar. Since he was dealing with a soldier, Nelson may have been tempted to exaggerate a little when Drinkwater asked him about the probability of an engagement. He replied, 'Very possible', and looking up at his broad pendant, added, 'But before the Dons get hold of that bit of bunting, I will have a struggle with them, and sooner than give up the frigate I'll run her ashore.' But although they were in a ticklish situation, they were not yet within range of sighting shots and, once clear of the Rock, it was odds on *La Minerve* to outrun the Spaniards. Although cleared for action, officers and men had not yet been summoned to quarters, so they all went to dinner, Drinkwater happily congratulating Hardy on his newly regained freedom – until a seaman fell overboard. 'The Officers of the Ship ran on deck; I, with others ran to the stern windows to see if anything could be observed of the unfortunate man; we had scarcely reached them before we noticed the lowering of the jolly boat, in which was my late neighbour Hardy, with a party of sailors; and before many seconds had elapsed, the current of the Straits, (which runs strongly to the eastward,) had carried the jolly boat far astern of the frigate towards the Spanish Ships.' Hardy, soon signalled that their search was fruitless and his crew turned to pull hard for their ship. With the current against them and *La Minerve* still under way, albeit with reduced sail, the boat's crew were in increasing danger from the leading French ship which was now almost within range of *La Minerve*. Nelson's response to the crisis was, 'By G—, I'll not lose Hardy; back the mizzen topsail.'[26] *La Minerve*'s progress was immediately checked. Boat and ship moved towards each other, until Hardy and his furiously rowing crew could be thrown a line. The captain of *Le Terrible*, totally disconcerted by Nelson's extraordinary manoeuvre, responded by also shortening sail, as if to allow himself time for thought or for his companion ship to draw closer to reinforce him. But now with Hardy and his men clambering on board, Nelson hoisted every stitch of sail *La Minerve* could wear and was soon well out of shot and by sunset out of sight.

In that moment of crisis Nelson had decided that his first priority was to save Hardy and his men, not to ensure that his frigate and the intelligence he possessed reached Jervis as quickly as possible. Had he lost his ship and been court-martialled it is unlikely that he would have been able to justify his action. By the same token his people's admiration for him was unbounded; his legend enlarged. At London dinner parties Drinkwater would tell the story time and time again.

Just how important it was that he find Jervis became more than ever apparent that same night when Nelson and Cockburn were gripped by the realization that they had blundered into the path of the Spanish fleet. Having been blown through the Straits it was now finding its way to its destination, Cadiz, which lay to the north-east. Quietly aligning *La Minerve* with the enemy course they sailed along with them, keeping well out of hailing distance until the enemy fleet turned north in the early hours of the morning and *La Minerve* was able to detach herself to the westwards and then steer north to make her way to her rendezvous with Jervis off Cape St Vincent. On 13 February Nelson sighted the British fleet and as soon as they drew near to the *Victory*, boats were launched to take Nelson, Elliot, Drinkwater, Culverhouse and Hardy on board the flagship. Nelson knew the importance of intelligence and wanted Jervis to have the benefit of first-hand accounts of everything that had transpired since last they had met.

The battle of Cape St Vincent that was about to begin was not billed to be Nelson's battle. In the cast list he was a relatively minor player, below his Commander-in-Chief Sir John Jervis, below the commanders of the fleet's three divisions, Vice-Admiral Thompson, Vice-Admiral the Honourable William Waldegrave and Rear-Admiral Parker. Although still flying his broad pendant as a commodore he was back in his own ship the *Captain*, simply one of fifteen captains.

In command of the Spanish ships was Teniente General José de Cordoba y Ramos who had unwisely accepted a command previously refused by two others, General Juan de Langara y Huarte and Teniente General José de Mazzaredo. Both had characters strong enough to back their personal assessment of the fleet's defects in manning and materiel, and to accept the personal consequences of their refusal. Cordoba's freedom to manoeuvre was further circumscribed by orders to convoy four urcas (armed merchant ships) laden with mercury, to Cadiz. Having been blown through the Straits and out into the Atlantic he had now to make his way to Cadiz, away to his north-east. Cordoba's misfortune was Jervis's luck, for he could reach Cadiz only by sailing across Jervis's path, and Jervis had just been reinforced by Rear-Admiral Parker in the *Prince George* and five ships-of-the-line.

The situation began to unfold on 9 February when the *Viper* brought Jervis news that the Spanish fleet had passed through the Straits four days previously. On the 10th the *Emerald* confirmed that the Spaniards were still at sea so there was the possibility of his intercepting them. On the 12th Jervis decided to move his fleet to the south-west. Early on the 13th came Nelson's intelligence and later in the day the *Bonne Citoyenne* reported the Spaniards to be some twenty miles to the south-east, moving east for Cadiz. At dinner on board *Victory* Jervis raised his glass to Elliot and Drinkwater in a jocund toast, 'Victory over the Dons in the battle which they cannot escape tomorrow.'[27] Many years previously he had written to the Secretary of the Admiralty after Keppel's action, 'I have often told you that two fleets of equal force can never produce decisive events, unless they are equally determined to fight it out, or the Commander-in-Chief of one of them misconducts his line.' He was determined that on this occasion there should be a battle.[28]

In the *Captain* Nelson was reunited with Ralph Miller and his former first lieutenant, Edward Berry, now promoted Master and Commander, but on board as a volunteer, not having yet been appointed to a ship of his own. Word of impending battle had spread through the fleet. Officers submerged any anxieties they may have felt by adopting an air of confident anticipation. Nelson himself was calm and ready.

At dawn on 14 February Jervis and his fleet were twenty-four miles west-southwest of Cape St Vincent. He had been awake all night and was on deck as the morning light moved across the ship. His frigates, *Niger*, *Lively*, *La Minerve* and the sloop *Bonne Citoyenne* were out like scenting pointers in the hazy dawn. At first the information that filtered back from them was of the crudest kind: occasional sightings with courses and positions in relation to himself, but nothing substantial about a fleet and its actual formation. Such fragmentary information caused him on two occasions to detach ships to chase small groups of reported enemy. It was only when the fleets were five or six miles apart that the *Bonne Citoyenne* signalled that she could see twenty-five ships-of-the-line. This was a testing moment for Jervis, his first experience of commanding in a major fleet action. Fully conscious that 'a victory is very essential to England at this moment', he was determined that this would be no abortive battle of the kind he had previously described. At 10.57 he signalled, 'Form line of battle as convenient.' This brought ships he had previously sent chasing into the line ahead of him. Troubridge in *Culloden* was leading, *Victory* was now seventh in the line and Nelson in *Captain*, twelfth.

With a full press of sail they bore down on the Spaniards. By 11.20 when they were almost on the enemy, the Spaniards had changed course. From his quarterdeck Jervis focused on a gap that had opened between the main body of the Spaniards moving to his right and a smaller group, perhaps a third of the total, following on behind. At 11.26 he signalled, 'The Admiral means to pass through the enemy's line.' Three-quarters of an hour later, he judged he had filled the gap sufficiently, and ordered his ships to tack in succession and pursue the main body of the Spanish fleet to his right. He had decided not to divide his force and chose to attack the main body of some eighteen ships to his right, rather than the nine to his left, which he did not know included four urcas. This opened up the possibility that he might find himself sandwiched between the two groups of the enemy. Having matched his fifteen against eighteen he must have concluded that he could fend off the others as he passed. *Culloden*, the leading British ship, tacked with such speed and verve that Jervis exclaimed, 'Look at Troubridge there! He tacks his ship to battle as if the eyes of England were upon him; and would to God they were! for then they would see him to be, as I know him, and, by heavens Sir, as the Dons will soon feel him.'[29]

About the same time as Troubridge tacked, the rear group of Spaniards under the command of Teniente General Joaquin Moreno in the 112-gun *Principe de Asturias* began to come up to attack the turning British line, making successive attempts to halt its progress, in the process maiming the *Colossus* sufficiently to bring her to a standstill, obliging the *Orion* to hold back and cover her, and together with the *Conde de Regla* firing in turn at the *Irresistible*, *Victory*, *Egmont* and *Goliath*. Moreno had engaged almost half the British ships but after about three-quarters of an hour broke off his action, no doubt judging that with his five battleships intact and his precious convoy still safe, the time had come for him to join up with the main body of the Spanish fleet, or alternatively make for Cadiz.

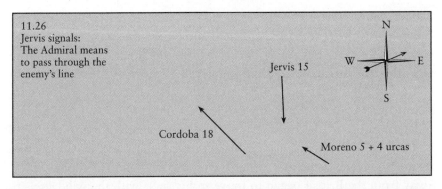

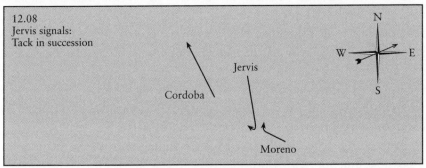

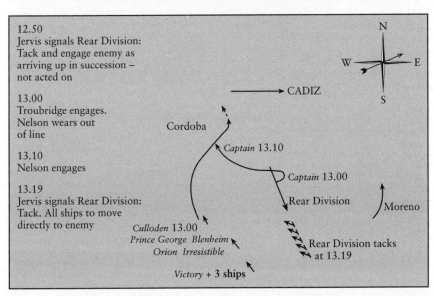

The Battle of Cape St Vincent, 14 February 1797

It was now 12.45 and the weakness of Jervis's battle plan was fast becoming evident: he had insufficient force near the main body he was seeking to attack. His single line of battle, the lateness of his signal to tack, the delays occasioned by running the gauntlet of Moreno's attacks had produced a situation in which only five ships ahead of him had actually tacked to pursue the enemy, while eight of his ships were behind him sailing steadily to the turning point. To make matters worse the wind had changed and was pushing his following ships further away from their objective. His enemy's scenario was also changing. Cordoba, sailing away from the British began to move to his right with the wind so as to pass behind Jervis's line of advance and head his ships for Cadiz. Moreno, held off by the British ships, began to move out of range and point his ships towards the rear of the British ships and Cadiz. The idea that Moreno beat against the wind, that is to the west-southwest in almost the opposite direction to Cadiz, to rejoin the main body being pursued, seems to have grown up in recent years. It is contradicted not only by common sense but by the eyewitness accounts of Miller, Drinkwater and Nelson himself who clearly saw Moreno sailing with the wind to make a possible junction with Cordoba.

Had Jervis had a bird's eye view he would have seen that the enemy ships to his right and left were on courses by which they might eventually join behind him, either to fight or to run for Cadiz. Moreno had done well in slowing the British line and Cordoba was responding intelligently to his disordered situation. It was time to improvise. Jervis saw that his five advanced ships were going to the right-hand side of the Spaniards and signalled his own division to go to the left to sandwich the Spaniards. He then signalled Vice-Admiral Sir Charles Thompson in the *Britannia*, commanding the rear division, which was still sailing steadily to the original turning point: 'Leading ship to tack and others in succession.' He then signalled all ships, 'Take up suitable stations for mutual support and engage the enemy as arriving up in succession.' The evident intention of these signals was to get the rear division to tack, make for the enemy by the most direct route and reinforce his five foremost ships without losing any more time. He had at last realized that he must abandon his single line and find a more direct way of getting at the enemy. To Jervis's intense chagrin *Britannia* neither acknowledged his signal nor altered course.

By now Jervis was on the point of failing to get the battle he wanted.

By 1 p.m. only *Culloden* had reached the rearmost ships of the Spanish fleet and had opened fire, although the *Blenheim* was up and likely to be in action soon. It was at this point that Nelson, appreciating the implications of Cordoba's change of course, reading the spirit of Jervis's two signals, understanding the vital need for speed, turned *Captain* to his left and sailing in a continuous leftwards arc, wore his ship out of the line past the two following ships *Namur* and *Diadem* to cross in front of the *Excellent* captained by his friend Collingwood and head directly for the enemy. None of these captains followed him, not even Collingwood. Ten minutes later, at 1.10, he was in action not far from Troubridge. Seeing this, Calder, Jervis's captain of the fleet and a Hotham at heart, wanted to recall *Culloden* and *Captain* as being dangerously isolated where they were. But Jervis, following the lead that Nelson had just given him, signalled at 1.19 for the entire rear division to come on to the larboard tack, thus causing them all immediately to turn towards the battle scene. At 1.45 Jervis signalled, 'Engage the enemy more closely', but this was an expression of hope rather than expectation, for distinctions between fast and slow ships were now showing. *Britannia*, *Namur*, *Goliath*, *Egmont* and *Barfleur* were at this stage tucked in behind *Victory* and in a sense more threatening than involved.

Nelson had placed *Captain* somewhat ahead of the *Culloden* with the 112-gun *San Josef* and the 84-gun *San Nicolas* opposite him; further ahead was Cordoba's flagship the 130-gun *Santissima Trinidada*. Within half an hour *Culloden* and *Captain* were both severely damaged. Although *Captain* had lost her fore topmast and her wheel was shot away, she was still fighting when Rear-Admiral Parker who had been following behind *Culloden* arrived on the scene in his flagship the *Prince George*, with *Blenheim* and *Orion*. Seeing Troubridge and Nelson heavily engaged around the enemy centre he sensibly ordered his ships to 'Fill and stand on', thus passing Troubridge and Nelson to get up with the Spanish leaders and new ships to fight. Nelson's ship by now was immobilized and *Blenheim* began to occupy his target.

Over on the windward side of the Spanish fleet was Collingwood, who following Jervis's general signal had ended up in front of the *Victory*. Now at 2.15 Jervis signalled *Excellent* to 'pass through the enemy line'. Collingwood made his way via the rearmost Spanish ship, the 112-gun *Salvador del Mundo* into which he poured rapid and well aimed broadsides, promptly causing her to lower her colours, only to put them up when it was seen that he was not waiting to take possession of her himself. The next in line was the 74-gun *San Isidro* which he likewise reduced to surrender, this time in the space of ten minutes. (It is not without reason that the gunnery school of the modern Royal Navy was named HMS *Excellent*.) At three o'clock he passed between the *Captain* and her two immediate opponents the *San Nicolas* and *San Josef*, which in their confusion promptly became entangled in each other as *Excellent* after emptying her broadside into them surged forward to grapple with the *Santissima Trinidada*.

The *Captain* was by now in tatters, sails and rigging shredded, wheel shattered, spars and masts severely damaged. After two hours of battle, dead and wounded were mounting to one in three. Nelson himself had been knocked sideways by a blow in the abdomen from a lump of wood, but in the smoke and noise, gripped with the madness of battle he was sufficiently alert to seize the moment offered by the collision of the *San Josef* and *San Nicolas*. Ordering Miller to take the *Captain* alongside, he shouted for boarders, sweeping aside Miller's attempt to lead them: 'No Miller I must have that honour.' The *Captain*'s cathead crashed into the stern gallery of the *San Nicolas* with a juddering crunch. Her bowsprit shot up and over the taffrail of the Spanish ship with a grinding lurch to entangle in her mizzen rigging. A marine clambered along *Captain*'s cathead on to the gallery of the Spanish ship and smashed a way into the enemy cabin with his rifle butt. Nelson, sword in hand and with a cry – whether 'Death or Glory' or 'Westminster Abbey or Glorious Victory' does not much matter – followed, his party of marines and seamen with cutlasses, axes and pikes pouring in behind. The door out of the cabin was locked. Frenzied axe strokes soon smashed it down. They charged on, some falling to the pistols of Spanish officers firing from the other side. A volley from his marines swept their path clear of Spaniards.

Meanwhile the dashing young Edward Berry, the first man into the Spaniard's mizzen chains, had taken a party of seamen by the high road: darting along the narrow bowsprit above the enemy taffrail, they leaped down like so many dervishes from above, hacking their way through any resistance, taking possession of the poop and hauling down the Spanish colours. For the Spaniards, one in three of whom was already dead or wounded, there was no incentive to fight on. They surrendered. At this point the boarding party became aware that they were being fired on from the stern gallery of the *San Josef* which lay alongside, half overlapping the *San Nicolas*. Nelson's response was instant. Shouting to his marines to return the fire, he yelled to Miller to send more men and calling to the men around him set off for yet another boarding. The three-decker which loomed above them was still being battered in her exposed front parts by the *Prince George*, and having lost over one in five of her crew killed or wounded and with her commander Don Francisco Xavier Winthuysen dying below with both legs shot off, there was no fight left in the remainder. When Nelson climbed into her main chains a Spanish officer called out in surrender. In the short and savage fight to capture the *San Nicolas* he had lost seven killed and ten wounded. By comparison the *San Josef* was a walkover: she was ready to surrender to the first caller, which in no way diminishes Nelson's mad courage in taking her on. Once down on her quarterdeck he accepted the captain's sword, and confirmed her surrender.

It was now about 3.30 p.m. Collingwood had moved on and had joined Frederick's *Blenheim* and Saumarez's *Orion* in battering the *Santissima Trinidada*. To them she seemed on the point of surrender, when at 4.22 Jervis signalled his fleet to wear and in effect terminated the engagement. Saumarez, no doubt feeling cheated of success, ruefully described the order as 'ill timed but doubtless necessary'.[30] He was probably right, for Jervis knew that sunset came early in February, four of his ships, *Blenheim*, *Culloden*, *Captain*, and *Colossus*, were damaged, and he sensed the possibility of a Spanish rally. Two Spanish ships that had become detached that morning, the *San Pablo* and the *Pelayo*, had appeared on the northern horizon and were making towards them and Moreno was not far away with his eight ships.

For once, Nelson, hater of all unfinished business, had nothing to say. At dusk he had been effusively welcomed by his relieved C-in-C on the quarterdeck of *Victory*. 'He said he could not sufficiently thank me, and used every kind expression which could not fail to make me happy.'[31] He had had his fill of fighting and a sufficient sense of personal achievement. On the other hand, Jervis had learned on this his sixty-fourth birthday that he lacked tactical genius. His plan had virtually failed; he had improvised too late in the day. If Nelson had not interpreted his orders in such an inventive way and made his marvellous dash to halt the flight of the Spaniards, there would have been no victory worth talking about. Jervis lacked neither courage nor determination. His own good instincts had prompted improvisation in the forming of his line. His decisive tactical insight pushed his ships into the gap between the enemy groups, but thereafter his signals came, not when they should have come, but only when their need had become obvious, and thus too late; Troubridge should have been asked to tack much earlier and what Nelson did should have been anticipated as an option much sooner by Jervis and signalled as a clear command to all his ships. More fundamentally he still saw himself as the conductor of an orchestra, conducting a battle as a set piece from the flagship. By comparison, Nelson was well on the way to realizing, intellectually as well as instinctively, that the variables involved in a fleet action were such that battles could not be fought by a method of centralized command and control. He would never fight his battles in this way.

Nelson had moved centre stage in a transcendent display of audacity and courage as *Captain* wore out from the line in a graceful curving motion and dashed at the towering Spanish three-deckers. Onlookers held their breath in awe as she came up alongside the enemy, her broadsides spouting flame and smoke. On board the *Captain* herself hearts and guts were variously filled with bravado, silent terror, prayer or quiet concentration, as they moved inexorably towards the monster Spaniards, jokes and expletives gave way to silence as men stood ready by their guns, close by their mates, under the eyes of their officer, gripped by the routines of preparation, releasing themselves into an orgy of cheers as the lanyards were pulled and their guns roared and leaped like wild things. One in four of them was about to die or be wounded. Later when it emerged that this now battered and sail-shredded ship had suffered almost a third of all the British battle casualties and that Nelson had personally led the boarding parties on to the *San Nicolas* and *San Josef* and had there received their surrender, he and they became instantly legendary. This was improvisation and opportunism on the grand scale. Crowned by success it was heroism of the highest order.

Full of exhilaration and joy Nelson felt he basked in the praise 'of every man from the highest to the lowest in the fleet'. His boarding of the *San Jose* from the *San Nicolas* was branded 'Nelson's Patent Bridge for Boarding First Rates'. Wits in the wardrooms of the fleet were hard at work and he sent home a copy of 'Commodore Nelson's receipt for making an Olla Podrida. . . . Take a Spanish first rate and an 80-gunship and after well battering and basting them for an hour keep throwing in your force balls, and be sure to let these be well seasoned.'[32]

On the other hand, Jervis's dispatch to the Admiralty mentioned no captain by name, other than the bearer of his dispatches, Calder Captain of the Fleet. It is open to question whether this was out of fairness, nicety or more dubious motives. As a captain participating in Keppel's battle off Ushant he had looked askance at self-publicity: 'I perceive it is the fashion of people to puff themselves, and no doubt you have seen, or will see, some of these accounts. For my part I forbade the officers to write by the frigate that carried the dispatches – I did not write a syllable myself except touching my health – nor shall I, but to state the intrepidity of the officers and people under my command.' But this was a different situation. Jervis was now a commander-in-chief. He was not usually worried about whether the opinions he entertained on the merits of individual officers were fair. Moreover he knew that notice was the oxygen of a sea officer's career.

One would be tempted to reach the more cynical conclusion, that this was the perfect way to take all public credit for himself, if it were not for the private follow-up letter he sent to Spencer on 16 February. This is so bizarre and such a travesty of events that it points to the true fact of the situation: a Jervis disorientated and overwhelmed by the emotional and mental overload of battle. Troubridge was given the most extravagant praise, 'led the Squadron through the enemy in masterly style and tacked the instant the signal flew', as though this was his major contribution. Nelson was bracketed with Collingwood and there was not a hint of his solo effort: 'Commodore Nelson contributed very much to the fortune of the day as did Captain Collingwood', a statement that by any standards was unjust to both. He next mentioned Berry, and somehow managed to give his leadership precedence over Nelson's: 'Captain Berry who served as a volunteer entered at the head of the boarders and Commodore Nelson followed immediately and took possession of them both.' He made a peculiar reference to Ben Hallowell, captain of the *Victory*, 'whose conduct aboard the *Victory* during the action has made him more dear to me than before'. His reference to Parker was offensive: 'I have omitted to notice Rear Admiral Sir William Parker ... who made his signals in a very officer like manner.' It was as though the greatest merit of a man who had commanded his division intelligently throughout, and had fought hard and suffered casualties, was to fly signals in an officer-like manner. In fact it was worse; consciously or unconsciously it was a classic case of damning with faint praise. He mentioned Admiral

Waldegrave only in terms of a conversation with him about whether he should take home a duplicate set of dispatches and the arrangements he was making to convey his baggage and suite home. There was no mention whatsoever of Frederick whose ship the *Blenheim* played a fine part in the action and had accounted for a fifth of the British casualties. His lack of mention of Thompson was no doubt intended; he was not inclined to forgive him for failing to acknowledge a crucially important signal.

Nicolas, the editor of Nelson's *Letters and Dispatches*, takes the view that Calder is the most likely person to have diluted Jervis's praise for Nelson's contribution, on the grounds that it might encourage others to disobey orders. This is preposterous. Jervis was a dominant, tough-minded man *par excellence*. He would have listened to Calder only if Calder's views had chimed with his own. It is more likely that in his state of mental overload he simply could not remember properly. He told Spencer, 'for the rest I beg leave to refer you to Captain Calder who is thoroughly master of the subject'.[33]

Although it is difficult to empathize with Nelson's by now over-whelming urge for self-promotion, we cannot blame him for his marvellous capacity to make himself legendary. In late February he produced his own narrative of the battle, *A Few Remarks relative to myself in the Captain, in which my Pendant was flying on the most Glorious Valentine's Day, 1797*. No writer of advertising copy or spin doctor could equal this succinct and vivid account. Exact clarity in his narrative is woven with strands of generous praise for others, which by a kind of alchemy makes his own achievement appear the greater: 'I was immediately joined and most nobly supported by the *Culloden*, Captain Troubridge . . . Collingwood, disdaining the parade of taking possession of beaten enemies, most gallantly pushed up, with every sail set, to save his old friend and messmate, who was to appearance in a critical state . . . Captain Miller was in the very act of going also, but I directed him to remain.' His account is studded with graphic vignettes, 'The *Excellent* ranged up within ten feet of the *San Nicolas*, giving a most tremendous fire. . . . A soldier of the 69th Regiment having broke the upper quarter gallery window, jumped in followed by myself . . . a Spanish Officer looked over the quarter-deck rail, and said, "they surrendered."'

He ended with a word picture as magically romantic as any filmic finale and as graphic in its delineation of a group as Benjamin West's *Death of General Wolfe*. 'On the quarter-deck of a Spanish First-rate, extravagant as the story may seem, did I receive the swords of the vanquished Spaniards, which as I received I gave to William Fearney, one of my bargemen, who placed them, with the greatest sang froid under his arm. I was surrounded by Captain Berry, Lieutenant Pierson 69th Regiment, John Sykes, John Thompson, Francis Cook and William Fearney, all old Agamemnons, and several other brave men, Seamen and Soldiers. Thus fell the Ships.' In his own autograph copy he added an heroic and theatrical coda, 'The *Victory* passing us saluted us with three cheers, as did every ship in the Fleet. . . . At dusk I went aboard the *Victory*, when the Admiral received me on the quarter deck and having embraced me, said he could not sufficiently thank me, and used every kind expression which could not fail to make me happy.'[34] His theatrical gesture to Captain Miller who was himself preparing to board, 'No Miller I must have that honour', was after the battle reinforced in his great cabin by a heartfelt, 'Miller I am under the greatest obligation to you', as with a flourish he took a ring, a rather large topaz set in diamonds, from his finger and placed it on one of Captain Miller's.[35]

The purpose of his graphic description was not for his private satisfaction or to remind himself what had happened. That might have been sufficient for many people but what he craved was public recognition and so copies were soon on their way to Locker, for publication in the newspapers, and to the Duke of Clarence as a stimulus for conversation in more exalted circles. What is printed becomes immortal, and so it was with Nelson's account. Published by Clarke and McArthur in their *Naval Chronicle* of 1799, it became for all time the Authorized Version.

Of course Nelson's account was biased. Battle involved an overpowering assault on the senses. The roar and blast of guns merged with the humming and whizzing of shot, the thump, crash, clang, ripping and twanging as the ship was hit, timber splintered, metal dinted and taut rigging parted; the shuddering of the ship as enemy broadsides found their target, the drunken heeling as their own guns fired; the bedlam of human sounds and activity, shouted orders, cries from wounded and dying men, the bustle of gun crews remustering as men were killed and wounded, the frenzy of carpenters' and boatswains' working parties as they hammered, cut and heaved shattered spars and rigging. And everywhere clouds of smoke blanked or distorted vision. It is amazing that with such distractions and such demand for focus on his own ship and its opponents Nelson noticed and remembered so much.

At the more normal end of the spectrum of reportage was Cuthbert Collingwood, who writing to his father-in-law a few days after the battle said, 'It is a very difficult thing for those engaged in such a scene to give details of the whole, because all the powers they have are engaged in their own part of it.' It is also particularly interesting to compare Collingwood's account with that of his friend. 'The ships longest and most engaged were *Culloden*, Captain Troubridge; *Captain*, Commodore Nelson; the *Blenheim*, Captain Frederick; and *Prince George*, Rear Admiral W Parker and Captain Irwin.' In this account to his wife Sarah three days after the battle the modesty with which he descibes his own encounters with the *Salvador del Mundo*, the *San Isidro*, the *San Nicolas* and the *Santissima Trinidada*, is striking. 'I had eleven men killed and many wounded; everybody did well.' He was fair to Nelson, fair to all the other major protagonists and played down his own achievements which were actually of critical importance. He himself made no distinction between Nelson and Troubridge, although he puts *Culloden* first in his list, which suggests that he shares the judgement of the ships' logs, that it was Troubridge who opened the action and not Nelson.

On the matter of the ships mainly engaged, Nelson had mentioned *Blenheim* in passing, but had said nothing about the *Prince George* which had clearly played a key role in moving ships up the line. That was to land him in trouble with Parker later. There was no doubt in Collingwood's mind however about Nelson's prime role, 'Let me congratulate my dear Commodore on the distinguished part he ever takes. . . . It added very much to the satisfaction I felt in thumping the Spaniards that I released you a little. The highest rewards are due to you and *Culloden*: you formed the plan of attack – we were only accessories to the Don's ruin.' He was thus both just and self-effacing. Nor was there any doubt in Nelson's mind about Collingwood's contribution, ' "A friend in need is a friend indeed," was never more truly verified than by your most noble and gallant conduct yesterday in sparing the *Captain* from further loss . . . I have not failed by letter to the Admiral, to represent, the eminent services of the *Excellent* . . . I could not come near you without assuring you how sensible I am of your assistance in nearly a critical situation.'[36] Part of Nelson's innate instinct for command was to be the author of commendation.

Nelson's great good fortune was that he did not have to rely on what either Jervis or Calder said about him or indeed what he had to say himself. The fact that his friends Elliot and Drinkwater had witnessed the battle from the frigate *Lively* was an advantage he was determined to make the most of. On the morning of the 15th, Nelson was rowed over to *Lively* to see Elliot but he had already gone to see Jervis. When Drinkwater remarked that, 'as the *Lively* would bear the glorious news to England, I should be obliged by his giving me as many particulars of the proceedings of his Ship, the *Captain*, and of his own conduct in the capture of the two Ships as he was disposed to communicate', he gave Nelson the perfect lead and when he asked, 'How came you Commodore, to get into that singular and perilous situation?' the stage had been set for his own naturally self-centred view of the battle. But Nelson nevertheless positioned himself properly, as well as astutely, as the man who saw what Jervis's intention was and did what he did because he had a better view of what the Spaniards were attempting than had Jervis.

When it came to prizes Drinkwater (who was taking pencil notes at the time) records Nelson as saying, 'I saw (and then he spoke with increased animation) that from the disabled state of the *Captain*, and the effective attack of the approaching British Ships, I was likely to have my beaten opponent taken from me; I therefore decided to board the *St Nicolas*, which I chiefly fought, and considered to be my Prize.' How indicative of Nelson's competitive, driven nature this is and how different from Collingwood's attitude that the actual taking of prizes was a mere formality. Not so Nelson – the *St Nicolas* was *my* prize. The overall result of this conversation was that the major contributions of Collingwood and Troubridge would be forever characterized merely as supporting Nelson and those of Frederick in the *Blenheim* and Parker in the *Prince George* would be totally overlooked.

The facts are that the casualty league (killed and wounded) was headed by *Captain* with 80, *Blenheim* with 61, *Culloden* with 57, *Excellent* with 23, *Irresistible* with 19 and *Prince George* with 15. No other ships got into double figures for casualties and seven ships had nobody killed. The same ships used the most powder. In essence the brunt of the battle had been borne by five British ships, *Captain*, *Culloden*, *Blenheim*, *Excellent* and *Prince George*. Between them they accounted for 89 per cent of the dead and 75 per cent of the wounded. Jervis underlined this in his private letter to Spencer: 'The Ships' returns of killed and wounded, although not always the criterion of their being more or less in Action is, in this instance correctly so.'

When Drinkwater happened to touch on the subject of honours and rewards for the admirals and ventured that Nelson would be made a baronet.

The words were scarcely uttered, when placing his hand on my arm, and looking me most expressively in the face, he said, 'No, no; if they want to mark my service, it must be in that manner.' 'Oh,' said I, interrupting him, 'You wish to be made a Knight of the Bath'; for I could not imagine that his ambition, at that time, led him to expect a Peerage. My supposition proved to be correct for he instantly answered me, 'Yes if my services have been of any value, let them be noticed in a way that the public may know me or them.' I cannot distinctly remember which of these terms was used, but from his manner, I could have no doubt of his meaning, that he wished to bear about his person some honorary distinction, to attract the public eye, and mark his professional services.[37]

Nelson's follow-up of this conversation was utterly single minded. When Elliot sent congratulations couched in hyperbole to match Nelson's own – 'Nothing in the world was ever more noble than the transaction of the *Captain* from beginning to end, and the glorious group of your ship and her two prizes, fast in your gripe, was never surpassed and I dare say never will'[38] – Nelson simply pressed his case: 'My Admiral and others in the Fleet think nearly the same as you do of my conduct . . . I conceive to take hereditary Honours without a fortune to support the Dignity, is to lower that Honour. . . . Baronetage is what I dread. . . . There are other Honours, which die with the possessors, and I should be proud to accept, if my efforts are thought worthy of the favour of my King.'[39] This was the story and message which Elliot, who had access to the Prime Minister and the highest levels of government, took home.

It did not particularly matter that Nelson soon began to have a few minor twinges about his claims, When he sent his *Remarks* to Locker on 21 February giving him *carte blanche* to publish them in the newspapers, 'inserting the name Commodore instead of I', he continued, 'I pretend not to say these Ships might not have fell, had I not boarded them; but truly it was not far from impossible but they might have forged into the Spanish Fleet as the other two Ships did.'[40] That was not how the record would stand.

The effect in naval circles of Nelson's achievement was immediate, and *preceded* that of his public relations campaign, as Fanny's letters to him in the second half of March show. On 11 March she wrote, 'Lady

Saumarez came running to tell me she had letters from her husband [captain of the *Orion*] . . . saying Com. Nelson's conduct was above praise'. Captain Andrew Sutherland, sometime Naval Commissioner at Gibraltar had written a very handsome letter which she quoted:

I have this instant heard of Sir John Jervis's battle in which Adm Nelson [he had been promoted Rear-Admiral on 22 February before news of the battle reached London on 3 March] bore a most conspicuous part, as he has in every service he was engaged in. The naval officers I heard speak on the subject in the course of yesterday and today all declare that, 'he has displayed more professional skill more zeal and more intrepidity than any officer who served this war,' and I think it impossible that he can escape being made a lord or at least a K.B. for such honours are sometimes bestowed on men who really deserve them. Be this as it may happen, yet it is the general wish! . . . Lord Hood wrote that he was astonished to hear you were there, that he congratulated us on the glorious share Adm. Nelson had in the late action . . . begs I will write him all you say about the action . . . Admiral Parker it seems had written the *Captain* and *Culloden* bore the brunt of action.

Fanny was warm and enthusiastic about Nelson's success but could not prevent herself from saying what was in her heart. 'I shall not be myself till I hear from you again. What can I attempt to say to you about boarding. You have been most wonderfully protected. You have done desperate actions enough. Now may I, indeed I do beg, that you never board again. Leave it for Captains.'[41] She returned to the theme in her next letter, 'you have acquired a character or name which all hands agree cannot be greater, therefore rest satisfied'. It would have been better had Fanny been able to contain her feelings and accept that when a husband is a soldier or sailor certain things are best left unwritten. There is an irreconcilable gulf between those who are motivated or obliged to take great risks, and those at home who cherish them and fear for them. Fanny cannot be blamed for her fear of loss, and nor can Nelson for the shafts of irritation he was likely to feel on reading her phrases.

In this following letter of 20 March Fanny was able to tell him that she had sent his account to Lord Hood who, 'when he returned it said a number of handsome things. "The glorious share Adm Nelson had in the action will immortalize his name in the pages of the history of

England." That he had an opportunity of shewing [it] where he knew it would be of service – that it was a most excellent clear account of the battle. He said a great deal more I assure you.' In thus circulating his *Remarks* she was not unaware of the potential danger. 'I hope I have not done wrong. I have lived long enough to dread envy.' A letter to his father from their grand relative, Lord Walpole assured him, 'nothing was yet talked of in London but Nelson. Everybody was loud in his praises', suggesting that many of society's dining rooms were being held in rapt attention by the eyewitness accounts of Elliot and Drinkwater or of those who had heard them. An extract from Collingwood's letter to his cousin Sir Edward Blackett had been brought to Fanny's notice. It had said that 'brave, honest Nelson with his little crew did wonders.' By now Nelson's art of cooking had appeared in *The Times*.[42]

In all this congratulation there was to be one discordant note. Rear-Admiral, and by now Sir, William Parker who had been notably generous in his praise for *Culloden* and *Captain* eventually got sight of Nelson's account, was dismayed, and wrote to him, 'I very readily admit that you have all the credit that belongs to an able officer and brave man.' What stuck in his throat was Nelson's lack of acknowledgement of the part played by the *Prince George*, *Orion* and *Blenheim*, although the latter had been mentioned *en passant*.

The essence of his own position was that *Culloden* had been firing for ten minutes before Nelson arrived on the scene, that Nelson had not been unsupported for an hour but more like ten to fifteen minutes, and that the *San Josef* had struck as a result of his own fire: he produced chapter and verse from his ship's log to prove his point. Nelson's egocentric presentation of the battle and his high and mighty assumption of a prerogative to hand out commendation had obviously irritated Parker vastly for he went on, 'The first ship that came within my observation, except the five ships alluded to, was the *Excellent*, *whose Captain neither requires your testimony or mine in proof of his bravery and good conduct*' (my italics). He then got to the heart of the matter. 'I am well aware that people in Action know but little of occurrences in their rear, yet when a letter is written to be exposed to public view, positive assertion should be made with great circumspection.'[43]

Nelson had dashed off his account, authenticated by the signatures of Miller and Berry (and of course it was in their interest as followers of his to do so), because on this occasion he was determined not to be overlooked. Recent research supports the accuracy of Parker's main contentions. He was not seeking to take credit from Nelson, or seeking notice for himself, for he had by then been made a baronet for his part in the action. He seems to have been motivated more by self-respect and recognition for the intelligent hard fighting of his own division. The importance of the episode however lies not so much in a wrangle between sailors about what actually happened on the day (an inevitability the moment a personal account was published) as in Nelson's response to Parker, which was very revealing. 'I must acknowledge the receipt of your Letter of the 25th July; after declaring that I know nothing of the *Prince George* till she was hailed from the forecastle of the *San Nicolas*, it is impossible I can enter into the subject of your letter.'[44] This was not the kind of letter one might have expected to be directed to a brother-in-arms six months after a battle in which they had shared the dangers of the day; not at all the diplomatic sort of letter that Nelson was very capable of writing. It was a letter that could have been penned by the most clinically focused of public relations executives, a ruthless closure of the debate, even though the letter, left behind with St Vincent to deliver, was accompanied in Parker's words by verbal assurances, 'that no offence was meant by him to me, and that he never thought it could be understood that both Ships had struck to him'.

There may already have been antipathy between Nelson and Parker. The hyperactive, and by now charismatic, self-absorbed and professionally brilliant Nelson would just as certainly repel some as he attracted others. It would seem that he had also repelled Sir James de Saumarez, captain of the *Orion*, which was in the leading group of ships. According to his biographer Ross, he reacted to aspects of Nelson's behaviour much as Parker did. 'When the captains met on board *Victory* Commodore Nelson said, "It was true Saumarez that the *Santissima* struck to you; the Spanish officers acknowledged it." Sir James supposing from the manner in which this was spoken that Nelson had doubted the truth of his report answered rather sharply, Who ever doubted it sir? I hope there is no need for such evidence to establish the truth of the report of a British officer!'[45] Nelson's effusiveness could easily set on edge the teeth of men who were on the proud side.

On the other hand there are strong hints in a letter of 6 April to brother William that whilst full of admiration for what Troubridge and Collingwood had done he was not quite so pleased about the rest: 'the others did their duty and some not entirely to my satisfaction. We ought to have had the *Santissima Trinidad* and the *Soberano 74*. They belonged to us by conquest, and only wanted some good fellow to get alongside them and they were ours. But it is well; and for that reason only we do not like to say much. Sir John Jervis is not quite contented, but says nothing publicly.'[46]

In the hard business of leadership, ruthless judgements of the performance of commanders have to be made and it seems as though Nelson was making such a judgement of others who had been engaged with the Spanish van. Collingwood had been willing to settle for, 'all have the merit of having done their utmost.' It was a measure of Nelson's superiority as a potentially supreme commander that he was unlike Collingwood in that respect.

The fall out of honours, when it came in March could hardly be said to have reflected Jervis's private letter to Spencer, or Nelson's views either. No nice distinctions were made as to who had done what. The handout was purely hierarchic. Jervis, who, although he did not know it, had already been elevated to the peerage a fortnight before the battle, was now elevated two further steps, made an earl (eventually taking the title Earl St Vincent) and awarded a pension of £3,000 a year. Admirals Thompson and Parker were both made baronets. Admiral Waldegrave, already the son of a peer and ranking above a baronet, got nothing immediately but his card was marked for a future Irish peerage. Nelson, due to the good offices of Elliot, was not made a baronet but a knight of the Order of the Bath as he had wished. Calder, bearer of the dispatches, was also knighted. All flag officers and captains received a gold medal. Then, as now, justice in the matter of honours was not to be hoped for. If there had been justice, neither Thompson, the ignorer of critical signals, nor Calder the hidebound defeatist, would have received anything; Troubridge, Collingwood and Frederick would have been made baronets, or at least knighted; and Nelson, in spite of his wishes, would have been elevated to the peerage with a very substantial pension, as the true begetter of Jervis's earldom.

11

Hubris

I have had flattery enough to make me vain and success enough to make me confident.

Nelson, July 1797

Having returned to sea four years previously in a mere 64, the lowest form of ship-of-the-line, an officer with no particular achievement to his name, having no more significance in the scheme of things than the single line he occupied in the Admiralty's list of 500 post captains, Nelson had, in the space of a single day, mutated into a glittering star. Moreover, St Valentine's Day served to bring sudden illumination to everything else he had done previously, in Corsica and Elba, along the Italian riviera, and against the *Ça Ira*. In retrospect they would be seen as the achievements of a hero in waiting. His legendary 14 February stamped him as one who could both make and seize the moment.

He was now a rear-admiral, a knight of the Honourable Order of the Bath. He had a gold medal to hang round his neck and the certainty that he would stay to command and prosper under Jarvis soon to become Earl of St Vincent. His father had been dazzled by the news and according to Fanny, repeating the words of Uncle Maurice Suckling, 'that he would live to see you an Admiral' Now he wrote,

The height of glory to which your professional judgement, united with a proper degree of bravery, guarded by Providence, has raised you, few sons, my dear child attain to, and fewer fathers live to see. Tears of joy have involuntarily trickled down my furrowed cheek. . . . The name and services of Nelson have sounded throughout the City of Bath, from the common ballad singer to the public theatre. . . . It gives me inward satisfaction to know, that the laurels you have wreathed spring from those principles and religious truths which alone constitute the Hero; and though a Civic Crown is all you at present reap, it is to the mind of inestimable value, and I have no doubt will one day bear a golden apple.[1]

True pride, mawkish sentimentality, pretentious moralizing, sharp perception of his son as a social and material asset, make an odd mixture, not unlike *mélanges* that are to be found from time to time in his distinguished son's effusions.

Over the coming weeks, praise continued to lap around his feet. He had sent the sword of the vanquished Spanish Rear-Admiral Don Xavier Francisco Winthuysen to the City of Norwich and in due course was rewarded with the Freedom of the City, the highest civic honour that a city can award. A clutch of other freedoms followed. When his knighthood came through in April he lost no time in writing to the Duke of Clarence, 'Your Royal Highness, who has known me for every hour upwards of sixteen years, will do me justice in saying, that at no one period of my life did my zeal and duty to my King and Country abate; and I must rejoice in having gained the good opinion of my Sovereign, which I once was given to understand I had no likelihood of enjoying. With every sentiment of the most dutiful attachment.'[2] When writing to the Duke of Clarence Nelson found it difficult to avoid sounding like Jane Austen's Mr Collins addressing Lady Catherine de Burgh.

In mid-March a letter was on its way to him from Lady Parker, who had been his surrogate mother in the West Indies in 1780: 'your mother could not have heard of your deeds with more affection, nor could she be more rejoiced at your personal escape from all the dangers to which you were exposed on that glorious day. Long may you live, my dear Nelson, an ornament to your Country and your Profession . . . your truly able and gallant Commander-in-Chief . . . shall henceforth be my Valentine . . . remember me to dear, good Collingwood . . . I am very happy at the glory he has gained.'[3]

Battle and a lucky escape from serious injury had by no means quenched Nelson's thirst for action. He volunteered to go up the Mediterranean to cover evacuation of the British troops left at Elba. He had made the suggestion because he now felt himself to be a close intimate of St Vincent. By boldly drawing attention to the fact he enlarged his influence: 'You have spoiled me by allowing me to speak and write freely.'[4] But both were playing the same game. Nelson was cleverly managing St

Vincent but was being equally cleverly managed himself. St Vincent, an acute judge of men, realized that Nelson's instinct was to please, that confidence and commendation from above were the oxygen of his life. He had grasped the paradox: although Nelson might seem to be self-willed and headstrong, he was in fact a wonderful subordinate. St Vincent felt confident he could ride him on a loose rein. He was also feeling under personal obligation to him and so chose Nelson to command a squadron to go off Cadiz, its object to intercept the Viceroy of Mexico's treasure, reported to be heading there with an escort of three ships-of-the-line.

St Vincent had shown an early and notorious penchant for plunder in the West Indies in his combined operations with General Grey, but had later adopted a Hood-like attitude towards those who were inclined to put prize money first. Nevertheless he maintained a keen interest in getting his share; a few years later he would have a dispute with Nelson over prize money which Nelson had to take to appeal to win.

Money was also on Nelson's mind. In March he drew up a memorandum of his right as a flag officer to share in prizes taken since 10 August 1796. Nineteen prizes were together valued at £537,500 (actually £437,500; as usual he added up incorrectly). He would share, with the other five flag officers, in the one-eighth share due to the Admiral. Nelson and Fanny were now wanting to buy a house. On 14 March he calculated that his current assets in the hands of his agents Marsh & Creed amounted to £1,470, to which he could add £432 flag pay, £400 marine pay and his share of prize money estimated at £5,000. He calculated his total assets at the time to be £7,304, out of which, '£2,000 can be spared for a home.' He was not expecting a pension with his Order of the Bath but, 'I do not say that if the government offered me £300 or £500 I would refuse on the contrary I should be obliged to them, but it is a thing I cannot ask. . . . My chains, medals and ribbons with a contented mind are all sufficient.'[5]

Included in Nelson's squadron was Saumarez's *Orion*. Saumarez wrote to his brother Richard, 'Be not surprised if, with our desperate Commodore, you hear of our taking the whole Spanish fleet, should we fall in with it.'[6] His use of the adjective 'desperate', that is 'reckless', 'staking all on a small chance', the rather pejorative hyperbole of his irony, reveals again his attitude to Nelson. Saumarez was at the careful, responsible and decent end of the leadership spectrum. There is little doubt that he was not captivated by Nelson. He could respect his achievement but being of a different personality was repelled by some of his behaviour. The hard fact is that to be a successful leader in war, or in any great enterprise, you have to be able to do the business; infinitely more important than being liked by everybody. Nelson did the business but also succeeded, to his enormous advantage, in being liked by most of those who worked with him. His famous contemporary, the Duke of Wellington, could do the business too, and was respected for it, but in his case few of his officers even thought of liking him, let alone loving him.

It was just as well that Nelson had pronounced himself happy with chains, medals, ribbons and a contented mind, for his dreams of riches from the Viceroy of Mexico's treasure were dashed. On returning with the Elba convoy he found that the Admiralty had sent another squadron to do the job, and he was required to concentrate on the blockade of Cadiz.

> We find to our mortification that Lord Hugh Seymour is cruising on our station to intercept the galleons which are momently expected at Cadiz. This we cannot but think a most cruel thing, leaving us here [off Cadiz] with so great an inferiority in numbers to the enemy and sending 4 sail of the line to reap the fruit of our toil which has been obtained by sweat of blood. This act of cruelty committed by one of our taskmasters. The whole [squadron] feel and are louder than myself, 'share our dangers, share our riches' but to obtain the latter at our expense is hitherto unprecedented. We cannot come to our families rich in ought [sic] but honour. How government can answer for this act I cannot guess but I have done.[7]

Despite his dissatisfaction with his earnings opportunities he gave Fanny *carte blanche* in buying a house and raised the price ceiling.

However the Viceroy of Mexico and his treasure was far from forgotten. St Vincent sent *Dido* and *Terpsichore* off to Tenerife in the Canary Islands to see whether the Viceroy was anchored at Santa Cruz. Nelson advocated a combined operation against Santa Cruz using the troops from the Elba garrison. He estimated the prize for such a heavyweight intervention as, 'six or seven millions sterling'. If the Army was unwilling there were still some 600 marines in the fleet, who, augmented with 1,000 more, 'would still insure the business, for Tenerife never was besieged, therefore the hills that cover the Town are not fortified to resist any attempt of taking them by storm; the rest must follow – a Fleet of Ships and money to reward the Victors'. These were the characteristic tones of Nelsonian advocacy, a nothing-could-be-easier optimism and in this case a juicy carrot to reward the victors, although disingenuously denied. 'But I know with you, and I can lay my hand on my heart and say the same – It is the honour and prosperity of our Country that we wish to extend.'[8]

However, for the time being a decision had to be postponed. St Vincent faced other challenges closer to home. There had been a naval mutiny at Spithead in April (and subsequently its domino effects at Plymouth and the Nore), and there was incipient rebellion in Ireland. The constant coming and going of ships made it impossible for him to build a cordon sanitaire around his own fleet and one in twelve of his seamen were Irishmen and open to agitation by members of the United Irishmen. There had been mutiny in the *Marlborough* on her way out from Portsmouth and on arrival the ringleader was court-martialled and sentenced to death. St Vincent decided to use the occasion to send a message to every man in the fleet. He ordered that the man be executed the next morning by his own shipmates, in spite of advice from the *Marlborough*'s captain that the men would refuse. He ringed the ship with boats from every other ship in the fleet armed with carronades and under orders to fire, and if necessary to sink the *Marlborough* if the slightest sign of resistance occurred. His will prevailed and the man was hanged. He suspected trouble was brewing in the *Theseus* and on Nelson's return to the fleet on 24 May ordered him to transfer to her. Nelson took Miller with him, and told him 'Such officers as wish to go with me are to get ready: Mids., "Hoste & Bolton, &c., and such men as came from *Agamemnon*, if they like it.'[9] The previous captain, fearful of the possibility of mutiny, had been accustomed to have a party of marines constantly at his side. Nelson, Miller, the officers, and not least the men who went with them, soon changed things. 'I have found a more orderly set of men,' Nelson told Fanny, and within a month a message from the lower deck dropped on the quarterdeck made that clear: 'Success attend Admiral Nelson God bless Captain Miller we thank them for the officers they have placed over us. We are happy and comfortable and will shed every drop of blood in our veins to support them, and the name of *Theseus* shall be immortalised as high as *Captain's* ship's company.'[10]

There were many straightforward judges of officer behaviour on the lower deck. Moreover there were no secrets in ships and the grapevine was always working at full speed. It is highly likely that a striking example of Nelson's behaviour quickly did the rounds. Two men were being held in irons on board the *Swiftsure*, suspected of simulating madness to obtain their discharge. Nelson reported to St Vincent that the sight of them 'affected me more than I can express'. He wanted Mr Weir [physician to the fleet] to see them. 'The youth may, I hope, be saved. . . . If any mode can be designed for sending him home, I will with pleasure pay fifty pounds to place him in some proper place for his recovery; the other I fear is too old.'[11] St Vincent was sceptical but Nelson faced up to him:

> I hope for the poor men's sakes, that they are imposing on me; but depend on it, that God Almighty has afflicted them with the most dreadful of all diseases. They do not sham; indeed, you will find I am not mistaken, and all the Commissioners in the World cannot convince me of it. For what purpose can these poor wretches attempt to destroy themselves? for what purpose can one of them have spoken to me as rationally as any person could do? Do let Mr Weir look at them: I am sure he will think with me, from the order to represent those who are objects unfit for the service, I could not do otherwise than I did.[12]

As commander of the inshore squadron Nelson's strategy was to keep his force in a state of constant activity to annoy the enemy and tempt them to come out. His aggressive attitude chimed perfectly with his belief that the devil makes work for idle hands. He set up an attack on Cadiz in the early hours of 4 July, but what began as a bombardment using the *Thunderer* bomb vessel, anchored 2,500 yards from the walls of Cadiz, turned into a desperate hand to hand fight. It was a moonlit night and the Spaniards, quickly alerted, were not minded to be humiliated. Very soon a flotilla of Spanish launches and gunboats was heading in the direction of the *Thunderer*, intent on boarding and capturing her. Nelson, having foreseen the likelihood of a Spanish counterattack had arranged with St Vincent for all the boats, launches and pinnaces in the fleet, to be manned and equipped with carronades as support for *Thunderer*. What Nelson, Rear-Admiral commanding the inshore squadron, was doing on board *Thunderer* in the first place is a question that can properly be asked, but given that he was there, it was not in his nature to be anything other than in command. Realizing that the Spaniards had to be stopped he ordered his assembled boats to attack them. Evidently Captain Miller did not succeed in getting them away quickly enough and Nelson, accompanied by Fremantle, leaped into his barge and set his ten-man crew rowing furiously in the direction of the enemy. His impulse to active leadership and his instinct to attack were phenomenal, and while it was unwise for him to abandon all capacity to control the operation, it was a wonderfully inspiring sight to all those whom he needed to emulate him.

Headlong propulsion took them alongside a Spanish boat containing Don Miguel Tyrason, commander of the Spanish flotilla, and thirty men. It was providential for Nelson that Miller was able to spot his predicament and come down to the other side of Don Tyrason's boat. Even more providential on that day was Nelson's boatswain Sykes. In a dreadfully bloody and deadly mêlée of slashing and stabbing he saved Nelson's life at least twice, at the cost of severe wounds to himself. In the small space of the three boats eighteen of the Spaniards were killed and the rest, including Don Tyrason, wounded before the Spaniards surrendered and the Spanish flotilla was routed. The aftermath was more plaudits from St Vincent, who reported to Spencer, 'Rear Admiral Nelson's actions speak for themselves; any praise of mine would fall short of his merit.'[13] Another layer was added to Nelson's reputation in the fleet when the story of his exploit was told, when it became known that not only had he shown much personal tenderness to the wounded Sykes in the aftermath of the action but he had bracketed his name in his dispatch with those of Miller and Fremantle, and sought promotion for him. The action was another milestone for Nelson. In his *Sketch of My Life* he said, 'perhaps my personal courage was more conspicuous than at any other part of my life', and spoke of 'a hand to hand service with swords'. He draws back from saying, 'I killed a man or men with my own hand thus', but the probability is that the parson's son had for the first time broken the sixth commandment.

While Nelson had been thus engaged there had been a further outbreak of mutiny, this time in the *St George*, Rear-Admiral Parker's flagship. Four mutineers were tried and sentenced to death. The court martial having continued till late in the evening, the men could not be executed immediately as St Vincent intended. The next day was Sunday and Vice-Admiral Thompson protested that to hang the men would profane the Sabbath. St Vincent set his face and had them hanged from the yardarm at nine o' clock on Sunday morning, again ordering their own shipmates to be the hangmen and boats' crews and marines from every ship to attend as spectators. As an additional message to his officers he demanded Thompson's immediate recall. Nelson, who was required to send twenty barges and pinnaces to witness the executions, was not without sympathy for the original complaints of the seamen at Spithead, as distinct from the more political objectives of the ring-leaders at the Nore, but was in no doubt where he stood on mutiny. 'Had it been Christmas Day instead of Sunday, I would have executed them.'[14]

When St Vincent received information that the *El Principe d'Asturias*, a rich Spanish merchantman bound from Manila to Cadiz, was at Santa Cruz, Nelson was able to reopen the idea of an attack on Tenerife. Nothing further seems to have been heard of the Viceroy of Mexico and his gold and the two scouting frigates which returned from Santa Cruz earlier in the year had found instead the *San Jose* from Manila and the *Principe Fernando* from Mauritius. They had cut out the *Principe Fernando* and its cargo worth £30,000. Now it was the *El Principe d'Asturias* that was being talked about. Against this background St Vincent's orders to Nelson read oddly:

> to proceed to the island of Teneriffe, and there make your disposi-
> tions for taking possession of the Town of Santa Cruz, by a sudden
> and vigorous Assault. In case of success, you are authorized to lay
> a heavy contribution on the inhabitants of the Town and adjacent
> district, if they do not put you in possession of the whole cargo
> of *El Principe d'Asturias* . . . and all the treasure belonging to the
> Crown of Spain; and you are to endeavour to take, sink, burn, or
> otherwise destroy, all vessels of every description, even those
> employed in the Fishery, on the coast of Africa, unless a just con-
> tribution is made for their preservation, by the inhabitants of the
> Canary Islands.[15]

Nelson's original proposition had been the capture of treasure ships carrying an estimated £6–7 million, in a combined operation involving

'3,700 men from Elba with cannon, mortars and every implement now embarked', and, 'a very small Squadron to do the Naval part'.[16] Now he was setting off with a very much smaller prize in sight, a much more diffuse objective and a force of 750 seamen and 250 marines, drawn exclusively from the seamen already in the ships of his squadron, *Theseus, Culloden, Zealous, Leander, Seahorse, Terpsichore, Emerald*, the mortar boat *Terror* and the cutter *Fox*. General O'Hara at Gibraltar had been as uninterested as De Burgh in a combined operation.

It is difficult to see how St Vincent could have justified an attack on such a small scale as bringing political and economic pressure on Spain. The only real practical justification for detaching three ships-of-the-line, four frigates, and a mortar boat from his blockading force off Cadiz was the possibility of prize money for St Vincent and a group of his favourite officers.

Surviving manuscripts show that on the way to Tenerife Nelson involved his captains in analysing tactical options, this or that objective by this or that route and that he also evolved a clear set of operational orders, but the papers suggest that their thinking and planning was focused entirely on what they were going to do and how they were going to do it. There is no sign that Nelson, on this as on any previous occasion, addressed contingencies, the important, 'what ifs'. Troubridge was to be in overall command of the landing party and would be supported by groups under Captains Hood, Fremantle, Bowen, Miller, the commander of the Marines Captain Oldfield and Lieutenant Baynes of the Royal Artillery. The curving bay on which Santa Cruz stood was protected by a string of beach-side gun batteries and the town itself by the Castillo de San Cristobal. They decided to land about a mile to the northeast of the town, their first objective a fort, the Castillo de Paso Alta, which when taken would provide a base from which they could fire on the town and from where they could move along the narrow coastal strip to storm the town or deliver a summons to surrender as Troubridge judged fit.

The landing party, embarked in three frigates, *Seahorse, Terpsichore* and *Emerald*, had got to within three miles of their disembarkation point by midnight, but such was the strength of the offshore current and wind that they were still a mile from the shore at daybreak. Nelson had known about this wind, the *alisios*, but evidently did not know enough about it, or think enough about it. Thus when he arrived with his big ships at 4.30

on the morning of 22 July the Spaniards were soon firing guns to sound the alarm. The absence of any plan for dealing with this situation became obvious when Troubridge recalled his boats and he, Bowen and Oldfield went on board the *Theseus* to consult with Nelson about what they should do next. They decided to adopt what had been their second option, to take the heights above the fort and storm it from there. In the meantime Nelson would batter the fort with his big guns. By mid-morning Troubridge began to land his men to the north of the fort leading them up the steep, rocky, and by now sun-baked Jurada Heights, only to find when they reached the top that they had misread the terrain. There was a parallel ridge between them and the fort, a steep chasm between the ridges, and on the ridge opposite Spanish defenders and field guns, who would have to be cleared before they could get at the fort, an impossible task. Meanwhile neither Nelson's big ships nor the mortar boat *Terror* had been able to get within three miles of the fort because of calms and contrary currents. Troubridge was in an impossible position and ordered a retreat to the boats. By eleven o'clock that night his hungry, thirsty, weary, and no doubt critical seamen were back on board.

Most naval historians have concluded that Troubridge might have had a fair chance of success had he pressed ahead with his first attack, bypassed the fort if necessary (a possibility envisaged in his orders) and made his way directly to Santa Cruz, relying on landed guns and the powerful back-up of the squadron to support his beachhead and advance. Nelson himself was in that camp. He subsequently wrote to Sir Andrew Snape Hamond, Comptroller of the Navy, 'Had I been with the first party, I have reason to believe complete success would have crowned our endeavours.'[17] This was his self-confidence speaking, not a hard-headed assessment of his actual situation. He was overlooking the impotence of his becalmed squadron to support Troubridge on that first day.

The unfolding of this inept and unlucky fiasco touched every officer and man in the squadron and placed an irresistible pressure on Nelson to do something to recover the situation. His reputation was at stake. St Vincent had listened to his passionate arguments for taking Tenerife, had authorized his venture and had expected 'a sudden and vigorous Assault'. Nelson hated the thought of letting him down or of failing his eager officers who looked to him to lead them to fame and fortune. After the action he would write to St Vincent, 'Thus foiled in my original plan, I considered it for the honour of our King and Country not to give over the attempt to possess ourselves of the Town, that our enemies might be convinced there is nothing which Englishmen are not equal to.'[18] Bastia and Calvi had ended up being credited to other men but Tenerife would be *his*.

Nelson now moved his ships to a position about eight to ten miles off-shore in blowing and squally weather, standing on and off, increasing and shortening sail, his squadron strengthened by the arrival of Captain Thompson and his 50-gun *Leander*. It did not take Nelson long to make his incredible decision to mount a night attack. His decision seems to have been crystallized by intelligence obtained from a Prussian deserter, interrogated by Fremantle and Miller, with Betsy Fremantle acting as interpreter. This intelligence was that, 'nothing could be easier than to take the place, only 300 men of regular troops, the rest are peasants who are frightened to death'.[19] It seems that Nelson did not critically examine this intelligence; it supported what he wanted to do. But if defenders had managed to turn up on the ridge to confront Troubridge it suggested at least that the Spaniards might be on the qui vive because of the cutting out of the *Principe Fernando* in January and the French frigate *Mutine* in May, and might have the strength and readiness to defend themselves. If the place was so weakly defended and the populace in such fear, where was the need for a night attack? The mole was the chosen landing place, a confined place on which a thousand men might overwhelm a defence by sheer weight of numbers, but only if the flow of men was delivered as an irresistible tide. What were his chances of delivering such an assault? A night operation might well have the advantage of surprise, might reduce the effectiveness of the gun batteries, but the problem of maintaining cohesion of a battle group in a strange place becomes par-ticularly challenging if you cannot see, and the unexpected occurs. Captain Thompson's personal knowledge of the layout of the place passed on at Nelson's council of war gave a certain reassurance, but could the information be recalled in the stress of action? And there was the weather to consider; Nelson had already one experience of the violent offshore wind. Thus, every atom of logic and military insight spoke against the wisdom or necessity of a night attack and yet Nelson went ahead. Strangely there is no mention anywhere in Nelson's Journal of the *El Principe d'Asturias*, except in the document he had prepared in advance for summoning the town. She was never mentioned again, nor were there any signs of plans being laid to cut her out. The most likely reason was that she was no longer there.

At 8 p.m. on the night of the attack he sent a message to St Vincent, 'we are not in possession of Santa Cruz . . . all has hitherto been done which was possible, but without effect; this night I, humble as I am, command the whole, destined to land under the batteries of the Town, and to-morrow my head will probably be crowned with either laurel or cypress. I have only to recommend Josiah Nisbet to you and my Country.'[20] It cannot have helped when Josiah turned up armed and equipped for the attack. He went so far as to remind Josiah of what it would do to Fanny if she lost both husband and son, but he did not order him to stay behind. Publicly he radiated calm and confidence. Betsy Fremantle, who had entertained Nelson to dinner that afternoon noted in her journal, 'the taking of the place seemed an easy and almost a sure thing'.[21]

So at eleven o'clock on 24 July close on a thousand men were embarked in the ships' boats, and formed into six divisions under Troubridge, Hood, Thompson, Miller and Waller. Fremantle and Bowen went along with Nelson, 'to regulate the attack'. They were followed by 180 men in the *Fox* cutter as a reserve. With oars muffled by pieces of canvas or kersey, they began their long row, a heavy swell helping to propel them shorewards for the next two and a half hours. At first darkness was their friend. They got to within half-gunshot, less than a hundred yards from the mole and the landing beach to its right, before surprise was lost, the alarm was sounded and defenders opened fire. The boats spurted forward to the beach and with a mad dash Bowen led his seamen and marines up on to the mole, overrunning the battery and spiking the guns at the seaward end. Fremantle also got men on to the mole but was wounded before he himself got there. Thompson following on with his detachment was also wounded. By now the Spanish defenders were organized and the British were caught in the narrow confines of the mole. The Spaniards needed only to point their cannon into the darkness ahead and grapeshot would do the rest. All who had gained the mole were pinned down. They rallied and charged, only to be swept away in a hail of grapeshot and musket balls. In one bloody moment Bowen and his first lieutenant were dead.

Troubridge and Waller were faring somewhat better, although their boats had missed the target and were arriving to the left both of the mole

and the Citadel. Troubridge later said that the night was so dark he could
not see the mole. The surf was wild, heavy boats smashed against the
rocks, men went under and those who managed to scramble ashore had
to rely on cold steel to brush through the light opposition they encountered. Guided by firing to their right they made for the Great Square of
the town immediately behind the Citadel, which Nelson had designated
as a regrouping point. Troubridge had achieved his objective, but without
the scaling ladders which had been lost with his boats and with all their
ammunition soaked, an immediate attack on the rear of the Citadel was
not an option.

Even further to the left Miller and Oldfield had likewise a chaotic
landing, having to leap almost up to their necks into the water and wade
thirty yards to the shore from their swamped and grounded boats. They
overran a nearby battery, again having to do so with cold steel. Soon
after they were joined by Hood, and were now a group of about fifty
men but in poor shape, many having lost their weapons in the struggle
to get ashore, most of them with wet powder; to make matters worse,
the seamen in the group were showing a decided lack of enthusiasm for
attacking the Citadel. Miller, a good man and humane commander, could
not summon up the means to inspire them further. So they set off in the
hope of linking up with Troubridge. They might as well have been in a
maze. They blundered straight on instead of turning to their right as
Troubridge had done. On their left they could hear musket volleys from
Spaniards, firing at boats not yet landed. Perhaps they were the boats
which Troubridge would speak of in his report, 'The surf was so high,
many put back', or perhaps they were stray boats from other groups.
Whoever they were we know that almost a third of Nelson's force never
even got ashore; Hoste noted that several boats unable to land returned
to the ship at about 4 a.m.; others were seen, still offshore at daybreak,
being fired on by the Spanish.

None of these outlying groups knew what had happened to Nelson.
He had been in the second wave, landing when Bowen was already on
the mole. Nelson's evidence of what happened is contained in his own
dispatch: 'Captains Fremantle, Bowen and myself, with four or five Boats
stormed the Mole, although opposed apparently by 400 to 500 men, took
possession of it, and spiked the guns; but such a heavy fire of musketry
and grape-shot was kept up from the Citadel and houses at the head of
the Mole that we could not advance, and we were all nearly killed or

wounded.'[22] This was an entirely misleading account of his personal part in the attack, mentioning neither his wound nor where he was when he was wounded. Betsy Fremantle's diary entry, presumably her husband's view, he being near Nelson at the time, said 'The Admiral was wounded as he was getting out of the boat.'[23] Miller's hearsay account tallied: 'The Admiral had reached the middle of the boat, and was drawing his sword to jump on shore when a musket ball shattered the bone of his right arm.'[24] As he felt the powerful thump of the musket ball, Nelson exclaimed, 'I am shot through the arm', his immediate reaction, 'I am a dead man.' Josiah, close by, tore a handkerchief from around his own neck, made a tourniquet, cut off the flow of blood from Nelson's severed artery and undoubtedly saved his life. Nelson had seemed at first completely felled by his wound, but now slowly recovering he insisted that Josiah and the seamen he had diverted to getting the boat afloat should attempt to save men from the *Fox* cutter. Hit below the waterline the *Fox* had sunk like a stone, leaving 180 men struggling and shouting in the water. Having done what they could, Josiah and his men rowed back in the direction of the ships. The first they encountered was the *Seahorse* but Nelson was unwilling to go aboard in case he alarmed Mrs Fremantle, of whose husband he had no news. At last, at two in the morning and alongside *Theseus* he had substantially recovered himself. He refused all assistance in getting on board. Midshipman Hoste saw him come over the side, 'his right arm dangling by his side, whilst with the other he helped himself to jump up the Ship's side and with a spirit that astonished everyone told the surgeon to get his instruments ready, for he knew he must lose his arm and the sooner it was off the better'.[25]

While Nelson was submitting with courage and calmness to Thomas Eshelby's knife, Troubridge was coping well with the unknowns that faced him. After waiting for an hour with no other troops arriving to join him he tried to bluff Don Antonio Gutiérrez, Commandant-General of the Canary Islands into surrender, sending a sergeant of marines and two Spanish gentlemen under a flag of truce with his surrender demand. No reply was forthcoming and he was forced to conclude that his sergeant had been killed.

Meanwhile Miller and Hood, harried by the hit and run tactics of marauding militias, had made their way further inland and had ended up to the rear of Troubridge's group in the Convento de Santo Domingo. Fortunately they succeeded in getting a message of their whereabouts to

Troubridge, who led his men to join them. It was now daybreak and although they could muster about 340 men between them, there was still no word from Nelson, Fremantle, Thompson or Bowen, and although they had some captured Spanish ammunition it was not much and they still had no ladders. The Convento was a strong, defendable position but Troubridge was now on the way to being surrounded himself. Enemy cannon were commanding the streets: his opposition seemed to be growing more numerous.

In his subsequent report to Nelson he would put the enemy at 8,000 Spaniards and 100 French. He had been taken in by Spanish bluff for he had no means of counting the enemy for himself. Spanish sources show conclusively that Gutiérrez had no more than 1,282 men, of which only 400 were regulars. The rest were militia or local people.[26] Thus the force directly facing Troubridge was probably less than twice his own, rather than the twenty-four times implied by his reported figures.

Troubridge tried another bluff. This time he sent Captain Oldfield under a flag of truce with a threat to burn the town if the Manila ship was not delivered up. Gutiérrez stayed cool. By now the struggle for the mole was over. Having taken twenty-eight prisoners and driven off the remainder, Gutiérrez felt under no impulsion to negotiate. It was stalemate. Troubridge concluded that the best he could achieve would be to save his remaining men and as much face as possible. So at seven o'clock, in the words of Nelson's dispatch, he sent Captain Hood with a message to Gutiérrez, 'that if he should be allowed, freely and without molestation, to embark his people at the Mole-head, taking off such of our boats as were not stove, and that the Governor should find others to carry off the people, the Squadron now before the Town should not molest it. The Governor told Captain Hood he thought they ought to surrender prisoners of war, to which he replied that Captain Troubridge had directed him to say, that if the terms he had offered were not accepted in five minutes, he would set the Town on fire, and attack the Spaniards at the point of a bayonet, on which the Governor instantly closed with the Terms.'[27] He had been quick witted enough to see that an ace had been handed to him, a British undertaking not to attack the town with the squadron.

Whether Nelson and the squadron could have summoned up the spirit to do anything more is very doubtful. They had been defeated as much by their own injudicious leader as by a more resolute than expected enemy. The full horror of their failure was becoming clear. Out of the 700 or so of his people who had succeeded in landing, more than a third were killed, drowned or wounded. He had lost a post captain and six lieutenants killed, and five other officers, including himself, wounded. The aftermath was even worse for Nelson personally. In the shock of that moment by the mole his aggression and forward impulse had deserted him. A wound to his arm had immobilized him; he had not struggled against being led away from the scene of battle; others had wanted to protect him, and that might have seemed right at the time. Even so the thought of that mortifying personal retreat must have haunted his mind in the days that followed: hardly the behaviour of a hero. There was some consolation to be found in the fact that Fremantle's wound had also obliged him to retreat, albeit some two hours after himself. And there was his missing arm, proof of shared danger, a talisman against blame, which none of the participants ever levelled against him a testimony to the generous and forgiving spirit of men who share danger.

Yet by one of those paradoxes of fate, the framing of Nelson's dispatch, exaggeration of enemy number and the number of guns brought to bear on them, their ill luck in the raging surf, the loss of men, the apparent resourcefulness of Troubridge in his game of bluff with Gutiérrez, the Governor's sporting and civilized behaviour when it was all over, and the loss of Nelson's arm, together conspired to transmute a disastrous attack into a magnificent failure.

Shocked, disconsolate, pained by his losses, armless, sick in his guts, enveloped in a sense of failure as a man and a leader, he opened his heart in a characteristically uncalculated and vulnerable way to St Vincent:

> I am become a burthen to my friends, and useless to my Country; but by my letter wrote the 24th, you will perceive my anxiety for the promotion of my son-in-law, Josiah Nisbet. When I leave your command, I become dead to the World; I go hence, and am no more seen. If from poor Bowen's loss, you will think it proper to oblige me, I rest confident you will do it; the boy is under obligations to me, but he repaid me by bringing me from the Mole of Santa Cruz. I hope you will be able to give me a frigate, to convey the remains of my carcass to England.[28]

On 16 August Nelson was in sight of the fleet. 'I rejoice at being once more in sight of your Flag, and with your permission will come on board the *Ville de Paris* to pay my respects. If the *Emerald* has joined, you know my wishes. A left handed Admiral will never again be considered as useful, therefore the sooner I get to a very humble cottage the better, and make room for a better man to serve the state.'[29] Nelson's uncomplaining vulnerability and concern for his stepson were touching and evoked a warm and fatherly response in St Vincent:

My dear Admiral, Mortals cannot command success; you and your Companions have certainly deserved it, by the greatest degree of heroism and perseverance that ever was exhibited. I grieve for the loss of your arm and for the fate of poor Bowen and Gibson, with the other brave men who fell so gallantly. I hope you and Captain Fremantle are doing well; the *Seahorse* shall waft you to England the moment her wants are supplied. Your Son-in-law is Captain of the *Dolphin* Hospital-ship, [he had promoted Josiah Master and Commander] and all other wishes you may favour me with shall be fulfilled, as far as is consistent with what I owe to some valuable Officers in the *Ville de Paris*. . . . Give my love to Mrs Fremantle. I will salute her and bow to your stump to-morrow morning, if you will give me leave.[30]

St Vincent, who had never been as sanguine of the outcome as Nelson, wrote to the Admiralty the same day, taking full personal responsibility for the attack and praising the efforts of Nelson and his men in a letter which was printed in the *London Gazette* of 2 September: 'Although the enterprise has not succeeded, his Majesty's arms have acquired a very great degree of lustre. Nothing from my pen can add to the eulogy the Rear-Admiral gives of the gallantry of the Officers and men employed under him.'[31] He had the presence of mind and thoughtfulness to write to Fanny, 'Sir Horatio Nelson has added very considerably to the laurels he had won before the assault on the town of Santa Cruz. . . . He is wounded but not dangerously and I hope your Ladyship will be soon made happy by his presence in England, whither he will proceed the moment the *Theseus* joins.'[32]

In everything he did St Vincent had struck the right note, but it has to be said that the image he had in his mind at this time was Nelson on the mole, sword in hand, leading the attack. This was still the impression given in a copy of the *Details* Nelson gave personally to Sir Gilbert Elliot later that year.

Just over a month later Nelson would write from Bath to Sir Andrew Snape Hamond, Comptroller of the Navy, his last words on the subject: 'You will see by my Journal the first attack on the 21st, under Troubridge, completely failed; and it was the 25th before it could be again attacked, which gave four days for collecting a force to oppose us. Had I been with the first party, I have reason to believe complete success would have crowned our endeavours. My pride suffered; and although I felt the second attack a forlorn hope, yet the Honour of our Country called for the attack, and that I should command it. I never expected to return and am thankful.'[33]

For such reasons he had sacrificed his men.

12

The Admiralty Dips for Nelson

The fittest man in the world for the command.

Lord Minto, 24 April 1798

From the moment he arrived at Spithead on 1 September 1797 and was formally ordered to strike his flag and come on shore, Nelson was bent on getting back to the Mediterranean and to St Vincent.

By this time the two men held immense attractions for each other. St Vincent, the most assiduous nurturer of talent in the Navy, was intent on surrounding himself with the best captains and flag officers he could find – and just as ruthlessly weeding out 'old women' and 'drivellers'. It had not taken him long to form decided views about Nelson, to recognize his capacity to bear and exercise the responsibilities of command; his ability to measure up to every situation he came across, and dominate all concerned. He had become very aware of the little commodore's talent for waging a one man war against the enemy – he dubbed him 'an excellent partisan.'[1] Above all he had seen with his own eyes, from his own quarterdeck, Nelson's inspired and aggressive improvisations on St Valentine's Day, when Nelson had transformed the stately progress of his own resolute but fading battle plan into an instinctively designed and suddenly executed death trap for the Spaniards. Having been thus upstaged in full view of the fleet it was a measure of St Vincent's quality that he wanted to hang on to his intrepid and headstrong virtuoso.

For his part Nelson had warmed to St Vincent's professional leadership. Fired and driven by his vision of a thoroughly professional and well officered Navy, St Vincent increased the performance and efficiency of the Mediterranean fleet by an order of magnitude. His recipe was simple. He set an impeccable personal example, and demanded very high standards which he communicated unambiguously to his officers. In all things great and small the Navy came first, but for deserving officers there was no shortage of understanding, sympathy and recognition. For Nelson these attitudes and traits were the foundations for good professional chemistry. There were also other deeper and more complex factors. Both men were blessed with inner self-confidence. They could recognize the talents and achievements of others without feeling in the least threatened.

Both were unlike the great mass of competitive, ambitious but unconfident men who abound in politics, commerce and the services, whose last aim in life is to acknowledge the talents of others, whose first aim in life is to take all the credit and who surround themselves with subordinates who provide no challenge to their personal sense of security. Even more important was the fact that St Vincent exercised a natural and confident dominance over everybody he met, and Nelson was no exception. Admirals like Hotham, Keith and Hyde Parker could not live with Nelson because Nelson dominated them. Each of them felt helpless when exposed to the full force of his motivation, will, energy and speed of thought. But St Vincent was very different. He was a basalt castle, not to be outsmarted nor faced down, even by Nelson, and Nelson did not try; his animal sensitivity and awareness immediately responded to an even more dominant animal. If it should come to a battle of wills Nelson would lose. And in any case he could see that he had much to learn from St Vincent, for Nelson possessed the professional humility evident in all exceptional men. He learned about the organization and efficiency of fleets and how to bear the hard and awesome responsibilities of high command – not least from St Vincent's handling of mutiny in the fleet. The lessons he learned stayed with him for life, and Nelson often referred to them.

The two men were fortunate in the marked difference in their ages (St Vincent being more than twenty years older than Nelson) and in their difference in rank, which together enabled a comfortable and acceptable master–pupil, father–son relationship. But there was also another, rather unlikely facet. St Vincent's was an organizing and controlling nature, yet he was also able to manage and employ Nelson successfully. He realized that Nelson was totally inner-directed and had his own motive power; his free spirit needed only opportunity and support to flourish and deliver results. St Vincent did not himself have the same restless urge to get at the enemy. He preferred to forge the instrument for Nelson to use.

Later, when Nelson's fame had greatly increased and his free spirit burst the bounds of convention in his very public private life, St Vincent acted somewhat less straightforwardly and Nelson perceived him less generously. But all this was in the future and for the moment the relationship was perfect. St Vincent's unequivocally generous and affectionate reaction to the Tenerife disaster was exactly what Nelson's kind and magnanimous nature required.

The journey home in *Seahorse* with the Fremantles lasted a month. Nelson had ample time to go through the normal cycle of depression, despair and anger about the loss of his arm. He had plenty of time to agonize over what seemed to be his dramatically foreshortened career prospects, to turn over his financial situation and reflect on another escape from death. In the letters he wrote to St Vincent[2] and Fanny,[3] he had mentioned retirement to 'the cottage', 'a humble cottage', an image he brought to mind throughout his life as an alternative to the stress or crisis of the moment, but it was more a symptom of the pressure and pain, never a real alternative. He had had six years 'on the beach' and the memory of it was unalluring to a man of vaulting ambition who needed action to feel alive. He must have worried about money, until he worked out that his half pay would be about £284 a year and with a pension for his service during the war, and the loss of his arm, he might be able to count on an income of say £900–£1,000 a year. Additionally, a rear-admiral of his quality, with St Vincent's patronage, could reasonably expect a shore-based appointment or sinecure to supplement his half pay.

Having thus quietened most of his worst fears – he had a future of some sort – and with resolution and confidence returning, he stepped ashore with his mind characteristically made up. Not for him a mouldering convalescence, or a shore-based appointment, or a cosy cottage, or domesticity and a genteel life of retirement as a former naval hero. His real family was at sea, the quarterdeck his stage. The confined world of his ship-of-the-line was his home, gossip about his superiors and his peers infinitely more real and important than gossip about neighbours or acquaintances on shore. Nothing in Fanny, their relationship or her tender care of his injured arm could compete with these things. Had he and Fanny had a child his feelings might have been different. But the evidence of the future would be that nothing was able to keep him from his life at sea. As ever he made nothing of his latest brush with death. He had learned to live with the idea of death and eliminate it as a concern in his mind. Here was an opportunity to retire honourably. He did not take it.

By the middle of September Nelson and Fanny had left Bath, where he had surprised her by appearing unheralded on the doorstep and had taken lodgings with Mr Jones at 141 Old Bond Street. In spite of his constantly inflamed and troublesome stump, he set about working his passage back to the Mediterranean. Whilst at Bath he had received the forerunners of much congratulation. He had handsome letters from Earl Spencer, First Lord of the Admiralty, and from Lord Hood who generally never had a good word to say about anybody. On this occasion what he said allowed Fanny 'to put aside the ill treatment of former years which my good man received from him.'[4]

Once in London Nelson soon made an opportunity to meet Lord Spencer and to make sure that Spencer understood his position and wishes. Spencer subsequently wrote to St Vincent, 'I have had great pleasure in making acquaintance with Sir Horatio Nelson and am very happy to have it in my power to inform you that he seems likely to recover entirely from the effects of his wound and to be again able to serve.'[5]

On 27 September the King invested him with the Order of the Bath at a levee at St James's Palace. Royal approval would be very helpful, for the King was involved in all senior military appointments and rewards and usually held decided views. Shortly before this Nelson had been received by Prince William, who had written to Nelson on his arrival with typical tact and sensitivity that he wanted to be one of the first 'to shake him by the hand'! No doubt he had managed to do so with some momentary confusion when Nelson's hand came at him from an unexpected direction. At the levee Nelson was in fine fettle. When the King, fully the equal of his son where tact was concerned, met Nelson he observed, 'You have lost your right arm.' Nelson, quick as a flash replied, 'But not my right hand as I have the honour of presenting Captain Berry to you; and besides may it please your Majesty I can never think that a loss which the performance of my duty has occasioned; and as long as I have a foot to stand on, I will combat for my King and Country.'[6]

Nicolas believes that this sounds too melodramatic to be true. The fact is that part of Nelson's stock in trade as a leader was a brand of hyperbole which in cold print does sound melodramatic, but in real life undoubtedly singularized him and won the hearts of his followers.

Waving his sword, rallying his boarding party to go over the side into the smoke and shot, with a cry of 'Victory or Westminster Abbey!' comes in the same category. It can't have been as pompous as it sounds. It may well have been done with a sort of laughing bravado, a flavour of Cyrano de Bergerac, but whatever the delivery it is an odds-on bet that the sailors, who probably did not have the faintest idea of what he was getting at, received it with a kind of 'There he goes again the little bugger. . . . Come on, lads!' At any rate the King got the message and trying his hand with his own brand of less effective jocularity replied, 'But your country has a claim for a bit more of you.' Game, set and match to Nelson. He had made his mark.

Nelson lost no time in following up with a letter to St Vincent himself. 'The moment I am cured I shall offer myself for service; and if you continue to hold your opinion of me, shall press to return with all the zeal, although not with all the personal ability I had formerly.'[7] Right on cue St Vincent wrote to Spencer, 'I am very glad your Lordship has had an opportunity of being personally known to Admiral Nelson, Pray send him back to me in the *Foudroyant*.'[8] Spencer did not get round to replying till early December but when he did he was ready to please both of them. 'I am better pleased with him the more I see of him and as he seems as desirous to return under Your Lordship's command as you are to have him I shall be very happy to promote the wishes of you both whenever the *Foudroyant* is ready and he is able to get on board.'[9] And so Nelson and St Vincent achieved their mutual objective.

Nelson was also moving prominently on to the public stage as one of the two current heroes on shore and available for public display. It was in his nature to communicate, and to wish his colleagues to share in the glory. He therefore sent an account of public reactions to his friend Miller in the *Theseus* (and no doubt his letter did the rounds of the fleet), particularly pointing out that 'Sir Horatio Nelson and the brave officers and men who fought on board the *Captain* on the 14 February' were being given the third place of honour after 'Lord Duncan and his recent victory' (Camperdown, 11 October 1797) and 'Earl St Vincent and the glorious 14th February'.[10] He wryly and realistically commented that the last victory was always the best and that they would have fared better had their own battle been in the Channel. His ambition was still hungry.

On 19 December he was invited to join the Board of Admiralty, other distinguished senior officers and many of the great and good in St Paul's

Cathedral, 'to return thanks to Almighty God for the many signal and important victories obtained by His Majesty's Navy during the present War'. Processions and the royal family drew the crowds and it is easy to imagine how they picked out the one-armed little hero and took him straight to their hearts.

Later, on 28 December when he received the Freedom of the City of London in a gold box to the value of 100 guineas, the Chamberlain (the celebrated John Wilkes) departed from the usual banalities of such occasions to single out Nelson in a striking way. 'In your case there is a rare heroic modesty, which cannot be sufficiently admired. You have given the warmest applause to your Brother-Officers and the Seamen under your command; but your own merit you have not mentioned, even in the slightest manner and the relation of the severe and cruel wounds you suffered in the service of your country is transmitted by your noble Commander-in-Chief.'[11]

Nelson's public image was being formed and he had a sufficiently keen ear to pick up the music the public wanted to hear and play to it. But whatever growth this might prompt in his thirst for even greater fame he was never less than delighted by the success of those who served under or alongside. He loved pushing his officers into the limelight and joining them into his fame as he did with Berry at the levee, even if paradoxically the effect was to enlarge his own reputation. This was an essential instinct and quality that never left Nelson and it generated a great flow of love and affection from those who served with him.

Interwoven with these public events, prevented neither by pain nor lionization, he was from the moment he stepped on shore active in the interests of others, ensuring that Captain Miller's wife knew her husband was perfectly well and longing to get home to his family;[12] reassuring the Reverend Dixon Hoste that his 'dear good son' William was now under the wing of Miller, who 'loves William and is the only true virtuous man I ever saw;'[13] lobbying Nepean, Secretary of the Admiralty Board to bolster the prospects of Lieutenant Withers, an 'old Agamemnon,'[14] asking St Vincent to smile on George Cockburn who, as his captain in *La Minerve* had so impressed Nelson with his skill and determination in their fight with the *Santa Sabina*. 'I now have a favour to beg of you. After George Cockburn's gallant action with the *Sabina*, I directed a gold-hilted sword to be made for him, which I had hoped to present to him myself in the most public and handsome manner but as Providence has decreed otherwise, I must beg of you to present it for me.'[15]

He was also active on behalf of his brothers. Using his newly acquired status as a lever and showing plenty of 'neck' and push, he intervened with the Lord Chancellor to get his younger brother one of his father's livings on the latter's retirement and was successful.[16] Prompted by his ambitious and 'eye on the main chance' elder brother, he tried to get him a stall at Norwich, but was unsuccessful.[17]

There were things he had to do on his own account. He had to chase up the ten shillings a day allowance which should have been paid to him from 4 April 1796 when St Vincent ordered him to hoist his broad pendant (St Vincent used to call it 'a ten shillings pendant)[18] to 11 August 1796 when he was paid as a rear-admiral. His claim had been lost in the mail or the Admiralty system.

In October he had to prepare a submission or memorial to the King to support a pension of £1,000 he was to be awarded. It required no padding and he provided none. The record spoke volumes. The arithmetic was formidable. In the four years 1793–97 he had been in action 120 times, an average of 30 times a year. This included four fleet actions, three actions with frigates and command of the batteries at the sieges of Bastia and Calvi. He had assisted at the capture of seven sail-of-the-line, six frigates, four corvettes, eleven privateers and fifty merchant vessels. That was the profit to the Navy and the country. The losses were all to his account: loss of sight in one eye, loss of an arm, other severe body wounds and bruises. His pension was cheap at the price, £712 with deductions,[19] but it almost doubled his pay.

By early December his arm had healed and with his usual command of gesture, he posted a notice in St George's, Hanover Square: 'An officer desires to return Thanks to Almighty God for his perfect recovery from a severe Wound, and also for the many mercies bestowed upon him.'[20] It was endorsed 'For Next Sunday' and was no doubt accompanied by a generous donation. On 13 December he was declared fit by the Navy doctors.

His life had by now taken on the accelerating tempo of professional concerns involved in preparing a ship for sea. Both Spencer and St Vincent had wanted him to have the brand new *Foudroyant*. But a gap opened up between intention and achievement and the Navy Board did not succeed in getting her launched for another four months. Nelson was in no mood to hang around drawing rooms month after month and so it was decided that *Vanguard* was to be his ship. In typical fashion there was to be a last minute scramble, or so it seemed. Nelson who had written to his chosen captain, Edward Berry, in his usual charming and personal way about Berry's intended marriage and 'becoming one of us', and of how *Foudroyant* would be launched in January,[21] suddenly had to alter tack and write urgently only ten days later, 'If you mean to marry I would recommend your doing it speedily, or the to be Mrs Berry will have very little of your company; for I am well and you may expect to be called for every hour. We shall probably be at sea before the *Foudroyant* is launched. Our ship is at Chatham, a seventy four and she will be choicely manned. This may not happen but it stands so today.'[22] His letter was marked 'Secret' but delightfully and winningly annotated, 'except to Dr Forster and Miss'. Berry would already have told them in detail of the way in which Nelson had introduced him to the King and turned the limelight on him. This latest piece of consummate tact, understanding and fun instantly recruited two new worshippers to the Nelson shrine. Happily, such were the ways of the Navy that Berry, who married four days later on 12 December, was to have three months of married bliss after he received the Admiralty Board Order of 28 February 1798 to cause *Vanguard* to be provisioned for foreign service, 'with the utmost dispatch.'[23]

Nelson himself kept a close eye on *Vanguard*'s progress and on 18 December, busy and urgent as ever, anxious not to lose a moment, called into the Admiralty at noon on his way home from Chatham and penned a note for the First Lord. '*Vanguard* will be out of dock at half past one this day and ready to receive men when your Lordship is pleased to direct her being commissioned.'[24] This over, Nelson and Fanny returned to Bath to say farewell to his father.

Towards the end of his stay there he wrote a very curious letter to Thomas Lloyd of May's Buildings in the City, saying he had been flattered by the Marquis of Lansdowne's 'kind notice of me' and asked Lloyd to, 'Tell him that I possess his place in Mr Palmer's box; but his Lordship did not tell me all its charms, that generally some of the handsomest ladies in Bath are partakers in the box, and was I a bachelor I would not answer for being tempted; but as I am possessed of everything which is valuable in a wife, I have no occasion to think beyond a pretty face.'[25] What prompted this observation? Are we really to conclude that it demonstrates Nelson was perfectly happy with his wife and marriage? Or was it a need to convince onlookers that the loss of an arm and an eye hadn't affected his virility? Or was he unconsciously reflecting that the aphrodisiac of fame and power was bringing with it inevitable female attention and suggestions of availability which were causing him to draw comparisons between what he had and might have? He also put on quite a performance for Lady Spencer.

> The day before he was to sail Admiral Nelson called upon me as usual, but on leaving he took a most solemn farewell, saying that if he fell, he depended upon my kindness to his wife – an angel whose care had saved his life! I should explain that, although during Lord Spencer's administration no sea captain ever returned [to sea] without being asked to dinner by us, I made it a rule not to receive their wives. Nelson said, that out of deference to my known determination, he had not begged to introduce Lady Nelson to me; yet if I would take notice of her, it would make him the happiest man alive. He said he felt convinced that I must like her. That she was beautiful, accomplished; but above all, that her angelic tenderness to him was beyond imagination. He told me that his wife had dressed his wounds, and that her care alone had saved his life. In short he pressed me to see her with an earnestness of which Nelson alone was capable. In these circumstances I begged that he would bring her with him that day to dinner. He did so, and his attentions to her were those of a lover. He handed her to dinner and sat by her; apologising to me by saying that he was so little with her, that he would not voluntarily lose an instant of her society.[26]

What a performance! That Nelson succeeded, and with the grand and highly sophisticated, very intelligent but tender-hearted Lavinia Spencer, speaks volumes for his personal impact, his sheer effrontery and ability to get what he wanted by emotional blackmail. More dubious however was the motivation for the performance, which places on Nelson a charge of gross insincerity. Perhaps he was feeling guilty about the haste with which he was dashing back to sea. Perhaps his well known (in the fleet and perhaps gossiped about back home) dalliance with Adelaide Correglia, the opera singer in Leghorn, required that he serve up a smoke-screen of husbandly devotion. Perhaps, noting how relatively unsociable Fanny was, he was trying to project her into a social setting where she might be able to help his career.

Whatever the case, their subsequent letters give no indications of any soft passages between them. Indeed, the judgement that their relationship was 'friendly quite unloverlike'[27] is probably very close to the mark. They had bought a house together, but Nelson seems to have invested little emotional capital in the process; he just wanted to get her settled. In spite of Fanny's being an angel, the problems of re-entry into 'normal' life after four years' absence, the frustration and pain of his circumstances, most likely produced a deal of anger, irritation and frustration in their life together. And perhaps the extravagance of Nelson's approach to Lady Spencer and his public professions were part guilt, part making up, part denial of the truth that he had made a mistake in marrying Fanny; a bitter pill for him to swallow.

Fundamentally theirs was a misalliance, foundering on a clash of personality, between his decisive, emotional, optimistic and active temperament and her pessimistic, negative inertia. Such a polarity of temperament must have made for a difficult relationship. Nelson's tendency to self-pity and her resentment at being left alone would not help – all culminating in letters from Spithead well laced with complaints. On 29 March 'with great difficulty found one pair of raw silk stockings. I suppose in some place or other I shall find my linen.'[28] On 3 April, 'I cannot find my black stock and buckle. I find the weights for your scales are on board this ship.'[29] On 5 April, 'Pray my dear Fanny did you put up the three Portugal pieces – joes? For if you did they cannot be found. If they are not sent so much the better. My black stock and buckle has not yet appeared, nor are the keys of my dressing stand sent. If they were left with the stand in London, the man has neglected to pack them up. I can do very well without these things, but it is a satisfaction to mention them.'[30] On 7 April, 'I have looked over my linen and find it very different to your list in the articles as follows: thirteen silk pocket handkerchiefs: only six new, five old. Thirteen cambric ditto; I have sixteen. Twelve cravats: I have only eleven. Six Genoa velvet stocks: I have only three. You have put down thirty huckaback towels, I have from 1 to 10. Eleven is missing from 11 to 22, that is Nos. 12 and 21; therefore there is missing No 11–22 and to 30: ten in all. I only hope and believe they have not been sent. I do not want them.'[31] On 8 April, there was at least a white lie: 'From my heart I wish it was peace, then not a moment would I lose in getting to my cottage'. And a twist of the knife: 'I have bought a new stock buckle at double the price of the old one.'[32]

Nelson began to feel ashamed of his behaviour. Irritation over his jumbled and incomplete kit reflected his frustration with Fanny, his wound-up pre-voyage state of mind, and over-reaction because tidiness and good order was not his own strong suit either. Fanny was more than anxious to meet him halfway. Nelson's 'I can only my dear Fanny repeat, what I hope you know, that you are uppermost in my thoughts'[33] brought a revealing 'I had written to you yesterday before I received your kind and affectionate letter. Indeed I have always felt your sincere attachment and at no one period could I feel it more strongly than I do at this moment and I hope as some years are past, time enough to know our dispositions, we may flatter ourselves it will last.'

She was very much reflecting, as indeed he was, a commitment to work at their marriage but there was no doubt of her total incapacity to mask attitudes incompatible with his own. 'As to peace I most ardently wish for it particularly as you will be satisfied to live quietly at home. I can't help feeling quite unsettled and a little hurried for when my spirits are not quiet you know I am but a poor creature.'[34] She brings forward Josiah as a surrogate son for Nelson, almost in the sense of 'he is your son' but meets with silence. They never speak of a child or wonder why they do not have one. They express no hopes.

While at Bath Nelson had been keeping St Vincent in touch with the *Vanguard*'s progress, telling him the ship was rigged, had her ground tier and nearly 400 men. 'I hope to be with you in early March.'[35] The formal notification from Spencer followed on 30 March. Events moved ahead at a quickening pace. Nelson took leave of the King at a levee on 14 March.

Meanwhile Berry had brought *Vanguard* from the Nore to Spithead. On 16 March Nelson was ordered to hoist his flag and he entered into his kingdom.

When the wind came favourable on 10 April Nelson was, on the face of it, routinely employed on convoy duty, rejoining the fleet after convalescence, but unknown to him deeper forces were shaping his destiny. He had played his part in getting back to sea as quickly as possible. The duet he and St Vincent had sung to Spencer had got him back to the Mediterranean fleet. The hour and the man had begun a slow but ineluctable convergence. But at this moment of sailing Nelson was unaware that discussions were in motion which, within a space of two months, were to make him the chosen instrument of new British strategy

for the Mediterranean, and within a further two months the toast of
Europe and the hero of the nation.

Even while Nelson was chafing at anchor, waiting for a fair wind, a
momentous discussion took place in Downing Street. British strategy was
undergoing an agonizing reappraisal. The sea victories over the Spaniards
off Cape St Vincent on 14 February and the Dutch at Camperdown on
12 October had been like beacons shining in the otherwise unrelieved
gloom of 1797. Nationally and strategically it had been an awful year.
Sandwiched between the naval victories were the mutinies at Spithead
and the Nore in late spring and early summer. The Bank of England had
suspended cash payments in February, 3 per cent government consols fell
to 48 and on 2 June Pitt was obliged to make his historic appeal for
national unity in the House of Commons. Gillray portrayed Pitt as a
sleepwalker descending, with guttering candle and fixed staring eyes, the
gaping stairway of a tottering ruin.[36]

Abroad, Bonaparte, still only a general and accountable to the
Directory, had exercised his genius on the near-defeated army of Italy
and with victories at Rivoli and Marengo had forced a triumphant 'peace'
on Austria at Campo Formio in October 1797. Britain stood alone and
the Directory was intent on crushing Britain. All members of Pitt's First
Coalition against the French were now at 'peace' with France. If that
corpse was to be revived it would require both British finance and British
military leadership.

The only British military instrument of any consequence in 1797 was
the Navy. Lord Grenville, the Foreign Secretary had several reasons for
wanting to send a fleet into the Mediterranean. The ever reluctant,
devious and difficult Austria demanded subsidies and a British fleet, 'to
protect her military flank in North Italy, and to support her protégé
Naples.'[37] Lord Grenville's motive was more active. The appearance of a
British fleet in the Mediterranean might well escalate the war because it
would need a Neapolitan base, and the French might retaliate against the
formally neutral Naples, in which case Austria would be forced to come
to the rescue. This is what Grenville hoped for.[38]

When Spencer rose from the Cabinet table the decision was all
but made, certainly in Pitt's mind. Spencer was unenthusiastic, caught

between the force of his colleagues' view that it was the only viable option they had, and his own knowledge of the worry of his naval lords about numbers of ships and supply lines. Pitt needed to get the argument on to a more factual base, to inch Spencer into a more supportive position, and ensure a full examination of the risks before a final decision was taken. He sent Spencer away with a list of questions. Can a fleet be stationed, victualled and refitted in the ports belonging to the Kingdom of Naples? What is the extra expense of maintaining a fleet in the Mediterranean? What is the Venetian and Neapolitan force? What is the French force in the Mediterranean? These were the right questions, to do with logistics, cash, and numbers of ships, ships sufficient to protect England and Ireland, blockade Cadiz and enter the Mediterranean when compared with the enemy.[39]

Spencer already had available a note prepared in the Admiralty the day before (5 April) 'State of Naval Preparations making by the Enemy in the Ports of France and Holland according to the latest Intelligence.'[40] The thrust of this document was that the whole Channel coast opposite England, from Flushing in the east to St Malo in the west, was alive with invasion boat building. Major concentrations of French ships-of-the-line leaped from the page – up to ten off Holland, twenty-two at Brest, nine split between Lorient, Rochefort and Ferrol, and thirty at Cadiz. Inside the Mediterranean there was a sizeable aggregate of nineteen, split more or less equally between Toulon, Cartagena, Corfu and Venice. Apart from the nerve-racking invasion preparations across the Channel there was a grand total of ninety enemy ships-of-the-line of which the great majority (seventy-one) were on England's doorstep, well positioned to attack England directly or indirectly via Ireland, and support invasion. To make matters worse, St Vincent's fleet off Cadiz relied on entry to the Tagus for provisioning and repair and this support system was sharply threatened by the possibility of 'peace' between France and Portugal. No wonder Spencer was dragging his feet. His colleagues wanted him to get a quart out of a pint pot and they needed to understand that something would have to give.

Spencer worked throughout the day with the Board Secretaries Nepean and Marsden and those Lords of the Admiralty who were in town, to produce a preliminary view. By eleven o'clock that evening he was able to share it with Grenville. His assessment was still not encouraging 'The answers did not tally very well with our wishes.'[41] He judged that the Channel including the coast of Ireland required thirty-five ships and that a further thirty-five would be needed to keep the Spanish fleet bottled up in Cadiz and command the Mediterranean. British resources currently stretched to only sixty-two ships (compared to the seventy required and the enemy's total of ninety) although there were eight more building which might be available in three months' time. But the key bottleneck was men. There was already a deficiency of about 1,000 men on the home station and the eight new ships would require 5,000 men, 'of which there is not the least prospect.'[42]

Then Spencer ran a proposition he had five months before put to St Vincent when considering options for his fleet if it was forbidden to use the Tagus.[43] This was to send St Vincent on a sweep through the Mediterranean to do what damage he could. If the Spanish fleet whose blockade would be thus lifted went north, Spencer felt the Channel fleet could deal with them. If the Spaniards pursued St Vincent he felt that he could readily deal with them himself, but he concluded: 'I cannot bring myself to making it stationary there [i.e. in the Mediterranean] because exclusive of the great expense [£1.5 million p.a.] it would leave the Spaniards too much at liberty'.[44]

At this moment of decision and while Nelson was still at Spithead waiting for his fair wind the French Directory was also reviewing its strategy. In February 1798 the victorious Bonaparte had been sent to inspect the Channel ports and preparations for invading England. How relieved the British Cabinet, and how much easier the decision making of the Admiralty would have been, had they known that he took a very dim view of the likelihood of success – 'It would be too much of a toss-up (un coup trop chanceux): I shan't risk it.'[45] – and set about steering the Directory against invasion and in the direction of Egypt. He had already expressed his own strategic vision in August of the previous year, that soon 'we will come to the conclusion that in order to really destroy England we must seize Egypt.'[46] Thus a few weeks before the Downing Street discussion the Directory decided to go for Egypt and Napoleon immediately focused his formidable energies on putting an expedition together. The news that filtered back to England was not of a change in French strategy but of accelerating naval and military preparations, especially at Toulon. French charades on the Channel coast and a campaign of disinformation kept the British guessing and sharpened the Cabinet's dilemmas. Was the French destination England, Ireland, Naples or Sicily? Most of the betting was on Naples and Sicily but Ireland could not be ruled out. Egypt did not enter minds till much later.

The Toulon armament focused minds and turned the spotlight on George, second Earl Spencer, the First Lord of the Admiralty. He had joined Pitt's administration in July 1794 at the age of thirty-six, first as Lord Privy Seal, becoming First Lord of the Admiralty in December 1794 when he exchanged office with Pitt's brother the Earl of Chatham, who had been failing conspicuously at the Admiralty. He was a remarkably likeable and intelligent man who was to take a huge personal risk in pinning his hopes on Nelson as the cutting edge of the Cabinet's new strategy. One of the inner circle of Whig aristocracy, owner of a great house and estate at Althorp, he was highly educated, well travelled, a bibliophile possessing a great private library and happily married to Lavinia, daughter of the Earl of Lucan. Their relationship was broad and deep and she was an intelligent and perceptive ally in his political and naval responsibilities. In those days when writing was as normal a way of communicating with one's nearest and dearest as speaking to them, she was eloquent and perceptive in her congratulations to him on gaining office – 'Well indeed may a country rejoice when virtue, integrity, firmness, talents, judgement, candour, piety and excellence of character steps forward, utterly against inclination but prompted by Duty to its service.'[47] – and on the difficulties which lay ahead. 'You may lament the inevitable checks and misfortunes attending human affairs and exalted situations, but the glorious certitude of having acted with virtuous intentions will forever support you whatever adverse circumstances may arise.' And on the next day she followed up with a perceptive view of what her 'dearest beloved fellow' would bring to the party. 'So angelick a heart never was accompanied before by so rational a mind'; she characterized him, with a great understanding of the process of politics, as 'the egg of their party and that without you the oyl and vinegar would have remained ever separate.'[48] Five weeks later she was painting an equally enchanting picture of domestic happiness after the birth of her third child: 'My little gold haired darling is thriving just as her mother is a doing on her part.'[49] This neither feels like, nor was in fact, mere wifely hyperbole. Seven years later when St Vincent, who had been on the receiving end of Spencer's work at the Admiralty for about as long, came to succeed him in February 1801, he wrote to Admiral Duncan: 'I come here to great disadvantage, the successor of an able and virtuous man with a princely fortune.'[50]

All Spencer's correspondence, with Lavinia or his colleagues, shows that he was not inclined to think that he knew all the answers and was not possessed of an ego that needed to dominate others. Secure in his estate, his happy marriage and his wide interests, he was well fitted to sit at the War Cabinet table with Pitt, Grenville the Foreign Secretary (an accomplished scholar and linguist but decidedly not good with people), and Henry Dundas the Secretary for War, a friend who as Lord Melville would be First Lord at the time of Trafalgar and described as 'highly convivial over the bottle'. Indeed, although 1797 was a grim year Lavinia had reported to her husband, then up to his eyes in the naval mutiny at the Nore, 'I hear Mr Pitt's Birthday is due to be kept with all due Bacchanalianism this day at Wimb'[ledon].'[51] The last of the group was William Windham, Secretary at War, scholar, mathematician, friend of Dr Johnson, brilliantly witty and sociable and gifted in his capacity to think things through. These were all men of consequence who could not be dominated. Grenville, Dundas and Windham had widely divergent positions on Britain's war aims and how the war should be prosecuted. Grenville's aim was the extirpation of Jacobinism, 'to save Europe and society itself' by a process of subsidized European coalition against France and war on the Continent. Dundas's aim was imperial, to make England 'the paramount commercial and naval power of the world', hence the colossal military efforts in the West Indies in 1796. Windham's aims were royalist, the restoration of the monarchy in France through support of émigré forces and insurrection in France, hence involvement in the Vendée and other projects off the coast of western France.[52] The British Navy would find itself having to respond to a confused multiplicity of war aims. At this point in the war Grenville's voice carried most weight.

Spencer's natural inclination was to seek a meeting of minds. However, he had also answering to him the Board of Admiralty composed at this point of three sea officer members, all rear-admirals, 'Neptunes' as St Vincent called them, and three Civil Lords supported by First Secretary Nepean and Second Secretary Marsden. Whatever his capacity for learning quickly, Spencer was up against his 'Department', not least the professionals with their 'experience', custom and practice, their specific axes to grind, and their highly developed personal networks of serving officers, which supplied them with red-hot gossip and made them a magnet for intrigue. As St Vincent wrote to Spencer in 1798 when he was Commander-in-Chief of the Mediterranean fleet, 'Your puisne Lords of Admiralty have got into an habitual gossiping correspondence with the inferior Admirals [and] Captains serving abroad and at home which does incredible mischief and should be put a stop to but it is arrived at such a pitch I really do not know how to advise the mode of preventing it.' There was a mass of work to be done, and the Admiralty Board Minutes for the year 1797 show the Board sitting daily, Saturdays and Sundays included. In the current situation Spencer had to rise above a departmental position which was chiefly preoccupied with the number of ships on each side, rather than by qualitative analysis; worries about logistics and supply lines which were real enough; and a conservative approach to risk. He had to cut through the perceived or actual dilemmas of resource allocation in order to meet the overwhelming political need urged by Pitt and Grenville and the increasing actual threat posed by the Toulon armament.

As far as Spencer himself was concerned the new strategy was not the only thing in gestation. Lavinia was expecting another child and being confident and optimistic about the outcome. Even so, no eighteenth-century father could be complacent about childbirth and it was with considerable relief that Spencer wrote to his mother the Dowager Countess on 14 April (at which point Nelson was halfway to Lisbon) to say that Lavinia had been brought to bed about four o'clock that morning, her birth pains having been very severe, which was he supposed occasioned by the great size and strength of the child, 'who is as fine a boy as ever was seen, remarkably large and fat and healthy with red hair and dark coloured eyes.'[53] A good omen indeed.

By the end of April, one day before Nelson arrived off Cadiz, the decision had been taken. Spencer had personally accepted the naval risks and had ensured that his War Cabinet colleagues understood them too, for which he would be greatly thankful in the agonizing summer months that were to follow. Now he set about communicating the strategy to St Vincent in a characteristically eloquent and empathetic way, so as to convince as well as order him.

You will by the present conveyance receive a letter from Nepean preparing you for orders to act upon a plan of operations very different from that which we have hitherto adopted, and which I have no doubt will appear to be attended with a considerable degree of risk. You will easily conceive that such an instruction would not have been in contemplation if the circumstances in which we now find ourselves did not in a manner oblige us to take a measure of a more decided and hazardous complexion than we should otherwise have thought ourselves justified in taking: but when you are apprised that the appearance of a British squadron in the Mediterranean is a condition on which the fate of Europe may at this moment be stated to depend, you will not be surprised that we are disposed to strain every nerve and incur considerable hazard in effecting it.[54]

Spencer left it to St Vincent to decide whether to go into the Mediterranean with his whole fleet, or send a detachment, because although the key objective was defeat of the Toulon armament, there was also the high desirability of keeping the Spaniards at Cadiz in check. He went on, 'If you determine to send a detachment into the Mediterranean I think it almost unnecessary to suggest to you the propriety of putting it under the command of Sir H Nelson whose acquaintance with that part of the world as well as his activity and disposition seem to qualify him in a peculiar manner for that service'.

Spencer also knew that he had to involve St Vincent in the strategic concept and inspire his resolution to outface the severe tactical challenge it would place on him and so he concluded,

I am as strongly impressed, as I have no doubt your Lordship will be, of the hazardous nature of the measure which we now have in contemplation; but I cannot at the same time help feeling how much depends upon its success, and how absolutely necessary at this time to run some risk in order if possible to bring about a new system of affairs in Europe which shall save us all from being overrun by the exorbitant power of France . . . if by our appearance in the Mediterranean we can encourage Austria to come forward again, it is in the highest degree possible that the other Powers will seize the opportunity of acting at the same time.

Knowing also of St Vincent's passionate concern for logistics, he made sure that two days later Grenville sent a 'Most Secret' letter to St Vincent which was in effect a highly desirable political umbrella. Basically it was permission for the detached squadron to treat as hostile anybody refusing to supply the ships. At the same time the commander of the detached squadron was not to behave like a bull in a china shop. He was 'to be instructed to use his discretion in the execution of his Orders in such a manner as may best contribute to the success of His Majesty's Arms or those of any Power in alliance with His Majesty in that part of Europe'. This requirement fitted Nelson like a glove. Furthermore he was to stay there as long as his provisions lasted or as long as he could get provisions. So the issue of staying in the Mediterranean was to be handled on a pragmatic English basis. If they could, they should. If they couldn't, they shouldn't. In the event they could – and did.

Spencer also made a further decision: to accept some heightened risk, closer to home in the Channel, by sending a detachment from the Channel fleet to reinforce Cadiz and so, on the same day as Grenville wrote, he sent a further 'Most Secret' letter to St Vincent to say that Sir Roger Curtis was being sent with nine ships-of-the-line and a fireship.[55]

The stage was set and the leading part was about to be given to a junior flag officer. The circumstances of Nelson's appointment need explanation for it is indicative of a far higher level of sophistication than we might imagine. St Vincent's strong suit was setting standards, monitoring performance and, as far as he was able amid the complications of patronage, getting rid of those officers who could not meet his standards. His philosophy was that his flag officers and captains were the key prime movers in the performance of the fleet. It was also characteristic of St Vincent to conduct a continuous, frank and intimate correspondence with Spencer about the performance and potential of individuals under his command, and to be energetic in reshaping his command structure. Although taking a decided view of individuals, he was never slow to revise his opinions nor at all hesitant in admitting that his own *élèves*, for example Saumarez and Berkeley, were not measuring up to specific tasks. Later on he was to express reservations about Nelson's fitness for the highest command. Clearly he was not always right and probably not always fair. Indeed in the business of selection and identification of potential it never will be possible to be always right and always fair. Fortunately Spencer had the knack of matching St Vincent's outspoken, high-handed and occasionally frankly outrageous comments. They could in effect 'level' with each other on professional matters, not least in the area of appointments.

So Spencer developed a high level of confidence in St Vincent's judgements. Nelson is a case in point. He came under St Vincent's command at the end of November 1795 and St Vincent had begun to mention him to Spencer in January 1796, sharing with him Nelson's ambition for flag rank, informing him that he had given him a distinguishing pendant as a commodore. Later in the year he was putting himself in Spencer's chair, reviewing as it were the talent bank of the Navy. 'You see my Lord how very few men are fit to command. Looking over the list of admirals with an impartial eye I cannot find many men on it qualified to command ten line-of-battleships on critical service.' He went on to mention his own blue-eyed boys, Commodore Nelson, Captain Frederick, Captain Troubridge, sowing seeds in Spencer's mind and then ducking out from under his *lèse-majesté* with a graceful 'Pardon these reveries'. Later, he told Spencer how Nelson had sorted out the evacuation of Corsica and 'by the firm tone he held soon reduced these gentlemen to order and quiet submission to the embarcation.'[56] Then came 14 February, when Nelson's critical manoeuvre earned St Vincent an earldom. Fortunately for Nelson, Gilbert Elliot (later Lord Minto) had been an eyewitness. His account not only counteracted Calder's spiteful and erroneous reports, but filled the gaps in St Vincent's dispatches and, equally important, won over Grenville (to whom he reported). Spencer, with the kind of reports he had had from St Vincent, the support of Grenville, the evidence of Gilbert Elliot, and the King's support, was able to take Pitt and the Cabinet with him in nominating Nelson. Nelson had suddenly become flavour of the month.

The choice was about to fall on a junior admiral because he was correctly judged to have superior talent and energy, local knowledge and diplomatic skills – and this would cause ructions. But Spencer's eyes were open. He had learned a lesson in October 1795 from his Cabinet colleague Henry Dundas, about appointing commanders. Spencer had wished to appoint the very young Rear-Admiral Christian (whose appointment Captain Nelson had applauded) to be joint commander of a West Indies expedition with General Abercromby, but feared the reactions of Admiral Laforey and his senior officers in the Leeward Islands, who would feel 'imprecedently and unjustly degraded in the eyes of the whole service.'[57] Dundas read him three lessons. First, 'It is really too deep a stake we are contending for to be put at risk by the etiquette of rank.'[58] Second, to anybody who objected to his own choices he would reply, 'I and not he was responsible for the person in whom I reposed the safety of His Majesty's troops and the safety of the State. It is impossible to sleep sound in one's bed on such occasions if any other principle is for a moment to be tolerated.' Third, 'It is a subject on which you cannot expect any Cabinet Minister will give an opinion. The responsibility rests with you, and you must act upon it.'[59] Spencer did so, with the result that when Sir Charles Middleton, one of his Sea Lords, would not sign the minute, and adopted a 'holier than thou' attitude, Spencer showed his steel and sacked him.[60]

This time Spencer was clear that he wanted Nelson and that his appointment would have St Vincent's approval – but he still left the final operational decision to St Vincent, although he made his own and the Admiralty's view quite clear. In a sense St Vincent had no choice. In fact he had, and he could have gone himself. St Vincent does not appear to have agonized. He had Nelson pigeon-holed as having the characteristics required for the job and he quite properly interpreted his orders as, 'We want you to send Nelson unless you wish to go yourself'. Here was an opportunity for glory, which the Admiralty could not forbid him to take for himself. Mahan takes the view that there was a key difference between St Vincent and Nelson, St Vincent being 'distinguished rather by tenacity and resolution in meeting difficulties and dangers when forced upon him; than by the sanguine and enterprising initiative in offensive measures which characterised Nelson.'[61] The strategy, with its logistical uncertainties, did not appeal to him either. He was in fact showing his age and character, strong in stamina rather than dash. He was happy to send Nelson.

Thus was Nelson launched. The process of his choice had been exemplary. The squadron he was to be given was the best St Vincent could muster. The strategy had been hammered out and agreed on at the highest level. Nelson had broad support, among those who mattered. The military and political objectives were clearly spelled out, the tactical issues were clearly delegated. The risks and repercussions had been evaluated and accepted. In what was to follow Nelson was to be the greatest single factor, but the supporting heroes of the Nile were undoubtedly Spencer and St Vincent.

13

The Hero Ascends

If they are above water I will find them out.

Nelson, July 1798

Making sure that Nelson first of all delivered his precious surplus of fresh water to the inshore blockading squadron off Cadiz harbour, St Vincent lost no time in sending him off on a mission of reconnaissance 'to endeavour to ascertain the real object of preparations making by the French.'[1] Nelson was delighted by his reception and 'found Lord St Vincent everything I wished him and his friends in England have done me justice to him for my zeal and affection'[2] – gossip travelled fast. The only cloud on the horizon was the unhappy thought of the possibility of losing his chief. 'I believe he has written to be superseded which I am sincerely sorry for. It will considerably take from my pleasure in serving here, especially if the command is for a month only, left with Sir William Parker, but I will hope for the best.' Having objected to Nelson's account of the battle of St Vincent Sir William was not one of his favourites. In this letter home Nelson had also to avoid the real purpose of his mission so as not to alarm Fanny, 'The Admiral will probably (secret is going) detach me with a small Squadron; not on any fighting expedition, therefore to not be surprised if it should be some little time before you hear from me again'. Four days later he was at Gibraltar casting an irritated and jaundiced eye on the proceedings of another fellow but more senior flag officer, Sir John Orde, 'here giving fetes etc., but I have no time for such things when we had better be alongside a Spaniard'. As to the latest Spencer baby, his reaction was deadpan 'I am glad to see that Lady Spencer is safe.'[3] Nelson was treading on glass. There were no spontaneous reflections or regrets on their own childless state.

On 8 May 1798 they sailed from Gibraltar Bay, not turning east till darkness covered their movements. The *Vanguard* was now accompanied by two 74s, *Orion* (Sir James de Saumarez) and *Alexander* (Alexander Ball) and the frigates *Emerald*, *Terpsichore* and *Bonne Citoyenne*; he sent orders to the frigates *Caroline* and *Flora* to station themselves to the west of Toulon. Berry later recalled their excited high spirits, how they were 'elated beyond description at being so fortunate as to be the detached squadron in the Mediterranean, and surrounded by Enemies, and but little chance of seeing anything else on these seas.'[4] The Nelson magic was already working, creating a sense of purpose, conveying confidence, engendering closeness. His own verdict 'The Squadron is as I wish them.'[5]

Two days later Spencer's dispatches reached St Vincent's hand and he immediately set about recalling Nelson. 'You and you alone can command the important service in contemplation; therefore make the best of your way down to me.'[6] Ten days later St Vincent did a rapid about-turn when further letters from Spencer told him that reinforcements were on the way. Hardy was sent away immediately in the fast-sailing brig *Mutine* to tell Nelson that he should not return and that reinforcements would instead be sent to him: 'I look for the re-inforcements every hour . . . Sir Roger Curtis with his whole squadron was ordered to join me from Cape Clear [Ireland] where he was cruising.'[7]

Nelson's mission was now to 'take, sink, burn and destroy' the Toulon armament wherever he might find it. He was to take special care not to let the enemy escape westwards, i.e. to the Straits, Ireland and England. He was given *carte blanche* to pursue them to any part of the Mediterranean, Adriatic, Morea (Peloponnese), or even into the Black Sea, 'should its destination be to any of these parts' – words which were to haunt Nelson in the weeks ahead. He was to open up lines of communication with diplomats at every court in Italy, Vienna and Constantinople and with consuls on the Mediterranean coasts. He had freedom to extract supplies from the nervous and unwilling and treat as hostile anybody refusing to supply him, although the Foreign Office had made it clear that Sardinia was excepted and he wasn't to go around upsetting 'allies': he was to make omelettes without breaking eggs. As Commander-in-Chief St Vincent added the lightest of touches: 'You will see the necessity of my being informed of your moves from time to time.'[8]

Having given Nelson these 'most secret' orders, St Vincent was then absurdly indiscreet in reassurances to Sir William Hamilton and the Neapolitan Court. To Sir William he gave chapter and verse:

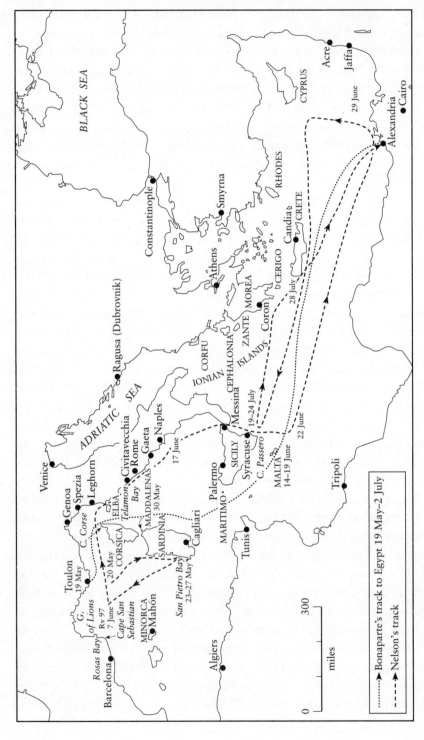

From Toulon to the Nile, 1798

Nature & Nurture

Nelson's mother, Catherine (1725–67).

Nelson's father, Edmund (1722–1802).

Uncle Maurice Suckling (1725–78).

Nelson's elder brother, William
(1757–1835).

Mentors & Patrons

Admiral Sir John Jervis, later Earl St Vincent, Commander-in-Chief Mediterranean Fleet 1795–99, First Lord of the Admiralty 1801–04.

Nelson's Sea Daddy, Captain Locker, later Lieutenant–Governor of Greenwich Hospital.

Admiral Lord Hood, Commander-in-Chief Mediterranean Fleet 1793–95.

Sir Gilbert Elliot, later Lord Minto, Viceroy of Corsica 1794–96, British minister in Vienna 1800.

Admiral Sir Peter Parker, Commander-in-Chief Jamaica 1778–82. As Admiral of the Fleet chief mourner at Nelson's state funeral.

Political Masters

George Spencer, 2nd Earl Spencer, First Lord of the Admiralty 1794–1801.

William Pitt, Prime Minister 1783–1801 and 1804–06.

Lord Grenville, Foreign Secretary 1791–1801.

Henry Dundas, Secretary of War 1794–1801. As Viscount Melville First Lord of the Admiralty 1804 to May 1805.

Henry Addington, Prime Minister 1801–04 and Lord president of the council January to June 1805.

The Real Nelson?

Nelson in 1781, by J. F. Rigaud.

Nelson in 1800, by Heinrich Füger.

Nelson in 1800, by Simon de Koster, framed in a gold locket worn by Emma Hamilton. Nelson described de Koster's engraving as 'most like me'.

Nelson in 1805, by Catherine Andras. Emma Hamilton found this likeness 'so great that it was imposssible for anyone who had known him to doubt or mistake it'.

Nelson by a Leghorn artist, 1794.

Marble bust of Nelson by
Lawrence Gahagan, 1798.

Nelson by Leonardo Guzzardi, 1799.

Nelson in a miniature by Robert Bowyer,
1800.

Nelson in an oil sketch by John Hoppner, 1800.

Nelson in an oil sketch by William Beechey, 1800.

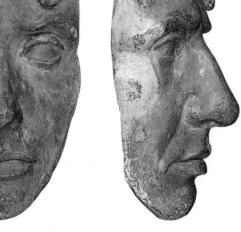

Life masks of Nelson, 1800.

Nelson's Wife

Watercolour drawing of Frances Nelson by Henry Edridge, sometime after 1801.

Frances Nelson, possibly in her wedding dress, in 1787, by an unknown artist.

Pencil drawing of Frances Nelson in 1798 by Daniel Orme.

Emma Hamilton dancing the tarantella in 1796 by Mariano Bovi after William Lock.

Emma Hamilton in 1788 by Angelika Kaufmann.

Emma Hamilton by George Romney.

Emma Hamilton as a Bacchante after George Romney.

Emma Hamilton as a Sibyl by J. H. W. Tischbein.

'reinforcements from the west of Ireland which is on its passage . . . Sir Horatio Nelson will command this force which is composed of the elite of the Navy of England'. To Lady Hamilton he was even more gallant. Being himself 'forbid to quit my post before Cadiz', he pronounced himself 'happy however to have a knight of superior power in my train who is charged with this enterprise', 'the succour of their Sicilian Majesties'; 'at the head of as gallant a band as ever drew sword or trailed pike.'[9] St Vincent's letters to the Hamiltons were never less than fulsome and flattering.

Right on cue on 24 May the topgallant masts of Sir Roger Curtis's squadron appeared over the horizon and as soon as their private signals were recognized St Vincent signalled Captain Thomas Troubridge in *Culloden* to make sail for the Mediterranean with nine of his fleet's best 74s; *Theseus*, Captain Ralph Willett Miller; *Minotaur*, Captain Thomas Louis; *Swiftsure*, Captain Benjamin Hallowell; *Audacious*, Captain Davidge Gould; *Defence*, Captain John Peyton; *Zealous*, Captain Samuel Hood; *Goliath*, Captain Thomas Foley; *Majestic*, Captain George Westcott, *Bellerophon*, Captain Henry D'E Darby; and Captain Thomas Thompson in the 50-gun *Leander*. Three months hence they, with Saumarez and Ball, would be immortalized by Nelson as his 'Band of Brothers'. The remainder of his squadron, the frigates *Flora*, *Terpsichore*, *Caroline*, *Emerald* and the sloop *Bonne Citoyenne* all intended as his fast, wide-ranging scouts were, by various strokes of misfortune, never to be an effective part of his force at all. Their captains could all qualify as among the unluckiest men in naval history.

As he set off to join Nelson, Troubridge was unaware that the French had already given him the slip. Even worse, Nelson had only just survived a major crisis. Having passed up the Mediterranean from Gibraltar in fine weather Nelson had kept his ships-of-the-line in close company until they reached Cape Sicie, between Marseilles and Toulon. On 17 May he learned from a captured ship out of Toulon that Bonaparte had arrived there; vessels were arriving from Marseilles, fifteen sail-of-the-line were ready for sea, troops were embarking, events were moving to a head. Nelson was himself cruising well below the horizon, keeping his ships out of sight. On the afternoon of the 17th he spotted three scouting French frigates but was not himself seen. As Berry said later: 'not discovered by the enemy, though close to their ports, we thought ourselves at the height of our glory.'[10]

By the early morning of 19 May 'the wind blew strong from the North West'[11] and Bonaparte, more ready than Nelson thought, took his chance. It seems incredible that this armada of more than 150 ships with 10,000 soldiers embarked, the main core of 'the greatest fleet seen in the Mediterranean since the days of the Crusaders,'[12] should have sailed out of Toulon unnoticed and escaped unseen. Nelson's 'mission of observation' could hardly have been a greater failure. He was positioned just too far to the south and west (about seventy-five miles from Toulon) and had evidently not deployed his frigates so as to provide an effective chain of surveillance and communication. The *Terpsichore*'s log shows her to have been sixty miles south of Toulon at the time. Nelson thought he had placed *Caroline* and *Flora* to the west of Toulon to counter a possible escape to the west but the orders he wrote to their captains were never delivered. *Flora* was in the Aegean off Candia and the island of Rhodes and *Caroline* was cruising off the North African Cape Pallas – altogether a very nice illustration of the hit or miss nature of naval warfare and communication in the eighteenth century.

So the north-west wind, whipping white caps on a rising sea, hurried Bonaparte's ships out of Toulon Roads and when they had sufficient sea room enabled them to steer east and make a rendezvous with more ships and men from Genoa and Civitavecchia – a perfect start for Bonaparte, who was no doubt fancying himself as fine an admiral as he was a general. Nelson and Berry, who had also been feeling rather pleased with themselves, now suffered a calamitous and near fatal setback. When the same wind that propelled Bonaparte out of Toulon freshened, *Vanguard* had to strike her topgallant masts and yards, it being a usual precaution in worsening weather to bring them down to the deck to reduce wind resistance and the top heaviness of the ship. The next day, Sunday 20 May, the wind moderated, they got their masts and yards aloft again, changed course and headed for Toulon, little knowing that the bird had flown. Again the weather worsened and once more the forty-five-foot-long topgallant yards were lowered to the deck.

The gale struck just before midnight on Sunday the 20th, a full blown howling mistral. Berry made frantic last minute efforts to reduce sail. Too late: the mistral was blowing with an appalling ferocity. At about two o'clock in the pitch of the night the sixty-foot-long main topmast snapped like a matchstick. The mast, its yard and the men on its yard crashed down. By a miracle only two men died. Robert Westcott went overboard to be lost immediately in the prodigious seas and Dinnis Neal was killed as he hit a boom on his fall to the deck 150 feet below. At half past two the forty-eight-foot mizzen topmast also went by the board, trailing torn rigging behind it. At a quarter past three the mighty foremast, ninety-six feet high, three feet thick and bound with iron bands, shattered into two pieces and hurtled down with a rushing crash. The wreckage of the fore topmast and the foremast was now hanging over the side beating time on the ship's bottom with every roll of the ship. Soon it was joined by the best bower anchor, which having come adrift from the cathead added its three-and-a-half-ton thumps to the battering of the ship's bottom. With every pitch and roll of the ship the tangled wreckage of masts and yards threatened the rigging supporting the main mast. In their crazily plunging and rolling ship, in driving spume-filled wind, they managed to get the ninety-six-foot-long main yard down to the littered deck, thus easing pressure on the mainmast and its rigging. At a quarter past three the sixty-nine-foot-long bowsprit cracked in three places but mercifully did not shatter. Within a space of three hours the gale had reduced *Vanguard* to a floating wreck of disintegrated masts, shattered yards and more than seven miles of standing rigging torn, tangled and streaming in the wind.

Mercifully they still had a working rudder and the sprung bowsprit could carry a scrap of spritsail. So, in the dawn light, with the ship labouring and heaving and shipping green sea, they managed to wear ship, turn *Vanguard* round and instead of being pushed eastwards in the dangerous direction of Corsica she was able to point her head and run to the south-west. *Orion*, *Alexander* and *Emerald* followed suit but *Terpsichore*, *Bonne Citoyenne* and a captured prize stayed where they were, riding out the storm under 'bare poles'. They had now been driven 150 miles away from Toulon.

Tuesday was a day of 'exceeding heaving gales and a great sea from the north.'[13] On board *Vanguard* the crew interrupted their struggles of salvage and repair to gather in the waist. Berry read the solemn and beautiful words of the burial service, 'Forasmuch as it hath pleased Almighty God of his great mercy to take unto himself the soul of our dear brother here departed we therefore commit his body to the deep . . .' and with the wind snatching away his words, the long overhanging crests of the sea patched with white foam, the bodies of Dinnis Neal and Thomas Meek, midshipman, who had been recommended by Nelson's brother

Suckling, slid over the side, each sewn in a hammock weighted at the feet with two 32-pounder cannon balls. 'Our situation on Tuesday night was the most alarming I ever experienced,'[14] wrote Berry. At midnight he could hear surf breaking on the rocky shore of Sardinia. Daybreak revealed them in a perilous position, in a bay a mere five miles or so from shore. At three o'clock in the afternoon the light wind was sufficient only to give the ship forward movement, and according to Berry, with a westerly swell driving them shorewards, the *Alexander* took *Vanguard* in tow. They continued in light airs, the *Alexander* with all possible sail set. At about seven on Thursday morning a moderate breeze came off the land to fill the *Alexander*'s sails and take them on out of danger until at eleven *Vanguard* was cast off and both ships came quietly to anchor 'in six fathoms and fine smooth water' off St Pierre's Island.[15]

Previous biographers and engravers have made much of the *Alexander* towing the *Vanguard*, claiming that Nelson categorically *ordered* Ball to cut the tow line and let *Vanguard* fend for herself because of the evident danger to Ball's ship, and that Ball *refused* to do so. This is no more believable than the implicit idea that Nelson was prepared to go down with his ship, depriving the squadron of its leader and himself of a future. It seems more likely that becoming more anxious than Ball, he discussed their options with him in two shouted conversations, ('spoke the Admiral' being noted in the *Alexander*'s log) and Ball's judgement was that they could make it. Although the ships' logs reveal that cables were prepared against the possibility of being able to anchor, there are no signs that other emergency measures were taken, such as launching of boats to tow the ships. More interestingly there is no mention in the ships' logs of a tremendous swell. Any master facing a combination of no wind, a lee shore with breakers and a heavy swell setting on shore would have made sure they were all mentioned in his log. Perhaps he who recounted the tale took a little poetic licence!

Once at anchor it was in character for Nelson immediately to call for his boat to take him over to *Alexander* to thank Ball in person. Fifteen years earlier in St Omer he had ostracized Ball on no stronger grounds than that he sported an epaulette in the French fashion, a 'coxcomb', Nelson thought; and that Ball had seemed to project the airs and graces of a fine gentleman, a judgement which reflected directly the young

Nelson's sense of insecurity. When greeting him at Gibraltar as a member of his detached squadron Nelson's prejudice was evidently still alive and well, if we are to believe Ball's later account that he was greeted with an ill-tempered 'What, are you come to have your bones broken?'[16] But now all was sweetness and light, now it was a case of 'A friend in need is a friend indeed'. Ball had earned a friend and supporter for life and Nelson had won over Ball.

On the other hand it must all have been a nightmare for Berry. Here he was the flag captain, under the eye of his Admiral with his masts and rigging blown to pieces. True, the *Alexander*'s main topsail had split and blown away and the frigate *Terpsichore* had lost a number of shrouds but none of the ships had suffered to anything like *Vanguard*'s degree. Nelson's response was characteristic. He did not blame Berry, as well he might. Nor did he blame the dockyard, which had after all refitted *Vanguard* only two months previously. Instead he blamed himself. To Fanny he wrote,

I ought not to call what has happened to the *Vanguard* by the cold name of accident; I believe firmly, that it was the Almighty's good-ness, to check my consummate vanity. I hope it has made me a better officer, as I feel confident it has made me a better Man. I kiss with all humility the rod. Figure to yourself a vain man, on Sunday evening at sun-set, walking in his cabin with a Squadron about him, who looked up to their Chief to lead them to glory, and in whom this Chief placed the firmest reliance, that the proudest ships, in equal numbers, belonging to France, would have bowed their Flags; and with a very rich Prize lying by him. Figure to yourself this proud, conceited man, when the sun rose on Monday morning, his ship dismasted, his Fleet dispersed, and himself in such distress, that the meanest Frigate out of France would have been a very unwelcome guest. But it has pleased Almighty God to bring us into a safe Port, where although we are refused the rights of humanity, yet the *Vanguard* will in two days get to sea again, as an English Man-of-War. The exertions of Sir James Saumarez and Captain Ball have been wonderful and if the ship had been in England months would have been taken to send her to sea. Here my operations will not be delayed four days and I shall join the rest of my fleet on the rendezvous. If this letter gets to you be so good as to write a line to

Lord Spencer telling him that the *Vanguard* is fitted tolerably for sea, and that what has happened will not retard my operations. We are all health and good humour. Tell Lady Saumarez Sir James never was in better health.[17]

Here is Nelson, casting himself in a role of almost biblical proportions, giving vent to a burst of exalted eloquence; instinctively confident in his powers of recovery and leadership, aware of his dangerous professional situation, intuitively defining and packaging it with inspired public relations skill. The letter did not reach Fanny's hands until 10 September (probably) and she sent it to Lord Spencer in its entirety on the 11th.[18] It had the desired impact and was copied by his great supporter Sir Gilbert Elliot now Lord Minto and by others many times. Nelson's letter of the same date to St Vincent was more factual, less extravagant, but equally full of confidence. This time events were classed as 'accidents'. He implicitly exonerated Berry and himself from fault, 'as the ship was prepared for gale my mind was easy.'[19] Typically, in heaping praise on his captains for getting *Vanguard* ready for sea in just three days, he also singled out for the special attention of the Board of Admiralty, Mr Morrison the carpenter of the *Alexander*, 'an old and faithful servant of the Crown, and who has been near thirty years a warranted Carpenter.'[20]

At dawn on 27 May, Nelson vented some exquisitely courteous and diplomatic contempt on the Sardinians for their unwillingness to help him: 'I could feel the sorrow which it must have been to his Majesty to have given such an order, and also for your Excellency, who has to direct its execution.'[21] Nelson signalled his ships to weigh and make for Toulon, some 300 miles to the north. The next day they spoke with a vessel out of Marseilles and received the staggering and dispiriting news that Bonaparte had sailed nine days previously. For another three days Nelson sailed north to his fixed rendezvous off Cape San Sebastian only to receive a further blow – an empty sea, no frigates. At daylight on 5 June when the *Mutine* joined with St Vincent's new orders Nelson learned from Hardy, who had fallen in with the frigate *Alcmene* off Barcelona, that Captain Hope had taken all Nelson's frigates off the rendezvous, assuming that the damage suffered by *Vanguard* would inevitably drive Nelson back to the dockyard at Gibraltar for repairs. In the case of most captains this was not an unreasonable assumption. Nelson's attitude to Hope's action was always more one of sorrow than of anger: 'I thought

Hope would have known me better.' But the news that Troubridge was on his way with ten sail-of-the-line was, according to Berry, 'received with universal joy throughout our little Squadron and the Admiral observed to him that he would then be a match for any hostile Fleet in the Mediterranean, and his own desire would be to encounter one.'[22]

Unfortunately the loss of his frigates virtually eliminated Nelson's capacity to explore different options for the track of the French armada. He would be virtually blindfold. From his masthead he could, on a clear day, see about twelve miles to the horizon. If an enemy ship allowed its topgallants to peep over that horizon, Nelson's lookout would see the mastheads of a ship about twenty-four miles away. He could increase this viewing range in any direction by placing his ships in a widely spaced extended line, but sightings would automatically produce dilemmas (to look or not to look) and without frigates how could he look without dividing his force? The fact was that in the vastness of the sea the capacity of fleets to miss each other was always easy. When Troubridge with his ten ships-of-the-line and *Leander* hove into sight on 7 June, the French were almost three weeks ahead and the operational flexibility of Nelson's powerful squadron was virtually zero.

Meanwhile, back in the fleet off Cadiz St Vincent had two very angry flag officers on his hands. Rear-Admiral Sir William Parker wrote a letter of protest to Spencer about Nelson's appointment expressing feelings of 'injury', 'degredation', 'feelings more hurt than I can describe.'[23] Then St Vincent discovered that Rear-Admiral Sir John Orde had been going behind his back to Spencer on the same subject and this led to an enraged and exasperated outburst: 'I learned from Sir John Orde yesterday that he had communicated his discontents to your Lordship – indeed there is such extreme and rooted jealousy, hatred and malice against Rear Admiral Sir Horatio Nelson that it becomes absolutely necessary for the carrying on His Majesty's Service here, to remove all the Admirals above him.'[24] Promotions and appointments have ever been great generators of passion and pain, particularly in a case like this when the second and third in command had been passed over in favour of a younger and less senior officer, to say nothing of personal dislike. But it is worth noticing here that while Orde and Parker failed to manage their disappointment and behaved like prima donnas, Nelson never, in the whole of his career, gave a superior officer anything like the hard time Parker and Orde gave Spencer and St Vincent. Spencer stood by his choice with the calm

and reasoned argument that it was 'very natural that a younger Rear
Admiral in a two-decker ship lately come out from Docks should be sent
with two sail of the line on a service of that nature'[25] and 'I have never
understood that it was looked upon as a Rule in the service that when a
Detachment was made from a Fleet the second-in-command had a right
to expect its being entrusted to his care. . . .'[26] Spencer's correspondence
with Orde went on for months. St Vincent became more and more furious
with his behaviour and announced that he intended to order Orde home
in the first available ship, 'coute qu'il coute.'[27] Sir William Parker eventually asked to be removed from St Vincent's command, accusing him of
having pretended to support his initial protests, and having implied
that Nelson's appointment had not been his own but Spencer's. That
was rather naughty of St Vincent, but passing the buck is not a modern
invention.

The French had steered east from Toulon, rounded Cape Corse, turned
south and sailed down the east coast of Corsica, having picked up the
Genoa and Civitavecchia contingents which British intelligence put at
about 12,000 men, 100 ships and a frigate. They arrived off the *east*
coast of Sardinia just as Nelson was off the *west* coast receiving the
news that they had sailed from Toulon. At this point there was little more
than the width of Sardinia, say 100 miles, between them. By 7 June when
Nelson met up with Troubridge the French armada had altered course
to the south-east and was passing through the Sicilian channel between
North Africa and Sicily, about 600 miles ahead of him. Nelson could
be pretty certain that the French had gone east and so he determined
to look into Genoa to see what had happened to the ships assembled
there and then establish whether Naples and/or Sicily were the targets.
Caught in calms, he did not himself pass Cape Corse until 12 June.
Mutine had found no signs of the French in Telamon Bay so he headed
south along the coast of Italy and on the 14th off Civitavecchia he
'spoke a Tunisian cruiser, who reported he had spoke a Greek, on the
10th who told him that on the 4th, he had passed through the French
Fleet of about two hundred sail, as he thought, off the NW end of
Sicily, steering to the eastwards'.[28] This intelligence was in fact accurate
but nevertheless unconfirmed. It suggested that Sicily might be the target,
but if not, Nelson's mind and intuition were working overtime: 'If they

pass Sicily, I shall believe they are going on their scheme of possessing
Alexandria and getting troops to India – a plan concerted with Tipoo
Sahib, but no means so difficult as might, at first view be imagined.'[29]
On the other hand, if they got a whiff of his whereabouts, the French
might seek shelter in Malta, and the seizure of Malta had been on the
French agenda for some time.[30] In Naples, Hamilton had evidently
received St Vincent's letter and sent Nelson one full of double-speak –
not least because Naples was formally neutral and the Court was split:
'the distressful situation of this country openly threatened to be invaded
by the powerful armament at Toulon . . . not . . . quite ready for an open
and declared rupture with the French republic, however well inclined to
it. . . . All Italy sir looks upon the King's Fleet that you have the honour
of Commanding as its Guardian Angel from the Ruin with which it has
been long menaced and without which sooner or later it must fall.'[31] The
key fact was that Acton had been removed as Prime Minister of Naples
at Bonaparte's insistence and the Marquis de Gallo who as Neapolitan
Ambassador in Vienna had taken part in the Campo Formio negotiations, had replaced him. Acton, who retained influence, was anti-French;
Gallo was an appeaser.

Nelson liked Sir William's phrase 'Guardian Angel'; it was to stick in
his mind and be applied subsequently by him to Sir William's wife. Nelson
sent Troubridge ahead to Naples hopeful that he would obtain active
Neapolitan support, frigates, pilots and intelligence. Troubridge returned
empty handed apart from a promise of assistance at Neapolitan ports,
sub rosa, and intelligence that the French were off Malta on the 8th and
were going to attack it. Nelson steered immediately for Malta leaving
behind a pleading but strongly worded private letter for Hamilton on the
necessity for positive Neapolitan support by way of supplies, gun and
mortar boats and fire ships in case the French got into port. As to frigates,
'My distress for Frigates is extreme; but I cannot help myself and no one
will help me. But thank God I am not apt to feel difficulties.'[32] Nelson
never spoke a truer word, but it did not subdue the anxiety and emotional
distress he was feeling. 'Tell her [Lady Hamilton] I hope to be presented
to her crowned with laurel or cypress. But God is good, and to Him I do
commit myself and our Cause.' Touching at Messina on his way to Malta
he fired off another long letter to Hamilton on the threat posed to the
Kingdom of the Two Sicilies by French command of Malta, and on the
ambivalent attitude of the Sicilians, 'plenty of good will towards us, with

every hatred towards the French; but no assistance for us – no hostility to the French'.[33] He was handling the Neapolitans, in fact between a rock and a hard place, with skill and intelligence, postponing the day when he would have to force his requirements on them.

All the same, he had virtually caught up with the French. Now, at a critical moment, Hardy gathered information from a vessel the *Mutine* intercepted near Cape Passero off the south-eastern tip of Sicily. He understood that the French had taken Malta on 15 June (correct) and had sailed on the 16th (false). Given that a strong fresh gale was blowing from west-northwest Nelson could only conclude that the French had sailed for Alexandria and were ahead of him. Before committing his squadron to the chase, leaving the gate to the west open and Sicily and Naples uncovered, he took the extraordinary but sensible step of consulting with four of his captains, Saumarez, Troubridge, Darby and Berry.

> The vessel spoke with this morning is from Malta one day, he says the two frigates in sight are French, that the French colours and garrison are in Malta, that the Fleet and transports left it six days ago, but they did not know where they were going, some said to Sicily. With this information what is your opinion? Do you believe under all circumstances which we know that Sicily is their destination? Do you think we had better stand for Malta or steer for Sicily? Should the armament be gone to Alexandria and get safe there our possessions in India are probably lost. Do you think we had better push for that place.[34]

He was not looking for consensus or a majority vote before he acted; that was always anathema to him. In any case his loaded final question conveyed his own views exactly, but the value of involving his senior captains came in their unequivocal response that the squadron should steer for Alexandria. Nelson had no information as to where the French had gone: He could only work on the balance of probabilities. And so it was a united squadron that set its course for Alexandria, 900 miles away. Nelson was thirsting to meet Bonaparte at sea and fearful that he might have to settle for second best and merely succeed in driving him into port. Yet, it was to be a case of 'so near, yet so far'. The frigates they had seen on the morning of the 22nd were indeed part of the armada's protective screen. Nelson had no frigates to give chase and could not afford to dispatch ships-of-the-line on a wild-goose chase and risk separating his squadron. After all, the French had left Malta almost a week ago (he thought) and were unlikely to be just over the horizon.

But they were. Bonaparte, sailing eastwards, had crossed ahead of Nelson on the afternoon of the previous day. By the evening of the 22nd when Nelson crossed the same point sailing south-east, they were on diverging courses. Dame Fortune seemed to be intent on dealing Nelson an excessively bad hand, and Bonaparte an excessively good one. First the storm, second the frigates, no help from the Neapolitans, catch them up and now miss them by about twenty-four hours. Rodger says that, 'had this squadron made contact with Brueys' unwieldy array on the high seas there would have been a victory of annihilation'.[35] In fact the outcome would most likely have been a dispersed French armada. It is clear from Berry's account that Nelson discussed tactics with his captains.[36] His intention was to divide the squadron into three parts: one of five ships plus *Leander*, and two of four ships. Two of the groups were to attack the French ships of war and the third was to pursue the transports and sink and destroy as many as it could. Nelson was determined that the invasion force should not escape and subsequently rendezvous. But when he wrote pleadingly to Hamilton for Neapolitan frigates he was fully aware of his key weakness: 'if I meet the Enemy at Sea, the Convoy will get off for want of Frigates'.[37] According to De la Jonquière, the French historian, the French warships were concentrated in two groups. Thus each of Nelson's two battle groups would be pitting itself against a bigger French group and the French groups would include *L'Orient* of 120-guns with Bonaparte on board, and the *Tonnant*, *Guillaume Tell* and *Le Franklin*, each of 80-guns. Nelson might see an opportunity to unite his force and take on each group separately but alternatively might himself be obliged to deal with a united French force. Whatever the scenario, some of Nelson's ships were bound to be damaged, possibly even immobilized. Meanwhile his other four ships were projected to deal with 300 transports divided into three groups. The problem here was the size and spread of the target. Each of Nelson's 74s had to destroy, disable, board or force into surrender some seventy-five enemy ships. Even supposing the most favourable weather conditions and French ships not too widely dispersed, the workload for each 74 was still enormous. No wonder Nelson himself forecast that the convoy would escape. Only a group of fast manoeuvrable frigates would have given him much hope of corralling the French transports but annihilation is as wide of the mark as Bonaparte's retrospective comment, 'if the English had really wanted to attack us during the voyage we should have defeated them handsomely'.[38]

Yet Bonaparte might have been captured (or killed and the history of Europe changed), his Army dispersed, his ambitions in Egypt dislocated, and a great shadow cast over his future. He was in retrospect very lucky, that quality he looked for in his commanders. But so too was Nelson. He was spared a highly complex and uncontrollable operation with a dubious outcome and his fame was founded on what happened when he did eventually meet the French.

Nelson headed south-east taking the swiftest course possible to Alexandria. Two hundred and thirty-three miles out he sent *Mutine* ahead with letters for George Baldwin, the Consul. 'Pray do not detain the *Mutine* for I am in a fever at not finding the French'.[39] He arrived there himself on 28 June, three weeks after taking up the chase, to find the coast and harbour empty of French ships. Bonaparte, who had crossed his path five days earlier heading east for the Gulf of Coron on the south-west of Greece was now heading for Alexandria from the north-west. Hardy returned without intelligence of any kind and Nelson sat down, sick at heart but candid and resolute to write to St Vincent:

> where success does not crown an Officer's plan, it is absolutely necessary that he should explain the motives which actuate his conduct, and therefore, I shall state them as briefly as possible. . . . To do nothing, I felt, was disgraceful: therefore I made use of my understanding, and by it I ought to stand or fall. . . . if under all circumstances, it is decided that I am wrong, I ought, for the sake of our Country, to be superseded; for, at this moment, when I know the French are not in Alexandria, I hold the same opinion as off Cape Passaro – viz, that under all circumstances, I was right in steering for Alexandria, and by that opinion I must stand or fall. However erroneous my judgement may be, I feel conscious of my honest intentions, which I hope will bear me up under the greatest misfortune that could happen to me as an Officer – that of your Lordship's thinking me wrong.[40]

The strength of Nelson's character, the power and resoluteness of his decision making, are displayed in every line of this dispatch. Its transparent honesty and breast-baring bravery are also highly disarming and seductive. Before sending the letter he showed it to Ball, whose powers of judicious and mature judgement had by now greatly impressed him. Ball's straight, worldly wise advice was not to send it: 'I should recommend a friend, never to begin a defence of his conduct before he is accused of error.'[41] Nelson sent the letter; he had to live with himself.

During this time, responsibility, risk and the loneliness of command were making substantial inroads into his inner resources. Saumarez his senior captain confided in his diary as early as 22 June, 'Fortunately I only act here en second; but did the chief responsibility rest with me, I fear it would be more than my too irritable nerves would bear.'[42] (Saumarez was the senior captain but Troubridge seems to have been intended as second-in-command by St Vincent. Saumarez had been destined to return home but in the event chose to stay on with the squadron.) But Nelson could draw energy from interchange with his captains. Having formed his concepts, he set about selling them to his captains, in the process opening himself to their 'what ifs' and 'why nots' exploring 'hows', using his enthusiasm and clarity of vision to create energy, to prompt and guide the discussions, enabling each of his captains to contribute to the extent of his talents, but at least drawing them into ownership of his battle plans.

Berry records the process:

It had been his practice during the whole of the cruize, whenever the weather and circumstances would permit, to have his Captains on board the *Vanguard*, where he would fully develop to them his own ideas of the different and best modes of attack, and such plans as he proposed to execute upon falling in with the Enemy, whatever their position or situation might be, by day or by night. . . . With the masterly ideas of their Admiral, therefore on the subject of Naval tactics, every one of the Captains of his Squadron was most thoroughly acquainted, and upon surveying the position of the Enemy, they could ascertain with precision what were the ideas and intentions of their Commander, without the aid of further instruction, by which means signals became almost unnecessary.[43]

We should not imagine that this was a modern process of 'group think' or that it was one in which careful paper plans were drawn up to meet every conceivable set of circumstances. Neither of these was in Nelson's nature and his experience of the battle of St Vincent prompted him to develop a new approach to fleet actions. He knew what he wanted to do and his key intention was to enable and empower his captains to deliver what he wanted. Thus he would concentrate on the principles he saw as appropriate for all sets of circumstances, not on detailed plans for each of a wide range of hypothetical possibilities. His principles were simple. Forget the Order of Battle and the Order of Sailing, we shall form up as most convenient at the time. We shall concentrate our whole force on one or two parts of the enemy line, which we shall isolate and double up on. We shall immediately attack the enemy and immediately get close to our target. We aim first for a knockout blow and then a mopping-up operation. We shall be ready with anchors to hold positions and with lights for night actions. If he succeeded in implanting these simple but clear intentions in the minds of his captains there would be no place for inertia or indecision. Whatever the conditions on the day minds would be prepared. The most recent research, based on examination of the ships' signal books, seems at first sight to deny Berry and undermine the whole thesis.[44] On only two occasions were three or more of Nelson's captains (in addition to Berry) on board the *Vanguard* on the same day. But Berry nowhere says that all Nelson's captains were on board simultaneously, and Nelson would instinctively have realized that a persuasive process is best conducted either one to one or in small groups where he could make maximum personal impact. The absence of written confirmation or minutes of the meetings also underlines that it was an informal process and part of Nelson's developing method. More seriously, Lavery's research indicates that five of the captains – i.e. a third of them if Hardy is included – were not signalled to come aboard *Vanguard* at all. Now, whatever the evidence of the signal logs, it is inconceivable that Berry's recollection should be so wide of the mark, or that Nelson actually failed to find an opportunity for a personal meeting or dinner with each of them, which might well have been arranged by unrecorded hailings between ships in close company.

His captains encountered a man who never for a moment lost sight of his core objective 'to sink, burn and destroy' the enemy, who was determined to make this happen, determined to dominate and shape events, but equally determined to release their own mental and professional energies. It was this modelling of the fighting commander and his process for building up to an action that made Nelson such a formidable man in charge of an élite force. He increased its deadly potential by an order of magnitude.

Now Nelson was increasingly desperate to find Bonaparte and as ever totally disinclined to find reasons for hanging around. A reason which did not see the light of day till 1802 was that if George Baldwin had been at Alexandria at the time he would, in Nelson's view, have persuaded the Turkish Governor to allow Nelson 'to remain a few days and get some water and refreshments' and thus he would have been there when the French arrived. In the event Nelson had not been able to enter the port. And so reasoning that his quarry might have been heading for Asia Minor and the overthrow of the Turkish empire, or rather that this was a possibility he must now explore, he set off northwards to Caramania, 600 miles away on the coast of Asia Minor. Three days later Bonaparte arrived off Alexandria and Nelson, finding no traces or intelligence of him off Asia Minor, turned west on 12 July to beat his way another 600 miles to Syracuse in Sicily where he arrived on the 19th/20th. 'The Devil's children have the Devil's luck', wrote a frustrated and exasperated Nelson to Hamilton. He had done a round 1,800 miles and 'I am as ignorant of the situation of the Enemy as I was twenty seven days ago. . . . In about six days I shall sail from hence, and if I hear nothing more from the French, I shall go to the Archipelago where if they are gone towards Constantinople I shall hear of them. I shall go to Cyprus and if they are gone to Alexandretta, or any other part of Syria or Egypt, I shall get information . . . I want to send a great number of Papers to Lord St Vincent, but I dare not trust any person here to carry them even to Naples. Pray send a copy of my letter to Lord Spencer. He must be very anxious to hear of this fleet.'[45]

On the same day he wrote to St Vincent: 'Every moment I have to regret the Frigates having left me'. He did not know that they were at that very moment scouting for him between Malta and the North African coast. 'To be so unsuccessful hurts me most sensibly. But if they are above water, I will find them out, and if possible bring them to Battle. You have done your part in giving me so fine a Fleet, and I hope to do mine in making use of them.'[46]

After reprovisioning his ships and with a last despairing 'No Frigates – to which has been, and may again, be attributed the loss of the French fleet',[47] Nelson again sailed east. On 28 July Troubridge was sent into the Gulf of Coron and on his return the next day he brought with him a captured French brig and information that the French fleet had been seen sailing to the south-east of Candia (by which they meant Crete) about four weeks before. Ball corroborated after speaking to another vessel on the same day and so with rising hopes and some foreboding that the French would be safe in harbour, Nelson 'immediately bore up, under all sail for Alexandria' and arrived there on 1 August two months (less two days) after he began the chase.

14

The Nile

Joy, joy, joy to you, brave, gallant, immortalized Nelson.

Lavinia Spencer, 1798

As they turned to run into Aboukir Bay Nelson's ships were sailing easy, rigging singing in a fine topsail breeze, ahead the French fleet about two miles distant, now very distinct in its outlines, its centre dominated by the great three-decker flagship *L'Orient*. It was a lovely evening, albeit still a touch sultry, with glittering blue skies, deep blue sea, sandy blue hazy shore in the distance beyond, sea birds wheeling and turning behind the ships. They had been cleared for action for some time, stripped from stem to stern, all partitions, furniture and possessions struck down into the holds. The sailors had dined, the officers had dined. All were now at their battle stations. *Zealous* had driven her ten live bullocks over the side.[1] In battle, frantic cattle stampeding around the deck could not be contemplated. The people were gripped by a strange mixture of apprehension, bravado, quiet contemplation, anticipation and fear. From the main chains the eager Nelson could see the French line curving away to right and left, almost a mile and a half from end to end, the ships moored about 160 yards apart.

The three French admirals, Vice-Admiral Brueys in overall command in *L'Orient*, Rear-Admiral Blanquet du Chayla in the *Franklin*, and Rear Admiral Villeneuve in the *Guillaume Tell*, had watched Nelson's approach since early afternoon. Brueys had considered and passed up his option to unmoor and put to sea. He had the edge in guns and thus in weight of metal he could throw at his attackers, but having twenty-five men from each ship detached for shore duties he judged that whilst he had enough men to fight his ships he had insufficient to fight *and* manoeuvre them at sea. He felt secure in his position, backed and flanked on the van as he was by shoals. So having made some abortive efforts to

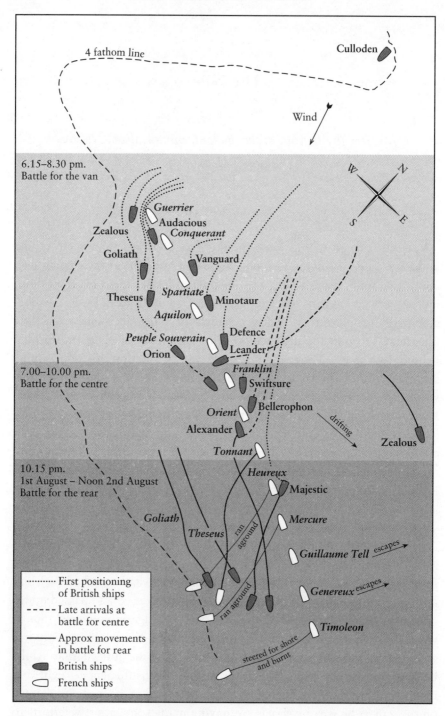

The Battle of the Nile, 1 August 1798

prepare for sea he decided at five in the afternoon to engage at anchor. Time and wind being what they were, he expected a parade of British ships along his line and an exchange of broadsides, a repetition being unlikely because darkness would fall at seven o'clock and the wind blowing down the French line would require the British to claw their way back to the start point to begin again. Each British ship would have to run the gauntlet of thirteen French ships including *L'Orient* which could deliver twice as much metal as any of the British ships. The British masts and rigging would be savaged and it would matter less if his own were damaged.

At five o'clock Brueys saw clearly that Nelson was coming at him. At thirty-four minutes past five he saw the signal flags fluttering on the British flagship but had no inkling as yet what they meant. But Edward Strode, master of the *Zealous* noted in his log: 'Admr^L mad Sig^L to engage the *Van* and Centre of ye Enemy.' Strode had already noted that they had 'Bent the sheet Cable thro the Stern port to the Sheet anchor'. Nelson had a different plan for the French fleet and they were about to find out about it. He intended to throw overwhelming force at the leading French ships to his right, aiming at their rapid elimination. Simultaneously he would attack the French centre with the rest of his force, again in superior numbers, thus creating a platform from which he might progressively roll up the whole French line. At worst he would secure victory, at best the French would be annihilated.

Like the *Zealous*, the rest of the British fleet had been ordered to prepare to anchor by the stern so that each ship might place herself in the most advantageous position alongside the enemy and subsequently make use of the wind blowing down the French line to move with it and congregate around fresh targets. An even more potent weapon in Nelson's armoury was psychological. Berry records: 'The Admiral's designs were as fully known to his whole squadron, as were his deter-mination to conquer *or perish in the attempt*.'[2] This was not mere histri-onics. Nelson was never hesitant to lay his life publicly on the line: it was part and parcel of his heroic attitude. Example was everything. The total, visible and audible commitment of the leader engendered in his more ordinary companions an awesome commitment. Thirteen years later when Hoste flew the signal 'Remember Nelson' at the battle of Lissa he was demonstrating the residual power of Nelson's leadership which placed at the forefront of his followers' hearts and minds, 'What will Nelson think of me?'

Meanwhile the French, undoubtedly brave and resolute as events were to prove, did not appreciate their own vulnerabilities, did not rig hawsers and springs which would have enabled them to manoeuvre their ships and bring more guns to bear on ships attacking them at angles to their stems and sterns,[3] did not appreciate that shoaling water did not frighten Nelson. Never had they contemplated such a headlong attack. The French saw an untidy bunch of ships transform itself into a double-headed strike. *Vanguard* was giving way to *Goliath*, *Zealous*, *Orion*, *Theseus* and *Audacious*, all peeling off to Nelson's right to surround the leading French ships *Guerrier*, *Conquérant* and *Spartiate* – five to three. They closed and at 5.30 in the afternoon the French hoisted their colours and opened fire at a range of about 500 yards.

The British ships held their course and fire, until at 6.15 Tom Foley in *Goliath* rounded *Guerrier*'s stem and poured a full double-shotted broadside through it, causing immense carnage as seventy cannon balls smashed, bounded and ricocheted along the full length of her gun decks killing and maiming men, gouging out showers of splinters, and over-turning guns; she then anchored by the second ship, the *Conquérant*, and engaged her. At 6.30 Sam Hood in *Zealous* went round, again mercilessly raking *Guerrier* through the stem, and anchored on her bow. Saumarez in *Orion* was next and passing both *Zealous* and *Goliath* on their outside, went on to anchor by the fifth French ship, the *Peuple Souverain*. The American Ralph Miller in *Theseus* followed, passed *Zealous* and *Goliath* on their inside and blasting the two French ships as she passed, came to anchor off the third, the *Spartiate*. At ten minutes to seven Davidge Gould in *Audacious* followed, raking the *Guerrier* as she passed to anchor between her and the *Conquérant*. At 6.30 Nelson anchored on the outside of the third French ship, the *Spartiate*. Thomas Louis in *Minotaur* and John Peyton in *Defence* passed him to go for the fourth and fifth French ships, the *Aquilon* and the *Peuple Souverain*. This gave Nelson total odds of eight to five in this half-mile of concentrated hell and the French found themselves having to fight both sides of their ships.

So far Nelson had gained the advantage of surprise. And instead of following the tactic of two ships against one on the *outside*, Foley had seen that he could get round to the inside and unprepared side of the French line and thus fulfil Nelson's penetrating understanding that 'where there was room for an enemy's ship to swing, there was room for one of ours to anchor'. Furthermore, Hood, Gould, Miller and Saumarez had the skill and discipline to extemporize on Foley's initiative. A log jam around the *Guerrier* was avoided.

It was a brilliant combination of individual talent and team effort, unleashed by the mesmeric simplicity of Nelson's concepts, and driven by his transfer of initiative and responsibility to individuals. In a real sense the Nile was neither planned nor commanded, nor directed, especially after darkness fell. The problems Nelson had at this stage were that Tom Troubridge, rashly endeavouring to get at the enemy as quickly as possible, had gone aground on the Bequier shoal, so Nelson was already missing a ship, and *Alexander* and *Swiftsure*, having been scouting off Alexandria, were lagging behind and could not get into action before eight o'clock, an hour after darkness had fallen. However, in the critical half an hour before nightfall the French van was all but crushed. The *Guerrier* had lost her masts in the first ten minutes to those raking broadsides; the *Conquérant* and *Spartiate* lost theirs some twenty minutes later. By half past eight the next two ships *Le Peuple Souverain* and *L'Aquilon* had struck their colours and were taken.

To begin with, the attack on the centre went less well. Just as night fell Henry Darby got *Bellerophon* alongside *L'Orient*. Under intense fire from the great three-decker *Bellerophon*'s masts came crashing down and with 49 men killed and 148 wounded Darby ordered his anchor cables to be cut and drifted out of the action. George Westcott in *Majestic* had sailed past to engage the *Tonnant*, *L'Orient*'s 80-gun neighbour but ended up against the next ship, the *Heureux*. At that point, contending as they were with two 80-gun ships, the odds were against Nelson, but at 8.20 the odds evened when Alexander Ball in the fresh *Alexander* arrived to take on *L'Orient*, and Ben Hallowell positioned the fresh *Swiftsure* to bring his guns to bear on *L'Orient* as well as on Blanquet's flagship the 80-gun *Franklin*. Thomas Thompson then bravely and smartly sailed his little 50-gun *Leander* into a position between the *Peuple Souverain* and the *Franklin*, from where he raked *Franklin* mercilessly through her vulnerable stem. Saumarez, having finished with the *Peuple Souverain*, also came down to lend a hand with the *Franklin* which was fighting with conspicuous courage and ferocity. The even odds, and French courage, explain why this phase of the battle lasted so long. The end came suddenly. *L'Orient* took fire at ten past nine and blew up at ten o'clock, just at the moment when the *Franklin* was dismasted. The French centre was now effectively broken although the wonderfully dogged and courageous *Franklin* with only three guns capable of firing did not lower her colours till half past eleven.

The scene of the battle now shifted to the French rear and beyond. Brueys had died on his quarterdeck virtually cut in two by British shot, Blanquet was severely wounded and Villeneuve situated to the rear of the French line had neither means nor capacity to reorganize the remainder of the ships. The *Tonnant* had cut her cable at a quarter past ten, and drifted south-east, still under fire from the *Majestic*. The *Alexander*, relieved of *L'Orient*, drifted south-east too. So did the two French ships *Heureux* and *Mercure*, which in the darkness of the night and bearing no distinguishing lights, caused French ships to fire into each other. *Majestic*, still engaging the *Tonnant*, had her main and mizzen masts shot away at 3 a.m., and lost her captain George Westcott killed. *Theseus* had got down to join in this phase of the action, much as Nelson had envisaged and the *Tonnant* was, in her turn, dismasted and run on shore.

When dawn arose on the shambles, Nelson, who had won a magnificent victory but who could never bear unfinished business, made every effort to revive the battle. He signalled *Goliath* and *Zealous* to join *Majestic*, *Alexander* and *Theseus*, who were already in the south-east quarter. They faced five French ships of the line, *Heureux*, *Mercure*, *Timoléon*, *Guillaume Tell*, *Généreux* and the two frigates *La Justine* and *La Diane* – even odds, excluding the frigates. The British were exhausted and except for *Zealous* their ships very badly knocked about. The French had no stomach for further fighting and the rallying of British force was sufficient to cause the *Tonnant* to strike; under renewed attack both the *Heureux* and *Mercure* ran aground and also hauled down their colours. At eleven o'clock *Timoléon* steered for the shore, was abandoned and set on fire. Simultaneously the *Guillaume Tell* and *Généreux* accompanied by the remaining two frigates *La Justine* and *La Diane* cut their cables and stood for the open sea. Only *Zealous* was in any position to block their progress or pursue. At noon she engaged and her log records the final shots of the battle. 'At noon engaged 2 line of battle and 2 frigates.

Received a broadside from each in passing.'[4] From the *Vanguard* Nelson signalled recall as the French survivors headed for the open sea.

Just as Nelson had lagged behind the French fleet so did news of the battle lag behind the event. Spencer was becoming extremely anxious about Nelson's progress, having to answer daily enquiries from his Cabinet colleagues for news. On 9 July, after Bonaparte had reached Alexandria and had landed with his Army, and Nelson was fruitlessly beating back to Syracuse, Spencer wrote to St Vincent: 'extremely anxious to hear something of them as the accounts we get through French are so very imperfect . . . our last account is that of the capture of Malta by Bonaparte [14 June]. . . . We are assured . . . that the ultimate object of their grand Expedition is Egypt; it appeared at first so improbable that it seemed almost absurd to act upon that speculation.' He tried hard to remain optimistic about the squadron's success but he was aware of the pressure of expectation: 'nothing ever was equal to the sanguine expectations which have been raised.'[5] Because of pressure of anticipation of news he told his mother that he had not been able to go to the Harrow Speech Day to hear his son Jack perform. 'I'm told he did very well'; he went on: 'it is unlucky that Bonaparte should have got into Malta and as to blockading him there, that is sad work and we have enough of it already.'[6]

St Vincent, who was protecting Nelson's back as best he could, immediately sent Spencer copies of Nelson's letters. He added a stern injunction: 'Although the enclosed copies of letters from Sir Horatio Nelson are not fit for the eye of a gossiping Board, it is proper your Lordship should see the innermost recesses of such a soul as Nelson's.'[7] There was plenty of gossip and tittle-tattle doing the rounds of clubs and dinner tables. Admiral Goodall later recalled to Nelson how he had 'often been obliged to stand in the breach against the senseless criticisms of the noble and ignoble of this Country; you know them well-governed by the tide of sure and immediate success. Knowing my attachment to you, how often have I been questioned, "What is your favourite Hero about? The French fleet has passed under his nose and etc etc."'[8]

At last Nelson was on Bonaparte's heels but Spencer's nervous tension was great and he was writing in full flow of his anxiety and concern to his mother. 'I have put [off] my journey to Bath for the present, as the Accounts we have received from the Mediterranean are so very critical that I cannot bring myself to retire from the Neighbourhood of London till I hear something further. In a very few days I hope we shall hear again, and God grant it may be satisfactory as much depends on it.'[9] Spencer's anxieties and stress mounted and he had intended to get to Bath for a cure, but 'I hope my stomach will rub on pretty well without it, though it has lately been rather out of sorts. . . . I mean to get a few days shooting at Creak with Jack before he returns to school.'[10]

Rumour and report added to the tension. By mid-August Spencer was telling his mother, 'The Hamburg Mail which arrived this morning brought us a Report said to have come from Venice to Dresden of Admiral Nelson having gained a complete victory over the French Fleet.'[11] And on 18 August he had to summon up all his even temper and self-control. 'I am afraid it is not yet in my power to confirm the various flattering Reports we have lately received from the Mediterranean. They as yet amount to nothing more than reports and the circumstances of the total silence of the French papers respecting them, though it does not amount to an absolute contradiction cannot but throw considerable doubt on their authenticity.'[12]

They were not to know that Nelson had written his dispatches on 2 August, entrusting one set to Captain Berry in the *Leander* which was subsequently captured by the *Généreux*, and one set to Captain Capel in the *Mutine* to take overland to London via Naples. The long-drawn-out transmission of the news was extraordinary. On 21 August Spencer was replying to a dispatch from St Vincent. 'I . . . am very anxious to hear from you as we have no news of Nelson that can be depended on since his being on the 21st June off Cape Passaro.'[13] On 4 September it was still a case of 'We still remain in the utmost anxiety about News from Nelson.'[14]

It was not only Spencer who was worrying. Dundas was very edgy and inclined to adopt a somewhat complaining note. After all it was now 16 September. 'I have not spirits enough on the subject of the late accounts from Sir Horatio Nelson to say a word on that business. I must in charity presume when he tells his own story he will be able to give a good reason for his leaving Alexandria after he had got there in so auspicious a manner.'[15] Spencer, loyal, decent and with his own reputation on the line, defended him stoutly. 'His missing the French fleet both going and return-ing was certainly very unfortunate; but we must not be too ready to censure him for leaving Alexandria when he was there till we know the exact state of the intelligence which he received on his arrival there.'[16] Lavinia was hard at work keeping up Spencer's spirits and looking on the bright side. 'Harrison says it is all that is wanted that Buona should be entrenched near Alexandria that he will not have a man alive in the course of a very little while – such is the death giving situation.'[17] As long ago as 16 August *The Times* had reported Bonaparte's landing in Egypt.

Still the suspense continued and Spencer, shooting at Creake, was besieged by a second report of a Nelson victory but in spite of the sanguine conclusions of friends set his face against premature celebration. He wrote to his mother on 24 September, 'I do not encourage myself to believe it notwithstanding the quarter from whence it comes which it should seem entitle it to some Credit lest I should subject myself to another disappointment.'[18] His sister Georgiana, Duchess of Devonshire, wrote from Chatsworth. 'We are all very anxious indeed for news.'[19]

Then on 2 October Capel arrived in England with Nelson's dispatches and the long pent up emotions and anxieties gave way to an explosion of relief, joy and triumph which from its epicentre in the Admiralty swept through the nation. Spencer reeled and fainted when his secretary incautiously blurted out the news but quickly recovered his wits to write heartfelt words of congratulation and thanks to the little Admiral who had so gloriously vindicated his trust.

> Most sincerely and cordially do I congratulate you on the very brilliant and signal Service you have performed to your country in the glorious Action on the first of August last which most certainly has not its parallel in Naval History . . . I have only now time to say thus much. In my next, I shall have the pleasing task of acquainting you with the measures which will be taken by Government to mark their sense of the merits of yourself, and your gallant Officers, on this memorable occasion. I wrote immediately a line to Lady Nelson, to tell her you were safe, and what you had achieved. I was happy to hear from Capel that your wound was doing well. God bless you, my dear Sir Horatio . . .[20]

By the same post Lavinia Spencer wrote Nelson a wonderful letter, full of grace, warmth and admiration, striking exactly the right note of Spencer gratitude and obligation:

Captain Capel just arrived! Joy, joy, joy to you, brave, gallant, immortalized Nelson! May that great God, whose cause you so valiantly support, protect and bless you to the end of your brilliant career! Such a race surely never was run. My heart is absolutely bursting with different sensations of joy, of gratitude, of pride, of every emotion that ever warmed the bosom of a British woman, on hearing of her Country's glory – and all produced by you, my dear, my good friend. . . . This moment the guns are firing, illuminations are preparing, your gallant name is echoing from street to street, and every Briton feels his obligations to you weighing him down. But if these strangers feel in this manner, who can express what We of this House feel about you? What incalculable service have you been of to my dear Lord Spencer! How gratefully, as First Lord of the Admiralty, does he place on your brow these laurels so gloriously won. In a public, in a private view, what does he not feel at this illustrious achievement of yours, my dear Sir Horatio, and your gallant Squadron's! What a fair and splendid page have you and your heroic companions added to the records of his administration of the Navy! And, as wife of this excellent man what do I not feel for you all, as executors of his schemes and plans! But I am come to the end of my paper, luckily for you, or I should gallop on for ever at this rate. I am half mad and I fear I have written a strange Letter, but you'll excuse it. Almighty God protect you! Adieu! How anxious we shall be to hear of your health! Lady Nelson has had an Express sent to her.[21]

And what of Fanny? During the long period of rumour and suspense she had been her usual anxious and fretting self. 'The newspapers have tormented and almost killed me in regard to the desperate action you have fought with the French fleet.'[22] There is no record of what she wrote to Nelson after she received the express from Lord Spencer. She must have written, but her letter was not one that he took evident pains to keep. It is unlikely that its histrionics would match those of Lavinia Spencer.

Congratulations flowed in. The Spencer family's had a proprietorial air. Georgiana from Chatsworth exclaimed, 'we are all mad here with joy . . . what Ld of the Admiralty could boast of such Victorys as yours? You have a right indeed to stand on tip toe.'[23] From Henrietta, 'my dearest brother I only write you one line to wish you joy of your glorious victory.'[24] Tom Grenville, brother of Lord Grenville architect of the return of the fleet to the Mediterranean, was fulsome: 'My dear good people – I cannot tell you how much in my heart and soul I am rejoicing at the glorious news I have just heard. I know too how much you are both triumphing in this grand and magnificent event having fallen to the lot of Nelson with his one lame arm and gallant spirit. I know Lord S will not be backward either in the rewards which should follow . . .' His own position was clear. 'What the right distinction is I feel it difficult to ascertain by any other measure than the greatness of the victory which in numbers and comparative force has, I am persuaded, never been exceeded.'[25] Later in October Lord Grenville underlined his own judgement: 'The more I hear and the more I think of this great event, the more its importance rises in my estimation.'[26] Of its importance there was no doubt.

The total action, from the first to last shot, had lasted for nineteen hours, the first eight and a half being most intensely fought. It had resulted in the virtual elimination of the French fleet – eleven out of thirteen taken, sunk or burnt – without the loss of a single British ship. It had, at a single stroke, removed French naval influence from the Mediterranean, severely blunted the French threat to the Levant and India, and secured all the desperately hoped for European strategic alliances. It was 'the end of the beginning, the hinge of fate'.[27] The Second Coalition against France could now be built.

From a purely British naval perspective it was the supreme naval victory of the war so far. Lord Howe's Glorious First of June 1794, in which seven French ships were taken, had been a tactical victory but had not prevented a strategically important grain convoy from reaching France. St Vincent's action on 14 February 1797 had lasted for five and a half hours and resulted in the capture of four Spanish ships, by comparison a minor action, but crucial to British morale in the dark days of 1797. Duncan's action at Camperdown on 11 October 1797, which lasted for only three and a quarter hours but resulted in the capture of eleven Dutch ships, was equal in size, decidedly a victory of magnitude, but not of equal strategic significance.

Spencer had to canvass opinion. Clever Windham gave him a clever answer which was equivocal: it muddled the issues of reward for the victory, which hinged on the magnitude of the victory, with the question of where Nelson ought to be positioned in the naval hierarchy, which hinged on where he should be placed in relation to St Vincent, an earl and Duncan, a viscount. He wrote, 'Though Nelson has fulfilled so magnificently all the hopes that could be conceived of him I cannot wish him to be put on a level with Lord St Vincent at the same time, that I conclude there is not a thought of placing him below Lord Duncan . . . he ought to stand somewhere between the two, if there were in fact any such intermediate degree . . . I hope there is no idea that his not having commanded in chief, is to place the victor of the 1st August below the author of the victory of the 11th October.'[28]

Of course, rewarding Nelson on the merits of his astounding victory was the right thing to do and he ought in all justice to have been advanced to Viscount at least. But the reaction of the King, who recalled that Nelson had rejected the idea of a Baronetcy the previous year after the battle of Cape St Vincent on grounds that he was not rich, was that Nelson should receive a handsome pension but no peerage. This critical intervention discouraged Spencer from pressing for a Viscountcy, and bolstering his own name with that of Pitt, proposed a Barony instead.[29] Spencer had to fall back on Windham's scorned excuse that Nelson had not been a commander-in-chief. Also it was, and had to be, a snap decision. By 6 October it was all done and dusted and Nelson was duly gazetted as Baron Nelson of the Nile and of Burnham Thorpe in the county of Norfolk. The next day Spencer wrote to him informing him of the King's pleasure but alas lapsing into a rather pompous and patronizing, not to say defensive formula: 'I have particular pleasure in remarking that it is the highest honour that has ever been conferred on an officer of your standing in the Service, and who was not a Commander-in-Chief.'[30]

Powerful voices were raised in public and private. In the House of Commons General Walpole put his finger on the weakness of the government's position: 'The argument that he commanded only a Detachment was absurd. It was the same as to say, that in the distinction of reward, more attention should be paid to rank than to merit.' Pitt countered that 'his glory did not depend on the rank to which he might be raised in the peerage. . . . Achievement would be perpetuated in the memory of his countrymen and all Europe . . . nor . . . the title of Baron, Viscount or Earl, that would enhance his consideration with Englishmen . . . claims to their gratitude and admiration would always rest on the intrinsic merits of his Victory . . . most splendid and useful that has hitherto signalised the Naval annals of their country . . . attention to the difference of rank in the distribution of Honours was not absurd . . . not a question for the consideration of the House . . . reserved entirely for the determination of the Crown . . . in no instance within his recollection where the merits of the achievements were equal, had an inferior Officer been distinguished by the same honour as an Officer of higher rank.'[31] This smokescreen of humbug served to get Pitt out of the House but did not answer General Walpole's point. And when the government moved to the question of pension, Nelson was again short-changed, being awarded £2,000 a year as opposed to the £3,000 awarded to both St Vincent and Duncan.

Nelson's nearest and dearest were thunderstruck. Maurice, serving in the Navy Office, was called in by Lord Spencer to be congratulated and asked for his opinion as to what title his brother would wish to take. Spencer hadn't mentioned 'what degree of peerage was to be conferred'[32] and Maurice hadn't liked to ask, but when he found out the next day he expressed himself forcibly to Fanny: 'I am by no means satisfied with it, and if I had been authorized I should have rejected it with contempt, but as I was not, I held my tongue. I only hope he may be better pleased with it than I am.'[33] And it was not self-interest speaking. He did not himself wish to be a successor to the title. 'I move in too humble a sphere to think of such a thing.' 'William may have all the honours to himself.'

Fanny became equally indignant. Writing to Lord Hood on 18 October she shared her feelings in no uncertain fashion: 'The honours which have been conferred on Lord Nelson is I am told the subject of conversation everywhere. It does not meet the approbation of the public, as to my own feelings, they were mortified in the extreme, so much so that I was going to direct my letter to my husband, as I usually did, but Mr Nelson requested I would give him every mark of distinction which his own title would allow.'[34] His father in a family letter declared, 'The Peerage is not what the Publick are fully satisfied with. But we are told it is only to begin with.'[35]

Equally important letters of congratulation were very quickly on their way to Nelson. From St Vincent off Cadiz came, 'God be praised, and you and your gallant band rewarded by a grateful Country, for the greatest Achievement the history of the world can produce . . .'. St Vincent did not know how Nelson had been rewarded. But Admiral Viscount Hood did and wrote:

No Officer, I will be bold to say, ever more highly merited the gracious notice of his Sovereign, and that of his Country. I am, therefore, extremely disappointed that your well-earned Honours are not
carried farther, particularly as Mr Pitt told me, the day after Captain
Capel arrived, that you would certainly be a Viscount, which I made
known to Lady Nelson. But it was objected to in a certain quarter,
because your Lordship was not a Commander-in-Chief. In my
humble judgement a more flimsy reason was never given. All remu-
nerations should be proportionate to the service done the public, let
the Officer who does it be first, second, or third in command. But
in fact your Lordship stood in the situation of Commander-in-Chief
off the Mouth of the Nile and could not possibly receive any advice
or assistance, at the distance of near a thousand leagues from Earl
St Vincent, and conquered from your own personal zeal, ability and
judgement. I do assure you, my dear and much loved Lord, I am not
singular in the sentiments I have stated. They are in unison with the
general voice of your grateful Country.[36]

Nelson's old friend Admiral Goodall of Mediterranean days under
Hood and Hotham wrote, 'I have just learnt you are made an English
Baron, by what Title I know not; but 'tis not enough: as you are in
the range of Titles which your Brother-Officers availed themselves of,
do you do the same. You have as just a claim. Go as far as you can –
Viscount at least. I shall clamour for more, but shall not rest till I hail
you Viscount.'[37]

But in spite of the threadbare and ungrateful decision of George III,
Pitt, Spencer and the Cabinet, Nelson had achieved the heroic fame he
sought. Both Houses of Parliament and the House of Commons of
Ireland recorded their thanks. The City of London, to whom he had sent
Admiral Blanquet's sword, in return presented Nelson with a 200 guinea
sword. The East India Company saw him as the saviour of its business
and would make him a gift of £10,000 (worth nearly half a million
today). The parson's son became the occasion for prayers and thanksgiving in churches throughout the land on 21 October. Peals of bells, *feux
de joie*, bonfires, illuminations, patriotic theatrical performances, balls,
ballads and poems galore – and collections for the widows and families
of the killed and for the wounded, were the order of the day. The Spencer
family was busy appropriating symbols of Nelson and the Nile for the

family china. 'Tell Lavinia I wish she would send me a service relating to the Victory for a copy for our new china,'[38] Georgiana wrote on 7 October.

The daily newspapers, now both numerous and influential and increasingly in a position to form and consolidate public opinion, made a popular hero of him. For more than a week he filled their pages. As he dined with his captains before the Nile Nelson had said, 'Before this time tomorrow I shall have gained a peerage or Westminster Abbey.'[39] He had gone much further and had established his claim to be an icon of the nation. But for the time being Nelson was ignorant of all this. The *London Gazette* announcing his elevation to the peerage would not reach him for three and a half months and Lord Spencer's letter not until four months after the battle.

Part IV

Finding Love

15

Hero Meets Heroine

No I wou'd not like to die till I see and embrace the Victor of the Nile

Emma Hamilton, 8 September 1798

Somewhere between eight and 8.30 p.m., at the height of the battle for the centre, a piece of stray metal from a langrel shot, a crude but lethal confection of bolts, nails and pieces of iron designed to shred *Vanguard*'s rigging, slashed suddenly across Nelson's temple. Like a bloody flap the severed skin fell instantaneously over his good eye. Blinded, with blood pouring down his face, with the shouts of battle and the crash of cannon all around him, he recognized his fate; he knew his hour had come. 'I am killed; remember me to my wife.'[1]

They helped him below to the orlop deck; the arms of Mr Jefferson the surgeon and his loblolly boys were stained with the blood of sixty or seventy of the wounded and dying who lay there, not in neat rows, but higgledy-piggledy as their mates had laid them tenderly down. Nelson resisted preferential treatment: 'No I will take my turn with my brave fellows.' When his head was bound, still convinced he was a dead man, he again called, this time on his chaplain Mr Comyn, to convey his dying remembrance to Lady Nelson. Quickly realizing the state he was in, Berry and the surgeon urged him to rest quietly in the bread room at the stern end of the same deck. But Nelson was hyperactive, his mind seized with sudden desire to lose no time in getting his name on the roll of fame. The battle was nothing like over but he called for his secretary, Mr Campbell, to join him and take down a dispatch for the Admiralty. Campbell was himself wounded and they must have made a macabre spectacle in the scarcely lit bread room. Campbell, in shock from his own wound, recoiled at the sight of his blind and suffering Admiral and was 'unable to write a word'. Nelson grasped the pen and managed a few ineffectual words himself. Then Berry came hurrying below to report fire in the French flagship *L'Orient* and once again on deck, Nelson with instinctive compassion for men caught between the horrors of death by fire or drowning, ordered their only seaworthy boat to help pluck survivors from the water.

By this time the fire had taken a furious hold and a yellow and red glow began to illuminate the sea, the masts of nearby ships, and the faces of watching men, held spellbound. Flames began to sprout from gun ports as from an infernal boiler. Fire ran up the masts and along the rigging, which began to melt away or fall, until deep below, the magazine ignited and the vast ship erupted and burst. A prodigious sheet of flame shot skywards, taking a thousand men to their end. There was barely an interval before the rushing wind of displaced air fanned watching faces, and then the cataclysmic roar was upon their eardrums. Instinctively hands went to heads as the slash and splatter of debris rained on the sea. It seemed incredible that such a towering presence as *L'Orient* could have vanished from the face of the sea, leaving no more than a tangled mound of floating wrack behind. In Alexandria and in the desert, men heard the sound and wondered. Nearby there were some muted cheers.

In the deadly silence that followed Nelson was with some difficulty persuaded to lie down, but ever restless he irrationally and prematurely set about signing Hardy's commission to replace Berry in *Vanguard*, as the latter would have to be sent home with Nelson's dispatches.

By the afternoon of the 2nd, Berry, who had temporarily taken over Nelson's correspondence with his captains, wrote to Miller. 'He is now more easy than he was the rage being over.'[2] Nelson had been temporarily unhinged, disorientated and irrational, after the shock of his wound, the accumulated stress of the long chase, the risk he had taken in attacking the French at nightfall, and the most apocalyptic and terrible example of sudden destruction he or his captains would ever witness. Berry looked after Nelson with a discreet and loving kindness and his narrative published after the battle simply portrays a wounded but ever active hero. A few months later Nelson acknowledged his debt to Berry: 'I shall never forget your support for my mind on 1st August'.[3]

On the evening of the 2nd a steady stream of boats brought him the warm and excited congratulations of his now exhausted captains. They included Miller of the *Theseus*, 'In the evening I went on board the Admiral, who I before knew was wounded. I found him in his cot, weak but in good spirits, and, as I believe every captain did, received his warmest thanks, which I could return from my heart, for the promptness and gallantry of the attack'.[4] With the boats came the lists of killed and wounded. George Westcott was dead and a third of *Majestic*'s people killed or wounded. *Bellerophon*, smashed by *L'Orient*'s guns, also had a third of her ship's company killed or wounded. *Vanguard* herself lost almost a fifth – 35 killed and 75 wounded. These three ships together accounted for 60 per cent of the 218 dead and more than half of the 677 wounded. Officers and midshipmen had paid a proportionately higher price, and besides himself, Saumarez, Darby and Ball were all walking wounded. For the French it had been catastrophic. Admiral Brueys and his flag captain Casabianca were dead, as were Thomas of the *Tonnant*, Thenard of the *Aquilon*, and Dalbarde of the *Conquérant*; in all the French had lost about eight times as many killed and more than twice as many wounded.

Nelson, now in full possession of his senses, acted with an innate sense of theatre. Two memoranda flowed from *Vanguard* to his fleet, now busy with the business of repairing ship, securing prizes and burying those who had died of their wounds; the remainder of the dead having been thrown over the side during the battle, as was the custom. 'Almighty God having blessed His Majesty's Arms with Victory, the Admiral intends returning Public Thanksgiving for the same at two o'clock this day; and he recommends every ship doing the same as soon as convenient.' His second carried public congratulations to 'The Captains Officers Seamen and Marines on their very gallant behaviour in this glorious battle. . . . It must strike forcibly every British Seaman how superior their conduct is, when in discipline and good order to the riotous behaviour of lawless Frenchmen.' The tone had been set and was mirrored in his dispatch to St Vincent and the Admiralty, which he had so excitedly attempted at the height of the battle. It could scarcely have had a more grandiose opening: 'Almighty God has blessed his Majesty's Arms in the late Battle by a great Victory over the Fleet of the Enemy, who I attacked at sunset on the 1st August off the mouth of the Nile.'[5] Later, in a letter to his father, the parson's son echoed the spirit of the Old Testament: 'The hand of God was visibly pressed on the French: it was not in the power of man to gain such a victory.'[6]

It is worth noting that the otherwise emotional Nelson expresses no particular sadness and certainly no remorse for the death and suffering caused by battle. If he felt such emotions his heart and mind were well armoured to contain them. He did not let them surface as did Wellington after Waterloo. His reactions were entirely practical: thoughtful letters of condolence and care and attention for the widows and children of his brother officers. For example, he took under his wing the fourteen-year-old son of his Captain of Marines, also in *Vanguard* when his father was killed. As for the enemy (apart from his instinctive gesture in attempting to rescue drowning sailors from *L'Orient*), his drive was to annihilate them.

He had demonstrated once again in his headlong attack and his desire to continue the battle after hours of hard fighting that his fund of aggression was of heroic proportions, that he was a professional of violence of the highest order, going beyond that element necessary in all successful commanders to impress both those they led and those they served, suggesting again subconscious needs and drives to be fulfilled, or inner inadequacies to be compensated for. Coexisting with this there was a deeply empathetic thoughtfulness, which Miller recounts with pleasure to his wife:

> I had enjoyed the pleasure of finding the Admiral much better on the 6th, and he had given into my care the fitting of the Tonnant, and told me I should not in the least be interfered with, and he hoped I should see her all the way to England; that after so many services to the public I owed it to myself to pursue my own happiness. Though I had thought this before, I was pleased to find a man of his activity think so likewise, and am infinitely obliged to him for his consideration in putting me unasked in a fair way to return to my long, long wished for home – but let me keep down the thousand emotions that rise in my soul till this narrative is finished.[7]

This was the high point of Nelson's life. Wounded, victorious beyond any other admiral in living memory, his judgement, preparation and tactics utterly vindicated, he was surrounded by admiring captains, who immediately formed an Egyptian club to commemorate the event and presented him with a sword. For a moment at least he must have felt his radiant orb all around him.

Then came anticlimax. They had to refit their ships and prepare their prizes for sea, tasks of enormous mundane graft. Nelson, his head 'ready to split' and 'always sick', struggled with the after-effects of traumatic shock. But the individual driving strengths of Saumarez, Ball, Hallowell and Hood, team spirit and eagerness to realize the prize money tied up in the captured French ships, took them forward. Miller records that, 'To encourage and enable all my people to do much work in little time, I ventured to make every day a meat day, and to give them an additional half allowance of wine' (i.e. increased to a pint and a half, or almost a litre a day).[8]

By 7 August Nelson was writing to Evan Nepean, Secretary to the Board of Admiralty to say that eight of his ships were ready for any service. By the 14th he was able to send Saumarez to Gibraltar with six French prizes. He had already sent Berry away on the 6th in *Leander* with his dispatches, but as he wrote at the time to Lord Spencer, 'Was I to die this moment, Want of Frigates would be found stamped on my heart.'[9] He could not send his duplicates overland to London via Naples and Vienna until his long-lost frigates, which had been searching fruitlessly for him since late June, appeared out of the blue on the 14th and enabled him to send Capel away in *Mutine* with his duplicates.

In spite of his head wound, Nelson had his wits about him. He was taking care that nobody stole his thunder. He had already sent Lieutenant Duval to the Governor of Bombay with a personal account of his victory. The sword of Admiral Blanquet was on its way to the Lord Mayor of London, and now he specifically requested Sir William Hamilton not to pre-empt him: 'You will not send by post any particulars of this Action, as I should be sorry to have any accounts get home before my Dispatches.'[10] He also had his wits about him as far as the delicate matter of the Prize Agency was concerned. He wrote to tell his friend Alexander Davison that he had been unanimously appointed sole agent: 'They rely on your established character and abilities for a speedy payment of their Prize-Money, which all Agents hitherto so studiously endeavour to keep from them.'[11] He wrote the same day to his brother Maurice in the Navy Office, 'Whatever assistance you may give Davison or whatever he may wish to serve you in, I beg that you may never be considered, directly or indirectly, as having anything to do with the Agency.' Unlike some, he was determined to make sure that he could never be accused of lining his own pocket, or the pockets of his family, out of the blood of his men. Nelson's wounded secretary might normally have expected to have had a part in the Agency but during and after the battle had not risen to the occasion. Nelson was sufficiently unsentimental to get rid of him in one of the returning prizes: 'My Secretary I have recommended to be Purser of the *Franklin*. He has not activity for me.'[12]

On 19 August he sent Hood with two ships-of-the-line and three frigates to cruise off Alexandria and keep Bonaparte's Army bottled up and as far as possible unsupplied. He himself was to set off for Naples in *Vanguard*, with *Culloden*, *Alexander* and *Bonne Citoyenne*. But before he could weigh anchor he had a problem to solve. 'Most secret Orders and letters' had just arrived from St Vincent about the intended conquest of Minorca. These required him to sail immediately, but three French prizes, the *Guerrier*, *Heureux* and *Mercure*, were not yet ready for sea. His conservative estimate of their value was £60,000. Shared out this would produce, according to his own calculations, £3,750 for St Vincent as Commander-in-Chief, £1,000 for each of his captains, £625 for himself as a junior admiral, £75 for each of the lieutenants, and £2 4s. for each of the seamen and marines.[13] These were handsome sums, worth about three and a half years' pay for a captain and two months' pay for an ordinary seaman. Nelson destroyed the ships, and informed Spencer that he hoped the Admiralty would back his assurance to the squadron that though the ships had been destroyed they would be paid for. The apparent anomaly of Nelson's meagre share arose from the fact that prize money was always weighted in favour of captains, who received three-eighths of the value of a prize. But if there was a Commander-in-Chief he took one of the captain's eighths. If the Commander-in-Chief had flag officers below him, and St Vincent had a number, he kept only half of his one-eighth, the remainder being shared equally among the other flag officers. So the oddity was that Nelson collected only as much as the flag officers he left behind at Cadiz. According to a note Davison made three years later in 1801, Nelson's total prize money from the Nile ships (those sent home as well as those destroyed) came to £2,358 4s 6d., exactly the same as for Orde who had been making St Vincent's life such a misery off Cadiz, although St Vincent would be somethat compensated by his own share of £14,149 13s. There would of course be other rewards for Nelson, some of which had already been decided in London.

For a further month they made their way to Naples, to all intents and purposes lost to the world. Nelson's Band of Brothers was dispersing, the battle, as transient as a theatrical performance, was over. In a squall off

Stromboli, 'the poor wretched *Vanguard*' lost masts and seamen and for the rest of the journey was towed by *Thalia*. Yet Nelson could not rest. He wanted to finish the job. He had immediately appreciated the vulnerability of Bonaparte's army to a knockout blow. A handful of bomb ships could wreak havoc among the French transports in the crowded confines of Alexandria harbour and destroy his supply lines. But he was absurdly optimistic in thinking, 'If the Grand Signior [of Turkey] will but trot an Army into Syria, Buonaparte's career is finished.'[14] In the months to come he would plead in vain for bomb vessels from Naples, the Grand Signior and the Admiralty. In the immediate future he had to think of Hood's blockading ships and how long their supplies would last. He tried fruitlessly to integrate into his scheme of things a Portuguese squadron of four 74s under Rear-Admiral the Marquis de Niza, which had recently arrived at Naples, but, as he confessed to Sir William Hamilton, 'I never expect any real service from that Squadron'. Hamilton would look intently at the bearer of that message, 'Captain Nisbet, who you remember a boy.'[15] Nelson's stepson had arrived in Aboukir Bay in *Bonne Citoyenne*, one of his lost and wandering frigates.

For no one was the anticlimax following the battle greater than for Troubridge. The whole squadron had witnessed his running aground and *Culloden*, intended to lead the line of battle, had not fired a shot. His failure would haunt him for months ahead and prompt an orgy of over-work; *and* he had just learned of the death of his wife. Nelson was suffering from the effects of his wounds. In the release of tension his emotionalism was rampant. He wrote to Sam Hood, 'Our friend Troubridge has lost his wife and is in much distress', described himself to St Vincent as 'your affectionate Nelson', wrote to St Vincent of 'dear Troubridge and Ball', and dwelling on the state of his health: 'my head is nearly well, but I am from various causes I believe going fast: my hectic cough is now at that pitch that I believe my lungs are at every hour coming through my mouth.'[16] Or, again to St Vincent: 'On the day Hoste left me I was taken with a fever which has very nearly done my business; for eighteen hours my life was thought to be past hope; I am now up, but very weak in body and mind, from my cough and this fever. I never expect my dear Lord to see your face again; it may please God, that this will be the finish to that fever of anxiety which I have endured from the middle of June; but be that as it pleases His goodness – I am resigned to his will.' Paradoxically, he was feeling insecure too. 'My first order was to pay the strictest attention to all the orders and regulations of the

Commander in Chief; and I can truly say, that I have endeavoured to support your orders with all my might. We shall do very well whilst you stay below, but if you should go home, I shall be unfit for this command, where I want so many indulgences.'[17] Never was Nelson's emotional distress more clearly displayed, or his lack of inhibition in communicating his sufferings and feelings to others, in this case to his Commander-in-Chief – almost like a child to its mother. Few heroes have had a less stiff upper lip.

It was in a broken and battered state that *Vanguard* limped into the Bay of Naples on 22 September 1798, bearing an Admiral who was exhausted, emotional, self-absorbed and vulnerable. He had had some indication of feelings in Naples, for he had already received letters from Sir William and Lady Hamilton. Hers was more like an aria than a letter, an extravaganza of images, emotion and colour, rampaging vividly down the page:

My dear, dear Sir, How shall I begin, what shall I say to you – 'tis impossible I can write, for since last Monday I am delerious with joy, and assure you I have a fervour caused by agitation and pleasure. God, what a victory! Never, never has there been anything half so glorious, so compleat. I fainted when I heard the joyfull news, and fell on my side and am hurt, but well of that, I shou'd feil it a glory to die in such a cause. No I wou'd not like to die till I see and embrace the Victor of the Nile. How shall I describe to you the transports of Maria Carolina, 'tis not possible. She fainted and kissed her husband, her children, walked around the room, cried, kissed, and embraced every person near her, exclaiming, Oh Nelson, Nelson, what do we not owe to you, Oh Victor, savour of Itali, Oh that my swolen heart cou'd now tell him personally what we owe to him!

You may judge, my dear Sir, of the rest, but my head will not permit me to tell you half the rejoicing. The Neapolitans are mad with joy, and if you wos here now, you wou'd be killed with kindness. Sonets on sonets, illuminations, rejoicings; not a French dog dare shew his face. How I glory in the honner of my Country and my Countryman! I walk and tread in the air with pride, feiling I was born in the same land with the victor Nelson and his gallant band. But no more – I cannot dare not trust myself for I am not well.

We are preparing your appartment against you come. I hope it will not be long, for Sir William and I are so impatient to embrace you. I wish you cou'd have seen our house the 3 nights of illumination. 'Tis, 'twas covered with your glorious name. Their were 3 thousand lamps, and their shou'd have been 3 millions if we had had time. All the English vie with each other in celebrating this most gallant and ever memorable victory. Sir William is ten years younger since the happy news, and he now only wishes to see his friend to be completely happy. How he glories in you when your name is mentioned. He cannot contain his joy. For God's sake come to Naples soon. We receive so many Sonets and Letters of congratulation. I send you some of them to shew you how your success is felt here. How I felt for poor Troubridge. He must have been so angry on the sandbank, so brave an officer! In short I pity those who were not in the battle. I wou'd have been rather an English powder-monkey, or a swab in that great victory, than an emperor out of it . . .

The Queen bids me to say that she longs more to see you than any woman with child can long for anything she takes a fancy to and she shall be for ever unhappy if you do not come. God bless you my dear, dear friend. My dress from head to foot is alla Nelson. Ask Hoste. Even my shawl is in Blue with gold anchors all over. My earrings are Nelson's anchors; in short we are be-Nelsoned all over. I send you some Sonets, but I must have taken a ship on purpose to send you all written on you.[18]

In his own way, Sir William was scarcely less extravagant: 'History, either ancient or modern, does not record an Action that does more honour to the Heroes that gained the Victory, than the late one of the first of August. You have now completely made yourself, my dear Nelson, immortal. . . . You may well conceive, my dear Sir, how happy Emma and I are, in the reflection that it is you – Nelson – our bosom friend, who has done such wondrous good.'[19] Nelson had certainly become their 'bosom friend' very quickly. To date he had spent precisely three days in Naples, five years previously. However, he soon realized their letters had been a mere prologue, that Naples was indeed in ecstasy. Boats and bands were coming over the sea to meet them, their distant murmuring becoming a wall of sound as they neared the *Vanguard*. The King himself was in one boat, in another Sir William and Lady Hamilton. Here before his eyes and all around him was the story book Return of the Hero.

The Emma who moved like a Grace across the deck, palms held to her face, searching his face with her shining eyes, breathing, 'Oh God is it possible?'[20] collapsing with sweet abandon against his good arm, was a formidable challenge to Nelson's senses. At thirty-three she was Romney's 'divine lady', a goddess at the height of her powers. The scent and touch of this soft and glowing creature invaded his being. Yet this was not an assault with sexual intention; it was simply Emma's way of being a celebrated beauty. Like many beautiful women what she needed was constant reaffirmation of her capacity to enchant and enslave. On the face of it, Nelson had nothing physical or biological to offer such a splendid woman – the little Admiral, pale, exhausted, suffering, one-armed, with a horrid gash across his brow – but he had an aura of transcendent celebrity, the charisma of heroism and power. He was a wonderful scalp to add to her belt, a wonderful foil for her exhibition-ism, and in his diminutive vulnerability, a perfect subject for her kind and mothering nature.

Nelson's knowledge of Emma's previous life was probably not all that extensive. He knew she was of humble origin; he knew she had been Hamilton's mistress and was now his wife; he may have known of a con-nection with Hamilton's nephew before she became the second Lady Hamilton. He certainly did not know, and was never to know, that seventeen years previously she had had an illegitimate child, the result of her first contact with the aristocracy. She had been picked up by Sir Harry Featherstonhaugh, a noted young rake, possibly at 'Mrs Kelley's', a cross between club and brothel in London's Arlington Street.[21] He had taken her to his mother's great house, Uppark in Sussex and installed her, a spirited and desirable sixteen-year-old, in a cottage in nearby South Hartington. From there she joined his set of young blades in sports, dis-sipation and frolics, one of which may well have been her legendary naked dance on the dining table. Inclined by nature to be giddy and unthinking, she had proceeded headlong to give all she had to offer. When Sir Harry lost interest and she found herself pregnant, she was cast out from this golden circle. And so she appealed to another of his set, Charles Greville, the thirty-two-year-old second son of the Earl of Warwick, and favourite nephew of Sir William Hamilton. In the first instance she was looking for help and guidance in her efforts to recover

Sir Harry, but when that failed, she implored Greville to take her as his own mistress. Luckily for her the appeal succeeded, Greville saw her through her confinement, and when baby Emma had been deposited with her grandmother in the far north-west, he installed her in a little house in Paddington Green, promising her a new identity and respectability as Mrs Emily Hart, a name she had assumed during her confinement. Her mother, Mrs Lyon, who was included in the ménage, also changed her name, to Mrs Cadogan.

Greville had a hidden agenda. Having no fortune, and with an income of little more than £500 a year, he desperately needed an heiress. In the meantime he saw an opportunity to capitalize on Emma's beauty. Within two months of setting her up in Paddington he had her sitting for his artist friend George Romney. Over the next five years she was to sit more than 300 times for him. Most likely Greville thought he could create a demand for Emmas by commissioning pictures of her from this very fashionable painter. Like all Greville's schemes it was half baked and came to nothing. He found himself without sufficient money even to buy the pictures, let alone speculate in them. Romney does not seem to have minded. Enchanted by Emma's youth, beauty and enthusiasm and by her prodigious talent for expressing every nuance of feeling, the forty-eight-year-old painter painted her to his heart's content. She, in turn, basked in his adoration and, never slow to learn, absorbed everything he had to say, especially about theatrical realism.

Greville's relationship with Emma had been much more complicated. There was a kind of perversity and shallowness of feeling in it. Everything he had put on offer was conditional on Emma's moderating her naturally emotional and turbulent temperament and becoming a submissive, well-trained courtesan. Pygmalion-like, he set about the task of changing Emma's behaviour with a regime of rigid control. Such was Emma's youth, gratitude, desire to please and lack of alternative that she conformed and to an amazing degree did learn to control herself. He had also a declared sexual preference for 'girls of the town', and chose later to highlight an attribute of Emma's which he was not used to encountering: 'she is the only woman I have ever slept with without having ever had any of my senses offended, & a cleanlier, sweeter bedfellow does not exist'.[22] Greville and his uncle, both avid collectors, had been close friends and regular correspondents for more than a decade, in fact ever since Greville had visited Naples in 1769. It was inevitable that when

Hamilton returned to England in 1783 to bury his first wife, Emma should be put on display. They quickly became cosy. He was eventually allowed his kisses, she a flirtatious familiarity. He acknowledged frankly that the beauty of 'the sweet tea maker of Edgware Road' often had its effect.[23] He returned to Naples, having purchased Romney's *Bacchante* as a souvenir of her, a more appropriate choice than he could possibly have guessed.

Three years later, in 1786, Greville transferred Emma to Sir William. Greville's motives were to rid himself of all encumbrance, as he put it, in his renewed search for an heiress, and by reducing the risk of Sir William's remarrying he would strengthen his position as his uncle's heir. This transaction they finally accomplished in a gentlemanly and civilized way, that is to say without loss of face for either of them. It revealed, as did many other incidents throughout Hamilton's life, that a man could have a remarkably urbane approach to life, could possess smooth manners, every social grace and great aesthetic judgement, and yet at the same time be of coarse moral fibre. And so in 1786 Hamilton took possession of Emma on a sale or return basis. Neither he nor his nephew gave Emma any hint of their intentions and Greville frankly misled both of them. She felt deeply betrayed. Greville had rescued her, and had at least brought security and order into her life. Whatever it meant to her, she said she loved him. Now her security was once again at hazard as she moved to a third 'protector'.

Emma had been accompanied to Naples by her mother, a shadowy figure who nevertheless must have played a significant part in Emma's life. It is tempting to see her simply as a necessary and compliant chaperon or even as her daughter's procuress, a woman who saw that her daughter's face and form was their only hope of fortune. Emma genuinely cared for her and never hesitated to acknowledge her as her mother. And indeed Mrs Cadogan must have been a credible person for she earned the good opinions of Hamilton himself, Nelson and the Dowager Lady Spencer, among many others. Whether it was Emma alone or the women together who plotted to hoist Hamilton with his own petard, the fact is that after eight months of refusing his bed, she not only became his mistress but led him meekly to the altar some five years later. From the beginning Hamilton set out to educate and develop, encourage and praise her, and he quickly came to dote on her. Now, when Greville had passed Emma to Sir William he had stressed the need for control, the need not to give her too much rope, 'Give her an inch and she'll take a yard.'[24] As Hamilton's consort Emma was given singing lessons and Italian lessons and opportunities to expand her horizons. Being of an energetic and talented disposition she made the most of them and, becoming subject to a considerable volume of flattery, began to believe she was as marvellous as people said she was. On the other hand there is not the slightest indication that notwithstanding the frank immorality and voluptuousness of the Neapolitan Court, propositions offered by travellers, or the attentions of middle-aged libertines like the notorious Earl Bishop of Derry, she was ever seduced again. The conclusion has to be that she did not have the inclination, and that what she enjoyed or did not enjoy with Sir William suited her very well.

In choosing to encourage her in her 'attitudes', Sir William was probably ministering as perfectly to her needs and drives as he was to his own. When she performed these famous poses she was never more than flimsily clad. The histrionic use of her body, the feeling that she was being ogled by every man in the room and envied by most of the women, the murmurs of indrawn breath and ripples of frank admiration, probably gave her most of the thrills she desired. Sir James Bland Burges, the Foreign Under-Secretary of State, saw the whole exercise as, 'a variety of the most voluptuous and indecent postures.'[25]

But under the guise of Art, voyeurism was totally sanctioned, and that pleased Sir William too. According to Goethe the celebrated German poet, who visited Naples in 1787, Hamilton the collector had other voyeuristic tendencies, like the naked boys he paid to disport themselves in the sea for his afternoon entertainment. And there had been his work describing the discovery of the continued existence at Isernia in the Abruzzo of the cult of Priapus, which he sent to Sir Joseph Banks in 1781. It was subsequently included in a volume published by the Society of Dilettanti, of which he was a member, with a Discourse on the worship of Priapus by Richard Payne Knight. Sir William had acquired some wax *ex votos*, 'representing the males parts of generation', as he put it. He explained that the local euphemism for a phallus was 'St Cosmo's big toe', and it was quite in character that Hamilton should end his letter with a wish that Sir Joseph's 'big toe' should never fail him. The publicly shocking aspect of the whole business was of course that those who presented the vows were chiefly women, and Sir William reported that one had handed over hers with the words, 'Blessed St Cosmo, let it be like this'. The rather unwise publication of this piece of porno-voyeurism caused a stir among those of a prudish, censorious and chauvinistic disposition but perhaps the greater significance lies in Hamilton's wanting to supply the information at all. He deposited his collection of waxen phalluses with the British Museum on the same visit that led to his encountering Emma for the first time. His instruction to Dr Paul Henry Maty, Keeper of Natural and Artificial Productions, was to 'keep hands off them'. They were of course very fragile.[26]

Sir William, now sixty-eight, was brought up with the future George III, chiefly because his mother had been the mistress of George's father Frederick, Prince of Wales. He was the youngest son of the seventh son of the third Duke of Hamilton. He had married Catherine Barlow in 1758, frankly trading his name for her money. After a few years of running her estate in Wales and four years as a Member of Parliament for Midhurst he accepted the post of Envoy Extraordinary to the Court of Naples, not least because moving to a drier, warmer climate seemed imperative for Catherine's health. Shy, retiring, introvert, religious, she seems to have been plagued with asthma and 'nerves'. Fortunately the Hamiltons had a common interest, both loving music, Catherine being pre-eminent at the harpsichord and pianoforte and quite up to playing before the young Mozart when he and his father Leopold visited Naples in 1770. The young William Beckford, smitten by her empathetic charm, rhapsodized, 'so sweetly soft was her touch she seemed as if she had thrown her own essence into the music'. Of her love for Hamilton, at least in the mind and heart, she wrote movingly during her final illness, in papers not discovered till after her death, 'But how shall I express my love and tenderness to you, dearest of earthly blessings. . . . You never have known half the tender affection I have borne you because it has never been in my power to prove it to you.'[27]

Poor Catherine had not been well matched with this energetic, hedonistic and worldly husband. She had sought quiet and reflection, he activity and action. Her invalidism and his frequent absences were the reflection of a marriage without passion of any kind on one side and passion in the head only, on the other. But they had managed to be companionable, friendly and well tempered. Otherwise Naples had presented a wonderful opportunity for Hamilton to indulge his multifarious talents and interests and within a few years of his arrival in 1764 he had become a well known European figure. Fascinated by Vesuvius, he ascended it more than twenty times in his first four years and with laborious and courageous effort made minute and careful observations of its activity, all of which found their way back to the Royal Society in London, of which he became a Fellow in 1776. Mad about collecting, he acquired pictures, statues, bronzes, cameos, intaglios, amuletic rings, brooches, jewellery and curiosities. In 1772 the Trustees of the British Museum bought his first collection of vases for £8,500 to form the basis of its Department of Greek and Roman Antiquities. The four magnificent folios he had produced at a personal cost of £6,000 to illustrate his collection had a profound effect on the aesthetic and commercial success of Josiah Wedgwood. Not surprisingly, he was elected, *in absentia*, President of the newly formed Royal Society of Arts. He was prodigiously energetic, spending weeks in the hunting field with King Ferdinand, of whom Beckford said, 'give him a boar to stab, a pigeon to shoot at, a battledore or an angling rod and he is better contented than Solomon in all his glory'. In addition to all his other accomplishments Hamilton was also a crack shot. 'Sensa adulazione avete sparato come un angelo.' (Without flattery you shot like an angel.)[28] Besides all of this, he was socially gifted, entertaining, full of anecdotes and small talk, stage-managing his entertaining with style and panache. He was a man with a supercharged inner drive, as he explained to Sir Joseph Banks when after the death of his wife, he began work on the Queen's English Garden at Caserta: 'I promise myself great pleasure in this new occupation. As one passion begins to fail, it is necessary to form another; for the whole art of going through life tolerably in my opinion is to keep oneself eager about anything. The moment one is indifferent on s'ennuie, and that is a misery to which I perceive even Kings are subject.'[29]

The five years of the French Revolutionary wars had been hectic, but given his declining energy and the intrigues of the court, Hamilton's impact as an envoy was also declining. Nevertheless, life in Naples had suited him and he had been well placed to pursue his interests: collecting, moneymaking, and self-indulgence. 'Nothing at home, or even in a higher station abroad, would allow me to pass my time so much to my own satisfaction as I do at present.' He did not like people to think of him as a dealer, but such he most certainly was, albeit of an unofficial and discerning kind. It is not possible to describe by any other name the horse trading he did with the Duchess of Portland over the lovely vase which came to bear her name, nor his many attempts to sell his Correggio, about which Horace Walpole wrote to Horace Mann, 'I have seen it, it is divine – and so is the price; for nothing but a demi-devil that is a Nabob, can purchase it. What do you think of three thousand pounds?'[30] Nor does he seem to have been over-scrupulous. When he was being shown Hamilton's 'secret lumber-vault of art', the German poet Goethe noticed two bronze candelabra. 'With a sign I drew Hackert's attention to this treasure and in a whisper asked him if they did not look like those at the Portici museum. In reply he signalled to me to hold my tongue; it was not impossible that they might have strayed here from the cellars of Pompeii. Perhaps because of these and other fortunate acquisitions the Knight might have had very good reason for only allowing these hidden treasures to his most trustworthy friends.'[31]

Elisabeth Vigée-Le Brun, the French painter, tells in her *Memoirs* that she painted Madame Hart as a bacchante and how, 'He bargained for a while for the portrait of his mistress and eventually I agreed to paint it for a hundred louis; he subsequently sold it in London for three hundred guineas. Later when I painted Lady Hamilton again as a sibyl for the Duc de Brissac I decided to make a quick copy of the head and send it as a present to Sir William, who without hesitating sold it.'[32] In the same vein she recounts, 'This summerhouse reminds me of another incident involving Sir William. One day I sketched two small heads in charcoal upon one of the doors; I was very surprised to find the same sketches in England at the home of Lord Warwick, for Sir William had had the surface of the door sawn off and had sold my sketches; I do not remember the exact sum he obtained for them.' Hamilton was a singularly mercenary gentleman, and it was not surprising that he should have struck up a friendship with Nelson, for Nelson had many ships under his command whose holds might be very useful some day for transporting works of art to England.

After the death of his first wife Catherine in August 1782, there had been other potential second wives, and it seems astonishing that he was in the end prepared to marry so much below his station. Maybe he did it as a reaction to his passionless, if companionable first marriage, maybe to bring a more piquant sauce to his fading appetites, the foolish last chance syndrome of older men, or more simply, as a collector, to possess an amazing piece of human art; or maybe his Enlightenment rationality departed him and he was bewitched by this lovely creature. However it was she must have made herself necessary to his life. Onlookers tended to be basic, for example James Byres writing to the Bishop of Killaloe, 'Our friend Sir William is well. He has lately got a piece [of] modernity from England which I am afraid will fatigue and exhaust him more than all the volcanoes and antiquities in Naples.'[33] The celebrated Casanova was predictably cynical: 'He was a clever man but ended by marrying a young woman, who was clever enough to bewitch him. Such a fate often overtakes a man of intelligence when he grows old. It is always a mistake to marry, but when a man's physical and mental forces are declining, it is a calamity.'[34] Among his oldest friends was the first Countess Spencer, mother of George, who was now Nelson's First Lord of the Admiralty. The Spencers had visited Naples and Hamilton had acquired works of art for the Earl, with whom he was on terms of rather lewd correspondence. With Lady Spencer he was on even more intimate terms, a rather coy, 'naughty', and above all flattering correspondent, writing sentimentally in January 1770, 'When I retire in my old age I hope we shall set by the fire side together, talk over old times, while your grand children are playing about.'[35] In 1782, she wrote to him on Catherine's death. She was now a grandmother, and it was a long, friendly, family, newsy letter. In 1784 it was his turn to sympathize with her on the death of her husband.

It was against such a long established background of intimacy that Hamilton, in London and about to marry Emma, wrote to her on 17 August 1791 in a much more measured tone:

I took Bath in my tour principally to have the pleasure of seeing your Ladyship and I was cruelly disappointed when I heard that you was not there, however upon the whole it may be better for as it is not probable that I shall ever visit England again the taking leave of so good a Friend with that idea would have given me pain. Your Ladyship must have heard from more than one quarter that I am anxious to preserve a place in your good opinion and indeed I am. A man of 60 intending to marry a beautiful woman of 24 and whose character on her first outset in life will not bear a severe scrutiny seems to be a very imprudent step and so it certainly would be 99 times in 100, but I flatter myself I am not deceived in Emma's present character. We have lived together five years and a half and not a day has passed without her having testified her true repentance for the past and ardent desire to behave in such a manner for the future as to deserve universal esteem. At Naples her conduct has been such as to have conquered all difficulties and the very best company of both sexes solicit her acquaintance. But as I am in a publick character there and as you know must receive many English Families Emma must naturally have been subject to frequent mortifications and her sensibility is so great that her health has often been affected by it. In short I have at length consented to take off those difficulties and as the world calls it make an honest Woman of her . . . I do assure your ladyship that Emma is out of the common line and considering that she came to me without the least education has with the help of an uncommon good understanding and great application improved herself to such a degree as to astonish everybody. I am ashamed of having dwelt so long upon a subject that concerned me chiefly but tho I feel awkward I am relieved by having made a full confession to an old friend and that your Ladyship may continue to enjoy every blessing. It is an odd world but we must make the best of it – at least I will endeavour to do so – We leave England the first week of Sept.[36]

Lady Spencer's draft letter of reply has been preserved in the Althorp Papers. She found it difficult to strike the right note. She was tempted to be frank with him – 'indeed the fear of being consulted upon it was one great motive for my avoiding you as I should have been unwilling to have promoted a Marriage in which the probability is so strong against the happiness of both parties and yet I am sure I would not without pain have seen so extraordinary a young woman continue in the humiliating position in which she was placed'[37] – but struck out her words. A draft of two days later made no mention of Emma at all. However, the marriage did not lead to a break in their relationship. Letters passing between the two old friends in 1794 reveal quite clearly that Emma and Mrs Cadogan had both earned Lady Spencer's good will: 'My best regards I beg to Lady Hamilton – I often think of the Whist evenings and the Handils Musick & Songs at Caserta . . . hers and Mrs Cadogans kind care of my poor little girl.'[38] Compliments passed to and fro and by September 1795 Lady Spencer was pressing Hamilton to make sure Emma was properly provided for, prompting him to reply, 'Knowing how little we can count upon the duration of this life be assured that I shall not delay doing what you so kindly advise.' There was even a hint that Lady Spencer herself intended to make some provision for Emma: 'and you can depend upon my keeping your secret and burning your letters.'[39] Indeed Countess Spencer's favourable reaction to Emma was generally shared, although like every other celebrated beauty, Emma was fated to be judged by the world and his wife and naturally she did not appeal to everybody.

In the early days judgements were almost invariably complimentary. Lord Palmerston (not the future Prime Minister), who was observing constitutional discussions in Paris, met the Hamiltons on their way back to Naples after their wedding. He took to Emma. 'She is certainly very handsome and there is a plain good sense and simplicity of character about her which is uncommon and very agreeable. I have seen her perform the various characters and attitudes which she assumes . . . and was pleased even beyond my expectation though I had heard so much.'[40] Lady Malmesbury, travelling through Naples soon after, was also warm in her reaction: 'She really behaves as well as possible, and quite wonderfully considering her origin and education . . . I believe all the English mean to be very civil to her, which is quite right.' She talked of 'Lady Hamilton who behaves incomparably', and found her attitudes charming: 'the most graceful statues or pictures do not give you an idea of them. Her dancing the Tarantella is beautiful to a degree.'[41] Goethe met her on his 1787 visit to Naples when he was thirty-seven. He was swept off his feet by her beauty:

Sir William Hamilton, who is still living here as an English ambassador, has now, after many years of devotion to the arts and the study of nature, found the acme of these delights in the person of an English girl of twenty with a beautiful face and a perfect figure. He has had a Greek costume made for her which becomes her extremely. Dressed in this, she lets down her hair and, with a few shawls, gives so much variety to her poses, gestures, expressions etc., that the spectator can hardly believe his eyes. He sees what thousands of artists would have liked to express realised before him in movements and surprising transformations – standing, kneeling, sitting, reclining, serious, sad, playful, ecstatic, contrite, alluring, threatening, anxious, one pose follows another without a break. She knows how to arrange the folds of her veil to match each mood, and has a hundred ways of turning it into a head-dress. The old knight idolises her and is enthusiastic about everything she does. In her, he has found all the antiquities, all the profiles of Sicillian coins, even the Apollo Belvedere. This much is certain: as a performance it's like nothing you ever saw before in your life.[42]

But there was a sting in the tail, since Goethe valued qualities of mind and sensibility as much as physical beauty. He considered her 'by no means richly endowed in respect of mind';[43] he needed to be impressed by more than physical beauty. On the other hand his companion Tischbein the painter was as fully satisfied by her looks as was Romney. Sir Gilbert Elliot saw her some years later, in 1797, the year before the Nile.

Her face is beautiful. She is all Nature, and yet all Art; that is to say her manners are perfectly unpolished, of course very easy, though not with the ease of good breeding, but of a barmaid; excessively good-humoured and wishing to please and be admired by all ages and sorts of persons that come in her way; but besides considerable natural understanding, she has acquired, since her marriage, some knowledge of history and of the arts, and one wonders at the application and pains she has taken to make herself what she is. With men her conversation and language are exaggerations of anything I ever heard anywhere.[44]

Naval captains could generally be relied upon to fall at her feet. Captain Thomas Fremantle of the *Inconstant*, involved with Nelson in the *Ça Ira* engagement of 1795, was at first no exception. However, he changed his tune when he experienced the full force of Emma's managerial capacity applied to organizing his betrothed Betsy Wynne and her family over the arrangements for their wedding. His new wife captured another aspect of 'the well known and much admired Lady Hamilton . . . she makes no secret of the meanness of her birth, and is so little intoxicated by the splendour of her present situation, that her mother is always with her . . . she loudly says . . . that before she married Sir William she had not a gown to put on her back'.[45] Emma lacked neither self-confidence nor self-esteem.

In another important sense Emma was no longer in the same position as when Nelson had met her fleetingly in 1793. Then she had been married for only two years and was still consolidating her position as Hamilton's wife. When Naples had been forced into peace and neutrality by Bonaparte's successes in Italy and was increasingly vulnerable to French subversion, she flowered in a new role. The politics of the Court were divided on strategies for survival. The King was under the influence of the pro-French Marquis de Gallo. The Queen, together with Prime Minister Acton, continued to believe that the power of England offered their only hope of resisting the French, for whom the Queen, sister of the guillotined Marie Antoinette, nourished a hatred of a passionate intensity: 'Je poursuiverai ma vengeance jusqu'au tombeau.' In this polarized situation Maria Carolina needed a back door to the British Envoy and the obvious conduit was Emma, 'Ma bien chere Miledy'. As a result Emma's sense of self-importance had escalated; she now felt herself to be a seasoned political performer in the full confidence of the Queen. The flattering applause of Maria Carolina gave her the illusion of being centre stage, a dangerous position for a woman with a marked lack of self-knowledge.

The genie Hamilton had let escape was one of colourful and charming chemistry with vitality to match. She established herself instantaneously as a power in Nelson's life – more bewitching to his senses than any woman he had so far encountered. Emma overwhelmed him with her energy, her desire to please, her instinct for knowing exactly what kind of medicine he needed. Three days later he was writing openly and naïvely to his Fanny, 'I hope one day to have the pleasure of introducing you to Lady Hamilton. She is one of the very best women in the world. How few could have made the turn she has. She is an honour to her sex and a proof that even reputation may be regained but I own it requires a great soul. . . . Her Ladyship if Josiah was to stay would make something of him and with all his bluntness I am sure he likes Lady Hamilton more than any female. She would fashion him in 6 months inspite of himself.'[46]

Three days later Nelson is again writing, this time, 'The goodness of Sir William and Lady Hamilton is beyond every thing I could have expected or desired.'[47] By the beginning of October he is even more

fulsome: 'The continued kind attention of Sir William and Lady
Hamilton must ever make you and I love them and they are deserving of
the love and admiration of all the world.'[48] Such was Nelson's capacity
for sudden judgement when his heart was touched that within a fortnight
foundations for a frankly extravagant admiration were in place, based it
should be said on the flimsiest of evidence, and in particular having no
regard to the motives the Hamiltons might have had in so lionizing him.

Nelson's reception at Naples had been all a hero could desire. 'His
Sicillian Majesty came out three leagues to meet me, and directly came
on board. His Majesty took me by the hand and said such things of our
royal Master, our Country, and myself, that no words I could use would
in any degree convey what so apparently came from the Royal heart.
From his Majesty, his Ministers, and every class, I am honoured by the
appellation of "Nostro Liberatore." '[49] He was fêted to the highest
degree.

> The preparations of Lady Hamilton [he injudiciously began another
> letter to Fanny] for celebrating my birthday to-morrow, are enough
> to fill me with vanity; every ribbon, every button has 'Nelson' & c.
> The whole service is marked 'H.N. Glorious 1st of August!' – Songs
> and Sonnetti are numerous beyond what I ever could deserve. I send
> the additional verse to God save the King as I know you will sing it
> with pleasure.
>
> > [Join we great Nelson's name
> > First on the roll of fame
> > Him let us sing
> > Spread we his praise around
> > Honour of British ground
> > Who made Nile's shores resound
> > God save the King.]
>
> I cannot move on foot, or in a carriage, for the kindness of the
> populace; but good Lady H preserves all the papers as the highest
> treat for you.[50]

From now on his incantation of Lady Hamilton's name would be an
omnipresent feature of correspondence with his wife.

16

Disappointments, Dilemmas and Disharmony

I receive as I ought what the goodness of our Sovereign and not my desserts, is pleased to bestow

Nelson, December 1798

Professionally speaking, Nelson had not suspended his judgement. Something caused a snappy letter to St Vincent the day after his wonderful birthday party. 'I trust, my Lord, in a week we shall all be at sea. I am very unwell, and the miserable conduct of this Court is not likely to cool my irritable temper. It is a country of fiddlers and poets, whores and scoundrels.'[1] On his birthday he had written to Saumarez, 'This is a sad place for refitting, the swell sets in so heavy. Never again do we come to Naples: besides the rest we are all killed with kindness',[2] and to Lord Spencer on the same day, 'This Marquis de Gallo I detest. He is ignorant of common civility. . . . He admires his Ribbon, Ring and Snuff box so much that an excellent Petit-Maitre was spoiled when he was made a Minister.'[3]

From the moment he arrived he had sensed that further opportunities for taking advantage of his victory were being lost. 'I keep till Sunday morning, in hope some news may arrive from Vienna. What precious moments the two Courts are losing: three months would liberate Italy; this Court is so enervated that the happy moment will be lost.'[4] Nelson himself had been clear where he should be positioned. On his way to Naples he had written to St Vincent, 'I detest this voyage to Naples: nothing but absolute necessity could force me to the measure. Syracuse in future, whilst my operations lie on the eastern side of Sicily, is my Port where every refreshment is to be had for a Fleet.'

It is extremely important to remember, when it comes to judging his future conduct, that others were of a different opinion about his priorities. Spencer was very clear with St Vincent that Naples was the priority:

In every point of view it seems preferable that their headquarters should be in the neighbourhood of the Two Sicillies. They are more secure of supplies and more centrally situated for any purpose which may occur of employing them: and the great object of giving courage and support to the Kingdom of Naples, which from the peculiarity of its present connection with the Court of Vienna stands in a rather higher rank in the scale of politics than on a superficial view might at first appear, will be much more effectually obtained by the presence of such a naval force which may at the same time be very usefully employed in distressing Malta or in intercepting the communication between France and Egypt.[5]

Both St Vincent's Admiralty orders and Nelson's actions would reflect Grenville's marshalling of the Second Coalition against France. Although not yet in being, its formation had already been encouraged by increasing revulsion against France which following Campo Formio, 'unashamedly claimed the right to interfere in the internal affairs of other countries in the name of the principles of 1789, and spread the principles by propaganda backed by bayonets'.[6]

So, at this stage there was absolutely no question of Nelson's taking the initiative to linger at Naples. He was very consciously positioned there by the Admiralty for clearly defined purposes: protection of the coasts of Sicily, Naples and the Adriatic; active co-operation with the Austrian and Neapolitan armies; cutting off France from Egypt; blockading Malta and co-operation with the Turkish and Russian squadrons in the Archipelago – a sizeable agenda for his reduced force. For the remainder of 1798 Nelson was energetically engaged on the Admiralty's priorities, personally intervening to encourage Neapolitan land action under the Austrian General Mack, fruitlessly seeking supplies for his besieging forces at Malta and preparing to link up with the Russian and Turkish fleets in Adriatic operations directed at the islands of Corfu and Zante. British naval supremacy in the Mediterranean was unchallenged, and Nelson briskly engaged in doing what he could to collect the dividend of victory.

In parallel his relationship with Emma was developing, not just the simple effect of propinquity to a beautiful woman mirrored in his relaxed and rather arch letter to St Vincent: 'I am writing opposite Lady Hamilton therefore you will not be surprised at the glorious jumble of this letter. Were your Lordship in my place I much doubt if you could write so well; our hearts and our hands must be all in a flutter; Naples is a dangerous place and we must keep clear of it.'[7] He was now in a working relationship with Emma. Queen Maria Carolina was playing a power game to keep the British in Naples. Her husband's main energies were escapist, devoted to hunting, fishing and fornication. Hamilton, close to the King, could not himself afford to intrigue openly with the Queen and so she came to rely on Emma as the conduit to Hamilton.

Nelson found Emma very congenial to work with, in fact one of his own sort, energetic, committed, decisive and resolute. Having to rely on her for translation he admired her fluency in French and Italian. Her innate desire to please ensured that she was constantly in tune with his own views, a perfect acolyte. A very twentieth-century office relationship was about to develop. By early October he was writing fully fledged political letters to her, expressed in the strongest possible terms as the 'firm and unalterable opinion of a British Admiral'.[8] His assessment of the situation was clear:

> I cannot be an indifferent spectator . . . I have seen in Sicily . . . the utmost detestation of the French and their principles. . . . At Naples all ranks eager for War with the French . . . who are preparing . . . to plunder these Kingdoms and to destroy the Monarchy . . . I am all astonishment that the Army has not moved a month ago. I trust that the arrival of General Mack will induce the Government not to lose any more of the favourable time which Providence has put in their hands; for if they do, and wait for an attack in this Country, instead of carrying the war out of it, it requires no gift of pro-phecy to pronounce that these Kingdoms will be ruined, and the Monarchy destroyed . . . and may the words of William Pitt, Earl of Chatham be engraved on the heart of every Minister of this country . . . 'The boldest measures are the safest.'[9]

Nelson had the bit between his teeth, but at the same time he hastened to reassure St Vincent, 'You will not believe I have said or done anything, without the approbation of Sir William Hamilton. His Excellency is too good to them, and the strong language of an English Admiral telling them plain truths of their miserable system may do good.' There is something of a flavour of 'fools rush in' about this, about the King being 'very attentive', about the Queen being 'truly a daughter of Maria Theresa'. His head was being turned and the full weight of Lady Hamilton's arch flirtation is sent in St Vincent's direction: 'Lady Hamilton commands me to say she longs to see you her true Knight.'[10] By 13 October he is writing to St Vincent again: 'The King of Naples . . . inducing the emperor, & c., to go to War, is my very greatest reward, and I desire no other . . . Lady Hamilton is an Angel. She has honoured me by being my Ambassadress to the Queen: therefore she has my implicit confidence, and is worthy of it.' In a completely unbuttoned PS he adds, 'I cannot write a stiff formal public letter. You must make one or both so. I feel you are my friend, and my heart yearns to you.'[11]

He had sent Ball away on 4 October in the refitted *Alexander* with two frigates and a fire ship, to command the siege of Malta. Arriving off Malta on 24 October to assess the situation he had discovered no signs of Neapolitan officers in the island, nor any supplies from the Governors of Syracuse or Messina. He felt totally let down: 'I was led to believe [by Acton and the Marquis de Gallo] that promises of protection, with supplies of arms, ammunition, and provisions had been given to the Inhabitants of Malta.'[12] He expressed himself passionately to Sir William: 'The total neglect and indifference with which they have been treated, appears to me cruel in the extreme . . . I have sent Ball this day to summon Gozo: if it resists, I shall send on shore, and batter down the Castle.'[13] Three days later the French garrison of Gozo capitulated but when Nelson left for Naples on 30 November the French still held the fortress of Valletta. The blockade of Malta was to prove a dismal chapter of wanton failure on the part of the Neapolitans to strengthen and supply the starving besiegers, and on the part of the British Army in the Mediterranean to deliver means to force the capitulation of an equally starving French garrison. None of the many appeals he made were listened to, and St Vincent's successor, the egregious Lord Keith, who blamed Nelson for neglect of the siege of Malta, showed not the slightest idea of what to do differently. Malta fell in September 1800 only when the British Army had at last been prevailed upon to become properly involved.

Nelson had been reflecting on his victory. 'The more I think the more I hear, the greater is my astonishment at the good consequences of our Victory.' A wider tapestry of congratulation was also about to unfold as the powers of Europe and Asia Minor rushed to acknowledge his fame. The Grand Signior of the Ottoman empire declared war on the French and a present was to follow. St Vincent had written to him, personally and warmly on 28 October, with his usual sureness of touch, 'You're great in the Cabinet as on the Ocean and your whole conduct fills me with admiration and confidence. I thank God that your health is restored and that the luscious Neapolitan dames have not impaired it. God bless you my dear Admiral and be assured no man loves or values you more highly than your truly affectionate St Vincent.'[14] But still effectively cut off from England, it was not until 17 or 18 November that Nelson received news of his elevation to the peerage, via a copy of the *London Gazette*. He did not receive Spencer's official letter until 7 December.

His reply was polite and decent, with only the barest tinge of bitterness:

On my arrival here from Leghorn I received your Lordships letter of October 7, communicating to me the Title his Majesty had been graciously pleased to confer upon me – an Honour, your Lordship is pleased to say, the highest that has ever been conferred on an Officer of my standing who was not a Commander in Chief. I receive as I ought what the goodness of our Sovereign, and not my desserts, is pleased to bestow but great and unexampled as this Honour may be to one of my standing, yet I own I feel a higher one in the unbounded confidence of the King, your Lordship, and the whole world, in my exertions.[15]

Perhaps Spencer felt a little ashamed when he received this letter. At any rate the first of a series of misjudgements he was to make in handling Nelson had been made. It was essential for Nelson to feel that he had been treated fairly. He was so absolutely punctilious himself in ensuring that those alongside and below him got their just deserts.

Currently it was a question as to whether Troubridge would receive, a Nile medal and his first lieutenant the customary automatic promotion. He praised Troubridge as unequivocally as he knew how: 'I am not surprised that you [St Vincent] wish him near you; but I trust you will not take him from me. I well know he is my superior; and I so often want his advice and assistance.'[16] He was very anxious that Troubridge should not be overlooked: 'He commanded a Division equally with Sir James Saumarez . . . ; and I should feel distressed if any honour is granted to one, that is not granted to the other . . . it was Troubridge that equipped the Squadron so soon at Syracuse . . . it was Troubridge who saved

Culloden, when none that I know in the Service would have attempted it – it was Troubridge whom I left as myself at Naples to watch movements – he is, as a Friend and an Officer, a non pareil!'[17] In the midst of his own disappointment he still had the greatness of mind and heart to press Troubridge's case with Spencer himself

> I observe what your Lordship is pleased to say relative to the presenting myself, and the Captains who served under my orders, with medals, and also that the First Lieutenants of the Ships engaged will also be distinguished by promotions, also the senior Marine Officer. I hope and believe the word 'engaged' is not intended to exclude the *Culloden*: the merit of that Ship and her gallant Captain are too well known to benefit by anything I could say. Her misfortune was great in getting aground . . . I am confident that my good Lord Spencer will never add misery to misfortune. Indeed no person has a right to know that the *Culloden* was not as warmly engaged as any Ship in the Squadron . . . In the midst of his great misfortunes he made those signals which prevented certainly the *Alexander* and *Swiftsure* from running on the shoal. I beg your pardon for writing on a subject which, I verily believe, has never entered your Lordship's head, but my heart, as it ought to be, is warm to my gallant friends.[18]

Nelson did not live his life by analytical impersonal reasoning, or indeed by *rules* of any kind. His personal values and feelings were always fully engaged to form the basis of his judgements. Naturally he did not sympathize with the judgements of those whose personalities worked in the opposite mode.

In his own case all surrounding him in Naples were up in arms. Lady Hamilton expressed herself in a characteristically unladylike fashion to Lady Nelson. 'Sir William is in a rage with ministers for not having made Lord N. a Viscount; for sure this great Action, greater than any other, ought to have been recompensed more. Hang them I say!'.[19] Earlier she was on the record as saying, 'If I was King of England I would make you the most noble puissant DUKE NELSON, MARQUIS NILE, EARL ALEXANDRIA, VISCOUNT PYRAMID, BARON CROCODILE, and PRINCE VICTORY, that posterity might have you in all forms.'[20] Now that he was also learning of the reaction of family and supporters such as Lord Hood, a note of injured and unreasonable irritation creeps in: 'I have not received a line from England since the 1st of October. Lord St Vincent is in no hurry to oblige me now; in short I am the envied man, but better that than to be the pitied one. Never mind: it is my present intention to leave this country in May.'[21] It cannot have helped his frame of mind to feel the note of pomposity in a letter from his royal 'friend', HRH the Duke of Clarence. 'On Captain Capel's arrival with the news of your glorious Victory, I was both astonished and hurt at not receiving a line from my old friend. But now being assured that you had written by *Leander* I take up my pen.'[22]

Spencer's next mismanagement of Nelson was his failure to recall him, to bring him home to sport his laurels before an adoring public and receive the homage of the nation that was his due. The naval war in the Mediterranean was self-evidently over; there was no need for Nelson to remain. It is not as though the possibility had never been raised. Spencer had sent one of Nelson's letters, probably that of 29 November, to Lavinia and she, in typical Lavinia fashion, was on to the point in a flash:

I enclose to you my best love your letter from Nelson and I return you my sincere thanks for having allowed me to see it. The dear little creature puts me into a fidgit about his health – surely you will let him come back when he asks it – he will be a longer time useful by a well timed respite than he can possibly be by working him to death 'toute d'un trait' [at one stretch] he is exactly like the thoroughbred Mail coach horses that one hears of now and then that go on drawing till they drop down dead having lost shoes hoofs and everything –[23]

Lavinia had clearly succumbed to Nelson's charm two years previously and the term 'dear little creature' must distinguish him from every other hero in the British Pantheon. It is doubtful whether any other eighteenth-century ministerial wife gave her husband such brutally succinct and elegantly expressed advice about the affairs of his department – no wonder Spencer's rackety sisters, Georgiana and Henrietta, did not take to her. Alas, Spencer was not listening.

Around this time tongues may have begun to wag at home concerning Nelson's continued absence and his evident admiration for Lady Hamilton. Even so, gossip must have sped back amazingly quickly if it was at all the cause of Alexander Davison's letter of 7 December. More likely his letter was chiefly motivated by Fanny's own growing impatience:

> I cannot help again repeating my sincere regret at your continuation in the Mediterranean; at the same time I would be grieved that you should quit a station, if it in the smallest degree affected your own feelings. You certainly are, and must be, the best and only judge. Yet you must allow your best friends to express their sensations. . . . Your valuable better half writes to you. She is in good health, but very uneasy and anxious, which is not to be wondered at. She sets off with the good old man tomorrow for Bath. Lady Nelson this moment calls and is this moment with my wife. She bids me say, that unless you return home in a few months she will join the standard at Naples. Excuse a womans tender feelings . . . they are too acute to be expressed.[24]

Crossing with this letter was Emma's to Fanny, written on 2 December, which would not have been at all pleasing to her with its familiar flavour and proprietorial air as far as her husband was concerned: 'by nursing and asses milk . . . quite recovered . . . the King and Queen adore him . . . we only wanted you to be completely happy . . . Josiah is much improved in every respect, we are all delighted with him . . . Sir William desires his kind compliments to your Ladyship, and to Lord Nelson's dear respected father.'[25]

Before these letters reached their destinations events in Naples had taken a dramatic turn. While he was in the process of moving his base to Syracuse Nelson was intercepted off the west end of Sicily by King Ferdinand and Prince Leopold who put pressure on him to return to Naples and 'be useful in the movements of their Army'. Nelson changed his plans. He wrote to John Spencer Smith, Minister at Constantinople, 'I was anxious to go to Egypt from this place . . . but the King of Naples has begged me so earnestly that I would be at Naples in the first week in November, the commencement of the war, that I could not refuse him, especially as my orders are to protect the Kingdom of the Two Sicilies.'[26] The King and Queen had been thoroughly alarmed by Nelson's intention to move to Syracuse and concentrate his attention on Malta and the Levant, and so when he got back to Naples the Queen, no doubt histrionically aided and abetted by Emma, seduced Nelson into a promise which he rather ruefully reported to St Vincent: 'I am, I fear, drawn into a promise that Naples Bay shall never be left without an English Man-of-War. I never intended leaving the Coast of Naples without one; but if I had, who could withstand the request of such a Queen?'[27] His promise chimed with his orders but his personal entanglement with personalities and events in Naples was beginning to create connections which would inevitably determine his future personal priorities.

Naples had been neutral and nominally at peace with France since October 1796 but was highly resentful of Jacobin influence and propaganda permeating its borders from adjacent French satellites. Driven by Maria Carolina's overwhelming hatred of the French and aided and abetted by Nelson and the Hamiltons, Naples decided on a pre-emptive strike and declared war. They could find justification in the support gathering around them. In May 1798 Austria had promised to provide 60,000 troops if Naples was attacked. In November Russia had agreed to cover Sicily. In December Britain had guaranteed full naval support and the Turks had offered 10,000 Albanians. Even now there were Russian and Turkish naval units in the Adriatic. However, at the critical moment, vital Austrian support would be withheld on the grounds that Naples the aggressor could not invoke a defensive treaty.

Nelson had been asked by the King to organize an offensive on the basis of presumed Austrian support. Nelson had initially characterized Mack, the Austrian General who had arrived there in early October 1798, as one 'who cannot move without five carriages'. However, under the influence of a dinner party given by the King and Queen who adjured the General 'to be by land, what my hero Nelson, has been by sea', Nelson changed his mind. 'He is active and has an intelligent eye, and will do well, I have no doubt.' The plan was that 4,000 infantry and 6,000 cavalry would take Leghorn. *Vanguard*, *Culloden*, *Minotaur*, two Portuguese ships and the *Alliance* store ship would convey the infantry, a Neapolitan ship the cavalry. Meanwhile Mack was to march on Rome with his 30,000, 'la plus belle Armee d'Europe'. The confident expectation was that the Emperor of Austria would attack the French rear. Then came the last-minute crisis. No help was to be forthcoming from the Austrians, who wanted the French to be identified as aggressors before

they would take up arms against them. Nelson threw the full force of his
character into this critical moment and as he put it to Lord Spencer, 'I
ventured to tell their Majesties directly that one of the following things
must happen to the King, and he had his choice, – Either to advance,
trusting to God for his blessing on a just Cause, to die with l'epée à la
main, or remain quiet and be kicked out of your Kingdoms.'[28] Admirably
aggressive though these sentiments were, they were unfortunately based
on a totally superficial appreciation of Neapolitan capability for fighting,
Ferdinand's capacity to lead, and Mack's capacity to command. He knew
that Mack had been outmanoeuvred during his own manoeuvres. He
knew that Neapolitans had run away at Toulon.

Nelson had put himself in a most dangerous position, exercising
influence and leadership without being in a position to command, and
having to communicate his dramatic sentences via the equally dramatic
Emma. He could not communicate sensitively and flexibly because his
only language was English. It was a highly political situation calling
for political skills and insight. Sir William, the man who ought to have
supplied them, had neither the energy nor the will to take command. He
had been unable or unwilling to make his voice heard in the councils of
war. Lord Grenville had warned him clearly that any plan to attack the
French would have to have the fullest support of Vienna. Yet he was
swept along by Nelson, Emma and the Queen, and probably devoting
more attention than he should to packing fourteen cases of pictures and
five cases of marbles and bronzes, his vases already being on their
way home in the *Colossus*. Given their joint political blunder in their premature declaration of war, 'It was not unreasonable for the Austrian
court to blame Nelson; and by an easy extension to blame the British
Government.'[29]

By 6 December Nelson's judgement was catching up with his ardour.
Writing to congratulate Commodore Duckworth on the capture of
Minorca, he was in a realistic mood. 'Naples is just embarked in a new
war: the event, God only knows; but without the assistance of the
Emperor, which is not yet given, this country can not resist the power of
France'.[30] By the 11th he was giving Spencer the bad news that the
Neapolitan Army was falling to pieces, 'The Neapolitan Officers have
not lost much honour, for God knows they had but little to lose; but they
lost all they had. . . . General St Philip had gone over to the French . . .
General Michaux . . . ran away, as did all the Infantry.'[31]

By the 15th the King was back in Naples. Crisis was in the air. *Vanguard* had shifted her berth out of gunshot of the forts and Nelson was urgently recalling Troubridge. To Spencer he adopted a breezily direct and confident tone, 'There is an old saying – that "when things are at the worst, they must mend". No the mind of man cannot fancy things worse than they are here. But, thank God, my health is better, my mind never firmer, and my heart in the right trim to comfort, relieve and protect those who it is my duty to afford assistance to'.[32] The prospect of activity in which he was to be the prime mover changed his mood. He was now caught up in headlong and secret preparations for a flight from Naples to Sicily.

The voyage to Sicily marked a new stage in Nelson and Emma's relationship. *Vanguard*, packed with the royal family and its court, ran into the worst storm Nelson had ever experienced. The royal family and its servants were hysterical with terror or prostrate with seasickness, the youngest royal child was having epileptic fits, Sir William, terrified of death by drowning, cowered in his cabin, pistol at the ready to blow out his brains should the ship founder. In the midst of this was Emma, sleeves rolled up, supporting, rallying, comforting and nursing. Her prodigious physical and mental energy, and devotion, showed Nelson a new side of her and by the time *Vanguard* at last lay alongside the mole at Palermo, Emma was in his eyes an equal partner; together they had brought the King and Queen to safety.

The Queen who went ashore was more *jolie laide* than conventionally beautiful, though she had a reputation for seduction and sexual appetite. Lieutenant Parsons, then a midshipman in *Foudroyant* and a veritable Cherubino in his susceptibility to ladies, describes her in glowing terms: 'This energetic woman, whose slender and perfect form seemed to tread on air, while the tender animation of her sparkling eyes expressed a warmth of heart that prompted her (at least in my imagination) to embrace all around her.'[33] Years previously Catherine Hamilton had described the Queen as 'quick, clever, insinuating when she pleases, hates and loves violently. . . . Her strongest and most durable passions are ambition and vanity, the latter of which gives her a strong disposition to coquetry, but the former which I think is her principal object, makes her use every Art to please the King in order to get the Reins of Government into her hands in as great a measure as is possible.'[34] Bonaparte said of her: 'C'est le seule homme de son royaume.'[35]

The Admiralty's orders of 3 October 1798 had clearly stressed that Nelson should give 'the most cordial and unlimited support and protection to His Majesty's allies . . . and most carefully to avoid giving to any of them the smallest cause for suspicion, jealousy, or offence'. These orders explain some of the excessive saccharin with which he surrounds references to the Queen, and the alacrity with which he responded to her every requirement. But, as a woman of energy, self-direction and aggression, she too chimed with Nelson's personality. Maria Carolina and Emma were a formidable team. Through her role as interpreter the lovely Emma had control of communication and with her dramatic nature was capable of playing the Queen to an even greater effect than the Queen herself. Romney's friend Hayley had likened Emma's features to the language of Shakespeare in their power to express 'all the gradations of every passion with the most fascinating truth'.[36] A man as susceptible as Nelson could not fail to respond. And there was also the satisfaction the socially obscure Nelson obtained from conducting an intimate and influential relationship with royalty.

Then came a third and astonishingly insensitive piece of Spencer mismanagement. Captain Sir Sidney Smith, a flamboyant young exhibitionist, arrived on the scene in the 80-gun *Le Tigre*, bound for the Levant. He announced that he would take Sam Hood and his ships under his command. Nelson, incandescent with rage and pain, poured them out immediately to St Vincent:

> My dear Lord, *I do feel for I am a man*, that it is impossible for me to serve in these seas, with the Squadron under a junior officer: – could I have thought it! – and from Earl Spencer! . . . The Swedish Knight [Sir Sidney Smith was a Knight Grand Cross of the Order of the Sword of Sweden] writes Sir William Hamilton that he shall go to Egypt, and take Captain Hood and his Squadron under his command. The Knight forgets the respect due to his superior Officer: he has no orders from you to take my ships away from my command; but it is all of a piece. Is it to be borne? Pray grant me permission to retire.[37]

The government was right to wish to take advantage of the Nile to make a positive impact on the Turks. The British Minister at the Porte in Constantinople was John Spencer Smith, Sir Sidney's brother, and this was the rationale for entrusting the mission to him. Fortunately St Vincent was no more enamoured of Sir Sidney and his behaviour than was Nelson, who received a swift reply to his *cri de coeur*:

> I am not surprised at your feelings being outraged, at the bold attempt Sir Sidney Smith is making to wrest a part of your Squadron from you. I have received much the same letter from him . . . a copy of which with my answer, you have enclosed, and orders for you to take him immediately under your command. I have informed Lord Spencer of all these proceedings, and sent him copies of the letters. The ascendance this Gentleman has over all His Majesty's Ministers is to me as astonishing, and that they should have sent him after the strong objection I made to him, in a private letter to Mr Nepean, passes my understanding.[38]

St Vincent had in fact been very direct with Spencer: 'An arrogant letter written by Sir Sidney Smith . . . has wounded Rear Admiral Nelson to the quick . . . affronted by his embassy and separate command . . . compels me to put this strange man immediately under his Lordship's orders . . . I experienced a trace of the presumptuous character of this young man during his stay at Gibraltar.'[39] He also knew exactly how to handle Nelson and tried to bind his wounds: 'I trust the greatness of your mind will keep up the body, and that you will not think of abandoning the Royal Family you have by your firmness and address preserved from the fate of their late Royal relations in France. Employ Sir Sidney Smith in any manner you think proper; knowing your magnanimity, I am sure you will mortify him as little as possible, consistently with what is due to the great characters senior to him on the List, and his superiors in every sense of the word. God bless you my dear Lord, be assured no man loves and esteems you more truly than your very affectionate, St Vincent.'[40] This time Spencer realized he had made a mistake but the damage was done and he could not retrieve the situation. Sir Sidney and Nelson were on a collision course which would in the end reveal that compared with Sir Sidney, Nelson was a model of modesty and obedience. He antagonized *everybody* in the Mediterranean, St Vincent spoke of his being 'completely absorbed in the importance of his ambassadorial character'. Nelson despised 'such frippery and nonsense as he is composed of'.

Troubridge recoiled. 'Sir Sidney talks so large, as a member of the divan and plennippo that he made me sick.' Keith, referred to him as 'that madman Sir S Smith'. When he arrived Nelson's reaction was composed; he placed him in command of the blockade of Alexandria (but by implication of none of his own ships).

New Year 1799 opened with a still irritated Nelson asking for leave. To Fanny he gave vent to his anger: 'The first week in March it is my intention if I get leave to quit this situation for, as a piece of my command is lopped off by the great S.S.S. there can be no occasion for a Nelson.'[41] To his brother William he grumbled, 'I shall rejoice if Ministry will do anything kind for my family but, believe me, I have no dependence on any of them.' He seemed even to be detaching himself from the Neapolitan royal family: 'the Imperial Court acts in such a way, that it's difficult to forsee what is to happen six months hence, but by May I hope to be in England to rest during the summer.'[42] He commented gloomily to St Vincent on the dismal performance of the Neapolitan Army, 25,000 strong against the French 8,000: 'Is not this a dream? Can it be real?'[43]

By the middle of January General Pignatelli had made a treaty with the French, who entered Naples on 23 January, resisted only by the *lazzaroni* (the ordinary people). On the 27th, the French General Championnet announced that the Neapolitan monarchy was at an end and the Parthenopean Republic established.

Amidst the military disasters Nelson's own feelings remained subdued and his health suffered. By the end of January plenty of people were to learn that he was unwell. Not even a congratulatory letter from the great Lord Howe, hero of the Glorious First of June, could greatly raise his spirits, although it was

> an honour the most flattering a Sea Officer could receive, as it comes from the first and greatest Sea-Officer the world has ever produced. I had the happiness to command a Band of Brothers; therefore night was to my advantage. Each knew his duty, and I was sure each would feel for a French ship . . . and had it pleased God that I had not been wounded and stone blind, there cannot be a doubt but that every Ship would have been in our possession. But let it not be supposed that any Officer is to blame. No, on my honour, I am satisfied each did his very best.[44]

His reply was wonderfully typical, and exemplified his generosity of spirit as well as his deep conviction that annihilation of the enemy is a commander's first objective.

It was when the Neapolitan situation was at such a catastrophically low ebb that a flood of congratulatory letters reached him in February, from Lord Minto, who enclosed a copy of his speech to the House of Lords, from the Lord Chancellor, the Lord Chancellor of Ireland, the Speaker of the House of Commons, the Speaker of the House of Commons of Ireland, the Mayor of Liverpool, the Lord Mayor of London, HRH the Duke of Clarence, and three old friends, Captain Locker, Lady Parker and Vice-Admiral Goodall. To Goodall he was very warm, 'It is the part of a friend to take care of the reputation of an absentee: you have performed that part and have my gratitude . . . I have to thank you for your hint of Supporters and Mottoes. Those things I leave to the Herald's Office as unworthy of our notice.' He chose on this occasion to mask his interest (for which there is plenty of evidence) in the detail of his coat of arms. He also displayed his seam of melancholy. 'For soon, very soon, we must all be content with a plantation of six feet by two, and I probably shall possess this estate much sooner than is generally thought; but whilst I live, I never shall forget the few real friends I have in this world.'[45] He returned to his theme with Lady Parker, who loved him like a son:

What shall I say to you and good Sir Peter for all your goodness to me; you who have known me from my youth even till now, know that Horatio Nelson is still the same – affectionate in his disposition and grateful to his friends. God knows, my dear friend, I have few indeed! When I go hence, and am seen no more, I shall have very very few to regret me. My health is such that without a great alteration, I will venture to say a very short space of time will send me to that bourne from which none return; but God's will be done. After the action I had nearly fell into a decline, but at Naples my invaluable friends Sir William and Lady Hamilton nursed and set me up again. I am worse than ever; my spirits have received such a shock that I think they cannot recover it. You who remember me always laughing and gay, would hardly believe the change; but who can see what I have and be well in health? Kingdoms lost and a Royal Family in distress; but they are pleased to place confidence in me, and whilst

I live and my services can be useful to them, I shall never leave this Country, although I know that nothing but the air of England, and peace and quietness, can perfectly restore me.[46]

Nelson recognized his changed state now that the euphoria of his welcome and the headlong action which followed the Neapolitan campaign had worn off. He had not the words to diagnose his condition as depression. He was still suffering from the aftermath of battle, exacerbated by a new set of anxieties, still stretched beyond his emotional capacity, temporarily succumbing to his vulnerability to emotional distress. By the time he came to reply to Locker he was back on an even keel, reminding his mentor that it was he, 'who always told [me] Lay a Frenchman close, and you will always beat him.'[47] But he continued uncharacteristically pessimistic with St Vincent on 13 February: 'I see but gloomy prospects, look which way I will. . . . At present I see but little prospect of the fall of Malta; several vessels with provisions are got in. In short, my dear Lord, everything makes me sick, to see things go to the Devil, and not to have the means of prevention.' Sicily itself was under threat from a potential French drive to the south through Calabria. He was not bearing up well under a cloud of ambiguity and uncertainty. Toleration of ambiguity was not his strong suit. Gordian knots were not there to be unravelled but to be cut through, hence his despairing letter to Davison about the end of the month: 'Thank you most heartily, my dear Davison, for your letter. Believe me, my only wish is to sink with honour into the grave, and when that shall please God, I shall meet death with a smile. Not that I am insensible to the honours and riches my King and Country have heaped upon me, so much more than any Officer could deserve; yet I am ready to quit this world of trouble, and envy none but those of the estate six feet by two.'[48]

Dangerous and difficult though his situation was, he was clearly mentally unwell. A sense of this must have conveyed itself to St Vincent, who expressed worries to Spencer about both of his favourites: 'Yet I am much more affected by the discontents of Lord Nelson and Captain Troubridge: the former continuing seemingly determined upon relinquishing his command and returning to England and the latter in such a state of despondency from the slight he has received which he terms an indelible disgrace that I really am put to my wits end how to act.'[49]

Just at this moment when Nelson really needed to leave, and when leaving would have altered the course of his personal history, Spencer not only did not remember Lavinia's shrewd advice, but wrote Nelson a letter which made it impossible for him to go home:

> I am much concerned to perceive that you so often allude to your health being in a bad state. I am aware that you must have undergone very great fatigues and anxieties, but I trust that the brilliant successes which have hitherto attended, and . . . will I hope, ever continue to attend, your exertions in the service of your King and Country will make you ample amends for all your labours; and the reflection of the great advantages derived by the Public from your presence in the Mediterranean, will induce you (unless it should be absolutely necessary for you to return), to postpone the idea of it till matters are in a state a little more settled.[50]

Six months after the battle of the Nile there was not the slightest dubiety in Spencer's mind that Nelson's focus on the affairs of Naples and his conduct there was highly approved of: he was expected to stay there until further notice. Thus he wrote to St Vincent on 12 April, 'We of this house are all anxious to get home, yet, in the present moment, cannot move. Indeed we have been the mainspring, joined with you, that have kept and are keeping this so much out of repair machine from breaking to pieces.'[51]

In April there was a further blow to his expectations. The Admiralty had paid a poor price for the French prizes destroyed at Aboukir, engendering more disappointment and disillusion. To Spencer he was diplomatic: 'I observe what your Lordship is pleased to say about the worst Ships being destroyed.' He gave way without animus on the question of promotion for his brother Maurice. 'It is natural, my dear Lord, that I should be anxious for the rise of a beloved brother, after thirty years' service, to something beyond a Clerk. A Commissioner's situation was my desire for him, but I submit, that it is not right at present for my wishes on this point being complied with.'[52] A fortnight later he was revealing his real feelings to Davison:

> Your observation respecting the Prizes destroyed in Egypt is most just; for so far from being the worst, but not so much beat to pieces as the others, whose sides a carriage might have been driven in. Lord Spencer's plan ['to allow a sum equivalent to the least valuable of

the other Prizes, as it is reasonable to suppose, that those which you were under the necessity of burning were the worst-conditioned Ships amongst those which were captured'[53]] is not fair to the captors. Suppose I had kept the Squadron to have fitted out those Ships: it would, on my honour, have cost the Nation 40,000 L., besides the services of the ships. I shall know better another time, and will from this very hard conduct, fit out at any expense all my Prizes.

He added, 'Poor Maurice seems forgot by both Mr Pitt and Lord Spencer, or worse than forgot. I feel it all.'[54] He was outspoken with Berry, feeling he had let down all those who had placed their trust in him. 'The conduct going to be pursued about the Ships I ordered to be burnt, is mean and unjust. All our friends here think as I do on that subject'.[55]

17

Neapolitan Affairs

Tria Juncta in Uno

Nelson, October 1799

Vice-Admiral Lord Keith, who had joined the Mediterranean fleet in December 1798 as St Vincent's second-in-command, wrote to his sister on 10 April 1799, 'It is here reported Lord Nelson is to go home immediately. Lord St V says he shall not go in the *Vanguard*. The world says he is making himself ridiculous with Lady Hamilton and idling his time at Palermo when he should have been elsewhere – so says G Hope and the officers who are come thence to me.'[1] George Hope was of course the officer who had taken Nelson's frigates off their rendezvous in 1798, and it is quite conceivable that he had received the rough end of Nelson's tongue for it when they finally met up in Aboukir Bay. Later in the month Keith has more gossip to pass on: 'A ship from Palermo brings the most wretched account of Sicily . . . the Queen, Lady Hamilton. General Acton and Lord N. . . . n cutting the most absurd figure possible for folly and vanity. They are the cabinet and ordered Mac [Mack] to march, now they call him traitor.'[2]

Keith, who was either ignorant of or discounted the Admiralty's orders to Nelson, had not the slightest compunction in spreading tasteless gossip about him. In fact, Nelson was mobilizing his force to take war to the enemy. On 10 March 1799 General Stuart had literally appeared out of the blue with 1,000 English troops, which stationed at Messina would secure Sicily against French attack: 'It will be an electrical shock to the good and the bad.'[3] This allowed Nelson to send Troubridge with five sail-of-the-line to blockade Naples and take possession of all the islands in the Bay of Naples. By 12 April Troubridge had taken Procida, Capri and the Ponza islands, was in contact with Royal forces under Cardinal Fabrizio Ruffo sweeping up though Calabria, and the local

Neapolitan *lazzaroni* were ready to overthrow the French Parthenopean Republic.

Far to the north-west, the French Admiral Bruix had escaped from Lord Bridport's blockade at Brest, was joined by five Spanish ships off Ferrol, and sailed south for the Mediterranean with twenty-five ships-of-the-line. In London the Admiralty tried to guess what the enemy intended. Admiral Young, one of the board's Neptunes, thought Italy.[4] Secretary Marsden opted for Naples,[5] but they were in any event confident that St Vincent would prevent the enemy from entering the Mediterranean.

In fact the Directory had a multiplicity of objectives: relief of Corfu, Malta, and Bonaparte in Egypt, support for the Army of Italy if necessary, as well as destruction of the British fleet now scattered around the Mediterranean. Keith had sixteen ships off Cadiz, Duckworth four off Minorca, Nelson nine off Palermo, Ball three off Malta and Smith three in the Levant – thirty-five in all. The Spanish fleet in Cadiz was to be part of the plan and the combined enemy fleet would be forty to forty-five ships-of-the-line. It was not just a question of picking off the scattered British detachments one by one. If the British could be tempted to concentrate their forces the sieges would automatically be raised for the time being.

On 4 May Bruix appeared off Cadiz, where Keith was blockading Mazzaredo and twenty-eight Spanish ships. The French, in sight of Keith, ran for the Straits, where St Vincent watched them enter the Mediterranean. Keith had taken the line that it was better for him to concentrate on keeping them out and the Spaniards in, rather than taking any initiative. Then St Vincent concluded that an attack on Minorca was the enemy's objective and called Keith to concentrate there. Cadiz was left uncovered. Bruix headed for Toulon and soon afterwards most of the now unguarded Spanish ships got out of Cadiz and into Cartagena. The last thing St Vincent expected was forty-two enemy ships sharing the Mediterranean with him. At this critical point, an ailing St Vincent seems neither to have felt fit enough to command the situation nor think beyond protecting Minorca; he promptly delegated his command to Keith.

When the *Espoir* arrived at Palermo on 12 May Nelson knew that the Brest squadron was at sea and that its targets could be Minorca and Sicily. He immediately decided to send ships to Duckworth at Minorca, 'to either form a junction with our great and excellent Commander-in-

Chief, or proceed down the Mediterranean and join him, as he may direct'.[6] On the same day he wrote to Troubridge and Ball, asking them for ships, in both cases assuming that Keith would deal with the enemy. He told St Vincent that he could not himself go: 'Nothing could console the Queen this night, but my promise not to leave them unless the battle was to be fought off Sardinia.'[7] The royal priority was now the reconquest of Naples.

When Nelson learned that the French had passed through the Straits he countermanded all his previous orders. Believing that he was now in the enemy's most likely path he ordered all his ships to rendezvous off Maritimo so as to protect Sicily and block the route to Malta and Egypt. It was at this time that he received a quite extraordinary present from Ben Hallowell of the *Swiftsure*: a coffin made from part of *L'Orient*'s mast. The theatrical Nelson much appreciated the gift, and for some time it stood behind his chair, although it was finally stowed below. Hallowell's gift was timely; it would be ten British ships against the French twenty-five, and the coffin might well come in handy.

Nelson was torn by conflicting instincts. To his extraordinary comment that he was kept at Palermo by the Queen, he now added a feverish,

Should you come upwards without a battle, I hope in that case you will afford me an opportunity of joining you; for my heart would break to be near my Commander-in-Chief, and not assisting him in such a time. What a state I am in! If I go, I risk, and more than risk, Sicily, and what is now safe on the Continent; for we know from experience, that more depends on opinion than on acts themselves. As I stay, my heart is breaking; and, to mend the matter, I am seriously unwell. God bless you. Depend on my utmost zeal to do as I think my dear friend would wish me; for believe me with real affection your faithful friend.[8]

The 28th of May saw him still stressed and he wrote to Sir William, 'To fight is nothing, but to be continually on the stretch for news and events of the greatest importance is what I find my shattered carcass unequal to.'[9]

However, the moment he began to focus on the enemy he was all resolution and determination, 'Your Lordship may depend that the

Squadron under my command shall never fall into the hands of the Enemy; and before we are destroyed, I have little doubt but that the Enemy will have their wings so completely clipped that they may be easily overtaken.'[10]

Nelson's list of ships showed how skeletal his force was. He talked of his squadron but it was a pale shadow of his original Nile force. At that moment he had off Maritimo five 74s. He expected that Ball would join him from Malta with three more and the *Lion* 64 would join him from cruising off Leghorn, in total nine ships-of-the-line he could count on, plus four Portuguese in whom he rightly had zero confidence. The real potential odds were at least two to one against, and whatever the Admiralty's chauvinistic assumption of British superiority, Nelson must have registered how bravely and with what bloody consequences the French had fought at Aboukir. And so after almost a month on the qui vive he still prepared and still waited.

By 5 June he learned that St Vincent had moved with twenty sail-of-the-line and was off Minorca, aiming to prevent the Spanish and French from joining up. He wrote excitedly, 'We are all on the tip-toe of expectation, that, in truth, we can think nor talk of anything but you.' To Lady Hamilton he expressed himself in rather different imagery: 'I long to be at the French fleet as much as ever a miss longed for a husband.'[11]

Less than a week later the blow came. 'We have a report that you are going home. This distresses us most exceedingly, and myself in particular; so much so, that I have serious thoughts of returning, if that event should take place. . . . We look up to you, as we have always found you, as to our Father, under whose fostering care we have been led to fame. If, my dear Lord, I have any weight in your friendship, let me entreat you to rouse the sleeping lion. Give not up a particle of your authority to any one; be again our St Vincent, and we shall be happy.'[12] But a letter was already on its way to Nelson. 'I have transferred the command to Lord Keith, not deeming it for the public good, or just to his Lordship, to hold a trust which I cannot exercise in person.'[13] Crossing with St Vincent's letter was another impassioned plea from Nelson as the enormous blow of losing his father figure sank in:

My dear Lord, our St Vincent! What we have suffered in hearing of your illness, and of your return to Mahon! Let me entreat you to come to us with a force fit to fight. We will search the French out, and if either in Leghorn, Espezia, or Naples we will have at them. We shall have so much pleasure in fighting under the eye of our ever great and good Earl. If you are sick, I will fag for you; and our dear Lady Hamilton will nurse you with the most affectionate attention. Good Sir William will make you laugh with his wit and inexhaustible pleasantry. We all love you. Come then to your sincere friends. Let us get you well; it will be such a happiness to us all, amongst the foremost to your attached, faithful, and affectionate . . .[14]

Not many commanders-in-chief in the history of war can have received such a passionate plea. But the die was cast.

Things were now coming to a head in the affairs of the Kingdom of Naples. The Second Coalition against the French was in being and by the end of May, General Suvorov, with an Austro-Russian army 120,000 strong, was sweeping the French before him. Moreau had been forced back from Verona. Under pressure the French had withdrawn MacDonald's army of Naples, evacuated Civitavecchia and Leghorn, and left only skeleton garrisons in Naples and the Papal States. Russia and Turkey had sent detachments to Cardinal Ruffo, who since 8 February had been sweeping up through Calabria with his irregulars and was now at the gates of Naples. Troubridge who had been set the task of repossessing the islands off the Bay of Naples was completing the encirclement from the seaward side. Repossession of Naples was now in sight.

The King, the Queen and the Hamiltons were now united in urging Nelson to return to Naples. The overarching nature of his orders from the Admiralty, not to mention the Treaty of 1 December 1798 which had made George III and Ferdinand allies, made it right for him to do so. But as he set out for Naples in the brand new *Foudroyant*, recently arrived to replace *Vanguard*, he received news from Keith which caused him to return to port immediately and disembark troops and passengers. Keith, with some prospect of overtaking Bruix, had been caught by a foul wind and had felt obliged by his orders to fall back to protect Minorca. Keith told Nelson that the wind which was foul for himself, 'is of course a fair wind for the Enemy, if bound towards you', and made the scarcely munificent gesture of sending Nelson two 74s, *Bellerophon* and *Powerful*.

Once again Nelson found himself awaiting a phantom French fleet, wanting to maintain his strategic grip on the gateway to Sicily, Corfu,

Malta and Alexandria, and yet deal with Naples. Hence the turbulence of his 'Most Secret' letter to Sir William Hamilton: 'I am agitated but my resolution is fixed. For Heaven's sake suffer not any one to oppose it. I shall not be gone eight days. No harm can come to Sicily. I sent my Lady and you Lord St Vincent's letter. I am full of grief and anxiety. I must go. It will finish the War. It will give a sprig of laurel to your affectionate friend.'[15] His dilemma was solved by news that Keith, having been reinforced from England by Rear-Admiral Cotton and twelve ships, now had thirty-one ships. Nelson could return to Palermo and restart his voyage to Naples.

Nelson was not impressed by Keith and was putting the worst interpretation on his decision not to attack the French fleet off Cadiz, and now the worst interpretation on his giving priority to Minorca rather than attacking Bruix. Keith was equally disparaging about Nelson. 'I have a letter from Lord Nelson, got into Naples. He is absurd with Lady H and vanity: I wish he would go home and her too.'[16] Nelson's problems with Keith or, some would say erroneously, Keith's problems with Nelson, began to multiply.

Lord Keith (formerly George Elphinstone) had been promoted Vice-Admiral in 1795, two years before Nelson was made Rear-Admiral. He used to say he had been sent to sea with a £5 note in his pocket and told to make his fortune. Certainly his chief motivation seems to have been to make money. This he did in sufficient quantities to enable him to purchase two large estates. His record shows that he was good on paper, energetic in self-justification, but allergic to risk. St Vincent's own approval of Keith was strongly prejudiced and ambiguously double edged. He told Spencer, 'You will never find an officer of that country [i.e. Scotland] figure in supreme command, they are only fit for drudgery. Lord Keith is by far the best I have ever met with by land or sea.'[17] As in all organizations, the reputation of senior officers was common currency. Although Nelson and Keith had never met they would know all about each other.

Keith had at first been doubtful about his reception by St Vincent, writing to his sister Mary, 'Nothing could be more agreeable or accommodating than the Earl; at the same time there seemed a tincture of jealousy that may make it just as well that we are at a distance.'[18] Maybe he was experiencing a reaction to his wealth, or maybe it was a case of Scottish over-sensitivity. At any rate by the end of March 1799 Keith was obviously impressing St Vincent with his organizational diligence, his strongest professional suit, and as a result earning the St Vincent treatment. 'He told me I was so like himself I was the only man in England fit for that command' (the Channel fleet – the 'best' job in the Navy).[19] Keith was being as expertly managed as Nelson had been. In June, when he was on the horns of his dilemma, to concentrate on the French fleet or protect Minorca, he wrote to his sister a long letter of self-justification: 'Although I shall be blamed I have no fault, but having gone further than I ought strictly speaking. The whole of our late proceedings has so affected my mind and body that I have written for leave to come away. I have the fullest confidence of Lord St Vincent but still as the acting man people naturally look to me, who am only obeying the orders of another.'[20] There could hardly be a sharper contrast with Nelson, who never required others to tell him what to do.

After he had given up the Mediterranean command on 17 June, St Vincent left strong words of advice with Keith: 'It will be advisable for Lord Nelson to detach from the squadron under his orders, a force to protect Minorca, for it is probable that some ships are left at Cartagena to cover the intended descent on that island.'[21] Keith acted on this advice and sent Nelson a perfectly reasonable set of orders (dated 27 June when Nelson was at Naples). 'Events which have recently occurred render it necessary that as great a force as can be collected should be assembled near the Island of Minorca; therefore if your Lordship has no detachment of the French squadron in the neighbourhood of Sicily, nor information of their having sent any force towards Egypt or Syria, you are hereby required and directed to send such ships as you can possibly spare off the Island of Minorca to wait my orders; and I will take care, so soon as the Enemy's intentions shall be frustrated in that quarter, to strengthen your Lordship as soon as possible.'[22]

Just before he received Keith's order, Nelson, quick to pre-empt the situation, had involved Spencer in his thinking. 'Lord Keith writes me, if certain events take place, it may be necessary to draw down this Squadron for the protection of Minorca. Should such an order come at this moment, it would be a cause for some consideration whether Minorca is to be risked, or the two Kingdoms of Naples and Sicily? I rather think my decision would be to risk the former.'[23] He wrote to Keith later on the same day, 'as soon as the safety of His Sicillian Majesty's Kingdoms is secured, I shall not lose one moment in making the detachment you are pleased to order.'[24] A further letter to Spencer followed immediately.

> You will easily conceive my feelings at the order this day received here from Lord Keith; but my mind . . . was perfectly prepared for this order; and more than ever is my mind made up, that, at this moment, I will not part with a single Ship, as I cannot do that without drawing a hundred and twenty men from each Ship now at the siege of Capua, where an army is gone this day. I am fully aware of the act I have committed; but sensible of my loyal intentions, I am prepared for any fate which may await my disobedience. Capua and Gaeta will soon fall; and the moment the scoundrels of French are out of this Kingdom, I shall send eight or nine Ships of the Line to Minorca. I have done what I thought right; others may think differently; but it will be my consolation that I have gained a Kingdom, seated a faithful Ally of his Majesty firmly on his throne, and restored happiness to millions. Do not think, my dear Lord, that my opinion is formed from the arrangements of any one. No; be it good, or be it bad, it is all my own.[25]

Nelson was now reacting to Keith's self-centred assumption that Nelson's role in supporting the Kingdom of the Two Sicilies for the last ten months was of little importance. He was determined to trust his own professional judgement that Minorca was in no serious danger from the Spaniards (for which he had absolutely no evidence) and he too would shelter behind *his orders*. This was a relatively high risk gambit to play with the Board. Perhaps at the age of forty and with the Nile behind him he had a growing realization that his standing and achievement were such that he did not have to be the creature of Lord Keith. But fundamentally, Nelson was responding to his dilemma in a characteristic way, making his decision and being honest and open about it. Whether the actual situation at Naples really required all his ships was debatable, but given the current chaos and uncertainty surrounding Naples, he must have thought it did, and that cannot simply be wished away by hindsight. On the other hand blind adherence to an order from above would have been equally misguided. The easiest way of responding to a dilemma is to take the line of least resistance, as Keith himself had just done in breaking off his pursuit of Bruix with no benefit other than conformity to orders, and had evidently regretted it. Nelson was prepared to take responsibility for his decision and let events and others decide whether he had been right or wrong. This was exercise of the responsibility of command to a high degree.

Nelson had been at Naples since 24 June and it was there that he received a surprising communication from Keith (dated 9 July), telling him that the Combined Fleet had left Cartagena, that the French had no intention of attempting an attack on Sicily, or of reinforcing their Army in Egypt, but would be aiming at Ireland. He Keith, would follow them. If Minorca, threatened by the Spanish, was not to fall, 'You must ... either come, or send Duckworth, to govern himself as circumstances offer, until I can determine to a certainty the intentions of the enemy.'[26] He had not of course received Nelson's first reply.

Nelson simply reiterated his position: 'I am perfectly aware of the consequences of disobeying the orders of my Commander-in-Chief; but, as I believe the safety of the Kingdom of Naples depends at the present moment on my detaining the Squadron, I have no scruple in deciding that it is better to save the Kingdom of Naples and risk Minorca, than to risk the Kingdom of Naples to save Minorca.'[27] Whilst he could expect that Keith, knowing of the orders the Admiralty had given both St Vincent and himself should have some respect for his view, he was on very thin ice. Again he was open with the Admiralty about his actions, and on the same day sent Nepean copies of the correspondence, and wrote another rather different letter to Keith: 'I grieve most exceedingly that you had not the good fortune to fall in with the French Fleet before they formed their junction with the Dons, although I am sure, when you are united with the Channel fleet, that you will send them to the Devil.'[28] The irony was palpable. He also wrote to Spencer on 19 July. 'I bitterly my dear Lord condole with you on the escape of the French fleet.' Again a not so heavily coded message – politicking of a sharp order.

Keith having gone, Nelson's action was instantaneous. He ordered Duckworth to take *Powerful*, *Majestic*, *Vanguard* and the corvette *Swallow* to Minorca, 'leaving it entirely to your well known abilities and judgement to act with them in the best manner for the protection of that Island'. Meanwhile Bruix passed the Straits on 14 July; the French and Spaniards joined and left Cadiz for Brest on 22 July; Keith passed the Straits on 30 July, arrived off Ushant on 18 August, continued to Spithead, and cruised with the Channel fleet before going on leave on

27 September. There was no action at all with the enemy, which having reached Brest settled down to be blockaded after perhaps the most ineffective campaign of the sea war. In the Mediterranean Nelson became *de facto* Commander-in-Chief.

The upshot was that there was Admiralty approval for Nelson's efforts in the Bay of Naples and disapproval for his having detached so large a force of seamen and marines to form part of an army at a distance, thus reducing the operational capacity of his squadron. Nelson was told not to do that again. As to disobeying Keith's orders, the bottom line after a good deal of waffle was, 'their Lordships do not, therefore, from any information now before them, see sufficient reason to justify your having disobeyed the orders you had received from your Commanding-Officer, or having left Minorca exposed to the risk of being attacked, without having any Naval force to protect it'.[29] This was the least the Admiralty could do. They could not pass over his conduct in silence, but this reproof could hardly be classed as the most weighty ever delivered for insubordination. Opinion on the Board of Admiralty was clearly split and Spencer wrote a mollifying letter ending, 'You have already, my dear Lord, done wonders. What remains for you to do, may not, perhaps, be quite so brilliant, but is no less useful to your Country.'[30]

Nelson has been strongly criticized for not following the copybook formula to concentrate his force with Keith, and for deploying valuable marines and seamen on shore. The fact is that Nelson was the only one who emerged with real achievement from the Bruix episode. Bruix himself had been timid and indecisive from the beginning and attacked nothing, and in the end, overwhelmed by his multiplicity of objectives and the fact that Keith was after him, turned tail and fled. Mazzaredo had done nothing about Minorca or anything else. Neither St Vincent nor Keith had in any shape or form managed to grasp the opportunity or dominate the situation. They had kept the French and Spaniards temporarily separated but nothing else. At a point of crisis St Vincent had given up his command. With all his opportunities, Keith had been unable to bring the combined fleet to battle and had been unable to prevent their junction or their subsequent escape from the Mediterranean. War is about results, not theory. Nelson had not concentrated his force with Keith but had maintained his strategic grip on the gateway to the eastern Mediterranean and had otherwise focused on a key actual objective, Naples. In terms of what Corbett has called the conflict between cohesion and elasticity, Nelson had not played his cards at all badly. The last word on the Minorca business can reasonably be given to Lord Grenville, the Foreign Secretary, who on 16 August wrote to Spencer: 'earnestly hope Lord Nelson will not think himself restrained by Lord Keith's orders to go and watch Minorca which nobody is thinking of attacking . . . trust that there can be no difficulty now in leaving Lord Nelson (as long as his health makes it possible) in the command of the Mediterranean fleet. He is infinitely fitter than Lord Keith (or any one else I believe) to act with our Allies.'[31]

This was a period of undeniable stress for Nelson, and so Keith, Nepean, Locker, Ball and Duckworth all variously heard that he had not the strength to write, that he was in a fever, that he could not sit up, that he was sick and tired out, that he was nearly blind. This went on from late July, through August and into September, when he announced 'We are all unwell', not very surprising after all they were going through in Naples.

Nelson and the Hamiltons, now effectively in charge of the restoration of the monarchy at Naples, were in an invidious position. The King at first, and the Queen, all the time, remained at Palermo, two or three days away by letter yet the supreme arbiters. Naples was in an uproar of vengeance, the *lazzaroni*, a veritable lynch mob, wreaking a terrible revenge on any known or suspected Jacobin sympathizers, Cardinal Ruffo's Calabrians likewise out of control. The King and Queen were bent on a purge of nobles and professionals who had collaborated with their conquerors in setting up the Parthenopean Republic. The *lazzaroni* had remained loyal to the King and wanted their heads.

The King and Queen, full of congratulation for Cardinal Ruffo's efforts in sweeping up from Calabria to the gates of Naples, were nevertheless alarmed by rumours of double dealing and so the King persuaded Nelson to take his fleet to Naples and act there as his *alter ego* and plenipotentiary, roles he had previously given to Ruffo. Nelson had fair warning of the situation he was likely to face. Although Troubridge was not short of callousness he had found it difficult to cope with the Neapolitans in his campaign to take the offshore islands. He resolutely refused to have anything to do with their summary vengeance trials, 'as they were not British subjects. The trials are curious; frequently the culprit is not present. . . . The odium I find is intended to be thrown on us.' He found the stress intolerable. 'I am really very ill. I must go to bed. This treachery fairly does me up.'[32]

When Nelson arrived on the scene on 24 June Cardinal Ruffo had not yet secured the surrender of the 500-strong French garrison in the St Elmo fort which dominated Naples, but together with the Russian and Turkish commanders of allied forces, and Captain Foote of the frigate *Seahorse* commanding the British ships in the Bay of Naples, had agreed generous capitulation terms with the Neapolitan rebels in the forts Nuovo and Uovo. They were to march out with colours flying, and accompanied by other supporters of the Parthenopean Republic who so wished, would be transported to Toulon. The individuals in question did not all bear arms and many might be better described as collaborators, who had served in the military or civil administration, and in various ways and to different degrees had aided and abetted the Parthenopean Republic.

It is vital in understanding what happened next to realise that Nelson knew that Ruffo had long-standing orders, repeated on many occasions by both King and Queen, not to negotiate with the rebels. The fate of those involved in the Parthenopean Republic was to be reserved for the King himself: he was determined that they should be judged by the extent of their involvement. Knowing this, Nelson had no freedom of action. He immediately denounced the armistice, as he then believed it to be, first on the commonsense grounds that an armistice could be broken by either side – 'the arrival of the British fleet has completely destroyed the compact, as would that of the French' – and second, on the grounds of what he knew of the King's stated position. 'As to rebels and traitors . . . they must instantly throw themselves on the clemency of their sovereign, for no other terms will be allowed them.'[33] As soon as Nelson learned from Foote that he was in fact dealing with a treaty of capitulation he saw no reason to change his mind. He issued a note to the Cardinal asking that it should be conveyed to the two forts. His message was clear. He would 'not permit them to embark or quit those places. They must surrender themselves to his Majesty's royal mercy.'[34] Ruffo refused to deliver his note.

Nelson was self-evidently within his rights in cancelling the armistice and on reasonably sound grounds in cancelling the capitulation, as *ultra vires*. The more serious charge against Nelson is that he then made a play of changing his mind in order to lure the Neapolitan Jacobins into awaiting polaccas, their intended transport to Toulon. This is where the real controversy lies.

The issue cannot be settled on existing evidence, especially since some Neapolitan sources are highly suspect and because pressure of events produced mistakes or irreconcilable contradictions in documents or letters otherwise of good provenance. What is clear and fully documented is that following Nelson's rejection of the capitulation there was a major and acrimonious confrontation between Ruffo and Nelson on board the *Foudroyant* which threatened to break the relationship wide apart. Hamilton later told his nephew, 'nothing but my phlegm could have prevented an open rupture on the first meeting between Cardinal Ruffo and Lord Nelson. Lord Nelson is so accustomed to dealings fair and open that he has no patience when he meets with the contrary which one must always expect when one has to deal with Italians, and, perhaps his Eminency is the very quintessence of Italian finesse.'[35] His more pithy description of Ruffo's position was 'rascality or imbecility'. The breakdown of these discussions led Nelson once again to reiterate his position in writing. The treaty as he now correctly called it could not be carried into execution, 'without the approbation of his Sicillian Majesty'.[36] Yet the meeting must have had some impact on Ruffo for Hamilton wrote to Acton on the same day, 'The cardinal I believe intends to let them know at the castle of St Elmo, Nuovo and dell'Uovo that he cannot answer for Lord Nelson's allowing of the armistice to continue.'[37] Also on the 25th Ruffo himself wrote to Nelson: 'The letter to the castles will have gone by this time, and if there is any hope of their surrendering at discretion, it may succeed.'[38]

With Ruffo seeming to accept to some degree Nelson's position, there came a sudden volte-face by Nelson himself. The next morning, the 26th, Hamilton wrote to Ruffo, 'Lord Nelson begs me to assure your Eminence that he is resolved to do nothing which might break the armistice which your Eminence has granted to the castles of Naples.'[39] There is in Nelson's Letter Book an undated and unsigned letter to Ruffo conveying precisely the same sentiments.[40] That same day the rebels came out of the forts and embarked in the polaccas and at 4 p.m. the log of the *Foudroyant* confirmed that British marines took over the forts. When Hamilton reported this to Acton on the next day the 27th, he said they had done what they did 'upon cool reflection'. The outcome he noted as, 'the rebels on board the polaccas from the castles cannot stir without a passport from Lord Nelson' and he added, 'However we shall now act perfectly in concert with the cardinal tho' we think the same as we did at first as to the treaty his Eminence made before our arrival. If one cannot do exactly as one could wish, one must make the best of a bad bargain and that Lord Nelson is doing. I hope the result will be approved by their Sicilian Majesties.'[41] It looked very much as though Nelson and Hamilton were matching Ruffo's finesse with some of the British variety.

On the morning of the 28th there were letters from Ferdinand to Nelson (missing), from Acton to Hamilton and from the Queen to Emma. Hamilton reported to Acton, 'Lord Nelson's finding that his Sicilian Majesty totally disapproved of what the Cardinal Ruffo has done contrary to his instructions with respect to the rebels in the castles and those rebels being still on board of 12 or 14 polaccas and it being in time to remedy that evil, thought himself sufficiently authorised to seize all these polaccas.'[42] He enclosed a letter in French, dated 25 June (which obviously should have been 28 June), which he said he had written to Ruffo at Nelson's request saying that 'in consequence of orders just received (*vient de recevoir*) from the King which totally disapproved of the capitulation he was going to seize and secure those who had come out and were on board the boats.' The *Foudroyant*'s log showed that while the polaccas were brought nearer to the fleet the day before (the 27th), the taking into custody of certain principal rebels did not take place until the day the letters from Palermo were received. The Nelson–Ruffo situation, which had been critical on the 25th, was now even more so. Having had Nelson placed over him, Ruffo was not surprisingly leaving all initiative to him. Civil order ashore was now on the point of total breakdown and Nelson and Hamilton urged the King to come to Naples to provide an unequivocal source of authority. He arrived there on 10 July and Troubridge secured the capitulation of the St Elmo fort on the next day.

In this game of double dealing it is impossible to pin down precisely how the rebels were enticed into the polaccas. It was obviously sensible for Nelson and Hamilton to keep the peace with Ruffo in the interests of military collaboration. They could afford to wait for vindication from Palermo, even if Nelson might have wished to move events ahead as rapidly as possible, to get the rebels out and avoid the greater evil of wholesale carnage if the forts had to be stormed. The worst complexion that can be put on the use of the word 'armistice' in Hamilton's note of the 26th is that although meaningless and conceding nothing, they were hoping it would be misunderstood and achieve the desired effect. Even so, if Nelson had that misleading intention, it would still require Ruffo, the only person in communication with the forts, to use it to mislead. On the other hand if Nelson was not worried by the likely consequences of storming the forts, and there was never any sign that he was, he had only to wait for the King's reaction to the situation, which would leave neither of them with any choice but to obey.

Ruffo was in a quite different position. Time was not on his side. His confrontation with Nelson must have reminded him forcibly of the many occasions on which the King and Queen had said there must be no deals with rebels, and how for the past weeks he had hidden his actions from them. He was in some danger. He had quickly to regularize his position, unless he wished to set himself up in open opposition to the King. Thus, he had a powerful motive to get the rebels out and into the King's hands, either by implying that Nelson's words meant what they did not say, i.e. that the rebels were free to embark, or by giving Chevalier Micheroux – the Neapolitan diplomat attached to the Russian forces, and his go-between with the castles – a misleading message for him to deliver about Nelson's intentions. Micheroux had his own motive too for misleading. Remembering his own advocacy of the treaty he wanted to place the onus for it on Ruffo, which he later did, and he had a personal interest in securing the release of a cousin being held hostage. He himself stated that he did not at any time use any document from Nelson. They had 'relied on my word alone'.

Both Ruffo and Micheroux knew exactly what Nelson's real position was and Nelson issued nothing directly to the castles to alter his position. An idea recently raised, that Hamilton was the driving force and Nelson's puppetmaster, is not really tenable. The possibility that Hamilton could have hoodwinked Nelson or that Nelson would have allowed him to is remote. The balance of probabilities is that the embarkation of the rebels was the work of Ruffo and or Micheroux, most probably the latter. Nelson believed that the rebels came out on his terms, and he was probably telling the truth, but whether he had consciously or unconsciously, with the connivance of Hamilton, enabled Ruffo and Micheroux to do what they most likely did, is another matter. There would be another episode some two years later at Copenhagen involving the inspired use of words and underlying motives.

By the 30th Nelson had received powers to arrest Ruffo if he refused
to recognize the cancelling of the capitulation. These he did not use but
kept under lock and key and, in Hamilton's phrase, they [Nelson and
himself] would in the meantime 'keep smooth with him'. He went on:
'The criminals will remain at the mercy of His Sicillian Majesty in the
midst of our fleet. Lord Nelson's manner of acting must be as his conscience and honour dictate. I believe his determination will be found best
at last.'[43] This seems to place the onus for events entirely on Nelson.
Nelson's reaction to his power over Ruffo was typically Nelsonian, but
a mite unbelievable. 'I really do not believe that his Eminence has a disloyal thought towards overthrowing your Majesty's monarchy, but that
his Eminence's wish was to have everything his own way.'[44]

Whether an action to lure the rebels into the polaccas was criminal or
immoral, or the lesser of two evils has to be a moot point. These were
rebels and collaborators and the aim was to bring them to justice. Nelson
had not gone to Naples as a mediator. He went to help restore the monarchy, which was what his political masters including Hamilton wanted
and which the King and Queen of the Two Sicilies and their Prime Minister, Acton most fervently wanted. Nelson's deep royalist convictions,
his anti-revolutionary sentiments and a certain chauvinistic indifference
were secondary. It would not have occurred to any of them to look at
the situation from the point of view of the rebels.

There is room for an arithmetical perspective on the official aftermath.
The number of Neapolitan Jacobins in the fourteen polaccas has been
estimated at about 2,000, with the same number imprisoned ashore.[45]
Of this total 162 (4 per cent) were executed, 500 (12.5 per cent) were
imprisoned for varying periods, and 3,332 (83.3 per cent) were freed to
sail from Naples into exile. In spite of their reputation the Bourbons do
not seem to have been been particularly bloody, and the sheer blood-
stained nastiness of the totalitarian regime that France was imposing on
Europe was hardly likely to encourage a gentle and decent approach
towards fellow travellers. In France itself tens of thousands of French men
women and children had been guillotined in the officially inspired Terror
of 1793. In the counter-revolution in the Vendée, French republicans mas-
sacred 250,000 of their royalist fellow countrymen in two departments.
Closer to home, after the Second World War, 'people wanted to settle
accounts with wartime collaborators. In some cases it was undertaken by
legal process. Pierre Laval, Vidkun Quisling, William Joyce (Lord Haw

Haw), and Father Tiso were among those sentenced and executed. . . . In Italy thousands of fascists were simply lynched or shot by partisans. In France, in an orgy of retribution, tens of thousands were killed, often on the flimsiest of accusations.'[46] No doubt there were people who thought it hard that the British executed William Joyce merely for broadcasting enemy propaganda, just as they feel the same about Eleonora Pimentel, the poetess and editor of the republican paper *Monitore* hanged after the Neapolitan counter-revolution. Such things were in twentieth-century Europe as they had been in eighteenth-century Naples. Retribution for traitors and collaborators seems to be one of the deepest instincts of society.

Nevertheless, the prominence and ambiguity of Nelson's position allowed his own countrymen to attack him at the time, and the Neapolitans subsequently to shelter behind him. In February 1800 in the British Parliament, Charles James Fox, on a motion for the Address thanking His Majesty for refusing to negotiate with the French Republic (which had put out peace feelers on Christmas Day 1799), would muddle the excesses of the *lazzaroni* with official retribution and refer to Naples as a case where atrocities did not belong exclusively to the French; he would go on:

> if I am rightly informed, it has been stained and polluted by murders so ferocious, and by cruelties of every kind so abhorrent, that the heart shudders at the recital . . . nay England is not totally exempt from reproach, if rumours which are circulated be true . . . I will mention a fact to give Ministers the opportunity, if it be false, to wipe away the stain that must otherwise affix on the British name. A part of the Republican inhabitants at Naples took shelter in the fortress of Castel del Uovo . . . demanded that a British officer should be brought forward, and to him they capitulated . . . they made terms with him under the sanction of the British name. . . . They were accordingly put on board a vessel; but before they sailed, their property was confiscated, numbers of them taken out, thrown into dungeons, and some of them I understand, notwithstanding the British guarantee, absolutely executed.[47]

Nelson was not mentioned by name, Fox did not dare, but the finger had been pointed, the smear made, the half-truths aired and subsequent drawing-room gossip can be imagined. Ever since, there has been a stain on Nelson's name.

Additional odium has attached itself to Nelson because of the fate of Commodore Caracciolo who had served alongside Nelson, in the *Tancredi* 74, in Hotham's abortive action of March 1795. After the flight to Naples, he received permission from Ferdinand to return to the city to save his property from confiscation. Willingly or unwillingly, he had gone over to the other side, had commanded republican gunboats, and had fired on the Neapolitan frigate *La Minerva*. Troubridge had mentioned Caracciolo a number of times in his April letters including, 'I enclose your Lordship one of Caracciolo's letters, as head of the marine. I hope he has been forced into this measure.'[48] Captain Foote of the *Seahorse* had also written from off Procida on 28 May, 'Caraccioli threatens a second attack with a considerable addition of force.'[49] Five days after Nelson arrived Caracciolo was dragged on board, a prisoner. Nelson immediately committed him to trial by a Sicilian court martial under Count Thurn, the commander of the Sicilian squadron. After two hours' deliberation it returned the only possible verdict – guilty, with a death sentence. On receipt of the judgment of the court Nelson ordered Caracciolo to be hanged that same evening from the yardarm of the Neapolitan frigate *La Minerva*. There were undoubtedly observers who thought that Nelson ought not to have used *Foudroyant* for the court martial but they miss the point that the ship was the *de facto* seat of government and the only place where Caracciolo was likely to get a trial of any kind. Others, including some of his officers, felt that Nelson acted mercilessly in ordering a summary hanging, paying no attention to pleas for a second trial, for death by firing squad, or for more time to prepare for death. In this Nelson's implacable hatred of all things French, of all things smacking of rebellion and treason, may possibly have come to the fore. But he was not alone. Hamilton wrote to Acton, 'Lord Nelson has ordered him for execution this afternoon at 5 o'clock at the foremast yard arm of the *Minerva*. Thurn represented it was usual to give 24 hours for the care of the soul. Lord Nelson's orders remain the same, although I wished to acquiesce with Thurn's opinion. All is for the best.'[50] It is also a fact that Hamilton thoroughly approved of the hanging: 'such an example is necessary for the future marine service of H.S Majesty and particularly as Jacobinism had prevailed so much in the Neapolitan marine'.[51] Nelson's role in the affair was to order the trial, approve the sentence, and have it carried out. There is not a scintilla of doubt that Caracciolo deserved his fate. Those who tend to higher moral views in hindsight and ignore the realities of counter-revolution and the need for Nelson quickly to stabilise a chaotic situation and show loyal Neapolitans that justice was being done, tend to think that Nelson did not really behave as they would have liked him to. But the idea that Nelson could have single handedly altered the inevitable processes of counter revolution is entirely illusory.

Naples under the Bourbons was rotten to the core and it is surprising that a man of Nelson's character could stomach it, even though his orders required him to. But in a political sense he had a very conventional mind; the right of kings was writ large in his mental furniture, even when he was dealing with a creature such as Ferdinand. The only time Nelson commented on his own performance in Naples was much later, in 1803, when he said in a self-interested and complacent way, 'I paid more attention to another sovereign than my own; therefore the King of Naples' gift of Bronte [Dukedom in Sicily] to me, if it is not settled to my advantage, and to be permanent, has cost me a fortune, and a great deal of favour which I might have enjoyed, and jealousy which I might have avoided. I repine not on those accounts. I did my duty to the Sicilifying my own conscience, and I am easy.'[52] That use of the word 'Sicilifying' might well signal a somewhat guilty conscience about not having been perfectly straight. But in January 1800 he was standing by Ferdinand in terms that are really incredible to any objective observer. 'I have before ventured an opinion on the character of their Sicillian Majesties. The King is a real good man but inclined to be positive in his opinion; the Queen is certainly a great Monarch and a true daughter of Maria Theresa.'[53] Occasionally Nelson gives real cause for doubt about his grip on reality, or his honesty.

For the whole of this Naples period, ten months or so, from October 1798 to August 1799, about a score of letters to Fanny survive and it is clear from internal evidence that more were written. None of them conveys any feeling that he needs her, that she is necessary to him; in short they are perfectly representative of their normal relationship. Indeed when he received letters from her in April 1799 (written in December 1798 and probably coincident with Davison's letter already quoted), expressing a wish to join him, he was very emphatic that it would not be practical:

> You would by February have seen how unpleasant it would have been had you followed any advice, which carried you from England to a wandering sailor. I could, if you had come, only have struck my flag, and carried you back again, for it would have been impossible to have set up an establishment at either Naples or Palermo. Nothing but the situation of affairs in this country has kept me from England; and if I have the happiness of seeing their Sicillian Majesties safe on their throne again, it is probable I shall yet be home in the summer. Good Sir William, Lady Hamilton, and myself, are the mainsprings of the machine, which manage what is going on in this country. We are all bound for England when we can quit our posts with propriety.[54]

Nelson knew how unadaptable and unrobust Fanny was. She would have been a distinct encumbrance. The winter in Palermo had been cold and dismal; they had all been ill; Fanny was notorious for catching cold.

His letters, with some exceptions, are short, frequently less than a dozen lines, yet the twenty-one that survive over a period of ten months of fairly continuous crisis can hardly be regarded as negligible. His excuses carry some weight: 'As mine is a truly active scene you cannot hope for long letters'; 'with more writing than two hands could get through you must take a line for a page and a page for a sheet of paper'. He was neglecting others to an even greater degree, frequently sending apologies to his family. He became decidedly irritated in response to Fanny's nagging for more letters, or about other people expecting replies to their letters. 'If I do not write to you so often, not such long letters as formerly I have done, pray attribute it to the true cause, viz, that in truth my poor hand cannot execute what my head tells me I ought to do. As to writing a line to anyone else, they may take it ill or well, as they please.' All this indicated a man overstretched and decidedly out of humour.

Josiah featured in the great majority of his letters to Fanny. Nelson had written to St Vincent in the month after the Nile, asking if Josiah could have *Thalia* and as usual had underwritten him honestly. 'Depend on it he is very active, knows his business, but is certainly ungracious in the extreme.' Although Nelson showed some resentment at the failure of the powers that be immediately to promote the hero's stepson, it was mingled with a settled sense of Josiah's total failure to bring anything but discredit on himself. St Vincent and Duckworth both reinforced his own opinion and Duckworth would eventually save Josiah from court martial by sending him home.

The dynamics of a step-relationship, always complex, were infinitely more so when the stepson had a hero for a stepfather, a successful, all-powerful presence standing between him and every other person he met in the Navy, and to make matters even more complicated, a stepfather who now appeared to fancy another woman, which woman had in turn entirely confused the nineteen-year-old by exerting her charms on him as well. Nor could Nelson, who always had such winning ways as a boy, understand one who was the exact opposite. Josiah seems to have got drunk at Nelson's birthday party and there had been loutish altercations between Josiah and Emma, and Josiah and his stepfather. Fanny must have wept to receive Nelson's spare, mainly unfriendly, and semiofficial reports of her son. It is as though Nelson no longer cared to empathize with either of them.

There are from time to time flashes of a more thoughtful Nelson. He had been generous with the award made to him by the East India Company, instructing Fanny to distribute 'five hundred to my father . . . five hundred to Mr Bolton . . . five hundred to Maurice and five hundred to William. And if you think my sister Matcham would be gratified by it, do the same for her.'[55] There was a sudden display of status consciousness:

> I must have a house in London if possible. I should like the one that was Captain Suckling's or one like it. The rooms must be light and airy, but this is supposing my pension is handsome. I wish you to think if Roundwood pleases you if not, look out for another . . . if we have money a neat house in London near Hyde Park, but on no account on the other side of Portman Square I detest Baker Street. In short do as you please you know my wishes and income. A neat carriage I desire you will order and if possible get good servants. You will take care I am not let down. The King has elevated me and I must support my station in short whether I am at home a month sooner or later a house in London must be furnished and ready for us.[56]

There was not much feeling of joy and delight in all that either – as basic as a set of orders for a boat's crew.

Whereas letters to Fanny reflected alienation his communication to Emma had moved into a new intimacy of tone, open, confiding, and mirroring the increasing effect of her own unguarded expression. Writing from *Vanguard* at sea on 19 May it was a case of, 'I am now perfectly the great man – not a creature near me. From my heart I wish myself the little man again! You and good Sir William have spoiled me for any place but with you. I love Mrs Cadogan. You cannot conceive what I feel, when I call you all to my remembrance.'[57]

From 25 June until 5 August 1799 Nelson and the Hamiltons lived together in *Foudroyant*. Nelson and Sir William were in double harness, dealing with Ruffo, communicating with Acton and the King, and managing their explosive situation as best they could until the King arrived on 10 July. Emma had only an occasional part to play since Hamilton was able to interpret for himself and Nelson, but she bore the burden of correspondence with Maria Carolina. All three had to carry the emotional burden of dealing with pleas for help from previous Neapolitan friends and acquaintances who were now on the wrong side, and whose fate could be decided only by the King and Queen. For Nelson and Emma this was a shared experience which could not help but deepen their already considerable emotional attachment, but in the crowded ship and under the press of bitter events they could be nothing more than spectators of each other.

Once returned to Palermo, Nelson was made Duke of Bronte by a grateful Ferdinand. With Keith out of the Mediterranean and himself in *de facto* command, a watershed had been reached. As he said to Troubridge, 'The Neapolitans must manage their own Jacobins. We thank God have done with them.' He was fed up. 'Our joint exertions have been used to get the King to go to Naples but of no avail: the Austrians will be there before him . . . I am sick and tired of this want of energy, and when I find the impossibility of being longer useful, I will retire from this inactive service.'[58] Mid-August also brought medals from Davison. Nelson gave a spare gold medal to Sir William Hamilton, 'the man that all Europe is obliged to for his encouragement of the Arts, as well as many other acts of a public benefit'. He saw that no medal had been included for Hardy so he sent him his own, 'confident it was not your intention to exclude Captain Hardy, who was a Captain in the Battle of the Nile.' The letter was continued on two further days when it touched on his feeling that his brother Maurice had been over-looked and the transience of his own fame: 'as Lord Keith will annihi-late the Combined Fleet, if he meet them, the name of Nelson will be forgot'.[59]

Within a month he was writing again to Davison, falling into a mood better described as bathetic than melancholy, 'In my state of what con-sequence is all the wealth of this world? . . . And my dear friend, if I have a morsel of bread and cheese in comfort, it is all I ask of kind Heaven, until I reach the estate of six feet by two, which I am fast approaching. I had the full tide of honour, but little real comfort. If the War goes on, I shall be knocked off by a ball, or killed with chagrin.' He who had been willing to risk his commission, even his life, by his disobedience, was now grumbling at the Admiralty's mild and formal reproof of his insubordi-nation, 'My conduct is measured by the Admiralty, by the narrow rule of law, when I think it should have been done by that of common sense. I restored a faithful Ally by breach of orders; Lord Keith lost a fleet by obedience, against his own sense. Yet as one is censured, the other must be approved. Such things are.'[60]

One bright spot was that his advocacy of Troubridge's merits had not fallen on deaf ears. He had now received Spencer's letter of 18 August. 'His Majesty has been pleased to signify his intention of conferring the honour of a Baronetage on him.'[61] Now he could write 'most affection-ately' to Commodore Sir Thomas Troubridge, 'How happy you have made us! My pen will not say what I feel.'[62]

Meanwhile in London, amid the flow of gossip, Dowager Countess Spencer had been hearing from Emma. Lord Spencer was very intrigued to find out what she had written: 'I shall be much obliged to you for a sight of Lady Hamilton's letter.' Three days later came his musing reac-tion: 'I return you Lady Hamilton's letter which is, (considering all cir-cumstances) a very curious Paper. I have no doubt but that she may have on many occasions during the late Troubles at Naples been of consider-able Service to the Royal Family but I am not without my Apprehensions that she has obtained more ascendancy than I could wish over the Mind of our gallant little Admiral and has drawn him perhaps into one or two demarches that are not quite so proper and consistent with his Duty as the Commander of a British Squadron.' By blowing her own trumpet and by linking her efforts to Nelson's she was unwittingly adding to perceptions that he was unduly influenced by her, and by 24 August Spencer was reaching a rather jaundiced, somewhat unworthy but typically upper-class English conclusion: 'The Fetes at Palermo are not quite to my Mind any more than the Dukedom of Bronti.'[63]

Nelson could hardly have refused to participate in these extravaganzas. After the great fête of 8 August to celebrate the return of the King from Naples, there were indeed more fêtes to come, the feast of St Rosalia on the 16th, and a great *fête-champêtre* on 3 September which would eventually be featured in *The Times* of 23 October, Nelson having sent Cornelia Knight's account to his brother Maurice for publication in the newspapers. This was an account of palace gardens lit by fairy lights, a glittering assembly of foreign ministers and courtiers, fireworks to represent the battle of the Nile, the performance of a new cantata, *Long Live the British Hero*, pavilions dedicated to each of the allies English, Portuguese, Turkish and Russian, and a temple whose vestibule was adorned with full-size waxworks of Nelson and the Hamiltons. Inside was a waxwork King Ferdinand mounted in a chariot backed by the figure of Glory on an altar. Following their joint homage to the King, little Prince Leopold crowned Nelson with laurel to the strains of 'God Save the King.'

Basking in the pleasure of being yet again the centre of attention he did not stop to think how those in England might interpret his position although he seemed aware of possible suspicions that his loyalty to Naples might have been bought. He wrote to Davison on 15 August, 'You will observe in a part of the King's letter [accompanying the present of his father's sword] an observation is made, that this present could not hurt my delicate feelings; that is, I might have before received money and jewels, but I rejected them, as became me, and never received one farthing for all the expenses of the Royal Family on board the *Vanguard* and *Foudroyant*. This I expect from the Board of Admiralty, and that they will order me a suitable sum. It has been my honour, and not money which I have sought, nor sought in vain.'[64]

In October 1799 Lord and Lady Elgin passed through Palermo on their way to Constantinople, where he, as Ambassador, would make use of his position to acquire marble sculptures from the Parthenon in Athens, and professionally speaking, display marked irresolution in dealing with the wilful Sir Sidney Smith. The Elgins' letters home were a mixture of observation and gossip. Neither found in Nelson the hero of their imagination. Elgin was evidently put off by his appearance: 'He looks very old, has lost his upper teeth, sees ill of one eye, and has a film coming over both of them. He has pains pretty constantly from his late wound in the head. His figure is mean, and in general, his countenance is without animation.' Lady Elgin was very hard on Emma: 'I must acknowledge she is pleasant, makes up amazingly. . . . She looked very handsome at dinner, quite in an undress – my father would say, "There is a fine woman for you, good flesh and blood." She is indeed a Whapper! and I think her manner very vulgar. It is really humiliating to see Lord Nelson, he seems quite dying and yet as if he had no other thought than her. He told Elgin privately that he had lived a year in the house with her and that her beauty was nothing in comparison to the goodness of her heart.' Lady Elgin was equally scathing about Maria Carolina. 'Such a complete old devil as the Queen is, I never met with; she flattered us beyond all credibility; to Lord N. it was the most fulsome thing possible. I never never saw three people made such thorough dupes of as Lady Hamilton, Sir William, and Lord Nelson. They made an amazing splutter with us, and asked us to a great fete today. . . . 'And again in a letter of 4 October to her mother, 'You never saw anything equal to the fuss the Queen made with Lady H. and Lord Nelson, wherever she moved, was always by her side. I am told the Queen laughs very much at her to all her Neapolitans, but says her influence with Lord N. makes it worth her while making up to her. Lady H. has made him do many very foolish things.'[65]

This latter was pure hearsay, and they were ignorant of the fact that the Queen had been very close to Emma for years before Nelson appeared on the scene. However, such insubstantial personal criticism says as much about the attitudes of the Elgins as it does about the possible silly behaviour of Nelson and Emma. The subsequent history of the Elgins' bizarre marital difficulties puts them in perspective as commentators. Following a difficult birth Lady Elgin, by letter, denied her husband further sexual intercourse; there were suggestions of marital rape. Soon afterwards Lady Elgin took a lover whom Elgin took to court in 1807 on grounds of criminal conversation. The resultant scandal ruined Elgin's career and reduced him to the butt of satirists.[66]

Suddenly it was all action. Nelson received information that thirteen

French and Spanish sail-of-the-line were off the coast of Portugal. He set out at once for Minorca determined to make for Gibraltar, 'and if I can but get a force to fight these fellows it shall be done quickly'.[67]

While away, he sent Troubridge a letter containing a very odd sentence: 'All my letters from the Marquis de Niza and Ball you will open but not those from Sir William Hamilton or Palermo, as there are many things in them which I do not wish anyone to be acquainted with.'[68] What could these things be that even dear Troubridge should be warned off? It is difficult to imagine any political or operational matters that Troubridge, his trusted friend and second-in-command could not be privy to. There can be only one conclusion, that Nelson expected that these letters would contain intensely personal matters. Interestingly enough Sir William *did* write to Nelson in a strangely agitated sort of way, from Colli in the woods to the west of Palermo, 'Emma is tired of the Colli . . . and we come back to Palermo tomorrow – for God's sake come back as soon as you can.' One senses drama rather than the hyperbole of friendship, a fraught situation that could be calmed only by Nelson's return. By 19 October the crisis appeared to have resolved itself for it was now a case of, 'Your appartment is cleaned and prepared and we are all with open arms ready to receive you at the Mole.'[69] There is no means of knowing for certain that Emma had told her husband of her growing love for Nelson and sought his agreement to an understanding about their future domestic arrangements. What is known is that Nelson arrived back on 22 October and two days later wrote to his old friend Lord Minto, 'I received your kind and friendly letter of 31st August which gave equal pleasure to Sir William Hamilton Lady Hamilton and myself, We are the real Tria juncta in uno.'[70] Indeed Hamilton may well have just agreed to a *ménage à trois*.

On 14 November 1799 *The Times* published the first public reference to Nelson and Emma:

> Lord Keith is going out immediately to take command in the Mediterranean. Upon his Lordship's arrival, Lord Nelson will return to England.

> *Perfidium ridens Venus & Cupido*

> These perfidious Gods have in all times spread their smiling snares for the first of mankind. Heroes and Conquerors are subdued in their

turn. Mark Anthony followed Cleopatra *into the Nile* when he should have fought with Octavius! and laid down his laurels and his power, to sail down the *Cyndus* with her in the dress, the character and the *attitudes* of Venus. What will not the eye effect in the bosom of a Hero?

As Russell says, 'No reader would have missed the association of the attitudes. They turned up again on November 28th. By a false point in one of the morning Papers, the admirable attitudes of Lady HAM-T-N are called *Admiral-attitudes.*'[71] From now on the popular press and cartoonists would be like salt in Fanny's wounds and Nelson himself would come to find that being in the public eye has its less than agreeable moments.

The pressure of events in Nelson's private life were accompanied by an increase in his capacity for anger. While at Naples he had clashed violently with the egregious Consul Lock who had tried to obtain a contract to supply the fleet with fresh beef and other provisions. When he failed, Lock insinuated corruption. The affair culminated in Nelson's terrifying Lock and sending magisterial rebukes to the Victualling Board in London, whose correspondence reduced him to incandescent rage and grandiosity. 'Nelson is as far from doing a scandalous or mean action as the heavens are above the earth.'[72] 'One of my proudest boasts is that no man can ever say I have told a lie.'[73] The episode showed how unbalanced Nelson had become.

He was further affronted in November by a letter from Nepean complaining that he was not keeping the Admiralty properly informed. After giving him chapter and verse of the arrangements he had made he felt obliged to be defensive:

As a Junior Flag Officer, of course without those about me, as Secretaries, Interpreters, &c., I have been thrown into a more extensive correspondence than ever, perhaps fell to the lot of any Admiral. . . . It is a fact which it would not become me to boast of, but on the present occasion, that I have never but three times put my feet on the ground, since December 1798, and, except to the Court, that till after eight o'clock at night I never relax from business. I have had hitherto, the Board knows, no one emolument – no one advantage of a Commander-in-Chief.'[74]

When Nelson came to relate all this to Duckworth he did so with the air of world-weariness he had begun to adopt towards his lords and masters. 'But my dear Admiral, when the object of the actor is only to serve faithfully, I feel superior to the smiles or frowns of any Board. Apropos, I have received a severe set down from the Admiralty for not having wrote by the *Charon* attached to a convoy, although I wrote both by a Cutter and Courier the same day. But I see clearly that they wish to show I am unfit for this command. I will readily acknowledge it, and therefore they need have no scruples about sending out a Commander-in-Chief . . . I am nearly blind but things go so contrary to my mind out of our profession that truly I care not how soon I am off stage'; and then with the lightest touch, since he had passed none of the blame to Duckworth, he added simply, 'Pray don't let the Admiralty want for letters of every occurrence.'[75] The next day he wrote more pitifully to Spencer, 'Do not my dear Lord, let the Admiralty write harshly to me – my generous soul cannot bear it, being conscious it is entirely unmerited.'[76]

Not only was he again distressed, fretting and worried by the guilt of his private intentions, he was also suffering from failing sight, a terrible threat to a one-eyed man. His state of mind reflected the low level of his activity. He confessed to Sidney Smith in early December, 'All our Mediterranean operations are pretty nearly at a standstill; for the enemy have no Fleet at this moment to make us keep a good look-out.'[77]

Spencer now compounded his error of not listening to Lavinia about bringing Nelson home; he also ignored Grenville's suggestion to leave him as Commander-in-Chief. Towards the end of 1799 Spencer allowed Keith to return to the Mediterranean. He failed to appreciate that in the absence of a French fleet in the Mediterranean the command would be absurdly top heavy.

Keith arrived in December, and Nelson would make his first report to him on 7 January 1800. The omens were not good. By now Keith would have the full story of Nelson's insubordination from his friend Admiral Young, a member of the 'gossiping' Admiralty Board. He would also be aware of Nelson's attitude to his failure to bring the enemy fleets to action either at Cadiz or off the Riviera or during his fruitless chase to Brest. To Keith himself Nelson had been ironic: 'I grieve most exceedingly that you had not the good fortune to fall in with the French fleet before they formed their junction.'[78] To Spencer Nelson had been childishly direct: 'I bitterly my dear Lord condole with you on the escape of the French fleet', and 'I cordially congratulate you on the happy arrival of the combined Fleets off Cadiz; for having escaped the vigilance of Lord Keith.'[79] Keith had probably received Nelson's letter of 1 August 1799 which would have followed him to England: 'I sincerely congratulate your Lordship on the entire liberation of the Kingdom of Naples from a band of robbers and am with the greatest respect' – formally correct but with unmistakable overtones for Keith of, 'See, *I* succeeded.'[80] Keith did not return to the Mediterranean with a friendly attitude towards such a subordinate. He would now take every opportunity to clip his wings and damage his reputation. Unhappily, Keith had no professional leadership to offer and no capacity to remotivate Nelson, even had he had the slightest inclination to try. Although he would make much of the importance of the siege of Malta, he had no new ideas on how to achieve the desired result beyond insisting that Nelson pay closer personal attention to it. His fundamental analysis was exactly the same as Nelson's, and as he wrote to Spencer, 'I am therefore under very great apprehension that Malta will be lost for I am convinced that nothing less than 6000 troops will reduce it and if it is not to be pressed with vigour it were better to give it up.'[81] His chief motivation was simply to make Nelson do what he, Keith, wanted.

Nelson was feeling increasingly hard done by. He had won the greatest sea victory in his nation's history. By his own standards he found his country ungrateful, the magnificent and curious honours heaped on him by foreign potentates and the celebrations at Naples and Palermo seeming to him to throw into relief the niggardliness of his own masters. Their cardinal blunder had been to award him a pension of £2,000 for the Nile, compared with £3,000 to St Vincent for St Valentine's Day and £3,000 to Duncan for Camperdown. As he had written to his brother on 21 August 1799, 'I am truly sorry that [the] Administration have neither done that for me or my family which might have been expected. Lords St Vincent and Duncan have £1000 a year from Ireland: I have heard of no such thing for Nelson.'[82]

Nelson was now forty-one. He was suffering from the cumulative stress of his hunt for the French, the battle of the Nile, the effects of his wound, the political struggles of the Neapolitan war, revolution and counter-revolution, the manifold frustrations of Malta and his divided loyalties. Nigel Hamilton describes how in modern times great commanders suffered in the aftermath of the intolerable stress of battle. After

Alamein, Rommel suffered a virtual mental breakdown. During his Sicilian campaign Patton struck hospitalized soldiers whom he accused of cowardice. Montgomery became distressingly mean and vindictive to his family.[83] Nelson's paranoia, insubordination emotionalism and self-pity may well have had similar origins. Professionally, he may have contemplated the downside of his unbelievable success, of being without a living equal as a fighting commander – what did he do for an encore? And now there was the inner turmoil caused by his deep attachment to Emma and his emotional abandonment of Fanny. He might have been unable to blank out the memory of his father's voice echoing from the pulpit at Burnham Thorpe, 'Thou shalt not commit adultery.'

So Nelson took Keith's return very badly and on 26 February 1800 confided in his friend Lord Minto, 'I have in truth serious thoughts of giving up active service – Greenwich Hospital seems a fit retreat for me after being evidently thought unfit to command in the Mediterranean.'[84]

18

Soulmates

Your own faithful Nelson lives only for his Emma.

Nelson, January 1800

O n 16 January 1800 Nelson sailed in *Foudroyant* for Leghorn and a first meeting with Lord Keith, who wrote to his sister, 'Lord Nelson has arrived. I am much employed. Of course he brings no news.'[1] Nelson's mind was indeed elsewhere and five days after they set sail on their return journey to Palermo he began a long and passionate love letter to Emma, the earliest that has survived.

> Separated from all I hold dear in this world what is the use of living if indeed such an existence can be called so, nothing could alleviate such a Separation but the call of our Country but loitering time away with nonsense is too much, no Separation no time my only beloved Emma can alter my love and affection for You, it is founded on the truest principles of honour, and it only remains for us to regret which I do with the bitterest anguish that there are any obstacles to our being united in the closest ties of this World's rigid rules, as We are in those of real love. Continue only to love Your faithful Nelson as he loves his Emma. You are my guide I submit to You, let me find all My fond heart hopes and wishes with the risk of my life I have been faithful to my word never to partake of any amusement or sleep on Shore. Thursday Janry 30th. We have been six days from Leghorn and no prospect of our making a passage to Palermo, to me it is worse than death. I can neither Eat nor Sleep for thinking of You my dearest love, I never touch even pudding You know the reason. No I would Starve sooner. My only hope is to find You have Equally kept your promises to Me, for I never made You a promise that I did not as strictly keep as if made in the presence of heaven, but I

rest perfectly confident of the reality of Your love and that You would die sooner than be false in the smallest thing to Your Own faithful Nelson who lives only for his Emma. friday. I shall run mad we have had a gale of Wind that is nothing but I am 20 Leagues farther from You than Yesterday noon. Was I master notwithstanding the weather I would have been 20 Leagues nearer but my Commander in Chief knows not what I feel by absence, last night I did nothing but dream of You altho I woke 20 times in the Night. In one of my dreams I thought I was at a large Table You was not present, Sitting between a Princess who I detest and another. They both tried to Seduce me and the first wanted to take those liberties with Me which no Woman in this World but Yourself ever did. The consequence was I knocked her down and in the moment of bustle You came in and taking Me in Your embrace wispered I love nothing but You My Nelson. I kissed You fervently And we enjoy'd the height of love. Ah Emma I pour out my Soul to You. If you love any thing but Me You love those who feel not like your N. Sunday Noon. fair Wind which makes me a little better in hopes of seeing You my love My Emma tomorrow. Just 138 Miles distant, and I trust to find You like myself, for no love is like Mine towards You.[2]

Nelson and Emma had taken their loving friendship to its natural conclusion. Emma, after twenty years' experience of men with ulterior motives felt herself loved and respected, a new and wonderful thing. Nelson found what he had been seeking for all his life, unequivocal and unrestrained adoration. Now they appeared to be on the brink of an even deeper commitment, the striking evidence of which appears in a letter Nelson wrote to Emma a year later from his cabin on board the *St George* as she lay in Torbay preparing to sail for the Baltic: 'Ah my dear Friend I did remember well the 12th February and also the two months afterwards. I shall never forget them and never be sorry for the consequences.'[3]

This date, 12 February, must have had magic about it to have been so etched on Nelson's memory, suggesting an anniversary of the greatest emotional significance, the date on which they gave themselves to each other as freely as man and wife. And what did the 'two months afterwards' refer to? Most likely the suspense of waiting to see if the child he wished them to have, had been conceived. The powerful thrust of his thinking in early January 1800 is unmistakable: 'it only remains for me to regret which I do with the bitterest anguish that there are any obstacles to our being united in the closest ties of this World's rigid rules as we are in those of real love'. Nelson wanted to think of Emma as his wife. Being Nelson, he had to persuade himself, with his egocentric logic, that because his motives were honest and pure, what he was doing was right. Their understanding had deepened to vows and promises; 'Forsaking all others' was already part of their commitment, hence his undertaking not to sleep on shore at Leghorn. A second Prayer Book injunction, 'Marriage was ordained for the procreation of children', chimed exactly with his own desire to cement their union with a child, a 'dear token of love', as he would subsequently call Horatia. The alternative is to believe that their child was a 'mistake', in spite of the fact that Emma had successfully avoided pregnancy during the previous eighteen years. Horatia would be born at the end of January 1801. Her conception must have been between 24 April and 23 May 1800, most likely in the great cabin of the *Foudroyant* (although if the indisposition Emma was suffering from, when she went on board *Foudroyant* on 24 April 1800 for their cruise to Syracuse and Malta, was morning sickness, the baby may have been conceived slightly earlier, in Palermo).

It was not so remarkable that Nelson and Emma did not become lovers until late 1799 or early 1800. Nelson's primary driving force was not an urgent, physical hunger but a deepening emotional dependence. Emma had lived by her body in her early years, but nothing in her subsequent life suggested powerful sexual motivation. Her four years of Greville and her fourteen years of Hamilton are stamped with sexual question marks, there being not the least hint of a child, or miscarriage, to indicate either a normal or an active sex life. There had not been the slightest suspicion of sexual adventure in the dissolute Court of Naples, or at the hands of British blades passing through. Now a thirty-four-year-old, married to a seventy-year-old, she had got into the arms of a forty-one-year-old, but it was not only the aphrodisiac of his fame that got her there. The foundations of Nelson and Emma's relationship were the bonds they formed by working together, and the congruence of their personalities. Both reacted to people and situations with their feelings. In Emma power of analysis and reflectiveness were totally absent. Nelson's seemed to have been applied exclusively to professional problems and in such an intuitive way as to be more in the nature of a gift than an ordinary

intellectual process. There were other important similarities. Both were
highly energetic to the point of being hyperactive. Both liked to decide
and settle things; neither was inclined to act as a restraining force on the
other. Emma's exhibitionism fed on Nelson's fame. Her managing nature
revelled in the feeling that he and his whole naval entourage were delightfully responsive to her wishes. Nelson's theatrical nature responded in
turn to her masterful and dramatic beauty. Socially speaking they were
very compatible. Her titled status and entrée, her European celebrity,
flattered him. Her inferiority of origin offered no challenge to his own
social insecurity. Neither of them had pronounced cultural or intellectual
pretensions, so there was nothing in the basic ordinariness of either to
intimidate or threaten the other. He was not offended, either by her
accent, or by her extrovert and good-natured noisiness. Her passionately
spendthrift nature was echoed in his own generosity and carelessness
about money. Their relationship was thus founded on solid rock. And
when, eventually, they made love it was for Nelson a revelation; afterwards thoughts of their *jouissance* were never far from his mind. His
friend Admiral Goodall could not have been wider of the mark in describing Nelson as Rinaldo in the arms of Armida the enchantress.[4] Nelson
loved Emma for herself. He admired her and was comfortable with her.
Her increasing roundness, and extravagance in thought, word and deed,
were to him irrelevant. She had become totally necessary to his existence.
Their choice of each other speaks volumes about both of them, especially
their need for reassurance and security.

Another vital consideration must have been surfacing. Hamilton's
return home was imminent, his life expectancy thereafter, conjectural. On
his death Greville would inherit and Emma could expect to be provided
for, but to what extent she could hardly tell. She and her mother must
have talked frequently about the future; not to put too fine a point on
it, about her next protector after Hamilton. Both would be acutely aware
of the risk in forming an unapproved extramarital connection. The great
unknown of the Nelson–Emma–Hamilton relationship has always been
whether Hamilton simply turned a blind eye, whether he signalled by
hints and behaviour that they had his blessing to be more than friends,
or whether there was an actual *menage-à-trois*. As the affair escalated
there was such an absence of friction that it had to be based on an explicit
understanding, which in effect gave each of them what they wanted.
Emma probably told Hamilton in October 1799 of her love for Nelson,

no doubt in tones of sadness and regret, with punctual but not excessive tears. She would continue to make him feel loved and needed, and never neglected. Sir William was no simpleton. He had always recognized that he would be in his dotage when Emma was in her prime. He had observed her growing attachment to Nelson and would readily have rationalized that at his age his creature comforts and pastimes were more important to him than a sexual monopoly of Emma. He admired and liked Nelson, treated him rather like a son and had grown accustomed to his presence. Having himself taken on his nephew's mistress he was hardly likely to be so fastidious as to be above handing her on to his younger 'best friend'. Financially he had something to gain; he owed his bankers £15,000, he had abandoned many possessions in the flight from Naples, his shipment of vases had gone down with the *Colossus* the previous December, and to cap it all there was Emma's inexhaustible capability for spending money. The benefit of spreading this female financial liability to the generous Nelson would appeal to his innate commercial instincts. If they all managed themselves discreetly, there would be no loss of face and he would continue to share Emma's company, and be looked after in his old age.

Nelson's marriage to Fanny, with whom he had spent only seven months in the previous seven years, was now merely an obstacle. It could not compete with a relationship which gave him everything he had been looking for. Being a father might have placed more obligation on him to be faithful, but in that sense Fanny was doubly unlucky. She had apparently failed to give him a child, and Josiah, whom Nelson had taken to sea as a surrogate son, had alienated him completely. Poor Fanny was guilty by association of that too. The fact is, Fanny *had* been fertile and had conceived Josiah in the first two months of her first marriage, although her subsequent child-bearing capacity may have been compromised by puerperal sepsis, minor enough to have gone unrecorded. She may have been fearful of giving birth again, and discouraged sexual relations. Nelson himself was fertile, as future events would prove. There is a wall of silence around their childlessness. Neither letters nor family tradition refer to it. There is no evidence of concern on Fanny's part or of efforts to search for cures, such as one would expect from a man of Nelson's active temperament.

Their start in married life had been inauspicious, living with Nelson's father in a cold Norfolk rectory, Nelson himself unemployed and on half pay. Having married Fanny 'out of esteem', he may not have been a very effective lover. Then after seven uninterrupted years 'on the beach' with Fanny, Nelson immediately set about making a fool of himself with Adelaide Correglia in Leghorn. When he went to bed with Emma he liked it very much, she being like Adelaide, a woman whose life had required her to be active in pleasing: 'those liberties with Me which no woman in this World but Yourself ever did.' Nelson's sister Catherine naturally blamed Fanny's frigidity. 'He had great excuses. . . . She was so very cold.'

Catherine's husband George put his finger on Nelson's need for love. 'Lauded admired and sought everywhere but at home where complaining and reproach formed a sad contrast to the merited reception he met elsewhere.' He went on, 'His warm heart eagerly strove to attach itself to some object of primary affection: if Lady Hamilton had not artfully endeavoured to inveigle it, some other female would.'[5] Lady Hardy, wife of Nelson's Hardy, knew Fanny at first hand and was not far from the George Matcham point of view:

> Lady Nelson was a good, well disposed woman, surprisingly tiresome and prejudiced and, though nothing could excuse her husband's conduct towards her, it was not surprising that, used to the gay and unrestrained conversation of Lady Hamilton, he should have been very much bored by his commonplace wife, who however retained to the last the most extraordinary devotion to his Memory and excused even his partiality to her Rival, owning how difficult it must have been to resist her, which I did not myself at all think, but Lord Nelson has never been in clever artful Women's Society and was completely humbugged by Lady Hamilton.[6]

Now Lady Hardy was a social animal of the highest order and therefore likely and well positioned to look down on Fanny and through Emma.

Nelson's entanglement and lifestyle and the gossip they occasioned were becoming increasingly upsetting to Troubridge, still suffering from his own accumulation of stress. The Nile had been a personal disaster. He had thrown himself into a frenzy of compensatory effort, had absorbed the hard blow of his wife's death, had undergone frustrating and distasteful duty in the liberation of Naples and was now engaged in the equally frustrating siege of Malta. He had observed Nelson's presence at junketings in Palermo and his dancing attendance on Lady Hamilton. Above all he had heard the talk, the idle gossip in the wardrooms of the fleet. If he had been less stressed, if he had loved his Admiral less, he might have handled things differently; with more worldliness and cynicism towards the reports of idle tongues. But he could not bear the contrast between his image of the hero of the Nile and what now came to his notice.

Pardon me, my Lord, it is my sincere esteem for you that makes me mention it. I know you can have no pleasure sitting up all night at cards; why then sacrifice your health, comfort, purse, ease, everything to the custom of a country where your stay cannot be long. Your Lordship is a stranger to half that happens and the talk it occasions. If you knew what your friends feel for you, I am sure you would cut out all the nocturnal parties. The gambling of the people of Palermo is publicly talked of everywhere. I beseech your Lordship leave off. I wish my pen could tell you my feelings, I am sure you would oblige me. Lady Hamilton's character will suffer; nothing can prevent people from talking. A gambling woman in the eyes of an Englishman, is lost.[7]

Clearly Troubridge was not well up on gambling women or he would have known that Lord Spencer's sister Georgiana, Duchess of Devonshire was one of the more notorious lady gamblers of her day, and that female members of Almack's had right of veto over aspiring male members. He was temporarily mollified by Emma's response on gambling, and 'most completely happy at your promise to play no more . . . the construction put on things which may appear to your Ladyship innocent, and I make no doubt, done with the best intention – still your enemies will, and do give things a different colouring. . . . I therefore risk your displeasure by telling you. I am much gratified you have taken it as I meant it – purely good.'[8]

Powerful and charismatic leaders generate equally powerful dependency feelings in their followers. Troubridge needed Nelson to be at the helm and was resentful that Nelson's attention was being diverted from himself. There is an insatiability about such dependency. Nelson had supported Troubridge staunchly, had got him his gold medal, his first lieutenant had been promoted and in October 1799 Troubridge had been created Baronet for his effort in securing the capitulation of Rome and Civitavecchia, a responsibility which Nelson had placed on Troubridge and for which he was given full credit. St Vincent never spoke of Troubridge other than in superlatives, 'capable of commanding the fleet of England' (something he would never allow Nelson), 'the ablest adviser and best executive officer in his Majesty's naval service with honour and courage bright as his sword', 'the greatest man in his walk that the English navy ever produced'. But here was an overwrought Troubridge, at the end of his tether about Malta, fearing for Nelson's reputation. He was frustrated by not achieving his mission because of factors outside his control, perhaps feeling some resentment at the distasteful tasks Nelson had asked him to perform, but still displaying his characteristic loyalty and protectiveness. In a series of passionate and rather unhinged letters to Nelson in early January 1800, from Malta, he poured it all out: 'I wish I was at your Lordship's elbow for an hour – all, all will be thrown on you, rely on it. I will parry the blow as much as is in my power; I forsee much mischief brewing. God bless your Lordship – I am miserable I cannot assist your operations more. . . . 'I curse the day I ever served the King of Naples. . . . We have characters my Lord to lose; these people have none. Do not suffer their infamous conduct to fall on us. . . . Such is the fever of my brain this minute, that I asure you, on my honour, if the Palermo traitors were here, I would shoot them first, and then myself.' . . . 'All I write to you is known at the Queen's: I suspect my letters are opened before they reach you . . . I pray your Lordship be cautious; your honest open manner of acting will be made a handle of. It is necessary to be very vigilant over the deceitful set you have to deal with: every nerve of mine shall be exerted to forward your Lordship's views and service. I cannot assist you so fast as I could wish, so little depends on me; that little you shall find well done.'[9]

Nelson was highly empathetic but did not get drawn in to Troubridge's emotion. He took the line of hard facts, that the King had made his required contribution in gold, that there was an undoubted shortage of corn and that he Nelson was doing everything he could. However, the invariable supporter of his subordinates, he advised Troubridge, 'You must in the last extremity seize vessels loaded with corn; the inhabitants cannot starve. If, unfortunately, you are forced to this measure, I am confident it will be exercised with great discretion.'[10] A few days later he backed Troubridge to the hilt when he ordered vessels carrying corn to be seized from the port of Girgenti and taken to the starving besiegers of Malta. Nelson described it to Hamilton as 'an act of the most absolute and imperious necessity. . . . I trust that the Government of this country will never again force any of our Royal Master's servants to so unpleasant an alternative.'[11] To Keith, Nelson said, 'I have been begging of his Sicilian Majesty small supplies of money and corn to keep the Maltese in arms and barely to keep from starving the poor inhabitants.'[12] Nelson knew that even if he positioned himself continuously before Malta it was extremely unlikely that he could have any impact without the troops he correctly judged to be necessary. General Fox was sitting on his hands in Minorca, unwilling to strengthen Graham at Malta. The Russians had moved their troops from Messina to Corfu and the only option he had was to renew his efforts to get Sicilian troops. The fact is that without Nelson's presence at Palermo, within reach of the King and Acton, there would probably have been no support at all from the Neapolitans.

When Nelson had set out to meet Keith at Leghorn on 16 January his frame of mind, which he hadn't minded imparting to Troubridge, had been to wash his hands of command. 'Lord Keith is gone to see what the Austrians are after on the coast of Genoa and from thence comes here; then I have nothing to do but obey.'[13] A complaint to Keith from Sir Sidney Smith winged its way to Nelson: 'Sir Sidney Smith complains much of want of provisions, salt particularly. If your Lordship has not sent him sufficient supplies, let it be done as soon as possible, requiring that he send me a state and condition of the ships & vessels under his orders.'[14] This was calculated to make Nelson feel like the office boy and was setting a scene in which Keith and Nelson would each do his best to marginalize the other. Arrived back at Palermo he sent a note to Emma which openly expressed his chagrin: 'Having a Commander-in-Chief, I cannot come on shore till I have made my manners to him. Times are changed but if he does not come on shore directly, I will not wait. In the meantime I send Allen to inquire how you are. Send me word for I am anxious to hear of you. It has been no fault of mine that I have been so long absent. I cannot command, and now only obey.'[15] Tucked inside would be that long, unsigned unaddressed, love letter which could now be safely delivered by the hand of his servant the trusty

Allen. There is in that 'no fault of mine', a very uncharacteristic note. Nelson was very much used to pleasing himself and not at all used to making excuses.

While in Palermo, Keith adopted a rather different line with the royals than the compliant Nelson was accustomed to deliver. 'His Majesty who dined on board yesterday (with the Queen and Royal family) asked when I intended to return. I replied when his Majesty intended returning to Naples I would endeavour to provide a suitable squadron, but that Palermo lay out of our way, and all the ships must necessarily be employed in conjunction with the allies against the enemy whenever the campaign opened.'[16]

Accompanying Keith to Palermo was another Scot, a very bright twenty-four-year-old, Lieutenant Lord Cochrane, heir to the ninth Earl of Dundonald but all the same,'without expectations other than those arising from my own exertions'. Having survived with some aplomb the inherent difficulties of joining the Navy as a seventeen-year-old midshipman and Lord, he was soon to show himself to be an officer of aggressive genius. A year after meeting Nelson, his tiny 158 ton sloop *Speedy* would fight and capture the Spanish frigate *El Gamo* of more than 600 tons, *Speedy*'s fourteen 4-pounder pop guns matched against twenty-two long 12-pounders, eight long 8-pounders and two 24-pounder carronades; his crew of fifty-four officers, men and boys pitted against 319 Spaniards. Having placed his ship under *El Gamo*'s stern, where he was below her guns and could elevate his own to fire up through her deck, he ordered the ship's Doctor Mr Guthrie to take the helm and lay *Speedy* alongside the Spaniard, while every other member of the tiny crew prepared to board, an event out-romancing even the most extravagant imaginings of fiction. He received plenty of encouragement from Nelson, which he recalled in his autobiography: 'The impression left on my mind during these opportunities of association with Nelson was that of his being the embodiment of dashing courage, which would not take much trouble to circumvent an enemy, but being confronted with one would regard victory so much a matter of course as hardly to deem the chance of defeat worth consideration.' And he recorded one of Nelson's frequent injunctions: 'never mind manoeuvres, always go at them'.[17] Like had been speaking to like, for as a dashing, aggressive, humane frigate captain, Cochrane would prove to be at least Nelson's equal.

It is the differences between them that are so illuminating. In spite of his great gifts Cochrane's career was to be spent in the shallows. He did not have the qualities necessary to be successful in an organization. Nelson, paradoxically it might seem in the light of his popular reputation as one of the great mavericks of the Navy, was in fact an instinctively committed and effective organization man. Always willing to work with the grain of the Navy, his instinct was always to collaborate, using his wonderfully persuasive and dominant personality, to convince and lead subordinates, peers and superiors alike. He was able to distinguish those situations where he could take a stand against authority, and succeed because of the ground he had chosen to fight on. He also knew when to give in. Cochrane was the very opposite. A man of high principles, great intelligence, humane feeling, wide sympathies, inventive professional brilliance, he could not appreciate that 'being right' was never the route to success in organizations. He pursued points even when they had been well and truly lost, perceived minor administrative oversights as personal slights, and became a crusader against incompetence and graft in the naval administration. Alas, hierarchies have a very low tolerance for being lectured at and Cochrane's crusade led him into the even more dangerous water of wearing two hats, those of naval captain and MP. In the long run he did undoubted public good, but brought on himself years of disillusion and disappointment.

It might appear inappropriate to compare Nelson with an officer who so evidently had a capacity to destroy his own career, but this brilliant and celebrated captain, hero of the Basque Roads fire-ship action of 1809, throws into sharp relief Nelson's critically important capacity, to be different, very assertive and yet remain credible. For example, Nelson's professional credibility was no more than slightly dented by his high-handed treatment of Keith, simply because of the way he communicated his intentions and disarmed potential critics. Cochrane's career also highlights Nelson's profound lack of real interest in reforming the organization and administration of the Navy. His whole motivation was as a fighting commander, a hero bent on fame and the enemy's destruction.

When Cochrane recalled in his autobiography how Keith put him in command of Nelson's prize, the *Généreux*, he made no further references to Nelson, nor to wardroom gossip about Nelson and Emma, nor to any comments from Keith. What happened with the *Généreux* was that three days after Keith and Nelson sailed from Palermo, Nelson, having parted from Keith, fell in with a small French squadron, under Rear-Admiral Perrée, in *Le Généreux* 74, one of the Nile survivors bound from Toulon to Malta with troops and supplies.

Lieutenant Parsons, an eyewitness, gives a graphic account of the encounter in his *Nelsonian Reminiscences*, of 1843.

'Ah! an enemy, Mr Stains. I pray God it may be Le Genereux. The signal for a general chase, Sir Ed'ard, (the Nelsonian pronunciation of Edward) make the Foudroyant fly!'

Thus spoke the heroic Nelson; and every exertion that emulation could inspire was used to crowd the squadron with canvas, the Northumberland taking the lead, with the flagship close on her quarter.

'This will not do, Sir Ed'ard; it is certainly Le Genereux, and to my flagship she can alone surrender. Sir Ed'ard, we must and shall beat the Northumberland.'

'I will do the utmost, my lord; get the engines to work on the sails – hang butts of water to the stays-pipe the hammocks down, and each man place shot in them – slack the stays, knock up the wedges, and give the masts play – start off the water, Mr James, and pump the ship'.

The Foudroyant is drawing a-head, and at last takes the lead in the chase. The Admiral is working his fin, (the stump of his right arm,) do not cross his hawse I advise you.'

The advice was good, for at that moment Nelson opened furiously on the quartermaster at the conn. 'I'll knock you off your perch, you rascal, if you are so inattentive. Sir Ed'ard, send your best quarter-master to the weather wheel.'

'A strange sail a-head of the chase!' called the look-out man.

'Youngster, to the mast-head. What! going without your glass, and be d——d to you? Let me know what she is immediately.'

'A sloop of war or frigate, my lord,' shouted the young signal-midshipman.

'Demand her number.'

'The Success, my lord.'

'Captain Peard; signal to cut off the flying enemy – great odds, though-thirty two small guns to eighty large ones.'

'The Success has hove-to athwart-hawse of the *Genereux*, and is firing her larboard broadside. The Frenchman has hoisted his tri-colour, with a rear-admirals flag.'

'Bravo – *Success, at her again*!'

'She has wore round, my lord, and firing her starboard broadside. It has winged her, my lord – her flying kites are flying away altogether. The enemy is close on the Success, who must receive her tremendous broadside.' The Genereux opens her fire on her little enemy, and every person stands aghast, afraid of the consequences. The smoke clears away, and there is the Success, crippled it is true, but, bull-dog like, bearing up after the enemy.

'The signal for the Success to discontinue the action, and come under my stern,' said Lord Nelson; 'she has done well for her size. Try a shot from the lower deck at her, Sir Ed'ard.'

'It goes over her.'

'Beat to quarters, and fire coolly at her masts and yards.'

Le Genereux at this moment opened her fire on us; and, as a shot passed through the mizzen stay sail, Lord Nelson, patting one of the youngsters on the head, asked him jocularly how he relished the music; and observing something like alarm depicted on his countenance, consoled him with the information that Charles XII ran away from the first shot he heard, though afterwards he was called 'The Great,' and deservedly, from his bravery. 'I, therefore,' said Lord Nelson, 'hope much from you in future.'

Here the Northumberland opened her fire, and down came the tri-coloured ensign, amidst the thunder of our united cannon.[18]

What is so striking about Parsons's eyewitness account is its revelation of Nelson as a competitive, hard driving, ruthlessly demanding commander – and how in the presence of sudden death his personality took on a calm and reassuring detachment.

When Nelson wrote to Emma he was in a sardonic mood, 'Had you seen the Peer receive me, I know not what you would have done; but I can guess. But never mind! I told him, that I had made a vow, if I took the *Généreux* by myself, it was my intention to strike my Flag. To which he made no answer.'[19] Nelson then took a quite extraordinary, and apparently childish step. He wrote to his brother Maurice at the Navy Office, 'I have written to Lord Spencer, and sent him my Journal, to prove that the *Généreux* was taken by me, and owing to my plan; that my quitting

Lord Keith was at my own risk, and for which, if I had not succeeded, I might have been broke. If I had not, the *Généreux* would never have been taken.'[20]

In the event Nelson's distrust of Keith was well enough founded. Keith's dispatch, which accompanied Nelson's letter, shows that he made his own priority the covering of the harbour to prevent troops being landed, but indicates clearly that he positioned Nelson and that Nelson 'conducted himself with skill, and great address, in *comprehending my signals*, which the state of the weather led me greatly to suspect'.[21]

A revelatory footnote to the *Généreux* affair is provided by Tyson, Nelson's secretary who had been appointed Prize Agent by the captains involved in her capture. He tells Emma that his news was received by Keith with 'a number of black looks and orders given respecting the prizes which I did not like'. Tyson very quickly appreciated where the problem lay and promptly gave Keith's brother, also his secretary, one half of the agency, which assured him of a cut and thus, 'brightened all up again and now I am one of the best fellows in the world with him. I have got orders from him to the officers at Mahon to purchase every thing she has got in, and supply me with storehouses etc.' He adds, 'I almost regret that I had not been born a Scotchman, and had not Lancashire produced a Lady Hamilton, whom I am so proud of calling my countrywoman I do not know but I might hail from the North of the Tweed.' Emma had insinuated herself into Nelson's naval affairs, which explains the familiar and sycophantic tone of Tyson's letter. He also felt free to discuss Nelson's health with her. 'I am exceedingly anxious to hear of our invaluable Lord Nelson, as in his last letter he mentions a return of the pain in his heart of which he suffered so much coming from Egypt.'[22] Ball was another who wrote direct to Emma for he too had felt the full weight of her charm. 'I find that you fascinate all the navy as much at Palermo as you did at Naples. If we had many such advocates, everybody would be a candidate for our profession.'[23]

In general the Nile captains, and those close to Nelson resented Keith, closed ranks and took Nelson's part against him. Alexander Ball wrote to Mr Macauley, Treasurer of Malta on 22 March, 'General Graham will not allow my Maltese to make false attacks, all I can urge will not do. I can perceive that he gives in to Lord Keith's prejudices, as he relates and repeats whatever is against our friends at Palermo. He does not do it to me knowing that my friendship revolts at it.'[24] Earlier in the year

Captain Blackwood had confided in Nelson, 'I must also confess to your Lordship that I did not wish to fall in with Lord Keith, who most probably would have changed the good orders your Lordship gave me.'[25] Troubridge in that January letter to Emma said, 'The new Admiral, I suppose will send us home – the new hands will serve them better, as they will soon be all from the north, full of liberality and generosity, as all Scots are, with some exceptions.'[26]

By 24 February Troubridge and Nelson were in still deeper water. It would seem that Nelson had at least given an impression of taking offence at some apparent want of attention on Troubridge's behalf, and Troubridge had replied:

> General Graham and Ball will tell your Lordship how ill I was, and did not reach my Ship till ten o'clock, much tired & etc., & etc . . . your letter of the 22nd, which I found on my return last night . . . has really so unhinged me, that I am quite unmanned and crying. I would sooner forfeit my life – my everything, than be deemed ungrateful to an Officer, and friend, I feel I owe so much to. Pray, pray, acquit me; for I really do not merit it. There is not a man on earth I love, honour, and esteem more than your Lordship . . . I beseech you hear the entreaties of a sincere friend, and do not go to Sicilly for the present. . . . Leave the Foudroyant out, and hoist your flag in the Culloden, to carry on the operations with the General. Everything shall be done to make it comfortable and pleasing to you: a month will do all. If you comply with my request I shall be happy, as I shall then be convinced I have not forfeited your friendship.[27]

Even when allowance is made for the fact that Troubridge was suffering from jaundice, the anguish of his letter leaves no doubt of the possessiveness he felt for Nelson, and his feeling that Emma was coming between them.

But Nelson was determined not to stay long. Keith had left him on 24 February, 'to attend to other services of public importance', and ordered Nelson to 'adopt and prosecute the necessary measures for contributing to the complete reduction of Malta'.[28] He left detailed instructions and ordered Nelson to shift his base from Palermo to Syracuse or Messina. All in all, it was a patronizing set of orders from a man who had himself nothing to add to the situation, who wanted to get away to a theatre

where there might be greater hopes of success and reward. Nelson immediately sent him a letter which amounted to a refusal to be thus treated:
'my state of health is such, that it is impossible I can much longer remain
here. Without some rest I am gone. I must therefore, whenever I find the
service will admit of it, request your permission to go to my friends at
Palermo, for a few weeks, and leave the command here to Commodore
Troubridge.'[29] He passed over in silence the business of moving his base
from Palermo. In fact Nelson stayed on, but gave Keith another health
bulletin four days later: 'My state of health is very precarious. Two days
ago I dropped with a pain in my heart, and I am always in a fever; but
the hopes of these gentry coming out shall support me for a few days
longer.'[30] On the 25th he wrote to Emma, ' by Lord Keith's order, to me,
Palermo is no longer to be the rendezvous of our ships . . . I long to give
it all up. Nineteen sail of the line, and four Admirals are enough for one
man; at the taking of sixteen I have borne my flag. My health has been
so bad, that yesterday I wrote a letter to Lord Keith for two or three
months leave of absence [a little white lie to Emma since he had asked
Keith for a few weeks] to go to Palermo, and quiet rest, but I found if I
went at this moment perhaps we might lose Malta, therefore for a very
short time I have given way, as I have often done to the public service;
but I really want rest and a great deal of your kind care.'[31]

Ball also wrote to Emma about their 'heaven-born Admiral, upon
whom fortune smiles wherever he goes'. He wanted to achieve the opposite of what Nelson desired. 'I do not think a short stay here will hurt
his health, particularly as his ship is at anchor and his mind not harassed.
Troubridge and I are extremely anxious that the French ships, (Guillaume
Tell in particular) and the French garrison at La Valetta, should surrender to him. . . . What a gratification it would be to us if you and
Sir William could pay us a short visit. We would make up a snug whist
party every evening for Sir William but we should fall very short in our
attempts to amuse you, when we consider the multiplicity of engagements
and amusements you have every day at Palermo.'[32] It was signed, 'Brother
and friend'.

Troubridge and Ball sensed a crisis and were pooling their influence to
keep Nelson away from Palermo, but they were not fated to succeed. It
is hard to believe that Nelson did not hear the messages they were giving
him but he was clearly not prepared to listen. On 8 March he simply
told Keith, 'I am sorry to tell you that my health continues to be so very

indifferent, that I am obliged, in justice to myself, to retire to Palermo
for a few weeks, and to direct Troubridge to carry on the service during
my necessary absence. I shall quit the station when matters are all put in
a right way.'[33] As Nelson departed he wrote to Goodall, whose Rinaldo
and Armida letter he had just received, 'I am now on my route to my
friends at Palermo. I shall rest there quiet for two weeks, and then judge
by my feelings whether I am able to serve well, and with comfort to
myself.'[34] Needless to say he did not refer to Rinaldo and Armida.

Paradoxically it would appear that Nelson was trying to appear in as
good a light as possible at the Admiralty as far as his relationship with
Keith was concerned. Admiral Young noted in a letter to Keith on 30
March 1800, 'I am very happy to find you and Nelson on such good
terms and him so reasonable. I have a letter from him in which he says
you may depend on all the execution he is master of to support your
measures, but he speaks of himself as not very well. You have made a
most judicious change of rendez-vous which nothing but the infatuation
you mention would have prevented being done before. I am grieved,
as everyone must be, that a man who on other occasions has done so
well should on this have so sadly exposed himself to ridicule and
censure.'[35]

Nelson was still melancholic on his return to Palermo and wrote rather
pathetically to Troubridge, 'As yet it is too soon to form an opinion
whether I ever can be cured of my complaint, which it appears to me
growing something like Oakes's [Captain George Oakes, who died in
1797]. At present I see but glimmering hopes, and probably my career
of service is at an end, unless the French fleet shall come into the
Mediterranean, when nothing shall prevent my dying at my post. I hope
my dear friend that your complaints are better. Pray do not fret at
anything. I wish I never had, but my return to Syracuse in 1798, broke
my heart, which on any extraordinary anxiety now shows itself, be that
feeling pain or pleasure.'[36] The same day Nelson sent Keith a similar bulletin. Even today, letters such as these would be regarded as unmascu-
line, to say the least. Then they must have been read with incredulity and
baffled helplessness by all who were not friends and aware of his mood
swings.

In mid-January Sir Sidney Smith had come again into the foreground.
He had decided to become the midwife of the Convention of El Arish,
signed on 24 January 1800 by himself, the French General Kléber, and

the Turks. The Convention would allow the French Army to evacuate Egypt with its baggage, artillery, ships and transports and effects, and with passports and convoys, 'necessary to secure its safe return to France'. Keith typically tried to find out what his masters wanted him to do before committing himself. He wrote on 1 March, hiding behind Lord Elgin, who he said 'not only concurred but strongly recomended the measure', and said he was inclined to support the Convention. (Elgin was in fact foaming at the mouth at Smith's wilful conduct.) He ended his letter, 'Under these circumstances I am exceedingly desirous of their Lord-ships' direction for my proceedings, as I am much inclined to do right.'[37] Nelson did not require the Admiralty's help in reaching a sound strate-gic judgement; it seemed so obvious to him and his view was subse-quently shared by Spencer. On 15 January he sent Smith an ominous note, 'I have wrote to Lord Keith and home, that I did not give credit that it was possible for you to give any passport for a single Frenchman, much less the Army, after my positive order of March 18th, 1799.'[38] This had been a brutally frank and unequivocal direction, 'I must therefore strictly charge and command you, never to give any French ship or man leave to quit Egypt . . . I shall not pay the smallest attention to any such passport after your notification; and you are to put my orders in force, not on any pretence to permit a single Frenchman to leave Egypt.'[39] Keith finally repudiated the Convention and Kléber ordered a renewal of hostilities. Smith came under heavy fire and on 9 May Grenville the Foreign Secretary wrote to Spencer, 'I have as I expected, received from Worontzow a heavy complaint against Sir Sidney Smith for his conduct in the negotiation of Kléber's capitulation. May I give him to understand in my answer that Sir Sidney Smith will by this time have been with-drawn from that station? If this has been done, it will be better proof of disavowal than all the assurances I could give.'[40] Spencer had in fact already opened up the possibility with Keith of pulling Smith out of the Levant, placing him, as he said to Keith, 'more under your own eye and direction' and replacing him with Nelson.[41] There is a kind of Olympian carelessness in the way he would allow Keith to dispose of an asset like Nelson, simply because the wilful Smith had become unacceptable to the Russians and the Foreign Office. Much later in the year, at the end of September, Henry Dundas gave the government's last judgement on El Arish: 'My words had almost stuck in my throat when I defended the measure in the House of Commons, and I am sure I see not the possibility of defending it when the whole business comes to be known in its full extent.'[42] Nelson's judgement had been vindicated.

Meanwhile, on 24 March the *Foudroyant* had returned without him to the blockade of Malta, and in company with *Lion,* and *Penelope*, Berry captured *Le Guillaume Tell*. Berry's brief account of the action concluded, 'All hands behaved as you would have wished. How we prayed for you, God knows. . . . Love to all.' There were two postscripts, 'Pray send this to my wife, or write Admiralty', and, 'Within hail before I fired'[43] – witness to Nelson's capacity to inspire those he led with a desire to emulate his own headlong attack and deadly purpose. For Nelson this was like the final verse of a song, and his reaction shows why his officers loved him so much. 'My dear Berry, I am sensible of your kindness in wishing my presence at the finish of the Egyptian Fleet, but I have no cause for sorrow. The thing could not be better done, and I would not for all the world rob you of one particle of your well earned laurels. Thank kindly for me all my brave friends in the *Foudroyant*; and whatever fate awaits me, my attachment to them will never cease but with my life. . . . My task is done, my health is lost, and the orders of the great Earl of St Vincent are completely fulfilled – thanks, ten thousand thanks, to my brave friends! . . .'[44] He then had pleasure in playing the same tune with virtually the same words to Lord Minto, but with an additional cadenza, 'May all orders be as punctually obeyed, but never again an Officer at the close, of what I must, without being thought vain, (for such I am represented by my enemies,) call a glorious career, be so treated! I go with our dear friends Sir William and Lady Hamilton; but whether by water or land depends on the will of Lord Keith.'[45] With Spencer he laid it on even more thickly:

I send you Sir Edward Berry's letter, and I am sure your Lordship will not be sparing of promotion to the deserving. My friends wished me to be present. I have no such wish; for a something might have been given me, which now cannot. Not for all the world would I rob any man of a sprig of laurel – much less my children of the *Foudroyant*! I love her as a fond father, a darling child, and glory in her deeds. I am vain enough to feel the effects of my school. Lord Keith sending me nothing, I have not, of course, a free communication. I have wrote him for permission to return to England, when you will see a broken hearted man. My spirit cannot submit patiently. My complaint, which is principally a swelling of the heart, is at times alarming to my friends, but not to, my dear Lord, your obliged and . . .'.

He added a PS: 'If I may again say it, what would I feel if my brother was a Commissioner of the Navy – for ever grateful.'[46] Keith got his letter too but Nelson noticeably withheld the formal but customary congratulation to his senior officer and instead rubbed in the salt. 'The conduct of these excellent Officers enabled Sir Edward Berry to place the *Foudroyant* where she ought, and is the fittest Ship in the world to be, close alongside the *William Tell* – one of the largest and finest two decked ships in the world . . . I thank God I was not present, for it would finish me could I have taken a sprig of these brave men's laurels: they are, and I glory in them, my darling children, served in my school, and all of us caught our professional zeal and fire from the great and good Earl of St Vincent.'[47] What is so striking about these letters is that they all tell exactly the same story: that Nelson was not in the business of taking credit due to others. Naturally this success soured his relations even more with Keith who in spite of his one-eighth share of the prize, indulged in more tit for tat, refusing to promote a surgeon recommended by Nelson (the one who had removed his arm at Tenerife) and disagreeing with a contract Nelson had entered into for Marsala wine.[48]

On 23 April Hamilton, having been superseded by Paget, presented his letters of recall. He had had to accept the inevitable and the next day *Foudroyant* sailed from Palermo with Emma, Sir William and a few friends to Syracuse and Malta, not returning to Palermo till 1 June. This voyage had no military purpose and no justification. It was more in the nature of a honeymoon or pleasure cruise. Its chief purposes were sightseeing and celebrating Emma's birthday, its main outcome Horatia's conception. Nelson was using *Foudroyant* as his personal yacht. At the same time as they were swanning around Sicily, Spencer was writing to Nelson, reflecting no doubt his reaction to the general flow of gossip and some irritation that Nelson had not worked a miracle at Malta, '. . . my extreme regret that your health should be such as to oblige you to quit your station off Malta, at a time when I should suppose there must be the finest prospect of its reduction. . . . If the Enemy should come into the Mediterranean, and whenever they do, it will be suddenly, I should be much concerned to hear that you learnt of their arrival in that Sea, either on Shore or in a Transport at Palermo.'[49] Spencer had now made up his mind and on 9 May wrote Nelson a private letter, at the same time as formal Admiralty permission went to Keith to allow Nelson to return home.

It is by no means my wish or intention to call you away from service but having observed that you have been under the necessity of quitting your station off Malta, on account of the state of your health which I am persuaded you could not have thought of doing without such necessity, it appeared to me much more advisable for you to come home at once, than to be obliged to remain inactive at Palermo, while active service was going on in other parts of the station . . . I am quite clear, and I believe I am joined in opinion by all your friends here, that you will be more likely to recover your health and strength in England than in an inactive situation at a Foreign Court, however pleasing the respect and gratitude shown to you for your services may be, and no testimonies of respect and gratitude fom that Court to you can be, I am convinced too great for the very essential services you have rendered it. I trust you will take in good part what I have taken the liberty to write to you as a friend . . .[50]

By 20 June Nelson had received Spencer's letters. The word 'inactive' had cut him to the quick. 'Your two letters of April 25th and May 9th, gave me much pain; but I trust you and all my friends will believe that mine cannot be an inactive life, although it may not carry all the outward parade of much ado about nothing.' With his usual assertiveness he announced his intentions: 'The extraordinary position in which we find ourselves at this moment makes it undetermined what measures may be proper for the Queen of Naples to pursue; and until I have safely got rid of my charge, nothing shall separate me from her. I should feel myself a beast could I have a thought for anything but her comfort.'[51]

After two years the curtain was about to fall on Naples, Palermo, and the last remnants of the Band of Brothers. Troubridge was moving on to be captain of the Channel fleet under St Vincent, who had been appointed Commander-in-Chief of that fleet at Spencer's instigation so that like the

Mediterranean fleet it might be revivified by St Vincent's organizing genius. Nelson wrote to Spencer on 5 June 1800, 'I only wish for the sake of our country, that Troubridge may recover sufficiently to undergo the fatigue of his high and honourable station.'[52] Troubridge's departure, the Queen's departure for Vienna, the Hamiltons' return to England, a sterile relationship with Keith, had brought this chapter of Nelson's life to a close. 'I am from various causes no longer of any use.'[53] He would also know by now that Emma was pregnant.

Meanwhile a new military challenge was about to appear. Bonaparte had abandoned his Army in Egypt, evaded the British blockade and landed in the south of France on 9 October 1799. Within a month he had become the instrument for political change. In the *coup d'état* of 18 Brumaire, Bonaparte overthrew the Directory, dispersed the legislative council and established a consulate of three, with himself the First Consul. With insurrection in western France, and rejection of his Christmas peace feelers by Britain, only military victory could consolidate his grip on France.

As usual, allied offensive operations in Italy had been a matter of fits and starts. Suvorov, having overrun Piedmont in summer 1799 had been diverted to Switzerland. However, the Austrians had reopened their offensive in early April 1800 with Melas pushing west along the Riviera, cutting off Masséna in Genoa and propelling Suchet back to the River Var. At sea Keith was focusing his attention on the blockade of Genoa. Then in June all changed. Bonaparte's reorganized Army appeared over the St Bernard pass. Melas retreated, was narrowly but sufficiently defeated by Bonaparte at Marengo, and forced into the armistice of Alessandria by which the whole of Liguria, Piedmont and Lombardy were given up to Bonaparte.

It was on 14 June, the day of Marengo, that Nelson sailed into Leghorn, about a hundred miles to the south of Genoa, with the Queen, three princesses, Prince Leopold, and Sir William and Emma in the *Foudroyant*, with *Alexander* and *Princess Charlotte* in company. Maria Carolina had not wished to return to Naples following the restoration of the monarchy. She had had enough of Naples and Neapolitans for the time being, and was out of charity with her husband. She had prescribed for herself a home visit to Vienna to see her daughter the Empress of Austria. It was on a project of this magnitude that Nelson was now engaged.

Sir John Moore, the future hero of Corunna, and ambivalent and uncon-
structive leader in Corsica, saw Nelson in Leghorn and commented on his
appearance. 'Nelson is covered with stars, ribbons and medals, more like
a prince of an opera than the conqueror of the Nile. It is really melancholy
to see a brave and good man, who has deserved well of his country, cut so
pitiful a figure.'[54] Sir John obviously had a great antipathy to medals and
decorations. It is a pity he was not at the Admiralty in November 1801 to
see Sir Sidney Smith arrive, 'attired in the Turkish dress, turban, robe,
shawl, and girdle round his waist, with a brace of pistols'.[55]

Nelson found himself having to respond immediately to the Queen's
alarmed reactions to the uncertain situation. He was also unwell. He
wrote to Spencer, 'the situation of the two Armies renders the Queen a
little anxious; but her great mind is superior to all difficulties. . . . Four
days out of seven I am confined to my bed, but I hope for better times.'[56]
Nelson did not, at least for the moment, appear fully to appreciate the
situation. He was untypically out of touch. On the 19th Keith brought
him up to date. All the forts and garrisons in the Genoese territories were
to be evacuated. Lord Nelson was to help in that operation. The French
would enter Genoa on 24 June. Leghorn and Tuscany would continue
under the Emperor's troops.

Notwithstanding the crisis, Keith, had orders to allow Nelson to
proceed home by land or sea and did not stand in his way. But he did
expressly forbid him to use any British ships to return the Queen to
Palermo in the event of her deciding not to proceed to Vienna. Keith was
evidently distracted and somewhat overwhelmed:

> . . . wretched situation to which we are reduced distracts me. . . . told
> from England there is not a Ship to be sent out . . . directed to under-
> take many and distant important services. . . . impossible to let the
> *Foudroyant* go to England . . . could not consent to yielding a
> Frigate to a lesser application than that of a King. . . . I think for the
> accommodation of those I love, who are with you, they should get
> to Mahon instantly . . . there the *Seahorse* is hourly expected . . .
> and, of course at their command. . . . As to yourself, the *Princess
> Charlotte* will take you, provided you persist in going home, of
> which I hope your health does not stand in need God knows, I wish
> more was in my power for you all; but really the late unfortunate
> events make me tremble for all Italy.[57]

Two days later, on 21 June, Keith wrote again as the level of his anxiety rose, 'I have seen a man who has come from Buonaparte. He, Buonaparte said, publicly, there's one Power still in Italy to be reduced, before I can give it Peace. . . . Let the Queen go to Vienna as fast as she can. If the Fleet gets the start of ours a day, Sicily cannot hold out even that one day.'[58]

Nelson had ordered the *Santa Dorotea* and *Alexander* to proceed immediately to the Gulf of Especia to carry out Keith's orders, but told him he was keeping *Foudroyant* and some Neapolitan vessels. He appears studiously to have avoided referring to Keith's private letters, although in writing to Berry on the 21st he tells him, '*Foudroyant* must be kept ready for sea, and is to proceed to Mahon: at present it is uncertain whether I can go in her. . . . His Lordship believes reports of the Brest Fleet, which I give not the smallest credit to.'[59] Clearly he judged that Keith was panicking, but equally clearly his own mind was firmly focused on his own affairs. On the same day he huffed and puffed unrealistically to Lord Minto, 'The shameful scandalous terms entered into with Buonaparte, must ever reflect disgrace on the Austrian arms, unless the signer and adviser are shot, for nothing can justify a General, at the head of 20,000 brave men for signing such a paper. I am mad. Our dear Queen of Naples is today unwell, agitated by these events. As soon as we see her safely off, Sir William, Lady Hamilton and myself, pursue our route to England.'[60] Nelson for the first and only time in his life appears to turn his back on action, subduing any thought that he might be needed, seeing no need to volunteer himself, refusing to take a hint from Keith that he might establish himself as senior officer at Mahon in Minorca, indeed refusing to give the present situation any kind of priority over his personal undertakings to the Queen, and his urgent personal concern to watch over the pregnant Emma.

Keith, making his way to Leghorn with his squadron, was justifiably fuming to Consul Paget: 'I must go to Leghorn with the wretched fugitives and to be bored by Lord Nelson for permission to take the Queen to Palermo and Princes and Princesses to all parts of the globe. To every request I have said my duty to the nation forbids it. God knows it is true.'[61] Arrived in Leghorn he met with a detached Nelson. 'If Sir William and Lady Hamilton go home by land, it is my intention to go with them; if by water we shall be happy in taking the best Ship we can get; but we are all pledged not to quit the Royal Family till they are in perfect secu-

Emma's Protector and Husband

Sir William Hamilton in 1788 by George Romney.

Tria Juncta in Uno

Emma in 1800 by Schmidt; hung in
Nelson's cabin – his 'guardian angel'.

Nelson in 1800 by Schmidt.

Sir William Hamilton after Grignion.

Paradise Merton & Nelson's Dear Token of Love

A watercolour of Merton Place, the house that Emma found for Nelson, which he bought in 1801 for £9,000. .

Horatia Nelson at Merton.

Horatia Nelson in a coloured drawing, which hung in Nelson's cabin.

Other Significant Characters

Alexander Davison, Nelson's agent and confidant.

Lavinia Countess Spencer, who called Nelson 'a dear little creature'.

Emma's mother, Mary Lyon, a blacksmith's widow, who later called herself Mrs Cadogan.

Admiral Lord Keith, the only commander-in-chief whose orders Nelson disobeyed.

Nelson's Royal Acquaintances

King William IV when Duke of Clarence.

King Ferdinand of Naples and Sicily.

Queen Maria-Carolina, wife of Ferdinand and sister of the guillotined Marie-Antoinette.

Bands of Brothers

Alexander Ball

James Saumarez

Edward Berry

Thomas Troubridge

Cuthbert Collingwood

Thomas Masterman Hardy

Thomas Foley

Thomas Fremantle

'The Hero of the Nile' by James Gillray, 1798.
A not unaffectionate swipe at Nelson adorned with his
orders, medals and gifts – and with a full purse in his
coat of arms.

'A Mansion House Treat – or Smoking Attitudes' by Isaac Cruikshank, 1800. A coarse and smutty portrayal of the relationship between Nelson and Emma.

'Dido in Despair' by James Gillray, 1801. From her husband's bed, Emma laments the departure of Nelson for Copenhagen – the floor littered with suggestive objects.

Homes in Norfolk, Naples and at Sea

Nelson's birthplace, Burnham Thorpe parsonage, where he lived with Fanny, 1788–93.

A view of Naples from a point near the Villa Emma at Posillipo.

Nelson's Flagships: *Agamemnon, Captain, Vanguard, Elephant* and *Victory*.

Battle

Nelson's 64-gun *Agamemnon* rakes the dismasted 80-gun *Ça Ira*, which later surrendered in Hotham's action of March 1795.

Mission Command

Nelson explaining the plan of attack before Trafalgar, published on the day of his funeral, 9 January 1806.

The Battle of Trafalgar.

Death

The Death of Nelson by Arthur Devis, 1807; a relatively authentic rendering, portraying the individuals involved in the actual scene.

Death of Nelson by Stephen Farthing, 1999, exemplifies the random chance of death in battle.

Nelson's funeral in St Paul's, 9 January 1806.

rity.' He also gave Keith his opinion that the Brest fleet was not likely to put to sea and would be no great threat if it did.

By now all Keith wanted was to be rid of Nelson. He sent him an order on 9 July that *Alexander* could be used to take the Queen to Palermo, Messina, or a port in the Adriatic. Nelson could leave *Alexander* and accompany the Queen, having struck his flag, or he could return to England in *Seahorse*, or from Malta in *Alkmaar* or any other troopship.

After a final flurry of fright by the Queen, because the violently anti-French populace of Leghorn had attempted to detain her, she set off for Florence and Ancona by land on 10 July and on the next day Nelson struck his flag and followed. A letter Cornelia Knight wrote on 2 July to Berry indicates that a decision to go overland to Vienna had already been made: 'the Queen wishes, if possible, to prosecute her journey. Lady Hamilton cannot bear the thought of going by sea; and therefore, nothing but impracticability will prevent our going to Vienna. Lord Nelson is well, and keeps up his spirits amazingly. Sir William appears broken, distressed, and harassed.'[62] Now that she was pregnant the sea held no charms for Emma, who had behaved so magnificently in the storm-tossed *Vanguard*. Besides, there was the added attraction of showing off in Vienna with her beloved Queen.

And so Keith and Nelson parted, and it has to be said, in a way that shows Nelson in a very poor light. However it is instructive to follow Keith for a few more years. By September 1800 he himself wanted to leave the Mediterranean. His friend on the Admiralty Board, Admiral Young, reported to Spencer, 'He writes as if he felt himself unequal to the command with which so much of politics is blended, complains of the slowness of all those he is concerned with, and says if anyone more equal to the task should be sent out, he should be well pleased to be quiet; but I fancy one more equal to the task will not be easily found.'[63] Keith was not finding the Mediterranean easy pickings, but had to stay there till June 1802.

Then there was the matter of the abortive combined operation against Cadiz in October 1800. Sir John Moore, who had spoken so disparagingly of Nelson's appearance at Leghorn, which did not after all matter very much, spoke even more cuttingly of Keith's performance, which did matter a great deal. 'I found him all confusion, blaming everybody and everything but attempting to remedy nothing. . . . The Admiral said it was impossible to anchor nearer the shore, so as to make a better arrangement, that the same confusion must occur tomorrow as did this day. He went on repeating much more incoherent nonsense. It was with difficulty I persuaded him to make the signal to the troops to re-embark.'[64] The Cadiz business caused Captain Sam Hood to write, 'I am sorry Lord Keith has been so unsuccessful. I wish Lord Nelson had been given the command; things I think, would have altogether gone more to our advantage. The former seems to be too great to consult people who are informed of the local situation of the country, which he himself does not appear to have a right knowledge of.'[65] Later, on the occasion of the landings in Egypt in 1801 with Generals Abercromby and Hutchinson, Keith displayed an almost infinite capacity to fall out with his captains. There were insinuations that Keith's agents were dishonest and he entered into a long and acrimonious correspondence with Ben Hallowell about the price charged for shoes. Three captains urged more vigorous measures for the supply of fresh meat and vegetables for the sick, and Keith, at his wits' end for supplies, chose to regard as improper their entirely reasonable advocacy, with the result that eleven captains demanded that he should comply. He even managed to have sharp altercations with them over firewood, of all things.[66]

Keith was indeed the antithesis of Nelson: mercenary, wooden in his relationships with his officers, unable to seek their help and advice or to mobilize their talents to produce solutions to their common problems. In all organizations there are people of relative mediocrity who somehow make their way upwards, as he did, rising to be Admiral of the Blue and to command the prestigious Channel fleet at the time of Waterloo. Alas, History remembers him only as the Commander-in-Chief whose orders Nelson disobeyed.

19

Public Fame and Private Pain

Let her go to Brighton or where she pleases, I care not: she is a great
fool and thank God you are not the least like her.

Nelson, January 1801

Their continental progress home was triumphal, Trieste to Laibach
(now Ljubljana in Slovenia), then via Klagenfurt to Graz, via Bruck
an der Mur to Wiener-Neustadt, via Baden to Vienna, then to Prague,
capital of Bohemia, down the Elbe to Dresden, capital of Saxony, thence
to Magdeburg in Prussia and finally to Hamburg, where, after four
months, the party crossed the North Sea to Yarmouth.

The hero's return Nelson had experienced at Naples in 1798 had been
the delirious welcome of a court euphoric at deliverance from the guil-
lotine at their gate. He now had his first experience of public fame. At
Trieste, 'he is followed by thousands when he goes out'.[1] From Vienna
itself Lady Minto reported, 'You can have no notion of the anxiety and
curiosity to see him. The door of his house is always crowded with
people, and even the street, whenever his carriage is at the door; and
when he went to the play he was applauded, a thing which rarely happens
here. On the road it was the same. The common people brought their
children to touch him. One he took up in his arms [*sic*], and when he
gave it back to the mother she cried for joy, and said it would be lucky
through life.'[2] Ladies sported their 'Nelsons', black capes with colourful
trimmings. Prague was illuminated for his forty-second birthday. At
Dresden, 'the fine bridge was crowded with spectators to see Lord Nelson
depart, as was the shore, and every window that commanded a view of
the river.'[3] In Magdeburg, 'the press to watch Lady Hamilton feeding her
one armed hero was so great that the doors of the dining room had to
be opened and the landlord charged a fee to look in'.[4] The educated and
aware knew who the Hamiltons were; ordinary mortals may well have

thought that Emma was Lady Nelson, but the cynosure of all eyes was undoubtedly Nelson. As usual the hero fell short of the ideal. An Austrian newspaper described him: 'His face is pale and sunk, with the hair combed onto the forehead; the loss of an eye is less noticeable than that of the right arm as he . . . fastens the empty sleeve across his buttoned tunic.'[5] Karoline Jagemann the actress saw 'a small thin man with one eye and one arm whose looks do not betray the hero'.[6] At Dresden Thomas Kosegarten, variously described as a Lutheran pastor or travelling writer and art expert from Hamburg, remarked, 'Nelson is one of the most insignificant looking figures I ever saw in my life. His weight cannot be more than seventy pounds. A more miserable collection of bones and wizened frame I have never yet come across. His bold nose, the steady eye and the solid worth revealed in his whole face betrays in some measure the great conqueror. He speaks little and then only English and he hardly ever smiles,'[7] – a far cry from the idealized, almost ethereal, presence recorded by the Füger portrait, painted in Vienna on that same journey, but not from the commanding head sculpted by Franz Thaller in 1801 at the same time and probably with the aid of life masks made by Matthias Ranson soon after the visit to Füger's studio.

Reputation had travelled ahead. Lord Minto, Nelson's friend and supporter, now Ambassador at Vienna, had been on the receiving end of effusive letters from Nelson, notably about the *tria juncta in uno*; and gushing letters from Emma: 'Glorious Nelson oh how he loves you. He keeps by him your friendly and eloquent speech in the House of Lords after the battle of the Nile and we often read it together and tears of friendship and gratitude run down his honoured face in speaking of you and to me that loves you and remembers with such satisfaction our happy days at Naples.'[8] This kind of thing did not appeal to Minto. Earlier in the year he had written in a regretful vein to his wife, that Nelson 'does not seem at all conscious of the sort of discredit he has fallen into, or the cause of it, for he writes still, not wisely, about Lady Hamilton and all that. But it is hard to condemn and ill use a hero, as he is in his own element, for being foolish about a woman who has art enough to make fools of many wiser than an Admiral.'[9]

Minto was much less of a stuffed shirt than many they would meet. He was more distressed by the thought of Nelson making a public exhibition of himself than he was about his relationship with Emma; nothing could reduce his admiration for Nelson the sea officer. When he wrote to tell Keith of Nelson's arrival in Vienna, he was as supportive as a good friend should be: 'Lord Nelson has been received here by all ranks with the admiration which his great actions deserve, and notwithstanding the disadvantage under which he presents himself to the public eye. They talk of proceeding in a few days towards England; and I who am a lover of naval merit and indeed a sincere friend of the man, hope we shall hear again of him on his proper element.'[10] As for Emma, Minto's feelings were more complicated. He was inclined to say one thing to his wife and other things to ladies he admired. In November 1799 he had written Emma a letter with a decidedly intimate flavour:

> But you & she [the Queen of Naples] are I believe both accustomed to make fools of wiser men. . . . I wonder whether I shall ever kiss her hand; I lost my opportunity once and that you know is seldom recovered with a lady. I hope by this time you think me sufficiently foolish still, especially for an old fat fool, for I am both more than ever, notwithstanding which I continue in love with my wife, & with Sir William's wife, & consumedly as Scrub [a character in Farquhar's Beaux' Stratagem] says, with our nameless friend and mistress, besides half a dozen small passions here in Vienna, for some of us are most beautiful & many most agreeable. PS You have probably heard that Col Drinkwater married Miss Congalton last summer and has moreover got her with child. . . . The Freemantles are a most happy couple & have been growing His Majesty subjects ever since they began in a corner of my cabin on board the Inconstant.[11]

So Minto was not beyond making a fool of himself either. He had an earthy strain in his make-up, and a soft spot for extrovert females, subsequently enjoying the entertainments of another rumbustious, noisy and risqué lady, Caroline, Princess of Wales. He was drawn to Caroline's unconventional directness, just as he had been attracted to Maria Carolina's sexiness and Emma's vitality. Although he likened Emma's easy manners to those of a barmaid, he probably liked the company of barmaids a great deal more than he found it politic to admit.

Lady Minto, who liked Nelson, was struck by the dynamics of Nelson and Emma's relationship: 'I don't think him altered in the least. He has the same shock head, and the same honest simple manners; but he is devoted to Emma; he thinks her quite an angel, and talks of her as such to her face and behind her back, and she leads him about like a keeper with a bear. She must sit by him at dinner to cut his meat; and he carries her pocket-handkerchief.'[12] When they got to Dresden the party encountered Lord Minto's brother, Hugh Elliot, who was British Ambassador there. The Elliots' guest, a young widow Melesina St George, was poisonously eloquent on the point that had struck Lady Minto. 'It is plain that Lord Nelson thinks of nothing but Lady Hamilton who is totally occupied with the same subject. . . . Lord Nelson is a little man, without any dignity . . . Lady Hamilton takes possession of him, and he is a willing captive, the most submissive and devoted I have seen. . . . She puffs the incense full in his face; but he receives it with pleasure, and snuffs it up very cordially.'[13] She too noted that he went off to Court 'a perfect constellation of stars and Orders', just as Lady Minto had described him: 'a gig from ribands, orders and stars'. Then there was a rather riotous supper, Emma calling for champagne, Nelson full of party spirit calling, 'more vociferously than usual for songs in his own praise', poor Elliot trying helplessly to curb the flow of champagne, until such time as 'the Lord and Lady, or as he calls them, Antony and Moll Cleopatra were pretty far gone'. Sir William, who had begun the journey 'broken, distressed and harassed', was now seemingly resurrected, dancing a wild tarantella with Emma, performing 'feats of activity, hopping round the room on his backbone, his arms, legs, star and ribbon all flying about in the air'. Fresh from their free and easy life in Palermo, above all used to enjoying themselves, they had not yet adapted to colder, northern behaviour; they carried on in the way they were used to. How alien this appeared in the world of the Elliots was best expressed by Elliot himself, in words which reflect the eternal dissonance between extrovert and introvert, between the confident and the insecure, 'Now don't let us laugh tonight; let us all speak in our turn: and be very quiet.'[14]

Remarkably, none of these acquaintances reported serious conversation with Nelson, or how he affected them. They recorded only his reaction on hearing that the Electress of Saxony was unlikely to wish to receive Emma because of her past. 'Sir if there is any difficulty of that sort, Lady Hamilton will knock the Elector down,'[15] – very much the kind of careless bombast typical of Emma. There is no hint of Nelson's dominating the party by force of character or conversation. For example, Nelson had arrived in Vienna in the wake of Austrian defeat at Marengo. He met the Emperor and it must have been an intriguing encounter,

Nelson the only man in Europe who had given Bonaparte a seriously bloody nose, but the same Admiral who Austria believed had been used by the British government to launch a premature Neapolitan attack in order to drag Austria into war. It would have been difficult to avoid discussing the current situation in which the Preliminaries of Peace, which the Austrians had signed on 28 July, were producing aggressive and threatening French negotiations. He may have been told that the French were attempting to include Britain in the negotiations. It is difficult to believe that no words were spoken on these subjects but there is no record of them.

There was evidently no repeat of the personal impact he had made on Lavinia Spencer. The likelihood is that he was not naturally gifted in social circles of an educated and fashionable kind; his stage was the quarterdeck and the Admiral's cabin, the practical world, not the fashionable drawing room. Outside the world of the Navy he seems to have been a man of limited ambition and horizons. It was his professional enthusiasm that excited the admiration of others, and this, according to Lord Broughton, was how Nelson's friend Lord Minto saw him. 'He was intensely given up to his profession and thought of little or nothing else – so much so that in talking of other matters, he was rather below than above the ordinary man.'[16] Cornelia Knight had written from Ancona, 'Lord Nelson talks often of the *Foudroyant*, whatever is done to turn off the conversation.'[17] Now, besotted and protective of his pregnant Emma, he was content to sit back on all informal occasions and give way to her energetic sociability, and Hamilton's constant stream of amusing anecdotes, witty observations and encyclopaedic knowledge.

Emma was distinctly taller and more substantial than the little five-foot-six-inch Admiral. There were those who described her as 'colossal', 'exceedingly embonpoint',[18] 'the fattest woman I ever laid eyes on'. But size alone was not the prime determinant of how most people reacted either to her, or to them. To Kosegarten in Dresden, Emma 'behaved like a loving sister towards Nelson; led him, often took hold of his hand, whispered something into his ear, and he twisted his mouth into the faint resemblance of a smile . . . she did not seek to win hearts for everyone's lay at her feet'.[19] Karoline Jagemann was impressed by her physical histrionics, her image, 'a tall imposing figure with the head of a Pallas'.[20] For most people, Emma's person proclaimed her a potent female; her shape and proportions still exciting admiration, the beauty of her head, her features, her expression still proclaiming loveliness, her grace of movement in performing her attitudes still supremely enchanting. At close quarters, her personality and behaviour might jar on the likes of Mrs St George who found her 'bold, daring, vain even to folly . . . stamped with the manners of her first situation much more strongly than one would suppose, after having represented Majesty, and lived in good company fifteen years. Her ruling passions seem to me vanity, avarice, and love for the pleasures of the table.' But judgements on beauty and behaviour are always at the mercy of the beholder's personality, as is singing to the ear and heart of the listener, and on Emma's singing, Mrs St George was in a distinct minority: 'After showing her attitudes, she sung and I accompanied. Her voice is good, and very strong, but she is frequently out of tune; her expression strongly marked and variable; and she has no shake, no flexibility, and no sweetness. She acts her songs, which I think the last degree of bad taste.'[21] All of this makes Mrs St George sound something of an expert. Suerstolpe, a Swedish diplomat, judged differently: 'In her are combined voice as well as method, sensitivity and musical knowledge, so as to bewitch the listener.' He thought he would never hear 'anything so heavenly'. She received rave notices from the *Magyar Hirmondo* when she sang Haydn's cantata *Arianna a Naxos*, at Eisenstadt during their visit to Prince and Princess Esterházy: 'One of her many rare qualities is her clear strong voice with which, accompanied by the famous Haydn, she filled her audience with such enthusiasm that they almost became ecstatic.'[22]

Nor were some of the comments about behaviour justified. James Harris, eldest son of Lord and Lady Malmesbury, reported, 'The princess . . . had got a number of musicians and the famous Haydn . . . to play, hearing Lady Hamilton was fond of music. Instead of attending to them she sat down at the Faro table, played Nelson's cards for him, and won between 300L and 400L . . . I could not disguise my feeling, and joined in the general abuse of her.'[23] But it has been demonstrated to the contrary: that Haydn would not have personally directed 'table' or 'conversation' music, and that Emma's relationship with Haydn was very warm. The composer's friend and biographer Griesinger recalled, 'In My lady Hamilton Haydn found a great admirer . . . for two days she never left Haydn's side.'[24] Haydn presented her with manuscripts of two of his songs, set Cornelia Knight's lines on the battle of the Nile to music, presented the music to Nelson, and accompanied Emma when she sang it. This hardly suggests that Emma was philistine in her behaviour towards Haydn. It suggests that Harris did not know what he was talking about, or, for whatever reason, was intent on character assassination. Perhaps it was the latter because he also wrote to his father, 'Lord Nelson and the Hamiltons dined here the other day; it is really disgusting to see her with him, but he personally is not changed, open and honest, not the least vanity about him.'[25] It was up to Elliot, with a flash of insight to bring an air of worldly reality into these personal judgements: 'She will captivate the Prince of Wales, whose mind is as vulgar as her own, and play a great part in England.'[26] By implication at least, he could acknowledge that all society was not as precious, proper and critical as theirs.

For four months Nelson was fêted on the gloriously decorated centre stage of the baroque courts of Europe, framed in crowds and public fame, and as autumn gave way to early winter they arrived in Hamburg. Reality was beginning to impose itself as Nelson brought coming-home presents, 'a magnificent lace trimming for a court dress for Lady Nelson and a black lace cloak for another lady, who, he said, had been very attentive to his wife during his absence'.[27] Till that moment Fanny had had to make do with one letter, more an administrative communication than a letter, written from Vienna on 20 September, asking her to await his arrival in the second week of October, in a house or good lodging in London, which he had asked Davison to rent for them. Events were to show that he did not even remember he had sent it.

Nelson's official fame might well be measured by the absence of a British frigate to take him across the North Sea. He had to make do with the *King George* packet which crossed the Yarmouth bar on Thursday, 6 November 1800. There was no official welcome, no member of the Board of Admiralty was present. Two years had elapsed since the Nile and enthusiasm for possible special arrangements or personal initiatives had been blunted by time and gossip. But although Nelson was in some danger of losing official support, British heroes were not exactly two a penny in late 1800 and British arms had not exactly glittered since the Nile. On the Continent Bonaparte still had the upper hand. Austria was having to make concessions to extend its armistice and less than a month after Nelson set foot in England Archduke Charles of Austria would be defeated at Hohenlinden with the loss of 17,000 men. Nelson had not been overshadowed and the British public was not about to forget him; he had caught their imagination with his amazing victory in the nation's darkest hour.

By a quirk of fate the people of East Anglia had been given the opportunity to welcome home their heroic son, instead of having to be content with hearing of his arrival in faraway Portsmouth or Plymouth. The newspaper-reading public was also in some excitement, having been treated to a rising tide of innuendo and speculation about Nelson's private life, which titillated those who could put two and two together but left the mass of the population unmoved. And so the good citizens of Yarmouth concentrated on getting the bunting out, the bells ringing, the militia parading, the Mayor and Corporation at the ready, and a group of high-spirited young fishermen gathered to propel the Admiral's coach to the Wrestlers Inn, it being rather immaterial that Emma and Sir William were his supporters and in his coach. On home ground, where he could at least understand what people were talking about, he was once again in charge. Yet what he did next suggests a man who had been pulled up short by a cold douche of reality, suddenly unsure how he was going to cope. After writing to tell Fanny that they would arrive at Roundwood in time for dinner on Saturday night (she being in London where he had asked her to meet him the second week in October and where she had been ever since) he wrote to the Board of Admiralty, 'I beg to acquaint their Lordships of my arrival here this day, and that my health being perfectly re-established, it is my wish to serve immediately; and I trust that my necessary journey by land from the Mediterranean will not be considered as a wish to be a moment out of active service.'[28] That might indeed have been the case but the two things really uppermost in his mind were, what to do about Fanny, and what to do about money. Public fame was not cheap. Even at Yarmouth he had found himself handing out, '£50 for His Worship the Mayor, to be distributed by him, 5 guineas for the Town Clerk, 1 guinea for the Officer.'[29] Maria Carolina might well have promised them an all-expenses-paid stay in Vienna, but progressing through the courts of Europe had still been ruinously expensive. Their total expenses had been an astronomic £4,575. Vienna had cost them £1,100; Prague, Dresden and Hamburg £1,406; and

Yarmouth and Colchester £377. Sir William had paid out a mere £255 and now owed Nelson the balance of his share, £1,349 2s. 4d. When what Hamilton had borrowed from him at Palermo was included, he owed Nelson £2,276.

Nelson's income was about £3,500 (including his Navy pension for the Nile, his pension for the loss of his arm and eye, and income from his capital). After settling debts of £8,000 in respect of Palermo and the journey home, deducting the £4,000 Fanny had brought to their marriage (reckoning that it was hers by right,) his real capital assets with Marsh & Creed were about £4,000.[30] On the face of it that made him comfortably off, but not well enough off to support Fanny *and* enable Emma to live the life to which she had become accustomed, and provide for their future child, *and* provide generously for his family, *and* present gifts to all and sundry. By the middle of January 1801 he would arrange for Fanny to have an allowance of £1,600 a year, almost half his income and characteristically generous. This would leave him about £1,900 to call his own, and of that residue about half was already spoken for. He needed prize money and he needed to win his court case with St Vincent in which £13,000 of Mediterranean prize money was at stake.[31]

Hamilton would see himself as in an even worse state, especially for a man who had never been able to curb either his own extravagance or Emma's. In addition to the £2,276 he owed Nelson he also owed his bankers Ross & Ogilvie £7,000. Against these debts he had capital of £13,000, derived from mortgaging his estate, so he and Nelson had roughly similar real capital assets.[32] Hamilton's pension would be fixed at £1,200 a year in February of the next year, and his estate income brought in a further £1,000. Unless some of the money he had raised from the mortgage on his estate had been invested his income would be £2,200 a year. Thus he was as poor as Nelson. True he had claims on the government of £10,000 for losses at Naples and £13,213 for additional expenses at Palermo but they would never be met.[33] Hamilton was not at all inclined to reduce his standard of living and when it came to moving into their house at 23 Piccadilly, Emma had to sell £2,500 worth of jewellery to furnish it, and the lease cost Hamilton another £1,000. To help make his extravagant ends meet, he would set about selling pictures, realizing a total of £6,478 at Christie's on 28 March and 13 November 1801. He also succeeded in selling his remaining collection of vases privately for £4,000.[34] If he managed to hang on to this capital it would, with consols yielding 5.26 per cent in 1801, add about £540 to his annual income. Clearly the Hamiltons' projected style of living in London would be totally unsustainable and he was going to have to rely on Nelson to bear his share of the financial burden.

The second reality that had to be faced was Fanny. Nelson, never a very analytical person, seems to have acted on an assumption that he could have his cake and eat it, that this irregular ménage could be transplanted from Palermo to Piccadilly, that he could pass off Emma and himself as just good friends, that his wife would tacitly accept the situation and that they could all rub along reasonably well together. Their arrival and the first meeting was at Nerot's Hotel at three o'clock on a gloomy November afternoon. Fanny, being Fanny and well aware of newspaper gossip, came to the meeting nervous about what she was to encounter and on edge because of Nelson's delayed arrival in London; she had been kept waiting for the best part of three weeks. She was no match for socialites like Emma and Sir William, and after Nelson's effusive introductions, the party was borne along in a charming and flattering way, Emma on her best behaviour, Hamilton, witty, anecdotal and agreeable, playing the ambassadorial gentleman and savant to perfection. Emma's warmth towards both men, especially towards Sir William, and both men's evident liking and respect for each other, reassured Fanny. She could begin to see what they meant by *tria juncta in uno*. Her regret at feeling an outsider mingled with relief; her husband was now actually home, and the bogeys that had tormented her seemed to lack substance. She had no means of knowing what was in Nelson's heart or what her fate would be. Emma drew comfort from the meeting; her competitor was not very substantial.

When, at last, the Hamiltons and Nelson's father had left and Nelson and Fanny were forced to settle down and talk to each other, Nelson made no confession. Whether either made a show of endearment will never be known and whether and to what degree she complained will never be known either. What she felt about Nelson is more difficult to imagine. Two years previously, when he had departed, the fragility of their relationship was clearly visible. For those two years she had lived with Nelson's father, an unexciting, socially restrained life, an uninterrupted celibate life. She had not shown herself to be a passionate woman in any sense. In all probability friendly civility was all she was looking for. We can reasonably assume that with anger inside she needed Nelson's embraces as little as he wished to offer them. During the days that followed he could be greatly absorbed with his packed programme, could avoid his wife by losing himself in the flood of calls on his time. 'He looks well, is active and cannot rest long in a place therefore I myself can only see him for a minute,' is how his father described it when writing to his daughter, Catherine Matcham, and as the month went by the same sense of perpetual motion is conveyed by his reports, 'Your Bro is so constantly upon the wing that I can but get a short glimpse myself.' On the other hand brother William was sticking like a limpet, hoping for preferment on his brother's back. 'Wm and Mrs Nelson have lodgings very near and mean to stay some time.'[35]

On Monday, the day after his arrival, Nelson called on Lord Spencer and expressed the strongest wish to serve again under St Vincent.[36] He also saw Admiral Young, who immediately passed the news to Keith: 'I have seen him for a few minutes only this morning. He seems to have recovered perfectly from his fatigues and to be very well. He will immediately hoist his flag in the Channel Fleet.'[37] Nelson had obtained a plum appointment. St Vincent, totally uninfluenced by gossip, and despite their dispute over prize money, had written to Spencer while Nelson was on his way home, 'I think Lord Nelson will wish to serve in this squadron and I shall be very glad to have him.'[38] Once again he would have both his favourites under his command.

On his way to the Admiralty Nelson had been mobbed in the Strand. In the afternoon came dinner at the Mansion House, to which his coach was propelled by yet another crowd of well-wishers. Inside, he was fêted, and taking his place under a triumphal arch, was presented with a splendid 200 guinea sword, 'and with this very sword, I hope soon to aid in reducing our implacable and inveterate Enemy to proper and due limits; without which, this country can neither hope for, nor expect a solid, honourable, and permanent peace.'[39] Tuesday he called on the Duke of Clarence. Wednesday came the levee, where the King rather offensively cut Nelson down to size. Nelson was not above sharing his anger and embarrassment with Collingwood, who later said that Nelson 'gave me an account of his reception at Court, which was not very flattering, after having been the adoration of that of Naples. His Majesty merely asked him if he had recovered his health; and then, without waiting for an

answer, turned to General – and talked to him near half an hour in great
good humour. It could not be about his successes.'[40] Another gentleman
noted that, 'he was coldly received by the King, who merely observed
that his Lordship had come to Town on Monday and was to hoist his
Flag in the Channel Fleet; then turned and spoke to another.' Nelson may
have offended against etiquette by attending the Lord Mayor's banquet
before paying his respects to the King. It is possible that the King disapproved of Nelson's wearing his foreign decorations, although Nelson
had sought advance guidance on that point. It is possible that the King's
behaviour presaged a further bout of madness, which was in fact imminent. The disgracefully dissolute behaviour of his own sons may have
impelled him to adopt a high moral tone over Nelson's behaviour so that
all might stand condemned. Whatever his reason or unreason, it was
monumental stupidity thus to snub Nelson.

Wounded to the quick, Nelson could make a distinction between his
King and his offensive ingratitude, and his country which was daily
demonstrating unbounded admiration for him. In such a mood Nelson
vented his anger and irritation on poor Fanny as they dined with the
Spencers that same evening, treating her 'with every mark of dislike and
even of contempt'. Fanny, seeking to ingratiate herself with her bad-
tempered husband, made the mistake of playing mother. She prepared
walnuts for Nelson, only to suffer the shame and embarrassment of
having them pushed roughly aside. In the withdrawing room, according
to Lady Shelley, Fanny, unable to hold back her pain, unburdened herself
to Lady Spencer.[41]

There were plenty of opportunities for the narcissistic hero to respond
to his admiring countrymen and ignore the pain closer to home. On 18
November the Nelsons and Hamiltons (the Nelsons were now at 17
Dover Street and the Hamiltons temporarily at William Beckford's
London house in Grosvenor Street) accompanied by his father attended
Covent Garden, prompting the notice of the press. 'The noble and gallant
Admiral as soon as he presented himself to the audience was received
with the most ecstatic and reiterated bursts of applause we ever recollect
to have witnessed on any similar occasion.' On 24 November the Nelsons
and Hamiltons attended Drury Lane for a performance of *Pizarro*
and on the appearance of the hero 'Rule Britannia' was sung, 'amid the
universal plaudits of the admiring crowd' and 'every opportunity was
eagerly seized by the audience to evince the high estimation in which they

held the valiant conqueror of Aboukir'. There was an audience of a different though no less welcome kind, when on 20 November, in the House of Lords, Baron Nelson of the Nile and of Burnham Thorpe was introduced between Lord Grenville and Lord Romney.

Although it soon became clear that Emma would never be accepted at Court, this by no means cut off the Hamiltons from social life. The Duke of Queensberry, Prince Augustus, Lady Augusta Murray (with whom they had close bonds from their Naples days) and Charles Greville, now Vice-Chamberlain of the King's Household, were often there. Had Emma felt embarrassed at bringing together three men all of whom had slept with her, she would have taken more care to prevent it happening. Lord Cathcart, another of Sir William's nephews, called or dined. Lord Palmerston, who had first seen Emma in Paris as a stunning young bride, renewed his acquaintance soon after they arrived and noted, 'She is grown much larger and her face broader and her features stronger than they were. . . . She has a little more conceit and affectation than she had, which is very natural, but she has the same good humoured manner that she used to have. Her attentions to Sir William do not seem to have relaxed in any degree and they both talk of Lord Nelson in every other sentence. His bust is in the room and Sir William says his friendship and connection with him is the pride and glory of his life.'[42]

It quickly became obvious how Nelson was going to play the high society question and it was not at all as St Vincent had prognosticated in a letter to Nepean: 'It is evident from Lord Nelson's letter to you on his landing, that he is doubtful of the propriety of his conduct. I have no doubt he is pledged to getting Lady Hamilton received at St James' and everywhere and that he will get into much brouillerie about it.'[43] Social climbing was the last thing on Nelson's mind. As soon as Emma herself accepted that she was not going to be received at Court, he was happy with whatever set she chose to congregate around her. His own social acceptability was never affected. Davison gave a lunch in his honour attended by the Prince of Wales, Spencer, Pitt and the Cabinet, a piquant addition to the party being Admiral Payne, who as Captain Payne and an early employer of Emma's is generally held to have deflowered her. After only one dinner, Cornelia Knight deserted them. She said that Troubridge got hold of her as she arrived, and warned her against continuing the relationship. 'He

advised me to go to my friend Mrs Nepean, whose husband was secretary to the Admiralty, and who on the following day made me take possession of a room in her house.'[44] She had flattered them all to the skies,
when it was to her advantage to do so, but now this very self-interested
and socially ambitious lady was quick to take a hint. She would turn up
later as a lady in-waiting to Queen Caroline and chaperon to Princess
Charlotte, from which post she was summarily dismissed in July 1814
for allowing her charge to be visited by Prince Augustus of Prussia, 'a
well known womanizer of thirty five'.[45] For this she blamed everybody
but herself. Nelson was probably not far from the mark when he referred
to her as 'that b—— Miss Knight'. If what she alleged about Troubridge
was true, his motivation was more obscure – he could hardly care too
much about the fate of a sycophant. Maybe his action was an attempt
to reclaim Nelson for himself by stripping him of his Palermo friends.
But to push her into the arms of Mrs Nepean would be to ensure that
all kinds of confidences and recollections would come to the ears of
Nepean and the Board of Admiralty and suggests another motive:
Troubridge was also a competitor.

For a time the foursome went to theatres, dined together and rubbed
along as Nelson had hoped. He decided to meet press comment and
gossip about Emma head on, and according to Cornelia Knight, 'felt irritated and took it up in an unfortunate manner by devoting himself more
and more, for the purpose of what he called supporting her'.[46] Fanny
could not help but realize that Emma was pregnant, and, although she
refrained from accusing her husband of being the father, she was demoralized and sick at heart. Nelson, in his guilt, could not refrain from being
unreasonably irritated by Fanny, and the upshot was that when an
invitation came from William Beckford, then forty and reputedly the
richest man in England, inviting the Hamiltons (and himself if possible)
to spend Christmas with him and see in the new century at Fonthill
in Wiltshire, he accepted. Fanny was left behind to spend Christmas
with Nelson's father, brother William and his wife. A more offensive
and unfeeling action could scarcely be imagined. The trio swept off on
21 December, stopping *en route* at Salisbury for Nelson to receive the
Freedom of the City, escorted by Yeoman cavalry and cheered by
members of his former ships' companies. Then it was on to a grand
arrival at Fonthill Splendens, this time with an escort of Beckford's
Volunteers, preceded by a thirty-man band playing 'Rule Britannia'. This

was high life, produced and directed by this strange young man. Walks on lawns surrounded by gaunt skeletal trees, entrances to dinners in semi-darkness, cowled monk-like figures bearing torches provided a background of Gothic splendour. Emma portrayed Agrippina, and brought tears to the eyes of the audience. (By now she was not the only one performing attitudes. In a crowded salon in Paris men stood on chairs to see Juliette Récamier perform similarly.) Beckford, an immensely rich and complicated fantasist, was a bisexual and at the time strictly persona non grata in the drawing rooms of England. The company he had brought together to meet the great sea hero and his celebrity mistress was decidedly miscellaneous. There was his lover/pimp Chevalier Franchi, the artist Benjamin West, his architect James Wyatt, the Alsatian Dr Erhard, one Abbé Macquin described as a 'gossipy old hanger on', and Madame Banti, Emma's opera singer friend. His own agenda and the essential purpose of the invitation was to involve Hamilton in a mad scheme. In return for £2,000 from Beckford, Hamilton was to apply for a peerage and would arrange for it to be remaindered to Beckford on his own death.

After Nelson's return events moved quickly. On 1 January he was promoted Vice-Admiral of the Blue (two further steps, via Vice-Admiral of the White and subsequently Red lay between him and full Admiral), alas too late to receive the congratulations of his old mentor Locker, who had died on Boxing Day: 'a man whom to know was to love'.[47] and whose funeral he loyally attended on 3 January. In the usual flurry of departure he was on his way. He had intended to visit his Uncle Suckling's widow in nearby Hampstead, but had to write expressing regrets; yet, mindful of his Suckling obligations, he wrote to his uncle's son, Lieutenant-Colonel Suckling to say he hoped soon to advance him £300: 'you may my dear Suckling, always rely on all the kindness in my power to show you, not only on your own account, but from my real affection to your dear good father'.[48]

His parting from Fanny was as sombre as that from Emma was emotional. His mistress had no more than a fortnight to go before she was due to give birth. According to Nelson's solicitor William Haslewood, the break with Fanny came at about this time, although reflections forty years after an event are by definition unreliable. He pictured the scene at breakfast, Lady Nelson demurring at Nelson's 'dear Lady Hamilton', giving Nelson an ultimatum that he must give up 'either her or me'. Nelson soothingly and calmly reminding her of his obligations to Lady

Hamilton, but finally, 'muttering something about her mind being made up, Lady Nelson left the room, and shortly afterwards drove from the house. They never lived together again.'[49] There is no other evidence for the idea that Fanny walked out on Nelson. He certainly never referred to such an event himself, either to Emma or to his confidant Davison, and Fanny was in no position either to threaten him, or to walk out on him, and she never hinted at having done so in her correspondence with Davison. What becomes clear from subsequent events is that neither had confronted the other. She could not deliver an ultimatum. There could be no question of threatening him with divorce. For eighteenth-century wives divorce was not a practical possibility and besides her whole motivation was to recapture her husband's affections. Nelson could do what he liked, but his peace of mind depended on Fanny's going along with what was happening. And so he was not frank with her. Like so many men in his position, he displayed moral cowardice.

Arriving in Southampton on the 13th with brother William in tow, he sent Fanny a short but not unfriendly note, 'My Dear Fanny, We are arrived and heartily tired, so tell Mrs Nelson [William's wife], and with kindest regards to my father and all the family, Believe me your affectionate Nelson.'[50] Three days later he writes, still calmly, 'Your letters I received this morning at Tor Abbey for which I thank you. I have only time to say God bless you and my dear father and believe me your affectionate Nelson.'[51] These were decidedly not the words of a man whose wife had walked out on him, or the words of a man who had told his wife that he was in love with another woman and that to all intents and purposes their marriage was over. But they were never to meet again.

They had stopped *en route* at the Hampshire home of George Rose, Secretary to the Treasury, so that the advancement-obsessed William might be introduced, but Rose was not at home. Nelson was in a state, and wrote to Emma, 'Anxiety for friends left and various workings of my imagination gave me one of those severe pains of the heart, that all the windows were obliged to be put down, the Carriage stopp'd, and the perspiration was so strong that I never was wetter and dead with Cold.'[52] This suggests either a state of acute anxiety or an attack of angina, probably the former, because he recovered quickly and there was no aftermath.

On the way he also called on Captain Westcott's mother, who had not received her son's gold medal, whereupon Nelson took off his own and gave it to her. They called on St Vincent at Tor Abbey. He did not like the Nelson he saw in front of him and wrote to Nepean, 'Poor man he is devoured with vanity, weakness and folly, was strung with ribbons, medals etc and yet pretended that he wished to avoid the honour and ceremonies he everywhere met with on the road.'[53] Tough-minded old St Vincent knew enough of men to know that the acid test of a man is not what he says but what he does.

On 17 January 1801 Nelson hoisted his flag in the *San Josef*, the ship he had boarded at the battle of Cape St Vincent and which St Vincent wanted him to have. Hardy would go as his flag captain. In informing Nepean that he had hoisted his flag, he rather cheekily asked for full pay to date, on the grounds that his journey from Italy was, in effect, a transfer from the Mediterranean to the Channel fleet. His request was refused.

He had shown his usual carelessness about what he would need on board and had displayed his congenital unwillingness to take responsibility for properly organizing his private possessions. There was an almost exact re-run of his reactions of March 1798: 'all my things are breaking open for only one key can be found. My steward says I have no one thing for comfort come, but a load of useless articles from Burgess's and a large chest of green tea.' The next day, 'Half my wardrobe is left behind and that butler, a French rascal, ought to be hanged and I hope you will never lay out a farthing with Mr Burgess . . . I am forced to buy everything. In short I find myself without anything comfortable or convenient. . . . In short I only regret that I desired any person to order things for me I could have done all in ten minutes and for a tenth part of the expense. . . . It is now too late to send my half wardrobe, as I know not what is to become of me, nor do I care.' He suddenly becomes 'Yours truly'. On the 3rd he writes to Fanny at Brighton, clearly having been made to feel that something of an apology is in order, but his possessions are still a chapter of woe, and he still childishly exclaims, 'but I shall direct what things I want in future'.[54] This is the voice of a man who knows his own weakness and cannot bear to be reminded of it by his wife's equal incompetence. It speaks volumes for his gross insensitivity that he failed to realize that Fanny's heart could hardly have been expected to be in packing for him after the Christmas he had just given her.

Some decisions had been taken. Nelson had been addressing his letters to Fanny at Dover Street, but in a postscript of 21 January he noted, 'Captain B tells me you have changed your house.'[55] Now that he was ordered back to sea the question of where she should live had been a live issue. Roundwood was so far away that it would be sold; a base in London was considered appropriate, not least because propinquity to Emma was of key importance to Nelson. He appears to have believed that once he was at sea Fanny would leave Dover Street and take 'good lodgings or a very small ready furnished house'.[56] But again they seem to have miscommunicated, not least because Nelson's mind was distracted by the knowledge that Emma was about to give birth. Fanny seems to have had an intention of going to Nerot's Hotel, at least temporarily. She said Davison had advised her not to do that, 'particularly as the house is taken for me at Brighton'.[57] This plan was evidently news to Nelson, for he wrote to Emma, 'Let her go to Brighton or where she pleases, I care not: she is a great fool and thank God you are not the least like her.'[58] Fanny's decision was an attempt, if not to draw Nelson away from London, at least to separate herself from the Hamiltons. She tried to get Mrs William Nelson to go with her and grovelled, 'I am sure I need not repeat my constant desire to do anything in my power to serve or accommodate my dear Lord's family',[59] but she declined, and Fanny waited in Brighton with Miss Locker. As an admiral, Nelson worked by communicating with his captains. With Fanny he seems to have issued orders and expected her to work out the meanings and detail for herself. She was not up to that, and so went off at a tangent, and in the case of the Brighton house, made no attempt to prepare him for what she intended, all of which increased the unfavourable comparison with the masterful and resourceful Emma.

By now both Nelson and Emma were showing their darker sides, choosing all the worst options for managing a situation, which might have been made less painful with more tact and discretion. Nelson, with uncharacteristic lack of moral courage and decision turned his back on Fanny while she continued with periodic attempts to mend fences and start again. He was simply hoping she would go away.

At this stage British coalition strategy was in tatters. The next month, February 1801, the Peace of Lunéville between Austria and France, would recognize French puppet republics in Lombardy, Liguria, Switzerland and Holland, and peace with Naples a month later would bring the whole of peninsular Italy under French control and with it access to Egypt and the Levant.

Meanwhile to the north a simmering dispute was about to boil over. For obvious commercial reasons the Danish government had been turning a blind eye to abuses of its neutrality and had indeed ordered the commanders of its convoys to resist British search for contraband war materiel. This was brinkmanship, gambling that the British would not use force to detain Danish ships for fear of driving them into the arms of the French. Between October 1798 and October 1799 there had been eight cases in which superior forces of British ships had encountered Danish convoys but only one had been forcibly searched. In March 1800 Grenville ordered search to be enforced and seizure of ships if they did not comply. In July 1800 an incident involving the Danish frigate *Freya* and her convoy led to dead on both sides and the *Freya*'s convoy was seized and taken to Deal. The British show of force produced the Convention of 29 August 1800, by which all convoys would be suspended until the right to search had been discussed. The Danes immediately set about gathering support, appealing to Russia for help. By now the mad Tsar Paul was seeking a *rapprochement* with France and had turned against the British because of the exclusion of Russians from Malta following its surrender in September 1800. The Armed Neutrality was signed in St Petersburg on 16 December 1800 by Denmark, Sweden and Prussia, all with conflicting aims and hidden agendas and all joined with an unreliable and menacing leader, Russia, who promptly created another crisis by placing an embargo on British ships in Russian ports. Denmark found herself hoist with her own petard and in the front line. The Admiralty had begun to make arrangements in late 1800 for a campaign in the spring of 1801 and in retaliation an embargo was now placed on Danish, Russian and Swedish ships in British ports.

Britain stood on its right as a belligerent to stop and search merchant ships of neutral countries for supplies destined for Britain's enemies. Vital supplies of timber, hemp, tar and grain from the Baltic countries to Britain had also to be safeguarded. The Danes were in effect bent on a policy of offensive neutrality and were clearly not prepared to compromise. On 15 January 1801 the King was in a bellicose mood when he minuted: 'The present situation of this kingdom with the Northern Powers requires every degree of exertion . . . I have long wished to bring it to an issue.'[60]

On the 16th, when Nelson was with St Vincent, the news came through of Admiral Sir Hyde Parker's appointment to the North Sea command.

Although Nelson would not receive his official orders as second-in-command until 17 February, the informal system was hard at work. Spencer had been sounding him out and Nelson jumped at the chance to go, but the situation needed to be discussed with St Vincent. Nelson handled him well and reported to Spencer, 'The Earl was very handsome to me, and hoped that, by a temporary absence of a few months, I should not lose my *St Josef*'.[61] Ironically, St Vincent's recommendation in December 1800 had been: 'in the case of a great Fleet acting in the Baltic, Sir Hyde Parker, who is in possession of all the information acquired during the last preparation for a Russian war, must I conceive be appointed to the command of it.'[62] Nelson was in no doubt after serving with Parker, when Parker was second-in-command under Hotham, why he had been appointed. 'I guess that Lord St Vincent recommended Sir Hyde Parker in the strongest manner because he wanted to get rid of him.'[63]

Part V

Winning and Losing

Copenhagen and the Baltic

20

Bitter-sweet Emotions

Sir William should speak out, and if the Prince is a man of honour
he will quit the pursuit of you I know his aim is to have you for a
mistress. The thought so agitates me that I cannot write. I had wrote a
few lines last night but I am in tears. I cannot bear it.

Nelson, February 1801

For the next two months the emotionally immature Nelson would go through a form of hell. Emma, practical, resourceful Emma, would cope with the secret birth of her child; but there would be no escape from postnatal emotions nor from the stress of secrecy. Nelson, still hot with passion, all inner doubts about his masculinity triumphantly laid to rest by Emma's pregnancy, was separated from her for the first time, without her undivided attention to appease his insecurity, and full of guilt at his betrayal of Fanny. In the final days of Emma's pregnancy he began to entertain dark fears of his own betrayal: 'I own I wonder that Sir Wm should have a wish for the Prince of Wales to come under your roof . . . even one visit will stamp you as his chere amie and we know he is dotingly fond of such women as yourself, and is without one [spark] of honour in those respects, and would leave you to bewail your folly. But my dear friend, I know you too well not to be convinced you cannot be seduced by any Prince in Europe.'[1]

His health declined rapidly in sympathy with his thoughts. His eyes were giving him trouble. The physician of the fleet had been called in. He was 'not to write . . . not to eat anything but the most simple food; not to touch any wine or porter; to sit in a dark room; to have green shades for my eyes – (will you my dear friend, make me one or two? – nobody else shall) – and to bathe them in cold water every hour. . . . What a fuss about my complaints,'[2] he rather shamefacedly admits.

Waiting for Emma to give birth he gave way to irritation. Suppressing entirely the memory of his boorish behaviour at the Spencers' dining table, he complained defensively to Davison, 'The Lady of the Admiralty [Lavinia Spencer] never had any just cause for being cool to me. Either as a public or private [man], I wish nothing undone which I have done.'[3] He carped at the charges being levied by Garter King of Arms: 'Pray tell Sir Isaac Heard that [I] cannot afford to pay for any Honours conferred on me ... paying those fees to Secretaries of State, Earl Marshals &c., &c.'[4]

Suddenly, on the first day of February his mood swung through 180 degrees. He heard of the birth of his daughter. 'I believe poor dear Mrs Thompson's friend will go mad with joy. He cries, prays, performs all tricks, yet dare not show all or any of his feelings, but he has only me to consult with ... I cannot write, I am so agitated by this young fellow at my elbow. I believe he is foolish; he does nothing but rave about you and her. I own I participate of his joy and can't write anything.'[5]

By now Nelson had begun the pantomime of writing to Emma as 'Mrs Thompson care of Lady Hamilton'. He himself wrote on behalf of Thompson, so that all endearments, all enquiries about the pregnancy and subsequently about the child would be clearly attributable to the Thompsons, the apparent parents. Sensitive to a degree about his image, he had no wish to unleash a storm of unfavourable publicity; he knew the newspapers would show no mercy should compromising material fall into their hands. Alas, Nelson could never have made a career as a spy for even the manipulation of such a modest subterfuge was beyond his powers of self-discipline. He could rarely manage to line up his personal pronouns. 'Hes' tended to mix with 'Is', 'Yous' popped in instead of 'Shes', 'Hers' gave way to 'Yours'; 'Mine' and 'His' tended to be interchangeable. Nelson's joy in becoming a father was unalloyed, untinged by uncertainty or guilt. Now irrevocably committed to Emma and their child, he spoke again, irrationally but reassuringly of marriage 'as soon as possible'. But now unsteady with emotion, it needed only a teasing remark from Emma to open the floodgates of his insecurity. He pointed the finger straight at Sir William: 'Sir William should speak out, and if the Prince is a man of honour he will quit the pursuit of you. I know his aim is to have you for a mistress. The thought so agitates me that I cannot write. I had wrote a few lines last night but I am in tears. I cannot bear it.'[6]

His mood began to swing violently. One moment he was nostalgic and escapist: 'Ah those happy times. Would to God we were at this moment in the Bay of Naples.' The next, he was practical about arrangements for the child: 'a small pension should . . . be promised if the secret is well kept . . . nothing should be given under handwriting . . . might be better to omit xtening [christening] the child for the present.' Then, in the manner of lovers, he was reassured and chastened. 'Saturday noon Mr Davison came . . . says you are grown thinner but look handsomer than ever. . . . He says you told him to tell me not to send you any more advice about seeing comp^y for that you are determined not to allow the world to say a word against you, therefore I will not say a word; I rest confident in your conduct.' None of which prevented his adding, 'I was sure you would not go to Mrs Walpole's, it is no better than a bawdy house.'[7] He could neither calm his fears nor empty his mind of ugly images. Two days later he was again pouring out his uncontrollable feelings: 'I do not think I ever was so miserable as this moment. I own I sometimes fear that you will not be so true to me as I am to you, yet I cannot, will not believe you false. No I judge you by myself; I hope to be dead before that should happen, but it will not. Forgive me Emma, oh forgive your own dear, disinterested Nelson . . . I cannot express my feelings. May God send me happiness.'[8]

Sir William, the complaisant husband was now being cast as betrayer and pander. 'I have a letter from Sir William, he speaks of the Regency as certain, and then probably he thinks you will sell better – horrid thought.'[9] Hopeful thoughts of Hamilton's demise began to make their way to the surface: 'if your uncle would die. . . .'[10] Emma, every bit as insecure and emotional, was contributing to the drama; her counter-accusations and demands show in Nelson's replies: 'Suppose I did say that the West country women wore black stockings, what is it more than if you was to say what puppies all the present young men are? You cannot help your eyes, and God knows I cannot see much . . . Mrs Kelly . . . Kingsmill's friend. . . . It is now 17 years since I have seen her. I have no secrets and never had but one, only one love in my life.' He even began to get on his high horse with her: 'If you see Mrs Thompson, say her friend has been a little fretted at her nonsense, but is better, as he is sure it can only proceed from her affection for him, but he desires me to beg of you never to harbour a doubt of his fidelity.'[11]

For a moment he saw clearly the emotional tangle they were in and made an effort at analysing it.

> As for the P of W, I know his character, and my confidence is firm as a rock till you try to irritate me to say hard things, that you may have the pleasure of scolding me; but recollect it must remain 4 days before it can be made up, not as before 4 minutes. Consider my dear friend, what you ought to say if I did not fire at your scolding letters, and suppose me if it is possible for a mom^t answering your scolds with a joke. I know I should fire if I thought that of you, that you was indifferent; but firing like the devil with vexation, anger and retorting can only proceed from conscious innocence. I defy the malice of anyone, and my mind is as pure as my actions. I never intend if I can help it to set my foot out of the ship.[12]

Deeply in love as they were they still did not trust each other. Nelson feared the glittering attraction of the dissolute Prince of Wales. His frenzied sexual insecurity nominated many of the Hamilton set as pimp, whore or bitch. Emma, equally insecure, knew all about the ways of men and was not inclined to take Nelson's words at face value; once more she made him promise to keep to his ship. For Emma there was always Fanny. It had not been a case of wife liking mistress and vice versa, as with Spencer's sister Georgiana, Duchess of Devonshire and her husband's mistress Lady Elizabeth Foster, 'dearest Bess', to both of them. Emma and Fanny had diametrically opposed personalities; there could be no coexistence. Emma badgered him constantly. He hated Emma to spoil things by reminding him of Fanny. A man used to being in command felt uncomfortable at feeling driven by her: 'Only rest quiet, you know that everything is arrainged in my head for all circumstances. You ought to know I have a head to plan and an heart to execute whenever it is right and the time arrives. That person [Fanny] has her separate maintenance, let us be happy, that is in our power.'[13]

For a time he could relive his salad days in the Mediterranean. Troubridge was on board as they swung at anchor off Spithead and at dinner in Nelson's cabin, Troubridge would toast Emma. 'Now comes the fourth and old toast, all our friends – the King – success to the fleet, and, though last, not least, Lady Hamilton'[14] – rather disingenuous behaviour if Troubridge really had warned Cornelia Knight away from the Hamiltons' company. Nelson was trying to reassure himself that nothing had changed, because in almost the same breath he was retailing a troubling new awareness of his friend, 'Our friend Troubridge is to be a Lord of the Admiralty, and I have a sharp eye and almost think I see it. No poor fellow, I hope I do him injustice; he cannot surely forget my kindness to him.'[15] Nelson had detected something in Troubridge's demeanour suggesting a change in their relationship and was setting him the impossible task of behaving always as a friend, never as a Lord of the Admiralty. And, for all the delights of mulling over memories of Naples and Palermo, a few days later he was pouring out yet another wild and pathologically jealous letter prompted by news of a projected dinner party with the Prince of Wales.

I am so agitated that I can write nothing. I knew it would be so, and you can't help it. What did you not tell Sir William? Your character will be gone. Do not have him en famille, the more the better. Do not sit long at table. Good God he will be next to you and telling you soft things. If he does, tell it out at table and turn him out of the house . . . I cannot write to Sir William but he ought to go to the Prince and not suffer your character to be ruined by him. Oh God that I was dead! But I do not my dearest Emma, blame you, nor do I fear your inconstancy. I tremble and God knows how I write. Can nothing be thought of? I am gone almost mad, but you cannot help it. It will be in all the newspapers with hints. Recollect what the villain said to Mr Nisbet, how you hit his fancy. I am mad, almost dead, but ever for ever yours till the last moment.

Nelson was terrified of losing her, 'Don't let him touch, nor yet sit next you; if he comes get up. God strike him blind if he looks at you – this is high treason and you may get me hanged by revealing it. Oh God that I were. . . . Oh God! why do I live? But I do not blame you; it is my misfortune. I feel nobody uses me ill. I am only fit to be second, or third, or 4, or to black shoes. I want no better part than I have. I see your determination to be on your guard, and am as fixed as fate. If you'll believe me don't scold me; I am more dead than alive, to the last breath yours. If you cannot get rid of this I hope you will tell Sir William never to bring the fellow again.'[16]

A day later his feelings reached new levels of frenzied intensity. 'Hush hush, my poor heart, keep in my breast, be calm. Emma's true! . . . I know I am almost distracted, but I have still sense enough to burn every word of yours. . . . Oh I could thunder and strike dead with my lightning. I dreamt it last night my Emma. I am calmer; reason I hope will resume her place, please God. Tears have relieved me; you never will again receive the villain to rot me.'[17]

Nelson's mind was full of hateful knowledge of the part Sir William and Charles Greville had previously played in Emma's life. Although he fought the thought, he was fearful that history was about to repeat itself. 'Does Sir William want you to be a whore to the rascal . . . Mr G must be a scoundrel; he treated you once ill enough & cannot love you or would sooner die;'[18] he might have added, 'than now act as a pimp for the Prince of Wales'.

For a time his lovesickness and jealousy could be in remission, buttressed by pacts and undertakings. 'On board again; have received your truly comforting letters. In doing what I wish you win my heart for ever. I am all soul and sensibility; a fine thread will lead me, but with my life I would resist a cable from dragging me . . . I will dine nowhere without your consent, although, with my present feelings, I might be trusted with 50 virgins naked in a dark room.'[19]

Sir William was also feeling the full force of the emotional storm. He had to cope with an hysterical Emma. But he was determined to have his way, although it was not his style to be either confrontational or emotional about it. He wrote diplomatically but firmly to Nelson on 19 February, 'Whether Emma will be able to write to you today or not is a question as she has got one of her terrible headaches.' He continued, gracefully treading the tightrope,

Among other things that vex her is that we have been drawn in to be under the absolute necessity of giving a dinner to the Prince of Wales on Sunday next. He asked it himself having expressed his strong desire of hearing Banti's [a well known singer] and Emma's voices together. I am well aware of the danger that would attend the Prince's frequenting our house, not that I fear that Emma could ever be induced to act contrary to the prudent conduct she has hitherto pursued, but the world is so ill-natured that the worst construction is put upon the most innocent actions. As this dinner must be, or the prince would be offended, we shall keep it strictly to the musical part, invite only Banti, her husband, and Taylor and as I wish to show a civility to Davison I have sent him an invitation. In short we shall get rid of it as well as we can and guard against its producing any more meetings of the same sort. Emma would really have gone any lengths to have avoided Sunday's dinner, but I thought it would not be prudent to break with the Prince who really has shown the greatest civility to us when we were last in England and since we returned, and she has at last acquiesced to my opinion. I have been thus explicit as I know well your Lordship's way of thinking and your very kind attachment to us and to everything that concerns us.[20]

Sir William was not himself unhappy at the thought of entertaining the Prince of Wales and his glitteringly disreputable set. He placed more priority on the Prince's utility than on any threat he might pose to Emma's reputation. Because of the King's madness a Regency was looming, and the hard fact was that if Sir William's financial claims on government were to be met he needed influence in high places. It was a clever move to tell Nelson he was inviting his confidant Davison. In the end the volatile Prince chose to glitter in another place, or Regency intrigue occupied him, for the dinner never took place.

On 23 February this fevered passage, which had lasted a full month, came to an abrupt end. Nelson received permission from St Vincent for three days' leave in London. His thoughts were then on the rather unrealistic prospect of resuming their ardent love life three weeks after Horatia's birth. 'I daresay twins will again be the fruit of your and his [Thompson's] meeting. The thought is too much to bear. Have the dear thatched cottage ready to receive him & I will answer that he would not give it up for a queen and a palace.'[21] Soothed by three days with Emma he arrived back on board the *San Josef* on the morning of the 27th and threw himself into embarking troops and their commanding officer, Lieutenant-Colonel the Honourable William Stewart, setting off from Portsmouth with seven sail-of-the-line to rendezvous off Yarmouth with his Commander-in-Chief, Sir Hyde Parker. To Emma he had written, 'Parting from such a friend is literally tearing one's own flesh; but the remembrance will keep up our spirits till we meet. My affection is, if possible, stronger than ever for you, and I trust it will keep increasing as long as we both live.'[22]

On 1 March he wrote to Emma three times, at eight o'clock in the morning, at noon, and again at nine o'clock at night. At eight o'clock his mind was quiet: 'I have read over twenty times your dear kind letters.' He was thinking of using his sister-in-law as Emma's chaperon: 'if you like to have Mrs Nelson up, say that I will pay their lodgings and then you can have as much of their company as you please; but Reverend sir you will find a great bore at times, therefore he ought to amuse himself all the mornings, and not always dine with you or Sir William may not like it.' He mused suggestively on his visit, 'Tell Mrs Thompson that her friend is more in love with her than ever, and I believe dreams of her. He is sorry that she was a little unwell when he was in London, as it deprived him of much pleasure, but he is determined to have full scope when he next sees her.'[23]

But his state was still curiously nervous and a few hours later at noon his shore-based confidential secretary, Oliver suddenly appeared over the side, 'and when he was announced by Hardy, so much anxiety for your safety rushed into my mind that a pain immediately seized my heart, which kept increasing for half an hour, that turning cold, hot, cold & etc I was obliged to send for the surgeon, who gave me something to warm me, for it was a deadly chill'. The letter Oliver had brought from Emma must have been emotional and upset, probably because the magnitude and dangers of the Baltic operation were dawning on her and frightened her. He was reassuring: 'Why my dear friend do you alarm yourself. Your own Nelson will return safe as if walking London streets. The troops are only 800 and are intended for the better manning of our ships [a white lie]. Recollect the more force we have the less risk.' Other parts prompted crude and harsh images to flood his mind. 'That Lady Aber is a damned bitch; she would pimp for her husband that she might get at her lovers, for I daresay not one satisfies her. . . . Would to God I had dined with you. What a dessert we would have had.'[24] By nine o'clock in the evening his tone was calm and loving:

Now my own dear wife, for such you are in my eyes and in the face of heaven, I can give full scope to my feelings, for I daresay Oliver will faithfully deliver this letter. You know my dearest Emma, that there is nothing in this world that I would not do for us to live together, and to have our dear child with us. I firmly believe that this campaign will give us peace, and then we will sett off for Bronte.

In twelve hours we shall be across the water and freed from all the nonsense of his [Sir William's] friends, or rather pretended ones. Nothing but an event happening to him could prevent my going, for I am sure you will think so, for unless all matters accord it would bring 100 of tongues and slanderous reports if I separated from her which I would do with pleasure the moment we can be united; I want to see her no more, therefore we must manage till we can quit this country or your uncle [Sir William] dies. I love, I never did love anyone else. I never had a dear pledge of love till you gave me one, and you, thank my God, never gave one to anybody else. . . . Let Sir Hyde have any glory he can catch – I envy him not. You, my beloved Emma, and my country are the two dearest objects of my fond heart – a heart susceptible and true. . . . My longing for you, both person and conversation you may readily imagine. What must be my sensations at the idea of sleeping with you! it setts me on fire, even the thoughts, much more would the reality. I am sure my love and desires are all to you, and if any woman naked were to come to me, even as I am at this moment from thinking of you, I hope it might rot off if I would touch her even with my hand. No my heart, person and mind is in perfect union of love towards my own dear, beloved Emma – the real bosom friend of her, all hers all Emma's. . . . My love, my darling angel, my heaven given wife, the dearest only true wife of her own till death. I know you will never let that fellow or any one come near you. . . . Kiss and bless our dear Horatia – think of that.[25]

In Nelson's letters there is no distance between what he feels and what he says, never a hint of cleverness, sophistication or literary effect. However tortured, bitter or jealous he may be feeling, there is always a parallel stream of kind and loving feeling, and the sense of his vulnerability.

There had been a conflict between them about the present operation, whether he should go to the Baltic or stay by Emma's side. He reopened the question when he wrote to Emma in early February, 'But my dear friend, I know you are so true and loyal an Englishwoman, that you would hate those who would not stand forth in defence of our King, Laws, Religion, and all that is dear to us. It is your sex that makes us go forth; and seem to tell us – "None but the brave deserve the fair!" and, if we fall, we live in the hearts of those females, who are dear to us. It is your sex that rewards us; it is your sex who cherish our memories; and you my dear, honoured friend, are, believe me, the first, and best of your sex.'[26]

This sounds as though Emma had played a magnificent Britannia, unlike Fanny, who had always fallen short of the requirements for the consort of a hero. But the poem he sent her later in the month suggests there had indeed been a conflict,

> 'A heart susceptible, sincere & true;
> A heart, by fate, and nature torn in two;
> One half to duty and his country due;
> The other better half to love and you.'
> Sooner shall Britain's sons resign
> The empire of the sea;
> Than Henry shall renounce his faith,
> AND PLIGHTED VOWS TO THEE![27]

A fortnight later later would come a cryptic message to St Vincent: 'my utmost exertions shall be called forth: for although I own, I have met with much more honours and rewards than ever my most sanguine ideas led me to expect, yet I am so circumstanced that probably this expedition will be the last service ever performed by your obliged and affectionate friend.'[28] St Vincent, electrified by his words, jumped to an obvious conclusion. 'I was appalled by the last sentence of your letter; for God's sake do not suffer yourself to be carried away by any sudden impulse.'[29] He had concluded that Nelson was about to give up the service for Emma. Much later, in 1813, Emma would claim, 'It was in consequence of my earnest entreaties, that Lord Nelson consented in 1801 to go to the attack of Copenhagen, second in command under Admiral Parker.'[30] The fact was that Nelson went to the Baltic because he wanted to. There was to be no 'All for Love' theme in Nelson's life; he wanted fame as much as he needed love. But, as we have seen, he did make efforts to persuade Emma that she *wanted* him to go.

Nelson's professional power base was enormously strengthened when St Vincent replaced Spencer as First Lord of the Admiralty in the Addington administration (following Pitt's resignation over union with Ireland) and appointed Troubridge to the Board. Nelson himself had no expectation of being appointed First Lord and probably no wish to be a member of the Board of Admiralty, for that was not his theatre and those were not his ambitions. His reaction to both appointments was matter-of-fact: 'When I have neither hopes or fears, it is perfectly indifferent to me who is there. I only hope they will do well for the Country.'[31] But Nelson would have been hurt to know of the limitations St Vincent had placed on his potential. 'He [Nelson] cannot bear confinement, to any object; he is a partisan; his ship always in the most dreadful disorder, [a judgement incidentally shared by Hardy] and never can become an officer fit to be placed where I am'[32] – the latter a very doubtful judgement, hallmarked with St Vincent's own limitations and prejudices. Having supported Hyde Parker for command of the Baltic operation because he wanted rid of him from the Channel fleet, St Vincent did nothing to change things when he became First Lord. Events were to show that a more disastrously unsound appointment could hardly have been made.

On 12 February Nelson shifted his flag to the *St George* in preparation for departure for the Baltic. His lawsuit with St Vincent was now a source of anxiety. St Vincent had already complained to Nelson's solicitors of Davison's manner of speaking as being offensive to him. There was a great deal of money at stake, for the Admiral's share of the prizes in question amounted to £13,000. Nelson had the good sense to realize that lawsuits invariably poison relationships and was determined to remain friendly with the Earl. In January when they had met on his way to Plymouth, 'the Earl never mentioned Prize money to me, during the twenty-four hours I was with him'.[33] Nelson was going to leave the tough talking to others. 'I shall not enter on the subject further with the Earl than I can help. I rely on your goodness, and on the abilities of Messrs Booth and Haslewood, and, lastly, on the justness of my cause.' The canny Earl was playing the same game: 'not a word has been dropped by him or me on the subject, nor shall I begin it. No good can arise, but harm to ourselves and the public Service may; and whether I get the cause or lose it, not a word shall come from me.'[34] On St Vincent's appointment the two men had a typical warm exchange of letters. Compliments flowed, Nelson's full of flatteringly nice touches, 'we have got such a driver who will make the lazy ones pull as much as the willing. . . .'[35] Nelson was certainly capable of seeing through St Vincent's capacity for sweet talk even if he did not acknowledge his own. He was not relaxing

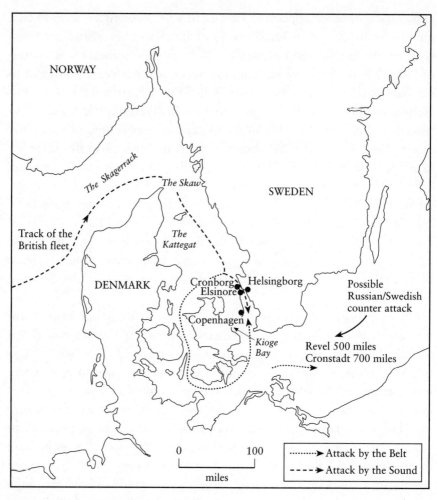

Options for the Attack on Copenhagen

his guard. 'I have just got a letter from the new Earl at the Admiralty, full of compliments. But nothing shall stop my lawsuit and I hope to cast him.'[36] With Davison he was more cynical: 'When I went to the Earl yesterday, you would have thought he would have overwhelmed me with civilities, nothing equal to me as an Officer. I hope he says true, but I will not spare him an inch in the point of law.' It must have caused him sorrow to realize and add, 'The Earl is nothing to either [of] us in his private character.'[37]

For the period 25 January to 12 March 1801, thirty-eight of his letters to Emma survive. On that evidence alone he wrote to her more frequently than every other day. Nevertheless the urgent distractions of a busy routine and his capacity to focus on the business in hand gave him as much refuge from his emotions as ceaseless activity does for any modern business tycoon. From the moment he arrived in Plymouth, delighted with the *San Josef*, 'the finest ship in the world . . . she works like a cutter', he was eager to be off. 'I hope there will be orders to complete our complement and the ship be paid on Saturday. On Sunday we shall get rid of all our women [most probably including 300–400 prostitutes], dogs, and pigeons, and on Monday, with the lark, I hope to be under sail for Torbay, where I trust *San Josef* will become a perfect Man-of-War.'[38]

Nelson's ambition was a battle with the combined French and Spanish fleets. So when St Vincent confirmed his Baltic appointment he responded with a clear message about his own wishes: 'to say the truth, I had rather been under your immediate command; my wish, and in which I hope you will assist me, is to keep *San Josef* for me to return to, if I outlive the Baltic. In ten weeks from sailing we must have finished, if not more shame for us, for I am convinced the Combined Fleet will put to sea.'[39] This constant assertiveness, and acuteness in Nelson's professional mind stand in great contrast to his bouts of inner turmoil; but having vented his emotions he was not immobilized by them. He was thoroughly impatient at the failure to man his ship promptly and the general slackness of the Channel fleet and confided in St Vincent, 'I did not wish to begin a scene here; I should perhaps have been thought impertinent and troublesome, for, except in two or three captains, I see such slackness that in the Mediterranean I have not been used to; and it requires a man of Collingwood's firmness to keep some of them to their duty.'[40]

In his private life the impending campaign prompted action to recognize his changed allegiance. The birth of his child had spelled Fanny's doom; she was to be ruled out of his life with an icy ruthlessness, whose only saving grace was financial generosity. He wanted to be rid of Josiah too. On 4 March he wrote to Fanny for the last time, 'Josiah is to have another ship, and to go abroad, if the *Thalia* cannot soon be got ready. I have done all for him, and he may again, as he has often done before, wish me to break my neck and be abetted in it by his friends, who are likewise my enemies; but I have done my duty as an honest, generous man, and I neither want nor wish for anybody to care what becomes of me, whether I return or am left in the Baltic. Living, I have done all in my power for you, and if dead you will find I have done the same, therefore my only wish is, to be left to myself: and wishing you every happiness, believe me that I am your affectionate . . .'[41]

He was as good as his word for in a codicil to his will, witnessed by Captains Hardy and Thesiger two days later, he directed that 'the sum necessary to pay Lady Nelson the sum of one thousand pounds a year (which I calculate will be twenty thousand pounds) be at her death equally divided as directed by will'.[42] He told Emma, 'I have given you by will £3,000, and three diamond boxes and the King of Naples' picture in trust to be at your disposal, so that is absolutely your own.' He was leaving her the money Sir William still owed him, 'nine hundred and twenty seven pounds lent him at Palermo in January 1799; also the sum of two hundred and fifty five pounds lent him between July and November 1800; also one thousand and ninety four pounds, being one half of our expenses from Leghorn to London in 1800.' He thus placed Hamilton's still unpaid debts in trust for Emma.

None of this was without its pain and his emotions were once again in turmoil, as he told Emma: 'I am really miserable; I look at all your pictures, at your dear hair, I am ready to cry, my heart is so full.'[43] Greville and Hamilton were back as *bêtes noires*: 'what pimps and bitches these people must be. I have always been taught that a pimp was the most despicable of all wretches. . . . God forbid that I should deprive you of innocent amusements, but never meet or stay if any damned whore or pimp bring that fellow [the Prince of Wales] to you. . . . Sir Wm has a treasure, and does he want to throw it away? That other chap [Greville] did throw away the most precious jewel that God Almighty ever sent on this earth.'[44]

Much to Nelson's intense frustration, they were wasting time at Yarmouth. The sixty-one-year-old Admiral Parker had got himself a new young wife, just eighteen. In his own celibate and frustrated state Nelson cried, 'Consider how nice it must be laying in bed with a young wife, compared to a damned cold, raw wind.' Lust for Emma mingled with his jealousy: 'I shall soon return and then we will take our fill of love. No we can never be satiated . . . the sight of my heaven-given wife will make me again a happy father and you a mother.'[45] The same frustration drove his complaints about Sir William to a crescendo. 'What can Sir William mean . . . Good God! my blood boils';[46] 'the iniquity of wanting you to associate with a set of whores, bawds and unprincipled lyars. Can this be the great Sir William? I blush for him.'[47]

Frustration gave a sharper edge to his politicking too. He was quick to imply to St Vincent that Parker was not up to the job: 'Our friend here is a little nervous about dark nights, and fields of ice.'[48] He fed information to Troubridge, 'I was in hopes that Sir Hyde would have had a degree of confidence but no appearance of it.' He implied confusion: 'Poor Domett [Captain of the Fleet] seemed in a pack of troubles.' He invited Troubridge to give Parker a push: 'Get rid of us dear friend, and we shall not be tempted to lay abed till 11 o'clock.'[49] Troubridge, evidently embarrassed, counselled him against committing his unhappy feelings on paper to St Vincent and he agreed. 'Why should I? as my own unhappiness concerns no one but myself, it shall remain fixed in my own breast.' But his unhappiness had to find an outlet; he fed information into the London gossip system via Davison. 'Sir H is onboard sulky. Stewart tells me, his treatment of me is now noticed. Dickson [captain of *Veteran*] came on board today to say all were scandalised at his gross neglect. I declare solemnly that I do not know [officially] I am going to the Baltic, and much worse than that I could tell you. . . . Burn this letter: then it can never appear, and you can speak as if your knowledge came from another quarter.'[50]

The Order of Battle was a sore point with Nelson. Parker had divided his twenty-two sail-of-the-line into three divisions, the starboard division of eight being placed under Nelson. However, Parker's allocation of ships had been so thoughtless and unbalanced and so much at odds with the judgement of his Captain of the Fleet Domett that Nelson wrote angrily to Troubridge, 'You may make your own comments, I feel mine. It was never my desire to serve under this man. . . . To tell me to serve on in this way is to laugh at me, and to think me a greater fool than I am. If this goes on I hope to be allowed to return the moment the fighting business is over.'[51]

Having at last prompted St Vincent to shake Parker out of his honeymoon idyll, they weighed anchor and sailed north on 12 March. Parker, Admiral of the Blue, led the way in the 98-gun *London* with Nelson, now Vice-Admiral of the Blue, in the 98-gun *St George*, and Rear-Admiral Thomas Totty in the 74-gun *Zealous*. The group of leaders would be completed with the later arrival of Rear-Admiral Thomas Graves in the 74-gun *Defiance*. In all there were two 98s, fourteen 74s, three 64s and two 50s, plus eleven frigates, seven bomb ships, two fire ships, nine gun brigs, two cutters and three schooners, a powerful force, equipped for all eventualities.

Nelson stayed frozen out of Parker's planning and on 16 March, with Denmark on the starboard beam, he sounded off again to Davison. 'I have not yet seen my Commander in Chief, and have had no official communication whatever. All I have gathered of our first plans, I disapprove most exceedingly.' Nelson was all for confrontation and intimidation. The thought of anchoring at Cronborg Castle, at least twenty miles from Copenhagen, filled him with dismay: 'The Dane should see our Flag waving every moment he lifted up his head.' He saw correctly that keeping the fleet out of sight was, 'to seduce Denmark into a war ... every good in the cause of humanity, and of honour to our country must arise by spirited conduct, and every ill to both from our delicacy'.[52] He was equally explicit with Troubridge, to the point of being contemptuous of his Commander-in-Chief: 'Bold measures from ministers and speedily executed meet my ideas. If you were here just to look at us I have heard of manoeuvres off Ushant but ours beat all ever seen. Would it were really over. I am sick of it.' He was being thoroughly disloyal but it is nevertheless difficult not to have sympathy with his situation. 'But as I am not in the secret, and I feel I have a right to speak out, not in the Fleet certainly, but in England and to England.'[53] He complained to Emma, 'I have had no communication yet with my Commander-in-Chief. Lord Spencer placed him here, and has completely thrown me in the background.'[54] Parker's fear of being upstaged by Nelson was intense. Never was there a truer judgement than Lady Malmesbury's, 'I feel very sorry for Sir Hyde ... no man would ever have gone with Nelson, or over him as he was sure to be in the background in every case.'[55] On this occasion there was every sign that Parker was aware of the danger and determined to keep Nelson there.

By the 19th, they were off the Skaw, the north-east tip of Denmark. The frigate *Blanche* was sent ahead carrying Vansittart, the British negotiator with dispatches for Drummond at Copenhagen. Parker's orders from the Admiralty were clear enough: to deal with Denmark either amicably or by hostilities, then to attack the Russians at Revel on the southern coast of the Gulf of Finland, or at Cronstadt, near to St Petersburg itself. Sweden was to be dealt with similarly, unless she chose to come into line, in which case she was to be offered protection against

Russia. He now sent an ultimatum: the Danes had forty-eight hours to give their reply to the British offer for negotiation.

They made their way down the Kattegat until they were in sight of the first obstacle in their passage to Copenhagen, the entrance to the narrow passage just three miles wide separating the north-east edge of the island of Zeeland on which stood Copenhagen further to the south, and the coast of Sweden. On the Danish side it was dominated by the great fortress of Cronborg whose guns they would have to pass. At this point Nelson succeeded in getting on board the flagship for a discussion with Parker and was pleased to find that Parker 'was determined to pass Cronborg and go off Copenhagen in order to give weight to our negotiator', but he added rather ominously in yet another of his private progress reports to Troubridge, 'Sir Hyde told me, on my anxiety for going forward with all expedition, that we were going to go no further without fresh orders.' Nelson's own mood was clear. His ship was already stripped for action, 'to prepare people's minds that we are going at it'.[56]

Three days later at about six in the evening the *Blanche* returned with Drummond, Vansittart, his secretary Dr Beeke, Talbot the British chargé d'affaires in Sweden, Fenwick the Consul at Cronborg and a group of British businessmen and their families. The Danes had refused to negotiate, their refusal tantamount to a declaration of war. Parker had no option other than to consider what to do next. He sent for Nelson, who interrupted a letter to Troubridge, 'The Commander-in-Chief has just sent for me and shall have my firm support and my honest opinion if he condescends to ask it.'[57] Nelson was at last involved and wrote to Emma, 'Now we are sure of fighting. I am sent for. When it was a joke I was kept in the background.'[58]

Unfortunately Nelson was now to have his worst fears realized. Events had already demonstrated the likelihood of Parker's unfitness for high command: his excessive dilatoriness in mobilizing his force, his seeming unconcern that time and melting ice could enable a Russian detachment to escape from Revel and come to the aid of the Danes, and his lack of interest in minimizing Denmark's opportunity to prepare her defence. Now his assessment of those defences relied purely on the unprofessional observations of Vansittart and Drummond. He ignored the special experience of officers attached to his force by the Admiralty. Worst of all he demonstrated that he was incapable of bearing the weight of responsibility placed on him; he was to show himself irresolute to the point of being a straw for every wind that blew. Nelson, being the man he was, could not sit in the wings. He could not avoid taking charge.

When Nelson appeared in the great cabin of the *London* for his meeting with Parker and Vansittart, he encountered a Commander-in-Chief who had changed his mind. Parker, greatly impressed by accounts of 'the immense preparations of defence against an attack made by the Danes' and by the difficulties put forward by his pilots in approaching Copenhagen directly by the Sound, or indirectly by the roundabout route of the Great Belt, was now minded to remain where he was and let the combined Danish, Russian and Swedish fleets come to him. Nelson, aghast, had to summon up every ounce of expression and will to persuade Parker to change his mind. It took him at least five hours. Nelson's instinct, let alone the Admiralty's orders, was diametrically opposed to Parker's spineless intentions. But Nelson's shrewd insight told him that if Parker was to be persuaded to take the offensive he must be given a choice, not just presented with a 'take it or leave it' Nelson plan.

Nelson's decision to commit to paper the gist of what he had said in Parker's cabin had a dual purpose, to force Parker to maintain his decision to attack and to dissociate himself publicly from Parker's plan. 'The more I have reflected, the more I am confirmed in opinion, that not a moment should be lost in attacking the Enemy: they will every day and hour be stronger . . . the only consideration in my mind is, how to get at them with the least risk to our own ships. . . . On your decision depends, whether our Country shall be degraded in the eyes of Europe, or whether she shall rear her head higher than ever.' The first option he put to Parker was 'taking the bull by the horns', in effect a frontal attack on 'the ships and Crown Islands' at the entrance to Copenhagen Roads. The natural issue of such a battle would be 'Ships crippled and perhaps one or two lost; for the wind which carries you in, will most probably not bring out a crippled ship.' But such an attack would 'not prevent the Revel ships, or Swedes, from joining the Danes [they would naturally approach Copenhagen from the south via the Baltic]; and to prevent this from taking effect, is, in my opinion absolutely necessary – and still to attack Copenhagen'. Thus, appreciating fully Parker's extreme apprehension at risking his ships, he implicitly ruled out a frontal attack and described two other options. The first was 'to pass Cronenburg, taking the risk of damage, and to pass up the deepest and straightest Channel above the

Middle Grounds; and coming down the Garbar or King's Channel, to attack their floating batteries &c &c., as we find it convenient'. This, the plan ultimately adopted, would position their ships to make their attack from a point to the south of Copenhagen and thus have 'the effect of preventing a junction between the Russians, Swedes, and Danes, and may give us an opportunity of bombarding Copenhagen'. The third option, avoiding the Sound and the guns of Cronborg altogether, would involve an anticlockwise circumnavigation of the island of Zeeland by the Great Belt, in effect again attacking Copenhagen from the south. This would take four or five days, with the attack then delivered in much the same way as in the second option, and also preventing junction with the Russians. A supplementary option, once the fleet was round the Great Belt, would be to detach ten ships with a bomb and two fire ships to destroy the Russian squadron at Revel. 'I do not see the great risk of such a detachment, and with the remainder to attempt the business at Copenhagen. The measure may be thought bold, but I am of opinion the boldest measures are the safest; our country demands a most vigorous exertion of her force, directed with judgement.'[59]

There was never any likelihood that Nelson would be able to persuade Parker that the Russians were the prime strategic target or that the Danes, intent on defence, were no great threat to his rear. Nor was Parker going to depart from the literal sequence of his orders; Denmark was to be dealt with first. So, *faute de mieux*, Nelson's overriding objective was to get Hyde Parker to attack the Danes, one way or another. Nelson played his cards well although there was no way that a man as irresolute as Parker could resist a Nelson in full flood, at least until he heard the next opinion forcefully expressed. Thus was Parker manoeuvred into acting, if only to select the less heroic option, the long, roundabout route by the Great Belt, which to him had the added attraction of enabling him to temporize a little longer.

And that was where the situation stood until the next day. Parker informed the Admiralty that with the support of Vansittart and Nelson he proposed to approach Copenhagen by the Belt. However, as soon as he ordered the course to be set he was immediately assailed by Domett, his Captain of the Fleet, Otway the captain of the flagship and Murray, captain of the *Elephant*, the leading ship of the fleet, none of whom had been involved in the discussions of the previous day. Parker with no will of his own and in a state of monumental indecision sent Otway to get

Nelson, whose immediate reaction according to Otway's later recollection was, 'I don't care a d——n, by which passage we go, so that we
fight them.'[60] Once on board the *London*, he used his unsent letter to
remind Parker of his position and noted in his journal, 'Sir Hyde told me
he was uneasy about going by the Belt in case of accidents and therefore
he thought of going by Cronborg, and which I cordially assented, and
the Fleet was tacked.'

The politically wide awake Nelson had also taken steps to make sure
that the Prime Minister and St Vincent knew who was actually devising
the plan of campaign. He took Vansittart aside and asked him to tell the
Prime Minister what had happened in Parker's cabin. Vansittart exceeded
Nelson's highest expectations: 'I gave a full account of what had passed
in Sir Hyde Parker's cabin on the 23rd ulto . . . he considers your readiness to take on yourself the responsibility attaching on a deviation from
your instructions, as not the least eminent of the services which you have
rendered your country . . . Mr Addington has since communicated the
whole affair to Lord St Vincent, who equally acquiesces in the propriety
of the determination so that whatever may be the event of the plan (which
Providence must decide) you will have the satisfaction of meeting with
the approbation of those who have the best right to judge of it.'[61]

By now Nelson knew that he was effectively in command. In deciding
after all to attack by the Sound, Parker had also agreed Nelson's
proposed mode of attack on Copenhagen and seems to have had no
difficulty in assenting to Nelson's request to be the man to command it.
Nelson at once began to form his team and sell his strategy. His Journal
entry for the 26th demonstrates his method, 'All day employed in arguing
and convincing to [*sic*] the different officers the mode of attack.' How
successful he was is shown in Fremantle's report to his wife: 'Lord Nelson
is quite sanguine, but as you may well imagine there is a great diversity
of opinion. In the mode of attack intended to be adopted and which is
planned by Lord Nelson there seems but one.'[62]

Now that Nelson felt in charge he could afford to be slightly more
relaxed about Parker. Writing to Troubridge on the 29th to warn him
that he was going to be surprised by what Vansittart had to say he went
on,

My last line to you before I left the *St George* was, if you recollect,
Now we are going to fight, I suppose I am to be consulted. Little

did I think it was to converse on not fighting. I feel happy I had so much command of myself, for I should have let out what you might have been sorry to see, especially fancying I had been, to say no worse, very unkindly treated by Sir Hyde; that is with a degree of haughtiness which my spirit could not bear. However, I have now every reason to believe that Sir H has found it not necessary to be high to me, and that I have his real honour at heart, and in having that I have the honour of my country. His conduct is certainly the very reverse of what it was.[63]

To Emma it was a case of, 'Sir Hyde Parker has by this time found out the worth of your Nelson, and that he is a useful sort of man on a pinch; therefore if he ever has thought unkindly of me, I freely forgive him. Nelson must stand amongst the first or he must fall.'[64]

On the 29th Nelson shifted his flag from the *St George* to the lighter draught *Elephant* commanded by his friend Foley, but the fleet was not able to enter the Sound until the morning of the 30th when a topsail breeze blew from the north-west. As in the case of everything Parker did, the risks of Cronborg had been greatly overestimated. Off Cronborg the Sound was two and a half miles wide. The effective range of a 36-pounder was one and a half miles. Sailing down the middle of the Sound and assuming 36-pounders on the Swedish side, their shot was going to strike the fleet in the final third of their effective range and both Danish and Swedish gunners would be firing at moving targets. The chances of sustaining heavy damage were not very considerable. In the event not a shot was fired from the Swedish shore (the Danes had not supported plans to construct batteries at Helsingborg in case the Swedes should demand a share in Sound dues levied on passing ships) and the fleet was able to move out of range of 200 guns blazing away ineffectually at them from Cronborg.

Having passed unscathed through the Sound, the fleet anchored about fifteen miles to the north of Copenhagen. That afternoon, 30 March, Parker and Nelson, together with some of the senior captains and the officer commanding artillery, went away in a schooner to inspect the Danish defences. They could see the entrance to Copenhagen harbour, heavily protected by the Trekroner fort and moored ships; then stretching away to the south a line of moored ships and gun platforms backing on to the land. In front of this line of guns was a deep channel, the King's

Channel, effectively about three-quarters of a mile wide. Then came the Middle Ground, an area of shallow water tapering at both ends about two miles long and about a mile wide at its broadest. Lying between the Middle Ground and Saltholm island came the Outer Deep, about three-quarters of a mile wide. The position of the channels and shallows was not evident, for the buoys marking them had been removed. Nelson, never a man to delegate where his vital interests were concerned, involved himself deeply in surveying and rebuoying. That night he wrote to Emma, 'I have just been reconnoitring the Danish line of defence. It looks formidable to those who are children at war, but to my judgement with ten sail of the line I think I can annihilate them.'[65] Events would prove his judgement wildly optimistic.

On the afternoon of the next day while the rebuoying and surveying work continued they held a council of war. Those present were Parker, Nelson, Graves, Domett, Fremantle, Foley, Murray, Riou and Stewart. It was now that Nelson really exerted himself. He pushed himself forward, undertaking to lead the attack with ten ships-of-the-line and all the smaller ships. It was an offer Hyde Parker could not refuse. Indeed he went further and added *Edgar* and much to Fremantle's delight *Ganges*. According to Colonel Stewart who was present at the council, Nelson talked down all the difficulties that were raised about the possible appearance of the Russians and Swedes. Of the former, 'So much the better, I wish they were twice as many, the easier the victory, depend on it.' Of the latter, 'The more numerous the better.'[66] Such was the mental energy, persuasiveness and personal domination of the little Admiral that Parker was quickly relegated to the role of follower; all hung on the words of Nelson. It was a further measure of Parker's unfitness for command that he asked Nelson, Graves and Domett to give their views in writing as to whether they should attack. Nelson and Domett were for it, Graves, ironically in view of his subsequent bravery, against.

Nelson's battle plan was simplicity itself. He would take his ships down the Outer Deep, round the far end of the Middle Ground, back into the King's Channel, spread them along the Danish line and batter it into submission. But it was immediately clear to Nelson that while getting into the King's Channel would be relatively easy, getting out would depend on winning. Unlike Parker, he did not fear shallow water, and he had been personally involved in rebuoying the channels. What he must do was ensure that his ships came to action in a controlled way and so avoid blocking the channel. He must also ensure that enough ships were deployed to engage the Trekroner fort, which unless stormed and taken by Stewart's soldiers, could effectively seal their exit. He knew that once his ships were in the King's Channel there would be no hiding place; the channel was only 1,100 yards wide at its narrowest point; any ship at any position in the channel would be in the killing field of the Danish guns.

During the morning of 1 April the whole fleet moved to within two miles of Copenhagen and the exit from the King's Channel. With a group of chosen captains Nelson made his final observations of the defences in Riou's *Amazon*. Back on board *Elephant*, he gave the signal for his detachment to weigh. *Amazon* led as they made their way slowly down the Outer Deep. They hove to and anchored in a closely packed group about two miles from the the enemy defences, vulnerable to mortar attack, but surprisingly not bombarded.

After a jovial and high-spirited eve of battle dinner with Hardy, Foley, Riou, Inman, Graves, Fremantle, and the two soldiers Stewart and Hutchinson who commanded a detachment of the 49th, Riou stayed behind and worked with Nelson and Foley to produce the Order of Battle and instructions for the following day. During the night Hardy set out in a small boat to establish the depth of water near the first of the Danish ships and, most importantly, to establish the edge of the Middle Ground.

Nelson had been working non-stop for two days, moving around, visibly exerting his powers of leadership and command; nobody was to be in any doubt as to who was in charge of the battle. He radiated personal commitment and enthusiasm, charging the spirits of those he would lead, personally supervising the buoying of the channels, seeking the views of others as he measured the facts of the tactical situation. Midnight passed. Foley and Riou felt he could leave to them what still remained to be done. It was not in the nature of Nelson's active brain to let go. His servant, the rough and ready Allen, no respecter of his Admiral's person, took him in hand and made him lie down. Nothing could prevent his continuing to dictate.

By about six o'clock in the morning when the orders had been transcribed, Nelson was up again and had breakfasted. At seven he signalled for all captains. Each got from Nelson himself his orders, words of encouragement and directions on matters of key importance. From his quarterdeck in the quiet morning light he saw the Danish defences,

stretching away for about two miles up the King's Channel, culminating in the Trekroner batteries and ships guarding the entrance to
Copenhagen harbour. Beyond that and supposedly in a position to
menace the defences at the harbour mouth was Hyde Parker with eight
ships-of-the-line.

21

Copenhagen

Foley has put me on a regimen of milk at four in the morning;
Murray has given me lozenges

Nelson, April 1801

Nelson had little scope for fancy tactics. He intended a controlled and disciplined battle. This time there was no reference in his orders to captains using their initiative. He hoped to position his biggest ships against the strongest opposition; to use his gunboats to rake the Danish positions from their flank; he hoped to puncture a hole in the Danish line that would enable him to use his bomb ships to rain shells on the arsenal and Citadel; to storm the Trekroner, once it had been bombarded, using troops in the flat boats, sheltered by his ships' sides until the moment of attack. With a favourable wind and current he expected his ships to move on to support others when they had subdued the immediate opposition; he expected the nearest end of the Danish line would be quickly subdued and that *Isis* and *Agamemnon* would cut their cables, and immediately make sail and take their station at the far Trekroner fort end of the line. It was clear from the beginning that this would not be a battle of boarding and close quarters but one of attrition depending on weight of metal, speed and consistency of firing, downright courage, and will to win; not a battle of manoeuvre or dash. It would be a fiendish, stationary slaughterhouse.

The action began on a false note. The pilots who would take responsibility for navigating the ships through the King's Channel were a group composed of mates of trading vessels from the ports of Scotland and the North of England to the Baltic, as well as several masters in the Navy. In the words of Colonel Stewart, 'A most unpleasant degree of hesitation prevailed amongst them all, when they came to the point about the bearing of the east end of the Middle Ground, and about the exact line of deep water in the King's Channel.'[1] Perhaps in the press of events and

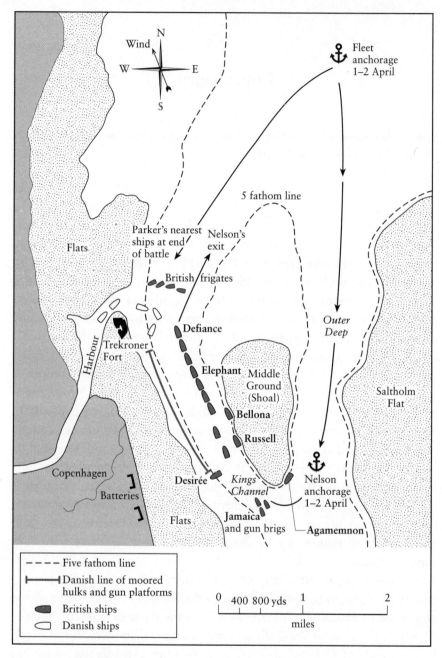

The Battle of Copenhagen, 2 April 1801

activity Nelson had not paid enough attention to this body of men and the vital part they had to play in such difficult waters. He later recalled with some heat, 'I have experienced in the Sound the misery of having the honour of our Country intrusted to Pilots, who have no other thought than to keep the Ship clear of danger, and their own silly heads clear of shot.'[2]

On the day, however, he showed no anger or anxiety. Nor did he choose at this late hour to share with the pilots the information Hardy had derived from his personal survey. He concentrated his whole force of character on the first and necessary objective: to calm their uncertainties and stiffen their resolve. The wind was fair, the signal made for action; the last thing Nelson needed was a debate about the exact dimensions of the channel or the depth of the water. As Stewart recounts, 'Lord Nelson urged them to be steady, to be resolute, and decide. At length, Mr Brierly [Briarly], Master of the *Bellona*, previously Davidge Gould's Master in the *Audacious* at the Nile, declared himself ready to lead the fleet.' Nelson himself later recalled his words, 'My Lord, if you will command each Ship to steer with the small red house open with a mill, until such a Church is on with a wood, the King's Channel will be open.'[3] Briarly's example was followed and the pilots rejoined their respective ships. Up to a point Nelson had succeeded. He had got his battle going, but Hardy's vital information that there was deep water right up to the enemy line was never appreciated by the pilots who took the ships no closer to the Danes than a cable's length, condemning Nelson to a battle of attrition fought at a range varying between 200 and 500 yards.

At half past nine the signal was given to weigh in succession. *Edgar* went off first, to take up her position a third of the way down the Danish line; this she achieved successfully, holding her fire till she arrived off her target. *Ardent* went off to sail beyond *Edgar*, and then *Glatton* to go beyond her, thus covering from a third to halfway down the Danish line. Having got this group into position, Nelson set about filling up the positions behind them. *Isis* went off first. *Agamemnon* should have followed but immediately went aground. Nelson quickly extemporized and signalled *Polyphemus* to take her place – his first forced change of plan. Then he set about filling up the far half of the line. His intention was that these ships should pass the first half of the British line on the side away from the enemy, thus being protected till they were almost in position. Disaster struck. *Bellona*, steering too far to the right, went aground opposite the second Danish ship, and *Russell* similarly went aground opposite the first. Nelson at once decided that he must personally show the way and following Hardy's advice, rather than that of the pilots, took *Edgar* between the British and Danish lines and was followed by *Ganges*, *Monarch* and eventually *Defiance*, all of whom took up positions ahead of him.

He appreciated at once his vulnerability at the far end of his line. His broadsides there amounted to some seventy-four guns; the Trekroner fort and the ships fronting it combined had more than twice as many, and the Trekoner's guns were all 36-pounders. Nor had Nelson's misfortunes ended. His nine gunboats, under Captain Rose in the *Jamaica*, were impeded by wind and current and never able to get into position to rake the Danish batteries, or fulfil Nelson's battle plan.

So there they were like two prize fighters toeing the line, a contest of brute force, each destined to throw lethal punches until one of the contestants was battered into submission. As Nelson himself said, 'Here was no manoeuvring: it was downright fighting.'[4] Weight of punch was therefore critical. The Danish main armament consisted of 24-pounders, except for the *Provesteenen*, and *Hialperen* which had 36-pounders. About half the guns of the British 74s were 32-pounders, including powerful carronades, 'smashers', not included in the nominal count of armament; the rest were mainly 18-pounders. After the battle the Danes claimed that the British outnumbered them and had heavier guns. In fact the forces facing each other, and actually in action (including *Bellona* and *Russell*, who though grounded were still able to fire), were broadly equal in terms of firepower (weight of metal). Each broadside could hurtle more than three tons of metal at the other. The Danes had an advantage in being able to supply and reinforce gun crews from the shore; the British were much more highly trained and their guns had superior muzzle velocity because of the superiority of their powder.[5]

The action began at five past ten and it took an hour and a half of slow but inexorable build-up before all the British ships were in position, each anchoring easily by the stern in the favourable current. A thousand guns were belching flame and smoke. The *Elephant*, in the centre, faced Commodore Fischer's *Dannebroge*, 200 yards away. A hundred yards astern was *Glatton* and 100 yards ahead was *Ganges*. Riou, whose frigates were intended as a flexible force, positioned himself to make up for the shortfall in guns at the head of the line. His frigates showed great courage but heavily outclassed could do little but draw fire.

After two and a half hours of savage pounding and carnage the battle was still at its height. According to Stewart *Elephant* fired forty broadsides in the first three hours and sixty in total. In the first two and a half hours more than 1,000 cannon balls must have thrashed through the air from each of the British ships, and much the same from the Danish side, crashing, smashing, embedding, clanging hideously on metal or ricocheting where they hit; carrying away guns, timbers, arms, legs, heads, mangling bodies, numbing minds. The Danes fought with desperate courage, the British with fierce application. Perhaps Nelson's chauvinism had disabled his insight and empathy for he had not appreciated how hard men would fight to defend the homes and families lying just behind them.

The battle was reaching a point of crisis. Nelson had managed to bring heavy force to bear on what he had judged to be the weakest part of the enemy line but success had not followed automatically. Five of his ships, including the two grounded, were firing at *Provesteenen* and *Wagrien*, the first two in the Danish line. Their combined firepower was significantly greater than that of the two Danes and Inman's 40-gun frigate *Desiree* had also managed to position herself so that she could rake them. Nevertheless the Danes were fighting so hard that *Isis* was to lose more than 100 of her men killed and wounded and *Bellona*, aground behind her, was also being mauled although most of her casualties resulted from two of her own guns exploding.

At the other end of the line *Monarch* was under heavy fire from two Danish ships and would lose more than 200 of her crew. Farther astern of Nelson, George Murray's *Edgar* was paying a heavy price; she would have the second-highest number of casualties, 136. Nelson's own ship with twenty-three killed and wounded was surviving well, as was *Ganges* ahead with only eight casualties. To his stern, *Glatton*, commanded by Captain Bligh (previously of the *Bounty*), had lost fifty-five. Nelson's intention to punch a hole in the Danish line so that his bomb ships could bombard the Citadel and arsenal had failed to materialize; the best they could manage was for two of them to get into a position near the Middle Ground and fire over the two fleets into the naval dockyards, but the range was too great; they did little damage.

What happened next is best left to Stewart.

Lord Nelson was at this time, as he had been during the whole Action, walking the starboard side of the quarter-deck sometimes much animated, and at others heroically fine in his observations. A shot through the mainmast knocked a few splinters about us. He observed to me with a smile, 'It is warm work, and this day may be the last to any of us at a moment;' and then stopping short at the gangway, he used an expression never to be erased from my memory, and said with emotion, 'but mark you, I would not be elsewhere for thousands.' When the signal, no 39 [to discontinue the engagement], was made, the Signal Lieutenant reported it to him. He continued his walk, and did not appear to take notice of it. The Lieutenant meeting his Lordship at the next turn asked, 'whether he should repeat it?' Lord Nelson answered, 'No, acknowledge it.' On the Officer returning to the poop, his Lordship called after him, 'Is no 16 [for close action] still hoisted?' the Lieutenant answering in the affirmative, Lord Nelson said, 'Mind you keep it so.' He now walked the deck considerably agitated, which was always known by his moving the stump of his right arm. After a turn or two, he said to me in a quick manner. 'Do you know what's shown on board of the Commander-in-Chief, no 39?' On asking him what that meant, he answered, 'Why to leave off Action.' 'Leave off Action!' he repeated, and then added, with a shrug, 'Now damn me if I do.' He also observed, I believe, to Captain Foley, 'You know Foley, I have only one eye – I have a right to be blind sometimes;' and then with an archness peculiar to his character, putting the glass to his blind eye, he exclaimed, 'I really do not see the signal.'[6]

Nelson's wonderful ability to create the phrases of history was equalled only by his more important capacity not to be panicked or to lose his resolution in front of others. His genius for inspiring others was at work, even when he was not physically present. When the wounded Riou, who had never met him before this action, saw the Commander-in-Chief's signal repeated by Rear-Admiral Graves in the nearby *Defiance* his immediate reaction was, 'What will Nelson think of us.'[7] In the next instant he died, cut in two by an enemy ball as *Amazon* turned away and exposed her stern to the enemy guns.

Nelson's judgement to continue the battle was undoubtedly correct. Parker's signal was tactically fatuous. It put Nelson in a quandary. Being a general signal it had to be obeyed by every ship that saw it, and had to be repeated by them. The frigates saw it and obeyed. Graves, like Nelson, saw it, repeated it, and then stayed where he was; he realized its nonsense and the following day wrote, 'If we had discontinued the action before the enemy struck we should have all got aground and have been destroyed.'[8] Nelson was of the same mind. He did not yet know for certain that he was winning but he instantly appreciated that the quickest way to lose would be to disengage. A force in retreat, its attention diverted from fighting to working badly damaged ships would be massively vulnerable to mishap; and Danish efforts would be redoubled at the sight of the retreating British. Nelson had no option but to continue the fight and win. The situation in his own ship was far from desperate; his casualties were comparatively light. His main opponent the *Dannebroge* had been on fire since 11.30 and was threatening to set alight other ships in the Danish line. Within another half-hour most of the Danish guns to his left had been silenced. To his right, *Monarch* and Graves's ship the *Defiance* were still hotly engaged, and taking great punishment; their combined casualties would make up a third of the British losses. Captain Mosse of the *Monarch* was already dead, but Graves had kept Nelson's signal flying and neither ship had shown the slightest inclination to break off the action. The Danish commander Fischer had abandoned *Dannebroge* when she caught fire, subsequently raised his flag in *Holsteen* (opposite *Monarch*) but now, at half past two, he abandoned her also and made for the Trekroner because *Holsteen* 'was so shattered, and had so many killed and wounded, and so many guns dismounted'.[9]

Within an hour of Parker's signal the battle, as a set piece, seemed to have swung decisively in Nelson's favour. Nevertheless its endgame posed many problems. The Danes were not following time-honoured procedure for giving up their surrendered ships, and land batteries behind the Danish line continued to fire over them. Nelson had three ships aground. It was becoming increasingly unrealistic to contemplate mounting an attack on the Trekroner fort; it had not been softened up and its guns still constituted a formidable obstacle, as the battered *Monarch* knew only too well. The original plan had been that Parker would protect Nelson's exit and engage the fort and the defensive ships about it but only two of his eight ships, *Defence* and *Ramillies*, had managed to claw their way against wind and tide and get into position to be of practical help. Parker himself was some four miles away. The state of Nelson's powder and shot had not yet become critical but if Stewart's reckoning of the number of *Elephant*'s broadsides was correct he must have used at least half his 5,000 rounds of heavy shot, an important consideration if the Russians and Swedes should turn up before shot could be replenished from England.

Uppermost in Nelson's mind was Danish behaviour. They were not playing the game according to the rules and he was not gaining the clear-cut victory he deserved. Irritation ignited into rage as he exclaimed menacingly, 'that he must either send on shore, and stop this irregular proceeding, or send in our Fire ships and burn them'.[10] He decided to send a message under a flag of truce. He did not break off the engagement. He showed no sign of loss of confidence or resolve. But he took great pains over his message. His conscious mind was about preventing irregular Danish firing because of the retribution he would otherwise have to deliver. He may or may not have consciously realized that even if he won the battle on the water he would still have to batter Copenhagen into submission, a form of total war. Whatever his conscious thought, his intuition led him to seek victory without more fighting. Nothing else can explain the inspired phraseology of his letter and the pains he took to present it properly. 'To the brothers of Englishmen, the Danes,' his message ran, 'Lord Nelson has directions to spare Denmark, when no longer resisting; but if the firing is continued on the part of Denmark, Lord Nelson will be obliged to set on fire all the Floating-batteries he has taken, without having the power of saving the brave Danes who have defended them.' He was inviting the Danes to end the contest. He demanded that the letter be sealed properly and as Stewart recounts, 'the person dispatched for the wax had his head taken off by a cannon ball'; which fact being reported to the Admiral, he merely said, 'Send another messenger for the wax.' It was pointed out to him that there were wafers on his table. 'Send for the sealing wax he said.' He wanted to give the impression that he had all the time in the world.

Captain Sir Frederick Thesiger, who had accompanied Nelson as a volunteer, went off with the message and at three o'clock the Danish Adjutant-General Lindholm came out, also under a flag of truce, to order the Trekroner to cease firing, at which point Nelson after some five hours of fighting ordered the British ships to cease fire too. Before Lindholm reached *Elephant* Nelson's instincts, if not his conscious intentions, were confirmed in a rapid consultation with Foley and Fremantle. They were not in favour of bringing forward the least damaged ships to attack the fort; they wanted him to get his ships out of the King's Channel while he had the chance. 'At this time he was aware that our ships were cut to pieces and it would be difficult to get them out.'[11]

Nelson was now fully aware that he had to transform the brief truce into a cessation of hostilities. So when he replied to the question Thesiger had brought from the Prince Regent about the purpose of Nelson's note his objective was to convey his conviction that he had won, in effect daring the Danes to continue the battle.

Lord Nelson's object in sending the Flag of Truce was humanity; he therefore consents that hostilities shall cease, and that the wounded Danes may be taken on shore. And Lord Nelson will take his prisoners out of the Vessels, and burn and carry off his prizes as he shall think fit. Lord Nelson, with humble duty to his Royal Highness the Prince of Denmark, will consider this the greatest victory he has ever gained, if it may be the cause of a happy reconciliation and union between his own most gracious Sovereign, and his Majesty the King of Denmark.[12]

The battle seemed to be over; the Danes were in no position to do other than accept Nelson's terms. Of the eighteen Danish vessels of all descriptions, sixteen were sunk or destined to be burned and *Holsteen* was taken as a prize. The frigate *Hiaelperen* alone escaped. The Danes had lost something approaching 40 per cent of their men. This annihilation, like that of the Nile, was again accomplished without the loss of a single British ship. But the human price had been greater. British casualties were higher than at the Nile, this time 943 killed and wounded out of about 6,800, nearly 14 per cent of those engaged. Nelson had come perilously close to fatally underestimating the Danes.

The diplomatic offensive that now opened was equally remarkable for the part played by Nelson. He was punctilious in recognizing that it was Parker's prerogative to negotiate terms with the Danes, and thus he sent Lindholm on to the *London*, while he concentrated his energies on getting his battered ships out of the channel. *Monarch* struck a shoal but *Ganges* coming up from behind gave her a controlled shove midships and got her off. *Glatton* made her escape, but *Defiance* and Nelson's *Elephant* both ran aground, about a mile from the Trekroner. Both

Bellona, and *Desiree* who had grounded trying to help her, seemed immovable. The unwisdom of Parker's signal could hardly have been better demonstrated than by this series of events which occurred when no shots were being fired. Leaving Foley to struggle for another four hours with the business of refloating *Elephant*, Nelson called for his boat and made for the *London*, where it was agreed that the suspension of hostilities should continue for another twenty-four hours.

The Danes were divided between those who would have fought on out of loyalty to their allies and fear of Russia, and those who felt they had done all they could. Neither Parker nor Nelson succeeded in getting the Danes to accept Parker's conditions for an armistice: Denmark's withdrawal from the Armed Neutrality coupled with an offer of British protection. The Danes were not granting Nelson the victory he had declared.

On 3 April Nelson was sent onshore for direct negotiations with the Crown Prince. The minutes of the meeting show Nelson dealing with the Prince with a wonderful open adroitness, always helping his opponent to save face, always being clear and decided about his own position but never boxing himself into a corner, always reserving Parker's position on issues requiring more thought or outside his own competence to agree. In short he proved himself to be a masterly negotiator – and with his sure instinct for preserving his reputation wrote to the Prime Minister following this first two-hour meeting with the Prince. However, subsequent negotiations aboard *London* were so difficult that Parker was in effect obliged to issue an ultimatum that the ceasefire would not be extended unless Denmark suspended its membership of the Armed Neutrality for the duration of the armistice, and he sent Nelson and Stewart on shore for further direct negotiations with the Crown Prince. During this meeting all changed but not as a result of anybody's negotiating skill. General Lindholm entered the room and whispered in the Crown Prince's ear, 'Tsar Paul has died.' By the end of the meeting the Crown Prince had agreed to an armistice of fourteen weeks with two months' notice, and suspension of Danish membership of the Armed Neutrality. On 9 April their agreement was signed, sealed, and delivered to Colonel Stewart who set off for England, still totally unaware of the death of the Tsar.

Again Nelson wrote to Addington, this time a masterly but egocentric account of what had been achieved, with thoughts on how to prevent future disputes over Danish trade. At the same time he seemed to have genuine worries about how it was all going to appear. 'A negotiator is certainly out of my line, but being thrown into it, I have endeavoured to acquit myself as well as I was able, and in such a manner as I hope will not entirely merit your disapprobation. If it unfortunately does, I have only to request that I now may be permitted to retire . . . all these matters have affected my mind, nor shall I have a moment's rest, till I know, at least, that I am not thought to have done mischief.'[13] Nor was he just fishing for praise. He also wrote to Minto, 'Before you condemn the Armistice, hear all the reasons: they are weighty, and most important. Without it we should have gone no further this year, and with it not half so far as I wished.'[14] He was perhaps beginning to sense what some newspapers would focus on, that an armistice diluted the quality of the victory and had been achieved at great cost.

However, his myth-making machine was hard at work. 'Sir Hyde having sent me on shore to talk with the Prince, I was received in the most flattering manner by all ranks, and the crowd was, as is usual, with me. No wonder I am spoilt. All my astonishment is that my head is not turned.'[15] That was how he put it to Davison, to all intents and purposes his London press agent. Stewart's account rings more realistically. 'The populace showed a mixture of admiration, curiosity and displeasure. A strong guard secured his safety, and appeared necessary to keep off the mob, whose rage, although mixed with admiration at his thus trusting himself amongst them, was naturally to be expected. . . . It perhaps savoured of rashness in Lord Nelson thus early to risk himself among them.'[16]

A few days later, on 12 April, there was still more attitudinizing, this time with Lindholm. 'Will you do me the honour to accept a medal of the action of the Nile. I have one ready for the Academy with a short account of my life, which may not be amiss for youths to study.'[17] Later, following his subsequent visit he justifiably turned up the volume for Emma: 'I received as a warrior all the praises which could gratify the ambitions of the bravest man, and the thanks of the nation, from the King downwards for my humanity in saving the town from destruction. Nelson is a warrior, but will not be a butcher. I am sure, could you have seen the adoration and respect you would have cried for joy; there are no honours can be conferred equal to this.'

He had other things to convey to her too. Whatever success he was having in his political management of the Danes he was still bound fast to her moods and suspicions. 'Having done my duty, not all the world

should get me out of the ship. No I owe it to my promise and not all the
world shall ever make me in the smallest article break it. . . . I will take
care your dear friend shall do no wrong. He [Thompson] has cried on
account of his child. . . . He desires me to say he has never wrote to his
aunt [Fanny] since he sailed. . . . He does not, nor cannot, care about her;
he believes she has a most unfeeling heart.'[18]

The flow of adrenalin from battle and diplomacy was receding, to be succeeded by anticlimax and frustration. He was angry that having carried
the campaign on his own shoulders the incompetent Parker was once
again in command. Nor was his lust for action at all assuaged. Now
the bloody business at Copenhagen was done he wanted to get after the
Russians. 'I but wish to finish Paul and then retire for ever.'[19] On the
12th Parker took the fleet in the direction of Revel. Nelson, delayed by
having to lighten the *St George* and by foul winds was, ironically, left
behind. He grumbled to Troubridge, 'I am trying to get over the Grounds
but Sir Hyde is slow, and I am afraid the Revel fleet will slip through our
fingers. Why we are not long since at Revel is past my comprehension.'
There was an undertone of worry about attitudes at home to his
armistice. 'Be it good or bad, it is my own; therefore, if blamable, let me
be the only person censured.'[20] He was also becoming much concerned
about his lawsuit and there was more than a tinge of self-pity directed
at Davison:

> You can gather from Nepean, or Troubridge, or the Earl, whether
> my leave is coming out; for here I neither can nor will stay. My health
> is ruined by fretting, and I will not kill myself to do the work of any
> Commander-in-Chief. I send home the Lawyer's opinion. Justice is
> all I want. My Commanders-in-Chief run away with all the money
> I fight for: so let them. I am content with the honour: there they
> cannot get a scrap. But damn me if I suffer any man to swindle me
> out of my property, whilst he is at his ease in England.[21]

St George never did get over the shoals but Nelson was briefly stimu-
lated by a panicky message from Parker about a Swedish squadron of
ten sail-of-the-line being at sea. He ordered his boat, and six men rowed
him for six hours to catch up. They arrived in the fleet about midnight,

Nelson again joining Foley in *Elephant*. Mr Briarly returned the follow-ing morning to retail stories of Nelson's amazing zeal and determination. The reaction onboard *Elephant* when Nelson arrived at midnight can be readily imagined. Of such behaviour are legends made.[22]

He was ill again and feeling neglected: 'my health is so indifferent – for I have a fever every night from fretting all day – that if the Admi-ralty would send me a commission as Commander-in-Chief, I would not now accept it'.[23] He wrote to congratulate Maurice on getting a better place, 'but the neglect shown me in not having placed you at the Navy Board is what I cannot forget. We shall see whether the new Adminis-tration treats me as ill as the old.' As for Sir Hyde, 'they may make him Lord Copenhagen if they please, it will not offend me. I only want justice for myself, which I have never yet had, and leave to go home for the re-establishment of my health.'[24] Poor Nelson could hardly think straight and Maurice never read his letter for he died on the 24th.

An account of the battle by the defeated Danish commander, Com-modore Fischer did not improve his frame of mind; what touched the rawest nerve was Fischer's damaging comment that, 'this hero himself, in the middle and very heat of the battle, sent a Flag of Truce onshore to propose a cessation of hostilities'.[25] Nelson fired off a detailed and heated refutation to Lindholm: 'He seems to exult that I sent on shore a Flag of Truce. Men of his description, if they ever are victorious, know not the feelings of humanity. You know, and his Royal Highness knows, that the guns fired from the shore could only fire through the Danish Ships which had surrendered, and that if I fired at the shore it could only be in the same manner. God forbid I should destroy a non resisting Dane. . . . Humanity alone could have been my object, but Mr Fischer's carcase was safe, and he regarded not the sacred call of humanity.'[26] Lindholm dealt gracefully with Nelson's outburst, and Nelson climbed down equally gracefully with a typically sweet reply: 'it is not in the interest of our Countries to injure each other. I am sorry I was forced to write you so unpleasant a letter.'[27]

He was now preoccupied with the business of the prizes. It was in a sense a repeat of the Nile. Only the *Holsteen* had gone to England as a prize. Parker had ordered the rest to be burned. 'In short, the wanton waste which has been made of our Prizes, which, God knows, we fought hard to get, has been hard upon the captors. Admirals,&c., may be rewarded, but if you destroy the Prizes, what have poor Lieutenants,

Warrant-Officers, and the inferior Officers and men to look to? . . . I by no means wish to prevent Commanders-in-Chief from destroying all Prizes; but in certain cases, I think, the Country is bound in honour to make it up to the brave fellows who have fought for her.'[28]

Nothing in Parker's conduct was praiseworthy. He had sent his favourite Otway home with his dispatches even though he had been nowhere near the action. In filling vacancies in Nelson's ships he promoted lieutenants from his own ship. Lieutenant Yelland who had commanded *Monarch* with distinction after Mosse's early death did not get the promotion that should have been his by custom and practice. Instead he was offered the position of First Lieutenant in the *London*, which he promptly refused. This was the high-water mark of Parker's monumental obtuseness and complacency.

Nelson was not to be outfaced and soon demonstrated his social dominance and leadership. On the day Otway arrived back in the fleet with the thanks of both Houses of Parliament Nelson arranged a party to celebrate Emma's birthday: Santa Emma, he called her. All who had served in the Mediterranean were invited, as were Graves and the pathetic Parker. 'I had 24 at dinner and drank at dinner in a bumper of champagne Santa Emma. . . . you are an angel upon earth. I am serious.'[29] Seeking to ingratiate himself with Nelson, Parker apparently tried to make out that he had seen Emma at the opera in Hamburg. Nelson stoutly denied the possibility, which cannot have added to Parker's comfort.

But Parker's days were numbered. Orders to hand over to Nelson and return home were on their way. Parker had not fulfilled his orders from the Admiralty and St Vincent had long been convinced that he had failed. His congratulations to Parker could not have been more brutally ironical. 'What a happiness it was that the impression made by the relation of Mr Vansittart did not long operate on your mind, for besides the hazard you would have run of losing some of your ships in the Belt, the delay might have been attended with the most disastrous consequences.'[30]

At home there was no doubt of the personal joy and acclamation that accompanied the victory. Lord Spencer, who could with justification look upon Nelson as his protégé, was quick to let Fanny hear of the account he had received from the Admiralty, 'of the glorious victory obtained under the Command of Lord Nelson . . . every one speaks in the highest terms of his Lordship's conduct on this occasion'.[31] On the same day Sir

William was sending an account of a more picturesque reaction in the Piccadilly ménage:

> We can only repeat what we knew well and often said before that Nelson was, is and to the last will ever be the first. . . . Emma did not know whether she was on her head or heels – in such a hurry to tell your great news that she could utter nothing but tears of joy and tenderness. . . . Davison . . . cried like a child. . . . Your brother, Mrs Nelson and Horace dined with us – your brother was more extraordinary than ever. He would get up suddenly and cut a caper rubbing his hands, every time that the thought of your fresh laurels came into his head. In short, except myself, and your Lordship knows I have some phlegm, all the company, which was considerable after dinner – the Duke, Lord William, Mrs Este, etc. were mad with joy – but I am sure that no one really rejoiced at heart more than I did. I have lived too long to have ecstasies but with calm reflection I felt for my friend having got to the very summit of glory – the 'Ne Plus Ultra,' that he has had an other opportunity of rendering to his country the most important service and manifesting again his judgement his intrepidity and humanity.[32]

Alas, on this occasion there was not the same unanimity of political and newspaper opinion. Britain's direct target had not been the hated enemy France, nor Russia the prime mover in the Armed Neutrality, but Denmark – a traditionally friendly power. Reaction was further confused by news of the assassination of Tsar Paul. The accession of Tsar Alexander suddenly transformed Russia into a friendly power. The government had been careless in not keeping Parliament fully informed of its plans. This showed in the House of Commons on the occasion of the Vote of Thanks to Hyde Parker, Nelson, Graves and Stewart, when Mr Grey remarked that 'this was perhaps, the only war in which this country had been engaged, where the first information received of it by the House, was a motion for a Vote of Thanks, in consequence of a brilliant and decisive Victory, without any previous communication whatever upon the subject'.[33]

Predictably, there was some failure of nerve by the government. Guns were fired but buildings were not illuminated. The newspapers sensed the opportunity for a field day and for the first time Nelson felt the pain of press criticism of his professional conduct. Not only did papers attack the government, the *Chronicle* and *Herald* published Fischer's account of the battle, and the *Chronicle* went further. 'The proposal of Lord Nelson appears to have been not a measure of humanity, but a ruse de guerre, and we are not quite sure if it be a justifiable one.' Both the *Post* and *Chronicle* thought an armistice no return for a battle. The *Chronicle* pinned the blame for the armistice on Nelson. Publicly the government stood by the expedition and its people, Addington in the Commons sounding all the notes that Nelson had gone to such lengths to implant in his mind. He spoke of the Flag of Truce and Nelson's humanity, of his negotiation with the Prince, in which 'Nelson had shown himself as wise as he was brave, and proved that there may be united in the same person, the talents of the Warrior and the Statesman', and he added, 'The manner in which he spoke of Admiral Graves, Colonel Stewart, and the rest of the Gentlemen who had co-operated with him, showed the kindness of his nature and the gallantry of his spirit.'[34]

All of this was absolutely true and even more could have been made of his resolute and inspiring behaviour. But he had also demonstrated a singular capacity for making sure that what he had done was not over-looked. However, when it came to rewards, the government, Admiralty and City were less than generous. Nelson was given a further step in the peerage to Viscount, a mean reward for his victory and peace-making. Graves, who had held firm in the bloodiest part of the battle, was knighted. Monuments were approved for Mosse and Riou in St Paul's. Hyde Parker justifiably got nothing. More degrading to those involved, medals were not awarded to the captains taking part in the action, lieu-tenants were not promoted, and the Admiralty did not deal generously over prize money, awarding £30,000 for the one ship salvaged and £60,000 for the burned ships. The City, in its wisdom, had marked down shares on news of the victory and could not summon up enough enthusiasm to pass a vote of thanks, though Lloyd's was generous in its contributions for the wounded. Bit by bit the news and newspapers filtered through to Nelson. It all stuck in his throat. He never forgave the City.

It was about this time that Nelson, pushed by Emma, took a decisive step as far as Fanny was concerned. And so on 23 April 1801 he wrote to Davison asking him to be brutal with Fanny on his behalf: 'You will, at a proper time, and before my arrival in England signify to Lady Nelson that I expect, and for which I have made such a very liberal allowance to her, to be left to myself, and without any inquiries from her: for sooner than live the unhappy life I did when I last came to England, I would stay abroad forever. My mind is fixed as fate; therefore you will send my determination in any way you may judge proper.'[35]

Having dismissed Fanny he repaid Emma on the same day with rapture: 'My dearest amiable friend, this day twelve months we sailed from Palermo on our tour to Malta. Ah! those were happy times, days of ease and nights of pleasure. How different, how forlorn!'[36]

The ambiguities of reactions at home to his victory were now bringing on a typical bout of self-pity: 'all must be finished by the middle of May and then I will not stay half an hour. Why should I? No real friend would advise me to it, and for what others say I care not a farthing. My health and other circumstances imperiously demand it. I have given up in reason everything to my country. The Commanders-in-Chief made fortunes by their victories, for which Ministers gave them £1,000 a year more than poor Nelson, higher title in the Peerage, and promoted their followers, while mine were all neglected.'[37] The Nile still rankled. To his old acquaintance of West Indies days, Captain Thomas Lloyd, he put it even more strongly. 'I know the envy of many, both in the late and present Ministry are upon me; but whilst my heart tells me I do my business like an honest man, I can smile at their dirty attempts to pull me down. . . . I am fixed as fate to go to England, and get, if possible, a little rest. The moment peace comes I shall go to Bronte and live under the shade of my great chestnut tree.'[38] Nelson's escape motif was sounding again. A letter Davison sent him by Stewart, who was returning to the fleet, was not calculated to make Nelson feel any better:

I am grieved to find . . . that you are not likely to obtain leave of absence as soon as expected. . . . It is said the service absolutely requires your aid in the Baltic . . . I hope it is not true, what I have heard, that it is the intention of the Government to offer you the dignity of Viscount. That you ought to have had long ago, and any distinction short of an Earldom in my humble opinion would be degrading. Your last act of service deserves every acknowledgement which a grateful country (whatever Ministers may think) can bestow. The nation would be gratified to see the highest mark of honour conferred on you.[39]

Indeed Stewart also brought the news that Parker was recalled and Nelson appointed Commander-in-Chief. The Admiralty was doing exactly what any organization in its situation would do; having decided to sack Parker it would move Nelson into his place. Parker was to be sacrificed but to bring both admirals home would have been seized on by unfriendly newspapers as a total admission of government failure. For Nelson it added insult to injury; had he been Commander-in-Chief in the first place, his victory would have brought him an earldom. The supreme irony was that Nelson's constant politicking had produced the desired result – which he did not now want.

To show that the fleet was under new management Nelson immediately made a signal to hoist in all boats and prepare to weigh. Getting off Bornholm he left a small detachment to keep an eye on the Swedes and sailed for Revel. His intention was to prevent the junction of the two Russian squadrons and get all English shipping and property restored, but as he told St Vincent, 'I will do nothing violently.' He then resumed his offensive to be relieved. 'As the business will be settled in a fortnight, I must entreat that some person may come out to take this command.'[40] Outwardly all was activity, all was punctiliousness towards their Lordships' commands, but to his confidant Davison he wrote, 'A Command never was, I believe, more unwelcomely received by any person than myself. It may be at the expense of my life; and therefore, for God's sake, at least, for mine, try if I cannot be relieved.' Now that Sir Hyde had left he could afford to sound sympathetic. 'Sir Hyde is just gone; he is very low.'[41]

But he was sharp with Addington about the pompous wording of the Secretary for War and the Colonies Hobart's letter to the Admiralty: 'I am sorry that the Armistice is only approved under all considerations. Now I own myself of opinion that every part of the all was to the advantage of our King and Country.' Nelson was a model of assertiveness, never hesitant in telling people, whatever their rank, what they should think of his actions. Nor was he slow to tell them how he was feeling so he also told Addington, 'My health is gone, and although I should be happy to try and hold out a month or six weeks longer, yet death is no respecter of persons. I own, at present, I should not wish to die a natural death.'[42] This was the nearest Nelson came to joking on paper. He was feeling an increasing need to get his side of the story on the record and wrote again to Addington, sending him a copy of a memorandum he had composed on his flag of truce and the armistice. It included an analysis and overview: 'I look upon the Northern League to be like a tree, of which Paul was the trunk, and Sweden and Denmark the branches. If I can get at the trunk, and hew it down, the branches fall of course; but I may lop the branches, and yet not be able to fell the tree, and my power must be weaker when its greatest strength is required. If we could have cut up the Russian Fleet, that was my object. Denmark and Sweden deserved whipping, but Paul deserved punishment.'[43] This was probably quite right at the time, although it underestimated the extent to which Denmark had been a prime mover in the Armed Neutrality: now it was out of date. News of the assassination of Tsar Paul had reached London and the new Tsar Alexander would aim to restore good relations with Britain, renounce his claim to Malta, and work for a European peace.

After neutralizing the Swedish fleet with threats couched in the most diplomatic language, Nelson proceeded up the Baltic towards the Gulf of Finland and Revel. The more he saw of Revel, the more Hyde Parker's lack of resolution and his own failure to persuade him of the right course of action rankled. They had missed an opportunity to get at fourteen sail-of-the-line.

Nelson's public fame followed him through the Baltic. Deputations came with public books of record for his autograph. Boats were constantly rowing round his flagship, the *St George*, full of people anxious to catch a sight of him, but Colonel Stewart noted his subdued state: 'He did not again land while in the Baltic; his health was not good, and his mind was not at ease: with him mind and health inevitably sympathised.'[44] Again, many were told of the state of his health, even though it seems to have had no adverse effect on his performance. He was rising early, breakfasting at about 5 a.m., usually with a gaggle of midshipmen, according to Colonel Stewart, working a full day till eight, keeping his fleet in very good order, up to the mark, properly provisioned and active, 'In short the Fleet shall always be in motion; and, as far as lies in my power, complete in every respect for real service.'[45] He had become peripherally involved in the negotiations and discussions with Russia and had scored a minor diplomatic success with Lord St Helens, the British negotiator who had accepted Nelson's canny view that the Russians should be allowed to give the impression that it was they who were taking the initiative in arranging peace in the North.

Nelson had now learned of the death of his brother Maurice, on the 24th and wrote generously to Davison, 'As the dead cannot be called back, it is of no use dwelling on those who are gone. I am sure you will do everything that is right for his poor blind wife. I hope he has left her well provided for; if not, I beg you will take the trouble to arrange a proper and ample subsistence, and I will make it up. It is the only true regard I can pay to his memory. He was always good and kind to me.'[46] With St Vincent he used Maurice as a lever to get home. 'The death of my dear brother, which I received only yesterday, has naturally affected me a good deal; and if I do not get some repose very soon, another will go. Six sons are gone, out of eight; but I hope yet to see you, and to cheer up once more.'[47]

At last, on 30 May 1801, St Vincent stirred himself and wrote to the King, 'unless his Lordship is immediately relieved, his life will be in danger'.[48] The contest over prize money had been settled in his favour five days earlier. The next day he wrote to tell Nelson that his wishes were about to be met:

> To find a proper successor, your Lordship well knows is no easy task; for I never saw a man in our Profession, except yourself and Troubridge, who possessed the magic art of infusing the same spirit into others, which inspired their own actions, exclusive of other talents and habits of business, not common to Naval characters. But your complaint demands prompt decision: we have therefore fixed on Admiral Pole. Your Lordship's whole conduct, from your first appointment to this hour, is the subject of our constant admiration. It does not become me to make comparisons: all agree there is but one Nelson. That he may long continue the pride of his Country, is the fervent wish of your Lordship's truly affectionate, St Vincent.[49]

The silver-tongued old Admiral could scarcely have written a more flattering note, no doubt highly relieved that Nelson had not been able to appear before the jury in person. Had he been less than scrupulous in keeping Nelson where he was? Nelson had himself been quite clear what would have happened had he appeared: 'I cannot doubt but if I could have appeared before a Jury, and told truth, that the Earl's cause would not have held water.'[50] In the end it did not; Nelson went on to win at appeal.

Nelson continued on his downward inner spiral. He can sound like a hypochondriac but most likely it was again a reflection of his mental state in physical symptoms. He sent a long and affectionate letter to his 'dear invaluable friend', Alexander Ball who had received neither a knighthood, nor been made a commissioner of the Navy for his efforts at Malta:

I know you will be sorry to hear that I have been even at Death's door, apparently in a consumption. I am now rallied a little, but the disorder is in itself so flattering that I know not whether I am really better, and no one will tell me, but all in the Fleet are so truly kind to me, that I should be a wretch not to cheer up. Foley has put me under a regimen of milk, at four in the morning; Murray has given me lozenges, and all have proved their desire to keep my mind easy, for I hear of no complaints, or other wishes than to have me with them. Hardy is as good as ever, and with Domett, join their kindest regards . . . if it ever should be in my power in any way to be useful, . . . nothing could give me greater happiness.[51]

He fretted and fretted to Davison, 'Why have I been kept here, when, for any thing which could be known, I ought long since to have been dead? unless, indeed, the Admiralty thought I had as many lives as a cat; or was it a matter of indifference to them whether I lived or died?'[52]

His last public act as Commander-in-Chief was to rig his quarterdeck as a stage on which to invest Admiral Graves with the red sash of the Order of the Bath. There was a guard of honour of Marines and Rifle Corps. The captains of all the ships in his fleet were there in full dress. Graves, flanked by Captains Hardy and Retalick, knelt before Nelson. In the name of the King he knighted him, using the sword his Band of Brothers had given him after the Nile. It was the charismatic public man who spoke from the heart of his own vision, 'I hope that these Honours conferred upon you will prove to the Officers in the Service, that a strict perseverance in the pursuit of glorious Actions, and the imitation of your brave and laudable conduct, will ever ensure them the favours and reward of our most gracious Sovereign, and the Thanks and gratitude of our Country.'[53]

He was now preparing himself for his public reception at home. There was a postscript marked 'Secret', in a letter to Davison: 'They are not Sir Hyde Parker's real friends who wish for an enquiry. His friends in the

Fleet wish everything of this Fleet to be forgot, for we all respect and love Sir Hyde; but the dearer his friends, the more uneasy they have been at his idleness, for that is the truth – no criminality. I believe Sir H.P. to be as good a subject as his Majesty has.'[54] This was a totally disingenuous and self-serving statement. Having succeeded in having his own position approved by the Prime Minister and St Vincent, and appreciating the critical attitude of some newspapers, he had no wish for a public raking over the coals. He chose to hide what must have been his deep professional contempt for Parker.

As he embarked in the brig *Kite* two days later to sail for England, Nelson did not forget those he was leaving behind. A final public flourish was published in General Orders to the Fleet: 'Lord Nelson cannot allow himself to leave the Fleet, without expressing to the Admirals, Captains, Officers and Men, how sensibly he has felt, and does feel, all their kindness to him, and also how nobly and honourably they have supported him in the hour of Battle ... if it pleases God that the Vice-Admiral recover his health, he will feel proud, on some future day, to go with them in pursuit of further glory.'[55]

22

Phoney War

A diabolical spirit is still at work. Every means, even to posting up papers in the streets of Deal, has been used to sett the Seamen against being sent by Lord Nelson to be butchered

Nelson, September 1801

Nelson reached Yarmouth on 30 June 1801, visited the hospitals where the Copenhagen wounded had been sent and made his way to London to call on St Vincent. The idyll he had looked forward to so eagerly, and the passionate encounters he intended it should involve, was to last precisely three weeks and four days. The first week, spent between Lothian's Hotel and 23 Piccadilly, was interrupted by the inevitable round of courtesy calls, professional discussions and correspondence. He fled to the country on a three-day excursion to Box Hill with the Hamiltons, 'a very pretty place and we are all very happy'. But still he could not escape. Anger and contempt at the City's silent response to his victory prompted a letter to Davison and a forlorn hope that three months after the battle and in vastly changed political and commercial circumstances, Davison might somehow through his connections prompt shame and second thoughts in the City:

> If the Victory on the 2nd was real, the Admirals, Officers, and Men, who fought and obtained the Victory, are from custom entitled to the Thanks of the City of London. Custom has never gone back to the first causers of Victories, but simply to the Victors. Lord St Vincent had no thanks given him for the Victory of the Nile, and Sir Hyde Parker, except being nearer the scene of action, had no more to do with that of Copenhagen than Lord St Vincent. I cannot object to any thanks or rewards being bestowed on any man; but I have a fair claim, from custom to be alone considered through the whole of the Battle as the Commander of the Ships fighting. The Thanks of Parliament went only to Sir Hyde's conduct in planning, not for

the fighting; therefore, I look forward with confidence to a Sword from the City of London; and their Thanks and the Freedom in a Gold Box to Graves. . . . I remember, a few years back, on my noticing to a Lord Mayor, that if the City continued its generosity, we should ruin them by their gifts, his Lordship put his hand on my shoulder and said – aye the Lord Mayor of London said – Do you find Victories and we will find rewards. I have since that time found two complete Victories. I have kept my word, and shall I have the power of saying that the City of London, which exists by Victories at Sea, has not kept its promise.[1]

It would continue to rankle.

They all returned briefly to London and then on 11 July made off again, this time for a fishing holiday at Staines. Once there he came down with a bout of diplomatic stomach ache to avoid having to go to town to dine with Lord Hobart who had pronounced so pompously on his armistice. Back in London on 25 July he was reunited with his father and on the same day appointed Commander-in-Chief of a special squadron to defend the Channel coast. The government had concluded that England was in danger of invasion; the evidence a reported build-up of troops and small craft at Boulogne. Now whilst it was true that in February Bonaparte had neutralized Britain's main ally Austria by the Treaty of Lunéville, Britain had countered with Nelson's destruction of the Armed Neutrality, had gained Russia as a friend, and General Abercromby had defeated the remainder of the French Army in Egypt at Alexandria. Three years earlier Bonaparte had declared invasion of England to be 'trop chanceux'. The years since then had seen British naval power triumphant at the Nile and Copenhagen. Bonaparte could hardly have viewed invasion as less risky in July 1801. At this juncture he needed a period of peace, and his invasion preparations were designed to pressurize the British into making greater concessions for a peace than would otherwise be the case. Such was the effectiveness of his propaganda machine that he succeeded in frightening the population and alarming the City.

The Admiralty understandably snatched at the opportunity to make a publicly reassuring appointment and Nelson did not think twice about accepting. Eloquent St Vincent made him feel that he would be centre stage, indispensable to the realm in its hour of need. And Nelson still needed to be employed, even though his pay as a vice-admiral was almost irrelevant in relation to the scale of his expenditure. The appointment would keep him in home waters, spells of leave or visits to London would be possible and Emma would be able to visit him, suitably chaperoned by Sir William.

At first, he was his usual marvel of activity as he confronted a fresh professional challenge. Two days before he hoisted his flag in the frigate *L'Unité* he had submitted to the Admiralty his *Observations on the Defence of the Thames*.[2] He had close on a hundred miles of southern coast to defend, from Beachy Head near Brighton to North Foreland, the easternmost tip of England, then another thirty-five miles almost due north, across the wide approach of the Thames estuary, to Orfordness near Ipswich.

Nelson's method for evolving plans was not analytical. He always despised 'pen and ink men'. He relied on his imagination and intuition to produce ideas, then applied intense mental energy in testing his ideas against the experience and insights of those whose judgement he trusted. The *Observations* which sprang direct from his pen, 'the rude ideas of the moment', as he called them, were disjointed, disordered, and in many respects unsound. The fundamental and not inconsiderable merit of his paper lay not in its content but in its demonstration to the Admiralty that he was immediately and energetically gripping his task. In this campaign however he would not have a group of seasoned captains around him.

Certain things seemed clear to him. The enemy's priority had to be to get on shore as soon as possible. Therefore the most likely thrust of invasion would be from Boulogne and Calais to attack London via Sussex and south Kent. A second and complementary attack would most likely come from Dunkirk and Ostend. Boulogne seemed to him to be the obvious launch point. He estimated that it would take twelve hours in calm weather to row the thirty miles from Boulogne to the south coast, which assumes a speed of about two and a half miles an hour. By the same reckoning crossings from Dunkirk to the coasts of Essex and Sussex, at least eighty-five miles, must take at least thirty-four hours.

He envisaged a total invasion force of 40,000 men, half landing to the west of Dover, the other to the east; each comprising about 250 craft, about eighty men per craft. He envisaged diversionary tactics by the Combined Fleet or the Dutch fleet, either by sailing or preparing to sail.

His tactical scenarios were undeveloped, apart from concentration on establishing the direction of the enemy flotilla and shadowing until sufficient British force was assembled. Tactics would then depend on the weather. If a breeze sprang up he envisaged ruthless destruction. In very calm seas, or if the British force was for any reason insufficient to attack the enemy in passage, whatever force there was would have to attack at the moment the invaders touched the shore, 'and the courage of Britons will never, I believe, allow one Frenchman to leave the beach'. But 'whatever plan may be adopted, the moment the Enemy touch our Coast, be it where it may, they are to be attacked by every man afloat and onshore: this must be understood. Never fear the event!' His attitude was typically aggressive, sanguine and confident but also accompanied by a subtler Nelsonian insight, that the situation called for captains who were prepared to collaborate, 'men of such confidence in each other should be looked for, that (as far as human foresight can go,) no little jealousy may creep into any man's mind, but to be all animated with the same desire of preventing the descent of the Enemy on our Coasts'.

His hurried and unsound appreciation fulfilled its purpose, and prompted an instant reaction from St Vincent, which resulted in Nelson calmly agreeing the exact opposite of his proposed tactics. 'Everything, my dear Lord, must have a beginning, and we are literally at the foundation of our fabric of defence. I agree perfectly with you, that we must keep the Enemy as far from our own coasts as possible, and be able to attack them the moment they come out of their Ports.'[3]

At first he was extremely energetic, consulting with his friend Admiral Lutwidge at Deal; sending Berry, now in *Ruby*, in Hosely Bay off Suffolk, gun-brigs to be trained, and revenue cutters as lookouts; requiring Vice-Admiral Graeme, Commander-in-Chief at the Nore, to direct 'such Ships, Vessels, and Revenue Cutters, as are or may be placed under my command, who have not received particular orders from me to proceed and put themselves under the command of the Senior Captains, either at the Squadron stationed off Hosely Bay, or the Squadron stationed to the southward of Margate Sand'. His young aide-de-camp, Commander Edward Thornborough Parker, who had served with him in *Foudroyant* in 1799 and more recently come to his attention in the Baltic now worshipped at his shrine and was overwhelmed by his capabilities. 'He is the cleverest and quickest man, and the most zealous in the world. In the short time we were in Sheerness, he regulated and gave orders for thirty of the ships under his command, made every one pleased, filled them with emulation, and set them all on the qui vive.'[4]

Having done all he could at Sheerness, he moved round to the Downs, to hoist his flag in the *Leyden*, on the way consulting with Captain Becher in command of the Sea-Fencibles (part-time volunteers for local defence against invasion) and with a rich merchant Mr Salisbury who had 'great influence amongst the Seafaring men on that part of the Coast, particularly about Whitstable'. Nelson needed men to man his stationed ships. The advice he got was that the sea-folk were very wary of Admiralty trickery, and would require an assurance that they would be able to return to their homes once the danger of invasion had passed. Nelson was not enamoured of having 'to get up and harangue like a Recruiting Serjeant',[5] but nevertheless got the assurance they required. 'I am authorized to assure the Fencibles, and other Sea-faring men who may come forth on this occasion, that they shall not be sent off the Coast of the Kingdom, shall be kept as near their own homes as the nature of the service will admit, and that the moment the alarm of the threatened Invasion is over, that every man shall be returned to their own homes; and also, that during their continuance on board Ship, that as much attention as is possible shall be paid to their reasonable wants.'[6]

Rapidly moving on, he hoisted his flag in *Medusa*, created the outline of a plan for a watching force off Flushing, formed contingency plans for dockyard men to be employed in his defence force and went off to Boulogne with Captain Fryers of the Artillery. He wanted to assess the chances of destroying vessels in Boulogne harbour. What he saw was a protective line of twenty-four armed vessels outside the port, batteries in the course of construction on both sides of the town and between fifty or sixty boats, all movable out of range. He also registered the impracticability of Boulogne as a source of invasion and told Lutwidge, 'of the Craft which I have seen, I do not think it possible to row them to England: and sail they cannot'. Nevertheless he continued energetically to build up his blockading force of frigates, brigs, sloops and cutters off the enemy shore, stretching them between Porte Point and Etaples. He was seeking to establish the enemy's strength in Dunkirk Roads, encouraging exploration of possibilities for attack, and proposing to send sloops, revenue cutters and gun-brigs in support. He was enlarging his force. The naval storekeeper at Deal had told him that twelve or fourteen flat-bottomed boats would be ready by the end of the week; these, fitted with eight-inch howitzers or 24-pounder carronades, would be used to harry harbours and ports by night. By 3 August he was confident that, 'with our present force from Dieppe to Dunkirk, certainly nothing can with impunity leave the coast of France one mile'.[7]

Ten days after assuming command, Nelson's bomb ships were in operation off Boulogne. Two floating batteries were sunk, a large gun-brig was forced to cut her cables and ran on shore. He saw others destroyed, 'but it is not my wish to injure the poor inhabitants, and the Town is spared as much as the nature of the service will permit'. At home there had been high expectations as to what the victor of the Nile and Copenhagen might do to the French at Boulogne and this resulting epiphenomenon generated disparaging comment in the newspapers. 'If there be anything to be regretted in this affair, it seems to be that so great a Commander as Lord Nelson should have been employed in a business of no great importance as now appears.'[8]

Eleven days after assuming command, Nelson had come to a clear conclusion which he did not hesitate to put to St Vincent. 'I pronounce that no embarkation can take place at Boulogne; whenever it comes forth, it will be from Flanders, and what a forlorn undertaking considering cross tides, &c.&c. As for rowing, that is impossible. It is perfectly right to be prepared against a mad Government; but with the active force your Lordship has given me, I pronounce it almost impracticable.'[9] St Vincent's objective was to keep the reluctant hero at his task. Nelson wanted to get away to see Emma; St Vincent with his typical hard driving determination wanted him at his post, but understanding Nelson so well he kept his iron fist well concealed in a velvet glove of flattery. 'The public mind is so much tranquillised by your being at your post, it is extremely desirable that you should continue there . . . let me entreat Your Lordship to persevere in the measures you are so advantageously employed in, and give up, at least for the present your intention of returning to town, which would have the worst possible effects at this critical juncture.'[10]

Nelson himself was unequivocal. He even went so far as to enquire after other appointments. 'I have no desire for anything else, than to get at a proper time clear of my present command in which I am sure of diminishing my little fortune, which at this moment does not reach £10,000. . . . Do you still think of sending me to the Mediterranean? If not I am ready to go.'[11]

St Vincent was happy to play for time and keep that discussion going: 'The moment Lord Keith signifies his intention of retiring from his command you shall be apprized of it'.[12] He went on to keep Nelson in touch with plans to reinforce the Mediterranean fleet from Cork and to send Vice-Admiral Pole and a detachment of the Baltic fleet to the Mediterranean too.

With the passage of time Nelson was coming to hate being confined to such a paltry command, although it contained at least one day of pure professional pleasure. Mr Spence the maritime surveyor proposed to take *Medusa* down from Harwich by a new channel. Nelson was enthusiastic and intrigued. 'I have been a tolerable Pilot for the mouth of the Thames in my younger days.' Mr Spence, 'took charge of the Medusa at high water and brought her over the Naze Flat, which was never yet navigated by a Ship of War of this size.'[13] It is known to this day as the Medusa Channel.

Nelson was pining for Emma. Not only had he been unable to get leave, but she had not yet been able to come to him. 'I wish that Sir William was returned [he was on a tour of Wales with Greville]; I would try and persuade him to come to either Deal, Dover, or Margate; for, thus cut off from the society of my dearest friends, 'tis but a life of sorrow and sadness. But patienza per forza!' His agreement with her not to leave his ship was still extant, 'But I will not dine there [with the Mayor and Corporation of Sandwich], without you say, approve.' He added, as in the fullness of time all do who court public attention, 'Oh! how I hate to be stared at.'[14]

For long solitary hours Nelson brooded on newspaper mockery of the invasion scare and the anticlimax of his bombardment of Boulogne. St Vincent did his best to nurse him along: 'Your mind is superior to the mischievous wit of the news writers, which is always directed at the great and good.'[15]

Quite why Nelson then undertook the Boulogne raid is a mystery. He had after all concluded that invasion would not come from that port. He was convinced that the port and its environs did not contain more than 2,000 men. It was not even his priority target. As he said to St Vincent, 'Flushing is my grand object, but so many obstacles are in the way, and the risk is so great of the loss of some Vessels, that under all circumstances, I could hardly venture without a consultation with you, and an arranged plan, with the Board's orders . . . this must be a weeks

Expedition for 4000 or 5000 troops. To crush the Enemy at home was the favourite plan of Lord Chatham, and I am sure you think it the wisest measure to carry the war from our own doors.' Then almost out of the blue, 'I purpose, if to be done, to take all the Gun Vessels outside the pier of Boulogne – I should like your approbation. I own, my dear Lord, that this Boat warfare is not exactly congenial to my feelings, and I find I get laughed at for my puny mode of attack.' He was unwell and despondent. 'I have all night had a fever, which is very little abated this morning; my mind carries me beyond my strength, and will do me up; but such is my nature. . . . I require nursing like a child . . . I shall be gone, God willing, to-morrow; but no attack for probably two nights, to throw them off their guard.'[16] The same day he told Davison, 'I am very much fagged, and from my soul wish it was all over, and I quiet in my nest again.'[17] For once his heart and mind were not fully engaged. He was in no fit state, physically or mentally, to direct the operation he had in mind.

Yet on the 15th he was off Boulogne and issuing his plan of attack. The assault was to be carried out by fifty-seven boats, carrying about 900 officers and men. Except for fifty-four marines who had muskets and bayonets and the 24-pounder carronade carried in each of their seven flat boats, the seamen were armed only with pikes, cutlasses and tomahawks. Their target was a line of twenty-four armed vessels. The boats were to be concentrated for the attack; three divisions, forty-two boats, would attack adjacent ships at the eastern end of the French line, the fourth division of fifteen boats would attack the western end, the plan then being to subdue the French, vessel by vessel. No bombardment would precede the attack because of the need for surprise, but a division of howitzer boats was positioned to fire into the shore batteries and camp once the attack had begun. A group of cutters was to stand in close to shore to tow out captured enemy vessels.

At half past ten the men climbed down into the boats. By 11.36 p.m. they were assembled and lanterns hung over the *Medusa*'s guns sent them on their way in pitch darkness and dead silence, oars muffled. Each division was roped together to form a concentrated force, with orders not to cut or separate till close to the enemy. As the darkness swallowed them they left behind an Admiral who hated the idea that men should be in action and risking their lives when he was not. That same night he confided to Emma, 'my mind feels at what is going forward this night; it is one thing to order and arrange an attack, and another to execute it; but

I assure you I have taken much more precaution for others, than if I was to go myself'.[18]

At one o'clock in the morning, far out of sight the action began but it was not until the cold light of day that his boats straggled back with their tale of failure and disaster. His report made melancholy reading: a hundred men killed and wounded, including the two young officers closest to him, 'dear little Parker, his thigh very much shattered; I have fears for his life. Langford shot through the leg.'

His force had failed to reach the battle zone intact; indeed the fourth division did not reach its objective till daybreak. Some, if not all, the enemy ships were moored to the shore or to each other by chains, others had rigged anti-boarding nets. Once the attackers were spotted they came under fierce musket fire from shore and cliffs. The desperate gallantry of men who stormed the sides of vessels after rowing through difficult waters for an hour and a half was not enough. The attack lost cohesion and momentum. Langford, himself shot through the leg, lost all his crew killed or wounded as they tried to help Parker, who had lost a third of his own people and had his own thigh shattered. Somerville's division suffered even more, almost 40 per cent casualties.

In his report to St Vincent Nelson shouldered the blame: 'No person can be blamed for sending them to the attack but myself; I knew the difficulty of the undertaking, therefore I ventured to ask your opinion. Your kind letter I received half an hour before the attack ... it was their misfortune to be sent on a service which the precautions of the Enemy rendered impossible to succeed in. After all this sorrow for me, my health is not improved; my fever is very severe this morning.'[19] Nelson was professionally shaken, and unlike Tenerife, had no wound to redeem his guilt.

The question remains. Why did Nelson attack Boulogne? Why did he not fully register the problems presented by tides and distance, and why did he ignore clear warnings from Troubridge that the French were aware of an impending attack? And what in any case was the military point of capturing a few unimportant ships off a port you are convinced will not be the source of invasion? A lightly armed cutting-out party, even one of 900 men, could not hope to take or destroy Boulogne's military camps and armaments; that would have required a properly organized combined operation of the kind he had envisaged for Flushing. Irrational subconscious motives were surely at work but we can only speculate whether a need for St Vincent's approval overrode his judgement; whether he wanted little Parker and the other young officers in his squadron who idolized him to have a chance to prove themselves; whether it was anger with the newspapers, frustration, or a boiling over of his seemingly inexhaustible store of aggression.

St Vincent, supportive as ever, did not cry over spilt milk and Nelson received a virtual repeat of his Tenerife letter: 'It is not given to us to command success: Your Lordship and the gallant officers and men under your orders most certainly deserved it, and I cannot sufficiently express my admiration of the zeal and persevering courage with which this gallant enterprise was followed up, lamenting most sincerely the loss sustained in it, more particularly the grievous wounds of Captain Parker and Mr Langford.'[20]

Lord Hood saw it more realistically. He wrote to Admiral Cornwallis, Nelson's friend, at the end of August, 'My friend Nelson, at his last attack at Boulogne, appears to have taken the bull by the horns, and to have sacrificed a great number of lives without an adequate object, for the bringing off of a few gun boats could not be one, for they could be replaced within a fortnight. This I am told is generally said in town where I go very seldom.'[21]

For the first time Nelson showed a heartfelt and poignant sadness for the waste of war. Loving Emma, becoming a father, growing older was making him more sensitive to loss. 'I have this morning been attending the Funeral of two young Mids: a Mr Gore, cousin of Captain Gore, and a Mr Bristowe. One nineteen, the other seventeen years of age. Last night I was all evening in the Hospital, seeing that all was done for the comfort of the poor fellows . . . I shall come in the morning to see Parker.' After Boulogne Emma imitated Fanny and begged him to be careful. Now he understood and did not repel her solicitude. 'You ask me, my dear Friend, if I am going on more Expeditions? And even if I was to forfeit your friendship, which is dearer to me than all the world, I can tell you nothing. For, I go out; [if] I see the Enemy, and can get at them, it is my duty: and you would naturally hate me, if I kept back one moment. I long to pay them, for their tricks t'other day, the debt of a drubbing, which, surely, I'll pay: but when, where, or how, it is impossible, your own good sense must tell you, for me or mortal man to say. I shall act not in a rash or hasty manner, that you may rely, and on which I give you my word of honour.'[22]

In mid-August he was still keen to attack Flushing, but was more circumspect and realistic after his bloody nose at Boulogne: 'I will go and look at them; but attack I cannot, without Pilots, nor without sanction. I own I shall never bring myself again to allow any attack to go forward, where I am not personally concerned; my mind suffers much more than if I had a leg shot off in this late business.' But his retrospective view of Boulogne was not short of characteristic Nelson bravado. 'Had our force arrived, as I intended, 'twas not all the chains in France that could have prevented our folks from bringing off the whole of the Vessels.'[23]

St Vincent while encouraging was also circumspect about Flushing: 'When Your Lordship has taken a view of it and furnishes us with your ideas, we shall be better able to form a judgement of the practicability of an attack. You will, I trust never harbour a doubt of my giving every possible support to your operations in thought word and deed.'[24]

But this time Nelson knew that he needed help and wrote direct to the Prime Minister:

> Lord St Vincent tells me he hates Councils, so do I between Military men; for if a man consults whether he is to fight, when he has the power in his own hands, it is certain that his opinion is against fighting; but that is not the case at present, and I own I do want good council. Lord St Vincent is for keeping the Enemy closely blockaded . . . Lord Hood is for keeping our Squadrons of Defence stationary on our own shore, (except light Cutters, to give information of every movement of the Enemy;) . . . When men of such good sense, such great Sea Officers, differ so widely, is it not natural that I should wish the mode of defence to be well arranged by the mature consideration of men of judgement? I mean not to detract from my judgement; even as it is, it is well known: but I boast of nothing but my zeal; in that I will give way to no man upon earth.[25]

Nelson knew very well the difference between joint decision making, that is abdication of personal responsibility, with which he would have nothing to do, and seeking advice, counsel and involvement, all of which were part of his normal method for working with his captains. In the aftermath of Boulogne he also knew that he must protect his back.

There is however an unusual caution beginning to appear in his thinking. His officer off Flushing was a Captain Owen and as Nelson reported to Admiral Lutwidge (Nelson's captain in the *Carcass*), 'His zeal, I am afraid, has made him overleap sandbanks and tides, and laid him aboard the Enemy . . . I admire his desire, and could join most heartily in it; but we cannot do impossibilities, and I am as little used to find out the impossibles as most folks; and I think I can discriminate between the impracticable and the fair prospect of success.'[26] And thus his conclusion to St Vincent, 'I look upon the attempt to be out of the question . . . I am convinced, from what I hear, that the thing is not to be done.'[27]

He was increasingly at odds with Troubridge, finding it difficult to adjust to the idea that a former subordinate and protégé should be exercising authority over him. He told Emma, 'You ask me what Troubridge wrote me? There was not a syllable about you in it. It was about my not coming to London; at the importance of which, I laughed; and then he said he should never venture another opinion. On which, I said – "Then I shall never give you one." This day, he has wrote a kind letter, and all is over. I have, however, wrote him, in my letter of this day as follows – viz "And I am, this moment, as firmly of opinion as ever, that Lord St Vincent and yourself should have allowed of my coming to Town for my own affairs; for every one knows I left it without a thought for myself."[28] This looks like childishness on both parts, but the likelihood is that Troubridge found himself uncomfortably caught between Nelson's demand to be dealt with as a friend and St Vincent's legendary determination to keep officers at their posts as a good example to the people they commanded. Troubridge would not dare to cross St Vincent in such a matter.

Emma, Sir William, and Nelson's boring brother had spent a fortnight in Deal with Nelson. While Emma had been there to love and nurse the little 'Nelsonite' as she called Parker, he had been 'easy, comfortable, cheerful', but following her return to London the fateful decision to amputate had been made and within a week he was on the point of death. Nelson was possessed by an extraordinary grief, writing to Dr Baird, 'he is my child, for I found him in distress'.[29] Parker lingered, Nelson sent him Madeira and wrote to Emma, 'You will [see] Parker is treated like an infant. Poor fellow!'[30] He wrote to Davison, 'Dear Parker has rallied again; he has taken new milk and jellies; there is a gleam of hope.'[31] Constant encouragement went to Dr Baird: 'I hope you will allow me to see my son, dear Parker; to you I shall always think I owe his life.'[32] To Parker's sister Nelson described him as, 'dear son and friend'.[33] By the evening of the 26th all hope had gone. When at last he died it was as if

Nelson had found grief for the first time. He abandoned his usual cool and stoical reception of death. 'My dear Parker left this world for a better at 9 o'clock this morning. It was, they tell me, a happy release; but I cannot bring myself to say I am glad that he is gone; it would be a lie, for I am grieved almost to death.'[34]

Grief distorts perspective; nothing could be too good for the memory of this youthful Commander whose gaiety and unconditional attachment had seized Nelson's heart. He wrote to St Vincent, 'not a creature living was ever more deserving of our affections . . . how well he has deserved my love and affection his actions have shown. . . . Pensions I know have sometimes been granted to the parents of those who have lost their lives in the service of their King and Country . . . I trust much to your friendship to recommend his father's case to the kind consideration of the King. I fear his loss has made a wound in my heart which time will scarcely heal.'[35] He asked Dr Baird that Parker's 'hair may be cut off and given to me; it shall remain and be buried with me'.[36] – and so it was. Parker was buried in Deal with full military honours; Nelson wept at his graveside.

It was part and parcel of his generosity, sense of brotherhood and penchant for emotional gesture that he should present Dr Baird with a silver vase inscribed, 'Presented to Andrew Baird Esq., M.D. as a mark of esteem for his humane attention to the gallant Officers and Men who were wounded off Boulogne on the 16th of August 1801. From their Commander-in-Chief, Lord Viscount Nelson Duke of Bronte.'[37]

During Emma's fortnight in Deal the lovers had found time to progress their plans for establishing themselves outside London. Emma had found a little farm at Merton in Surrey, which in spite of a thoroughly dismal survey had fired Nelson's imagination. They needed to find the money. He was quick to tell Davison of his proposed purchase and with it a tale of woe: 'I am used and abused; and so far from making money I am spending the little I have. I am after buying a little Farm at Merton – the price £9,000; I hope to be able to get through it. If I cannot, after all my labour for the Country, get such a place as this, I am resolved to give it all up, and retire for life. I am aware none of the Ministry care for me, beyond what suits themselves.'[38] Davison, as ever, was ready to offer assistance. Nelson was grateful but worried about his stretched finances. 'It is true it will take every farthing I have in the world, and leave me in your debt, and also in Tyson's . . . should I really want your help, and know that I have enough in the world to pay you, I shall ask no one else. The Baltic expedition cost me full £2,000. Since I left London it has cost me, for Nelson cannot be like others, near £1,000 in six weeks. If I am continued here, ruin to my finances must be the consequence, for everybody knows that Lord Nelson is amazingly rich!'[39]

Emma and Merton provided a spur for him not only to try again to be relieved from his present command but also to sound a less enthusiastic note about the Mediterranean to St Vincent:

> This Boat-business must be over: it may be a part of a great plan of Invasion, but can never be the only one; therefore, as our Ships cannot act any more in lying off the French Coast, I own I do not think it is now a command for a Vice-Admiral. Turn it in your mind. It is not that I want to get a more lucrative situation – far from it: I do not know, if the Mediterranean were vacant tomorrow, that I am equal to undertake it. You will forgive me if I have said too much; they are my feelings, which for several years you have allowed me to throw before you, not in an impertinent manner, but with all the respect due to your great character and exalted situation.[40]

This must have tried St Vincent's patience for he had told Nelson only a week earlier, 'I differ from Your Lordship in toto as to the importance of the command you fill and I am of the opinion it is not unworthy of an Admiral of the Fleet was he in a state of health and activity to fill it.'[41]

Nelson was having to absorb many reverberations of the Boulogne affair. At first it was the newspaper comment that had most nettled him. St Vincent had done his best to soothe him. 'Sarcasm in Newspapers are [sic] a tribute every man who is placed in a high situation must submit to: it is evident that those I have read are levelled at the Administration of the Government and intended to deprive the Country of your eminent services.'[42] But there was worse to follow. He was being crudely blackmailed by a Mr Hill, who had sent him a paper, 'Remarks by a Seaman on the Attack at Boulogne', critical of his official dispatch, and asked for £100 to avoid publication in the newspapers. Nelson must have been mortified but his reply was predictable: 'Very likely I am unfit for my present command, and whenever Government change me, I hope they will find no difficulty in selecting an Officer of greater abilities; but you will, I trust, be punished for threatening my character. But I have not been brought up in the school of fear, and, therefore, care not what you do. I defy you and your malice.'[43]

Then he began to get the wind of something infinitely more worrying than press comment and the odd blackmailer. He confided to St Vincent on 23 September,

> The people at the watering-places have been very free in their conversations, and I believe the Mayor of Deal either put a vagabond in prison, or sent him out of town, for arraigning my conduct in being careless of poor Seamen's lives; but I trouble not my head on these matters; my conscience tells me that I do my best. . . . The Wardrooms will prate, I believe, none of us can doubt, and it has its bad effects. The Boat service I believe is got very unpopular. G—— flogged some of his chaps severely for some very improper expressions. They belonged to the *Unite*, who was, I fancy, in very bad order. I assure you, my dear Lord, that I do not believe any Admiral could be better supported than I am by all the Captains under me.[44]

Later on in September Nelson wrote even more disturbingly to Nepean,

> A diabolical spirit is still at work. Every means, even to posting up papers in the streets of Deal, has been used to sett the Seamen against being sent by Lord Nelson to be butchered, and that at Margate it was the same thing; whenever any boats went on shore, ' What, are you going to be slaughtered again.' Even this might be got over, but the subject has been fully discussed in the Wardrooms, midshipmen's berths &c &c and it must give me more pain to mention a subject which the Admiralty have decided against, that no promotion should take place for the gallant but unsuccessful attempt at Boulogne; this matter I now find has been discussed in such a manner that its influence has spread through the whole fleet under my orders. It seems to be a matter of some doubt whether, if I was to order a boat expedition it would be obeyed, certainly not in such a zealous manner as to give me either pleasure or confidence.[45]

The factual context for these letters to St Vincent and Nepean was a proposed operation against the Dutch, the emotional context a kind of suspicious paranoia which seemed again to have taken over Nelson. It seems amazing that in spite of the failure of the Boulogne operation he should believe that the lieutenants involved should have been promoted. Yet, in his desperation to have his followers rewarded he concluded the Admiralty was not on his side and Troubridge was not delivering as he ought to have done for a friend. Troubridge was driven to protest, 'I feel much distressed at the part of your letter, which I construe that this Board would envy any success your Lordship might have, and feast on your failure, if I am right I will venture to say that never was a charge so unmerited on your real Friends, and I cannot persuade myself but some person has been poisoning your mind against us.'[46] Nelson, feeling he had gone too far, tried to put himself in the right with St Vincent: 'you will I trust give me credit that I never could have meant that the thing was possible for either the Board of Admiralty or any Member of it to be envious of any success attending my endeavours. As our friend Troubridge supposed, the thing was impossible.'

Now he went on to profess extreme sensitivity to having any part in the Dutch operation:

> If success attended it, it would be said, 'Aye the Admiralty gave from partiality this to their favourite,' (for I do flatter myself I am a favourite) If it miscarried, then it would be said – 'That vain man, Nelson, thought he could do what no one else could, and his friends at the Admiralty had folly enough to believe his impossible schemes.' I feel myself, my dear Lord, as anxious to get a Medal, or a step in the Peerage as if I never had got either, – for, 'if it be a sin to covet glory, I am the most offending soul alive,' – I could lose only a few Boats. If I succeeded and burnt the Dutch Fleet, probably Medals and an Earldom. I must have had every desire to try the matter, regardless of the feelings of others; but I should not have been your Nelson that wants not to take honours or rewards from any man; and if ever I feel great, it is, my dear Lord, in never having, in thought, word, or deed robbed any man of his fair fame.

In a further letter to Nepean following the one quoted above he virtually disengaged himself from the proposed operation: 'If I might be allowed to recommend, Lord Nelson should not command the present enterprize . . . if the thing succeeded the hatred against me would be greater than it is at present, if it failed I should be execrated . . . and as I must probably be, from all the circumstances I have stated, not much liked by officers or men, I really think it would be better to take me from this Command.'

This was not special pleading designed to obtain relief from a hated command. To say what he was saying must have caused Nelson intense pain and must have represented the very nadir of his professional life, almost a sudden lack of confidence. However, in confronting the situation, in not bottling up or concealing his injury the effect was probably therapeutic. But the episode tells us that those who worshipped at the shrine of the Nelson myth have obscured the fact that actual opinions about Nelson must have varied widely. There is no evidence to suggest that charismatic characters are universally loved, respected and trusted, especially those who are accustomed to take great risks in war.

Although the three months of his command had seemed like an eternity to Nelson, his view was not shared in London. In the end the Prime Minister himself had to enter the fray. Although flexible, he was firm: 'if you wish to remain chiefly on shore, or even to remove to London or elsewhere for a few days, you may, I know, rely on the acquiescence of the Board of Admiralty; but I owe it to my regard to your Lordship, and to my Public duty, to declare it to be my opinion, that it is of the utmost importance to your own high character, and to the interests of the Country, that your Flag should be flying till the Definitive Treaty [of peace with France] has been signed.' [47] His letter was a measure of the fuss Nelson had been making and his rationale a perfectly reasonable one for Prime Minister and Admiralty to hold. Nelson would not acknowledge that they were acting in good faith; he preferred conspiracy theory. However, now that peace was rapidly approaching he had to become more realistic. 'I am trying to get rid of my Command, but I am to be forced to hold it, to keep the Merchants easy till hostilities cease in the Channel. I must submit; for I do not wish to quarrel with the very great folks at the Admiralty, the last moment.'[48] Peace had a double edge for those who earned their living at war. 'I cannot get the Admiralty to set me free. They wish to put some pounds into my pocket, I suppose, by keeping me on full pay; but I am so ungrateful as not to thank them. But we shall all soon be adrift.'[49] His apparent change of heart has much to do with being forced to think about his future employment and earning capacity.

His mood was low even though the Channel coast was bathed in October sunshine. He wrote to Emma, 'This being a very fine morning, and smooth beach, at eight o'clock, I went with Sutton and Bedford and landed at Walmer, but found Billy [Pitt, the previous Prime Minister] fast asleep, so left my card; walked the same road that we came, when the carriage could not come with us that night; and all rushed into my mind, and brought tears into my eyes.' Just as the range of his emotions had been widened to include jealousy and grief so was the power of his recollection of shared intimacies. Self-pity he still had. 'Troubridge has so completely prevented my mentioning anybody's service, that I am become a cipher, and he has gained a victory over Nelson's spirit. I am kept here; for what, he may be able to tell – I cannot but long it cannot – shall not be. . . . I am, in truth, not over well. I have a complaint in my stomach and bowels, but it will go off.'[50] A day later his mood was not helped when Pitt came on board to return his call and sympathized with his feelings at being kept there: ' now all is over . . . I told Dr Baird yesterday that I was determined never to mention to Troubridge's unfeeling heart whether I was sick or well . . . I am so disgusted that this day I care but little what becomes of me. . . . If I am cross you must forgive me. . . . I have reason to be so by great Troubridge.'[51] A week later, 'My cold is still very troublesome – I cannot get my bowels in order. In the night I had not a little fever. But never mind; the Admiralty will not always be there. Every one has their day.'[52]

Nelson was working himself up into a mood to lash out at everybody, Emma included. He had been invited by Lord Pelham, Secretary of State for the Home Department to contribute to Cabinet consideration of some matter or other and Emma had unwisely made reference to time-serving, which caused Nelson to explode,

> My intention was to show them I could be as useful in the Cabinet as in the Field. My idea is, to let them see that my attendance is worth soliciting. For myself, I can have nothing; but, for my brother, something may be done. Living with Mr Addington a good deal, never, in your sense of the word, shall I do it. What, leave my dearest friends to dine with a Minister? D——n me if I do, beyond what you yourself shall judge to be necessary! Perhaps it may be once,

and once with the Earl; but that you shall judge for me. If I give up all intercourse, you know enough of Courts, that they will do nothing: make yourself of consequence to them, and they will do what you wish, in reason; and out of reason I should never ask them. It must be a great bore to me, to go to the House. I shall tell Mr Addington, that I go on the 29th to please him, and not to please myself.'[53]

Troubridge was in trouble again. 'Troubridge writes me, that, as the weather is set fine again, he hopes I shall get walks on shore. He is, I suppose, laughing at me; but, never mind.' A second letter on the same day: 'I dare say Master Troubridge is grown fat. I know I am grown lean with my complaint; which, but for their indifference about my health, would never have happened; or, at least, I should have got well long ago in a warm room, with a good fire, and sincere friends. I believe I leave this little Squadron with sincere regret, and with the good wishes of every creature in it.'[54]

By now the Preliminaries of Peace (outline peace treaty) had been signed and hostilities beween Britain and France had ceased. The Peace of Amiens would not be signed until March of the following year, by which time the British would have been comprehensively out-negotiated by the French, but just now the nation was sick and tired of war, and progress to peace was highly popular.

Nelson was at last able to write briefly to Nepean, 'Be pleased to acquaint the Lords Commissioners of the Admiralty, that it is my intention to set off this evening for Merton, agreeably to the leave of absence their Lordships have been pleased to grant me.'[55]

23

Fame without Fortune

Whenever it is necessary, I am your Admiral

Nelson, March 1803

From the moment he first stepped on board *Raisonnable* thirty years previously, Nelson spent less than seven years on shore; amost half of it accounted for by his first six years of marriage when he was unemployed and living under his father's roof. By comparison with the lack of interest he had shown in the purchase of Roundwood he was enthusiastic about Merton. He was certain, 'I shall like Merton.'[1] In his eyes Emma could do no wrong, and he happily busied himself with lists of domestic impedimenta. He was thinking of using his cot as a spare bed. 'I must leave my cot here till my discharge, when it shall come to the farm, as cots are the best things in the world for our Sea friends.' He was thinking about pictures: 'Why not have the pictures from Davison's, and those from Dodd's.'[2] But he had not conceived Merton as a hideaway love nest; public appearances would be kept up; the *ménage à trois* would have to be installed there. Even so he was determined to be lord and master; 'nothing but what is mine should be there . . . Sir William should always be my guest.'[3] 'I think you had better not have Sir William's books . . . not a servant of Sir William's, I mean the cook, should be in the house.'[4] In spite of his enthusiasm he was not as in command of himself as in the midst of a battle. He had difficulty in being realistic. His need to be master conflicted with his anxieties about money. 'I trust my dear friend, to your economy for I have need of it. To you I may say my soul is too big for my purse but I do earnestly request that all may be mine in the house, even to a pair of sheets, towels &etc.'[5] The Prince of Wales popped again into his thoughts; the house would be on his way to Brighton. He entertained irrational thoughts of getting away from it all, 'Do you think we shall soon go to Bronte? I should be very happy, but

I must first settle all my affairs in this country, and Merton may become a dead weight on our hands, but more of this hereafter.'[6] Then just as suddenly he switched to complaining at his solicitor's not having got possession: 'I wish I could get up for four or five days. I would have roused the lawyers about.'[7]

In the wings, awaiting his summons were brother William, his wife Sarah and two children; elder sister Susannah, her husband Thomas Bolton and seven children; youngest sister Catherine, her husband George Matcham and five children. Catherine's eventual tally would be fifteen and her continuing motherhood would prompt Susannah's tasteless and disloyal observation to Emma, 'I am afraid she will breed herself to death, which was the case with our poor mother.'[8] All would be drawn into his orbit: William because he saw his younger brother as the means for advancement, the others because Emma was determined to gather them in – a ready-made family on whom she could exercise her masterful and generous dominance. Nelson entered into these family connections with equally generous enthusiasm; for a younger son, fame *en famille* was a sweet commodity and their frequent visits bolstered his illusion that he and Emma were living a normal married life.

From the moment her baby had been born Emma's prime objective had been to alienate Nelson's family from Fanny. With shrewd instinct she made up to brother William's wife. 'It is such a pain to part with dear friends and you and I liked each other from the moment we met. Our souls were congenial. Not so with Tom tit for there was an antipathy not to be described.'[9] Her campaign to debase Lady Nelson produced many more disparaging references to Tom tit: 'Tom tit does not come to Town. She offered to go down [to Plymouth] but was refused. She only wanted to go to do mischief to all the great Jove's [Nelson] relations.'[10] Josiah came in for the same rough treatment: 'Tom tit at the same place Brighton. The Cub [Josiah] is to have a frigate. . . . So I suppose he will be up in a day or so. I only hope he will not come near me. If he does "not at home" shall be the answer.'[11] And yet four days later, 'Tom tit is at B[righton]. . . . The Cub dined with us, but I never asked how Tom tit was.' . . . 'Oh how I long to see you. Do try and come for God's sake do.'[12]

Meanwhile Susannah Bolton was still writing sympathetically to Fanny, assuring her that she had only just learned from Catherine that she was at Brighton:

Will you excuse what I am going to say? I wish you had continued in town a little longer, as I have heard my brother regretted he had not a house he could call his own when he returned. Do, whenever you hear he is likely to return, have a house to receive him. If you absent yourself entirely from him, there can never be a reconciliation. Such attention must please him and I am sure will do in the end. Your conduct as he justly says is exemplary in regard to him and he has not an unfeeling heart . . . I hope in God one day I shall have the pleasure of seeing you together as happy as ever, he certainly as far as I hear is not a happy man. . . . Keep up your spirits as well as you can and all will do well. . . . Excuse whatever I have said as I most sincerely wish you happy.[13]

By the time Susannah Bolton wrote again on 14 May 1801 she still had hopes that the marriage might be saved, but was also fully aware of Emma's campaign to separate them. 'Do not say you will not suffer us to take too much notice of you for fear it should injure us with Lord Nelson. I assure you I have a pride, as well as himself, in doing what is right, and that surely is to be attentive to those who have been so to us . . .'.[14]

No outsider ever knows the truth of another marriage. There was nothing she or anybody could do to alter the implacable coldness in Nelson's heart. Fanny tried, for after the news of Copenhagen she wrote, 'I cannot be silent in the general joy throughout the Kingdom. . . . What my feelings are your own good heart will tell you. Let me beg, nay intreat you, to believe no wife ever felt greater affection for a husband than I do. And to the best of my knowledge I have invariably done everything you desired. If I have omitted any thing I am sorry for it. . . . What more can I do to convince you that I am truly your affectionate wife?'[15] To Nelson this letter was an accusatory finger which he could not bear. He had told Davison to tell her to leave him alone. For once Davison had not obeyed and having to confront his omission about a fortnight after Nelson's return from the Baltic, addressed a less than frank note to Fanny, 'A few days quiet retreat in the Country I trust may be of use to Him. I hardly need to repeat how happy I should have been to have seen Him and You the Happiest. His Heart is so pure and so extremely good that I flatter myself he never can be diverted from his affection. I have the same opinion I ever had of his sincere respect for you. I have no right to doubt it.'[16] He was unwilling to be as brutal as Nelson wished him to be. At about the same time Fanny received her first quarterly payment and felt impelled to write again to her husband. 'Your generosity and tenderness was never more shown . . . your very handsome quarterly allowance, which far exceeds my expectations. . . . Accept my warmest, my most affectionate and grateful thanks. I could say more but my heart is too full. Be assured every wish, every desire of mine is to please the man whose affection constitutes my happiness. God bless my dear husband.'[17]

A major difficulty for Emma was that Nelson's father felt greatly obliged to Fanny for her kindness and support. He was distressed by the thought of having to choose between daughter-in-law and son. He tried to find a middle way. He announced his intention of travelling from Bath to meet his son in London, and sent peace offerings from Bath, 'recollecting that Sir William and Lady Hamilton seemed to be gratified by the flavour of a cream cheese'.[18] Nelson himself had been inclined to 'take not the smallest notice of how he disposes of himself',[19] but Emma was in an entirely different frame of mind. Her desire to see Fanny banished and to get the Matchams and Boltons to toe her line knew no bounds. While Nelson was still absent on his Channel command, she wrote in uncontrolled frenzy to William's wife, 'You and your husband are the only people worthy by him to be beloved. His poor father is unknowing and taken in by a very wicked, bad, artful woman, acting a bad part by so glorious a son. . . . A wicked false malicious wretch who rendered his days wretched and his nights miserable . . . I am afraid the Boltons are not without their share of guilt in this affair. Jealous of you all they have, with the Matchams, pushed this poor dear old gentleman to act this bad and horrible part, to support a false proud bad woman.'[20] Emma's insecurities were legion.

Fanny had become aware of the pressures her father-in law was under and after visiting him at Burnham wished to make things easy for him, 'The impression your situation has left on my mind is so strong that I cannot delay any longer offering my opinion on the subject of living with me, which from your conversation makes it impracticable; the deprivation of seeing your children is so cruel . . . I am not surprised for I knew Lord Nelson's friends could not like it . . . I told Mrs M at Bath that Lord

Nelson would not like your living with me. "Oh! my dear Lady Nelson. My brother will thank you in his heart for he knows no one can attend to my father as you do." I had seen the wonderful change pass belief. She had not."[21] And so the old parson wrote with pathetic dignity to his son,

possibly you may tell me where it is likely your general place of residence may be, so that sometimes we may have mutual happiness in each other, notwithstanding the severe reproaches I feel from an anonymous letter for my conduct to you, which is such, it seems as will totally separate us. This is unexpected indeed. . . . If Lady Nelson is in a hired house and by herself, gratitude requires that I should be sometimes with her, if it is likely to be of any comfort to her. Everywhere age and my many infirmities are very troublesome and require every mark of respect. At present I am in the parsonage, it is warm and comfortable. I am quite by myself, except the gentleman who takes care of the churches . . . I cannot do any public duty nor even walk to the next house, but my dearest son, here is still room enough to give to you a warm a joyful and affectionate reception, if you could feel an inclination to look once more at me in Burnham parsonage.[22]

If Edmund Nelson had received an anonymous letter about his conduct, Emma alone could have been motivated to arrange it.

On the very day that his father had written to Fanny, Emma received one from Nelson addressed to his father but left open for her to read and post. Heightening the drama with a flavour from her days of Neapolitan political intrigues, she promptly shared extracts with William's wife, 'This is an extract what do you think of it? When you and Mr Nelson has read it, pray burn it.' When he wrote it Nelson was suffering. 'The toothache torments me to pieces',[23] which may go some way to explain, but hardly excuses the injured grandiosity and self-justification of his letter. It shows him no different from many others involved in broken marriages. The untruths he told about how Fanny had reacted to his allowance must have been planted by Emma. He had believed Emma in spite of the contrary evidence of Fanny's letter. 'I have received your letter,' he said to his father, and of which you must be sensible I cannot like for as you seem by your conduct to put me in the wrong it is no wonder that they who do not know me and my disposition should. But Nelson soars above them all and time will do that justice to my private character which she has to my public one. I that have given her, with her falsity and his [Josiah's], £2,000 a year and £4,000 in money and which she calls a poor pittance, and with all that to abandon her son bad as he is and going about defaming me. May God's vengeance strike me dead if I would abandon my children. If he wants reformation who should reclaim him but the mother? I could say much more but will not out of respect to you, my dear father, but you know her, therefore I finish.

That having been said, he went on to issue the warmest possible invitation. 'On the 23rd I shall be at Merton with Sir William and Lady Hamilton and them with myself shall be happy, most happy to see you, my dear beloved father, that is your home.'[24]

Within the month Nelson's father had visited them all at Merton and had reported with evident pleasure to Catherine Matcham, his favourite daughter, 'Your good brother is truly in better health and happier in himself than in good truth I have in any passed time observed him to be.'[25] He went on to winter in Bath, while Fanny significantly stayed in London. As Christmas approached she tried again with Nelson: 'It is some time since I have written to you. The silence you have imposed on me is more than my affections will allow me and in this instance I hope you will forgive me in not obeying you. . . . Do my dear husband, let us live together. I can never be happy till such an event takes place. I assure you again I have but one wish in the world to please you. Let everything be buried in oblivion, it will pass away like a dream.'[26] But Nelson would have nothing more to do with her. The letter had been addressed to him at Davison's house and was returned to her by Davison, 'Opened by mistake by Lord Nelson, but not read.'[27]

By March of the following year Nelson's father seems to have become settled in his mind and wrote to wish him 'an abundance of internal peace such as you have never yet enjoyed much of', and to express 'hopes I shall with the assistance of the May sunshine get able to travel and smell a Merton rose in June'. He granted them his benediction: 'God bless you and all who dwell under your roof.'[28] This was to be the last letter he ever wrote to his son. There were to be no Merton roses for the old man. He died in Bath on 26 April, in his seventy-ninth year. Nelson did not see him at the last; Fanny did.

Mrs Bolton wrote to her, 'Your going to Bath my dear Lady Nelson was of a piece with all your conduct to my beloved father.' But, conscious of her own family's need for Nelson's patronage, she had at last submitted to Emma. (Nelson would spend £150 a year on the education of her boys.) She was candid with Fanny: 'I am going to Merton in about a fortnight, but my dear Lady N. we cannot meet as I wished for every body is known who visits you.²⁹ Fanny now knew that she would be cast out of the family. The nearest she came to meeting any of them again was in January of the next year, 1803, when she left her card at Catherine Matcham's house but did not seek to speak with her; in George Matcham's words, she 'rolled off as she came, in Lord Hood's carriage and four'.³⁰

Poor deserted Fanny had done the best she was capable of in her unenviable situation. She had communicated continuing affection to her husband and had made no secret of it to Nelson's confidant Alexander Davison who unknown to her had been expressly charged with fobbing her off. In March 1801, she began to address Davison in desperation, her 'My dear Sir' giving way to 'My Dear Friend'. Her handwriting previously neat and clear became markedly less so, her letters rambled as she opened her heart to him and revealed the depths of her anguish. The refrain of her letters was simple, 'I love him I would do anything in the World to convince him of My affection.' She did not draw back in pride from consulting Davison about what she should or should not do. She did not revolt at Nelson's contemptible command of June 1801 that if the King conferred any honour on him she was to go to St James's, "Support My Rank and do not let me down." She reacted submissively to Davison, "I have strictly adhered to my Lord's injunctions – no one ever felt so anxious to please & make him happy as I did."³¹ She wanted Nelson back at any price. Nelson's settlement would have enabled Fanny to live without him but she did not want to. Her need for Nelson was deep and reflected her insecure and dependent nature. But she was turning to the wrong man. Eventually she realized that Davison's first loyalty was towards her husband and once he and Emma were installed at Merton there was nothing Davison or anybody could do for her. Fanny remained faithful to Nelson and carried a torch for him for the rest of her life.

Nelson's relationship with his father was characterized by fine words and much emotional carelessness. George Matcham had written from Bath on 24 April to tell him that his father's life was in danger. Nelson had made no attempt to visit him and had written back to Matcham, 'From your kind letter of yesterday describing my Father's situation I have no hopes that he can recover. God's will be done. Had my Father expressed a wish to see me, unwell as I am, I should have flown to Bath, but I believe it would be too late, however should it be otherwise and he wishes to see me, no consideration shall detain me for a moment.'[32] The funeral was fixed for 11 May at Burnham Thorpe. Nelson did not attend. Emma appears to have set the scene and William writing to Nelson on 4 May was clearly reacting to what Emma had told him: 'I am quite alarmed, my dear brother, at the account my Lady gives of your indisposition. As it seems to be a surgical case surely you had better call in the assistance of Mr Hawkins or Mr Home or some other eminent surgeon and let them examine ye part.'[33] It is difficult to believe that unheroic concern for his own health led him to avoid his father's deathbed and funeral. It is more likely that he feared a father's last wish, or that he might encounter Fanny, and could face neither prospect. It is astonishing that Nelson did not feel obliged to be involved in these most sombre rites of passage. But whatever the reason, this is an indication of inner coldness and emotional emptiness in a man who was otherwise so public in displaying his feelings.

If there was turmoil around him in his private life his public life was hardly more successful, although it began agreeably enough with his reintroduction in the House of Lords on 29 October as a viscount. One of his two supporters was his former Commander-in-Chief, Admiral Viscount Hood. Now that he was Hood's equal in the peerage, and had greater victories to his credit, he could forget those unrewarded Corsican days. The next day, when he seconded St Vincent's motion for thanks to one of his Nile captains, now Rear-Admiral Saumarez, 'for his gallant and distinguished conduct in the Action with the Combined Fleet of the Enemy off Algeziras on the 12th and 13th of July', Nelson not only spoke effusively of Saumarez but with his characteristic grace complimented both his former chiefs.

When it came to speaking on behalf of the government in support of the Preliminaries of Peace with France, he was not on such firm ground. Minorca he described as 'an island of little value to us, as at too great a distance from Toulon to serve as a station to watch the Fleets of France'. Malta 'was of no sort of consequence to this country'. The Cape of Good Hope was 'merely a tavern on the passage (to India) which served to call at, and thence often to delay the voyage. Ministers had acted with prudence and economy in giving up the Cape and making it a free port.' In describing the Preliminaries on the table as 'honourable and advantageous to this country', Nelson had taken his political cue from St Vincent. It was left to his old political master, but now political opponent, Lord Spencer, to put the opposite view: 'no single object of the war had been obtained . . . in every part of the world . . . cessions of countries which the valour of our forces by land and sea had conquered'.[34] Under the weight of party flattery and pressure, Nelson's robust common sense had deserted him. Peace might in all senses have been socially and politically desirable but he had not spoken in character. His authentic feelings emerged in a letter to his friend Hercules Ross. 'I pray God we may have peace, when it can be had with honour; but I fear that the scoundrel Buonaparte wants to humble us, as he has done the rest of Europe – to degrade us in our own eyes, by making us give up all our conquests, as proof of our sincerity for making a Peace, and then he will condescend to treat with us. He be d——d, and there I leave him.'[35] It must have seemed sensible for the government to rope in the country's hero to speak on its behalf. Huskisson (latterly Under-Secretary at War) thought otherwise and wrote to his previous master, Henry Dundas, 'How can Ministers allow such a fool to speak in their defence?'[36]

On 12 November he supported a Vote of Thanks to Lord Keith and the officers under his command, for their services in Egypt. The next day he spoke approvingly but with chauvinistic and bloodthirsty hyperbole on the Convention with Russia. 'It has put an end to the principle endeavoured to be enforced by . . . the late combination of the northern powers that free ships made free goods – a proposition so monstrous in itself, so contrary to the law of nations, and so injurious to the maritime rights of this country, that, if it had been persisted in, we ought not to have concluded the war with those powers while a single man, a single shilling, or even a single drop of blood remained in the country.'[37] And that was all the House of Lords was to hear from him, until about the same time the following year. This second flirtation with politics confirmed that it was not his business. He did not see the House of Lords and party politics as a route to advancement, power, self-esteem, attention and applause, even though it offered great opportunities in each of them. The only theatre that interested him was the theatre of battle, the only part he wanted to play was the part he had written for himself.

Seven months after Copenhagen he was still deeply offended by the City's mute reaction. He seized on its Vote of Thanks to the Army and Navy for their campaign in Egypt, to fire off a letter to the Lord Mayor:

> From my own experience, I have never seen, that the smallest services rendered by either Navy or Army to the Country, have missed being always noticed by the great City of London, with one exception – I mean my Lord, the glorious Second of April – a day when the greatest dangers of navigation were overcome, and the Danish Force, which they thought impregnable, totally taken or destroyed by the consummate skill of the Commanders, and by the undaunted bravery of as gallant a Band as ever defended the rights of this Country. For myself, I can assure you, that if I were only personally concerned, I should bear the stigma, now first attempted to be placed upon my brow, with humility. But, my Lord, I am the natural guardian of the characters of the Officers of the Navy, Army, and Marines, who fought, and so profusely bled, under my command on that day. In no Sea-action this war has so much British blood flowed for their King and Country.

He concluded with what for him was an article of faith: 'It is my duty my Lord, to prove to the brave fellows, my Companions in dangers, that I have not failed, at every proper place to represent, as well as I am able, their bravery and meritorious services.'[38]

To read such a lesson to the powerful, self-satisfied and self-interested City of London might be thought naïve and unwise but it is a measure of Nelson's sense of honour, justice and national pride. It is also an example of the deep disappointment he felt when other actors in his play failed to perform their parts properly. Falling clearly into that category was the pusillanimous reply he received from an evidently dumbfounded

and ashamed Lord Mayor, one Sir John Eamer, 'I have only to assure
your Lordship, that I shall give the subject a proper and early consideration.'[39] Nelson had had the good sense to give the Prime Minister a sight
of his intended letter. He added, 'Lord St Vincent, in July, made me truly
happy in the assurance that the King would grant Medals to those who
fought on that day, as has been usual in other great Naval victories.'[40]
Surprisingly, Addington took a week to reply. The impatient Nelson
waited three days and sent off his letter to the Lord Mayor. Four days
later he received Addington's worldly advice: 'I acknowledge my anxiety,
that, on the subject in question, no letter, be the terms of it what they
may, be written by your Lordship to the Lord Mayor. It could be pro-
ductive of no good and might, and (I firmly believe) would lead to serious
embarrassments. . . . They are not merely of a public nature, but are connected with the interest I shall ever take in your well earned fame.'[41] The
message could scarcely have been spelled out more clearly, and there was
no reference to medals. In parallel Nelson had sent a copy to St Vincent,
'for approval. . . . Your expanded mind must see the necessity of my stepping forth, or I should ill deserve to be so supported on any future occasion.' He went on, 'Your Lordship's opinion of the services of that day
induced you to hold [out] hopes amounting to certainty. I believed that
the King would grant those who fought that day Medals, as had been
done for other great Victories, and I have been, I own, expecting them
daily since the King's return from Weymouth.'[42]

The reason for Addington's delay now became abundantly clear.
Addington and St Vincent had put their heads together and decided that
Addington would deal with the Lord Mayor and St Vincent with the
medals. St Vincent sent two separate letters: the first merely acknowledged the copy of the letter 'you have judged fit to send to the Lord
Mayor'; the second flatly denied Nelson's contention on medals and protected Addington's position: 'I have given no encouragement to the other
subject therein mentioned, but, on the contrary, have explained to your
Lordship, and to Mr Addington, the impropriety of such a measure being
recommended to the King.'[43] This curt, flat denial leaves us having to
decide who to believe, St Vincent or Nelson. Of course, one party can
always believe that it has heard what it wanted to hear, the other party
that they have given the contrary impression. Now, it is interesting that
St Vincent's record in dealing with other individuals over the years displays a distinct tendency towards half-truth in order to smooth matters,

for example in his dealings with Sir William Parker over the choice of Nelson in 1798. On that occasion his habit badly misfired. On this occasion the ambiguity he created when he spoke with Nelson after he arrived home from the Baltic was probably much as Nelson described it. And now it was misfiring again. In all the present circumstances, the changed political climate and the personal position of Parker, neither Addington nor the King was minded to support medals. The only option St Vincent judged he had was flat denial, knowing that he could neither explain nor justify what he meant by, 'the impropriety of such a measure'. He clearly felt unable to disclose real reasons to Nelson.

Nelson's immediate reaction rings true:

I was this morning thunderstruck by the reading your Lordship's letter, telling me that you had never given encouragement to the expectation of receiving Medals for the Action of April 2nd. Had I so understood you, I never should, the same day, have told Mr Addington how happy you had made me, by the assurance that the King would give us Medals; and I have never failed assuring the Captains, that I have seen and communicated with, that they might depend on receiving them . . . I could not, my dear Lord, have had any interest in misunderstanding you, and representing that as an intended Honour from the King, which you considered as so improper to be recommended to the King. . . . The conduct of the City of London is to me incomprehensible; for Lord Keith, who has not been engaged, has been Thanked, &c., and Sir Hyde Parker for not fighting might, for what matters to me, have been Thanked too; but surely, my dear Lord, those who fought ought not to have been neglected for any conduct of others. I am truly made ill by your letter.[44]

The next day St Vincent replied. 'That you have perfectly mistaken all that passed between us in the conversation you allude to, is most certain; and I cannot possibly depart from the opinion I gave your Lordship in my last. At the same time I am extremely concerned that it should have had so material an effect upon your health.'[45] Nelson did not believe him and told Sutton who had commanded the frigate *Alcmene* and had nineteen of his men killed or wounded, 'Lord St Vincent, who in contradiction to what I thought a most positive assurance that we were to have Medals, now tells me, that he has always thought it improper to recommend it to the King. You may judge my feelings: the result you shall know; but I am fixed never to abandon the fair fame of my Companions in dangers. I may offend and suffer; but I had rather suffer from that than my own feelings. I am not well and this thing has fretted me.'[46]

Nelson's success at the Nile had been under-rewarded by Spencer because he had not been a commander-in-chief, this time by St Vincent because his commander-in-chief had been useless and could not be rewarded. In any case the whole episode was something the government now wanted to forget. This denial left its mark on Nelson, not for the trivial reason that he wanted another medal to hang around his neck but for the sake of the officers and men who had fought and died or been maimed for life. An ungrateful King and country had not figured in his concept of heroism. Although he could not bring himself to denounce St Vincent he said bluntly to Davison on the 28th, 'Either Lord St Vincent or myself are liars.'[47] Many men could have cynically shrugged off the situation in an ultimately self-serving way but in these matters Nelson was as a wounded child.

To his great credit Nelson never wavered in his attitude to the City, and never gave up trying to get medals for his captains. Noticing a newspaper report that the City was to vote him thanks for commanding the anti-invasion forces he again wrote to the Lord Mayor, 'I entreat that you will use your influence that no Vote of approbation may ever be given to me for any services since the 2nd of April 1801.'[48] When the Sultan sent him a red ribbon and medal to celebrate the battle, Nelson coolly told Addington, 'I own, my dear Sir, that great as this honour would be, that it would have its alloy, if I cannot at the same time wear the Medal for the Battle of Copenhagen.'[49]

He was increasingly worried about money. Forced into selling diamonds given to him after the Nile, but unhappily not at a good price, he had to keep Davison in the picture: 'The valuation of the diamonds is, as far as I have been told shameful; therefore, although I am naturally very anxious not to obtrude more on your goodness than necessity obliges me, yet I wish to talk to you on the subject of being even a little longer in your debt.'[50] By March 1802 he had begun to realize that if he was not careful he would end up in Queer Street and he took the quite extraordinary step of writing to Addington to reopen the question of his Nile pension, claiming once again, and not unreasonably, that having won victories of greater consequence than either St Vincent or Duncan he deserved the extra £1,000 on his pension which they had received. He had been elevated to Viscount but there had been no recognition of a financial kind to help either himself or his heirs support the rank. To bolster his case he included a remarkable statement of his income, outgoings and assets.

My Exchequer Pension for the Nile	£2,000
Navy Pension for loss of one arm and one eye	923
Half-pay as Vice-Admiral	465
Interest of £1,000 3 per cents	30
	£3,418

To Lady Nelson	£1,800
Interest of money owing	500
Pension to my Brother's Widow	200
To assisting in educating my Nephews	150
	£2,650

He showed the difference between Income and Expenditure as £768 and concluded,

Therefore Lord Nelson is free of House-rent, but has to pay charities necessary for his station in life, taxes, repairs, servants, and live upon £768 per annum.

To complete the statement he went on to detail 'Property of Lord Nelson':

Merton House, Land Plate and Furniture	£20,000
In 3 per cents £1,000 stock	

His debts followed:

By Mortgage on Merton to assist in the purchase	6,000
Fitting out for the Baltic, and again for my Command on the Coast in Summer 1,801	4,000

He concluded his statement of assets,

Real Property of Lord Nelson, £10,000,
In Three per cents £1,000 Stock[51]

A month later on 23 April, as he was preparing for sea, he took up the cudgels again with Addington. He reckoned St Vincent had made £100,000 and Duncan £50,000 by the time they were elevated, whereas he had realized only £5,000. Although Nelson had always believed and stated that glory was more important to him than money, Copenhagen had brought no Vote of Thanks from the City, and no medals from the King. It hardly seems unjustified for him to point out, and no pension either. He followed up with a meeting with Addington and on the same day persuaded George Rose (Secretary to the Treasury), with whom he had evidently had many previous conversations, to take his side. The hard financial facts of Copenhagen were that he would make no more than his personal share of the one-eighth of £65,000, i.e. £8,125, half of which was due to be shared by the four admirals (five, if Colonel Stewart was included as a junior admiral as Nelson recommended) less agent's fees. Two years after the battle they had not yet received a penny, although £30,000 head-money for the prisoners they took had been shared out and would have brought Nelson about £750. The supreme irony in all this was that as the second anniversary of the battle approached Nelson found himself informing Davison that 'Sir Hyde has given up the management of this matter to me.'[52] Just as he had left Nelson to do the fighting and then most of the the negotiating, he now left him to chase up the prize money too.

Nelson had every reason to feel hard done by, but it is hard to see what an extra thousand on his pension could do to mitigate the financial haemorrhage caused by Emma whose housekeeping was running at a rate of about £4,400 a year, if her accounts for September to October that year were anything to go by. To a degree the financial outflow was offset by Sir William's half share, but on the other hand, increased by Nelson's own generosity. Even his brother-in-law George Matcham, thanking Nelson for a 'sett of china', felt moved to gentle protest, 'we should be sorry to see your liberality further shown to us. I am confident my Lord, your income is not, nor ever will be, equal to your generosity.'[53] Whatever Nelson's worries about money, they were not allowed to get in the way of his wish to buy an adjacent estate of 115 acres belonging to a Mr Axe, at an asking price of £8,000. This was to be financed by borrowing half from George Matcham, to be precise from his sister Catherine's marriage settlement, with Davison putting up the rest.

Sir William's position was equally precarious. For him Merton was an extra since neither he nor Emma had wished to give up their house in Piccadilly; 'as it is we spend neither more nor less than we did'.[54] Sir William was feeling under pressure too, but as he explained to Greville it was not only a question of money. 'It is but reasonable after having fagged all my life, that my last days should pass off comfortably and quietly. Nothing at present disturbs me but my debts, and the nonsense I am obliged to submit to here to avoid coming to an explosion which wou'd be attended with many disagreeable effects, and would totally destroy the comfort of the best man and the best friend I have in the world. However I am determined that my quiet shall not be disturbed let the nonsensicall world go on as it will.'[55] And whatever Sir William's worries about money or lifestyle, it did not occur to them to curtail a trip to Milford Haven, an exercise in public relations. Their plan was to arrive on the anniversary of the battle of the Nile, and with the hero present, sell the advantages of the port of Milford Haven and boost the value of Sir William's investment there.

Five days before they set off Sir William's feelings came to the boil, and he erupted like Vesuvius. Something he appears to have said to Oliver had been passed on to Emma and had caused her to rocket off in an explosion of 'passion humour and nonsense, which it is impossible to combat with reasoning while the passion lasts'. Somehow his generosity and their expenses had been called into question. 'I am an old sinner I confess – but I am not the hard hearted man you do not scruple to make me. Your Ladyship is exactly what your old aunt told you, so noble, so generous, so beautiful, that you would give away your A – and H thro' your ribs – it is all well and so would I if I could afford it, and our Dear Ld. N. is noble, generous, open and liberal to all and I wish to God he could afford it.' What he intended for her in his will had also come up: 'You charge me with having by my Will left you to poverty and distress, that is by no means my intention.' (He had in fact left her by a will of May 1801 a lump sum of £300 and £800 a year and her mother was to get £100, and £100 a year if she survived Emma.) But what he intended to leave, although a very reasonable sum naturally disappointed Emma, especially when she thought of the £1,800 a year that Nelson was paying out to Fanny.

The proposed legacy reflected Sir William's fundamental ambivalence towards Emma, his natural class sense in rating Greville's claims so much more highly, and of course his mercenary expectation that having taken

Nelson into her bed, she would have to rely on him. He also knew that however much he left her it could never be enough. 'It is not my fault if by living with a great Queen in intimacy for so many years that your ideas should so far outrun what my means can furnish.' And then came the outright threat: 'But my Dear Emma let us cut this matter short. I am the old Oak and by God I can not give way to nonsence. Do not strain the bow too tight, as the Duke of Grafton said to Ld Ossory, lest the string should break.' He went on, 'I love Ld. Nelson. I know the purity of your connection with him. I will do everything in my power not to disturb the quiet of my best Friend, and his heart, God knows, is so sensible that a sudden change from his present peace and tranquility might prove fatal too him.' A threat to divorce her by seeking damages against Nelson for criminal conversation (here described ironically as purity of connection) could hardly have been made in a more elegantly veiled way. For a moment he allowed the bitterness of a cuckolded old husband to peep through. 'Would to God I could enjoy all that is mine and which I know to be superior to what any other person on Earth possesses, but one can not have eaten one's Cake and have one's cake. Ponder well my Dear Emma these lines, let your good sense come forward – as to me it is perfectly indifferent what may happen!'[56]

With that on the table and like a cloud between them, for Emma must have shared the letter with Nelson, they all set off on 21 July 1802 on the first leg of their journey. They were accompanied by brother William, his wife and son Horatio on holiday from Eton and were met in Oxford by Catherine and George Matcham. Nelson, greeted by crowds was given the Freedom of the City in a gold box at the Town Hall and the following day he and Sir William were made Doctors of Civil Law and brother William a Doctor of Divinity. Moving on to Blenheim they were greatly put out by the refusal of the Duke to receive them, Emma the probable reason. From then on, for the next ten days it was crowds, shouting and cheering all the way as they passed through Burford, Gloucester, where Catherine and her husband left the party, Ross-on-Wye and from there twenty miles upriver to Monmouth.

The scale of their welcome increased as the news of their coming travelled ahead. At Monmouth they were met by Mayor and Corporation and the band of the Monmouth and Brecon Militia playing 'See the Conquering Hero Comes' and 'Rule Britannia'. Nelson was astonished and thrilled by the scale of his welcome. 'Had I arrived at any of the great sea port towns in the kingdom, I should not have been much surprised at this token of attachment from my Jolly Jack Tars, but to be known at such a little gut of a river as the Wye fills me with astonishment.'[57] On they went into Wales, to a warm welcome in Brecon with a band and crowds of onlookers, a tumultuous reception in Merthyr where Nelson was proudly shown round the great Cyfatha Iron Works. Then to Llandeilo, Llandovery and Carmarthen, where the crowds were every bit as big but the official welcome more inhibited because of Emma's reputation. Then on through Haverfordwest and down to Milford Haven. There to welcome them Greville masterminded a grand dinner and Nelson made a major speech. He did everything expected of him: paid tribute to Foley his friend, companion in arms and a native of Pembrokeshire, extolled the virtues of Milford Haven and paid tribute to Sir William and Greville. Sir William presented the New Inn with the odd-looking Guzzardi portrait of Nelson which now hangs in the boardroom of Admiralty House in Whitehall. Their stay, extended beyond the three days of festivities, included a return visit to Haverfordwest, where the Freedom of the Town and County was conferred on both Nelson and Foley, as well as a visit to the well known seaside resort of Tenby.

Then return home could be delayed no longer and back they went through Carmarthen, where the populace towed the carriages to the King's Arms to change horses. There they forked south to Swansea to be met by seamen, who hauled their carriages into town through cheering crowds. Freedom having been conferred, this time on both Nelson and Sir William, Lady Hamilton sang 'Rule Britannia'. On they went to Cardiff and Chepstow, till once again they arrived in Monmouth. There were crowds, breakfast with the Mayor and Corporation, and a civic banquet when Nelson displayed once again his knack for choosing exactly the right words. To bring the house down Emma had only to perform Cornelia Knight's additional Nelson verse to 'God Save the King', and sing 'Rule Britannia'. Once more in Ross-on-Wye, they entered through a triumphal arch of oak and laurel and for three days stayed at nearby Rudall Manor, where the entertainment included fireworks and a ball. At this point the party made a major diversion. Instead of continuing east and taking the shortest route home, they headed due north, no doubt influenced by civic leaders come down from Hereford to invite him there.

The news of Nelson's progress was being noted and the *Morning Post* observed, 'It is a singular fact that more eclat attends Lord Nelson in his provincial rambles than attends the King.' In Hereford he was yet again granted Freedom of the City. He gave his standard speech. He had to a superb degree that knack of praising others in such a way that the whole credit still redounded on himself – the honour and renown for the brilliant victories which the fleets under him had obtained were not attributable to him but first to the Deity and next to the undaunted courage, skill and discipline of those officers and seamen which it had been his good fortune to command. And he was good at praising the people: 'Should the nation ever again experience a similar state to that from which it has been recently extricated, I have not the slightest doubt, from the results of my observations during this tour, that the native, the in-bred spirit of Britons, whilst it continues as firmly united as it is at present, is fully adequate successfully to repel any attack, either foreign or domestic which our enemies may dare to make. You have but to say to your fleets and armies "Go ye forth and fight your battles, whilst we, true to ourselves, protect and support our wives and little ones at home." '58 He had instinctively grasped the importance of the home front in times of total war and of communicating direct with the mass of the people. Ludlow was typical, his carriage dragged to the Crown Inn where he stood at an open window with the Hamiltons to acknowledge the crowd. Then they pulled aside to spend a few days with Richard Payne Knight, Sir William's old friend and fellow dilettante who had caused such a stir by publishing the study of the Priapic cult. It was here that Nelson, caressed by fame and triumph, told Payne Knight of his 'I will be a hero' experience on board the *Dolphin* twenty-seven years previously and it was from Payne Knight that Clarke and McArthur got the story for their 1809 biography of Nelson.

After so long on the road and so much continuous time in each other's company all was not sweetness and light for the *tria juncta in uno*. Sir William was tired and fractious, irked by the realization that his sole purpose in life was to be Emma's chaperon. The tour was demonstrating all too clearly that having once been a notable figure in cultured Europe he was now, in the dazzling light of Nelson and Emma's public celebrity, a background figure, an insignificant nonentity. Once the object of visiting Milford Haven had been accomplished he wanted to get home; the others were enjoying the limelight; he was playing gooseberry. Perhaps Emma relented her ruthless pursuit of self-gratification, for it was she who had written to Payne Knight to arrange the visit to Downton. There Sir William could rest and enjoy his fishing and cultured conversation, leaving Emma and Nelson free to visit his old friend Richard Bulkeley at Ludlow, where by now predictably Nelson was granted the town's Freedom. From Ludlow they swung east, church bells ringing as they passed through the countryside, cathedral bells when they arrived at Worcester. Here, having entered Chamberlain's china factory through a decorated entrance they placed an extravagant order. The Freedom inevitably followed as did his standard speech that he had only the good fortune to command heroes. Then, with crowds and bells all the way, they went via Droitwich and Bromsgrove to Birmingham. There was dinner before the theatre with the local great and good, with songs from Emma and some of the gentlemen present. Their coaches were dragged to the theatre and their appearence greeted with 'Rule Britannia'.

W.C. Macready, the future famous actor and at this time the nine-year-old son of the theatre manager, was there:

> The shouts outside announced the approach of the carriage; the throng was great, but being close to my father's side, I not only had a perfect view of the Hero's pale and interesting face, but listened with such eager attention to every word he uttered, that I had all he said by heart, and for months afterwards was wont to be called on to repeat, 'what Lord Nelson said to your father.' Nothing of course passed unnoticed by my boyish enthusiasm: the right arm empty sleeve attached to his breast, the Orders upon it, a sight to me so novel and remarkable; but the melancholy expression of his countenance, and extremely mild and gentle tones of his voice impressed me most sensibly. . . . When with Lady Hamilton and Dr [William] Nelson, he entered his box the uproar of the house was deafening and seemed as if it would know no end . . . in the hall of the hotel were several sailors of Nelson's ship waiting to see him, to each of whom the great Admiral spoke in the most affable manner, inquiringly and kindly, as he passed through to his carriage.[59]

There were crowds of thousands and Nelson was mobbed. The next
day they inspected and toured nine factories and moved on to Warwick
where Lord and Lady Warwick (Sir William's sister) were away but they
were greeted by the whole populace, Mayor and Corporation. After an
overnight stop at Coventry they went on to Althorp to meet Lord
Spencer. Whether they renewed their acquaintance with the Dowager
Lady Spencer and talked over days in Naples is not known, but Sir
William would at least see items he had supplied to the present Earl's
father. Now they were on the home straight, Towcester, Dunstable, St
Albans and home to Merton, arriving on Sunday, 5 September. They had
been away for six weeks and the cost, to be shared equally between
Nelson and Sir William, amounted to £481 3s. 10d., roughly equivalent
to a year's half pay for Nelson.

For Nelson the whole thing had been a triumphal progress. He had
attained unimaginable public fame and recognition. He thought it justified his feelings about how he had been treated by government. 'Our tour
has been very fine and interesting, and the way in which I have been
everywhere received most flattering to my feelings, and although some
of the higher powers may wish to keep me down, yet the reward of the
general approbation and gratitude for my Services is an ample reward
for all I have done, but it makes a comparison fly up to my mind, not
much to the credit of some in the higher offices of state.'[60] Nelson was
now moving beyond his need for recognition from King, government and
profession into dependency on the love of the masses. Perhaps buoyed
up by his experience he did not hesitate for a moment in turning down
an invitation to dine with the Lord Mayor as the City attempted to climb
on to a very evident Nelson bandwagon. 'Whenever, my dear Sir John,
you cease to be Chief Magistrate of the City of London, name your day,
and I will dine with you with satisfaction; but never till the City of
London think justly of the merits of my brave Companions of the 2nd
April, can I, their Commander, receive any attention from the City of
London.'[61] In November he would take exactly the same line with the
Lord Mayor elect. Catherine Matcham had been reading newspaper
accounts of their reception. She may have read *The Times* which said,
'Lord Nelson and his party returned on Sunday to Merton from their
tour through a part of the west of England . . . if on the one hand, the
Country owes his Lordship a large share of gratitude for the brilliant
Services he performed during the war, no man ever had it repaid in a

more ample degree.'[62] Sir Joseph Banks', in his rather silly and probably envious comment to Greville – 'I think you have done very wisely in preferring a route through Cornwall, where nature would arouse you at every step, to the artificial satisfaction of feasts, Mayors and Aldermen, freedom of Rotten Boroughs &c'[63] – was missing the point. Public adulation, based on indisputable achievement, was taking Nelson to another level of public recognition.

Soon after they had returned home Sir William and Emma went off to Ramsgate so that she might enjoy sea bathing. There is circumstantial evidence to suggest that little Horatia was taken in the same direction by Mrs Gibson, but to Margate, and that Nelson, incognito of course, Emma and Horatia met there. In any event the episode probably gave rise to another exchange between Sir William and Emma, who scribbled him an undated note, 'As I see it is a pain to you to remain here, let me beg of you to fix your time for going. Weather I dye in Picadilly or any other spot in England, 'tis the same to me; but I remember the time when you wish'd for tranquillity, but now all visiting and bustle is your liking. However, I will do as you please, being ever your affectionate & obedient.'[64] He replied, again undated, but clearly a riposte to Emma, 'I neither love bustle or great company, but I like some employment and diversion. I have but a very short time to live, and every moment is precious to me. I am in no hurry, and am exceedingly glad to give every satisfaction to our best friend, our dear Lord Nelson. The question then, is what we can do that all may be perfectly satisfied. Sea bathing is useful to your health; I see it is, and wish you to continue it a little longer; but I must confess that I regret whilst the season is favourable, that I cannot enjoy my favourite amusement of quiet fishing. I care not a pin for the great world, and am attached to no one so much as you.' She scribbled on the back, 'I go when you tell me the coach is ready.' His reply, 'This is not a fair answer to a fair confession of mine.'

Sir William was being tested hard by Emma's behaviour and was pushed to another ultimatum. He was well experienced in Emma's temper, and wanted Nelson to know exactly where he stood, and so he again resorted to writing to her.

I have passed the last forty years of my life in a hurry and bustle that must necessarily attend a public character. I am arrived at the age when some repose is really necessary, and I promised myself a quiet home, and although I was sensible, and said so when I married, that I should be superannuated when my wife would be in her full beauty and vigour of youth. That time is arrived, and we must make the best of it for the comfort of both parties. Unfortunately our tastes as to the manner of living are very different. I by no means wish to live in solitary retreat, but to have seldom less than 12 or 14 at table, and those varying continually, is coming back to what was become so irksome to me in Italy during the latter years of my residence in that Country. I have no connections out of my own family. I have no complaint to make, but I feel that the whole attention of my wife is given to Lord Nelson and his interest at Merton. I well know the purity of Lord Nelson's friendship for Emma and me, and I know how very uncomfortable it would make his Lordship, our best friend, if a separation should take place, and am therefore determined to do all in my power to prevent such an extremity, which would be essentially detrimental to all parties, but would be more sensibly felt by our dear friend than by us. Provided that our expences in housekeeping do not encrease beyond measure (of which I must own I see some danger) I am willing to go on upon our present footing; but as I cannot expect to live many years, every moment to me is precious, and I hope I may be allowed sometimes to be my own master, and pass my time according to my own inclination, either by going [on] my fishing parties to the Thames, or by going to London to attend the Museum, R. Society, the Tuesday Club and Auctions of pictures. I mean to have a light Chariot or post Chaise by the month, that I may make use of it in London and run backwards and forwards to Merton or to Shepperton &c. This is my plan, and we might go on very well, but I am fully determined not to have more of the very silly altercations that happen but too often between us and embitter the present moment exceedingly. If realy we cannot live comfortable together, a wise and well concerted separation is preferable; but I think considering the probability of my not troubling any party long in this world, the best for us all would be for us to bear those ills we have rather than flie to those we know not of. I have fairly stated what I have on my mind. There is no time for nonsence or trifling. I know and admire your talents and many excellent qualities, but I am not blind to your defects, and confess to having many myself; therefore let us bear and forbear for God's sake.[65]

All of this was true. Emma, a woman of phenomenal energy, was running hither and thither in her tutelage of the William Nelson's children, entertaining hectically and doing so with an excess of language, letters and song. There was worse to come. Far from Emma's housekeeping not being increased beyond measure, it was out of control. Coutts her bankers had given her the bad news, 'the present balance of your money in our hands is twelve shillings and eleven pence'. Sir William was having to bail her out. 'I have given her an additional credit on Coutts for £130, so that of the £700 wanting to clear all, having had £120 before, I am to pay £450. [Clearly she had personal debts outside the housekeeping.] Sir William was feeling the pain: 'If I am not paid soon by the Treasury I am determined to apply to Mr Addington myself'.[66]

But they did not have to bear and forbear for very long. On 6 April 1803 at the age of seventy-two Sir William died in Emma's arms, Nelson holding his hand. Thus came to an end one of the more notorious relationships of the time. Hamilton and Nelson were as different as chalk and cheese. They had no common interests to unite them, yet seemed to have a genuine liking for each other. Their ability to share a woman depended not only on Nelson's utility to Hamilton and on their marked difference in age but also on Nelson's innate tact and diplomacy and Hamilton's collector's mentality, in which Emma's transfer was little different to that of a valued piece of goods being directed into favoured hands. Both men were good at superficial relationships, both at getting what they wanted. Hamilton was an intensely sociable, urbane character, but of a cynical and ironic turn of mind, a man who liked to please himself but who went out of his way to be liked by the right people. Nelson liked to be liked too and Sir William knew how to flatter. Sir William's problems were with Emma, her temper and the inevitable weakening of her resolve to look after him. On his death Sir William left Emma no more than her due, the going rate as it were, but well short of Nelsonian generosity. The portrait of Emma which he bequeathed to Nelson was accompanied by a poisonous comment from a master of irony, 'The copy of Madame Le Brun's picture of Emma in enamel by Bone, I give to my dearest friend Lord Nelson, Duke of Bronte, a very

small token of the great regard I have for his Lordship, the most virtuous, loyal, and truly brave character I ever met with. God bless him, and
shame fall on those who do not say amen.'[67]

In late 1802 the Peace of Amiens which had been so joyously received
in England was being revealed as fraudulent. By late 1802 the bad faith
of France was clearly emerging. Bonaparte had not evacuated Holland,
the Swiss revolt against the Helvetian puppet republic was crushed. Elba,
Piedmont and Parma were annexed. Nelson saw St Vincent and Addington a number of times. 'We felt our importance in the scale of Europe
degraded if Buonaparte was allowed to act as he has lately done; and
that it was necessary for us to speak a dignified language, but when where
and to whom all this was to be done I know no more than your Plough-
man.'[68] On 16 November Nelson seconded the King's speech. He had
been purposely chosen and what he said this time was in character. He
spoke as he put it in a 'plain seaman-like manner'. His was a warning
call: 'I my Lords, have in different countries seen much of the miseries
of war. I am therefore in my inmost soul a man of peace. Yet would I
not, for the sake of any peace, however fortunate, consent to sacrifice
one jot of England's honour.' His chauvinistic sentiments were given full
expression. 'Hitherto there has been nothing greater known on the continent than the faith, the untarnished honour, the generous public sympathies, the high diplomatic influence, the commerce, the grandeur, the
resistless power, the unconquerable valour of the British nation. Wherever I have served in foreign countries, I have witnessed these to be the
sentiments with which Britons were regarded.'[69] As ever he had struck
the right note. Emma, who naturally thought he spoke 'like an angel',
may have had a hand in rehearsing his words. By 8 March 1803 a
message from the King revealed that 'very considerable military preparations are carrying on in the ports of France and Holland'.[70]

  Nelson was now centre stage. Whatever enemies he might have, whatever thoughts there might be in some elevated circles about his conduct,
the revelation of his public popularity and his availability to second the
King's address led to increased access to power in those early months of
1803. He passed a message to Addington in the Lords, 'Whenever it is
necessary I am your Admiral.'[71] War was in the air. The Cabinet made
sure he was appointed to the Mediterranean command. Steps to mobi-

lize were being taken. He was working overtime. He had chosen Sam Sutton to command *Victory* and by 22 March he was already fitting her out. She would be commissioned in early April. He was gathering people round him, sending Sutton the names of six lieutenants, arranging for John Scott to be made available as his secretary. As Captain of the fleet he had his eye on George Murray, who had supported him so splendidly at Copenhagen in the *Edgar*. Nelson was in a buoyant mood, handling with the utmost judgement Sutton's situation as actual captain of *Spartiate* and first captain elect of *Victory*, at the same time sending him congratulations on the birth of a son, 'if one of his names is not Baltic, I shall be very angry with you indeed'.[72]

In May Britain presented France with an ultimatum. Agree to Britain possessing Malta for ten years, evacuate Holland and Switzerland, and Britain will recognize the current position of France in Italy. The net result: England declared war on France on 18 May 1803. Two days previously, on 16 May 1803, some eighteen months since he had entered the gates of Merton for the first time, and after a year on half pay, Nelson achieved the pinnacle of his ambition. He was appointed Commander-in-Chief of the Mediterranean fleet. Two days later he hoisted his flag in the *Victory*.

Part VI

The Road to Trafalgar

24

Commander-in-Chief

I have met with no character equal in any degree to his Lordship, his penetration is quick, judgement clear, wisdom great and his decisions correct and decided, nor does he in company appear to bear any weight on his mind, so cheerful and pleasant, that it is a happiness to be about his hand.

John Scott, Nelson's Secretary, July 1803

The thing that strikes one most about the Nelson of this final period is the power resting in his face. His figure might be slight, his height might be no more than average, but his was now a fully matured face of command. He sat for Catherine Andras in 1805 and her waxwork of a year later makes this abundantly clear. The prominent nose, the wide, powerfully sculpted mouth, confront you; the face pronounces a willingness to make decisions and bear responsibility. His string of victories have invested him with charisma; it becomes a moving experience just to catch sight of him. Meeting him is all the sweeter, for this great man has a talent for making *you* feel special. And like any great performer, having learned that his audience delights in how he is, and what he says, he gives them more of what they want.

Nelson's orders were wide ranging. He was to link up with Sir Richard Bickerton off Malta, concert with the Governor, his friend Alexander Ball, arrangements for protecting the island, deliver Hugh Elliot, Lord Minto's brother, to Naples as Minister, and then proceed to join his fleet off Toulon. He was to 'take, sink, burn or otherwise destroy' all French ships he might encounter. He was to detain all Dutch ships. He was to be on the lookout for threats against Egypt, Turkey, Naples, Sicily and Corfu and thwart any attacks on them. He was not to infringe Spanish neutrality but was to prevent the French, Spanish and Dutch from joining forces. By means of a detachment at Gibraltar he was to prevent French troopships from the West Indies from entering the Mediterranean. All in all, it was a very sizeable agenda.

He champed at the bit. 'If the Devil stands at the door the Victory shall sail tomorrow forenoon.'[1] He had longed for this command, but gaining one of his heart's desires meant losing another. He could not disguise the pang of separation. 'Believe me my dear Emma, although the call of honour separates us, yet my heart is so entirely yours and with you. ... Kiss our dear god [sic] child.'[2] He went off in a heavy shower of rain and a northerly wind, St Vincent's praise ringing in his ears: 'Your Lordship has given so many proofs of transcendent zeal in the Service of your King and Country, that we have only to pray for the preservation of your invaluable life, to insure everything that can be achieved by mortal man.'[3]

By the afternoon of 22 May the Victory was standing on and off stormy Ushant, Nelson looking for his friend Admiral Cornwallis, Commander-in-Chief of the Channel fleet. Nelson was under orders, 'on no account to pass Admiral Cornwallis, so as to run any chance of his being deprived of the service of the Victory if he should judge it necessary to detain her'. Cornwallis was not on the rendezvous and Nelson was unable to discover his whereabouts from other ships in the vicinity. Desperate not to lose the good north wind, he lingered only one night before impatiently shifting into the Amphion. Then he was on his way. Infuriatingly, his fair wind failed and it was a week before he arrived at Gibraltar. He stayed only long enough to replenish his water and assign convoy escorts, then pushed on for Malta. From the great cabin of the Amphion he began to link up with his political contacts, writing to Acton at Naples about Elliot, to Jackson, Minister at Turin about support for the King of Sardinia; and to William Drummond at the Porte about the situation in the Ottoman empire. At Malta he spent two days being briefed by his friend Alexander Ball, the Governor.

By now he was fully engrossed in Mediterranean problems. He was annoyed that a British ship had jeopardized the situation at Naples by seizing a French vessel in the Bay. Naples and Sicily were poised in such a state of uneasy neutrality that the last thing he wanted to do was provoke the French. For that reason he had decided not to move pre-emptively on Messina; he had political clearance and troops allocated by the War Department but he judged that by making such a move he would bring the French down on Naples. Nevertheless he took sensible precautions in stationing ships to keep a weather eye open for French troop movements and he left a frigate off Naples to evacuate the royal family should the need again arise. Flowery language to Acton was still the order of the day but his eyes were wide open; he knew how unreliable the Neapolitans were and how difficult their balancing act would be. To the south there was a sudden and unexpected crisis on the North African coast. The Dey of Algiers had dismissed Mr Falcon, the British Consul. Nelson, aware of the Dey's piratical harrying of foreign vessels, was naturally inclined to take a robust line: 'Should the business be left to me, I shall go to Algiers, and if the Dey refuses a complete acquiescence in our demands, instantly take all his Cruizers.'[4]

The *Amphion* sailed north, up the east coast of Sardinia with all the urgency the driven Nelson could muster. 'I am miserable at not having joined the Fleet.'[5] He switched his mental energy to assembling a political and military overview of his sphere of operations – Gibraltar, Malta, Naples and Sicily, Sardinia, Rome, Tuscany, Genoa and the Morea. A lengthy summary was soon on its way direct to Prime Minister Addington. As a commander-in-chief Nelson regarded himself as an instrument of government concerned with reading the direction of political and military movement across the whole of the Mediterranean. He was convinced that Bonaparte had designs on the Morea, his object the downfall of the Turkish empire, the invasion of Candia (Crete) and Egypt, 'when, sooner or later, farewell India'.[6] Events would show that he could not have been more wrong but he was never inhibited by having to base his strategic views on intuition and guesswork. A commander has to take a view.

At last, more than a month after he had left Gibraltar, he came across his fleet off Toulon. His nine sail-of-the-line, his one frigate and two sloops were undermanned and needed their bottoms scraped, but otherwise to his proud and proprietorial eye, 'they look very well'. The French, bottled up in Toulon, amounted to seven ships-of-the-line and five frigates, the flags of two admirals and one commodore flying over them.

Battle with the French was Nelson's ultimate aim, but battle was no more than a brief punctuation mark in the life of a fleet. Day after day men had to be fed and clothed, their health and spirits kept up, their ships in good repair. Even for a fleet of this modest size, the management task was vast, involving a ceaseless flow of logistical, administrative and personnel matters.

What mattered most to Nelson soon became apparent. First and foremost, his ships were engines for consuming food. Though he could, in theory, rely on his base requirements coming from England by transport, fresh food had to be sourced locally. The requirement he placed on Gibert, the British Consul at Barcelona was for 'live bullocks, onions, and a few sheep now and then, on an average of fifty bullocks a week'.[7] By the autumn, when war with Spain seemed imminent, he would have to think of getting his Spanish supplies in neutral ships, via Malta. Malta itself had proved useless as a source of supplies. He told Addington he had not been able to obtain there, 'one morsel of fresh beef or any vegetables'.[8] Besides, Malta was a six- to seven-week round trip from Toulon. And so he would detach his ships to the Maddalena Islands on the north-east corner of Sardinia, a mere twenty-four hours from Toulon where they could take on water and rendezvous with transports. By November 1804 he was arranging with Archibald Macneil in Naples for the supply of a hundred head of prime cattle, a month's supply of hay, and twelve tons of onions. He simultaneously authorized Richard Bromley, purser of the *Bellisle* to take the opportunity of their visit to the Maddalenas to procure as many live bullocks as he could find and 200 head of sheep for the sick. He insisted on quality as well as quantity; no detail was too minor for his attention. He set up a random sampling process to compare the quality of local and Admiralty-supplied provisions. The masters of all his ships were assembled, required to make random selections from supplies of pork, tongue, hog's lard, pease and wheat, have them cooked there and then, judge the results, and report to him.[9] Nelson knew that food was everything to sailors, the single greatest foundation of their health, happiness and morale, their mealtimes points of solace in a hard and demanding life. Bonaparte might have said that an Army marched on its stomach, but unlike Bonaparte, Nelson exerted personal effort to make sure that his men's stomachs were well filled.

Always conscious of his own health, he was equally aware of the health of his men. The Admiralty's seagoing medical service and shore-based hospitals were actuated by a spirit of enlightened self-interest: ill health reduced the efficiency of ships, epidemics could decimate their crews and wounded men needed surgeons. Nelson's interest was more personal, imaginative and detailed. In February 1804 he received from Dr Moseley, former Surgeon-General in the West Indies, a copy of the fourth volume of his *Treatise on Tropical Diseases*. The second volume had covered the expedition to San Juan and Nelson had himself contributed to it. In his reply he spoke of another aspect of his leadership credo:

> The great thing in all Military Service is health; and you will agree with me, that it is easier for an Officer to keep men healthy, than for a Physician to cure them. Situated as this Fleet has been, without a friendly Port, where we could get all the things so necessary for us, yet I have, by changing the cruizing ground, not allowed the sameness of prospect to satiate the mind – sometimes by looking at Toulon, Ville Franche, Barcelona and Rosas; then running round Minorca, Majorca, Sardinia, and Corsica; and two or three times anchoring for a few days, and sending a Ship to the last place for onions, which I find the best thing that can be given to Seamen; having always good mutton for the sick, cattle when we can get them, and plenty of fresh water. In the winter it is the best plan to give half the allowance of grog instead of all wine. These things are for the Commander-in-Chief to look to.[10]

These were not mere words. At that very moment he was asking Richard Ford, the agent victualler to the fleet, for 'two hundred pipes [of wine] together with thirty thousand oranges, and twenty tons of onions for the respective Ships' Companies, and also fifty good sheep for the use of the sick and convalescent Seamen of the Squadron'.[11] He was aware of psychological as well as physical health. He knew that the volume of sickness in the fleet was a prime indicator of its morale; he was proud to be able to say that the sick bays of his fleet were empty. When it was decided to re-establish a naval hospital at Malta he told John Snipe, physician to the fleet, that he should 'endeavour to procure a convenient and well appointed house, in an airy and healthy situation'.[12] Some six months later he told the Admiralty 'a certain space of ground attached to the said building is also indispensably necessary for a garden, a place for the convalescent Seamen and Marines to enjoy a little exercise and fresh air'.[13] He was called upon to arbitrate in a dispute between Mr Schaw, surgeon of the *Madras* and Dr Franklin, physician of the Military Hospital at Malta, who declared that a seaman in the *Madras* suffering from an inflammatory fever had been sent to hospital too late by the ship's doctor. He realized the difficulty he was in – 'When Doctors differ who shall decide?'[14] Nevertheless, undeterred, he was at his formidable best as a conciliator, not taking sides, but helping to evolve a pragmatic process for resolving such issues, and by his own attitude, building bridges for the future. 'I trust that this little asperity in a professional judgement, between two professional men, will not prevent the reception of our Seamen in future and the former kindness of the Gentlemen of the Hospital towards them.'[15] Following an intervention by Dr Snipe, he issued an order that men sent on wooding and watering parties onshore in the marshy areas of Sardinia should be given a dose of Peruvian Bark (quinine) mixed in two gills (one pint) of wine, before they went ashore and after they returned, this in addition to their normal daily allowance. Naturally he was very anxious to keep this extra vinous medication under control and while approving the policy required a return be made to himself of its application.[16] When the agent to the contractor for prisoners of war at Malta decided to feed them salt beef rather than fresh, Nelson was insistent that their health be safeguarded in their long and close confinement, by allowing them wine. 'I take the liberty of mentioning to their Lordships (that as Frenchmen are in the habit of drinking small wine in their own Country) the propriety of allowing Prisoners of War a certain quantity each per day.'[17] Little wonder that with such championing of the medical service, such attention to detail, and such care for individuals he was able to tell Hugh Elliot on 8 September, 'I never experienced anything like the health of this Fleet. We have literally not a real sick man in it.'[18]

Fresh food and careful attention to his men's health did not of themselves guarantee a trouble-free fleet. From the beginning he had to contend with desertion. He was realistic and philosophical: 'such is the love for roaming of our men, that I am sure they would desert from heaven to hell, merely for the sake of change'.[19] His fleet was undermanned. He had to grasp this nettle. As ever, he chose to be positive. He dictated a spirited memorandum to be read out to each ship's company: 'When British Seamen and Marines so far degrade themselves in time of War, as to desert from the Service of their own Country, and enter into that of Spain; when they leave one shilling per day, and plenty of the very best provisions, with every comfort that can be thought of for them – for two-pence a-day, black bread, horse beans and stinking oil for their food ... to put himself under the lash of a Frenchman or Spaniard must be more degrading to any man of spirit than any punishment I could inflict on their bodies.'[20] At first Nelson was sanguine, explaining to St Vincent a few weeks later, 'all the Ships have expected every day before the War, to go to England. . . . However, a good deal of that fever is wore off, and we are really got to a state of health which is rarely witnessed.'[21]

His appeal did not succeed and less than two months later he was obliged to send another memorandum to his captains: 'Lord Nelson is very sorry to find that notwithstanding his forgiveness of the men who deserted in Spain, it has failed to have its proper effect. . . . Therefore Lord Nelson desires that it may be perfectly understood, that if any man be so infamous as to desert from the Service in future, he will not only be brought to a Court-Martial, but if the sentence be Death, it will be most assuredly carried into execution.'[22] A month later he was sending out another warning signal. Robert Dwyer a marine private had been sentenced to the appalling punishment of 500 lashes for disobedience of orders and insolence to his superior officer. Nelson announced that he had remitted the rest of the sentence (probably four further bouts of 100 lashes each) because it was the first offence of its kind since he had taken over and his captains had made him aware of 'the very orderly conduct and good behaviour of their Ships' Companies'.[23] He was trying to establish an understanding with his men. His was not to be a reign of terror. He expected his men to respond to his evident wish to be fair and merciful. He knew that a policy of warning, of judging cases on their merits, of accepting pleas in mitigation on grounds of previous good conduct, would make severe punishment more acceptable, should the need for it arise. Brutality was institutionalized in the eighteenth-century Navy; the Navy's harsh laws were there to sustain its authority and, something that is often overlooked, to dominate nasty and vicious elements in ships' companies. Nelson knew what he was dealing with, what the rules of the game were, and in the last resort would not hesitate to enforce them; but he was always concerned to make discipline acceptable and the whole thrust of his nature was to be merciful and encourage that quality in others. He was also wise enough to know that the discipline of the Navy had to be administered by officers and petty officers, mostly men of their time, variable in their moral and behavioural quality and each to a greater or lesser degree confident and competent in exercising authority. He did not attempt to change the system and would not have succeeded had he tried. The Navy would change only as the mores of society as a whole changed. Therefore it is to be expected that men were flogged in Nelson's ships and this is indeed what the record shows. During his time in the West Indies Nelson and his friend Cuthbert Collingwood were having men flogged at a rate of two a month (Prince William's rate for the year 1787 was four a month).[24] Later when Nelson was captain of *Agamemnon*, by any standards a happy and effective ship, floggings were still being handed out at the same rate of two to three a month but the master's log for the period 1793–96 shows that no individual needed to be punished twice, that many of the punishments were incurred when the ship was in port and inactive, that half the punishments might be regarded as short sharp shocks of three to six lashes, heavier punishments of twelve lashes or more being reserved for serious crime. Two men and a boy given thirty-six lashes each for sodomy were by the standards of the day being treated leniently, since the Articles of War described theirs as a crime punishable by death.[25] Punishment was accepted as long as it was administered fairly, was not disproportionate to the offence or sadistic in intent. During his life as a captain in *Agamemnon* it would seem that Nelson made a real effort to make the punishment fit the crime. Now, as Commander-in-Chief, what Nelson could and did, was to encourage his officers by his own example. Thus these public displays of his values were matched by advice he gave his officers in specific cases. When Captain Corbet of the *Bittern* requested a court martial on five seamen who had deserted at Messina more than a year previously, he wrote to Corbet's senior officer, Captain Cracraft, 'I am inclined to think that Captain Corbet, from the said men's long confinement, and their late exertions in capturing *L'Hirondelle*, French Privateer, may be inclined to forgive them. You will therefore signify the purport of this letter to Captain Corbet, that if he is disposed to forgive them, I have no objections under the present circumstances.'[26] Corbet took Nelson's hint.

Nelson's concept of discipline had a clear moral base; each demonstration of care for his men reinforced it. After a boat action against enemy vessels in Hyères Bay on the night of 10 July 1804 he showed meticulous care for the personal and material needs of the wounded: 'A regular list will be sent to the Patriotic Fund at Lloyds and the Captains are to give each man a certificate before he leaves the Ship, describing his wound, signed by the Captain and Surgeon. The wounded men to be sent to the three Flag-Ships, as they will probably find better accommodation than in a Frigate.'[27] The news soon got round, as it did when he recommended that the Admiralty pay the extra postage for letters coming overland from Lisbon or Faro. Many were lying unclaimed because of the expense. Nelson knew that, next to food, letters from home were of the first importance to his men.

As far as his officers were concerned he had himself to exercise the broad personnel or human resources function, which would today in similar-sized enterprises occupy large bodies of managers and staff and frequently be accomplished less well. He had the senior officers under his command to judge and report on. He had quickly formed a good opinion of Sir Richard Bickerton and Captain Keats of the *Superb* and told St Vincent so. 'The *Superb* is in a very weak state; but her Captain [Keats] is so superior to any difficulties, that I hear but little from her. *Triumph* and *Renown* complain a good deal. Sir Richard Bickerton is a very steady, good Officer, and fully to be relied upon; George Campbell you know.'[28] Then there were young officers of quality whose interests he felt impelled to push. A Lieutenant Hillyer, previously promoted by Nelson for bravery, declined command of the *Ambuscade*, which would have given him promotion to Master and Commander. Paradoxically, it would probably have led to the earlier termination of his career because of the glut of commanders awaiting promotion to Post Captain. Being responsible for a mother, sisters and brother, the prospect of life on half pay horrified him and so he declined the appointment. Nelson interceded with St Vincent and asked that the *Niger*, a fast sailing frigate should be more heavily armed, so as to make her a post ship. St Vincent promptly agreed and sent out Hillyer's commission as a post captain.

His support for Captain Layman (actually a lieutenant at the time) court-martialled for the loss of the sloop *Weazle*, was another case in point. Layman was a young, active, confident officer and a firm favourite of his Commander-in-Chief. Nelson interceded with St Vincent and Layman was given another command, the sloop *Raven*. This had been a close run thing, for during his interviews at the Admiralty Layman had performed in character. As Nelson reported to Emma 'it was his venturing to know more about India than Troubridge, that made them look shy upon him; and, his tongue runs too fast. I often tell him, not to let his tongue run so fast, or his pen write so much';[29] an interesting insight into Nelson as a mentor and the personal feedback he would give to his protégés. The next time Nelson saw Layman was on 7 March 1805 when a Spanish cartel flying Spanish colours at its fore, the Union Jack at the main and the Stars and Stripes at the mizzen arrived in the squadron with a load of prisoners. The *Raven* had been driven into Cadiz in a gale and captured. The subsequent court martial found, 'a great want of necessary caution in Captain Layman, in approaching the land'. He was severely reprimanded and put at the bottom of the list of commanders. Nelson was not the man to desert his protégés in their hour of need, even though a court martial of his own officers had judged Layman. Just as he had gone the extra mile to obtain a Nile medal for Troubridge so he now pulled out all the stops for Layman. He wrote to Lord Melville (Formerly Henry Dundas) the current First Lord,

> Notwithstanding the Court-Martial has thought him deserving of censure for his running in with the land, yet, my Lord allow me to say, that Captain Layman's misfortune was, perhaps conceiving that other people's abilities were equal to his own, which, indeed, very few people's are. I own myself one of those who do not fear the shore, for hardly any great things are done in a small ship by a man that is; therefore, I make great allowances for him. Indeed, his station was never intended to be from the shore in the Straits: and if he did not every day risk his Sloop, he would be useless upon that station. Captain Layman has served with me in three Ships, and I am well acquainted with his bravery, zeal, judgement and activity; nor do I regret the loss of the *Raven* compared to the value of Captain Layman's services, which are a National loss. You must, my dear Lord, forgive the warmth which I express for Captain Layman; but he is in adversity, and therefore, has the more claim to my attention and regard. If I had been censured every time I have run my Ship or Fleets under my command, into great danger, I should long ago have been out of the Service, and never in the House of Peers.[30]

Perhaps those words, 'conceiving that other people's abilities were equal to his own', indicate some truth in the story that when Nelson, confident of acquittal, was talking over his coming trial with Layman, he counselled him against making a severe reflection on his officer of the watch: 'If this is laid before the Court, they will hang the Officer of the Watch.'[31] Thus he might have felt himself to some degree responsible for the outcome. In any event his efforts got nowhere. Layman's career was finished.

Less obvious, but equally indicative of Nelson's generally benign and forbearing approach, was the case of another young lieutenant, son of an eminent and respectable captain, who, 'from an unfortunate desire to travel, and perhaps an imprudent attachment to an Italian female, quitted the *Hydra* when she was last at Malta, without, I fear, the smallest inclination of ever returning to his duty in that Ship'. He went on in his letter to Marsden, 'and I must beg that you will interest their Lordships, in favour of this unfortunate young Officer . . . whose youthful imprudence I trust their Lordships will take into consideration, and, on account of his worthy and respectable father . . . allow his name to remain on the list of Lieutenants'.[32] The stony hearts of the Admiralty were touched and Nelson's intercession was successful.

It was not just high-flying officers whose interests he was anxious to support. He knew that honest, hard-working officers of limited potential, doing vital but unglamorous jobs, were the backbone of the Navy. He did his best for men like Lieutenant Pemberton, 'an old and experienced officer', who had been agent of transports at Malta. In asking the Admiralty to confirm his appointment as Governor of the Naval Hospital at Malta, he did so, 'until something more to his advantage shall offer'.[33]

He was under constant pressure from highly placed individuals, who wanted their sons, nephews, or the sons and nephews of friends, to be promoted either to Lieutenant, or to Master and Commander, or to Post Captain. Pressure came from members of his own family on behalf of relatives and friends, and not least from Emma, and the Admiralty had its own list. He told his brother on 18 October that he had sixty on his list for promotion to Lieutenant and twenty-six on his list of lieutenants for promotion to Master and Commander or Post Captain. But nothing was going to stand in the way of Sir Peter Parker's grandson. 'I have kept him as Lieutenant of the Victory, and shall not part with him until I can make him a Post Captain; which you may be assured I shall lose no time in doing. It is the only opportunity ever offered me, of showing that my feelings of gratitude to you are as warm and alive as when you first took me by the hand: I owe all my Honours to you, and I am proud to acknowledge it to all the world. Lord St Vincent has most strongly and kindly desired your grandson's promotion; therefore I can only be the

instrument of expediting it.'[34] He had a great sense of naval family obligation to those who had previously served with him and to the sons of
officers. On 20 March 1804 he commissioned Midshipman Faddy of the
Victory as a lieutenant in the *Triumph*. He was the son of Captain Faddy
of the Marines killed in the *Vanguard* at the Nile. Nelson added in his
letter to the Admiralty, 'I beg leave also to observe that his widowed
mother is alive, with the charge of a large family unprovided for, and
naturally looks up to him for assistance.'[35] As far as the sons of officers
were concerned he had no doubt. 'I consider the near relations of Brother
Officers, as legacies to the service,'[36] he said in relation to the son of Lord
Duncan. On the other hand Emma had clearly pushed forward a son of
Mrs Voller, whom Nelson did not know from Adam. 'What can I do for
a child that has never been to sea . . . Captain Hardy has been so good
as to rate him Mid . . . I know Mrs Voller's uniform kindness to you . . .
I have had the lad to dinner.'[37] Nelson could not avoid patronage, but it
is easy to show that he did not embrace the absurd nepotism of Admiral
Rodney. He judged men on their merits. Layman was clearly in the stream
of Nelson's professional patronage just as any young manager might be
in that of his senior today. As he told Davison after Layman's court
martial, 'I would employ Layman tomorrow if I could.' Hillyer was likewise a promising young man in exactly the same category, as indeed were
Hoste and the unfortunate Parker. They were all Nelson's high-flyers,
young men he thought well of, worked easily with, men of potential
whom he would be happy to have around him on future occasions. None
of them had families who could do the least thing for Nelson. And like
St Vincent, he believed that it was 'absolutely necessary merit should be
rewarded on the moment; and that the Officers of the Fleet should look
to the Commander-in-Chief for their reward: for that otherwise the good
or bad opinion of the Commander-in-Chief would be of no consequence'.[38] Fundamentally, Nelson was working on entirely modern principles. To him track record and potential were just as important for
operational appointments as they are seen to be today. The eighteenth-
century Navy's idea of followers is still practised today when a highly
placed executive leaves a City firm and takes his or her team along too.
The only thing that is different today is the vast amount of effort that
goes into producing no better outcome than the eighteenth-century navy
– a handful of brilliant and successful men, a great leavening of mediocrity, many unlucky, and vast numbers of unsung heroes.

A man whose first instinct was invariably to give his officers support and trust, Nelson could be hard and demanding in his judgements when the occasion demanded it. He took a hard line with Lieutenant Harding Shaw of the brig *Spider*. A flogging had just been completed. A shot was thrown and fell near Shaw and his master. Shaw then made an awful blunder; he threatened his whole ship's company with punishment if the offender did not declare himself, and ended up by having to give each member of his crew a dozen lashes. Nelson wrote him an icy note, totally disapproving 'of a measure so foreign to the rules of good discipline and accustomed practice'.[39] His card was marked. A master and commander of a sloop under quarantine came on board *Victory* and earned himself a monumental rocket for 'endangering the health of the *Victory*'s Ship's company, and that of the whole Fleet under my command ... highly reprehensible and unofficerlike ... you will hold yourself ready to answer (when called upon) for it accordingly'.[40] On another occasion he formed a bad opinion of a certain Captain Pearse of the *Halcyon* and asked Captain Gore to keep him on the alert, 'as I am sorry to observe that the Service has not derived that benefit from her which might have been expected from so fine a vessel'.[41] Gore subsequently defended Pearse, and Nelson, who had considerable respect for Gore's own unwearying efforts, was quick to adjust his view. 'The inactivity of that Sloop reached me through different channels; but I am satisfied, from your account of the state of the *Halcyon*, the blame is not imputable to her Commander, and I request you will tell him so.'[42] When one lieutenant asked to be transferred to another ship Nelson's reply to him was wonderfully magisterial and thoughtful: 'I have just received your letter, and I am truly sorry that any difference should arise between your Captain, who has the reputation of being one of the bright Officers of the Service, and yourself, a very young man, and a very young Officer, who must naturally have much to learn; therefore the chance is that you are perfectly wrong in the disagreement. However, as your present situation must be very disagreeable, I will certainly take an early opportunity of removing you, provided your conduct to your present Captain be such, that another may not refuse to receive you.'[43] When asked by an admiral to intercede on behalf of a young officer facing court martial for behaving badly to his captain, Nelson replied that if the officer in question wrote a very contrite letter acceptable to the captain, who then wrote to Nelson requesting cancellation of the order for the trial, he would accept it, but the letters and reprimand would still be published through the fleet. 'The young man has pushed himself forward to notice, and he must take the consequence. We must recollect, my dear Admiral, it was upon the Quarter-deck, in the face of the Ship's Company, that he treated his Captain with contempt; and I am in duty bound to support the authority and consequence of every Officer under my command. A poor ignorant Seaman is for ever punished for contempt to his superior.'[44]

He was not all sweetness and light and was very ready to tell his officers to watch their manners. On 30 March 1805 he wrote to Commissioner Otway at Gibraltar, 'I am very sorry that Captain – should have so far forgot himself, as to write you such an improper letter; but these young gentlemen sometimes think they have no superiors, and that their mandates are to be a law. I shall write him a public letter upon the subject, and you will receive also a public letter from me.'[45] He was also prepared to work the system to rid himself of bad apples. Captain Gore of the *Medusa* had problems with his gunner. 'With respect to Mr Ford, the Gunner, whom you represent as a worthless man and incapable of doing his duty, I have only to observe that if you can invalid him, I will appoint either the Gunner of *Halcyon* or *Sophie*, if you particularly desire it.'[46] The business of invaliding people, that is retiring them on medical grounds, was as notoriously difficult then as it is today. He knew it was 'too frequently done to get clear of bad and worthless characters',[47] but he was prepared to trust the judgement of a first-class officer like Gore. Invaliding was preferable in this case to court martial.

His officers soon realized that Nelson was eternally alert to value for money. At the end of December 1803 Captain William Parker would sense the all-seeing eye of his Commander-in-Chief when he received a communication: 'I have this moment received a set of vouchers for five live bullocks, 300 pounds of onions, and six bags of hay, procured for the Company of his Majesty's Ship, *Amazon*, under your command; and I must desire to acquaint you that the onions ought not to have been purchased without my particular orders for so doing; and I see no reason for the purchase of hay for bullocks which have been killed so immediately.'[48]

Captain Ryves of the *Gibraltar* was similarly challenged that 'between the 21st September 1803, and the 6th instant [May 1804] at Naples, there appears a charge of upwards of a hundred pounds sterling, for onions, cabbages, leeks and pumpkins, for the people during the said time . . . inform me with the reason of this very extraordinary charge'.[49] On the subject of clothing for his men he was as assiduous as any hard-up mother shopping for her children, and as demanding on the matter of quality and wearability. He thundered to the Admiralty about a batch of 'frocks and trowsers'. Instead of the good Russian duck they were used to, they were made of what he described as 'coarse wrapper-stuff', and more expensive than previously, twopence in the case of the frocks and thruppence in case of the trowsers. He sent a pair of each to the Board so that they could see for themselves, together with his decided opinion: 'the Contractor who furnished such stuff ought to be hanged; and little less, if anything, is due to those who have received them from him'.[50] Conversely, he wrote commending the latest issue of Guernsey jackets. Their general quality he thought 'most excellent', but 'they are considerably too narrow and short to be tucked in the Men's trowsers. It is, therefore, my opinion, that they ought to be three inches wider and six longer. Indeed if they were ten inches or a foot, it would be so much better, as they shrink very considerably in washing; and when the Seamen are on the yards, reefing or furling sails, the jacket rubs out of their trowsers, and exposes them to great dangers of taking cold in their loins. . . . Perhaps the Guernsey jacket, in its present state, might answer the largest of the boys.'[51] All of the shore-based naval storekeepers were kept constantly on their toes. Nathaniel Taylor at Malta was one of them. 'I herewith transmit you an account of the prices of cordage and other naval stores at Smyrna, and desire you will compare it with the prices paid for the like articles in the Adriatic, and send me your remarks thereupon.'[52]

In all of this Nelson was the apex of the triangle of command, absorbing data and information, monitoring and, as we have seen, taking a very personal interest in his priority areas. Yet he delegated sensibly and intelligently. The orders he sent to Captain Schomberg reflected his delegating style. His priorities were always made clear and explicit but, 'At this distance it is impossible for me to regulate every thing with exactness; therefore I can only repeat to you, Captain Cracraft and any other your Seniors, that it is my earnest desire to give every possible expedition in getting our Trade safe to and from the Adriatic and Levant, and affording Sir Alexander Ball and general Villettes Convoys for bullocks and corn. . . . We must all in our several stations exert ourselves to the utmost, and not be nonsensical in saying, "I have an order for this that or the other," if the King's service clearly marks what ought to be done. I am well convinced of your zeal.'[53] Within the scope of his imposed agenda he was always seeking to set his officers free to do their best. In this he was remarkably different from both Wellington and Napoleon, both of whom were chess players, their officers and men pieces.

He was never gratuitously offensive or arrogant. He was uniformly courteous, collaborative, free with praise and commendation and yet never less than clear about what he wanted. If you were Commissioner Otway at Gibraltar and Nelson said, 'You are so attentive to all our wants, that I am sure you will very soon procure canvas for us,'[54] it was very likely that you would. He quickly worked out who he could and could not trust. He wrote of a certain Mr Eaton, 'my opinion of him was formed some years ago; and from all I hear, I have no reason to alter it. He is, as Burke said of a noble Marquis, "a giant in promises, a pigmy in performances." '[55] As a peacekeeper and conciliator he was outstanding; he did not like disputes to be swept under the carpet to fester. He discovered that Captain Keats of the *Superb* and his Captain of the Fleet, Rear-Admiral Murray, were at loggerheads on the subject of hammocks. He wrote a 'Most Private' note to Keats:

> I felt most exceedingly last night, at finding your friend Admiral Murray so exceedingly hurt at some conversation which had passed between you and him about hammocks. I can solemnly assure you that far from Admiral Murray withholding any stores from the *Superb*, that he would stretch the point to comply with your wishes, well knowing that in our scanty supplies you would take no more than was absolutely necessary for present use. The *Superb* upon every consideration, whether I consider the value of her Captain as an Officer, or the importance of preserving her Ship's company . . . I have therefore desired that Admiral Murray will get from you an account of the number of hammocks wanted to complete the *Superb* for Channel Service, that I may send to Naples to purchase them; and I again assure you that Admiral Murray would stretch any length which you could desire, to meet your wants and wishes. The situation of First Captain is certainly a very unthankful Office, for if there is a deficiency of stores, he must displease, probably the whole Fleet; for no ship can have her demands complied with. I wish

my dear Keats, you would turn this in your mind, and relieve Admiral Murray from the uneasiness your conversation has given him; for I will venture to say, that if he could (or ought to) show a partiality, it would be to the *Superb*, because her Captain husbands the stores in a most exemplary manner. You will readily conceive what I must feel upon this occasion, being most truly your most obliged and faithful friend.[56]

Nothing could demonstrate more graphically the lengths to which Nelson would go to reinforce team spirit, his quickness in picking up signals and his unusual sensitivity in dealing with inter-personal problems, even if of an apparently trivial nature.

What is so striking about his performance of the managerial aspects of his command is his demonstation of an all-encompassing, all-round capacity. It extended from his firm grasp of priorities to his capacity to be flexible in the achievement of his aims, this management of individuals and sensitive situations, his capacity to apply himself where his influential intervention would be of most value and his infinite care and grasp of detail. He used this mastery of detail to spread his influence and personal example to all corners of the fleet. 'Keep a strict watch during the night, and have your guns loaded with grape,'[57] he told Captain Pettet. 'I would recommend you, in standing over to Toulon, not to keep more to the Northward than N.W. b N., as the wind at this season hangs very much to the North-West,'[58] he told Captain Parker. Above all there was his constant consciousness that his fleet was not a machine but a collection of human beings who needed to be encouraged, motivated, and kept on their toes. Always he had his fingers on the pulse of his fleet.

Two further aspects of his role absorbed an enormous amount of his time: protection of Britain's seaborne trade by convoys and extension of Britain's power and influence by diplomacy. 'If they find Trade, it is my business to find Convoy.'[59] He had to find means of defending trade routes at the entrance to the Mediterranean, between Malta and Sicily, up and down the Adriatic, taking in Trieste, Venice, Fiume, Patras and Zante, and along the Italian coast. Of course that did not prevent masters of merchantmen chancing their arm as 'Runners', as they were picturesquely called, without applying or waiting for convoy and sometimes paying the price: capture by privateer. Arranging convoys was not a pain-free operation. Ships had to be herded over long periods so that convoys could be formed. There would be allegations that Nelson favoured some merchants above others, and allegations of insufficient protection against privateers. The record shows the tremendous energy he devoted to the pursuit of his commercial responsibilities.

He was surrounded by diplomatic and political issues, which he handled with confidence and decision. He had developed his habit of corresponding directly with the Prime Minister, still Henry Addington. He was not above taking the odd swipe at those with whom he had to collaborate: 'General Villettes, although a most excellent Officer, will do nothing but what he receives, "You are hereby required and directed"; for to obey, is with him the very acme of discipline.'[60] Villettes had unfortunately disregarded Nelson's view that Neapolitan troops should not be returned to Messina. At times it is as though he thought he merely had to assert something for it to be true. Occasionally he strikes a note of grandiose disproportion. He began one of his reports to the Prime Minister on the occasion of the murder of Lord Kilwarden in Dublin,

I assure you, that I wish I only knew how I could serve my Country more effectually than in my present command. I attach no value to the high rank I at present hold, and if any, even the lowest situation is thought to be fittest for me in these times, I should feel prouder to be so placed than in any elevation of rank; all I ask is, to be allowed to be one of the men to be placed in the breach to defend my King and Country. I have but one arm, it is true, but believe my heart is in the right trim – therefore only consider how I can best be employed. But I trust, my dear Sir, that you know me, therefore I will not say more, for fear it should be suspected that I arrogate to myself more merit than, I believe, will be found in 999 of every 1000 in the United Kingdom. These lines have almost involuntarily flowed from my pen as they have done from my heart; pardon the effusion.[61]

Addington could not have been blamed for wondering whether his Commander-in-Chief had been over-indulging.

The Dey of Algiers's dismissal of Consul Falcon had landed back on Nelson's plate. He was well aware of the possibility of conflagration and confided in Villettes, 'Government at home should decide and not lay an Algerine War at my door; I shall be careful of beginning, but whatever on mature reflection shall be determined upon, shall be vigorously carried into execution.'[62]

It is frequently said that no man is a hero to his valet, and that might go for his chaplain and secretary too. The Reverend Alexander Scott's first impressions of Nelson were pronounced in a letter to a friend of 10 June 1803 when they had just sent Elliot on his way to Naples in the *Maidstone*, 'I think him one of the purist [*sic*] and most disinterested beings I ever yet met with – I speak of him thus without either praising him for his heroism or blaming him for what the idle mob does – but I think of him as having a mind free from envy, hatred and malice even of thinking evil of another of the most charitable nature, charity in its most comprehensive sense (not that of mere almsgiving by the by as the meanest part of it) which includes every good quality spiritualized. To finish with him I am convinced that he has abilities and judges the state of the parties in England and the relative politics in Europe with great discrimination.' He then goes on to comment on Nelson's shrewd world-liness and political graces in dealing with others. 'With all this he is acquainted with the World which notwithstanding his purity of mind is paradoxical and able to play a game at Politics with anyone. – What makes him able to do so is his honesty of mind the most refined way of doing anything nowadays and against which no rogue is upon his guard.'[63]

A few weeks later, his secretary, confusingly Mr John Scott, was writing to Emma. Given the identity of the recipient we must take this evidence carefully, but it nevertheless rings true: 'I have heard much of Lord Nelson's abilities as an officer and statesman, but the account of the latter is infinitely short. In my travels throughout the service I have met with no character equal in any degree to his Lordship; his penetration is quick, judgement clear, wisdom great, and his decisions correct and decided, nor does he in company appear to bear any weight on his mind, so cheerful and pleasant, that it is a happiness to be about his hand; in fact he is a great and wonderful character, and very glad and happy shall I be if, in the discharge of my duty, private and public, I have the good fortune to meet his Lordship's approbation.'[64] A few days earlier, when telling her about the state of Nelson's health he remarked, 'every one about him appears more anxious than another for his welfare'.[65]

Chaplain Scott in his *Recollections of Dr Scott* recalled an incident when a master's mate, who had jumped over the side to save a seaman, had been presented with his commission. This had caused the assembled midshipmen to cheer. 'Putting up his hand for silence, and leaning over to the crowd of Middies, he said with a good-natured smile on his face – "Stop, young Gentlemen! Mr Flin has done a gallant thing today, and he has done many gallant things before, for which he has got his reward. But mind you I'll have no more making Lieutenants for servants falling overboard".'[66] He had the knack of saying the right thing, at the right time, in the right way.

In parallel with this outer life, which could accurately be described as a miracle of management, his inner and intimate life continued, invisible to all. During his long and tediously slow journey from Plymouth to Toulon by way of Malta, Naples and Cape Corse, he had been writing to Emma, merely to say, 'Here I am and There I am', fearing that his letters would 'be read by every Post Office from Naples to London'. Once off Toulon his letters could go by sea, which would make them more secure if less frequent. Return to Capri had been enchanting in its evocations. 'Close to Capri the view of Vesuvius calls so many circumstances to my mind, that it almost overpowers my feelings.'[67] Both had been hoping for a generous response to his thinly disguised begging letter to the Queen. Nelson had played it for all it was worth: 'You will be sorry to hear that good Sir William did not leave her in such comfortable circumstances as his fortune would have allowed. He has given it amongst his relations.' The Queen's reply had not so much as mentioned Emma. 'I trust, my dear Emma, she has wrote to you. If she can forget Emma I hope God will forget her.'[68] As usual Emma was spending money she did not have. He, as ever, was entirely indulgent, 'whilst I have sixpence, you shall not want for fivepence of it! . . . I hope the Minister has done something for you. [Before he left England both he and Emma had sought Lord Melville's help to intercede with Addington to obtain financial recognition for Emma.] But never mind we can live upon bread and cheese. Independence is a blessing; and although I have not yet found out the way to get Prize money – what has been taken has run into our mouths – however, it must turn out very hard if I cannot get enough to pay off my debts, and that will be no small comfort.'[69]

He did not allow these personal circumstances to conflict with his professional duty. He needed to keep on good terms with his banker and agent friend Davison, who had just opened a banking house (Davison, Noel, Templer, Middleton, Johnson & Wedgewood at 34 Pall Mall) and to whom he felt very indebted. He would have liked to have been able to deposit £50,000, but as he said, 'My name shall stand in it if only for £10.' He would have liked Davison to be the agent for all the prizes the *Victory* might take but that was not in his gift. If they took a French fleet he might have the chance to nominate the agent but in that case he had also to think of the position of his secretary, Mr Scott. They might be able to share the agency money, 2 per cent to Scott for doing the business in the Mediterranean and 3 per cent to Davison for managing the distribution of the proceeds. Generally speaking he was not able to decide how the captures made by others in his fleet should be handled. 'They are all nearly strangers to me, and have their own friends and connexions.'[70] He was being straight with Davison.

On the arrival of the *Victory* on 30 July, Nelson shifted back into her, taking Hardy as his flag captain and saying goodbye to Sutton who transferred to the *Amphion*. In the *Victory* Nelson and Secretary Scott continued their private *Amphion* ritual, raising their glasses to a portrait of Emma, 'drinking a bumper to the health of the original, as our Guardian Angel'.[71] A first letter from Emma brought her very near. 'You will readily conceive my dear Emma, the sensations which the sight and reading even your few lines [occasioned]. They cannot be understood, but by those of such mutual and truly sincere attachment as yours and mine. Although you said little, I understood a great deal, and most heartily approve of your plans and society for next winter: and next spring I hope to be rich enough to begin the alterations at dear Merton. It will serve to amuse you; and I am sure, that I shall admire all your alterations, even to planting a gooseberry bush.'[72] On 26 August he received a further batch of letters dating from 20 May to 3 July. He was now seemingly master of his jealousy, keeping himself cool and unprovoked:

All your letters, my dear dear letters, are so entertaining! and which paint so dearly what you are after, that they give me either the greatest pleasure or pain. It is the next best thing to being with you. I only desire, my dearest Emma, that you will always believe, that Nelson's your own; Nelson's Alpha and Omega is Emma! I cannot alter; my affection and love is beyond even this world! Nothing can shake it, but yourself; and that I will not allow myself to think, for a moment, is possible. I feel that you are the real friend of my bosom, and dearer to me than life; and that I am the same to you. But I will neither have P's [Princes] nor Q's [Queensburys] come near you! no; not the slice of Single Gloucester! But if I was to go on, it would argue that want of confidence which would be injurious to your honour.

Her mention of a trip to Norfolk invokes his hope 'one day to carry you there by a nearer tie in law, but not in love and affection, than at present'. He rambles happily about plans for Merton, with the lightest touch on the need for a plan and for economy; William Bolton's prospects; the prospects of others of his followers and individuals recommended to him; his servants Chevalier and Gaetano (whom he had allowed ashore at Naples to visit his wife and family); Dr Scott his chaplain and interpreter and Mr Scott his secretary, 'a very excellent good man', who was grateful for news from Emma of his wife's having given birth. He talks of help that he would give to the education of his sister, Mrs Bolton's son; and his hope that Addington would grant Emma £500 a year: 'But your purse, my dear Emma, will always be empty; your heart is generous beyond your means.' He himself was just the same. There was wine on its way for Davison and William. 'Send it entirely free, even to the carriage. You know doing the thing well, is twice doing it; for sometimes carriage is more thought of than prime cost.'[73] His entirely practical view had somehow become entangled with a mistily remembered Latin tag: 'He gives twice who gives soon.'

He did not mention that he had been been corresponding about Bronte with Abraham Gibbs, a banker and former friend of their Palermo days. He had reached a decision. He would not spend another sixpence on Bronte; he now wanted it to show a return either in the form of a lump sum for handing it back, or if that was impossible, he wished Gibbs to appoint an agent to receive the full rentals regularly and remit them to London. In his first flush of enthusiasm as a duke and landowner he had allocated the first two years' rents for improvements and fitting up a house. Now that Sir William was dead and he had his house at Merton he had no need for a bolt hole at Bronte, nor for the additional drain on his resources. Underlying these practicalities was the disillusion he felt as a result of Queen Maria Carolina's royal amnesia over Emma, now that she had no direct use for her. It was at this point that he made his

famous remark to Gibbs about 'Sicilifying his conscience'.[74] His investment, his Sicilifying his conscience, had not paid off; it was time to write
it off.

Winter was now approaching, the Algerine Cruisers were putting into
port, the French sail-of-the-line, frigates and corvettes popped out from
time to time to exercise themselves but looked like settling down for the
winter. Nelson himself, blown well off station by the winds, had to be
careful: 'I must not in our present state, quarrel with the North Westers
– with crazy masts and no Port or spars near us. Indeed in the whole
station there is not a topmast for a Seventy-four.'[75] The mistral continued to blow three days out of seven – 'I am – don't laugh – dreadfully
sea sick this day' – but he was in a confident and upbeat mood when he
wrote to Davison on 4 October. 'I am truly sensible of your good wishes
for my prosperity. I believe I attend more to the French Fleet than making
captures. . . . This thought is better than Prize-money; – not that I despise
money – quite the contrary, I wish I had one hundred thousand pounds
this moment, and I will do everything consistent with my good name to
obtain it.'[76] On 6 October he was confident the French would soon be
out and told Addington so. 'Till the Battle is over I hope to write to you
no more; whether I survive it or not, my name shall never bring a blush
on the cheeks of my friends.'[77]

Emma, in her restless way, had been agitating to join him in the
Mediterranean. 'My dearest beloved Emma . . . I see so many obstacles
in the way of what would give us both such supreme felicity, that good
sence is obliged to give way to what is right . . . I am more likely to be
happy with you at Merton than any other place, and that our meeting
at Merton is more probable to happen sooner than any wild chase into
the Mediterranean.' He went on in a way that would have been inconceivable in a letter to Fanny, 'I am forever, with all my might, with all
my strength, yours only yours. My soul is God's let him dispose of it as
it seemeth fit to his infinite wisdom, my body is Emma's.'[78]

His letters to Addington were bearing fruit; they had been influential.
A letter from Lord Hobart indicated that the Admiralty would order him
to blockade Genoa and Spezia, as he had recommended. His policy on
Naples was approved and Lord Hawkesbury would be writing to him.
Furthermore the government was taking a jaundiced view of Algerine
hostility towards Maltese vessels and he was authorized to demand the
freeing of all captured Maltese and take a strong line. He was being very

positively supported by the government, not least because he was bypassing the Admiralty filter and always couching his missives to leave no doubt as to where he himself stood. He was never a man to delegate upwards by weakly seeking instructions. He was particularly pleased to hear that Elliot would be told by Whitehall to keep him informed.

His personal feelings about Elliot were generally equivocal and when the wind blew and action lacked, he was inclined to take it out on him. In September he wrote slightingly to Ball of Elliot's pay and perks, 'Your advice to Mr Elliot will be good, and I think he will attend to it; but Diplomatic men think of course, they know much better than any one else, and Mr E. is the oldest Minister we have. He got a better appointment than any Minister ever sent to Naples: he got £3,000 for plate money, and £4,500 a-year, being little [less than] Ambassador's pay – no bad hit, Mr Elliot.'[79] In October it was his judgement he questioned. 'Mr Elliot, I find, thinks Sicily quite safe, and Naples almost fit to bid defiance to all Buonaparte. I laugh at what I read. I know them well and so do you.'[80] When Elliot unfortunately suggested that Nelson employ French royalists he earned a direct rebuke: 'I would not, upon any consideration, have a Frenchman in the Fleet, except as a prisoner. I put no confidence in them. You think yours good: the Queen thinks hers the same: I believe they are all alike. Whatever information you get me I shall be thankful for; but not a Frenchman comes here. Forgive me; but my mother hated the French.'[81] This bizarre statement suddenly reveals the power of his mother's influence as the original source of his own hatred for the French.

In mid-October he had a tremendous scare. Gales and wind were incessant: 'you know I am never well in bad weather . . . I am at this moment confoundedly out of humour. A Vessel has been spoke that says she has seen a Fleet six days ago off Minorca; and it is so thick that we cannot get a look into Toulon, and blowing at this moment a Levanter. Imagine my feelings.'[82] The weather was 'thick as butter-milk'. He was 'in a fever of the mind'. He opened up his feelings to the Duke of Clarence: 'I cannot bring my mind to believe they are actually out; but to miss them-God forbid! . . . If I should miss these fellows my heart will break; I am actually only now recovering the shock of missing them in 1798, when they were going to Egypt. If I miss them I will give up the cudgels to a more fortunate Commander; God knows I only serve to fight these scoundrels; and if I cannot do that, I should be better on shore.' However, the next day *Seahorse* brought him news that the French were still snug in Toulon. 'I believe this was the only time in my life, that I was glad to hear the French were in Port.'[83]

Almost as soon as that scare was over his focus had again to switch, to North Africa. The Pasha of Tripoli, a friend of England, had made an indirect application for gunpowder and grapeshot. Tripoli was currently at war with the United States and Nelson was not inclined to help, balancing the Pasha's entitlement to kind treatment against the risk of upsetting the Americans. The Falcon affair was again on his mind and he was becoming increasingly aware of the ambiguities surrounding Falcon's conduct. He had also teased away at obtaining clear information about seizures of Maltese vessels and was not satisfied by the sketchy information he had received from Ball; he wanted chapter and verse. He was proceeding circumspectly and judiciously. If he proved the case he told Hobart he would hit the Dey hard. 'I shall if possible not resort to actual hostilities, until I can strike a blow, the same day, on all his vessels, from one end of the Mediterranean to the other.'[84]

It was not just the French or the Dey of Algiers who could put Nelson in a fever. He had just received another batch of Emma's letters, no doubt in that careless and provoking style which had produced so much pain for him in the Baltic. What she said produced a stream of outrage in him, 'Mrs D—— is a damned pimping bitch! What has she to do with your love? She would have pimped for Lord B——, or Lord L——, or Captain Mc N——, —— of —— or anybody else. She is all vanity; fancies herself beautiful; witty; in short, like you. She be damned!' Emma provoked another set of savage comments about their financial expectations. 'There will be no Lord Bristol's table. He tore his last will, a few hours before his death . . . I wish he may have given Mrs Dennis anything; but I do not think it: and, as for you my dear Emma, as long as I can, I don't want any of their gifts. As for old Q. he may put you into his will, or scratch you out, as he pleases. I care not. If Mr Addington gives you the pension, it is well; but do not let it fret you. Have you not Merton? . . . . one of these days you will be my own Duchess of Bronte; and then, a fig for them all.'

He had also to deal again with wild suggestions that Emma, possibly with Charlotte and Horatia, should join him in *Victory*, or at Malta, or in Sicily. She got a flat refusal: 'It would kill you; and myself to see you. Much less possible, to have Charlotte, Horatia, etc., on board ship! And

I, that have given orders to carry no women to sea in the *Victory*, to be the first to break them! . . . if you was at Malta, I might absolutely miss you, by leaving the Mediterrranean without warning. . . . As for living in Italy, that is entirely out of the question. Nobody cares for us there; and, if I had Bronte – which thank God I shall not – it would cost me a fortune to go there, and be tormented out of my life. I should never settle my affairs there.' Emma's reference to Horatia had resonated. 'Aye! she is like her mother; will have her own way, or kick up a devil of a dust. But you will cure her; I am afraid I should spoil her; for I am sure I would shoot any one who would hurt her.' Now he had to deal with Emma as though she were indeed still a child:

> I know, my own dear Emma, if she will let her reason have fair play, will say I am right; but she is, like Horatia, very angry if she cannot have her own way. Here Nelson is called upon, in the most hon-ourable manner, to defend his country! Absence to us is equally painful; but if I had either stayed at home, or neglected my duty abroad, would not my Emma have blushed for me? She could never have heard of my praises, and how the country looks up. I am writing, my dear Emma, to reason the point with you; and, I am sure, you will see it in its true light. But I have said my say on this subject, and will finish.

His strain of dissatisfaction and irritation continued; he referred to 'Mr Elliot, who knows more of Naples than any of us; God help him!. . . . Our friend, Sir Alexander, is a very great diplomatic character; and even an Admiral must not know what he is negotiating about . . . I hate such parade of nonsense . . . somehow my mind was not sharp enough for prize-money – Lord Keith would have made twenty thousand pounds, and I have not made six thousand.'[85] Perhaps these were the inevitable private reactions of a man who tried to be agreeable to those he met during the day. When alone he was forced to find an equivalent to kicking the cat.

Three days later he wrote direct to little Horatia. He could hardly have expected a two-year-old to read let alone understand his letter. But he was anxious to have it on record that he was Horatia's father. 'Receive this first letter from your affectionate father,' was unequivocal. So was, 'I have left Lady H your guardian. I therefore charge you my Child, on the value of a Father's blessing, to be obedient and attentive to all her kind admonitions and instructions.'[86] He told her he had left her £4,000 in his will, the interest to go to Lady Hamilton for Horatia's maintenance and education. The will itself described Horatia differently, as his adopted daughter. It went on, 'This request of guardianship I earnestly make to Lady Hamilton, knowing that she will educate my adopted child in the paths of religion and virtue, and give her those accomplishments which so much adorn herself, and I hope make her a fit wife for my dear nephew, Horatio Nelson [his brother William's son], who I wish to marry her, if he should prove worthy, in Lady Hamilton's estimation, of such a treasure as I am sure she will be.'[87]

Then he would be back on deck, once more the Admiral, perhaps on this occasion ordering a reduction in the setting of the sails as the wind freshened, or taking charge of some other aspect of the ship's management, a rather irritating aspect of his behaviour since ship management was not his responsibility but that of *Victory's* captain. Hardy, a self-contained imperturbable man and in all respects a stickler for doing things properly never demurred, and when Nelson once asked him, 'How is it that you and I never disagree, for my other captains Berry etc, never let me do a thing I wanted without at first resisting?' Hardy had replied, 'It is sir from my always being first Lieutenant when you like to be captain, and Flag captain when you have a fancy for being Admiral.'[88]

25

Waiting

*I have had a good race of glory, but we are never satisfied, although
I hope I am duly thankful for the past; but one cannot help, being at
sea, longing for a little more.*

Nelson, September 1804

The winter weather which had caused him to position himself under
Cape San Sebastian, rather than face the full blast of the mistral in
the Gulf of Lions; the weight of responsibility, his constant expenditure
of mental and physical energy, frequent seasickness, the battering his
ships were taking and their slow but palpable decay, were all bearing
down on Nelson and his interior mood. Private letters were his only
therapy. He wrote to Davison, 'But my time of service here is nearly over.
A natural anxiety must attend my station; but my dear friend, my eyesight fails me most dreadfully. I firmly believe that in a very few years, I
shall be stone blind. It is this only, of all my maladies, that makes me
unhappy; but God's will be done. If I am successful against the French,
I shall ask my retreat; and if I am not, I hope I shall never live to see it.'[1]
A few days later, writing to his brother William he conveyed an even
deeper sense of physical and mental dissolution: 'The mind and body
both wear out.' He was working himself into a confused and belligerent
mood about what might or might not be done for him in case of his
living or dying in the event of a battle. If he died, he told William,
'you will get an early seat in the House of Lords', and continued, 'If Mr
Addington does not give me the same Pension as Government gave to
the rich Lord St Vincent and Duncan, I shall consider no great favour
done me, and the Country never could avoid giving the Pension to you:
therefore unless the other [peerage] is tacked to it, I would not give
thanks or sixpence to have it [notice of the battle?] brought before
Parliament to benefit Lord St Vincent's heirs, and certainly, from
circumstances, not mine.'[2] Whatever the obscurities of this passage, his
expectation is clear: he and his family will be done down.

The New Year 1804 opened with Nelson reaching a conclusion about the Dey of Algiers. He dispatched Keats in the *Superb* to return Falcon, with a demand for his reinstatement and a further demand for restitution and compensation for Maltese and Neapolitan vessels captured by Algerine Cruisers while bearing British passports. He gave Keats a memorandum on his negotiating position and tactics. If the Dey tried to turn the discussion to any complaints of his own, 'you are never to reply, but always to answer by telling him that you were come for reparation of an insult, and not to attend to his complaints, which he had sent to England and settled'. If the Dey conceded only part of his demands and tried to get Keats to accept that they were now at peace Keats was equipped with his sticking points and fallback position: 'Never appear satisfied with what has been granted, but demand what has not; and leave the question of Peace or War entirely open, so that it may hang over his head.'[3] His mind was sharp again: the framework Nelson prepared for the mission was impeccable in its precise illumination of negotiating limits, and in preparing Keats for the wily Dey.

Keats bore away and the same day, 9 January 1804, brought Nelson a cornucopia of nine letters from Emma. Yet again they caused sensations of jealousy and fear. Emma had apparently been tricked by a hostess Nelson referred to as 'Lady Bitch' into visiting a house where the Prince of Wales had been present. His response syndrome played itself out on paper: jealous emotion preceded their need to have confidence in each other, and was followed by an account of his own behaviour as a model for Emma: 'It is not all the world that could seduce me, in thought word or deed, from all my soul holds most dear. Indeed if I can help it, I never intend to go out of the ship, but to the shore of Portsmouth.' He finds himself having to be defensive and ingratiating. 'If my dear Emma, you are to mind all the reports you may hear, you may always be angry with your Nelson.' He jumped at the thought that she intended to move out of London. 'This spring if you like the house altered you can do it . . . all I request, if you fix to have it done . . . Mr Davison's architect . . . must take care that it does not exceed the estimate. . . . If it is done by contract, you must not alter; or a bill is run up, much worse than if we never contracted.'[4]

Fortunately, mid-January also brought a letter from Davison. The Court of King's Bench had found for Nelson in his lawsuit with Lord St Vincent and awarded him entitlement to the Admiral's share, amounting to £13,000 of the prizes taken by Lord Digby in October 1799. 'This event will put me out of debt, and I hope to build my room at Merton, and leave my income, whatever it may be, unclogged.'[5] His spirits temporarily lifted, he shot over to the North African coast to see if Keats needed assistance in his mission. He soon learned that the Dey was not prepared to meet his demands. Nelson informed Lord Hobart that Keats's conference with the Dey was, 'rage and violence on the part of the Dey and firmness on the part of Captain Keats.'[6] He therefore decided that from 28 April every ship under his command would be ordered to take, sink, burn and destroy every Algerine they encountered and the ports of Algiers would be blockaded. In providing for a delay before he took action he was shrewdly allowing leeway for Lord Hobart to change his mind.

Nelson had returned to Cape St Sebastian. His winter of misery continued: 'from the 26th of January, we have not been twenty four hours without a gale'.[7] He was very worried that a French invasion of Sardinia would rob him of his excellent anchorage and watering point in the Maddalena Islands. He wanted to get some troops ashore to keep them under his power. 'We may prevent: we cannot retake.'[8] It was feared that the enemy squadrons at Brest and Ferrol would sail to join the Toulon fleet. There were 12,000 men ready for embarkation at Toulon and another 16,000 at Nice. He wrote to Captain Gore in *Medusa*, 'If they come up the Mediterranean and you have a mind for a shooting party, come with your frigates.'[9] On edge, under the weight of these multiple threats, he suffered from his recurrent feeling of neglect. He wrote to Dr Moseley, 'We seem forgotten by the great folks at home . . . I must not be sick until after the French Fleet is taken. Then I will hope to take you by the hand, and have further recourse to your skill for my eye.'[10]

It was not only potential enemy movements that had put him on edge. Emma, now thirty-eight, had made him a father for a second time. He wrote on 25 February, 'I am anxious in the extreme to hear that you are perfectly recovered from your late indisposition.'[11] He was deeply worried to hear that Horatia was also ill. 'Kiss dear Horatia for me, and the other. Call him what you please, if a girl Emma.'[12] On 14 March, 'All I long for, just now is to hear that you are perfectly recovered; and then, I care for nothing: all my hopes are, to see you, and be happy, at dear Merton again.'[13] On the 19th, 'I have been very restless my dearest

Emma, for these several days and nights, and shall not be better till I hear you are quite recovered.' He was suffering from what he described as, 'A kind of rheumatick fever in my head'.[14] Two months later it was this he probably described at length in the course of a letter to Dr Baird: 'I have had a sort of rheumatic fever, they tell me; but I have felt the blood gushing up the left side of my head, and the moment it covers the brain I am fast asleep: I am now better of that; and with violent pain in my side, and night sweats, with heat in the evening, and quite flushed. The pain in my head, nor spasms, I have not had for some time.'[15] Again there is evidence of an anxiety state. The sensation of blood rushing and heart beating is a common symptom, and common experience is that it goes away. But he may also have had a urinary tract infection or a transient incarcerated hernia relating to the blow he received at the battle of St Vincent. As ever, he was not incapacitated.

Money was also on his mind. There were the projected improvements at Merton to be decided on. Additional rooms and a new entrance were his priorities. For the time being they could make do with a barn to house their coach. They could also make do with a temporary lodge, and a common white gate. Top of all priorities was a three-foot barrier of netting to be placed the length of the Nile (Nelson's name for the ornamental canal running through the grounds), 'that the little thing may not tumble in . . . I shall be very anxious until I know this is done'. There was no possibility of these costs being met from income and he wanted Emma to make sure that they were aggregated into a separate fund so that he could arrange the financing. He wanted to be generous to his dead brother's blind widow and settle her debts. He wanted to help with his nephews' education, both Tom Bolton and William's son Horace Nelson. He had already told Emma that he had willed her part of the income from Bronte, 'whether Mr Addington gives you anything, or not, you will want it', and he wanted to settle £4,000 in trustees' hands for Horatia: 'she shall be independent of any smiles or frowns'.[16]

Nelson was a naturally generous man, a great present-giver who loved to play the universal benefactor. But just as his restraint in language had given way under the influence of Emma's outrageously thoughtless style, there was now no sensible woman in his life to put a brake on his generosity. It was a hopelessly spendthrift man who wrote to a woman who could spend money like a drunken sailor, 'I must make my arrangements so as not to run in debt.' His arrangements were inevitably with his friend Davison. He wrote to him on 18 March 1804, 'I have not only personal obligations to you out of number, but also a load of pecuniary debt. This latter I must manage and pay off; therefore I beg that you will let me know how the account stands. . . . At all events I must try and get out of your debt for money. There is not one farthing of Prize-money stirring here.'[17]

His mental maelstrom was eased on 2 April when another clutch of letters from Emma produced one undated which, 'thank God, told my poor heart, that you was recovering, but that dear little Emma was no more! and that Horatia had been so ill – it altogether upset me. But it was just at bedtime; and I had time to reflect, and be thankful to God for sparing you and our dear Horatia. I am sure, the loss of one – much more, both – would have drove me mad. I was so agitated, as it was, that I was glad it was night, and that I could be by myself.'[18]

And so this dual interior/exterior life continued. His captains saw evidence only of his ceaselessly active brain. 'As it is my determination to attack the French Fleet in any place where there is a reasonable prospect of getting alongside them,' he recommended that they arm themselves with information about a range of anchorages from Hyères Bay to the Gulf of Ajaccio where such an encounter might take place, and sent them a chart he possessed of Gourjean Bay. He made recommendations about having anchors ready to let go. 'The Ships will anchor in such a manner as to give each other mutual support for the destruction of the enemy.'[19]

It was not long before he was again in a bad way with himself, driven to respond to Emma's gossip, accounts of her conquests and wishes for more money with the terse and disjointed observations of an unrelaxed mind. 'Old mother L—— is a damned bitch; but I do not understand what you mean, or what plan. I am not surprised at my friend Kingsmill admiring you, and forgetting Mary; he loves variety and handsome women. You touch upon the old Duke; but I am dull of comprehension; believing you all my own. I cannot imagine any one else to offer, in any way. We have enough, with prudence; and without it, we should soon be beggars, if we had five times as much.'[20] He was a man who could be easily tortured by the careless outpourings of his lover. Yet one must also try to empathize with Emma, and sympathize with her needs for attention and support, having again to give birth in secret far from her lover. She was in a truly unenviable position.

Nelson felt his opponent Admiral Latouche Tréville was playing a game with him too. On 4 June, having left the remainder of his fleet with Bickerton some sixty miles out of sight, he himself took five sail-of-the-line off Cape Sicie to play cat and mouse. Latouche Tréville came out with five sail-of-the-line and two frigates, keeping three others with their yards raised, evidently ready for sea. Nelson formed up his ships to receive an attack, but as he told Acton on the 18th, it was 'merely a gasconade'. The next day Latouche sent out a frigate. Nelson wanted to see eight out and far enough out for him to attack. He hoped 'to shame Latouche out of his nest . . . my first object must ever be to keep the French Fleet in check; and if they put to sea, to have force enough with me to annihilate them.'[21] In August 1804 his thoughts about Latouche became positively murderous when a letter by him was published. In it he alleged that given the presence of several British ships which seemed about to cut off the retreat of his own two frigates, he had taken his whole squadron out of Toulon, upon which, 'l'Amiral Anglais ne tarda pas à renoncer à son projet, rappela son vaisseau et ses deux frégates engagés dans les îles et prit chasse. Je l'ai poursuivi jusqu'à la nuit; il courait au sud est. Le matin, au jour je n'en eu aucunne connoissance.'[22] Writing to Davison about his conviction for bribery at the Ilchester election and his twelve months in the Marshalsea prison, and displaying a rather different perspective on financial skulduggery than he would in his fleet affairs ('"Directly or indirectly, every man has his price." So said Sir Robert Walpole. Never mind. Do not take it to heart') he made sure Davison had the right story about Latouche, 'I am expecting Monsieur La Touche (as he has wrote a letter that I ran away) to come out of his nest. The whole history was too contemptible for my notice . . . perhaps sovereign contempt is the best.'[23] Sovereign contempt did not prevent Nelson from sending Marsden at the Admiralty a full account of the incident and extracts from *Victory*'s log, copying it all to Ball. Such was the level of his concern for his reputation.

On 1 August their blockading life was momentarily enhanced by letters and new commissions for Nelson and his senior officers. On 28 April there had been a promotion of admirals, Nelson himself to Vice-Admiral of the White. There were now only four steps to the pinnacle of Admiral of the Fleet, but unfortunately a hundred or so vice-admirals and admirals of the Blue, White and Red above him. Equally important was the news that there was now a new Board of Admiralty to deal with. On 12 May Pitt had succeeded Addington as Prime Minister and Viscount Melville (Henry Dundas) had replaced St Vincent as First Lord. Troubridge was no longer on the Board. The very next day Nelson dashed off a letter to Melville on the subject of Copenhagen medals. This produced a clinching argument. Whatever might have passed between Nelson and St Vincent, it would be impossible to award medals at a time when the government was intent on healing the wounds between England and Denmark. Nelson had to be satisfied with that.

At sea, incessant gales and winds were still the order of the day. He had received news from Rear-Admiral Alexander Cochrane, commanding off Ferrol, that the French fleets at Brest, Rochefort and Ferrol were ready for sea. Knowing from his own experience that the French at Toulon were also ready for sea, Nelson concluded that an attempt was about to be made to push a superior force into the Mediterranean. Nelson so wanted to fight and annihilate the French that he was sure they would come in his direction. Little did he know that Bonaparte's complex and ever changing tactics were addressed to one end only: to provide sufficient French force in the Channel to enable an invasion of England.

This was a contest of constant waiting, 'the uniform sameness, day after day, and month after month – gales of wind for ever'.[24] In the middle of August he was telling Emma, 'I have had, for two days, fires in the cabin, to keep out the very damp air.'[25] In June he had told her, 'I have little to say – one day is so like another, and having long ago given you one day, there is no difference but the arrival of a letter or newspaper, the same faces and almost the same conversation.'[26] Against this he had by constant exertion of his will to create movement and mission for his subordinate officers, a constant alertness for change in his enemy's intentions, a constant psychological toughness towards the seemingly eternal bad weather that was slowly battering his ships to pieces. 'I have always made it a rule never to contend with the gales; and either run to the Southward to escape its violence, or furl all the sails and make the Ships as easy as possible.'[27] If, for a moment, he relaxed his hold or reduced the power of his own dynamo he would insidiously sap the momentum of his officers and men.

The weather had given them seventeen days of gale in July, so much that he believed the Mediterranean weather had changed. He had not been out of his ship since he left home and was reaching the conclusion that he could not hold out another winter, although he hoped desperately that La Touche would give him a battle before then. Nevertheless, early in August, Nelson took what was for him a dreadful step. He set about stage-managing his departure. He wrote to Secretaries Nepean and Marsden stressing the positive aspects of his command: 'No Command ever produced so much happiness to a Commander-in-Chief, whether in the Flag-Officers, the Captains, or the good conduct of the Crews of every Ship in the Fleet ... the constant marks of approbation for my conduct which I have received from every Court in the Mediterranean ... every person of all ranks and descriptions, seem only desirous to meet my wishes, and to give me satisfaction.'[28] He wrote in the same vein to Lord Melville but pushing additionally the idea that he might be granted leave, the command being left pro tem with his second-in-command, Bickerton.

The die having been cast, he could not prevent himself from speculating who might actually succeed him. For the moment he was strangely detached about giving up a life's ambition, for he also wrote to Davison on 9 August, 'I expect that the Admiralty will give this Command to some other Officer, and not allow of my return, if I am able, in the Spring. But I must say, as the famous De Witt said, "my life I will freely risk for my Country, but my health I must take care of." '[29] He told Elliot, 'I may very possibly be laid upon the shelf',[30] and lobbied him to get the King of Naples to ask for his return. That worked; Elliot subsequently told him they intended to ask for his return and indeed offered Naples or Palermo as locations for rest and recuperation. Nelson was not seduced. Naples and Sicily no longer had charms for him. He was banking on Bickerton being left in command. To General Villettes he expressed more of his feelings. Talking about where the French might go if they escaped his blockade he said he was prepared to follow them to the West Indies if necessary, 'but I fear this is reserved for some happier man. Not that I can complain; I have had a good race of glory, but we are never satisfied, although I hope I am duly thankful for the past; but one cannot help, being at sea, longing for a little more.'[31] This elegiac note suggests a strong but possibly waning addiction, perhaps brought on by the sudden death of his immediate opponent, La Touche. Although growing convinced of a French attack on the West Indies, his usual certainty seemed to have deserted him. 'I may be wrong. It is at best but a guess, and the world attaches wisdom to him that guesses right.'[32]

His thoughts were not all on the French. In August he had learned that Horatia had just been inoculated against smallpox. 'My beloved, how I feel for your situation and that of our dear Horatia, our dear child . . . I wish I had all the smallpox for her, but I know the fever is the natural consequence. I dreamt last night I heard her call papa, and point to her arm just as you described. Give Mrs Gibson a guinea for me and I will repay you. Dear wife, good adorable friend, how I love you and what would I not give to be with you this moment.'[33] No father could have felt himself closer to his daughter, nor more concerned about her upbringing. Later the same day he is talking again of Horatia, now two and a half, 'She is become an age when it is necessary to remove her from a mere nurse and to think of educating her. . . . My earnest wish is that you would take her to Merton . . . at Merton she will imbibe nothing but virtue, goodness, and elegance of manners, with a good education to fit her to move in that sphere of life she is destined to move in . . . I am most anxious for the child's being placed under your protecting wing.'[34] His birthday, 29 September, came and went. 'Forty six years of toil and trouble! How few more the common lot of mankind leads us to expect; and therefore it is almost time to think of spending the last few years in peace and quietness!' He was mellowing, thinking of other things. 'Kiss dear Horatia. I hope she is at Merton, fixed.' He felt a kind of satisfied regret at leaving the fleet: 'Indeed we all draw so well together in the Fleet, that I flatter myself the sorrow for my departure will be pretty general.'[35]

By mid-October a rather shocking thought had entered his head: the possibility that Lord Keith would be the man to replace him. He began to show Emma the first signs of being torn: 'I should, for your sake, and for many of our friends, have liked an odd hundred thousand pounds; but never mind. If they give me the choice of staying a few months longer, it will be very handsome; and for the sake of others, we would give up, my dear Emma, very much of our own felicity. If they do not, we shall be happy with each other, and with dear Horatia.'[36] In a letter to Ball he had a different list of contenders for his job. 'Sir John Orde I am told is likely. Lord Radstock is trying; so is Sir Roger Curtis: and if a Spanish War comes, Lord Keith loves a little money, and a great deal much better.'[37] Nelson, for all his love of glory, might well have been envious of Keith's undoubted capacity to make money, which had to date enabled him to finance two Scottish estates.

Dr Lambton Este, private secretary and physician to Charles Lock (previously Consul at Naples and now dead) in his mission as Consul-General to Egypt and the Levant had been on board the *Victory* for some months awaiting a passage home. He made notes of his observations of Nelson's behaviour, which he provided for Nicolas. Being a doctor he heard all about Nelson's current state of health. 'He complained of frequent pains in his right side, from former injuries, – that many warnings and inabilities made him conscious of his shattered frame, and anxious for repose.' He noted the deterioration in Nelson's good eye. Apparently accepted by Nelson into his inner circle, Este was able to hear him thinking aloud about his future: 'His thoughts, his ambition, evidently tended to the Admiralty – to the management of the Naval Service of his Country. In his cabin, with his confidential friends, he occasionally alluded to what he would do if he were in power.'

This is the first mention anywhere of Nelson's thinking about his future in this way, of moving off the fighting stage towards directing from the shore. Previously he had not appeared to be at all envious when Troubridge had joined the Board, but now he was evidently imagining himself as First Lord of the Admiralty. Surrounded by all his known and trusted friends, he chaffed Dr Scott in his flattering way, 'Ah, my dear Doctor! give me knowledge practically acquired – experience! experience! experience! and practical men!' St Vincent's judgement had been that Nelson could never be fit to do his job, but here was Nelson getting it in his sights and musing on how he would do it.

Este had naturally formed the view that Nelson was determined to go home, because he had told Este that he wanted him to remain in *Victory* and return with him. Some two months later, on 1 November, Nelson sent for him and announced after breakfast, 'Oh my good fellow! I have abandoned the idea of going to England at present. I shall not go yet and when I may go is quite uncertain – must depend upon events, and upon my own precarious health.'[38] What had changed? His health was no better. War with Spain seemed imminent, but it had seemed so for some time. He had not yet received permission to return from the Admiralty. But Gore and his captains were out looking for Spanish treasure ships and he meant to give them more time to make him a rich man. Perhaps he had also realized that, lacking a political power base, he was unlikely to find the position of First Lord of the Admiralty thrust upon him. Perhaps too he was feeling that it was more likely that Orde or Keith, both senior to himself, would supersede him rather than Bickerton being left to keep his place warm. Whatever the cause, the underlying emotions provoked a disconcerting change in his usual friendly attitude. When Este gallantly demurred, saying, 'My Lord if I could be of further use, I should prefer remaining in uncertainty with your Lordship, to—' he was cut short: 'But my wish is that you should go, – I am anxious that you should go, and without further delay.' According to Este his manner was short, sharp and emphatic. 'Uneasy and embarrassed', Este was reduced in a moment from being someone fit to share the Commander-in-Chief's confidences to a mere cipher. He felt he had put his foot in it and after an awkward pause replied, 'My Lord I am ready to start at this moment's notice.' Nelson recovered his poise and countered, 'Oh not quite so soon as that! I shall want a day or two at least to prepare for you; but the point is settled, and being settled we shall both know what to be at; I shall set to work accordingly, and forthwith.' He went on to flatter Este, 'Should I retain my command in the Mediterranean, with the powers already conceded to me, I shall demand your re-appointment, and require your assistance in Italy, Naples, Sicily, and in the Islands, and perhaps in your former scenes of action to the Eastward.... If in the course of events, I should return to England and realize my anticipations, you must let me see you at Merton as soon as you know of my arrival there.' Did Nelson see before him another Drinkwater to press his claims for the Admiralty? What otherwise could he have meant by the phrase, 'my anticipations'?

It was settled that Este would return as far as Lisbon with Captain Pettet in the sloop *Termagant*, carrying with him the dispatches, letters and papers Nelson had intended taking himself. Este also retailed how, on hearing from Ball that he was to join Nelson in the fleet off Toulon, he assumed they would welcome additions to their table and assembled from his aborted mission's stores 108 dozen bottles of the finest English beer, tongues, Bayonne hams and some India pickle, all of which Nelson had seemed to receive with less than enthusiasm. '"What's all this lumber? What the devil have you got here?" Este said he seemed hurt at the explanation, "Only a little ammunition for the Fleet my Lord."' Nelson ordered Gaetano his servant to stow the goods and look after them carefully but as the weeks passed, none of Este's offerings appeared either in the Admiral's cabin or in the wardroom. However, when Este was onboard *Termagant*, whose captain, Pettet, Nelson had previously described as 'risen from humble origin by his own merits, with a little of my assistance', Este received a note from Nelson, which he recalled as being along the following lines:

> I have tasted and reserved some of your princely and delicious presents. Had we returned together in the *Superb*, these should have afforded consolation to all onboard that ship on our homeward voyage. As our destinies are altered, I have taken the liberty of sending them to Captain Pettet, to whom they will prove highly acceptable; and before you have been long onboard, I trust you will think with me, that they could not have been more worthily bestowed. I have added a few bottles of fine Marsala, lately sent me by Woodhouse from Sicily, that you may have the pleasure of drinking my health in my absence.'[39]

Nelson was to be the fount of favours; no one else. Consciously or unconsciously, he seems also to have understood that in keeping people guessing he could add a pleasant piquancy to human relationships, as well as providing subject matter for gossip and anecdote.

On 8 November Nelson received news from Captain Gore that on 5 October off Cape St Mary's, near Cadiz, his two frigates, *Medusa* and *Amphion*, had met up with two of Admiral Cornwallis's frigates *Indefatigable* and *Lively*. Because of Spain's evident support for France, all were now under Admiralty orders to intercept and detain as a preemptive measure, a group of Spanish frigates bound for Cadiz laden with South American treasure and merchandise. This they tried to do but the Spanish Admiral, Don Joseph Bustamente, refusing to be detained by such an equal force, decided to resist. In the ensuing combat, *La Mercedes* blew up, taking down with her most of her crew and many women and children passengers. *La Medee*, *La Fama* and *La Clara*, were captured. Spain was still formally at peace with England but this incident encouraged a chain reaction, albeit of surprisingly slow pace. A Spanish decree of 27 November would order reprisals against British property but war would not be declared until 12 December.

Nelson wrote a 'Most Private' letter of congratulation to Gore: 'From

my heart do I congratulate you on your share of the capture of the
Spanish Frigates; but I own it is mixed with regret that you did not
command. However it is a good thing and I hope before this time you
have taken more of them. The Lima ships are loaded with gold.'[40]
On 20 October Captain Sam Sutton who had arrived in England with
Amphion was very explicit in writing to Emma, 'They are very valuable
having on board nearly one million sterling in specie. I hope it will turn
out a good thing for that great and good man Lord Nelson as well as
for myself.' He went on, 'Bolton told me his Lordship meant to leave the
fleet a few days afterwards in the *Superb* for England so that if this
Spanish business does not prevent him from quitting the command his
arrival may be shortly looked for.' He continued, 'Two of the frigates
present on this occasion belonged to Admiral Cornwallis, the other two
to Lord Nelson, so that it prevents any dispute as to right to share prize
money.'[41] Emma quickly circulated the news; the family were soon like
bees round a honey pot. Catherine Matcham talked of his coming home,
'rich with dollars'; Susannah Bolton, salivated, '30,000 L to my Lord's
share will be a pretty thing', and went on to hope for more, 'I think it
very likely that if he falls in with the *Medora* he may cruize a little off
Cadiz just to skim a little of the cream and bring you home a bushell of
dollars. I hope the golden ships will not slip through his fingers.'[42] Part
of this was playing up to Emma, who in her generous and thoughtless
present-giving way had been buying their love, to such an extent that
Susannah Bolton was driven to write, 'But indeed I do not like to receive
so many presents. Nothing can make me love you better, but so many
handsome things as you do for me and mine make me feel uncomfortable. Be assured I have now everything I want, and do not send me more.
I shall be afraid you think me a mercenary wretch who has a price, but
surely you have a poor opinion of yourself and me.'[43]

In the event there was to be no prize money as such. War not having
been declared, the ships and treasure were a droit of the Crown and
so 'A grant was made to the captors which according to one account
amounted to quarter of a million sterling.'[44] One-eighth of this shared
by the commanders-in-chief the flag officers on both Nelson's and
Cornwallis's stations would have been £31,250.

In spite of his encounter with Este, Nelson was still maintaining that
he wanted to go home, confiding in Davison, 'Why my successor is not
arrived, I cannot guess. A Spanish War I should have thought would be

a spur to him.'[45] He had been raising Emma's expectations ever since October and she had complained to Davison about his non-arrival. Davison, ironically enough, was in the same position of defending Nelson to Emma as he had defended him to Fanny. Nelson was getting himself into a feverish state, fearful that the ship bearing his recall had been lost, 'for they never would, I am sure, have kept me so long in the dark'. He was winding himself up. He could think only of his successor, and about Emma's focus on money. He complained to her, 'Ministers could not have thought that I wanted to fly the service, my whole life has proved the contrary; and, if they refuse me now: I shall most certainly leave this country in March or April; for a few months' rest I must have, very soon. If I am in my grave, what are the mines of Peru to me!' He was again anxious about his health, evidently troubled by his hernia. 'My cough is very bad; and my side, where I was struck on the 14th of February, is very much swelled; at times a lump as large as my fist, brought on, occasionally, by violent coughing, but I hope and believe my lungs are yet safe.'[46]

On 1 December he had not heard anything from London for seventy-two days. Then Sir John Orde appeared on the scene, more precisely off Cadiz, which caused Nelson to write to Keats, 'I may very soon be your troublesome guest.' He began to prepare by shipping some of his wine over to the *Superb*, 'fourteen casks and about eleven or twelve cases; but my dear Sir, there are so many things I have to intrude upon your good-ness for, that I hardly see how to make you any amends for the trouble I shall give'.[47] By 5 December he was feeling injured and writing in cynical vein to Ball, 'No Sir John Orde, no orders, no letters from England; very extraordinary. I almost begin to think that he is sent off Cadiz by Cornwallis (by orders from Admiralty) to reap my sugar harvest. It's very odd, two Admiralties to treat me so; surely I have dreamt that I have "done the State some service." But never mind; I am superior to those who could treat me so. When am I to be relieved ? . . . I shall not trouble you with all my conjectures about Sir John Orde's never communicating with me for the three weeks he has been off Cadiz.'[48] Orde's message, delayed in reaching Nelson off Sardinia, was civil enough: 'Should it be in my power, during my stay to be useful to your lordship in promoting the King's service, or your particular views, I beg you will command me without ceremony.'[49] Nelson's response was hardly justified but reflected his pent-up emotion. He was not in the mood to be soft soaped by Orde.

His reply was pointed and frosty. He merely asked Orde to let him know in good time when he [Orde] was likely to leave the station, 'that I may . . . place a proper Squadron on that part of the Station hitherto under my orders'.[50] He was explicit with Elliot: 'the sending an Officer to such a point, to take, if it is a Spanish War, the whole harvest, after all my toils (God knows unprofitable enough! for I am a much poorer man than when we started in the *Amphion*) seems a little hard; but patienza. I suppose Sir John in the end will command here. . . . It is now ninety days since I have heard from England; it is rather long at these critical times. . . . Such things are.'[51] He was more openly contemptuous with Emma, talking of 'the great John Orde . . . he will get all the money and your poor Nelson all the hard blows, am I to take this as a proof of Lord Melville's regard for me . . . is Sir John after he has got riches to come here and get glory'.[52] This is one of those episodes that dent our image of Nelson. Wanting it all his own way, he behaves like a spoilt child.

It was on Christmas Day 1804 that he received from the *Swiftsure* a letter dated 6 October giving him permission to return to England and leaving Bickerton in command during his absence. He announced that he would take up their kind offer the moment another flag officer came out to replace Campbell who had been invalided home earlier in the month, 'unless the Enemy's Fleet should be at sea, when I should not think of quitting my Command until after the Battle'.[53] He decided to keep the permission to himself. A confident forecast that the French would be out in a fortnight turned out to be yet another case of his tendency to wishful thinking. He swore Elliot to secrecy, explaining that 'I have kept my permission a profound secret in the Fleet. Every body expects that it will come.'[54] The arrival of *Swiftsure* had also brought him formal notice of Orde's appointment as a commander-in-chief of a squadron off Cadiz and of the confinement of his own command to the Mediterranean. His instinctive reaction was one of childish practicality. In sending his dispatches home by Lisbon, he determined to avoid the vessel that carried them being diverted to Orde's purposes. He gave Captain Parker private instructions: 'Bring to for nothing, if you can help it; hoist the signal of Quarantine, and that you are Charged with Dispatches. If you are forced to speak by a Superior Officer, show him only my order for not interfering with you; and, unless he is an Admiral superior to me, you will obey my orders instead of any pretended order from him.'[55] At least to the south there was good news. Keats's latest visit to Algiers had succeeded in its objectives. Nelson heaped praise on him in a dispatch to Lord Camden, and recommended Crown livings for his two interpreters, Dr Scott and the Reverend Mr Evans.

Early in 1805 Dr Gillespie, the new physician of the fleet, joined the *Victory* as she made her way to Maddalena. He noticed immediately the ambience, 'the best possible order as to health, discipline, spirits and disposition towards our gallant and revered commander, Lord Nelson'. Nelson had not been exaggerating, as we might have been inclined to think, about the state of his men's health. Gillespie found, 'the company of this ship, which consisting of 840 men, contains only one man confined to his bed from sickness, and the other ships (twelve of the line), of from eighty four to seventy four guns, are in a similar situation as to health, although the most of them have been stationed off Toulon for upwards of twenty months, during which time very few of the men or officers (in which number Lord Nelson) have had a foot on shore.' He went on to tell his sister how, on the strength of the recommendations which had preceded him, 'I immediately became one of the family.' He had observed Nelson's 'noble frankness of manner, freedom from vain formality and pomp (so necessary to the decoration of empty little great men) . . . and the watchful and persevering diligence with which he commands the fleet'. He enlightened his sister on the daily routine of the great ship:

> At six o'clock my servant brings a light and informs me of the hour, wind, weather and course of the ship, when I immediately dress and generally repair to the deck. . . . Breakfast is announced in the Admiral's cabin, where Lord Nelson, Rear-Admiral Murray, the Captain of the Fleet, Captain Hardy, Commander of the *Victory,* the chaplain, secretary, one or two officers of the ship, and your humble servant assemble and breakfast on tea, hot rolls, toast, cold tongue, &c. . . . Between the hours of seven and two there is plenty of time for business, study, writing and exercise. . . . At two o'clock a band of music plays till within a quarter to three, when the drum beats the tune called 'The Roast Beef of Old England,' to announce the Admiral's dinner, which is served up exactly at three o'clock, and

which generally consists of three courses and a dessert of the choicest fruit, together with three or four of the best wines, champagne
and claret not excepted; and what exceeds the relish of the best
viands and most exquisite wines, if a person does not feel himself
perfectly at ease it must be his own fault, such is the urbanity and
hospitality which reigns here, notwithstanding the numerous titles,
the four orders of knighthood worn by Lord Nelson, and the well-
earned laurels he has acquired. Coffee and liqueurs close the dinner
about half past four or five o'clock, after which the company generally walk the deck, where the band of music plays for near an hour.
At six o'clock tea is announced, when the company again assemble
in the Admiral's cabin, where tea is served up before seven o'clock,
and as we are inclined, the party continue to converse with his lordship, who at this time generally unbends himself, although he is at
all times as free from stiffness and pomp as a regard to proper
dignity will permit, and is very communicative. At eight o'clock a
rummer of punch with cake or biscuit is served up, soon after which
we wish the Admiral a good night, who is generally in bed before
nine o'clock.[56]

26

French Diversions

*I would allow no man to take from me an atom of my glory, had I
fallen in with the French Fleet, nor do I desire any man to partake of
any of the responsibility – all is mine, right or wrong.*

Nelson, February 1805

It was on to such a scene on 19 January 1805 that the frigates *Seahorse*
and *Active* arrived at Maddalena. The French fleet had put to sea the
previous day.

Nelson immediately ordered his ships to sail, and to hoist lights ready
for a night action or chase in company. His frigates had been in sight of
the enemy until ten o'clock the previous night and had continued in
contact with one of them till two in the morning, the enemy's reported
course causing Nelson to deduce that they were intending to sail round
the southern end of Sardinia. He detached *Seahorse* to scout ahead
and, keeping the rest of his twelve sail-of-the-line and the frigate *Active*
together, he followed. At half past seven *Active* signalled a strange
sail but it turned out to be *Seahorse*. He next detached *Spencer* and
Leviathan, placing both these fast sailers on his weather beam, so as to
be ready to throw their weight where most needed, made signals to
'Prepare for Action,' and formed his ships into two close-knit lines.
Nelson had been absolutely certain from the direction of the winds that
the enemy was bound south round Sardinia, but 'whether to Cagliari,
Sicily, the Morea, or Egypt, I am most completely in ignorance'. He
believed there were 6–7,000 troops on board the enemy vessels. His
mind was working overtime. He sent one frigate ahead to Sicily in the
hope that Acton would also warn Naples. He calculated that with
the present winds the enemy would not be able to hold a course for
the Morea or Egypt. He had no frigate to alert Ball at Malta or to get a
message to Schomberg and his small ships in the Adriatic; both could
have been a considerable help in scouting the eastern Mediterranean.

At the same time he could not believe that the French had passed him and made for Naples. 'I am at this moment in the best possible position for intercepting them, should that be their destination.'[1] Intelligence from *Seahorse*, which had seen a French frigate off Pula at the mouth of the Gulf of Cagliari, confirmed Nelson in his view that the enemy was hereabouts. Hampered still by lack of information, Nelson was, as usual working himself up into a state. He wrote to Acton, 'You will believe my anxiety. I have neither ate, drank or slept with any comfort since last Sunday.' He finished his letter, 'I hope the Governor of Augusta [on the east coast of Sicily to the north of Syracuse and south of Messina] will not give up the port to the French Fleet; but if he does, I shall go in and attack them, for I consider the destruction of the Enemy's Fleet of so much consequence, that I would willingly have half of mine burnt to effect their destruction. I am in a fever. God send I may find them.'[2]

The French were not at Cagliari and Nelson pushed north-eastwards so that by the 29th he was to the north of Sicily, having flanked the Lipari Islands. Once in sight of the flaming island of Stromboli, he headed south for the Faro of Messina. From there he reached a logical conclusion and reported to the Admiralty, 'One of two things must have happened, that either the French Fleet must have put back crippled, or that they are gone to the Eastward, probably to Egypt, therefore I find no difficulty in pursuing the line of conduct I have adopted. If the Enemy have put back crippled, I could never overtake them, and therefore I can do no harm in going to the Eastward; and if the Enemy are gone to the Eastward, I am right.'[3] He now knew that the *Hydra* had seen three big ships apparently running for eastern Corsica on the 22nd, but unaware that the French were out she thought them likely to be Nelson's. He sent ships far and wide, *Morgiana* to look into Elba and St Fiorenzo and go on to Malta, *Bittern* to Tunis and Panteleria (an island between Sicily and Tunis) and also go on to Malta, *Seahorse* around Cape Corse or Maddalena to Toulon, *Hydra* round the southern end of Sardinia to Toulon, *Active* round either end of the islands or through the Strait of Bonifaccio to Toulon, *Termagant* to cruise off Toro Island (Sardinia) for a fortnight, and *Phoebe* around Coron and Candia (on Crete). 'Celerity in my movements may catch these fellows yet.'[4] *Termagant* had captured Toulon vessels and been told that the French now had eleven sail-of-the-line, nine frigates and corvettes. Nelson himself was now heading eastwards to the western tip of Crete with the possibility of looking into Alexandria before making his way back westwards. It must all have felt very familiar. By 7 February *Victory* was twenty-one miles off Alexandria. Nelson still did not know where the French were but remained convinced that Egypt was their destination. He was mustering his defence once again, sharing it with his friend Ball, as he had done in the late summer of 1798. 'When I call all the circumstances which I know at this moment, I approve (if nobody else does) of my conduct, in acting as I have done. We know the success of a man's measures is the criterion by which we judge of the wisdom or folly of his measures. I have done my best. I feel I have done right; and should Ministers think otherwise, they must get somebody else of more wisdom; for greater zeal I will turn my back on no man.'[5]

He need not have felt so defensive. There was nothing wrong with his analysis. The French had had a fortnight of favourable easterly winds which they could have taken advantage of to leave Toulon, had they intended to go west. They had in fact come out on the 17th with the wind coming gently from the north-northwest; had their objective been Naples it would have been better for them to have gone eastwards in the first instance, hugging their friendly coast. Nelson clung to his diagnosis that 'Egypt was the original destination of the Toulon Fleet, when they sailed January 17th, 1805', and protested rather too much in all quarters. He wrote to the First Lord in characteristic vein, 'I find no difficulty at this moment, when I am so unhappy at not finding the French Fleet, nor having obtained the smallest information where they are, to lay before you the whole line of the reasons which induced me to pursue the line of conduct I have done. I have consulted no man, therefore the whole blame of ignorance in forming my judgement must rest with me. I would allow no man to take from me an atom of my glory, had I fallen in with the French Fleet, nor do I desire any man to partake of any of the responsibility – all is mine, right or wrong.'[6] Even though he had a marvellous gift for being able to take others along with him he never had the slightest doubt about where the responsibility lay. The bravery of his standing up to be counted is equalled only by an overwhelming need both to be right and to be judged right.

Arrived back at Malta on 19 February he found out what had happened. The French fleet had gone nowhere and had put back into Toulon in a crippled state. But though he knew what the French had done, he was none the wiser about what they had intended. Their intention had been to attempt a junction with the Spanish squadron at Cartagena, then to sail out of the Mediterranean, join with Gravina off Cadiz and sail for the West Indies. Still struggling to beat his way back to Toulon against northwesterly gales and contrary seas, Nelson was now in a trough of depression. He told Emma, 'nothing can be more miserable, or unhappy, than your poor Nelson ... I know my dear Emma, that it is in vain to repine; but my feelings are alive to meeting those fellows, after near two years' hard service. What a time! I could not have thought it possible that I should have been so long absent; unwell and uncomfortable, in many respects ... I send you a trifle, for a birth-day's gift. I would to God, I could give you more; but I have it not. I get no Prize-money worth naming ... but if I have the good fortune to meet the French Fleet, I hope they will make me amends for all my anxiety; which has been and is, indescribable.'[7] He believed that the French soldiers had not yet disem-barked and so wrote to the First Lord, 'I would die ten thousand deaths, rather than give up my command when the Enemy is expected every day to be at sea.'[8] News from home brought other complexities. He needed Davison to finance Emma's interior decoration at Merton: 'She will not be extravagant; therefore, if you will let her have the money for it, I shall feel much obliged.'[9] Davison, now released from prison, worried Nelson by an apparent inclination to use Nelson's indebtedness to further his own interest, to which Nelson reacted with honest distress, 'and my dear Davison, your letter has hurt me not a little. It conveys to my mind an intimation, that I might have made you Agent for the Mediterranean Fleet. If I have that power, it is a power I am unacquainted with; nor do I see how it is possible. . . . There is nothing my dear Davison, that I could do to meet your wishes, that I should not rejoice in doing; and I only regret I cannot do impossibilities. I am truly sensible of all the obliga-tions I owe you ... I must not omit to mention that Sir Richard Strachan is the only Captain who, when stationed outside the Straits, wrote me, that he should, if he sent any ship to England, make you his agent.'[10] Nelson was being consistent. This is exactly what he had said to Davison in the previous December.

Orde continued to rankle with him. He told Collingwood, 'We are in a sad jumble with Sir John Orde off Cadiz; but let him do as absurd things as he pleases ... I shall never enter into a paper war with him, or anyone else.'[11] This did not of course inhibit him from bad-mouthing

Orde in all directions. The whole situation had been exacerbated by the fact that when Orde was appointed the Admiralty was under the impression that Nelson wanted to come home and was sending him permission to do so. Nelson was hoist with his own petard as he saw his command truncated and a potentially rich source of prizes removed from his grasp. Orde had been given the task of blockading Cadiz and was unwilling to divert resources to convoys emerging from the Straits. Nelson was increasingly of the view that Gibraltar should be part of Orde's command, with Orde responsible for supporting its logistical needs. He told Ball on 29 March, 'But this cannot go on. I have on January 7th wrote home of what would happen; and I dare say Orde has a trimmer before this time. He will not be suffered to remain much longer; he will go to the Channel: he will be the richest Admiral that England ever had, and I one of the poorest. Bravo!'[12] For his part Orde had complained about Nelson's ships being outside the Mediterranean. Orde brought the dispute to a head, writing to the First Lord two days earlier than Nelson's letter to Ball. After airing his complaints about Nelson's trespass and the insufficiency of his resources to protect convoys to Gibraltar he concluded, 'I now feel myself unequal to perform with satisfaction to my employers, and to my own feelings, extemely hurt by recent treatment. May I then request of your Lordship permission to retire.'[13]

In an ideal world Nelson and Orde might have been expected to find ways of collaborating effectively around the boundaries of their commands. Different men might have managed it, but these two egocentric and determined characters were in reality robber barons fighting a turf war, not least because Head Office (the Admiralty) had not thought carefully enough about the implications of its organizational arrangements. Although disappointing that Nelson and Orde both adopted such childish attitudes, it was not surprising that they fell out. It was also clear that Nelson was envious of Orde, as a letter of 1 April to Lord Radstock shows: 'As my station was to be lopped to give Sir John Orde a fortune and to keep me poor . . . I wish it had fallen to you, for you had at least done as much service as Sir John Orde, or any other man in the Service. Report says that Sir John Orde will be the richest Admiral that England ever saw. It cannot be pleasing to me to have every person tell me this; but my soul soars above this consideration, although I cannot help thinking that I could have made as good a use of a large fortune as Sir John Orde or any other Admiral. I should like to have tried.'[14]

On 26 March Nelson was joined by the Admiralty's replacement for Rear-Admiral Campbell. He was Rear-Admiral Louis, who as Captain Louis had commanded *Minotaur* at the Nile. Louis shifted out of the *Ambuscade*, and hoisted his flag in the *Canopus*, taking with him Jane Austen's brother, Captain Francis Austen. Now that Nelson had Louis and the Admiralty's consent to return in his pocket, and Bickerton nominated to hold the fort, he could begin to think again about going home. His analysis of what the enemy would do fitted conveniently: 'if they defer it [coming out] one month from this time, they will not come forth this summer'.[15]

Promptly on 4 April the *Phoebe* appeared over the horizon with news that the French, with eleven sail-of-the-line, seven frigates and two brigs, had left Toulon on 30 March and were steering south. Nelson at the southern end of Sardinia, cleared for action, stood to the westwards and waited. They would be evenly matched. Nelson, supposing them to have turned eastwards or continued southerly, positioned himself midway between the Barbary coast and Sardinia. From the morning of 1 April he noted the winds to have been variable and mostly from the south or east. His report had told him that, 'At noon [on 31 March] the wind came to the N.N.W., and they hauled to the Westward, as wishing not to let our Frigates near them.'[16] Here was a fact he might have paid more attention to. But he was thinking about Sardinia, Sicily or Naples, all to the east. He seems to have got himself into a state of the highest nervous tension. He told Ball, 'I am in truth half dead' and 'I am very uneasy and unwell.' He was trying to curb the urge to make a precipitate decision: 'I must not make more haste than good speed.'[17] He had dispatched ships to Tunis and to the east side of Corsica, and was on the point of sending to Naples and San Sebastian. He would himself take position off Ustica, ready to push for Naples or Sicily. He told Davison, 'I can neither eat, drink, or sleep. It cannot last long what I feel.'[18] On the 7th he told Elliot, 'I am most unlucky, that my Frigates should lose sight of them; but it is vain to be angry or repine . . . I shall neither go to the Eastward of Sicily or to the Westward of Sardinia, until I know something positive.'[19] He sent a frank message to Captain Sotheron in the *Excellent* off Naples, 'I am entirely adrift by my Frigates losing sight of the French Fleet so soon after their coming out of port.'[20] Three days later he was off

Palermo and proposing to stand northwards back to Maddalena and Cape Corse, writing to Ball, 'I am sorely vexed at the ignorance in which I am kept.'[21]

As with the previous French breakout, Bonaparte was intent on bringing to a climax his plan for invading England. First put in motion in September 1803, it involved the construction of a vast flotilla of troop carriers, the selection and modification of ports, fortification of the coastline to mitigate the effect of British attacks; and the assembly of an army, their housing and feeding, a monumental task in which he succeeded in joining the whole French people. Departments and towns sponsored the production of invasion craft, to the tune of 24 million francs. Napoleon knew that he had to command the Channel for at least eight hours. For this he endlessly formulated and reformulated his strategy and tactics. The concept was simple enough. It involved the breakout of his forces at Brest, Toulon, Rochefort and Ferrol. This was easy enough to accomplish, as Nelson's own experience showed; winds that allowed French ships out generally blew the blockaders off their station. Once at sea Bonaparte's ships would make for the West Indies, inflict what damage they could, draw off the British, and make for the Channel in a combined force of some fifty ships to brush aside the opposition. Diversionary attacks in South America, St Helena, Cape Town or Ireland figured in some of his plans. The Mediterranean theatre had never for a moment featured. But Bonaparte's strategy laboured under great difficulties: he changed his mind frequently; he made no real attempt to understand the state of his Navy, especially inadequacies in its readiness for action and its leadership; he did not factor into his plans the difficulties and unreliability of communication, and he treated the various elements of his Navy as a series of chess pieces able to be moved at will. His seventh plan, of 13 April 1805, envisaged Villeneuve's joining with Gravina off Cadiz. They would sail with a total of eighteen ships to Martinique, be joined by Ganteaume and his twenty-one ships from Brest, making a total of thirty-nine. With 12,400 troops under General Lauriston they were to conquer Britain's West Indian possessions. If after thirty-five days Ganteaume had not arrived, Villeneuve was to return by the most direct route to the coast of Spain, release the fifteen French and Spanish ships at Ferrol, thus increasing his numbers to thirty-three, break the blockade of Brest, release Ganteaume and his twenty-one ships and with a total of fifty-four sail up the Channel to rendezvous with

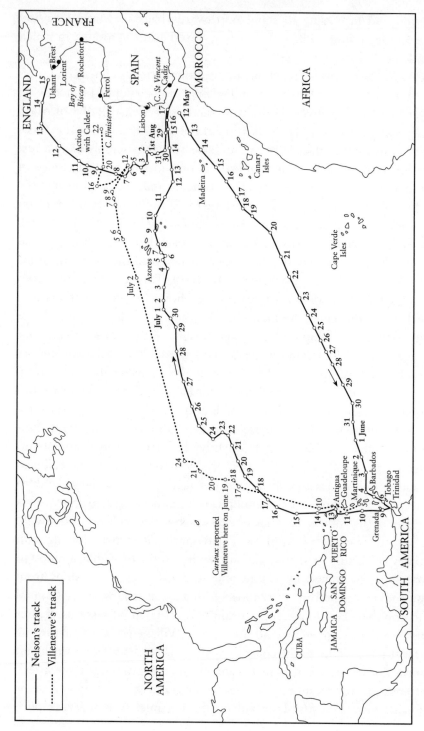

The Chase to The West Indies, 1805

Napoleon off Boulogne. To deceive the British he would leave some ships in Cadiz to attract a blockade and would order the six ships of the Spanish squadron at Cartagena to sail to Toulon to imply a target in the eastern Mediterranean.

Nelson did not even learn the direction the French had taken until 16 April, when *Victory* hailed the *Leviathan* and learned that a vessel she had encountered had seen a fleet on 7 April off Cape de Gata (the southeast tip of Spain), with the wind easterly, steering to the west. Nelson was sickened by the news: 'If this account is true, much mischief may be apprehended. It kills me, the very thought.'[22] The wind was now against him and as he laboured towards Gibraltar he had a decision to make. What should he do next ? First, as ever, was his need to justify himself, 'It may be thought that I have protected too well Sardinia, Naples Sicily, the Morea, and Egypt, from the French; but I feel I have done right, and am, therefore, easy about any fate which may await me for having missed the French Fleet.'[23] In truth, given the intelligence situation and the isolation of command, Nelson could hardly have been blamed for his focus on the Mediterranean.

In nine days he made only twenty miles a day. He heard at the bottom of Sardinia that the French had passed the Straits on 8 April. He was still ten days behind but not wasting his time. He made careful contingency plans for the protection of trade and for watching out for any French attack from Toulon against Sardinia, Naples, Sicily or Egypt, and for communication. He was guarding his back as well as he could against the possibility that he was being decoyed away. But he cursed his luck: 'My good fortune seems flown away. I cannot get a fair wind, or even a side wind. Dead foul! – dead foul! But my mind is fully made up what to do when I leave the Straits, supposing there is no certain information of the enemy's destination.'[24] By the 19th he realized that the French (as per Napoleon's plan) had joined up with Spanish ships at Cadiz. His mind was now working overtime, as revealed by what he wrote to Marsden,

The circumstance of their having taken the Spanish Ships which were for sea, from Cadiz, satisfies my mind that they are not bound to the West Indies, (nor probably the Brazils;) but intend forming a junction at Ferrol, and pushing direct for Ireland or Brest, as I believe the French have Troops on board; therefore, if I receive no intelligence to do away my present belief, I shall proceed from Cape St Vincent, and take my position fifty leagues West from Scilly. . . . My reason for this position is, that it is equally easy to get to either the Fleet off Brest, or to go to Ireland, should the Fleet be wanted at either station.[25]

And, true to form, he would send to tell Lord Gardner off Ireland, and Cornwallis, what he was about.

Having resolved his course of action, he was easier in his mind. He wrote to Lord Melville, 'I am not made to despair – what man can do shall be done. I have marked out for myself a decided line of conduct, and I shall follow it well up . . . I shall pursue the Enemy to the East or West Indies, if I know that to have been their destination, yet if the Mediterranean Fleet joins the Channel, I shall request with that order permission to go on shore.'[26] But notwithstanding all this ratiocination, his fleet was not yet at Gibraltar; he had still no decent wind from the east. It was 1 May before he was in sight of Ceuta and the 4th before he could anchor off Tetuan to take on water and cattle. He had expected that Sir John Orde off Cadiz would have been able to track the passage of the French and send him news; there was nothing awaiting him. How he must have fumed.

Sure enough, Orde had seen them and sent intelligence by a nearby merchant ship to Lord Robert Fitzgerald, Minister at Lisbon, 'Where their destination may be after this junction (which I am not astonished at) I cannot tell, but I judge westward. Where Lord Nelson is I cannot hear, but I am told he is likely to return to Egypt on hearing of the French fleet being at sea. Pray forward this intelligence in all directions, with every possible dispatch,'[27] and calmly left it at that. He neither sent a message into the Mediterranean, nor did he attack (for which he could not be blamed) nor did he make arrangements to shadow the enemy, for which he was culpable. His two intelligent actions were to send the frigate *Mercury* to warn the West Indies and to sail north himself to add his weight to the squadron off Ushant, guarding the entry to the Channel. He had after all sent in his resignation some time previously, on 27 March, and this decision would take the gout-troubled Admiral closer to home. However, his actions in neither checking nor following the enemy roused the commercial classes of England to the kind of indignation that only the potential loss of large sums of money can induce. Later, off

Ushant on 30 April he reiterated his desire, 'When the present alarm is over', to 'repair to Town for a few days'.[28] Not surprisingly he received instead his permission to retire, and was later refused a court martial to defend his actions.

The French were now a month ahead. The general opinion was that they must have made for the West Indies. Yet, even as Nelson's ships finally sailed through the Straits on 6 May, the die was not yet cast. As he sailed towards Cape St Vincent Nelson had other news to digest. Lord Melville had left office under a cloud as a result of the *Tenth Report of the Naval Inquiries*. 'Now we have to look forward to some one else.'[29] This was hardly the best time to be faced with a new First Lord. Pushing closer to Cape St Vincent on 7 May he recorded, 'I still am as much in the dark as ever.'[30] On the 9th he met up with *Amazon* and a letter from Captain Hill of the *Orpheus* with information gathered from the Master of the *Louisa* of Baltimore that eleven French sail-of-the-line had appeared off Cadiz on 9 April. By noon on the 10th they and their attendant frigates had been out of sight. Both Spanish and French ships were carrying troops and their destination was rumoured to be Ireland or the West Indies. Nelson immediately cleared his accompanying transports, provisioned his ships for five months, and on 11 May set sail for the West Indies. Although he knew the enemy had a month's lead he reasoned optimistically: 'chance may have given them a bad passage, and me a good one'.[31] Nobody in England would know until the end of May where either Nelson or the French fleet had vanished to.

As Nelson put his ten ships on course for the Canaries we might be inclined to think that Napoleon's ruse was working, but the fact was that Villeneuve was being pursued, without British forces off the Channel being diverted. Nelson was not receiving alarm signals from Cornwallis's sector; Ganteaume was still bottled up in Brest. Only Missiessy, who had slipped out of Rochefort in bad weather on 17 January, was on the loose. Actually Missiessy had been under orders to ravage British possessions in the West Indies, and was now on the way home (not having received Napoleon's latest orders to wait for Villeneuve). Nelson was acting on the principle that the Toulon fleet was his responsibility and that it was his job to take care of them. The potential weaknesses of his strategy did not, as usual, enter his reckoning. He did not agonize over what the enemy might do if they eluded him, nor where he might have positioned himself if he did not find them. His instinct was to get at the French, rather than immobilize himself with 'what ifs'.

Two days later Nelson was 108 miles out from Madeira, and Calder off Finisterre was receiving news that Missiessy's squadron was once again in sight, heading for Rochefort. Nelson, hurrying south before sweeping to the west on the trade winds, was shepherding his flock, in particular concerned that Keats should not feel embarrassed by his slow-sailing *Superb*. 'I know and feel that the *Superb* does all which it is possible for a Ship to accomplish; and I desire that you will not fret upon the occasion'[32] – words which would inevitably encourage a captain of Keats's character to strive even harder to keep up. Nelson had been doing his calculations: 'Our passage, though not very quick has been far from a bad one. They started from Cadiz thirty one days before we did from St Vincent, and I think we shall gain fourteen days upon them in the passage; therefore, they will only arrive seventeen days before us at Martinico.'[33]

His energetic mind was now focused on what he would do to the French when he found them. A surviving document, obviously a draft since it is neither clear nor particularly well written, displays in characteristic phrases the principles of his thinking:

> The business of an English Commander-in-Chief being first to bring the Enemy's Fleet to Battle, on the most advantageous terms to himself, (I mean that of laying his ships close on board the Enemy, as expeditiously as possible;) and secondly, to continue when there, without separating, until the business is decided . . . Admirals and Captains . . . will . . . knowing my precise object, that of a close and decisive Battle, supply any deficiency in my not making signals; which may, if extended beyond these objectives, either be misunderstood, or, if waited for, very probably, from various causes, be impossible for the Commander-in-Chief to make. . . . If the two Fleets are both willing to fight, but little manoeuvring is necessary; the less the better; a day is soon lost in that business. . . . Suppose that the Enemy's Fleet is to leeward . . .[34]

This piece of paper has the air of an *aide-mémoire* composed by a Nelson hard at work, thinking his way through his own principles and their practical application. It is highly original in terms of his own role as

Commander-in-Chief. He would define aims and options for handling the fleet but not control every subsequent contingency. The role of his subordinate admirals and captains would be to understand his broad aims and desired means and deliver victory. His portrayal of the battle situation is reduced to its key simplicities: laying ships close onboard the enemy, in stage one concentrating all his force on part of the enemy, in stage two dealing with the enemy's rear. But the numbers used in this draft show it to have been produced in 1803–1804 when he faced an enemy of equivalent strength at Toulon. The present numerical challenge would be to attack their seventeen with his own ten. The odds are that he would still have thrown his whole force aggressively at part of the enemy, had an opportunity arisen.

Nelson arrived off Barbados on 4 June after a passage of twenty-four days. At a council of war, Rear-Admiral Cochrane and Lieutenant-General Sir William Myers, Commander-in-Chief in the Leeward Islands, pressed on him their strong belief that the enemy's objectives were Tobago and Trinidad lying to the south of Barbados. They showed him a letter from Brigadier-General Brereton on St Lucia (to the north-west of Barbados). This was dated six days previously and read, 'I have received a report from the Windward side of Gros Islet that the Enemy's Fleet, of 28 Sail in all, passed there last night. Their destination, I should suppose, must be either Barbadoes or Trinidad.'[35] Pausing only to embark General Myers and 2,000 troops, Nelson sailed south with eleven ships, *Spartiate* having now joined him. On the afternoon of the following day they were off Tobago, where by a stroke of fate a misread signal from a schooner and misinformation from an American merchant-brig indicated that the enemy was at Trinidad. Cleared for action, they arrived off Trinidad on the 7th only to find the French had been nowhere near. News then came to Nelson that the French had captured Diamond Rock on 2 June and that the French and Spanish were still at Martinique and had been there since 29 May. He also had information from French sources that the Ferrol squadron of six French and eight Spaniards had arrived at Fort Royal on 4 June. Nelson wrestled with the data. Events had proven Brereton's information to be incorrect. The arrival of the Ferrol squadron he assessed as French disinformation. He told Lord Seaforth, Governor of Barbados, 'powerful as their force may be, they shall not with impunity, make any great attacks. Mine is compact, theirs must be unwieldy; and although a very pretty fiddle, I don't believe that either Gravina or Villeneuve know how to play upon it.'[36]

Nelson now turned north and by 9 June he was anchored in St George's Bay, Grenada. There he found that all was safe at Grenada, St Vincent and St Lucia. His enemy had not moved from Martinique. But on the afternoon of the same day he learned that the French fleet of eighteen sail-of-the-line had been seen near the Saints and was standing north-wards, whether to attack Antigua or St Kitts or to return to Europe, he could not tell. By the 11th he himself had passed to the west of Dominica, and was passing Montserrat, where he got only 'vague and very unsat-isfactory intelligence'. He was now putting the best gloss on his exploits. He reported to Marsden, 'I feel, having saved these Colonies, and two hundred and upwards of sugar-loaded Ships, that I must be satisfied they have bent their course for Europe before I push after them, which will be to the Straits' mouth.'[37] By the morning of the 12th off Antigua he learned that the Enemy had passed Antigua the previous Saturday (the 8th), standing to the northward after landing all their troops and stores at Guadeloupe. He determined to land his own troops at St John's and sail immediately for Europe. Villeneuve, originally required to wait in the West Indies for Ganteaume, now received new orders by the frigate *Dido* to return, link up with the ships at Ferrol, next with Ganteaume at Brest and sail up the Channel. Then on the 7th when he captured a British convoy of fifteen rum and sugar ships Villeneuve learned that Nelson was in the Caribbean. He and Gravina decided to return to Ferrol immedi-ately. Nelson's mind had still not penetrated Bonaparte's strategy, as a letter to Ball shows: 'In this diversity of opinions I may as well follow my own, which is, that the Spaniards are gone to Havannah, and that the French will either stand for Cadiz or Toulon – I feel most inclined to the latter place; and then they may fancy that they will get to Egypt without any interruption.'[38] He wrote to the Duke of Clarence. There were no reminiscences of their time together in the West Indies, but he was anxious to let the Duke know 'the misery I am feeling, at hitherto having missed the French Fleet; and entirely owing to false information sent from St Lucia', and to take on the mantle of Rodney: 'Our battle, most probably, would have been fought on the spot where the brave Rodney met De Grasse. I am rather inclined to believe they are pushing for Europe to get out of our way.' He posed: 'But I must not move, after having saved these Colonies and 200 and upwards of sugar-laden Ships, until I feel sure they are gone . . . I feel I have done my duty to the very utmost of my abilities. . . . My heart is almost broke, and, with my very serious complaints, I cannot long expect to go on.'[39]

Nelson's insatiable curiosity would not let him cease worrying at what the French were really up to. He was getting around to thinking about what they had been doing in the West Indies in the first place. If they had not been able to mount attacks in the first three weeks after their arrival, they could hardly have hoped for greater success after British reinforcements arrived and their own strength was diminished by disease. The French had known he was coming; a corvette had watched them for two days as they made for Madeira and a frigate arrived from France on 31 May; 'from that moment all was hurry'. The penny was dropping. He wrote to Nepean, 'My opinion is firm as a rock, that some cause, orders, or inability to perform any service in these seas, has made them resolve to proceed direct to Europe, sending the Spanish Ships to Havannah.'[40] He still did not know that the enemy's gambit was in aid of the invasion of England.

Carrying every sail he could, Nelson reckoned on 19 June that he was no more than 240 miles behind. Two days later he noted in his Private Diary, 'Midnight, nearly calm, saw three planks, which I think came from the French Fleet. Very miserable, which is very foolish.'[41]

On Wednesday, 18 July their long voyage was over. Cape Spartel was in sight, but there was no sign of the enemy, 'nor any information about them; how sorrowful this makes me, but I cannot help myself!' The previous day he had calculated that their journey out from Cape St Vincent had been 3,227 miles and back from the West Indies 3,459, a round trip of 6,686 miles.[42] He soon sighted Collingwood blockading Cadiz who immediately sent him a warm message of welcome: 'how truly dear you are to my friendship'. He told Nelson that he believed Ireland was the target. Collingwood was reading Napoleon's mind well. He believed the Toulon fleet would return, do the rounds of Ferrol, Rochefort and Ushant, liberating and joining up the separate squadrons, ultimately facing Cornwallis off Ushant and his thirty ships with some fifty-four. He interpreted what was happening as a pattern of concentration, the plan, 'some rash attempt at conquest'. He could not see that Bonaparte would subject his fleets to losses, 'without the hope of an adequate reward'. He felt a climax was approaching: 'The summer is big with events. We may all perhaps have an active share in them.' He hoped that Nelson was physically strong enough. 'I wish your Lordship strength of body to go through – and to all others your strength of mind.'[43] Sailing on, Nelson finally cast his anchor in Rosia Bay, Gibraltar on 19 July and for the first time in two years, less ten days, he put a foot on dry land.

Nelson was now actively working on what to do next. His first thoughts were to reprovision his ships, eradicate signs of scurvy, and hold himself ready to act on any orders Bickerton might have received in his absence. Brereton was a recurring theme and to Davison he spoke what was in his heart: 'But for General Brereton's damned information, Nelson would have been, living or dead, the greatest man in his Profession that England ever saw. Now, alas! I am nothing – perhaps shall incur censure for misfortunes which may happen, and have happened. When I follow my own head, I am, in general, much more correct in my judgement, than following the judgement of others. I resisted the opinion of General Brereton's information till it would have been the height of presumption to have carried my disbelief further.'[44] Nelson could not avoid personalizing all events he was involved in and he could not allow himself to be wrong, except when he wanted to be. None of this agony had been apparent at the time; no intelligent person would have done differently, and Nelson never reveals the grounds he had for thinking that the enemy had gone north, not south; it was all hindsight. His malevolent reverie on Brereton was interrupted by the *Decade* arriving from Collingwood, but still with no news of the enemy. He weighed and made his way towards Cadiz.

On the next day he learned from the *Curieux* brig that the enemy fleet had been seen sailing northwards on 19 July. Off he went, heading first for Cape St Vincent. He was sailing on a fresh Levanter, being blown out to the west, and since Collingwood faced a westerly wind, there was no prospect of the old friends meeting, 'I must forgo the pleasure of taking you by the hand till October next . . . I feel disappointed, my dear friend, at not seeing you; so does Admiral Murray and many, I am sure, in this Fleet.'[45] He sent ahead to his 'dear friend', Admiral Cornwallis, telling him that he was making his way towards him with eleven sail-of-the-line. 'I shall only hope, after all my long pursuit of *my* Enemy, that I may arrive at the moment they are meeting you; for my wretched state of health will force me to get on shore for a little while.'[46] He also wrote to Lord Gardner of the possibility that he might arrive off Ireland. He was going to strain every nerve to catch his prey. Off Lisbon the winds from the north were foul, forcing him westwards as he tried to make progress towards Ushant. He had been a mere eight days behind Villeneuve at the Azores but from that point their courses had been constantly diverging. Villeneuve, taking a more north-easterly course, had passed to the north of the Azores, while Nelson heading for the Straits had sailed due east. His quarry had been aiming for Cape Finisterre and Ferrol. Nelson's advance intelligence about the approach of the enemy fleet had reached Cornwallis. He, in turn, alerted Calder off Ferrol and Sterling off Rochefort that Villeneuve with his combined Fleet was coming in their direction. But what, he asked himself, was their intention?

On 22 July, while Nelson was weighing anchor at Gibraltar, Calder encountered the Combined Fleet 117 miles west off Ferrol. The warm light airs were hung with fog, the sea, a sickly swell. With only intermittent sight of each other and ignorant of their relative strengths, they went through a surreal performance of preparing for battle. Calder's fleet of fifteen formed a close line, likewise Villeneuve's twenty. They were seven miles apart, ready for action but with insufficient wind to enable early engagement. It was not until six and a quarter hours after the enemy had been sighted that the first shots were fired. Clouds of gunsmoke added to the obscurity of the day. The battle became blind man's buff, impossible to command or co-ordinate, as ships groped for each other, sure of nothing but the din and flash of enemy guns to aim at. With the approach of nightfall the situation worsened. Ships became as dangerous to friend as foe. Ships on both sides had been severely damaged; two Spanish ships had been taken. Overnight Calder learned of his casualties – 194 killed and wounded; their captured Spaniards had suffered much more heavily. At daybreak the fleets found themselves approximately eight or nine miles apart, but neither Calder nor Villeneuve took any steps to renew the action. Villeneuve was to windward and, the wind having freshened a little, might have been expected to swoop down on Calder. Instead they both sat like two staring animals, each rooted in its own territory. The next day continued in the same vein, both seemingly immobilized. On the 25th they tacitly declared the battle over by each sailing his separate way. No greater contrast to Nelson could have been found. As at St Vincent, Calder had shown himself fearful of numbers and cautious in spirit. Ships from Rochefort and Ferrol might come out to join Villeneuve; if they did it would increase the odds. Calder feared that an outlying group of enemy ships might come down, take the disabled *Windsor Castle* and recapture his prizes. He judged it right not to risk his victory by a second engagement, a not unreasonable risk assessment. However, when the news reached home, Calder had a very bad press. Even the *Naval Chronicle* was less than enthusiastic: 'The French fleet certainly did not run away; but on the contrary, owing to the particular manoeuvres of the action, they may be said even to have pursued us,' and went on ominously: 'The account which the French have published in the *Moniteur*, allowing for their natural boasting and vanity, contains a greater portion of truth than usual.'[47]

The truth was that Nelson had spoiled the public for anything other than complete victory. At the court of inquiry, which was not held until after Trafalgar in December 1805, it would be useless for Calder to cite in his defence the examples of Howe and St Vincent, both of whom had broken off engagements. By then Nelson had bequeathed a legacy of success that it would be impossible for anyone to live up to, and there must have been the thought in the minds of the Board of Inquiry that the man standing before them had been more anxious to vindicate his half-hearted efforts than stay behind to fight with Nelson. Calder was severely reprimanded for not having done enough to renew the action. At the time of Calder's action the Nelson legend had taken such a hold on the public mind that even the *Naval Chronicle* in its July–August issue of 1805 went on record as lamenting 'that ill-judged, and over-weening popularity, which tends to make another Demi-god of Lord Nelson, at the expense of all other officers in the service, many of whom possess equal merit, and equal abilities, and equal gallantry with the noble Admiral'.[48] The final twist in this rather sorry episode was that Villeneuve limped into Vigo and later when Calder was blown out to sea by a storm he moved along the coast and into Ferrol. Combined with the Spaniards there, he was a force of twenty-nine sail. Calder, with a mere nine sail-of-the-line, could not face such odds. He decided to abandon the blockade and join Cornwallis off Ushant.

Nelson was also making for Ushant. On 15 August *Victory* came in sight of the Channel fleet. At six in the evening some twenty-seven miles off Ushant *Victory* hove to and her salute boomed out over the evening sea. With night coming on, Cornwallis did not detain Nelson and in less than two hours he was on his way with only *Superb* and Keats for company, having left behind the rest of his ships with Cornwallis. He was now reading newspapers full of Calder's pusillanimous victory, the talk of the fleet. He confided rather ruefully in Fremantle, 'Who can, my dear Fremantle, command all the success which our Country may wish? We have fought together, and therefore know well what it is. I have had the best disposed Fleet of friends, but who can say what will be the event of a Battle? and it most sincerely grieves me, that in any of the papers it should be insinuated that Lord Nelson could have done better. I should have fought the Enemy, so did my friend Calder; but who can say that he will be more successful than another? I only wish to stand upon my own merits, and not by comparison, one way or the other, upon the conduct of a Brother Officer.'[49] There is in this a certain wisdom and restraint we have rarely heard before. Something of the truth and uncertainty of the fame he has so assiduously sought is beginning to make itself felt. Three days later *Victory* was making her majestic progress past Spithead to anchor off the Motherbank.

At nine o'clock on the 19th Nelson set out for Merton, arriving in the early morning of the 20th. The shouts and cries of a man-of-war, its creaking timbers, the wind in the rigging and the rush of the sea gave way to the profound silence of rural England, scents of new-mown grass and earth. The Merton roses had gone over, but the garden was full of the luxuriance of mid-August, still full of summer blooms. For the first time in two years he could relax in the privacy of his own home, feeling that special deceleration of time that comes with the quietness of a domestic interior, could surrender himself to the passionate warmth of his meeting with Emma, could carry out an indulgent survey of the modifications she had managed in his absence and then make a happy domestic tour of the newly laid gardens, hand in hand with Horatia. With Nelson such an even tenor of life could not last long. The next day he hurried off to London, to call at the Admiralty and on Mr Pitt in Downing Street and of course to meet with his agents, Marsh & Creed. Crowds followed him everywhere. After a day at Merton he was again in town, calling on Lord Castlereagh and Mr Addington. Telling Captain Keats of his meeting with Lord Castlereagh, who had recently become Secretary of State for War and the Colonies, he mused in the same manner as he had to Fremantle. They had all been full of the enemy's fleet. 'I am now set up for a Conjuror, and God knows they will very soon find out

I am far from being one.' In this kind of situation the natural political skills noted by Scott were fully deployed. He had had no compunction in putting Calder out of the running as a possible contender for his command: 'I was asked my opinion, against my inclination, for if I make one wrong guess the charm will be broken; but this I ventured without any fear, that if Calder got fairly alongside their twenty-seven or twenty-eight Sail, that by the time the Enemy had beat our Fleet soundly, they would do us no harm this year.'[50] Calder would not get alongside, would not risk a beating to stop the French. The music they would hear was the unspoken implication that he, Nelson, would get alongside and would not be beaten.

Paradise Merton was hardly rest and recuperation. Susannah Bolton had written breathlessly to Emma on 10 August, 'What a Paradise he must think Merton to say nothing of the Eve it contains. I need not give you joy for I am sure you have it. . . . When you give the hint I will come.'[51] Soon everyone came flooding there, bidden by his indefatigable social secretary. Merton was full of Nelsons, Boltons and Matchams, nephews and nieces. Sir Peter Parker and Lord Minto were early visitors and from soon after his arrival the house was always full. The Duke of Clarence dined; Lord Errol with him. Young George Matcham described the conversation, deference to Nelson and violence against Pitt, as 'Heavy'. Nelson was a godfather to Colonel and Mrs Suckling's child; they came to Merton for the christening. Sir Sidney Smith visited and talked of Acre. William Beckford came and treated them to extempore playing on the harpsichord, 'I thought it a very horrible noise,'[52] noted George Matcham. Lord Minto felt buoyed up by his old friend's positive attitude: 'He looks remarkably well and full of spirits. His conversation is a cordial in these low times.' Having heard from Nelson about all the wonderful things Emma had accomplished in his absence, Minto, who had always had a soft spot for Emma, was impressed by her competence: 'Lady Hamilton has improved and added to the house and the place extremely well without his knowing she was about it. He found it already done. She is a clever being after all.' He added, 'the passion is as hot as ever'. Two days later he met Nelson in Piccadilly surrounded by a mob. 'It is really quite affecting to see the wonder and admiration and love and respect, of the whole world; and the genuine expression of all these sentiments at once, from the gentle and simple the moment he is seen. It is beyond anything represented in a play or a poem of fame.'[53]

Everybody crowded to pay court to him including Lord Hood, the Neapolitan Ambassador Prince Castelcicala, and a deputation of West Indian merchants. Emma and he went out and about. Nelson's connection with the Spencers continued in a curious way. He met Lady Elizabeth Foster, the dear Bess of the Devonshire *ménage à trois*, at Fish Craufurd's. Nelson asked her to share a glass of wine with him. She in turn asked him if he would do her the favour of delivering a letter to her son Clifford in the *Tigre*, with his own hand. 'Kiss it then, and I will take that kiss to him.'[54] Lady Morgan saw Emma do her attitudes and heard her sing a laudatory ode at the top of her great 'Poll of Plymouth' voice, with Nelson bending over her, 'beating time to his own panegyric and joining in the chorus'.[55]

And so it went on. Nelson was as much a human dynamo on shore as he had been at sea. Berry was still in search of a ship and Nelson promised to put in a good word for him with the new First Lord. There were prize money questions to be argued, about vessels taken outside the Straits by captains under his command. There was Davison to be written to about his still shaky financial affairs. He wrote to Beckford to say another visit would be impossible. He sent Lord Minto his correspondence with government about Sardinia. He continued to push the interests of his unfortunate protégé, Lieutenant Layman. He tried to get his brother-in-law Bolton a commissionership in the Customs, Excise or Navy Office. The West India merchants had written to express their gratitude for his having chased the enemy to the West Indies and away again, and had to be answered. His neighbour Mr Perry, editor of the *Chronicle*, and intimate at Merton, was being used as Nelson's mouthpiece when his paper made a scoop announcement on 29 August: 'We are happy to state that the gallant Lord Nelson will very speedily hoist his Flag on board the *Victory*. His Lordship is again to have the Command in the Mediterranean, but we understand that the Cadiz Station is to be included within the limits of that Command.'[56]

On Sunday, 1 September all this activity halted with the sudden arrival at Merton of the Honourable Henry Blackwood, captain of the frigate *Euryalus*. He was on his way to the Admiralty with news that the Combined Fleet was in Cadiz, and had stopped off to give prior information to the man who mattered most. Two thoughts must have flashed through Nelson's mind. Would he actually be summoned? *Would* the boundaries of his command be redrawn to cover Cadiz? His public face announced what Blackwood expected: his motivation to finish the business himself rather than give up to another the culmination of his two years of toil. Blackwood went off, inspired by Nelson's determination and enthusiasm. Nelson soon followed, to be on hand as the information was digested in Downing Street. In fact, the die was cast. Pitt, who had been through a prodigiously turbulent year and whose strength was beginning to fail, had no thoughts of overlooking Nelson, nor for that matter had a relatively new, although highly experienced, First Lord of the Admiralty, Lord Barham. Nelson's popularity, fanned by the press, was by now almost tangible. There was clamour wherever he was seen in London. In spite of any feelings that might have existed in high places about his domestic arrangements, despite the powerful interest of other admirals and notwithstanding a family tradition that he at first declined the command and suggested to Pitt that it be left with Collingwood, he was immediately appointed. He was the obvious choice, and was given *carte blanche* by the First Lord to choose his own officers. It was as Bulkeley wrote to him, 'You have put us out of conceit with all other Admirals. Look into your own acts and read the public papers for the last four months, then judge if John Bull will consent to give up his sheet anchor.'[57]

He accepted. However much he might long to stay with Emma and Horatia, he could not let himself down. He could not let Blackwood, Hardy, Keats or Collingwood down. What would be the value of the Nelson touch, his formula for annihilating the enemy, if he found reasons for not putting it to the supreme challenge? His words to Davison summed up exactly his position, 'I have much to lose, but little to gain; and I go because it is right.'[58] Emma, even allowing for her histrionic Britannia-like attitudes, was bereft. She wrote to Lady Bolton, Nelson's niece on the 4th, 'I am again broken-hearted, as our dear Nelson is immediately going. It seems as though I have had a fortnight's dream, and am awoke to all the misery of this cruel separation. But what can I do? His powerful arm is of so much consequence to his country. But I do, nor cannot say more. My heart is broken.'[59] Later, in 1813, she would claim in a Memorial that 'somewhat against his own notions and presentiments, I prevailed on him to offer himself to command. . . . If, then, either or both of these battles [Copenhagen was mentioned too] were gained by his superior zeal,vigilance, skill and valour, I have proof that he would never have been at the one or the other but at my instance.'[60]

If anything, this was a tribute to Nelson's management of Emma in pursuing his own objectives.

Having got the command, he felt an urge to make Emma as happy as he could under the circumstances He knew that she wanted marriage and lived in hopes that Fanny would die and release him. He, as ever, needed to square his deeds with his conscience. And so before his departure he arranged for them to take Holy Communion together. Either before or after this service, they privately exchanged rings. When the service was over, Nelson, taking Emma by the hand, declared before the priest, 'Emma I have taken the Sacrament with you this day, to prove to the world that our friendship is most pure and innocent, and of this I call God to witness.'[61] Nelson's capacity for self-delusion seemed to have reached its apogee but such was the power of their performance that it convinced the devout Dowager Lady Spencer, the old friend of Sir William Hamilton, who was present and retailed her experience to her daughter-in-law, Lavinia Spencer. 'Lavinia, I think you will now agree that you have been to blame in your opinion of Lady Hamilton.'[62]

On 6 September he had made a remark to Davison which we should not take casually: 'I do not believe the Admiralty can give me a force within fifteen or sixteen Sail of the Line of the Enemy; and therefore, if every Ship took her opponent, we should still have to contend with a fresh Fleet of fifteen or sixteen Sail of the Line.'[63] Nelson knew that, for all his contempt for the French, these odds were powerfully against him. He was in a state of heightened and conflicting emotions. When his sister Catherine Matcham remarked on his tired and depressed look he replied, according to family tradition, 'Ah! Katty, Katty, that Gypsy', reminding her of the gypsy who telling his fortune had closed it at that very year with the words, 'I can see no further.'[64]

Fate had once again placed Collingwood and Nelson in close proximity. On the 7th he wrote from the Admiralty, 'My dear Coll, I shall be with you in a very few days, and I hope you will remain Second in Command. You will change the *Dreadnought* for the *Royal Sovereign*, which I hope you will like.'[65] He also knew that in late August Admiral Cornwallis, who had maintained his long vigil off Brest and kept Ganteaume bottled up for twenty-seven long months, had detached twenty of his sail-of-the-line, including eight of Nelson's Mediterranean fleet and sent them with Calder, Rear-Admiral Louis and Rear-Admiral the Earl of Northesk, to join Collingwood off Cadiz. On 21 August Collingwood's three ships had had to make themselves scarce on the appearance of Villeneuve and Gravina and thirty-six sail-of-the-line. Calder would reach Cadiz a month later, on 21 September, and Collingwood's force would be further augmented by the arrival of Rear-Admiral Knight and five more ships, bringing his total to twenty-six. The scene was being set.

Nelson spent much of his final few days of leave in London. Waiting to see Lord Castlereagh, he bumped into both Sidney Smith and Wellington. According to John Wilson Croker, Wellington was not at first impressed by Nelson:

> He entered at once into conversation with me, if I can call it conversation, for it was almost all on his side and all about himself and, in reality, a style so vain and so silly as to surprise and almost disgust me. I suppose something that I happened to say may have made him guess that I was somebody and he went out of the room for a moment, I have no doubt to ask the office-keeper who I was, for when he came back he was altogether a different man, both in manner and matter . . . he talked of the state of the country and of the aspect and probabilities of affairs on the Continent with a good sense and a knowledge of subjects both at home and abroad . . . for the last half or three-quarters of an hour, I don't know that I ever had a conversation that interested me more. Now if the Secretary of State had been punctual . . . I should have had the same impression of a light and trivial character that other people have had, but luckily I saw enough to be satisfied that he was really a very superior man; but certainly a more sudden or complete metamorphosis I never saw.[66]

This is all rather puzzling. Of course Wellesley, as he then was, was by no means lacking in competitive instinct, a sense of personal superiority, arrogance and snobbery. Indeed he was well known for all these characteristics. He also had a tendency to misremember.[67] It would not be at all out of character for him to retail many years later to Croker (who had made his own career on the back of Wellesley influence) such a patronizing and *de haut en bas* view of Nelson, which after all hinges

around his own alleged statement, '*I was somebody.*' The story is diametrically at odds with the behaviour we could confidently expect from
Nelson in Lord Castlereagh's waiting room. In such circumstances he was
simply not that kind of a fool.

On Friday, 13 September Nelson and Emma returned to Merton at
half past five to find Lord Minto there, a friend, but superfluous at that
time. He lingered on till ten, noting, 'Lady Hamilton was in tears all yesterday; could not eat, and hardly drink, and near swooning, and all at
table. It is a strange picture. She tells me nothing can be more pure and
ardent than this flame. He is in many points a really great man, in others
a baby.'[68] His last day at Merton was spent in quietness with Emma and
Horatia and as the early evening approached he prepared himself to
leave. His goodbye to Emma accomplished, and with the memory of his
sleeping Horatia and the perfumed embrace of Emma uppermost in his
mind, he set out in the darkness of the fading year for Portsmouth. His
Private Diary recorded his feelings:

> At half-past ten drove from dear, dear Merton, where I left all which
> I hold dear in this world, to go to serve my King and Country. May
> the Great God whom I adore enable me to fulfil the expectations of
> my Country; and if it is His good pleasure that I should return, my
> thanks will never cease being offered up to the Throne of His Mercy.
> If it is His good providence to cut short my days upon earth, I bow
> with the greatest submission, relying that He will protect those so
> dear to me, that I may leave behind. – His will be done: Amen,
> Amen, Amen.[69]

He arrived at the George Inn in Portsmouth's High Street at about six
o'clock the next morning. He was joined there by George Rose, Vice-
President of the Board of Trade, and George Canning, the Treasurer of
the Navy, who were to accompany him to dine on board *Victory*. News
of his arrival had produced a large crowd and Nelson, uncharacteristically one might think, decided to leave by the back door, eventually fetch-
ing up not at the sally port, but a few yards further, on Southsea beach
itself, from where he could look directly across to the Isle of Wight and
the distant bulk of *Victory* anchored at St Helens.

He had not succeeded in evading the crowds, and may have excited
them all the more by his evading path. An American, Benjamin Silliman

saw him: 'by the time he had arrived on the beach some hundreds of people had collected in his train, pressing all around and pushing to get a little before him to obtain a sight of his face'.[70] Some were naturally awestruck, others shouted and waved; among then were wives and children of sailors. It was another intense moment for Nelson. 'I had their huzzas before – I have their hearts now.' He was loved by the people.

27

Dame Fortune's Last Favour

God bless you Blackwood, I shall never speak to you again

Nelson, 21 October 1805

At eight o'clock on Sunday, 15 September the *Victory* weighed and set sail. Sailing past Portland, Nelson was dealing with home affairs, including the rescheduling of his debt to Davison. There were still alterations to be done at Merton, 'the kitchen, ante-room, and for altering the dining room . . . the alteration will cost three times as much as if it had been done at first'.[1] He was again shouldering the debts of his brother Maurice's blind wife. Off Plymouth on the 17th he wrote to Emma, 'I intreat, my dear Emma, that you will cheer up; and we will look forward to many, many happy years, and be surrounded by our children's children. God Almighty can, when he pleases, remove the impediment. My heart and soul is with you and Horatia.'[2]

As he proceeded south past Lisbon he placed an embargo on all news of his approach and sent ahead that no salutes should signal his arrival in the fleet, nor colours be hoisted. On 28 September in the afternoon he joined Collingwood's fleet of twenty-six sail-of-the-line. There were another six out of sight forming the inshore squadron directly off Cadiz, making thirty-two in all. They were facing a combined fleet in Cadiz harbour of thirty-five or thirty-six, much better odds than Nelson had expected, although he knew that there were two or three French ships at Toulon and eight Spanish at Cartagena, who might be expected to attempt to join Villeneuve and Gravina. Generally speaking, six of his own ships would be detached occasionally to Gibraltar and Tetuan for supplies and to cast an eye over Cartagena.

Once arrived, he began in typical fashion to energize the fleet, 'The present force is at present not so large as might be wished. But I will do my best with it; they will give me more when they can, and I am not come forth to find difficulties, but to remove them,'[3] he told Ball. His spirit was calm now as he wrote to Davison,

> Day by day my dear friend, I am expecting the Fleet to put to sea – every day, hour and moment; and you may rely that, if it is within the power of man to get at them, that it shall be done ... I must think ... that, let the battle be when it may, it will never have been surpassed. ... If I fall on such a glorious occasion, it shall be my pride to take care that my friends shall not blush for me. These things are in the hands of a wise and just Providence, and his Will be done! ... Do not think I am low spirited on this account, or fancy anything is to happen to me; quite the contrary – my mind is calm, and I have only to think of destroying our inveterate foe.[4]

'I know neither the time nor the manner of my death,' had been wonderfully internalized.

One of his first tasks had been to deliver the First Lord's letter to Sir Robert Calder about the Inquiry into his conduct on 23 and 24 July. Although ordered to return in another ship, Calder recoiled from the loss of face this would incur. Nelson did not insist that he leave his 90 gun ship, the *Prince of Wales*. 'I trust that I shall be considered to have done right as a man, and to a Brother Officer in affliction – my heart could not stand it, and so the thing must rest,'[5] he explained to the First Lord. Nelson's sentimentality and need to be loved had led him into a grave misjudgement. Fully aware of his need for ships, fully aware of how hard pressed the Admiralty was to supply them, mistakenly tolerant of Calder's crass indifference to Nelson's need for his big ship, his decision was incredibly bad. Calder also asked Nelson to release three captains as witnesses. Two went, but one Durham of the *Defiance*, to his credit declined and fought at Trafalgar. Nelson could be a soft touch.

On 2 October he would tell Emma of his distressing scene with Calder: 'I have given him the advice as to my dearest friend. He is in adversity, and if he ever has been my enemy, he now feels the pang of it, and finds me one of his best friends.'[6] So great was his need to be admired that he could persuade himself that he had won over an enemy. He might also, with such a great weight of public expectation settled on his own shoulders, have been thinking, 'There but for the grace of God go I.' There was great compassion and fellow feeling among these men. Ten days later

Collingwood would write to Nelson, 'I am grieved whenever I think of Sir Robert's case. I think he must be aware of his situation, and feels more about it than he chooses should appear. I wish he was in England, because I think he wants a calm adviser.'[7] Alas, Calder does not seem to have been able to take advice. Nelson's last words to Collingwood were, 'I am glad Sir Robert Calder is gone; from my heart I hope he will get home safe, and end his inquiry well. I endeavoured to give him all the caution in my power respecting the cry against him; but he seemed too wise.'[8]

The preoccupations of his command prevented his writing to Emma until 1 October. First he told her the bad news, 'It is a relief to me, to take up the pen, and write you a line; for I have had, about four o'clock this morning, one of my dreadful spasms, which has almost enervated me. It is very odd; I hardly ever felt better than yesterday. Fremantle stayed with me till eight o'clock, and I slept uncommonly well; but was awoke with this disorder. My opinion of its effect, some one day [ultimately], has never altered. However, it is entirely gone off, and I am only quite weak. The good people of England will not believe that rest of body and mind is necessary for me! But perhaps this spasm may not come again these six months.'

Here was an episode similar to others in the past yet his description was not quite the same. There is always insufficient objective data on which to make a conclusive diagnosis. Since the Nile he had appeared to be obsessed by his health, yet his pain and discomfort although seemingly real enough never incapacitated him. Of course his history of physical damage had left its effects, the malaria and tropical sprue of his early days, loss of sight in one eye at Calvi and progressive deterioration in the other, recurring symptoms from the traumatic hernia caused by the blow to his belly at St Vincent, amputation of his right arm with a cold knife and no anaesthetic at Tenerife followed by four months of painful post-operative complications, and a nasty head wound at the Nile. He had surmounted them all and survived St Vincent, the Nile and Copenhagen, an unequalled exposure to battle and command, in which his mental, physical and immune systems must have been stretched to breaking point. A parallel history of somatic symptoms, accompanied by actual pain, could have arisen from his anxieties, responsibilities, emotional distress, and at times accompanied his boredom and depression, or signalled his need for love and attention. His present symptoms could be indicative of the weight of responsibility and expectations the whole nation had placed on him.

The good news was his reception in the fleet,

> I believe my arrival was most welcome, not only to the Commander of the Fleet, but also to every individual in it; and, when I came to explain to them the 'Nelson touch,' it was like an electric shock. Some shed tears, all approved – 'It was new – it was singular – it was simple!'; and, from Admirals downwards, it was repeated – 'It must succeed, if ever they will allow us to get at them! You are, my Lord, surrounded by friends whom you inspire with confidence.' Some may be Judas's; but the majority are certainly much pleased with my commanding them.[9]

A letter to an unidentified recipient said, 'The reception I met with on joining the Fleet caused the sweetest sensation of my life. The Officers who came on board to welcome my return, forgot my rank as Commander-in-Chief in the enthusiasm with which they greeted me. As soon as these emotions were past, I laid before them the Plan I had previously arranged for attacking the Enemy; and it was not only my pleasure to find it generally approved, but clearly perceived and understood.'[10] He had lost no time in taking his captains by storm. What was so enthralling for them in the outline of his plan was the level of trust he would place in them and the freedom of action he would bestow. Above all, it was the clarity of his intention, the opening of his mind to them, that provided a foundation for their confidence.

On 3 October he sent six of his ships off to Gibraltar to take on stores and water, including *Canopus* the flagship of Rear-Admiral Louis whose captain, Francis Austen, was enjoying a farewell dinner with Nelson. On their taking leave Austen recorded Admiral Louis as saying, 'You are sending us away, my Lord – the Enemy will come out, and we shall have no share in the Battle.' Nelson replied in that infinitely charming way he now had, 'My dear Louis, I have no other means of keeping my Fleet complete in provisions and water, but by sending them in detachments to Gibraltar. The Enemy will come out and we shall fight them; but there will be time for you to get back first. I look upon *Canopus* as my right hand [she was his second astern in the line of battle]; and I send you first to insure your being here to beat them.'[11]

Nelson was convinced that a battle was imminent. He now stationed *Mars*, *Defence* and *Colossus* nine to twelve miles between the fleet and Cadiz, to repeat any signals his inshore frigates might make of the enemy's emergence. The main body of the fleet would be kept around fifty miles west of Cadiz. Duff of the *Mars* had dined with Nelson on 30 September and reported to his wife, 'I dined with his Lordship yesterday and had a very merry dinner. He certainly is the pleasantest Admiral I ever served under.'[12] Ten days later he wrote, 'He is so good and pleasant a man, that we all wish to do what he likes, without any kind of orders. I have been myself very lucky with most of my Admirals, but I really think the present the pleasantest I have met with; even this little detachment is a kind thing to me, there being so many senior officers to me in the Fleet, as it shows his attention, and wish to bring me forward.'[13] Hoste, who had arrived in command of *Eurydice*, was back on board *Victory* and told his father, 'I . . . have seen Lord Nelson, who is as good and friendly as ever.'[14]

Nelson was particularly intent on maintaining his good relationship with Blackwood who commanded his frigate screen, 'the eyes of the fleet', upon which he depended for intelligence. He continued to press the Admiralty for more eyes, and had no hesitation in going to the top. In a powerful communication to George Rose he made his point: 'I verily believe the Country will soon be put to some expense for my account, either a Monument, or a new Pension and Honours . . . a very few days, almost hours, will put us in Battle; the success no man can ensure, but the fighting them, if they can be got at, I pledge myself. . . . it is as Mr Pitt knows, annihilation that the Country wants, and not merely a splendid Victory of twenty-three to thirty-six, – honourable to the parties concerned, but absolutely useless in the extended scale to bring Buonaparte to his marrow bones; numbers only can annihilate.' He went on, 'If Mr Pitt would hint to Lord Barham, that he shall be anxious until I get the force proposed, and plenty of Frigates and Sloops in order to watch them closely, it may be advantageous to the Country; you are at liberty to mention this to Mr Pitt, but I would not wish it to go farther.'[15] He treated Blackwood as a partner, 'you estimate, as I do, the importance of not letting these rogues escape us without a fair fight, which I pant for by day, and dream of by night', ending this letter seductively, 'I send you two papers; I stole them for you.'[16] He was determined to keep his officers on friendly terms with each other as tension mounted. On another occasion he dealt gently with Blackwood: 'I see you feel how much my heart is set on getting at these fellows, whom I have hunted so long; but don't my dear Blackwood, be angry with anyone; it was only a laudable anxiety in Admiral Louis, and nothing like complaining.'[17] He developed the closest working relationship with Collingwood: to Nelson he was invariably 'My dear Coll'. He finished one of his letters to him, 'Telegraph upon all occasions without ceremony. We are one and hope ever shall be.'[18]

Aware that the Combined Fleet in Cadiz had re-embarked its troops and the ships at Cartagena had hoisted their topsail yards, he had now to be careful about his positioning. He had to be well up to Cadiz to cope with easterly winds but not so close that westerlies could force his big ships through the Straits. There was nothing he could do about his detached ships; the fleet had to have supplies, or be forced to go *en masse* into the Straits. He was obviously steeling himself for he knew what he intended. He wrote to his old friend, Brigadier-General Stewart, 'I have thirty six Sail of the Line looking me in the face; unfortunately there is a strip of land between us, but it is believed they will come to sea in a few days. The sooner the better, I don't like to have these things upon my mind; and if I see my way through the fiery ordeal, I shall go home and rest for the winter, and shall rejoice to take you, my dear Stewart by the hand.'[19] He knew very clearly that a fiery ordeal, above all for the leaders, was implicit in his plan.

A month previously, on 10 September, Nelson had stopped off at Richmond Park to talk with the previous Prime Minister Henry Addington, who as Lord Sidmouth had come back into government in January 1805. According to Sidmouth's recollections Nelson went to a small table and with his finger described diagrammatically how he intended to defeat the Combined Fleet: 'Rodney broke the line in one point; I will break it in two.'[20]

On 9 October, having already accustomed his officers to the broad concept of his plan, Nelson published it in a written memorandum.[21] It was the final flowering of a method that had been growing and developing in his mind since the battle of St Vincent and its outdated concept of command and control. He was anticipating by 200 years today's concept of Mission Command, whereby the commander makes his intention clear and his subordinate commanders are relied upon to internalize his broad intention and in the actual circumstances of battle extemporize, so as to achieve his objective. Nelson knew that no plan could cope with the chance, uncertainty, confusion and contingencies of war, to say nothing of the vagaries of weather. His Memorandum was very clear about his overall intention: 'bringing the enemy to battle' in all weather conditions without the loss of time involved in forming a line of battle and 'in such a manner as to make the business decisive'. His verbal discussions with his captains always emphasized that his overriding aim was annihilation of the enemy.

He then painted a general picture of how the fleet would be deployed. They would form two lines of sixteen ships, headed respectively by himself and Collingwood, with an advanced squadron of eight of the fastest two-deckers, which could be directed to reinforce whichever line was necessary. He assumed an enemy of forty-six sail-of-the-line and probably so extended 'that their Van [leading ships] could not succour their Rear'. His own line would attack the enemy centre, Collingwood's about twelve ships from their rear, the advanced squadron about three or four ships ahead of the centre, 'so as to ensure getting at their Commander-in-Chief on whom every Effort must be made to Capture. The whole impression of the British Fleet must be to over-power from two or three ships ahead of their Commander-in-Chief, supposed to be in the Centre, to the Rear of their Fleet.' He went on, 'I will suppose twenty Sail of the Enemy's Line to be untouched, it must be some time before they could perform a manoeuvre to bring their force compact to attack any part of the British Fleet engaged, or to succour their own Ships, which indeed would be impossible without mixing with the Ships engaged.'

Within these strategic intentions he gave the greatest freedom to his subordinates. Collingwood, Nelson's second-in-command, 'will after my intentions are made known to him, have the entire direction of his Line to make the attack upon the Enemy, and to follow up the blow until they are captured or destroyed'. 'The remainder of the Enemy's Fleet, 34 Sail, are to be left to the management of the Commander-in-Chief, who will endeavour to take care that the movements of the Second in Command are as little interrupted as possible.'

As for contingencies he was equally clear in his Memorandum. His general prescription could not have been more explicit: 'Captains are to look to their particular line as their rallying point. But in case Signals can neither be seen or perfectly understood, no Captain can do very wrong, if he places his Ship alongside that of an Enemy.... Some Ships may not get through their exact place, but they will always be at hand to assist their friends.'

The words of modern military doctrine as laid down in the current handbooks of the British Army and Navy echo to an uncanny extent what Nelson had created: 'Commanders who are in each other's minds and who share a common approach to the conduct of operations are more likely to act in concert.' The succession of captains who had been rowed over to the *Victory* had been left in no doubt as to what was in Nelson's mind: a headlong assault on the enemy, cutting off its rear with a force never less than a quarter stronger, an overpowering of its centre and destruction of its capacity for command and control, readiness to meet a counterattack from the van, above all a fight at close quarters, with the ultimate objective the annihilation of the enemy. He was confident that the superior fighting qualities of British captains, officers and men, and superior training, would bring victory. He had adopted a strategy whereby his units had to fight. Personally, he would be able to do no more than convey his intentions and set up his opening gambit. Thereafter the battle would be outside his control. To Collingwood he was entirely open and emphatic:

> I send you my Plan of Attack, as far as a man dare venture to guess at the very uncertain position the Enemy may be found in. But, my dear friend, it is to place you perfectly at ease respecting my intentions, and to give full scope to your judgement for carrying them into effect. We can, my dear Coll have no little jealousies. We have only one great object in view, that of annihilating our Enemies and getting a glorious Peace for our Country. No man has more confidence in another than I have in you: and no man will render your services more justice than your very old friend.[22]

The issue of his Memorandum, which was extraordinary in the public delegation and trust he placed in 'Dear Coll', brought him a swift reply from the undemonstrative and extremely competent fifty-four-year-old. 'I have a just sense of your Lordship's kindness to me, and the full confidence you have reposed in me inspires me with the most lively gratitude. I hope it will not be long before there is an opportunity of showing your Lordship that it has not been misplaced.'[23]

On 9 October, in a letter to Abbé Campbell in Naples there was another stab from his subconscious, 'Dr Scott desires his best respects, and my brother hopes I shall meet the Enemy's Fleet, that some how or other he may be a Lord.'[24] At home Emma was missing him. She wrote about Horatia, 'our dear girl', saying that she addressed Mrs Cadogan as 'Mrs Candogging'. She addressed him fervently: 'You are my whole of good. . . . My dearest life.'[25]

And so they waited. Nelson told Blackwood he did not wish there to be longer intervals between his reports than forty-eight hours. The French, as Nelson referred to the Combined Fleet, had bent (attached) their topgallant sails. On the 10th he told Coll that the Enemy was all but emerging from Cadiz. His flow of work was never-ending. On the same day he sent five letters to the Admiralty, three to Collingwood and fourteen circulars 'To All Captains' covering various aspects of supply and administration in the fleet; few have the air of being drafted for him, either by his secretary or by the Captain of the Fleet. There was one to Blackwood about signals he should make if the enemy came out: 'I rely on you, that we can't miss getting hold of them, and I will give them such a shaking as they never yet experienced; at least I will lay down my life in the attempt. We are a very powerful Fleet, and not to be held cheap.'[26] He told Ball of the trap he was laying, 'five frigates, a Brig, and a Schooner watching them closely, an Advanced Squadron of fast sailing Ships between me and the Frigates, and the body of the Fleet from fifteen to eighteen leagues West of Cadiz'.[27] He was determined not to be caught, as he had been in 1798 and 1804, by the French slipping out under his nose.

On 13 October his spirits were greatly raised by the appearance of the madcap Sir Edward Berry in dear old *Agamemnon*. Berry, in characteristic fashion, had fallen in with the French Rochefort squadron, six ships-of-the-line, two frigates and a brig, off Cape Finisterre. After a hair-raising chase of more than seventy miles in seven hours, the notably fast *Agamemnon* only just escaped a three-decker and another 80-gun ship after losing her main topgallant sheet. Nelson did not miss his opportunity, 'Here comes Berry; now we shall have a Battle.'[28] That evening Calder left the fleet in the *Prince of Wales* with the two captains he had asked to accompany him. The same day *Amphion* and Hoste sailed for Gibraltar and Algiers. He would not return till 15 November. On 16 October Nelson spent the morning organizing the fleet into the order of sailing. Somewhere to the north the Rochefort squadron was prowling. He hoped that Sir Richard Strachan had them in his sights. The October days were sun lit and Nelson exclaimed on the 19th to Coll, 'What a beautiful day! Will you be tempted out of your Ship? If you will, hoist the Assent and Victory's pendants.'[29] It was not to be. Under such idyllic conditions came the news they had all been waiting for – the signal from Blackwood that the enemy was out.

This, in a sense, was something of a miracle. After the fiasco of his grand strategy for invading England, Napoleon had turned his Army east, marching to his eventual victories against the Austrians and Russians at Ulm and Austerlitz. He had ordered Villeneuve to break out into the Mediterrranean and support the under-flank of his armies. Villeneuve's fleet was in dire straits, needing repairs and provisions, for which Spanish contractors, rightly distrustful of the French, were demanding payment in cash. He was 2,000 men short and his officers were split by dissension; he knew the size of the British fleet and that Nelson was on his way. However, when Villeneuve's orders arrived at the end of September his Council of War decided that they required a more favourable moment; they failed to take advantage of poor weather on 10 October. On the 18th, however, Villeneuve gave a sudden order to sail. He had heard on the grapevine that fifty-three-year-old Vice-Admiral Rosily had arrived at Madrid, seven to ten days away, and was on his way to replace him. He also knew that six of Nelson's ships had been sighted near Gibraltar.

The Combined Fleet began its move out of harbour early on the 19th but it took until the morning of the next day for the whole fleet to assemble outside Cadiz. Meanwhile, as soon as the news had been received by Nelson, some fifty miles to the west of Cadiz at half past nine on the 19th, he made the signal 'General Chase S.E.' His ships stood for the Straits to cut off the enemy from entering the Mediterranean.

The flurry of immediate activity over, he went to his cabin to give Emma the news: 'My dearest beloved Emma and the dear friend of my bosom – The signal has been made that the enemy's combined fleet are coming out of port. We have very little wind, so that I have no hopes of seeing them before tomorrow. May the God of Battles crown my endeavours with success! At all events I shall take care that my name shall ever be most dear to you and Horatia, both of whom I love as much as my own life, and as my last writing before the battle will be to you, so I hope in God that I shall live to finish my letter after the battle. May Heaven help you prays your Nelson & Bronte.'[30] Having for the moment finished with his letter to her mother, he wrote also to Horatia: 'I was made happy by the pleasure of receiving your letter of September 19th, and I rejoice to hear that you are so very good a girl, and love my dear Lady Hamilton, who most dearly loves you. Give her a kiss for me. The Combined Fleets of the Enemy are now reported to be coming out of Cadiz; and therefore I answer your letter, my dearest Horatia, to mark to you that you are ever uppermost in my thoughts.... Receive my dearest Horatia, the affectionate parental blessing of your Father.'[31]

With Nelson virtually permanently on deck, *Victory* was off the Straits by daybreak on the 20th. Having got away so quickly, there were no signs of the enemy. He turned back and stood to the north-west to search them out. They were still to his north, closer to the coast of Spain. At this point he wanted to shadow them and at the same time keep his advantageous position to windward. When reports came of ships to the north-east, he turned his ships again, sailing once more towards the Straits. At four o'clock in the afternoon of the 21st he decided to get closer and moved his ships towards the land. At dawn the two fleets were about twelve miles apart, and Nelson's positioning was well nigh perfect. His enemy were sailing for the Straits in a ragged line ahead. Then at eight o'clock, Villeneuve, faced by the choice of sailing on into the Mediterranean and his first objective Naples, with options *en route* to find shelter in Cartagena or Toulon, decided, amazingly, to turn his fleet towards the British. He had now two options only: fight or fly for Cadiz. As the fleets inexorably closed on each other, Villeneuve sailing north, Nelson coming down on him from the north-west, Villeneuve was well aware of what Nelson would try to do. Before sailing he had said in his orders, 'The enemy will not limit their tactics to forming the usual battle line parallel to ours ... [rather] they will endeavour to surround our rear guard, and cross through in order better to envelop and defeat us, carrying away those of our vessels they will have isolated.'[32]

Nelson would have been astonished to know that his tactics would come as no surprise to Villeneuve. It never seems to have entered into his calculations that his opponent might be thoughtful and clever and have learned from his experience at the Nile. He would also have been surprised to know that Villeneuve had also formed a *corps de reserve*, or *escadre d'observation* of twelve ships under Admiral Gravina and Rear-Admiral Magon, supposedly to be used as reinforcements. But the orders Villeneuve issued as they had prepared to sail were very unlike Nelson's in one crucial respect, 'Should it come to a battle, any commanding officer not under fire will not be considered to be at his post, and a signal from me pointing this out will be taken as a stain upon his honour.'[33] There was a vast difference between Villeneuve's command by threat, and the implicit low expectations he had of his captains and Nelson's confident trust in his officers and men. Yet in spite of all his previous hesitations, in spite of the inherent difficulties of commanding his dual nationality force, Villeneuve felt impelled by pride to fight; he did not frustrate Nelson by ordering his ships to make for Cadiz. But though his intelligence and previous experience had given him more than an inkling of Nelson's likely plan, he seems not to have formed any concept of how to counter it. He did not use the slow approach of the British to concert a counterattack by his van, or organize his *corps de reserve* properly; it existed, but was all over the place. He had only the serendipitous effect of his bunched ships to hinder Nelson. It is possible he thought that would be enough and appreciated from the very beginning the magnitude and dangers of the task Nelson had set himself. In thinking about this we have perhaps been blinded by our perception of 200 years that Nelson was the wolf and the Combined Fleet the sheep.

At 8.30 Nelson knew the Combined Fleet had turned to face him and began to match the spirit of his broad-brush battle plan with unfolding reality. He had made only two assumptions about the enemy: that they would form a line and that they would either be upwind (to windward) or downwind (to leeward) of himself. They were revealed in a straggly line about nine miles long and downwind. He was moving sluggishly across a broad swell, every sail he could wear catching at the weak wind. Because Louis and six ships were at Gibraltar he had to abandon his idea of a fast sailing observation-reserve squadron and concentrate on his two-pronged attack. Neither prong could be of sixteen ships as envisaged. His own was twelve ships, with two of them, *Africa* and *Orion*, way out of position; Collingwood's was fifteen. He had wanted Collingwood to be a quarter more powerful than the enemy's rear when he cut the line at the twelfth ship, but the partial double line of enemy ships actually meant that Collingwood would be outnumbered by two ships.

As for Nelson, he was left with sixteen enemy ships divided equally between centre and van; he was outnumbered by only four ships, not for him a very worrying proposition. He was leading his ships directly at the enemy and short of their scattering madly, he must oblige them to fight, his essential aim. There would still be about four enemy ships between himself and Collingwood. But as he sailed on with Collingwood's line a mile and a half away on his right, he was beginning to see more clearly the length of the French line, its irregularity and its concave curving form. Both he and Collingwood took steps to reorder their ships, bringing their faster ships to the head of the line to ensure that the first succession of blows followed each other without delay. On deck there was a certain amount of by-play as Blackwood, egged on by Dr William Beatty the surgeon and others, fiercely protective of their little Admiral, sought to persuade Nelson to transfer his flag to *Euryalus*, ostensibly to enable him to command the battle better, but covertly to protect him from his vulnerability in approaching the enemy head on; every gun in the enemy fleet that could be brought to bear on the *Victory* would fire at her. This was an offer which Nelson had no difficulty in refusing; he knew that once battle was joined, command and control could achieve little. Then there was a discussion about the position of *Victory* in the line. Her official place was third and though Nelson seems to have reluctantly agreed that the *Téméraire* should go ahead he proved remarkably unwilling to allow her to pass.

About this time he went below and in the heightened mood of imminent battle, took up his pen. After detailing the movements of the enemy fleet in his Private Diary he continued, 'May the Great God, whom I worship, grant to my Country, and for the benefit of Europe in general, a great and glorious Victory; and may no misconduct in any one tarnish it; and may humanity after Victory be the predominant feature in the British Fleet. For myself, individually, I commit my life to Him who made me, and may his blessing light upon my endeavours for serving my Country faithfully. To Him I resign myself and the just cause which is entrusted to me to defend. Amen. Amen. Amen.'[34] He then went to work on a codicil to his will in which he wrote of Emma's eminent services at Naples, when she had obtained the King of Spain's letter to the King of Naples which indicated his intention to declare war on England and had thus enabled the country to be warned, and also when she had obtained supplies for his own fleet at Syracuse in 1798. He continued,

Could I have rewarded these services I would not now call upon my Country; but as that has not been in my power I leave Emma Lady Hamilton, therefore a Legacy to my King and Country, that they will give her an ample provision to maintain her rank in life. I also leave to the beneficence of my Country my adopted daughter, Horatia Nelson Thompson; and I desire she will use in future the name of Nelson only. These are the only favours I ask of my King and Country at this moment when I am going to fight their Battle. May God bless my King and Country, and all those I hold dear. My relations it is needless to mention; they will of course be amply provided for.[35]

He called for Hardy and Blackwood to come and witness it. It is unlikely that either would have read what they were witnessing. Wills must have been written all over the ship on that day.

His codicil is a quantum leap from his thinking of himself as Captain Suckling's legacy. It demonstrates the height of the pedestal on which he had now placed Emma, prompted to such a grandiose gesture by the reality of what lay ahead, his feeling that the odds against him were shortening, now that he had so much to live for – Emma, his only child Horatia, and dear Merton. But nothing could now change his path. In his mind he and Emma had been married before he left and now, in his deeply emotional state, she was integrated into his golden orb, the heroine alongside the hero.

Now back on deck, where it was 11.30, he presented to all who saw him a calm and untroubled exterior. With tension mounting and battle inescapable he proposed a signal, he said to amuse the fleet, *England confides that Every Man will do his Duty*. The signal lieutenant, Pasco, was quick to realize that *confides* would increase the number of flags required because the word was not included in Sir Home Popham's signals vocabulary. He proposed substituting *expects* for *confides*. 'Make it so,' said Nelson. And so it was that the most famous signal in maritime history was born and hoisted, even though the signal as sent substituted patriotic grandeur for the original feeling of personal trust and confidence on which Nelson's leadership was founded. When the telegraph flag, a red and white diagonal, fluttered at the masthead, a host of telescopes throughout the fleet pointed towards *Victory*. For about four minutes thirty-two flags, generally in groups of three numeral flags, broke successively at the mastheads and on the yards. Numbers 253, 269, 863,

261, 471, 958, 220, 370 for the first eight words were followed by a single flag 4 and then three pairs of flags 21, 19 and 24, spelling out the word D-u-t-y. His ships slowly sailed on at about one and a half miles an hour. Two signals would follow, *Prepare to Anchor*, number 63, and *Close Action*, number 16. In half an hour or so his leading ships would enter their period of maximum vulnerability when they would be raked before they could themselves fire a shot. For the enemy, the sight of columns of warships, more numerous than expected, making directly for them, ready to take punishment without hesitation, would be extremely challenging, given that Nelson's reputation was by now as fearsome to the French and Spanish as it was inspiring to the British.

At 11.40 he was already having to contemplate a change of plan. He had been unable to locate his point of attack. Villeneuve had not hoisted his flag. He signalled to Collingwood, who was himself just coming under fire, 'I intend to push or go through the end of the enemy's line to prevent them from getting into Cadiz.'[36] If he went for the van he might still make his way down to the centre on what little wind there was, but equally the French and Spanish centre would have time to turn on Collingwood. His dilemma was solved when Villeneuve broke his flag and Nelson could revert instantly to his original plan, to make his hammer blow in the centre. It was now 11.50 and Nelson sent Blackwood and Prowse of the *Sirius* away to relay his intentions to the ships behind. Blackwood, like Riou before him, had become totally seduced by Nelson. He recoiled in horror as Nelson, seeing him over the side, said 'God bless you Blackwood I shall never speak to you again.'[37] These instinctive words came like an actor's ad lib, uninvited to his lips, the expression of an inner stream of consciousness. They were like other words on other occasions but seem less calculated to inspire, more private and intimate in their direction, more an acceptance of a personal fate. They may have reflected sudden insight into the death and horror his plan was about to visit on so many of his officers and men and a need to share it; or may reveal like the codicil to his will a highly charged emotional state, a man ready to go over the top. The fact that he wore a coat emblazoned with stars is neither here nor there; it was his usual habit to convey confidence and courage to others. It was not an indication, as some have believed, that on this occasion he intended to be killed. Whatever their inner genesis both his codicil and his words to Blackwood were gestures of the highest theatricality.

Nelson, now passing the enemy van, met with a solid wall of fire from the French centre as he probed for an opening. As *Victory* approached the French fleet, her upper deck was crowded with officers, marines and seamen, clumps of blue and gold, scarlet and white, bronzed bodies and red kerchiefs glinting in the sun, white sails billowing above the spotless decks. There was a small space where Nelson and his flag captain, Hardy walked, their immediate staff relatively close at hand. From just after noon *Victory* was a virtually helpless target, coming on inexorably, but very slowly, all sails set, borne forward as much by the great oily swell as by the wind. *Bucentaure* fired sighting shots, the first falling short, the ships being about a mile and a quarter apart. Further shots fell closer, spouting in the nearby sea. Soon holes appeared in *Victory*'s sails and now the fire of seven or eight French ships poured at the advancing ship. With 500 yards to go *Victory* was undergoing a terrible hammering. Before she could fire a shot in return, her wheel was shot to pieces and she had to be steered from the cockpit. Her marines on the upper deck were decimated by hails of double-headed shot. The masts and yards, the chief point of aim for the enemy, suffered terribly; her sails were riddled. By 12.15 as the *Victory* turned to enter the enemy line she was raked through her stem.

The awful gamble of life and death had begun. Some died swiftly and easily, their heads taken off by a cannon ball, hearts pierced by a sharp-shooter's ball or impaled by shards of torn timber. Some were not so lucky. They suddenly saw no hand where one had been, had no leg on which to stand, no sight in an eye. Others saw mates lose their guts, or legs, or arms; boys became blotches of stained matter against a mast, bodies now and then hitting the deck with a soft murmur. By now fifty men had been killed and wounded without a shot being fired in return. To the south of them in Collingwood's line the second lieutenant of the *Revenge* saw death enter the gun deck:

The shot entered the 3rd lower deck port from forward on the star-board side and struck the gun (32 pounder) in which it made a large dint, then altering its direction struck the foremast in a vertical posi-tion and scooped out a large proportion of the mast, which again altering its direction, it took a horizontal position and after decap-itating a young midshipman by the name of Green, it struck the seven men at the foremost tackle of the first gun forward on the star-

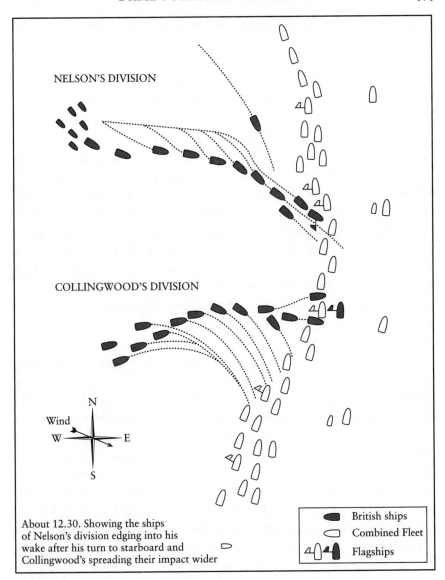

NELSON'S DIVISION

COLLINGWOOD'S DIVISION

N

Wind

W——————E

S

About 12.30. Showing the ships
of Nelson's division edging into his
wake after his turn to starboard and
Collingwood's spreading their impact wider

British ships
Combined Fleet
Flagships

The Battle of Trafalgar, 21 October 1805: The Blows are delivered

board side who were running out after loading, and killed the whole
of them by severing them nearly in two. It then stuck in the ship's
side in a horizontal position, just above the waterway nearly under
the breech of the gun.[38]

Nelson himself was splattered by the blood of his secretary Scott, who, standing nearby poised to do his Admiral's bidding, dropped to the deck, decapitated. A shot smashed its way into the woodwork and filled the air with splinters, one of which tore the buckle from Hardy's shoe. Even Nelson was appalled by the carnage around him. 'This is too warm work, Hardy, to last long.'[39]

Such was the pitifully slow pace of their approach that it was not until 12.35 that *Victory* could fire her first shots. Her 68-pounder forecastle port side carronade sent its ball and a keg packed with 500 musket balls through the *Bucentaure*'s stern cabin. Then as she sailed past she brought her 50-gun broadside, double and treble shotted, to bear with pulverizing effect on *Bucentaure*'s stern. That broadside alone cost the French flagship 400 dead and wounded and disabled twenty guns. This sudden hell for *Bucentaure* matched an equal hell for Nelson and Hardy. They had not found a way through but had ventured into a deadly *cul-de-sac*. Directly ahead was the French *Neptune*, raking them from a perfect position, on their right the *Redoutable* whose broadside could fire directly at them. *Victory* was hemmed in and fast losing way. Hardy had no option other than to decide which enemy ship he should crash into. He chose the *Redoutable* and locked her in a lethal embrace of unimaginable closeness, ferocity and horror. Sailors, fired by an unworldly detachment, summoned up the strength of men in extremity, fought like staring automatons, toiled unceasingly as they went through their gun drills, firing directly into the adjacent enemy, interrupted only when death shook some of their number like rag dolls or squashed others into pulp, or left others minus limbs, crying out, moaning and whimpering in pain on blood slopped decks. *Victory* swept her enemy's deck with her 68-pounder starboard carronade. *Redoutable* fought on, her main deck guns still active, her tops full of sharpshooters.

Further to the south Collingwood, who had come under massive and sustained fire as he approached the enemy line, had rapidly found himself in a similar position. At 12.10, fifteen minutes before Nelson fired a shot, he passed the stern of the *Santa Ana*, the 112-gun flagship of Vice-Admiral Ignacio María de Álava y Navarrete, and poured his broadside into her crying out to his captain, 'Rotherham, what would Nelson give to be here!'[40] But just as Nelson was to be hemmed in, so was he. He found himself being fired on from all sides, by the *Fougeux* which raked his stern, by the *San Leandro*, which raked him through his bow, by the *Indomptable* and *San Justo* off to his starboard as well as the *Santa Ana*, the ship he was closely engaging to port. He had also found himself entangled in the double line. The tables were completely turned. It was not a case of Nelson and Collingwood and their ships breaking through to surround their enemy: having broken through, they were surrounded. In Collingwood's case it was not until *Belleisle*, *Mars* and *Tonnant* came up, firing in turn into the *Santa Ana*'s stern and going on to combine against the *Fougeux*, that his own ship could concentrate on the *Santa Ana*. Collingwood's broadsides reduced her masts to stumps, shredded her rigging and sails and killed or wounded 300 of her men. When the *Santa Ana* surrendered at 2.15 after two hours of fighting the *Royal Sovereign* had also been reduced to an unmanoeuvrable wreck; two of her masts crashed down and she had to be taken in tow by Blackwood.

Trafalgar was not taking its expected course. Two mighty blows had been delivered much where Nelson had wanted them. Several of Nelson's division, the *Téméraire*, the British *Neptune*, *Leviathan* and *Conqueror* had all followed in his wake, creating a massive entry into the enemy centre, but his attack had been blunted not only by the exposure his strategy had imposed on his leading ships, but also by the unexpected pattern of the enemy ships, and the courage of his enemy. He was particularly fortunate that what little wind there was, held; had it not, his leading ships might have been sacrificed before supporting ships could get up. Collingwood's division had done things differently: each ship moved on a line of bearing towards an individually designated target, matching ship against ship in order to overpower the whole of the enemy rear. Thus help did not reach Collingwood as quickly as it had Nelson. After she got among the enemy, *Victory* cut through nothing, nor did the *Royal Sovereign*, and from this point onwards there was no pattern to the battle of Trafalgar.

Pell-mell is an accurate description of the battle's disorderliness and promiscuity; many were killed and maimed by friendly fire as the battle fragmented into a series of disjointed actions, the French and Spaniards at first frequently outnumbering the British, doubling and trebling on them, until other British ships came up. After supporting Collingwood the *Belleisle* was herself boxed in. Totally dismasted she was saved only by the arrival of *Polyphemus*, *Defiance* and *Swiftsure*. Gunnery soon emerged as the critical difference between the fleets. The British ships were by far the more efficient killing machines. In this Collingwood was pre-eminent; his crews were trained to fire three broadsides in five minutes and had been known to accomplish three broadsides in three and a half minutes. For thirty critical minutes the French and Spanish had been unable to take full advantage of the sitting targets provided by the slow-moving British ships before they eventually closed. Subsequently, Nelson's slower ships constituted a kind of reserve, a drip feed of fresh ships, each committed to find a fight. This constituted the second and most important critical difference. In approaching the extended mêlée, these captains would choose where to place themselves to best advantage. They were active in manoeuvring their ships to help each other and get alongside the enemy, several deliberately running their ships into their opponents. This was not just a question of the highly practised seamanship of the British officers and men. Each of the captains was fully motivated by Nelson's orders, each was aware of the plot. They were more effective because they knew what they had to do. This was in stark contrast to Villeneuve's tactical inertia.

Courage was not an essential difference, apart from the behaviour of Dumanoir and his van division. Several French ships fought as well as the best of the British. The *Intrépide*, Captain Louis Infernet, alone of Dumanoir's van had turned to help the centre and began to engage at about two o'clock. She was fired on by the *Africa*, smashed to pieces by *Orion*, cut off by the *Ajax* and *Agamemnon*, saw *Minotaur*, and *Spartiate* coming at her and surrendered only after losing 320 men. The *Achille*, Captain Gabriel Denieport, fought four British ships and eventually caught fire and blew up with the loss of most of her crew. The *Redoutable*, Captain Jean Jacques Etienne Lucas, sandwiched between the *Victory* and the *Téméraire*, fought with unimaginable bravery and resource, parts of her lower deck blown in, her stern pulverized and 522, 82 per cent of her crew, killed or wounded. The *Aigle*, Captain Pierre Gourrège, fought at least six British ships and had 270 killed and wounded.

At twenty-five minutes past one, Nelson was pacing his quarterdeck, seven paces forward to the raised border (coamings) of the cabin ladder, seven aft to the stanchions of the wheel. He had turned aft, slightly ahead of Hardy, when the thumping blow of a musket ball fired at him from the mizzen top of the *Redoutable* some forty feet above pushed him down on his knees into the pools of Scott's blood. Hardy turned, his face instantly concerned, 'Are you all right?' Nelson's words came out, his head bent close to the deck: 'They have done for me at last, Hardy.' He heard Hardy say, 'I hope not.' He heard himself answering, 'Yes my backbone is shot through.' Sergeant-Major Secker and seamen took hold of him to raise him from the deck. Hardy had called, 'You and You . . . lift . . . below . . . cockpit.' His own place was on deck.

It is said that when Nelson was carried below he had the presence of mind to cover his face and medals with his handkerchief. A handkerchief would have been hard to locate, even if his arm was free. Barely crouching under Nelson's light weight the seamen passed down through the indescribable noise of the upper, middle and lower gun decks to the sanctuary of the cockpit situated on the orlop deck below the waterline, normally the living quarters of the midshipmen, but now rigged as a casualty post and operating theatre. 'Ah Mr Beatty,' he said, as the surgeon and Mr Burke the purser placed him in a semi-sitting position on the hard planked deck, his back against one of the massive knees in the midshipman's berth. 'You can do nothing for me. I have but a short time to live: my back is shot through.' Emerging from the gloomy recesses was his chaplain, Dr Scott. Nothing in his Holy Orders had prepared him to cope with the horrific scenes he had been encountering before Nelson's arrival; they would invade his dreams for the rest of his life. The arrival of his dear chief steadied him and from that moment he did not leave his side. Asked by Dr Beatty what his sensations were, Nelson said, 'he felt a gush of blood every minute within his breast; that he had no feeling in the lower part of his body: and that his breathing was difficult, and attended with very severe pain about that part of the spine where he was confident that the ball had struck'. The gush of blood and the weakness of Nelson's pulse told Beatty that his case was hopeless.

It took Nelson three and a quarter hours to die and for most of that time he was in command of his speech and senses. At first, believing himself on the point of death, he was hurried, 'Remember me to Lady Hamilton! Remember me to Horatia! Remember me to all my friends. Doctor, remember me to Mr Rose: tell him I have made a will and left Lady Hamilton and Horatia to my Country.' According to Scott, when he realized he was still alive, his mind became calmer and he asked for Hardy. He noticed cheering from the gun deck above and asked what it was for. Pasco, his signals lieutenant, lying wounded nearby, told him an enemy ship had struck. This was the *Redoutable*. They had all felt the crash as the captain of the *Téméraire*, Elias Harvey, had brought his ship alongside the other side of the *Redoutable* and pounded her to pieces until Lucas had at last struck. Up came the *Fougeux*, and the *Téméraire*'s devastating broadsides killed the French captain and caused the now helpless ship to crash into the *Téméraire*, where she was lashed to the *Téméraire*'s other side. Their part of the battle was now over, leaving *Victory* and the fighting *Téméraire* with close on 300 dead, wounded and dying between them, Nelson included.

Hardy's absence agitated Nelson. He was troubled by his growing thirst and the close heat of the airless cockpit. Scott and Mr Burke, who had stationed themselves at his side, gave him sips of lemonade or watered wine from time to time. The surgeon and his assistants went about their dreadful business. Both men tried to jolly him along as best they could. 'It is nonsense Mr Burke, to suppose I can live; my sufferings are great but they will be all soon over.' Nelson, still the Admiral, was impatient to see Hardy: 'Will no one bring Hardy to me? He must be killed: he is surely destroyed.' Nelson managed to create such a fuss about Hardy that many messages had been sent up to the quarterdeck. Eventually Midshipman Bulkeley came below with a message that Hardy would come as soon as he was able. In his account of Nelson's death, Dr Beatty goes on, 'On hearing him deliver this message to the Surgeon, his Lordship inquired who had brought it. Mr Burke answered, "It is Mr Bulkeley, my Lord" – "It is his voice," replied his Lordship: he then said to the young gentleman, "Remember me to your father."'

An hour and ten minutes after Nelson was taken below, that is about 2.35 in the afternoon, Hardy appeared and stayed with him for about ten minutes. The verisimilitude of Beatty's account speaks for itself,

They shook hands affectionately and Lord Nelson said: 'Well Hardy, how goes the battle? How goes the day with us?' – 'Very well my Lord,' replied Captain Hardy: 'we have got twelve or fourteen of the Enemy's Ships in our possession; but five of their van have tacked, and show an intention of bearing down on the *Victory*. I have therefore called two or three of our fresh Ships round us, and have no doubt of giving them a drubbing.' – 'I hope,' said his Lordship, 'none of our Ships have struck Hardy.' – 'No my Lord,' replied

Captain Hardy, 'there is no fear of that.' Lord Nelson then said, 'I am a dead man, Hardy. I am going fast: it will be all over with me soon. Come nearer to me. Pray let my dear Lady Hamilton have my hair, and all other things belonging to me.'

Hardy looked to Beatty to give him hope, but Nelson cut him off.

Villeneuve had at 1.45 signalled Rear-Admiral Pierre Dumanoir Le Pelley in his flagship the *Formidable*, commanding his van division to come back immediately. Dumanoir did not begin to turn till 2.30 and it was three o'clock before he was approaching the battle area and when he arrived he calmly sailed on to the south, taking the *Duguay Trouin*, *Mont Blanc* and *Scipion* with him. He was blamed for the defeat by Villeneuve's flag captain Magendie and by three of the French captains who fought so bravely, Villemadrin of the French *Swiftsure*, Lucas of the *Redoutable*, and Infernet of the *Intrépide* who had turned at his own initiative.

Following Hardy's departure Nelson lay back quietly, visited by waves of pain and thought. He dismissed the surgeons to attend the other wounded with the words, 'You can do nothing for me.' A little while later he became aware of a change in his own state. He had now lost all movement and feeling below his chest and Beatty was forced to confirm what Nelson already knew to be true, 'Nothing can be done for you.' There was no anger or struggle in Nelson now. He had thought frequently of this moment, rehearsed it on previous occasions, and now it had arrived. There was no 'Remember Me'; all egoism had gone. The only acknowledgement he made of the sweetness of life, the only recognition that he would be absent from the victory celebrations and the prize giving, was that in spite of his pain 'I should have liked to live a little longer.' Some minutes later he thought again of Emma. 'What would become of poor Lady Hamilton if she knew my situation!'

About fifty minutes after he had first visited Nelson, that is about 3.25, Hardy returned and stayed with him for about eight minutes. This time Hardy bore the news of victory, ' "certain however of fourteen or fifteen having surrendered". His Lordship answered, "That is well but I bargained for twenty." ' (The actual total would be nineteen.) Beatty went on, 'and then emphatically exclaimed, "Anchor Hardy, Anchor!" ' Hardy very injudiciously said, 'I suppose my Lord, Admiral Collingwood will now take upon himself the direction of affairs,' which brought upon him,

'Not while I live, I hope Hardy,' and he repeated, 'Do you anchor Hardy,' to which Hardy replied, 'Shall we make the signal Sir' – 'Yes for if I live I'll anchor.' Nelson's conscious life of command, with its preoccupations of the battle, ship movements and anchoring, gave way to his internal life and into the stream of consciousness came his only shaft of fear, 'Don't throw me overboard Hardy', and then his thoughts again of Emma, 'Take care of my dear Lady Hamilton.' Perhaps feelings about Emma or his mother were really at the edge of his conscious mind, but they were feelings which he could not now precisely articulate in his state of exsanguination. Something caused him to ask, 'Kiss me Hardy.' Hardy, who had not previously been as seducible by Nelson's charm or so responsive to it as some others, kissed the dying Admiral's forehead. Then stubborn Hardy kissed him again, this time of his own free will. Nelson asked, 'Who is that?' For a moment he may have believed it was Emma or his long-lost mother, who perhaps had kissed him infrequently in his childhood. When Hardy replied, 'It is Hardy,' Nelson said, 'God bless you, Hardy.'

After about eight minutes Hardy left and when he had gone Nelson asked Chevalier, his steward, to turn him on his left side; his breathing was difficult and his voice faint and low. He lingered for another fifteen minutes or so. Freud had the idea that our instinct is to die in our own fashion. Nelson's revealed a gentle, resigned being. Brief stabs of guilt touched him. 'I wish I had not left the deck for I shall soon be gone.' Then a phantom touch of his boyish charm as he felt the imminence of Judgment: 'Doctor, I have not been a great sinner.' Even now he was not going to face the fact that he had broken at least three of the ten commandments. Then came a return to his most cherished feelings, before these witnesses, 'Remember that I leave Lady Hamilton and my daughter Horatia as a legacy to my country.' and, 'Remember. . . . Never forget Horatia.' Even in death he was imposing his will on others. And ironically, in view of how succeeding generations felt, it was not the Navy he left to the nation. There was no proclamation of *si monumentum requiris*. Uppermost in his mind were not ideas of honour, glory or fame, but the sense that he had not flinched, had lived up to his reputation and had let nobody down: 'Thank God I have done my Duty.' Uppermost in his heart were his dearly loved. And then ever fainter and inarticulate calls for 'drink, drink', 'fan, fan' and 'rub, rub', interrupted by 'Thank God I have done my Duty' repeated as a last refrain of his dying. Dr

Scott said the last words he heard from Nelson's lips were, 'God and my Country'. He became speechless in the semi-recumbent posture to which Scott and Burke had raised him against the great knee timber of the ship's side. After five minutes of silence, Scott and Chevalier called Beatty. Nelson's hand was cold, the pulse had gone from his wrist, his forehead was cold, his eyes opened for the last time and closed and within five minutes he was dead.[41]

Chance had dealt with him in the same way as it had dealt with 449 of his officers and men. They would soon be joined by many of the 1,214 who were wounded. His own death was mere chance. A French sharp-shooter, high above the deck, fumbling clumsily with his musket, his sweaty fingers pulling the trigger at figures on the smoke-filled deck below. At this moment there was a composite of two moving figures in the frame. He hit the outer edge of it, Nelson's shoulder, but in his fearful urgency to reload would not stop to register which of the men crumpled and fell to his knees. Nelson lived long enough to know of his stupendous victory. He was a dying hero, surrounded by worshippers, secure at last in his fame. Not for him future challenges, indignities or falls from grace. Not for him uselessness and decay. This was indeed Dame Fortune's last Favour.

Exeunt Omnes

In the scene of his death Nelson revealed spontaneously the dimensions of his charismatic personality. In it there is something for all of us. To leave Emma as a legacy to the nation seems to some ridiculous, to others a gesture of true romance. 'Kiss me Hardy' appeals wonderfully to some, revealing the gentleness and love among comrades jointly engaged in horror, to others it is an example of the charismatic Nelson's drive to seduce. *Kiss me Hardy*, and *England Expects*, have, like certain phrases from the Bible and Shakespeare, become part of the nation's consciousness. No onlooker could remain untouched by Nelson's human preoccupations as he quietly and stoically approached his end. Remember me to your father . . . Don't throw me overboard . . . I have not been a great sinner. His instinct for keeping control of the stories told about him was uncannily present, even in the extended scene of his death.

The Hero had departed, yet had not left the stage. Such was the aura he already wore, such was the poetry of Trafalgar to distant observers, that he became an instant icon. His myth endures because the emotions of victory were intensified by the poignancy of his death in the hour of victory, because the feelings he evoked among those he led were so tender, because of his love for one of the most celebrated beauties of the age, and because what he had accomplished was indisputable and of infinite value to the morale and self-identity of a nation under present threat of invasion. Nelson became the most tangible hero in England's history. There is no other great leader whose funeral has caused a remotely comparable outpouring of grief. His column in Trafalgar Square soars infinitely higher than the statue or monument of any other individual in Britain's history.

For Emma a process of disintegration lay ahead. She was deserted only by Nelson's brother William, of whom it is impossible to speak too contemptuously. Other family and friends helped and supported her. There were no further protectors, no amorous skirmishes with the Prince of Wales, only a certain flaunting before the old Duke of Queensberry which brought her a legacy of £500 when he died, and quietly companionable letters and consignments of game from her second seducer, Sir Harry Fetherstonhaugh. But the turbulence of her emotions, the death in January 1810 of her mother who had been the sheet anchor of her life, her need for attention, her insatiable need to spend, her retreat into victimhood as the world paid no attention to Nelson's final wishes, determined an inexorable downward course. Arrested for debt, she could well have spared Horatia the experience of a sponging house and sent her to the Matchams as they wished. Instead she kept Horatia with her, venting anger and unhappiness on a twelve-year-old child. On 31 October 1813 Emma addressed Nelson's dear token of love, 'Horatia Your conduct is so bad, your falsehoods so dreadfull, your cruel treatment to me such that I cannot live under these afflicting circumstances; my poor heart is broken. If my poor mother was living to take my part, broken as I am with grief and ill health, I should be happy to breathe my last in her arms.'[1] Following her release creditors poured forward. In confusion and haste she fled to Calais with Horatia in June 1814. She never told Horatia that she was her mother and died on 15 January 1815, whether from dropsy, drink or a virus will never be known. Horatia was rescued by the Matchams and lived with them until she married the Reverend Philip Ward in 1822.

Nelson's posthumous recognition passed to the egregious William who received £99,000 to purchase an estate and a grant of £5,000 a year to support his titles as Viscount Merton of Trafalgar and Earl Nelson of Trafalgar. Susannah and Catherine each received a grant of £15,000. William's son, Viscount Merton died early in 1808, and William knew that on his own death (in 1835, when he was seventy-eight) the title Earl Nelson would go to Tom Bolton. They, like the Matchams, had prepared for the eventuality by adopting the name Nelson for their children. The Bronte title passed to William's daughter Charlotte who married Viscount Bridport in 1810, and thus joined Bronte to Bridport. Fanny, as Nelson's wife, was awarded a pension of £2,000, never remarried and spent the rest of her life quietly, always in close contact with Josiah and his family. He, having left the Navy, was out of the shadow of his stepfather and became a successful businessman. Fanny died in May 1831.

The great St Vincent was spared till 1823 when he died at the age of eighty-eight. He was an active seventy-five when Nelson died but his name is missing from the list of mourners present at the funeral, although the much older Sir Peter Parker was chief mourner and Admiral Viscount Hood one of his supporters. In his later years St Vincent must have pondered on the fate of his two protégés. Nelson had gained enduring fame, and Troubridge, of whom St Vincent thought more highly, went down with all hands in his ship the *Blenheim* on passage from India to Cape Town in 1807. He had always been unlucky.

Alexander Davison, in spite of constant promptings, kept Fanny waiting until 1814 before he transferred to her the deed of trust of which he and Maurice Nelson had been the original trustees and which in part involved the £2,000 Nelson had allocated to Fanny.[2] Davison enjoyed a further spell in prison, this time for embezzlement, before he died in 1829.

Nelson's enemy did not yet leave the stage. England had been fighting for twelve long years a war for survival against an enemy of megalomaniac appetite. Trafalgar had eliminated the threat of invasion and set the seal on a century of British sea supremacy. But still supreme on land, Bonaparte, who had crowned himself Emperor Napoleon I in Notre Dame on 2 December 1804, had already struck his camp at Boulogne and marched eastwards to the Rhine and then onwards to the Danube to defeat Mack at Ulm five days before Trafalgar, and then an Austro-Russian army at Austerlitz in December. Europe would have to endure another ten years of war before his hold was broken by a land battle at Waterloo in 1815.

The Goddess of Fame was the figurehead of Nelson's ornate and wonderful funeral car. Nelson had found undying fame. But the love he had as urgently sought had been forfeit. The poignancy of his death in the hour of victory sums up an essential outcome of war, the parallel personal tragedy. Nelson's calling had obliged him to sacrifice what he held most dear for what he wanted most. His victory inspired a nation and would be a continuing inspiration, but it broke the heart and hastened the ruin of the woman he loved.

Notes

For abbreviations used in the notes, please see the Bibliography.

1: FOUNDATIONS FOR LIFE

1 C.J. Britton, *New Chronicles of the Life of Lord Nelson* (1947), p. 14.
2 Nelson to Dr Allott, 14 May 1804, H.N. Nicolas, *The Dispatches and Letters of Vice-Admiral Lord Viscount Nelson* (1846), VI, p. 18.
3 D. Goldberg and P. Huxley, *Common Mental Disorders* (1992).
4 N.F. Dixon, *Our Own Worst Enemy* (1987), p. 98.
5 M. Eyre Matcham, *The Nelsons of Burnham Thorpe* (1911), p. 37.
6 Ibid., p. 8.
7 Ibid., p. 25.
8 N.F. Dixon, *On the Psychology of Military Incompetence* (1976). M. Kets de Vries, *Prisoners of Leadership* (1989).
9 E.H. Moorhouse, *Nelson in England: A Domestic Chronicle* (1913), p. 58.
10 Eyre Matcham, p. 8.
11 J. Harrison, *The Life of the Right Honourable Horatio, Lord Viscount Nelson* (1846), I, p. 9.
12 Ibid., I, p. 8.
13 J.S. Clarke and J. McArthur, *The Life of Admiral Lord Nelson KB from His Lordship's Manuscripts* (1809), I, p. 8.
14 Ibid.
15 Nicolas, VII, p. 261.
16 Clarke and McArthur, I, p. 7.

2: CAPTAIN SUCKLING'S LEGACY

1 Harrison, I, p. 12.
2 G.L. Newnham Collingwood, *A Selection from the Public and Private Correspondence of Vice-Admiral Lord Collingwood Interspersed with Memoirs of his Life* (5th edn, 1827), p. 7.
3 Log of the *Raisonnable*, PRO ADM 52/1937.
4 Clarke and McArthur, I, p. 4.
5 N. A. M. Rodger, *The Wooden World* (Fontana edn, 1988), pp. 40–41.
6 Clarke and McArthur, I, p. 4.

7   Ibid.
8   D. Murray Smith, *Arctic Expeditions* (1880).
9   B. Lavery, *Nelson's Navy* (1989), p. 219.
10 Clarke and McArthur, I, p. 4.
11 Court Martial of Lieutenant Drummond, 30 May 1774, PRO ADM/5306.
12 Ibid.
13 Master's log of HMS *Seahorse*, ADM 52, PRO, ADM 52/1991.
14 Court Martial of Lieutenant Thomas Henery, 19 Feb. 1776, PRO ADM/5307.
15 Ibid.
16 Clarke and McArthur, I, p. 4.
17 Ibid., I, p. 14.
18 Ibid., I, p. 5.
19 Nicolas, I, p. 22.
20 Nelson to William Nelson, 14 Apr. 1777, Nicolas, I, p. 21.
21 Clarke and McArthur, I, Appendix ii.
22 Nelson to Locker, 12 Aug. 1777, Nicolas, I. p. 22.
23 Clarke and McArthur, I, p. 5.
24 Ibid.
25 T. Pocock, *The Young Nelson in the Americas* (1980), p. 32.
26 Nelson to his father, 24 Oct. 1778, BL Add. MS. 34,988.
27 D. Syrett, *Shipping and the American War 1775–83* (1970), p. 21.
28 Nelson to William Suckling, 5 July 1786, Nicolas, I, p. 186.

3: FIVE FRUSTRATING YEARS

1   Nelson to Locker, 23 Jan 1780, Nicolas, I, p. 32.
2   Pocock, *Young Nelson*, p. 82.
3   Nicolas, I, p. 9.
4   Pocock, *Young Nelson*, p. 65.
5   Ibid., p. 92.
6   Ibid., p. 129.
7   Nicolas, I, p. 9.
8   Ibid.
9   Dalling to Nelson, 30 May 1780, ibid.
10 Clarke and McArthur, I, pp. 22–3.
11 Pocock, *Young Nelson*, p. 152; A.M. Hills, 'Nelson's Illnesses', *Journal of the Royal Naval Medical Service*, Vol. 86, no. 2. (2000).
12 Pocock, *Young Nelson*, p. 153.
13 Ibid.
14 Nelson to Locker, 15 Feb. 1781, Nicolas, I, p. 38.
15 Nelson to William Nelson, 7 May 1781, ibid., p. 42.
16 R. Walker, *The Nelson Portraits* (1998), p. 38.
17 Nelson to Locker, 21 Feb. 1781, Nicolas, I, p. 39.
18 Nelson to Locker, 22 Dec. 1781, ibid., p. 49.
19 Nelson to William Nelson, 9 Sept. 1781, ibid., I, p. 44.
20 Nelson to William Nelson, 24 Aug. 1781, ibid., p. 43.
21 Nelson to William Nelson, 18 Dec. 1781, ibid., p. 49.
22 Nelson to William Nelson, 8 Feb. 1782, ibid., p. 57.

23 Nelson to Locker, 16 Apr. 1782, ibid., p. 62.

24 Nelson to Locker, 19 Oct. 1782, ibid., p. 66.

25 Nelson to his father, 19 Oct. 1782, ibid., p. 67.

26 Pocock, *Young Nelson*, p. 178.

27 Clarke and McArthur, I, p. 52.

28 Nelson to his father, 19 Oct. 1782, Nicolas, I, p. 67.

29 Clarke and McArthur I, p. 52.

30 Ibid., p. 53.

31 Nelson to Locker, 17 Nov. 1782, Nicolas, p. 68.

32 Nelson to Locker, 25 Feb. 1783, ibid., p. 72.

33 Nelson to Lord Hood, 9 Mar. 1783, ibid., p. 73.

34 C. Lloyd and R.C. Anderson (eds) *A Memoir of James Trevenen 1760–1790* Navy Records Society (1959), p. 56.

35 Nelson to Locker, 26 June 1783, Nicolas, I, p. 75.

36 Nelson to Hercules Ross, 9 Aug. 1783, ibid., p. 80.

37 Nelson to Locker, 12 July 1783, ibid., p. 76.

38 Nelson to Locker, 2 Nov. 1783, ibid., p. 83.

39 Nelson to William Nelson, 10 Nov. 1783, ibid., p. 86.

40 Nelson to Locker, 2 Nov. 1783, ibid., p. 83.

41 Nelson to Locker, 26 Nov. 1783, ibid., p. 89.

42 Nelson to William Nelson, 4 Dec. 1783, ibid., p. 91.

43 Nelson to William Suckling, 14 Jan. 1784, Nicolas, II, p. 479.

44 Nelson to William Nelson, 3 Jan. 1784, Nicolas, I, p. 93.

45 Nelson to Locker, 19 Jan. 1784, ibid., p. 94.

46 Nelson to William Nelson, 31 Jan. 1784, ibid., p. 98.

47 Nelson to Locker, 23 Jan. 1784, ibid., p. 97.

48 Nelson to William Nelson, 31 Jan. 1784, ibid., p. 98.

49 A. Foreman, *Georgiana, Duchess of Devonshire* (1998), p. 75.

4: TRYING TO GET NOTICED

1   Nelson to William Nelson, 29 Mar. 1784, Nicolas, I, p. 101.

2   Nelson to Locker, 21 Apr. 1784, ibid., p. 104.

3   Nelson to William Nelson, 23 Apr. 1784, ibid., p. 105.

4   Nelson to Locker, 7 June 1784, ibid., p. 109.

5   Nicolas, I, p. 124.

6   Nelson to Locker, 24 Sept. 1784, Nicolas, I, p. 110.

7   Nelson to Locker, 5 Mar. 1786, ibid. p. 156.

8   Nelson to Locker, 24 Sept. 1784, ibid., p. 110.

9   Nelson to Locker, 23 Nov. 1784, ibid., p. 112.

10 Nelson to Locker, 15 Jan. 1785, ibid., p. 113.

11 Nelson to Hughes, 11/12 Jan. 1785, ibid., p. 114.

12 Nelson to Locker, 15 Jan. 1785, ibid., p. 113.

13 Nelson to Lord Sydney, 20 Mar. 1785, ibid., p. 129.

14 Nelson to William Suckling, 25 Sept. 1785, ibid., p. 140.

15 Nelson to Fanny, 25 Mar. 1786, G.P.B. Naish, *Nelson's Letters to his Wife and Other Documents 1785–1831*, Navy Records Society (1958), p. 25.

16 Nelson to Locker, 5 Mar. 1786, Nicolas, I, p. 156.

17   Nicolas, I, pp. 171–86.
18   Nelson to William Nelson, 20 Feb. 1785, ibid., p. 123.
19   Nelson to William Nelson, 3 May 1785, ibid., p. 131.
20   Nelson to William Nelson, 20 Feb. 1785, ibid., p. 123.
21   Ibid., p. 133.
22   Clarke and McArthur, I, p. 37.
23   Nelson to William Nelson, 28 June 1785, Nicolas, I, p. 133.
24   Nelson to William Nelson, 15 Dec. 1785, ibid., p. 150.
25   Nelson to Fanny, 11 Sept. 1785, Naish, p. 19.
26   Nelson to Fanny, 19 Aug. 1786, ibid., p. 33.
27   Nelson to William Nelson, 29 Dec. 1786, Nicolas, I, p. 204.
28   Nelson to Fanny, 13 Jan. 1787, Naish, p. 41.
29   Nelson to Fanny, 6 Aug. 1786, ibid., p. 32.
30   Nelson to Fanny, 25 Feb. 1786, ibid., p. 21.
31   Nelson to Fanny, 23 Apr. 1786, ibid., p. 30.
32   Nelson to Fanny, 19 Aug. 1786, ibid., p. 33.
33   Nelson to Fanny, 24 Feb. 1787, ibid., p. 44.
34   Nelson to Fanny, 4 May 1786, ibid., p. 31.
35   Nelson to Fanny, 11 Sept. 1785, ibid., p. 19.
36   Nelson to William Suckling, 14 Nov. 1785, ibid., p. 53.
37   Nelson to Fanny, 3 Mar. 1786, ibid., p. 22.
38   Nelson to William Suckling, 9 Mar. 1786, Nicolas, I, p. 160.
39   Nelson to Fanny, 25 Feb. 1787, Naish, p. 45.
40   Nelson to William Suckling, 9 Mar. 1786, Nicolas, I, p. 160.
41   Nelson to William Nelson, 15 Dec. 1785, ibid., p. 150.
42   Nelson to William Suckling, 9 Mar. 1786, ibid., p. 160.
43   S. Homer and R. Sylla, *A History of Interest Rates* (Rutgers University Press, 3rd edn, revised, 1996), Table 13, p. 161.
44   Nelson's draft account of meeting Prince William, Dec. 1786, Naish, p. 56.
45   Nelson to Fanny, 12 Dec. 1786, ibid., p. 38.
46   Ibid., p. 57.
47   Nelson to William Nelson, 29 Dec. 1786, Nicolas, I, p. 204.
48   T. Pocock, *Sailor King: The Life of King William IV* (1991), p. 100.
49   Ibid., p. 85.
50   B.Lavery (ed.) *Shipboard Life and Organization 1731–1815*, Navy Records Society (1988), p. 104.
51   Nicolas, I, p. 209.
52   Prince William to Hood, 9 Feb. 1787, *Naval Miscellany*, IV, Navy Records Society (1952), p. 270.
53   Nelson to William Nelson, 9 Feb. 1787, Nicolas, I, p. 213.
54   Nelson to Locker, 13 Feb. 1787, ibid., p. 214.
55   Nelson to Fanny, 24 Dec. 1786, Naish, p. 39.
56   Nelson to Fanny, 12 Dec. 1786, ibid., p. 38.
57   Nelson to Fanny, 27 Feb. 1787, ibid., p. 46.
58   Pocock, *Sailor King.*, p. 91.
59   Nelson to Fanny, 24 Dec. 1786, Naish, p. 39.
60   Nelson to Fanny, 13 Jan 1787, ibid., p. 41.
61   Nelson to Fanny, 6 Mar. 1787, ibid., p. 50.

62 Prince William to Hood, 15 Mar. 1787, ibid., p. 58.
63 Pocock, *Sailor King*, p. 195.
64 Prince William to Nelson, 13 May 1787, Nicolas, I, p. 245.
65 Nelson to Prince William, 7 May 1782, ibid., p. 233.
66 Ibid.
67 Nelson to William Nelson, 9 Feb. 1787, Nicolas, I, p. 213.

5: BLACK MARKS AND 'ON THE BEACH'

1   Nelson to Stephens, 10 July 1787, Nicolas, I, p. 242.
2   Nelson to Stephens, 4 July 1787, ibid., p. 240.
3   Ibid.
4   Nelson to Stephens, 29 Aug. 1787, Nicolas, I, p. 255.
5   Nelson to Prince William, 27 July 1787, ibid., p. 250.
6   Prince William to Nelson, 3 Dec. 1787, Naish, p. 59.
7   Prince William to Hood, 26 Dec. 1787, *Naval Miscellany*, IV, p. 290.
8   Hood to Prince William, 1 Jan. 1788, ibid., p. 291.
9   Hood to Prince William, 8 Jan. 1788, ibid., p. 293.
10 Howe to Hood, 2 July 1787, ibid., p. 287.
11 Nelson to Locker, 12 Aug. 1787, Nicolas, I, p. 251.
12 Nelson to Locker, 3 Oct. 1787, ibid., p. 259.
13 Nelson to Locker, 27 Jan. 1788, ibid., p. 266.
14 Nelson to William Nelson, 3 Jan. 1788, ibid., p. 265.
15 Nelson to Ross, 6 May 1788, ibid., p. 273.
16 Lady Nelson's Memorandum of 1806, Naish, p. 61.
17 Eyre Matcham, p. 57.
18 Ibid., p. 45.
19 Nelson to William Nelson, 23 Sept. 1787, Nicolas, I, p. 258.
20 Eyre Matcham, p. 45.
21 Clarke and McArthur, I, p. 24.
22 Nelson to Fanny, 26 Aug. 1788, Naish, p. 51.
23 Nelson to Stephens, 8 May 1790, Nicolas, I, p. 287.
24 Nicolas, I, p. 294.
25 Eyre Matcham, pp. 45–87.
26 Nelson to Locker, 10 Sept. 1789, Nicolas, I, p. 281.
27 Eyre Matcham, pp. 45–87.
28 E. Burke, *Reflections on the Revolution in France* (1790).
29 Nelson to Duke of Clarence, 3 Nov. 1792, Nicolas, I, p. 292.
30 Nelson to Duke of Clarence, 10 Dec. 1792, ibid., p. 294.
31 J. Ehrman, *The Younger Pitt* (1983), II, p. 31.
32 S. Schama, *Citizens* (1989), p. 687.
33 Nelson to Stephens, 21 Sept. 1787, Nicolas, I, p. 257.
34 Nelson to Locker, 21 Feb. 1793, ibid., p. 301.
35 Nelson to Fanny, 14 Apr. 1793, Naish, p. 76.
36 Joseph Emmerson to his brother, 9 May 1793, *Nelson Dispatch*, Vol. 6, Part 10
    (April 1999), p. 434.
37 Nelson to William Nelson, 18 Apr. 1793, Nicolas, I, p. 304.

38 Nelson to Fanny, 18 May 1793, Naish, p. 80.
39 Nelson to Fanny, 12 Mar. 1793, ibid., p. 73.
40 Edmund Nelson to Fanny, 13 Dec. 1793, ibid., p. 176.
41 Nelson to Fanny, 12 Mar. 1793, ibid., p. 74.
42 Nelson to Fanny, 15 Mar. 1793, ibid.
43 Nelson to Fanny, 9 Apr. 1793, ibid., p. 76.

6: MELPOMENE, MINERVE, LA FORTUNE

1   Nelson to Fanny, 14 June 1793, Naish, p. 82.
2   Nelson to Fanny, 23 June 1793, ibid., p. 83.
3   Nelson to Edmund Nelson, 20 Aug. 1793, Nicolas, I, p. 319.
4   Hood, quoted in J.M. Thompson, *Napoleon Bonaparte* (1952), p. 31.
5   Nelson to Edmund Nelson, 20 Aug. 1793, Nicolas, I, p. 319.
6   F. McLynn, *Napoleon* (1997), p. 72.
7   Nelson to Fanny, 7 Sept. 1793, Naish, p. 89.
8   Nelson's Journal, 16 Sept. 1793, ibid., p. 135.
9   Ibid.
10 Nelson to William Nelson, 24 Sept. 1793, Nicolas, I, p. 327.
11 Nelson's Journal, 16 Sept. 1793, Naish, p. 135.
12 Nelson to Fanny, 7 Oct. 1793, ibid., p. 92.
13 Nelson to Fanny, 12 Oct. 1793, ibid., p. 93.
14 Nelson to Hood, 22 Oct. 1793, Nicolas, I, p. 334.
15 Nelson's Journal, 18–21 Oct. 1793, Naish, p. 139.
16 Nelson to Linzee, 24 Oct. 1793, Nicolas, II, p. 480.
17 Nelson's Journal, 24 Oct. 1793, Naish, p. 139.
18 Nelson's Journal, 1–6 Nov. 1793, ibid.
19 Nelson to Fanny, 1 Dec. 1793, ibid., p. 94.
20 Nicolas, I, p. 340.
21 Nelson to Fanny, 1 Dec. 1793, Naish, p. 94.
22 Nelson to Locker, 1 Dec. 1793, Nicolas, I, p. 337.
23 Ibid.
24 Nelson to William Suckling, 5 Dec. 1793, Nicolas, I, p. 340.
25 Nelson's Journal, 17 Dec. 1793, Naish, p. 141.
26 Nelson to Fanny, 27 Dec. 1793, ibid., p. 97.
27 Nelson to Fanny, 27 Sept. 1793, ibid., p. 91.
28 Nelson to William Suckling, 11 Oct. 1793, Nicolas, I, p. 331.
29 Nelson to Fanny, 12 Oct. 1793, Naish, p. 93.
30 Nelson to Fanny, 1 Dec. 1793, ibid., p. 94.
31 Nelson to Fanny, 27 Dec. 1793, ibid., p. 97.
32 Edmund Nelson to Fanny, 13 Dec. 1793, ibid., p. 176.

7: TOTALLY NEGLECTED

1   Nelson to Fanny, 16 Jan. 1794, Naish, p. 99.
2   Nelson to Fanny, 13 Feb. 1794, ibid., p. 102.
3   Nelson to Hood, 8 Feb. 1794, Nicolas, I, p. 352.

4   Hood to Nelson, 12 Feb. 1794, *Naval Miscellany*, IV, p. 366.

5   Nelson to Hood, 13 Feb. 1794, Nicolas, I, p. 354.

6   Nelson's Journal, 19 Feb. 1794, Naish, p. 146.

7   Nelson to Fanny, 28 Feb. 1794, ibid., p. 103.

8   Nelson to William Nelson, 1 Mar. 1794, Nicolas, I, p. 364.

9   Nelson to Fanny, 28 Feb. 1794, Naish, p. 103.

10 Nelson's Journal, 3 Mar. 1794, ibid., p. 148.

11 Nelson to Fanny, 4 Mar. 1794, ibid., p. 105.

12 Nelson's Journal, 6 Feb. 1794, ibid., p. 145.

13 Nelson to Hood, 6 Mar. 1794, Nicolas, I, p. 369.

14 Hood to Dundas, 6 Mar. 1794, *Naval Miscellany*, IV, p. 370.

15 Hood to Nelson, 8 Mar. 1794, ibid., p. 372.

16 J.F. Maurice, *The Diary of Sir John Moore* (1904), 13 Mar. 1794, p. 69. Hereafter Moore's Diary.

17 Moore's Diary, pp. 65–6.

18 Nelson to Hood, 18 Mar. 1794, Nicolas, I, p. 373.

19 Moore's Diary, 21 Mar. 1794, pp. 76–7.

20 Nelson's Journal, 20–24 Mar. 1794, Naish, p. 150.

21 Nelson to William Nelson, 26 Mar. 1794, Nicolas, I, p. 375.

22 Nelson to Hamilton, 27 Mar. 1794, ibid., p. 377.

23 Nelson's Journal, 11 Apr. 1794, Naish, p. 155.

24 Moore's Diary, 3 May 1794, p. 85.

25 Nelson's Journal, 24 May 1794, Naish, p. 159.

26 Nelson's Journal, 3 May 1794, ibid., p. 157.

27 Nelson to Hood, 24 Apr. 1794, Nicolas, I, p. 386.

28 Nelson to Hood, 25 Apr. 1794, ibid., p. 387.

29 Hood to Nelson, 24 Apr. 1794, *Naval Miscellany*, IV, p. 389.

30 Hood to Nelson, 29 Apr. 1794, ibid., p. 390.

31 Nelson to Fanny, 1–4 May 1794, Naish, p. 109.

32 Nelson's Journal, 19–24 May 1794, ibid., p. 158.

33 Moore's Diary, 31 May 1794, p. 98.

34 Hood to Nelson, 22 May 1794, *Naval Miscellany*, IV, p. 400.

35 Nelson to William Nelson, 30 May 1794, Nicolas, I, p. 403.

36 Nelson to Fanny, 20 May 1794, Naish, p. 111.

37 Nelson to Fanny, 30 May 1794, ibid., p. 112.

38 Stuart, 22 May 1794, *Naval Miscellany*, IV, p. 400.

39 Hood to Elliot, 25 June 1794, Naish, p. 171.

40 Stuart to Nelson, 4 July 1794, *Naval Miscellany*, IV, p. 405.

41 Hood to Admiralty, 24 May 1794, Nicolas, I, p. 399.

42 Nelson to Fanny, 8 July 1794, Naish, p. 116.

43 Nelson to William Suckling, 16 July 1794, Nicolas, I, p. 438.

44 Nelson to Fanny, 1–4 May 1794, Naish, p. 109.

45 Nelson to Fanny, 20 May 1794, ibid., p. 111.

46 Nelson to Hood, 7 July 1794, Nicolas, I, p. 423.

47 Nelson to Fanny, 8 July 1794, Naish, p. 116.

48 Nelson's Journal, 10 July 1794, ibid., p. 164.

49 Nelson's Journal, 12 July 1794, ibid., p. 165.

50 Moore's Diary, 13 July 1794, p. 110.

51 Nelson to Hood, 12 July 1794, Nicolas, I, p. 432.
52 P.J. Gray, 'Turning a Blind Eye', *Trafalgar Chronicle*, 2002, p. 44.
53 Nelson to Fanny, 14 July 1794, Naish, p. 117.
54 Nelson to Hood, 12 July 1794, Nicolas, I, p. 432.
55 Hood to Nelson, undated, ibid., p. 433.
56 Nelson to Hood, 18 July 1794, ibid., p. 445.
57 Hood to Nelson, 18 July 1794, ibid., p. 444.
58 Nelson to Hood, 19 July 1794, ibid., p. 446.
59 Nelson to Hood, 20 July 1794, ibid., p. 448.
60 Hood to Nelson, 21 July 1794, *Naval Miscellany*, IV, p. 411.
61 Nelson to Hood, 22 July 1794, ibid., p. 412.
62 Hood to Nelson, 24 July 1794, ibid., p. 413.
63 Nelson to Hood, July 1794, ibid., p. 413.
64 Hood to Nelson, 25 July 1794, ibid., p. 414.
65 Nelson to Hood, 26 July 1794, ibid.
66 Nelson's Journal, 29 July 1794, Naish, p. 118.
67 Nelson to Hood, 31 July 1794, Nicolas, I, p. 462.
68 Nelson to Elliot, 4 Aug. 1794, ibid., p. 464.
69 Nelson to Duke of Clarence, 6/10 Aug. 1794, ibid., p. 475.
70 Nelson to Fanny, 1 Aug. 1794, Naish, p. 118.
71 Nelson to Hood, 10 Aug. 1794, Nicolas, I, p. 477.
72 Nelson to Fanny, 11 Aug. 1794, Naish, p. 118.
73 Nelson to Fanny, 18 Aug. 1794, ibid., p. 119.
74 Nelson to Fanny, 1 Sept. 1794, ibid., p. 121.
75 Nicolas, I, p. 473.

8: 'MY DISPOSITION CAN'T BEAR TAME AND SLOW MEASURES'

1   Nelson to William Suckling, 20 Sept. 1794, Naish, p. 121.
2   Ibid., p. 123.
3   Nelson to Fanny, 1 Sept. 1794, ibid., p. 121.
4   Nelson to Fanny, 3 Oct. 1794, ibid., p. 125.
5   Nelson to Fanny, 10 Oct. 1794, ibid., p. 126.
6   Nelson to Fanny, 12 Oct. 1794, ibid.
7   Nelson to Fanny, 12 Nov. 1794, ibid., p. 187.
8   Nelson to Fanny, 15 Nov. 1794, ibid., p. 188.
9   Nelson to Fanny, 28 Nov. 1794, ibid., p. 189.
10 Nelson to Fanny, 5 Dec. 1794, ibid., p. 190.
11 A. Fremantle (ed.) *The Wynne Diaries 1789–1820* (1952), pp. 254–5.
12 The Huntington Library, San Marino, California HM34180.
13 Nelson to Fanny, 5 Dec. 1794, Naish, p. 190.
14 Nelson to Fanny, 27 June 1794, ibid., p. 114.
15 Nelson to Fanny, 1/4 May 1794, ibid., p. 109
16 Nelson to Fanny, 27 June 1794, ibid., p. 114.
17 Nelson to Fanny, 28 June 1794, ibid., p. 115.
18 Nelson to William Suckling, 7 Feb. 1795, Nicolas, II, p. 5.
19 Nelson to Fanny, 7 Feb. 1795, Naish, p. 196.
20 Nelson to Fanny, 10 Mar. 1795, ibid., p. 199.

21 Nicolas, II, p. 12.
22 Ibid., p. 13.
23 Ibid., p. 14.
24 Ibid., p. 16.
25 Nelson to Duke of Clarence, 15 Mar. 1795, ibid., p. 19.
26 Nelson to Locker, 21 Mar. 1795, ibid., p. 20.
27 Hotham to Admiralty, ibid., pp. 13–15.
28 Nelson to William Nelson, 25 Mar. 1795, ibid., p. 23.
29 Nelson to Fanny, 14 Mar. 1795, Naish, p. 199.
30 Nelson to Fanny, 28 Mar. 1795, ibid., p. 202.
31 Nelson to Fanny, 1 Apr. 1795, ibid., p. 203.
32 Nelson to Fanny, 12 Apr. 1795, ibid., p. 205.
33 Ibid.
34 Nelson to William Nelson, 8 June 1795, Nicolas, II, p. 42.
35 Nelson to Fanny, 7 June 1795, Naish, p. 210.
36 Nelson to Fanny, 15 June 1795, ibid., p. 211.
37 Nelson to Fanny, 22 June 1795, ibid., p. 212.
38 Nelson to Revd Hoste, 22 June 1795, Nicolas, II, p. 45.
39 Nelson to Fanny, 9 July 1795, Naish, p. 215.

9: 'IT IS ACTIVE YOUNG MEN THAT ARE WANTED, NOT DRONES'

1 Nelson to Locker, 19 Aug. 1795, Nicolas, II, p. 69.
2 Nelson to Fanny, 18 July 1795, Naish, p. 216.
3 Nelson to Fanny, 24 July 1795, ibid., p. 217.
4 Ibid.
5 Nelson to Spencer, 19 July 1795, Nicolas, II, p. 56.
6 Nelson to Locker, 19 Aug. 1795, ibid., p. 69.
7 Elliot to Nelson, 7 Aug. 1795, ibid., p. 67.
8 Nicolas, II, p. 73.
9 Nelson to Fanny, 1 Sept. 1795, Naish, p. 221.
10 Nelson to Collingwood, 31 Aug. 1795, Nicolas, II, p. 77.
11 Nelson to Elliot, 13 Aug. 1795, ibid., p. 67.
12 W. James, *Old Oak: The Life of John Jervis, Earl of St Vincent* (1950), p. 20.
13 Ibid., p. 54.
14 Nelson to Fanny, 13 Nov. 1795, Naish, p. 227.
15 Nelson to Fanny, 2 Dec. 1795, ibid., p. 228.
16 Ibid.
17 Nelson to Grenville, 23 Nov. 1795, Nicolas, II, p. 103.
18 Nelson to Fanny, 2 Dec. 1795, Naish, p. 228.
19 Nelson to Fanny, 18 Dec. 1795, ibid., p. 230.
20 Nelson to Fanny, 20 Jan. 1796, ibid., p. 281.
21 Nelson to Fanny, 27 Jan. 1796, ibid., p. 282.
22 Nelson to Fanny, 12 Feb. 1796, ibid., p. 283.
23 Nelson to Fanny, 17 Feb. 1796, ibid.
24 Nelson to Trevor, 2 Mar. 1796, Nicolas, II, p. 128.
25 Nelson to Jervis, 18 Mar. 1796, ibid., p. 137.
26 Spencer to Nelson, 15 Jan. 1796, Naish, p. 333.

27   Nelson to Fanny, 25 Mar. 1796, ibid., p. 286.
28   McLynn, p. 109.
29   Nelson to Fanny, 24 Apr. 1796, Naish, p. 290.
30   Nelson to Jervis, 18 May 1796, Nicolas, II, p. 172.
31   Jervis to Nelson, 22 May 1796, Naish, p. 336.
32   Nelson to Jervis, 3 June 1796, Nicolas, II, p. 180.
33   Nelson to Jervis, 5 June 1796, Nicolas, VII, p. lxxx.
34   Ibid., p. lxxxi.
35   Nelson to William Nelson, 20 June 1796, Nicolas, II, p. 186.
36   Jervis to Nelson, 13 July 1796, Naish, p. 337.
37   Nelson to William Nelson, 20 June 1796, Nicolas, II, p. 186.
38   Nelson to Jervis, 10 July 1796, ibid., p. 208.
39   Nelson to Fanny, 11 Aug. 1796, Naish, p. 300.
40   Nelson to Fanny, 2 Aug. 1796, ibid., p. 298.
41   Nelson to Elliot, 5 Aug. 1796, Nicolas, II, p. 233.
42   Elliot to Nelson, 6 Aug. 1796, Naish, p. 343.
43   Jervis to Elliot, 25 July 1796, ibid., p. 339.
44   Jervis to Elliot, 22 Aug. 1796, ibid., p. 240.
45   Nelson to Jervis, 15 Aug. 1796, Nicolas, II, p. 240.
46   Nelson to Jervis, 11 Sept. 1796, ibid., p. 264.
47   Nelson to Jervis, 20 Aug. 1796, ibid., p. 248.
48   Nicolas, II, p. 270.
49   Nelson to Fanny, 19 Sept. 1796, Naish, p. 303.

10: INTO THE LIMELIGHT

1   Jervis to Nelson, 25 Sept. 1796, Naish, p. 338.
2   Nelson to Fanny, 13 Oct. 1796, ibid., p. 305.
3   Jervis to Elliot, 26 Sept. 1796, ibid., p. 340.
4   Nelson to Jervis, 15 Oct. 1796, Nicolas, II, p. 288.
5   Nelson to Jervis, 19 Oct. 1796, ibid., p. 291.
6   Nelson to Fanny, 7 Nov. 1796, Naish, p. 307.
7   Nicolas, II, p. 292.
8   Nelson to Locker, 5 Nov. 1796, ibid., p. 298.
9   Nelson to Fanny, 22 Nov. 1796, Naish, p. 308.
10 Nelson to William Suckling, 29 Nov. 1796, Nicolas, II, p. 306.
11 Nicolas, II, p. 311.
12 Nelson to Fanny, 9 Dec. 1796, Naish, p. 309.
13 Nelson to William Nelson, 13 Jan. 1797, Nicolas, II, p. 326.
14 Nelson to Jervis, 20 Dec. 1796, ibid., pp. 312–15.
15 Nelson to Don Miguel Gaston, 24 Dec. 1796, ibid., p. 315.
16 Nelson to Don Juan Marino, about 24 Dec. 1796, ibid., p. 316.
17 Nelson to Jervis, 24 Dec. 1796, ibid., p. 317.
18 Nelson to William Nelson, 13 Jan. 1797, ibid., p. 326.
19 Nelson to Elliot, 24 Dec. 1796, ibid., p. 318.
20 Nelson to De Burgh, 29 Dec. 1796, ibid., p. 322.
21 Nelson to Spencer, 4 Jan. 1797, Nicolas, VII, p. cxxvii.
22 Nelson to Spencer, 16 Jan. 1797, ibid., p. cxxviii.

23 Nelson to Fanny, 27 Jan. 1797, Naish, p. 312.

24 Ibid.

25 Nelson to Edward Hardman, 11 Feb. 1797, Nicolas, II, p. 331.

26 Bethune J. Drinkwater, *A Narrative of the Battle of St Vincent with Anecdotes of Nelson, before and after that Battle* (1797) in Nicolas, II, p. 331.

27 C. White, *1797: Nelson's Year of Destiny* (1998), p. 37.

28 J.S. Tucker, *Memoirs of Admiral the Right Honourable the Earl of St Vincent* (1844), p. 258.

29 White, *1797*, p. 69.

30 Ibid., p. 71.

31 Nelson's *A Few Remarks relative to myself in the Captain, in which my Pendant was flying on the most Glorious Valentine's Day*, 1797, Nicolas, II, p. 346.

32 Nelson to Fanny, 22 Feb. 1797, Naish, p. 315.

33 Nicolas, II, p. 335.

34 Nelson's *Remarks*, Nicolas, II, pp. 344–6.

35 Nicolas, II, p. 342.

36 Nelson to Collingwood, 15 Feb. 1797, ibid., p. 347.

37 Drinkwater's *Narrative* in Nicolas, II, pp. 347–8.

38 Elliot to Nelson, 15 Feb. 1797, Nicolas, II, p. 349.

39 Nelson to Elliot, 16 Feb. 1797, ibid., p. 350.

40 Nelson to Locker, 21 Feb. 1797, ibid., p. 353.

41 Fanny to Nelson, 11 Mar. 1797, Naish, p. 350.

42 Fanny to Nelson, 20 Mar. 1797, ibid., p. 352.

43 Parker to Nelson, 1 Sept. 1797, Nicolas, II, p. 470.

44 Nelson to Parker, 19 Aug. 1797, ibid., p. 438.

45 J. Ross, *Memoirs and Correspondence of Lord de Saumarez* (1838), I, p. 175.

46 Nelson to William Nelson, 6 Apr. 1797, Nicolas, II, p. 369.

11: HUBRIS

 1 Edmund Nelson to Nelson, 23 Feb. 1797, Nicolas, II, p. 354.

 2 Nelson to Duke of Clarence, 2 Apr. 1797, ibid., p. 369.

 3 Lady Parker to Nelson, 15 Mar. 1797, ibid., p. 377.

 4 Nelson to Jervis, about 12 Mar. 1797, ibid., p. 362.

 5 Nelson to Fanny, 2 Apr. 1797, Naish, p. 321.

 6 Saumarez to Richard Saumarez, 6 Mar. 1797, Ross, p. 177.

 7 Nelson to Fanny, 27 May 1797, Nicolas, II, p. 324.

 8 Nelson to Jervis, 12 Apr. 1797, ibid., p. 378.

 9 Nelson to Miller, 24 May 1797, ibid., p. 386.

10 Nelson to Fanny, 15 June 1797, Naish, p. 326.

11 Nelson to Jervis, 9 June 1797, Nicolas, II, p. 394.

12 Nelson to Jervis, 10 June 1797, ibid., p. 395.

13 Jervis to Spencer, 5 July 1797, ibid., p. 404.

14 Nelson to Calder, 9 June 1797, ibid., p. 409.

15 Jervis to Nelson, 14 July 1797, ibid., p. 413.

16 Nelson to Jervis, 12 Apr. 1797, ibid., p. 378.

17 Nelson to Hammond, 8 Sept. 1797, ibid., p. 443.

18 Nelson to Jervis, 27 July 1797, ibid., pp. 423–8.

19 White, *1797*, p. 112.
20 Nelson to Jervis, 24 July 1797, Nicolas, II, p. 421.
21 Fremantle *Wynne Diaries*, pp. 184–7. Vol. II (1934 edn), quoted in A. Guimerá, *Nelson and Tenerife 1797*, 1805 Club (1999), p. 10. Also quoted in C. White, *1797*, p. 119.
22 Nelson to Jervis, 27 July 1797, Nicolas, II, p. 427.
23 White, *1797*, p. 119.
24 K. Buckland (ed.) *The Miller Papers*, 1805 Club (1999), p. 31.
25 Nicolas, II, p. 422.
26 A. Guimerá, *Nelson and Tenerife, 1797*, 1805 Club (1999), pp. 5 and 35.
27 Nelson's Journal, 25 July 1797, Nicolas, II, p. 432.
28 Nelson to Jervis, 27 July 1797, ibid., p. 434.
29 Nelson to Jervis, 16 Aug. 1797, ibid., p. 435.
30 Jervis to Nelson, 16 Aug. 1797, ibid.
31 Jervis to Admiralty, 16 Aug. 1797, ibid., p. 434.
32 Jervis to Fanny, 16 Aug. 1797, Naish, p. 371.
33 Nelson to Hammond, 8 Sept. 1797, Nicolas, II, p. 443.

12: THE ADMIRALTY DIPS FOR NELSON

1   H.W. Richmond, *Private Papers of George, Second Earl Spencer, First Lord of the Admiralty 1794–1801*, Navy Records Society (1913), II, p. 42.
2   Nelson to Jervis, 16 Aug. 1797, Nicolas, II, p. 435.
3   Nelson to Fanny, 3/16 Aug. 1797, ibid., p. 436.
4   Fanny to William Suckling, 6 Sept. 1797, ibid., p. 441.
5   Spencer to St Vincent, 29 Sept. 1797, BL Althorp Papers, G199.
6   Nicolas, II, p. 448.
7   Nelson to St Vincent, 6 Oct. 1797, ibid., p. 448.
8   St Vincent to Spencer, 24 Oct. 1797, BL Althorp Papers, G199.
9   Spencer to St Vincent, 4 Dec. 1797, ibid.
10 Nelson to Miller, 11 Dec. 1797, Nicolas, II, p. 456.
11 Nicolas, II, p. 453.
12 Nelson to Manley, 8 Sept. 1797, ibid., p. 442.
13 Nelson to Revd Dixon Hoste, Sept. 1797, ibid.
14 Nelson to Nepean, 9 Oct. 1797, ibid., p. 448.
15 Nelson to St Vincent, 18 Sept. 1797, ibid., p. 444.
16 Nelson to Lord Chancellor, 12 Oct. 1797, ibid., p. 449.
17 Nelson to Lord Chancellor, 2 Dec. 1797, ibid., p. 455.
18 D. Bonner Smith (ed.) *Letters of Admiral of the Fleet the Earl of St Vincent whilst First Lord of the Admiralty 1801–1804* Navy Records Society Vols I and II (1922 and 1927), II, p. 254.
19 Nelson to St Vincent, 6 Oct. 1797, Nicolas, II, p. 448.
20 Nicolas II, p. 455.
21 Nelson to Berry, 28 Nov. 1797, ibid., p. 453.
22 Nelson to Berry, 8 Dec. 1797, ibid., p. 456.
23 Admiralty Board Minutes, 28 Feb. 1798, PRO, ADM 3/120.
24 Nelson to Spencer, 18 Dec. 1797, Nicolas, II, p. 461.

25 Nelson to Lloyd, 29 Jan. 1798, Nicolas, III, p. 4.

26 E.M. Keate, *Nelson's Wife* (1939), p. 120.

27 C. Wilkinson, *Nelson* (1931), p. 142.

28 Nelson to Fanny, 29 Mar. 1798, ibid., p. 388.

29 Nelson to Fanny, 3 Apr. 1798, ibid., p. 390.

30 Nelson to Fanny, 5 Apr. 1798, ibid.

31 Nelson to Fanny, 7 Apr. 1798, ibid., p. 391.

32 Nelson to Fanny, 8 Apr. 1798, ibid., p. 392.

33 Nelson to Fanny, 3 Apr. 1798, ibid., p. 390.

34 Fanny to Nelson, 5 Apr. 1798, ibid., p. 423.

35 Nelson to St Vincent, 10 Jan. 1798, Nicolas, III, p. 3.

36 A. Bryant, *The Years of Endurance* (1942), pp. 200–8.

37 P. Mackesy, *Statesmen at War: The Strategy of Overthrow* (1974), p. 15.

38 Ibid., p. 19.

39 Spencer Papers, II, p. 435.

40 PRO, ADM 3/140.

41 Spencer to Grenville, Spencer Papers, II, p. 443.

42 Ibid.

43 Spencer to St Vincent, 4 Dec. 1797, BL Althorp Papers, G119.

44 Mackesy, *Statesmen*, pp. 38–9.

45 Thompson, *Napoleon Bonaparte*, p. 94.

46 C. Barnett, *Bonaparte* (1978), p. 56.

47 Lavinia Spencer to Spencer, 8 July 1794, BL Althorp Papers, G292.

48 Lavinia Spencer to Spencer, 9 July 1794, ibid.

49 Lavinia Spencer to Spencer, 16 Aug. 1794, ibid.

50 St Vincent Letters, I, p. 378.

51 Lavinia Spencer to Spencer, 28 May 1797, BL Althorp Papers, G292.

52 P. Mackesy, *War without Victory: The Downfall of Pitt 1799–1802* (Oxford, 1984), pp. 12 and 67.

53 Spencer to his mother, 14 Apr. 1798, BL Althorp Papers, F2.

54 Spencer to St Vincent, 29 Apr. 1798, Spencer Papers, II, p. 437.

55 Spencer to St Vincent, 2 May 1798, BL Add. MS. 34,933.

56 St Vincent to Spencer, 23 Oct. 1796, Spencer Papers, II, p. 61.

57 Spencer to Dundas, 12 Oct. 1795, Spencer Papers, I, p. 166.

58 Dundas to Spencer, 12 Oct. 1795, ibid., p. 168.

59 Dundas to Spencer, 20 Oct. 1795, ibid., p. 178.

60 Middleton to Spencer, 26 Oct. 1795, ibid., p. 183.

61 A.T. Mahan, *The Life of Nelson: The Embodiment of the Sea Power of Great Britain* (2nd edn, 1899), p. 273.

13: THE HERO ASCENDS

1 St Vincent to Spencer, 1 May 1798, Nicolas, III, p. 11.

2 Nelson to Fanny, 1 May 1798, Naish, p. 395.

3 Nelson to Fanny, 4 May 1798, ibid., p. 396.

4 Berry to Dr Foster, 29 May 1798, Nicolas, III, p. 17.

5   Nelson to St Vincent, 17 May 1798, ibid., p. 16.
6   St Vincent to Nelson, 11 May 1798, ibid., p. 15.
7   St Vincent to Nelson, 21 May 1798, Naish, p. 406.
8   T.J. Pettigrew, *Memoirs of the Life of Vice Admiral Lord Nelson, KB*, Vols I and II (2nd edn 1848), I, p. 19.
9   Ibid., pp. 117–18.
10 Berry to Dr Foster, 29 May 1798, Nicolas, III, p. 17.
11 Nelson to St Vincent, 24 May 1798, ibid., p. 20.
12 Thompson, p. 99.
13 Master's log of the *Alexander* , PRO, ADM 52/2653.
14 Berry to Foster, 29 May 1798, Nicolas, III, p. 19.
15 Ibid.
16 Nicolas, III, p. 21.
17 Nelson to Fanny, 24 May 1798, ibid., p. 19.
18 Fanny to Nelson, 11 Sept. 1798, Naish, p. 448.
19 Nelson to St Vincent, 24 May 1798, Nicolas, III, p. 20.
20 Nelson to St Vincent, 28 May 1798, ibid., p. 22.
21 Nelson to Viceroy of Sardinia, 26 May 1798, ibid., p. 21.
22 Nicolas, III, p. 27.
23 Parker to Spencer, 28 May 1798, BL Althorp Papers, G206.
24 St Vincent to Spencer, 19 June 1798, ibid.
25 Spencer to Orde, 18 July 1798, ibid.
26 Spencer to Parker, 18 July 1798, ibid.
27 St Vincent to Spencer, 12 Aug. 1798, Spencer Papers, II, p. 452.
28 Nelson to St Vincent, 12 June 1798, Nicolas, III, p. 29.
29 Nelson to Spencer, 15 June 1798, ibid., p. 31.
30 Thompson, p. 92.
31 Hamilton to Nelson, 9 June 1798, BL Add. MS. 34,907.
32 Nelson to Hamilton, 18 June 1798, Nicolas, III, p. 33.
33 Nelson to Hamilton 20 June 1798, ibid., p. 35.
34 National Maritime Museum, MS 9960, quoted Naish, p. 407.
35 A.B. Rodger, *The War of the Second Coalition 1798–1801* (Oxford, 1964), p. 44.
36 E. Berry, *An Authentic Narrative of the Proceedings of His Majesty's Squadron under the command of Rear Admiral Sir Horatio Nelson from its sailing from Gibraltar to the conclusion of the glorious Battle of the Nile drawn up from the Minutes of an Officer of Rank in the Squadron* (1798), Nicolas, III, pp. 48–56.
37 Nelson to Hamilton, 17 June 1798, Nicolas, III, p. 32.
38 Thompson, p. 125.
39 Nelson to Baldwin, 24 June 1798, Nicolas, III, p. 36.
40 Nelson to St Vincent, 29 June 1798, ibid., p. 39.
41 Clarke and McArthur, p. 69.
42 Ross, I, p. 207.
43 Berry's *Narrative*, Nicolas, III, p. 49.
44 B. Lavery, *Nelson and the Nile* (1998), p. 156.
45 Nelson to Hamilton, 20 July 1798, Nicolas, III, p. 42.
46 Nelson to St Vincent, 20 July 1798, ibid., p. 45
47 Nelson to Hamilton, 23 July 1798, ibid., p. 47.

14: THE NILE

1   Log of *Zealous* , PRO, ADM 52/3550.
2   Berry's *Narrative*, Nicolas, III, p. 50.
3   Translation of Rear-Admiral Blanquet's Account of the Battle of the Nile, Nicolas, III, p. 68.
4   Log of *Zealous*, PRO, ADM 52/3550.
5   Spencer to St Vincent, 9 July 1798, BL Althorp Papers, G206.
6   Spencer to Dowager Countess Spencer, 9 July 1798, BL Althorp Papers, F2.
7   St Vincent to Spencer, 15 July 1798, BL Althorp Papers, G206.
8   Goodall to Nelson, 3 Oct. 1798, Nicolas, III, p. 85.
9   Spencer to Dowager Countess Spencer, 28 July 1798, BL Althorp Papers, F2.
10 Spencer to Dowager Countess Spencer, 6 Aug. 1798, ibid.
11 Spencer to Dowager Countess Spencer, 14 Aug. 1798, ibid.
12 Spencer to Dowager Countess Spencer, 18 Aug. 1798, ibid.
13 Spencer to St Vincent, 21 Aug. 1798, BL Althorp Papers, G206.
14 Spencer to St Vincent, 4 Sept. 1798, ibid.
15 Dundas to Spencer, 16 Sept. 1798, Spencer Papers, II, p. 462.
16 Spencer to Dundas, 23 Sept. 1798, ibid., p. 469.
17 Lavinia Spencer to Spencer, 21 Sept. 1798, BL Althorp Papers, G292.
18 Spencer to Dowager Countess Spencer, 24 Sept. 1798, BL Althorp Papers, F2.
19 Georgiana Devonshire to Spencer, 29 Sept. 1798, BL Althorp Papers, G287.
20 Spencer to Nelson, 2 Oct. 1798, Nicolas, III, p. 73.
21 Lavinia Spencer to Nelson, 2 Oct. 1798, ibid., p. 74.
22 Fanny to Nelson, 11 Sept. 1798, Naish, p. 448.
23 Georgiana Devonshire to Spencer, 4 Oct. 1798, BL Althorp Papers, G287.
24 Henrietta Bessborough to Spencer, 17 Oct. 1798, BL Althorp Papers, G288.
25 Tom Grenville to Spencer, 2 Oct. 1798, Spencer Papers, II, p 475.
26 Grenville to Spencer, 30 Oct. 1798, Spencer Papers, IV, p. 56.
27 A.B. Rodger, p. 58.
28 Windham to Spencer, 4 Oct. 1798, Spencer Papers, III, p. 7.
29 See T. Coleman, 'Nelson The King and his Ministers,' *Trafalgar Chroniele*, 2003, p. 6.
30 Spencer to Nelson, 7 Oct. 1798, Nicolas, III, p. 75.
31 Nicolas, III, p. 80.
32 Maurice Nelson to Fanny, 4 Oct. 1798, Naish, p. 453.
33 Maurice Nelson to Fanny, 5 Oct. 1798, BL Add. MS. 34,988.
34 Fanny to Hood, 18 Oct. 1798, Naish, p. 458.
35 Edmund Nelson to Catherine Matcham, 8 Oct. 1798, Eyre Matcham, p. 160.
36 Hood to Nelson, 15 Oct. 1798, Nicolas, III, p. 85.
37 Goodall to Nelson, 3 Oct. 1798, ibid.
38 Georgiana Devonshire to Spencer, 7 Oct. 1798, BL Althorp Papers, G287.
39 Clarke and McArthur, II, p. 77.

15: HERO MEETS HEROINE

1   Nicolas, III, p. 55.
2   Berry to Miller, 3 Aug. 1798, ibid., p. 67.

3   Nelson to Berry, 10 Dec. 1798, ibid., p. 192.

4   Captain Miller's Narrative to his wife, Nicolas, VII, p. cliv.

5   Nicolas, III, p. 61.

6   Nelson to his father, 25 Sept. 1798, ibid., p. 131.

7   Miller's Narrative to his wife, Nicolas VI, p. clix.

8   Ibid., p. clx.

9   Nelson to Spencer, 9 Aug. 1798, Nicolas, III, p. 98.

10   Nelson to Hamilton, 8 Aug. 1798, ibid., p. 93.

11   Nelson to Davison, 11 Aug. 1798, Nicolas, VII, p. clxi.

12   Nelson to Maurice Nelson, 11 Aug. 1798, ibid., p. clxi.

13   Nelson to Spencer, 7 Sept. 1798, Nicolas, III, p. 115. For Davison's note of Nelson's total share in Nile prize money, see Sotheby's catalogue *Nelson: The Alexander Davison Collection*, p. 87.

14   Nelson to St Vincent, 1 Sept. 1798, ibid., p. 113.

15   Nelson to Hamilton, 13 Sept. 1798, ibid., p. 120.

16   Nelson to St Vincent, 14 Sept. 1798, Spencer Papers, II, p. 477.

17   Nelson to St Vincent, 20 Sept. 1798, Nicolas, III, p. 128.

18   J. Russell, *Nelson and the Hamiltons* (New York, 1969), p. 54.

19   Hamilton to Nelson, 8 Sept. 1798, Nicolas, III, p. 71.

20   Nelson to Fanny, 25 Sept. 1798, Naish, p. 401.

21   F. Fraser, *Beloved Emma* (1986), p. 7.

22   Russell, p. 22.

23   Fraser, p. 39.

24   Ibid., p. 100.

25   B Fothergill, *Sir William Hamilton, Envoy Extraordinary* (1969), p. 250.

26   I. Jenkins and K. Sloan, *Vases and Volcanoes*, British Museum (1996), p. 238.

27   Fothergill, pp. 178–80.

28   Jenkins and Sloan, p. 16.

29   Ibid., p. 18.

30   Ibid., p. 279.

31   Fothergill, p. 232.

32   M.L. Vigée-Lebrun, *Souvenirs* (1867), p. 102.

33   Fothergill, p. 218.

34   Russell, p. 26.

35   Hamilton to Lady Spencer, 6 Apr. 1774, BL Althorp Papers, F111.

36   Hamilton to Lady Spencer, 17 Aug. 1791, ibid.

37   Lady Spencer to Hamilton, 23 Aug. 1791, ibid.

38   Lady Spencer to Hamilton, 6 Nov. 1794, ibid.

39   Hamilton to Lady Spencer, 22 Sept. 1795, ibid.

40   Fraser, p. 169.

41   Nina, Countess of Minto, *Life and Letters of Sir Gilbert Elliot first Earl Minto from 1751–1806*, Lady Malmesbury to Lady Elliot, 27 Dec. 1791, 3 and 11 Jan. 1792, I, p. 402.

42   Fraser, p. 121.

43   Fothergill, p. 233.

44   Fraser, p. 206.

45   Ibid., p. 209.

46   Nelson to Fanny, 25 Sept. 1798, Naish, p. 400.

47 Nelson to Fanny, 28 Sept. 1798, ibid., p. 401.

48 Nelson to Fanny, 1 Oct. 1798, ibid., p. 403.

49 Nelson to Spencer, 25 Sept. 1798, Nicolas, III, p. 128.

50 Nelson to Fanny, 28 Sept. 1798, Naish, p. 401.

16: DISAPPOINTMENTS, DILEMMAS AND DISHARMONY

1 Nelson to St Vincent, 30 Sept. 1798, Nicolas, III, p. 138.

2 Nelson to Saumarez, 29 Sept. 1798, ibid., p. 136.

3 Nelson to Spencer, 29 Sept. 1798, ibid., p. 137.

4 Nelson to St Vincent, 27 Sept. 1798, ibid., p. 133.

5 Spencer to St Vincent, 16 Sept. 1798, Spencer Papers, II, p. 459.

6 A.B. Rodger, p. 70.

7 Nelson to St Vincent, 4 Oct. 1798, Nicolas, III, p. 144.

8 Nelson to Emma, 3 Oct. 1798, Nicolas, VII, p. clxiii.

9 Nelson to Emma, 3 Oct. 1798, ibid.

10 Nelson to St Vincent, 4 Oct. 1798, ibid., p. clxiv.

11 Nelson to St Vincent, 13 Oct. 1798, ibid., p. clxvii.

12 Nelson, Memorandum, 25 Oct. 1798, Nicolas, III, p. 156.

13 Nelson to Hamilton, 27 Oct. 1798, ibid., p. 161.

14 St Vincent to Nelson, 28 Oct. 1798, ibid., p. 145.

15 Nelson to Spencer, 7 Dec. 1798, ibid., p. 187.

16 Nelson to St Vincent, 27 Sept. 1798, ibid., p. 133.

17 Nelson to St Vincent, 19 Oct. 1798, ibid., p. 149.

18 Nelson to Spencer, 7 Dec. 1798, ibid., p. 18.

19 Emma to Fanny, 2 Dec. 1798, ibid., p. 138.

20 Emma to Nelson, 26 Oct. 1798, Naish, p. 420.

21 Nelson to Fanny, 11 Dec. 1798, Nicolas, III, p. 194.

22 Nicolas, III, p. 83.

23 Lavinia Spencer to Spencer, 21 Jan. 1799, BL Althorp Papers, G292.

24 Davison to Nelson, 7 Dec. 1798, Nicolas, III, p. 138.

25 Emma to Fanny, 2 Dec. 1798, ibid.

26 Nelson to John Spencer Smith, 26 Oct. 1798, ibid., p. 158.

27 Nelson to St Vincent, 7 Nov. 1798, ibid., p. 166.

28 Nelson to Spencer, 13 Nov. 1798, ibid., p. 170.

29 Mackesy, *Statesmen*, p. 56.

30 Nelson to Duckworth, 6 Dec. 1798, Nicolas, III, p. 186.

31 Nelson to Spencer, 11 Dec. 1798, ibid., p. 195.

32 Nelson to Spencer, 18 Dec. 1798, ibid., p. 205.

33 G.S. Parsons, *Nelsonian Reminiscences* (1843), p. 46.

34 Fothergill, pp. 180–1.

35 H.C. Gutteridge, *Nelson and the Neapolitan Jacobins*, Navy Records Society (1903), p. xvii.

36 Fraser, p. 29.

37 Nelson to St Vincent, 31 Dec. 1798, Nicolas, III, p. 215.

38 St Vincent to Nelson, 17 Jan. 1799, ibid., p. 215.

39 St Vincent to Spencer, 16 Jan. 1799, Spencer Papers, IV, p. 57.

40 St Vincent to Nelson, 17 Jan. 1799, Nicolas, III, p. 215.

41 Nelson to Fanny, 2 Jan. 1799, Naish, p. 480.
42 Nelson to William Nelson, 2 Jan. 1799, Nicolas, III, p. 219.
43 Nelson to St Vincent, 7 Jan. 1799, ibid., p. 22.
44 Nelson to Howe, 7 Jan. 1799, ibid., p. 230.
45 Nelson to Goodall, 31 Jan. 1799, ibid., p. 246.
46 Nelson to Lady Parker, 1 Feb. 1799, ibid., p. 248.
47 Nelson to Locker, 9 Feb. 1799, ibid., p. 260.
48 Nelson to Davison, about end Feb. 1799, ibid., p. 272.
49 St Vincent to Spencer, 13 Feb. 1799, Spencer Papers, IV, p. 45.
50 Spencer to Nelson, 12 Mar. 1799, Nicolas, III, p. 335.
51 Nelson to St Vincent, 12 Apr. 1799, ibid., p. 325.
52 Nelson to Spencer, 6 Apr. 1799, Nicolas, VII, p. clxxvii.
53 Spencer to Nelson, 24 Dec. 1798, Nicolas, III, p. 115.
54 Nelson to Davison, 21 Apr. 1799, Nicolas, VII, p. clxxx.
55 Nelson to Berry, 10 Apr. 1799, Nicolas, III, p. 30.

17: NEAPOLITAN AFFAIRS

1 Keith to Mary Elphinstone, 10 Apr. 1799, Bowood Archive, Bowood, Wiltshire.
2 Keith to Mary Elphinstone, 19 Apr. 1799, ibid.
3 Nelson to St Vincent, 10 Mar. 1799, Nicolas, VII, p. clxxvi.
4 Young to Spencer, 4 May 1799, Spencer Papers, III, p. 63.
5 Marsden to Spencer, 4 May 1799, ibid., p. 65.
6 Nelson to Duckworth, 12 May 1799, Nicolas, III, p. 352.
7 Nelson to St Vincent, 12 May 1799, ibid., p. 354.
8 Nelson to St Vincent, 13 May 1799, ibid., p. 355.
9 Nelson to Hamilton, 28 May 1799, in A Morrison, *The Hamilton and Nelson Papers*, Vols I and II privately printed (1893–94).
10 Nelson to St Vincent, 23 May 1799, Nicolas, III, p. 364.
11 Russell, p. 95.
12 Nelson to St Vincent, 10 June 1799, Nicolas, III, p. 377.
13 St Vincent to Nelson, 11 June 1799, ibid., p. 378.
14 Nelson to St Vincent, 12 June 1799, ibid., p. 379.
15 Nelson to Hamilton, 20 June 1799, Nicolas, VII, p. clxxxv.
16 Keith to Mary Elphinstone, 13 July 1799, Bowood.
17 St Vincent to Nepean, 1800, Spencer Papers, IV, p. 4.
18 Keith to Mary Elphinstone, 3 Jan. 1799, C. Lloyd (ed.) *The Keith Papers selected from the Papers of Admiral Viscount Keith*, Vol. II, Navy Records Society (1950), p. 36.
19 Keith to Mary Elphinstone, 30 March 1799, ibid. p. 37.
20 Keith to Mary Elphinstone, 8 June 1799, ibid., p. 39.
21 St Vincent to Keith, 7 July 1799, ibid., p. 42.
22 Keith to Nelson, 27 June 1799, Nicolas, III, p. 408.
23 Nelson to Spencer, 13 July 1799, ibid., p. 406.
24 Nelson to Keith, 13 July 1799, ibid., p. 408.
25 Nelson to Spencer, 13 July 1799, ibid.
26 Keith to Nelson, 9 July 1799, ibid., p. 415.
27 Nelson to Keith, 19 July 1799, ibid., p. 414.
28 Nelson to Keith, 19 July 1799, ibid., p. 415.

29 Nepean to Nelson, 20 Aug. 1799, ibid., p. 409.

30 Spencer to Nelson, 19 Aug. 1799, Nicolas, VII, p. clxxxix.

31 Grenville to Spencer, 16 Aug. 1799, Spencer Papers, III, p. 93.

32 Troubridge to Nelson, 18 Apr. to 7 May. 1799, Nicolas, III, pp. 357–8.

33 Nelson Memorandum, Nicolas, III, p. 886.

34 Ibid.

35 Hamilton to Charles Greville, 14 July 1799, Morrison, II, p. 53.

36 Nelson's Opinion, 26 June 1799, Nicolas, III, p. 388.

37 Hamilton to Acton, 25 June 1799, Gutteridge, p. 214.

38 Ruffo to Nelson, 25 June, BL Add. MS. 34,944, Gutteridge, p. 212.

39 Hamilton to Ruffo, Gutteridge, p. 231.

40 Nelson to Ruffo, undated, Nicolas, III, p. 394. Add. MS. 34,963. Gutteridge, p. 221.

41 Hamilton to Acton, 27 June 1799, Naish, p. 503.

42 Hamilton to Acton, 28 June 1799, ibid., p. 505.

43 Hamilton to Acton, 27 June 1799, ibid., p. 503.

44 Gutteridge, p. 287.

45 C. Knight, 'The British at Naples in 1799', The Trafalgar Chronicle, 1805 Club (2001), p. 15.

46 N. Davies, Europe: A History (1996), p. 1060.

47 Nicolas, III, p. 509.

48 Troubridge to Nelson, 13 Apr. 1799, Nicolas, III, p. 333.

49 Foote to Nelson, 28 May 1799, ibid., p. 360.

50 Hamilton to Acton, 29 June 1799, Gutteridge, p. 279.

51 Hamilton to Acton, 27 June 1799, Naish, p. 504.

52 Nelson to Gibbs, 11 Aug. 1803, Nicolas, V, p. 149.

53 Nelson to Spencer, 23 Jan. 1800, Nicolas, IV, p. 182.

54 Nelson to Fanny, 10 Apr. 1799, Naish, p. 482.

55 Nelson to Fanny, 14 July 1799, Nicolas, III, p. 411.

56 Nelson to Fanny, 2 Jan, 1799, Naish, p. 479.

57 Nelson to Emma, 19 May 1799, Nicolas, III, p. 361.

58 Nelson to Troubridge, 31 Aug. 1799, Nicolas, III, p. 472.

59 Nelson to Davison, 15 Aug. 1799, Nicolas, VII, p. clxxxix.

60 Nelson to Davison, 23 Sept. 1799, ibid., p. cxci.

61 Spencer to Nelson, 18 Aug. 1799, ibid., p. clxxxviii.

62 Nelson to Troubridge, 1 Oct. 1799, Nicolas, IV, p. 34.

63 Spencer to Dowager Lady Spencer, 15 Aug. 1799, BL Althorp Papers, F2.

64 Nelson to Davison, 15 Aug. 1799, Nicolas, III, p. 441.

65 Russell, pp. 123–4. Fraser, pp. 251–252.

66 J.A. Hodge, Love Against the Rules (1996), pp. 78–9.

67 Nelson to Troubridge, 4 Oct. 1799, Nicolas, IV, p. 43.

68 Nelson to Troubridge, 17 Oct. 1799, ibid., p. 58.

69 Russell, p. 125.

70 Nelson to Minto, 24 Oct. 1799, Nicolas, IV, p. 63.

71 Russell, p. 132.

72 Nelson to Victualling Board, 14 Nov. 1799, Nicolas, IV, p. 100.

73 Nelson to Victualling Board, 5 Dec. 1799, ibid., p. 129.

74 Nelson to Nepean, 26 Nov. 1799, ibid., p. 110.

75 Nelson to Duckworth, 27 Nov. 1799, ibid., p. 113.

76 Nelson to Spencer, 28 Nov. 1799, ibid., p. 115.

77   Nelson to Sidney Smith, 8 Dec. 1799, ibid., p. 131.
78   Nelson to Keith, 19 July 1799, Nicolas, III, p. 415.
79   Nelson to Spencer, 1 Aug. 1799, ibid., p. 427.
80   Nelson to Keith, 1 Aug. 1799, ibid., p. 428.
81   Keith to Spencer, 23 Dec. 1799, Spencer Papers, IV, p. 105.
82   Nelson to William Nelson, 21 Aug. 1799, Nicolas. III, p. 456.
83   N. Hamilton, *Monty, Master of the Battlefield* (1983), p. 136.
84   Nelson to Minto, 26 Feb. 1800, Nicolas, IV, p. 193.

18: SOULMATES

1   Keith to Mary Elphinstone, 18 Jan. 1800, Bowood.
2   Nelson to Emma, 29 Jan. 1800, *The Nelson Dispatch*, Vol. 3, Part 7 (July 1989). In the collection of Mr and Mrs Harry Spiro, New York. See T. Coleman, *Nelson: the Man and the Legend* (2001), Note 33, p. 386.
3   Nelson to Emma, 17 Feb. 1801, Morrison, II, p. 115.
4   Goodall to Nelson, 15 Nov. 1799, Nicolas, IV, p. 204.
5   Eyre Matcham, pp. 183 and 288.
6   J. Gore, *Nelson's Hardy and his Wife* (1935), p. 149.
7   Troubridge to Nelson, 14 Jan. 1800, Russell, p. 129.
8   Troubridge to Emma, 14 Jan. 1800, Pettigrew, p. 339.
9   Troubridge to Nelson, 1, 5, 7, Jan. 1800, Nicolas, IV, pp. 166–7.
10   Nelson to Troubridge, 8 Jan. 1800, ibid., p. 172.
11   Nelson to Hamilton, 10 Jan. 1800, ibid., p. 175.
12   Nelson to Keith, 7 Jan. 1800, ibid., p. 170.
13   Nelson to Troubridge, 14 Jan. 1800, ibid., p. 176.
14   Keith to Nelson, 8 Jan. 1800, Keith Papers, p. 205.
15   Nelson to Emma, 13 Feb. 1800, Nicolas, IV, p. 185.
16   Keith to Spencer, 9 Feb. 1800, Spencer Papers, IV, p. 108.
17   Thomas, Tenth Earl of Dundonald, *Autobiography of a Seaman* (1859), I, p. 36.
18   Parsons, pp. 12–15.
19   Nelson to Emma, 20 Feb. 1800, Nicolas, IV, p. 190.
20   Nelson to Maurice Nelson, *c.* 20 Feb 1800, ibid., p. 191.
21   Keith to Admiralty, 20 Feb. 1800, ibid., p. 187.
22   Tyson to Emma, 21 Feb. and 23 Mar. 1800, Pettigrew, p. 335.
23   Ball to Emma, 23 Feb. 1799, ibid., p. 210.
24   Ball to Macauley, 22 Mar. 1800, ibid., p. 341.
25   Blackwood to Nelson, 4 Jan. 1800, ibid., p. 302.
26   Troubridge to Emma, 14 Jan. 1800, ibid., p. 339.
27   Troubridge to Nelson, 24 Feb. 1800, Nicolas, IV, p. 195.
28   Keith to Nelson, 24 Feb. 1800, ibid., p. 191.
29   Nelson to Keith, 24 Feb. 1800, ibid.
30   Nelson to Keith, 28 Feb. 1800, ibid., p. 196.
31   Nelson to Emma, 25 Feb. 1800, Pettigrew, p. 312.
32   Ball to Emma, 27 Feb. 1800, ibid., p. 331.
33   Nelson to Keith, 8 Mar. 1800, Nicolas, IV, p. 19.
34   Nelson to Goodall, 11 Mar. 1800, ibid., p. 204.
35   Young to Keith, 30 Mar. 1800, Keith Papers, p. 214.

36 Nelson to Troubridge, 20 Mar. 1800, Nicolas, IV, p. 206.

37 Keith to Spencer, 1 Mar. 1800, Keith Papers, p. 209.

38 Nelson to Sidney Smith, 15 Jan. 1800, Nicolas, IV, p. 1.

39 Nelson to Sidney Smith, 18 Mar. 1799, Nicolas, III, p. 296.

40 Grenville to Spencer, 9 May 1800, Spencer Papers, IV, p. 77.

41 Spencer to Keith, 29 Mar. 1800, ibid., p. 114.

42 Dundas to Spencer, 27 Sept. 1800, ibid., p. 126.

43 Berry to Nelson, 30 Mar. 1800, Nicolas, IV, p. 218.

44 Nelson to Berry, 5 Apr. 1800, ibid., p. 219.

45 Nelson to Minto, 6 Apr. 1800, ibid., p. 221.

46 Nelson to Spencer, 8 Apr. 1800, ibid., p. 224.

47 Nelson to Keith, 8 Apr. 1800, ibid., p. 226.

48 Nelson to Keith, 3 June 1800, ibid., p. 245, and Keith Papers, p. 169.

49 Spencer to Nelson, 25 Apr. 1800, Nicolas, IV, p. 225.

50 Spencer to Nelson, 9 May 1800, ibid., p. 242.

51 Nelson to Spencer, 20 June 1800, Nicolas, VII, p. cxcviii.

52 Nelson to Spencer, 5 June 1800, ibid., p. cxcvi.

53 Nelson to Spencer, 5 June 1800, ibid.

54 Moore's Diary, 15 July 1800, p. 367.

55 *The Times* 11 Nov. 1801, Keith Papers, p. 238.

56 Nelson to Spencer, 17 June 1800, Nicolas, IV, p. 253.

57 Keith to Nelson, 19 June 1800, ibid., p. 255.

58 Keith to Nelson, 21 June 1800, ibid., p. 256.

59 Nelson to Berry, 21 June 1800, ibid., p. 258.

60 Nelson to Minto, 21 June 1800, ibid.

61 Keith to Paget, 20 June 1800, Keith Papers, p. 62.

62 Knight to Berry, 2 July 1800, Nicolas, IV, p. 263.

63 Young to Spencer, 11 Sept. 1800, Spencer Papers, IV, p. 291.

64 Moore's Diary, quoted in Keith papers, II, p. 132.

65 Sam Hood to Lord Hood, Nov. 1800, *Naval Miscellany*, I, p. 255.

66 Keith Papers, II, pp. 234–6.

19: PUBLIC FAME AND PRIVATE PAIN

1   Cornelia Knight to Berry, 9 Aug. 1801, Nicolas, IV, p. 265.

2   Russell, p. 157.

3   E.C. Knight, *Autobiography* (1861), I, p. 154.

4   Russell, p. 162.

5   *Gratzer Zeitung*, 18 Aug. 1800, quoted O.E. Deutsch, *Admiral Nelson and Joseph Haydn* (1982; Nelson Society, 2000), p. 69.

6   Deutsch, p. 85.

7   T. Blumel, 'Nelson's Overland Journey', *The Nelson Dispatch*, Vol. 7, Part 3 (July 2000), p. 166.

8   Emma to Minto, 6 Mar. 1800, Naish, p. 522.

9   Minto, III, pp. 114–47.

10 Minto to Keith, 30 Aug. 1800, Naish, p. 526.

11 Minto to Emma, 2 Nov. 1799, Morrison, II, p. 76.

12 Russell, p. 157.

13 Ibid., p. 160.

14 Ibid., p. 162.

15 Ibid., p. 161.

16 Broughton, *Recollections of a Long Life* (1849), quoted in the entry for Nelson in *The Complete Peerage*, House of Lords.

17 Knight to Berry, 24 July 1800, Nicolas, IV, p. 264.

18 Russell, p. 159.

19 Walker, p. 113.

20 Deutsch, p. 85.

21 E. Hallam Moorhouse, *Nelson's Lady Hamilton* (1906), p. 265.

22 Fraser, p. 269.

23 Ibid., p. 268.

24 Ibid.

25 Deutsch, p. 94.

26 Russell, p. 272.

27 Fraser, p. 164.

28 Nelson to Nepean, 6 Nov. 1800, Nicolas, IV, p. 267.

29 Nelson to Marsh & Creed, 7 Nov. 1800, ibid., p. 267.

30 Russell, p. 180.

31 Nicolas V, p. 370 note.

32 Russell, pp. 181–2.

33 Fothergill, pp. 392–3.

34 Ibid., pp. 401–2.

35 Eyre Matcham, p. 181.

36 Spencer to St Vincent, 28 Nov. 1800, Spencer Papers, IV, p. 273.

37 Young to Keith, 10 Nov. 1800, Keith Papers, p. 146.

38 St Vincent to Spencer, 8 Sept. 1800, St Vincent Letters, I, p. 317.

39 Nicolas, IV, p. 268.

40 Collingwood Letters, p. 110.

41 R. Edgcumbe, *Diary of Frances, Lady Shelley* (1912), I, pp. 78–9.

42 Fothergill, p. 391.

43 St Vincent to Nepean, *Naval Miscellany*, II, p. 329.

44 Fothergill, p. 389.

45 F. Fraser, *The Unruly Queen* (1996), p. 246.

46 Knight, p. 162.

47 Nelson to John Locker, 27 Dec. 1800, Nicolas, IV, p. 270.

48 Nelson to Col. Suckling, ibid., p. 271.

49 Haslewood to Nicolas, 13 Apr. 1846, Nicolas, VII, p. 391.

50 Nelson to Fanny, 13 Jan. 1801, Naish, p. 573.

51 Nelson to Fanny, 16 Jan. 1801, ibid., p. 618.

52 Russell, p. 191.

53 St Vincent to Nepean, Naish, p. 562.

54 Naish, pp. 618–19.

55 Nelson to Fanny, 21 Jan. 1801, ibid., p. 619.

56 Nelson to Davison, 24 Jan. 1801, ibid., p. 573.

57 Fanny to Mrs William Nelson, 22 Jan. 1801, ibid.

58 Nelson to Emma, 25 Jan. 1801, Morrison, II, p. 108.

59 Fanny to Mrs William Nelson, 22 Jan. 1801, Naish, p. 573.

60 St Vincent Letters, p. 52.

61 Nelson to Spencer, 17 Jan. 1801, Nicolas, IV, p. 274.
62 St Vincent to Spencer, 7 Dec. 1800, Spencer Papers, p. 319.
63 Nelson to Emma, 17 Mar. 1801, Pettigrew, p. 445.

20: BITTER-SWEET EMOTIONS

1 Nelson to Emma, 26 Jan. 1801, Morrison, II, p. 109.
2 Nelson to Emma, 28 Jan. 1801, Nicolas, IV, p. 279.
3 Nelson to Davison, 28 Jan. 1801, Nicolas, VII, p. cc.
4 Nelson to Davison, 28 Jan. 1801, Nicolas, VII, p. cc.
5 Nelson to Emma, 1 Feb. 1801, Morrison, II, p. 110.
6 Nelson to Emma, 4 Feb. 1801, ibid., p. 111.
7 Nelson to Emma, 6 Feb. 1801, ibid., p. 112.
8 Nelson to Emma, 8 Feb. 1801, ibid., p. 113.
9 Ibid.
10 Nelson to Emma, undated, ibid.
11 Nelson to Emma, 11 Feb. 1801, ibid.
12 Nelson to Emma, 14 Feb. 1801, ibid., p 114.
13 Ibid.
14 Ibid.
15 Nelson to Emma, 17 Feb. 1801, ibid., p. 115.
16 Nelson to Emma, 17 Feb. 1801, ibid., p. 117.
17 Nelson to Emma, 18 Feb. 1801, ibid.
18 Nelson to Emma, 19 Feb. 1801, ibid., p. 118.
19 Nelson to Emma, 22 Feb. 1801, ibid., p. 120.
20 Hamilton to Nelson, 19 Feb. 1801, Naish, p. 576.
21 Nelson to Emma, 1 Mar. 1801, Morrison, II, p. 122.
22 Nelson to Emma, 27 Feb. 1801, ibid., p. 121.
23 Nelson to Emma, 1 Mar. 1801, ibid., p. 122.
24 Ibid.
25 Ibid., p. 123.
26 Nelson to Emma, 8 Feb. 1801, Nicolas, IV, p. 284.
27 Nelson to Emma, 16 Feb. 1801, NMM.
28 Nelson to St Vincent, 1 Mar. 1801, Nicolas, IV, p. 290.
29 St Vincent to Nelson, Clarke and McArthur, p. 258.
30 Document by Emma, Mar. 1813, Morrison, II, p. 360.
31 Nelson to Davison, 14 Feb. 1801, Nicolas, VII, p. cci.
32 *Naval Miscellany*, II, p. 329, quoted in C. Oman *Nelson* (1947), p. 406.
33 Nelson to Davison, 17 Jan. 1801, Nicolas, VII, p. cxcix.
34 Nelson to Davison, 28 Jan. 1801, ibid., p. cc.
35 Nelson to St Vincent, 20 Feb. 1801, Nicolas, IV, p. 287.
36 Nelson to Emma, 16 Feb. 1801, NMM.
37 Nelson to Davison, 2 Feb. 1801, Nicolas, VII, p. cci.
38 Nelson to St Vincent, 22 Jan. 1801, ibid., p. ccxxvii.
39 Nelson to St Vincent, 24 Jan. 1801, ibid.
40 Nelson to St Vincent, 28 Jan. 1801, ibid., p. ccxxviii.
41 Nelson to Fanny, 4 Mar. 1801, Morrison, II, p. 125.
42 Document by Nelson, 6 Feb. 1801, ibid.
43 Nelson to Emma, 4 Mar. 1801, ibid.

44   Nelson to Emma, 6 Mar. 1801, ibid., p. 126.
45   Nelson to Emma, undated, ibid., p. 129.
46   Nelson to Emma, 10 Mar. 1801, ibid., p. 127.
47   Nelson to Emma, 11 Mar. 1801, ibid., p. 128.
48   Nelson to St Vincent, 1 Mar. 1801, Nicolas, IV, p. 290.
49   Nelson to Troubridge, 7 Mar. 1801, *Naval Miscellany*, I, p. 415.
50   Nelson to Davison, 11 Mar. 1801, Nicolas, VII, p. cciii.
51   Nelson to Troubridge, 11 Mar. 1801, *Naval Miscellany*, I, p. 419.
52   Nelson to Davison, 16 Mar. 1801, Nicolas, IV, p. 294.
53   Nelson to Troubridge, 16 Mar. 1801, *Naval Miscellany*, I, p. 420.
54   Nelson to Emma, 17 Mar. 1801, Pettigrew, I, p. 445.
55   Mahan, p. 462.
56   Nelson to Troubridge, 20 Mar. 1801, *Naval Miscellany*, I, p. 427.
57   Nelson to Troubridge, 23 Mar. 1801, ibid., p. 423.
58   Nelson to Emma, 23 Mar. 1801, Pettigrew, I, p. 448.
59   Nelson to Parker, 24 Mar. 1801, Nicolas, IV, p. 295.
60   Nicolas, IV, p. 301.
61   Vansittart to Nelson, 8 Apr. 1801, Morrison, II, p. 135.
62   Fremantle to Betsy Fremantle, 29 Mar. 1801, Fremantle (ed.) *Wynne Diaries*, p. 37.
63   Nelson to Troubridge, 29 Mar. 1801, *Naval Miscellany*, I, p. 424.
64   Nelson to Emma, 26 Mar. 1801, Pettigrew, I, p. 449.
65   Nelson to Emma, 30 Mar. 1801, ibid., p. 132.
66   W. Stewart, *Narrative of Events connected with the Conduct of Lord Nelson in the Baltic, 1801*, Nicolas, IV, p. 303.

21: COPENHAGEN

1   W. Stewart, *Narrative*, Nicolas, IV, p. 307.
2   Nelson to St Vincent, *c.* 29 Sept. 1801, Nicolas, IV, p. 449.
3   Nelson to St Vincent, 29 Sept. 1801, ibid.
4   Nelson to Lindholm, 22 Apr. 1801, ibid., p. 344.
5   C. N. Parkinson, *Britannia Rules* (1977), p. 10.
6   Stewart, *Narrative*, p. 308.
7   Ibid., p. 309.
8   Graves to John Graves, 3 Apr. 1801, J. K. Laughton (ed.) *Logs of the Great Sea Fights*, II, pp. 101–3.
9   Commodore Fischer's account, Nicolas, IV, p. 321.
10   Stewart, *Narrative*, p. 310.
11   Fremantle to Betsy Fremantle, 4 Apr. 1801, Fremantle (ed.) *Wynne Diaries*, p. 313.
12   Nelson to Prince of Denmark, 2 Apr. 1801, Nicolas, IV, p. 312.
13   Nelson to Addington, 9 Apr. 1801, ibid., p. 339.
14   Nelson to Minto, 9 Apr. 1801, ibid., p. 342.
15   Nelson to Davison, 4 Apr. 1801, Nicolas, VII, p. ccv.
16   Stewart, *Narrative*, Nicolas, IV, p. 326.
17   Nelson to Lindholm, 12 Apr. 1801, Morrison, II, p. 137.
18   Nelson to Emma, 9 Apr. 1801, ibid., p. 135.
19   Nelson to Sir Brooke Boothby, 9 Apr. 1801, Nicolas, IV, p. 342.
20   Nelson to Troubridge, 9 Apr. 1801, Morrison, II, p. 476.

21 Nelson to Davison, 15 Apr. 1801, Nicolas, VII, p. ccvi.

22 *Naval Chronicle*, Vol. 5, p. 542 quoted in Nicolas, IV, p. 344.

23 Nelson to Davison, 13 Apr. 1801, Nicolas, VII, p. ccv.

24 Nelson to Maurice Nelson, 15 Apr. 1801, Morrison, II, p. 138.

25 Commodore Fischer's account, Nicolas, IV, p. 321.

26 Nelson to Lindholm, 22 Apr. 1801, ibid., p. 344.

27 Nelson to Lindholm, 3 May 1801, ibid., p. 351.

28 Nelson to Davison, 22 Apr. 1801, Nicolas, VII, p. ccvii.

29 Nelson to Emma, 27 Apr. 1801, Morrison, II, p. 170.

30 St Vincent to Parker, 17 Apr. 1801, St Vincent Letters, I, p. 90.

31 Spencer to Fanny, 16 Apr. 1801, Naish, p. 584.

32 Hamilton to Nelson, 16 Apr. 1801, Russell, p. 239.

33 Nicolas, IV, p. 330.

34 Ibid., p. 329.

35 Nelson to Davison, 23 Apr. 1801, Nicolas, VII, p. ccix.

36 Nelson to Emma, 23 Apr. 1801, Morrison, II, p. 142.

37 Nelson to Emma, 20 Apr. 1801, ibid., p. 139.

38 Nelson to Thomas Lloyd, 24 Apr. 1801, Pettigrew.

39 Davison to Nelson, 22 Apr. 1801, Morrison, II, p. 140.

40 Nelson to St Vincent, May 1801, Nicolas, IV, p. 354.

41 Nelson to Davison, 5 May 1801, ibid., p. 353.

42 Nelson to Addington, 8 May 1801, ibid., p. 360.

43 Nelson to Addington, 5 May 1801, ibid., p. 355.

44 Stewart, *Narrative*, p. 386.

45 Nelson to Nepean, 23 May 1801, Nicolas, IV, p. 383.

46 Nelson to Davison, 22 May 1801, ibid., p. 378.

47 Nelson to St Vincent, 22 May 1801, ibid., p. 379.

48 St Vincent to George III, 30 May 1801, St Vincent Letters, I, p. 92.

49 St Vincent to Nelson, 31 May 1801, ibid., p. 100.

50 Nelson to Davison, 12 May 1801, Nicolas, IV, p. 369.

51 Nelson to Ball, 4 June 1801, ibid., p. 400.

52 Nelson to Davison, 11 June 1801, ibid., p. 407.

53 Nicolas, IV, p. 415.

54 Nelson to Davison, 15 June 1801, ibid., p. 416.

55 Nelson Memorandum, 15 or 18 June 1801, ibid., p. 418.

22: PHONEY WAR

1 Nelson to Davison, undated, Nicolas, V, p. 21.

2 Nicolas, IV, p. 425.

3 Nelson to St Vincent, 28 July 1801, ibid., p. 430.

4 Mahan, p. 519.

5 Nelson to St Vincent, 30 July 1801, Nicolas, IV, p. 432.

6 Nelson to Captains Shiels, Hamilton, Schomberg and Edge, 6 Aug. 1801, ibid., p. 443.

7 Nelson to Nepean, 3 Aug. 1801, ibid., p. 437.

8 Russell, p. 259.

9   Nelson to St Vincent, 7 Aug. 1801, Nicolas, IV, p. 446.

10 St Vincent to Nelson, 8 Aug. 1801, St Vincent Letters, I, p. 133.

11 Nelson to St Vincent, 10 Aug. 1801, Nicolas, IV, p. 449.

12 St Vincent to Nelson, 11 Aug. 1801, St Vincent Letters, I, p. 134.

13 Nelson to Nepean, 10 Aug. 1801, Nicolas, IV, p. 450.

14 Nelson to Emma, 11 Aug. 1801, ibid., p. 454.

15 St Vincent to Nelson, 14 Aug. 1801, St Vincent Letters, I, p. 135.

16 Nelson to St Vincent, 13 Aug. 1801, Nicolas, IV, p. 456.

17 Nelson to Davison, 13 Aug. 1801, ibid., p. 458.

18 Mahan, p. 521.

19 Nelson to St Vincent, 16 Aug. 1801, Nicolas, IV, p. 464.

20 St Vincent to Nelson, 17 Aug. 1801, St Vincent Letters, I, p. 136.

21 G. Cornwallis-West, *Life and Letters of Admiral Cornwallis* (1927), p. 368.

22 Nelson to Emma, 18 Aug. 1801, Nicolas, IV, p. 473.

23 Nelson to St Vincent, 17 Aug. 1801, ibid., p. 470.

24 St Vincent to Nelson, 18 Aug. 1801, St Vincent Letters, I, p. 137.

25 Nelson to Addington, 21 Aug. 1801, Nicolas, IV, p. 474.

26 Nelson to Lutwidge, 24 Aug. 1801, ibid., p. 477.

27 Nelson to St Vincent, 24 Aug. 1801, ibid., p. 478.

28 Nelson to Emma, 18 Aug. 1801, ibid., p. 473.

29 Nelson to Baird, 20 Sept. 1801, ibid., p. 491.

30 Nelson to Emma, 21 Sept. 1801, ibid., p. 493.

31 Nelson to Davison, 21 Sept. 1801, ibid.

32 Nelson to Baird, 24 Sept. 1801, ibid., p. 495.

33 Nelson to Miss Parker, 24 Sept. 1801, ibid., p. 494.

34 Nelson to Davison, 27 Sept. 1801, ibid., p. 497.

35 Nelson to St Vincent, undated, ibid.

36 Nelson to Baird, 26 Sept. 1801, ibid.

37 Nicolas, IV, p. 505.

38 Nelson to Davison, 31 Aug. 1801, ibid., p. 481.

39 Nelson to Davison, 14 Sept. 1801, ibid., p. 489.

40 Nelson to St Vincent, 29 Sept. 1801, ibid., p. 499.

41 St Vincent to Nelson, 22 Sept. 1801, St Vincent Letters, I, p. 145.

42 St Vincent to Nelson, 5 Sept. 1801, ibid., p. 142.

43 Nelson to Mr Hill, 6 Sept. 1801, Nicolas, IV, p. 485.

44 Nelson to St Vincent, 23 Sept. 1801, Nicolas, VII, p. ccxxix.

45 Russell, p. 272.

46 Troubridge to Nelson, 20 Sept. 1801, ibid.

47 Addington to Nelson, 8 Oct. 1801, Nicolas, IV, p. 507.

48 Nelson to Davison, 9 Oct. 1801, ibid., p. 506.

49 Nelson to Lutwidge, 9 Oct. 1801, ibid., p. 507.

50 Nelson to Emma, 12 Oct. 1801, ibid., p. 509.

51 Nelson to Emma, 13 Oct. 1801, Morrison, II, p. 174.

52 Nelson to Emma, 19 Oct. 1801, Nicolas, IV, p. 514.

53 Nelson to Emma, 20 Oct. 1801, ibid., p. 515.

54 Nelson to Emma, 20 Oct. 1801, ibid., p. 516.

55 Nelson to Nepean, 22 Oct. 1801, ibid., p. 518.

23: FAME WITHOUT FORTUNE

1 Nelson to Emma, 26 Sept. 1801, Naish, p. 590.
2 Nelson to Emma, 19 Oct. 1801, Nicolas, IV, p. 514.
3 Nelson to Emma, 28 Sept. 1801, Morrison, II, p. 168.
4 Nelson to Emma, 29 Sept. 1801, ibid., p. 168.
5 Nelson to Emma, 5 Oct. 1801, ibid., p. 171.
6 Ibid.
7 Nelson to Emma, 7 Oct. 1801, ibid., p. 172.
8 Susannah Bolton to Emma, Feb./Mar. 1803, ibid., p. 206.
9 Emma to Sarah Nelson, 20 Feb. 1801, Naish, p. 577.
10 Emma to Sarah Nelson, 24 Feb. 1801, ibid., p. 579.
11 Emma to Sarah Nelson, 26 Feb. 1801, ibid.
12 Emma to Sarah Nelson, 2 Mar. 1801, ibid.
13 Susannah Bolton to Fanny, 8 Mar. 1801, ibid., p. 582.
14 Susannah Bolton to Fanny, 14 Mar. 1801, ibid., p. 587.
15 Fanny to Nelson, undated draft, Apr. 1801, ibid., p. 585.
16 Davison to Fanny, 12 July 1801, Russell, p. 254.
17 Fanny to Nelson, undated draft, July 1801, Naish, p. 588.
18 Revd Edmund Nelson to Nelson, 16 July 1801, ibid., p. 589.
19 Nelson to Emma, 28 Sept. 1801, Morrison, II, p. 168.
20 Emma to Sarah Nelson, Sept. 1801, Naish, p. 592.
21 Fanny to Revd Edmund Nelson, Oct. 1801, ibid., p. 593.
22 Revd Edmund Nelson to Nelson, 8 Oct. 1801, ibid., p. 594.
23 Nelson to Emma, 15 Oct. 1801, Morrison, II, p. 175.
24 Nelson to Revd Edmund Nelson, 17 Oct. 1801, Naish, p. 595.
25 Revd Edmund Nelson to Catherine Matcham, Naish, p. 596, note.
26 Fanny to Nelson, 18 Dec. 1801, Naish, p. 596.
27 Ibid., p. 596, note.
28 Revd Edmund Nelson to Nelson, 23 Mar. 1802, ibid., p. 598.
29 Susannah Bolton to Fanny, 15 May 1802, ibid., p. 599.
30 George Matcham to Nelson, 9 Jan. 1803, ibid., p. 601.
31 Fanny to Davison ?27 July 1801. Auctioned at Sotheby's London, 21 Oct. 2002, in lot 85 of 72 letters from Fanny to Davison, sold to NMM.
32 Nelson to George Matcham, 25 Apr. 1802, Russell, p. 307.
33 William Nelson to Nelson, 4 May 1802, Morrison, II, p. 188.
34 *The Parliamentary History of England*, Vol. XXXVI, 29 Oct. 1801–12 Aug. 1803, cols 185–260.
35 Nelson to Ross, 12 Sept. 1801, Nicolas, IV, p. 487.
36 Huskisson to Dundas, Russell, p. 294.
37 *Parliamentary History*, col. 1262.
38 Nelson to Lord Mayor, 20 Nov. 1801, Nicolas, IV, p. 524.
39 Lord Mayor to Nelson, 20 Nov. 1801, ibid.
40 Nelson to Addington, 20 Nov. 1801, ibid., p. 525.
41 Addington to Nelson, 27 Nov. 1801, ibid.
42 Nelson to St Vincent, 20 Nov. 1801, ibid., p. 526.
43 St Vincent to Nelson, 21 Nov. 1801, ibid., p. 527.
44 Nelson to St Vincent, 22 Nov. 1801, ibid., p. 528.

45 St Vincent to Nelson, 23 Nov. 1801, ibid., p. 530.
46 Nelson to Sutton, 22 Nov. 1801, ibid.
47 Nelson to Davison, 28 Nov. 1801, ibid., p. 533.
48 Nelson to Lord Mayor, 21 June 1802, Nicolas, V, p. 17.
49 Nelson to Addington, 31 Jan. 1802, ibid., p. 3.
50 Nelson to Davison, 21 Dec. 1801, Nicolas, IV, p. 536.
51 Nicolas, V, p. 47.
52 Nelson to Davison, 8 Feb. 1803, ibid., p. 42.
53 George Matcham to Nelson, 14 Feb. 1802, Morrison, II, p. 185.
54 Russell, p. 297.
55 Hamilton to Greville, 24 Jan. 1802, Morrison, II, p. 182.
56 Russell, p. 310.
57 E. Gill, *Nelson and the Hamiltons on Tour* (1987), p. 23.
58 Ibid., p. 65.
59 Ibid., p. 77.
60 Nelson to Davison, 11 Sept. 1802, Nicolas, V, p. 29.
61 Nelson to Lord Mayor, 8 Sept. 1802, ibid., p. 28.
62 Russell, p. 317.
63 Banks to Greville, 30 Sept. 1802, Morrison, II, p. 197.
64 Emma to Hamilton, undated, ibid., p. 195.
65 Hamilton to Emma, undated, ibid., p. 197.
66 Hamilton to Greville, undated, ibid., p. 202.
67 Morrison, II, Appendix E, pp. 418–24.
68 Nelson to Davison, 20 Oct. 1802, Nicolas, V, p. 32.
69 *Parliamentary History*, Vol. XXXV, col. 936.
70 Ibid., col. 1162.
71 Russell, p. 332.
72 Nelson to Sutton, 13 Apr. 1803, Nicolas, V, p. 58.

24: COMMANDER-IN-CHIEF

1 Nelson to St Vincent, 19 May 1803, Naish, p. 403.
2 Nelson to Emma, undated, Morrison, II, p. 212.
3 St Vincent to Nelson, 19 Mar. 1803, Nicolas, V, p. 57.
4 Nelson to Nepean, 22 June 1803, ibid., p. 94.
5 Nelson to Elliot, 25 June 1803, ibid., p. 95.
6 Nelson to Moira, 2 July 1803, ibid., p. 115.
7 Nelson to Gibert, 10 Oct. 1803, ibid., p. 242.
8 Nelson to Addington, 27 Sept. 1803, ibid., p. 215.
9 Nelson to ships' masters, 22 Oct. 1804, Nicolas, VI, p. 250.
10 Nelson to Moseley, 11 Mar. 1804, Nicolas, V, p. 437.
11 Nelson to Ford, 27 Sept. 1804, ibid., p. 432.
12 Nelson to Snipe, 25 Nov. 1803, ibid., p. 294.
13 Nelson to Marsden, 10 May 1804, Nicolas, VI, p. 8.
14 Nelson to Villettes, 29 Aug. 1803, Nicolas, V, p. 189.
15 Ibid.
16 Circular, 21 Dec. 1803, ibid., p. 318.
17 Nelson to Marsden, 7 Aug. 1804, Nicolas, VI, p. 141.
18 Nelson to Elliot, 8 Sept. 1803, Nicolas, V, p. 198.

19   Nelson to Villettes, 6 Sept. 1804, Nicolas, VI, p. 189.

20   Circular, 13 Sept. 1804, Nicolas, V, p. 201.

21   Nelson to St Vincent, 27 Sept. 1803, ibid., p. 214.

22   Circular, 7 Nov. 1803, ibid., p. 284.

23   Circular, 10 Dec. 1803, ibid., p. 303.

24   J.D. Byrn, *Crime and Punishment in the Royal Navy: Discipline on the Leeward Islands Station 1784–1812* (1989), Appendix B. Master's Log of HMS *Pegasus*, PRO ADM/52 2442.

25   Master's log of HMS *Agamemnon*, 1793–96, PRO ADM/ 52 2710, 2707, 2632.

26   Nelson to Cracraft, 8 June 1804, Nicolas, VI, p. 61.

27   Nelson to Donnelly, 12 July 1804, ibid., p. 108.

28   Nelson to St Vincent, 12 Dec. 1804, Nicolas, V, p. 307.

29   D. Sladen *Lord Nelson's Letters to Lady Hamilton* (1905) Nelson to Emma, 2 Apr. 1804, p. 107.

30   Nelson to Melville, 10 Mar. 1805, Nicolas, VI, p. 353.

31   Nicolas, VI, p. 348.

32   Nelson to Marsden, 11 Apr. 1805, ibid., p. 403.

33   Nelson to Nepean, 15 Mar. 1804, Nicolas, V, p. 442.

34   Nelson to Sir Peter Parker, 14 Oct. 1803, ibid., p. 245.

35   Nelson to Marsden, 20 Mar. 1804, ibid., p. 463.

36   Nelson to St Vincent, 11 Jan. 1804, ibid., p. 364.

37   Nelson to Emma, 13 Aug. 1804, Morrison, II, p. 238.

38   Nelson to St Vincent, 11 Jan. 1804, Nicolas, V, p. 364.

39   Nelson to Shaw, 4 Oct. 1804, Nicolas, VI, p. 211.

40   Nelson to unidentified officer, 16 Sept. 1803, Nicolas, V, p. 205.

41   Nelson to Gore, 12 May 1804, Nicolas, VI, p. 10.

42   Nelson to Gore, 6 Aug. 1804, ibid., p. 137.

43   Nelson to unidentified lieutenant, Nov. 1803, Nicolas, V, p. 298.

44   Nelson to unidentified admiral, *c.* Jan. 1804, ibid., p. 385.

45   Nelson to Otway, 30 Mar. 1805, Nicolas, VI, p. 385.

46   Nelson to Gore, 2 Aug. 1804, ibid., p. 128.

47   Nelson to Gore, 7 Aug. 1804, ibid., p. 143.

48   Nelson to Parker, 30 Dec. 1803, Nicolas, V, p. 339.

49   Nelson to Ryves, 19 May 1804, Nicolas, VI, p. 25.

50   Nelson to Marsden, 12 Aug. 1804, ibid., p. 153.

51   Nelson, probably to the Commissioners of the Navy, 20 Nov. 1804, ibid., p. 275.

52   Nelson to Taylor, 10 Feb. 1804, Nicolas, V, p. 410.

53   Nelson to Schomberg, 7 Oct. 1803, ibid., p. 228.

54   Nelson to Otway, 24 Nov. 1804, Nicolas, VI, p. 279.

55   Ibid.

56   Nelson to Keats, 30 Mar. 1805, ibid., p. 386.

57   Nelson to Pettet, 31 Jan. 1804, Nicolas, V, p. 339.

58   Nelson to Parker, 8 Feb. 1804, ibid., p. 401.

59   Nelson to Elliot, 8 Oct. 1803, ibid., p. 237.

60   Nelson to Addington, 24 Aug. 1803, ibid., p. 173.

61   Nelson to Addington, 25 Aug. 1803, ibid., p. 177.

62   Nelson to Villettes, 29 Aug. 1803, ibid., p. 189.

63   Alexander Scott to Revd Thomas, 10 June 1803, NMM AGC S/19, framed letter.

64   John Scott to Emma, 8 July 1803, Morrison, II, p. 214.

65   John Scott to Emma, 3 June 1803, ibid., p. 212.
66   Nicolas, VI, p. 199.
67   Nelson to Emma, 2 June 1803, Morrison, II, p. 213.
68   Nelson to Emma, 5 July 1803, Nicolas, V, p. 117.
69   Nelson to Emma, 8 July 1804, ibid., p. 119.
70   Nelson to Davison, 12 Dec. 1803, ibid., p. 305.
71   John Scott to Emma, 3 July 1803, Morrison, II, p. 212.
72   Nelson to Emma, 1 Aug. 1803, NMM, Phillipps MSS Collection, NMM, 30.
73   Nelson to Emma, 26 Aug. 1803, ibid., NMM, 34.
74   Nelson to Gibbs, 11 Aug. 1803, Nicolas, V, p. 159.
75   Nelson to Ball, 16 Sept. 1803, ibid., p. 203.
76   Nelson to Davison, 4 Oct. 1803, ibid., p. 218.
77   Nelson to Addington, 6 Oct. 1803, ibid., p. 224.
78   Nelson to Emma, 6 Oct. 1803, Morrison, II, p. 219.
79   Nelson to Ball, 16 Sept. 1803, Nicolas, V, p. 203.
80   Nelson to Ball, 6 Oct. 1803, ibid., p. 226.
81   Nelson to Elliot, 8 Oct. 1803, ibid., p. 237.
82   Nelson to unidentified person, 14 Oct. 1803, ibid., p. 246.
83   Nelson to Duke of Clarence, 15 Oct. 1803, ibid., p. 247.
84   Nelson to Hobart, 16 Oct. 1803, ibid., p. 250.
85   Nelson to Emma, 18 Oct. 1803, ibid., p. 253 and Sladen p. 90.
86   Nelson to Horatia Nelson Thompson, 21 Oct. 1803, Nicolas, V, p. 260.
87   Nicolas, V, p. 260.
88   Gore, p. 18.

25: WAITING

1   Nelson to Davison, 12 Dec. 1803, Nicolas, V, p. 305.
2   Nelson to William Nelson, 14 Dec. 1803, ibid., p. 311.
3   Nelson to Keats, 9 Jan. 1804, ibid., p. 349.
4   Nelson to Emma ,13 Jan. 1804, Sladen, p. 98.
5   Nelson to Davison, 13 Jan. 1804, Nicolas, V, p. 370.
6   Nelson to Hobart, 20 Jan. 1804, ibid., p. 381.
7   Nelson to St Vincent, 26 Feb. 1804, ibid., p. 429.
8   Nelson to Jackson, 10 Feb. 1804, ibid., p. 406.
9   Nelson to Gore, 17 Feb. 1804, ibid., p. 422.
10   Nelson to Moseley, 11 Mar. 1804, ibid., p. 437.
11   Nelson to Emma, 25 Feb. 1804, Morrison, II, p. 225.
12   Nelson to Emma, undated [March 1804], ibid., p. 226.
13   Nelson to Emma, 14 Mar. 1804, Nicolas, V, p. 439.
14   Nelson to Emma, 19 Mar. 1804, Morrison, II, p. 227.
15   Nelson to Baird, 30 May 1804, Nicolas, VI, p. 41.
16   Nelson to Emma, 14 Mar. 1804, Nicolas, V, p. 439.
17   Nelson to Davison, 18 Mar. 1804, ibid., p. 454.
18   Nelson to Emma, 2 Apr. 1804, Sladen, p. 107.
19   Nelson to his captains, 28 Apr. 1804, Nicolas, V, p. 519.
20   Nelson to Emma, 27 May 1804, Sladen, p. 119.
21   Nelson to Acton, 18 June 1804, Nicolas, VI, p. 75.

22 Nicolas, VI, p. 132.
23 Nelson to Davison, 9 Aug. 1804, ibid., p. 148.
24 Nelson to Duke of Clarence, 15 Aug. 1804, ibid., p. 156.
25 Nelson to Emma, 20 Aug. 1804, ibid., p. 166.
26 Nelson to Emma, 27 June 1804, Morrison, II, p. 234.
27 Nelson to Duke of Clarence, 15 Aug. 1804, Nicolas, VI, p. 156.
28 Nelson to Marsden, c. 15 Aug. 1804, ibid.
29 Nelson to Davison, 9 Aug. 1804, ibid., p. 148.
30 Nelson to Elliot, 28 Aug. 1804, ibid., p. 175.
31 Nelson to Villettes, 6 Sept. 1804, ibid., p. 189.
32 Nelson to Ball, 6 Sept. 1804, ibid., p. 191.
33 Nelson to Emma, 13 Aug. 1804, Morrison, II, p. 239.
34 Ibid.
35 Nelson to Emma, 29 Sept. 1804, Nicolas, VI, p. 205.
36 Nelson to Emma, 13 Oct. 1804, ibid., p. 243.
37 Nelson to Ball, 22 Oct. 1804, ibid., p. 249.
38 Nicolas, VI, p. 257.
39 Ibid., p. 258.
40 Nelson to Gore, 9 Nov. 1804, Nicolas, VI, p.267.
41 Sutton to Emma, 20 Oct. 1804, Morrison, II, p. 241.
42 Susannah Bolton to Emma, 25 Oct. 1804, ibid., p. 243.
43 Susannah Bolton to Emma, 31 Oct. 1804, ibid., p. 245.
44 R. Hill, *Prizes of War* (1998), p. 89.
45 Nelson to Davison, 23 Nov. 1804, Nicolas, VI, p. 277.
46 Nelson to Emma, 23 Nov. 1804, ibid., p. 278.
47 Nelson to Keats, 3 Dec. 1804, ibid., p. 283.
48 Nelson to Ball, 5 Dec. 1804, ibid., p. 285.
49 D. Orde, *Nelson's Mediterranean Command* (1997), p. 156.
50 Nelson to Orde, 16 Dec. 1804, Nicolas, VI, p. 288.
51 Nelson to Elliot, 19 Dec. 1804, ibid., p. 289.
52 Nelson to Emma, 19 Dec. 1804, Nelson Museum Monmouth MS, quoted in Orde, p. 156.
53 Nelson to Marsden, 30 Dec. 1804, Nicolas, VI, p. 307.
54 Nelson to Elliot, 13 Jan. 1805, ibid., p. 320.
55 Nelson to Parker, 30 Dec. 1804, ibid., p. 308.
56 Gillespie to Mrs Hall, 7 Jan. 1805, *Nelsoniana*, Nelson Society (1999), p. 31.

26: FRENCH DIVERSIONS

1 Nelson to Acton, 22 Jan. 1805, Nicolas, VI, p. 327.
2 Nelson to Acton, 25 Jan. 1805, ibid., p. 330.
3 Nelson to Marsden, 29 Jan. 1805, ibid., p. 332.
4 Nelson to Ball, 31 Jan. 1805, ibid., p. 333.
5 Nelson to Ball, 11 Feb. 1805, ibid., p. 338.
6 Nelson to Melville, 14 Feb. 1805, ibid., p. 342.
7 Nelson to Emma, 9–10 Mar 1805, ibid., p. 349.
8 Nelson to Melville, c. 9 Mar. 1805, ibid., p. 352.
9 Nelson to Davison, 11 Mar. 1805, ibid., p. 354.

10 Nelson to Davison, 13 Mar. 1805, ibid., p. 357.

11 Nelson to Collingwood, 13 Mar. 1805, ibid., p. 359.

12 Nelson to Ball, 29 Mar. 1805, ibid., p. 382.

13 Orde to Melville, 27 Mar. 1805, Orde, p. 174.

14 Nelson to Radstock, 1 Apr. 1805, Nicolas, VI, p. 391.

15 Nelson to Elliot, 27 Mar. 1805, ibid., p. 375.

16 Nelson to Ball, 6 Apr. 1805, ibid., p. 399.

17 Ibid.

18 Nelson to Davison, 6 Apr. 1805, ibid., p. 400.

19 Nelson to Elliot, 7 Apr. 1805, ibid., p. 401.

20 Nelson to Sotheron, 7 Apr. 1805, ibid., p. 402.

21 Nelson to Ball, 10 Apr. 1805, ibid.

22 Nelson to Elliot, 16 Apr. 1805, ibid., p. 405.

23 Nelson to Elliot, 18 Apr. 1805, ibid., p. 407.

24 Nelson to Ball, 19 Apr. 1805, ibid., p. 410.

25 Nelson to Marsden, 19. Apr. 1805, ibid., p. 411.

26 Nelson to Melville, c. 20 Apr. 1805, ibid., p. 414.

27 Orde to Fitzgerald, 10 Apr. 1805, Orde, p. 169.

28 Nicolas, VI, p. 383.

29 Nelson to Davison, 7 May 1805, ibid., p. 427.

30 Nelson to Nepean, 7 May 1805, ibid., p. 428.

31 Nelson to Ball, 10 May 1805, ibid., p. 431.

32 Nelson to Keats, 19 May 1805, ibid., p. 442.

33 Nelson to Keats, 27 May 1805, ibid., p. 443.

34 Nicolas, VI, p. 443.

35 Ibid., p. 446.

36 Nelson to Seaforth, 8 June 1805, ibid., p. 449.

37 Nelson to Marsden, 12 June 1805, ibid., p. 452.

38 Nelson to Ball, 12 June 1805, ibid., p. 454.

39 Nelson to Duke of Clarence, 12 June 1805, ibid., p. 455.

40 Nelson to Nepean, 16 June 1805, ibid., p. 457.

41 Nicolas, VI, p. 468.

42 Ibid., p. 471.

43 Collingwood to Nelson, 18 July 1805, ibid., p. 472.

44 Nelson to Davison, 24 July 1805, ibid., p. 494.

45 Nelson to Collingwood, 25 July 1805, ibid., p. 497.

46 Nelson to Cornwallis, 27 July 1805, ibid., p. 500.

47 N. Tracy (ed.) *The Naval Chronicle* (consolidated edn, 1999), III, p. 156.

48 Ibid.

49 Nelson to Fremantle, 16 Aug. 1805, Nicolas, VII, p. 5.

50 Nelson to Keats, 24 Aug. 1805, ibid., p. 15.

51 Susannah Bolton to Emma ,10 Aug. 1805, Morrison, II, p. 260.

52 Eyre Matcham, p. 230.

53 Russell, p. 393.

54 G. Masters, *Georgiana* (1981), p. 262.

55 M. Villiers, *The Grand Whiggery* (1939), p. 188.

56 Russell, p. 395.

57 Bulkeley to Nelson, 26 Aug. 1805, Morrison, II, p. 262.

58 Nelson to Davison, 6 Sept. 1805, Nicolas, VII, p. 30.

59 Emma to Lady Bolton, 4 Sept. 1805, ibid., p. 28.

60 Morrison, II, p. 360.

61 Fraser, p. 320.

62 Ibid., p. 321.

63 Nelson to Davison, 6 Sept. 1805, Nicolas, VII, p. 30.

64 Eyre Matcham, p. 233.

65 Nelson to Collingwood, 7 Sept. 1805, Nicolas, VII, p. 32.

66 J. Jennings (ed.) *Correspondence and Diaries of J. W. Croker* (1885), II, pp. 233–4.

67 A. Roberts, *Napoleon and Wellington* (2001), passim.

68 Russell, p. 397.

69 Nicolas, VII, p. 33.

70 C. White, *Nelson's Last Walk*, The Nelson Society (1996).

27: DAME FORTUNE'S LAST FAVOUR

1 Nelson to Davison, 16 Sept. 1805, Nicolas, VII, p. 38.

2 Nelson to Emma, 17 Sept. 1805, ibid., p. 40.

3 Nelson to Ball, 30 Sept. 1805, ibid., p. 54.

4 Nelson to Davison, c. 30 Sept. 1805, ibid., p. 55.

5 Nelson to Barham, 30 Sept. 1805, ibid., p. 56.

6 Nelson to Emma, 2 Oct. 1805, Morrison, II, p. 267.

7 Nicolas, VII, p. 115.

8 Nelson to Collingwood, 14 Oct. 1805, ibid., p. 121.

9 Nelson to Emma, 1 Oct. 1805, ibid., p. 60.

10 Nelson to unidentified person, 3 Oct. 1805, ibid., p. 66.

11 Nicolas, VII, p. 63.

12 Ibid., p. 71.

13 Ibid.

14 Ibid., p. 98.

15 Nelson to Rose, 6 Oct. 1805, ibid., p. 80.

16 Nelson to Blackwood, 4 Oct. 1805, ibid., p. 73.

17 Nelson to Blackwood, 8 Oct. 1805, ibid., p. 87.

18 Nelson to Collingwood, 7 Oct. 1805, ibid., p. 83.

19 Nelson to Stewart, c. 8 Oct. 1805, ibid., p. 87.

20 *Nelsoniana*, Nelson Society (1999), pp. 38 and 44.

21 *Nelson's Memorandum*, Nicolas, VI, pp. 89–92.

22 Nelson to Collingwood, 9 Oct. 1805, Nicolas, VII, p. 95.

23 Collingwood to Nelson, 9 Oct. 1805, ibid., p. 93.

24 Nelson to Abbé Campbell, 9 Oct. 1805, ibid., p. 92.

25 Emma to Nelson, 8 Oct. 1805, Morrison, II, p. 268.

26 Nelson to Blackwood, 10 Oct. 1805, Nicolas, VII, p. 110.

27 Nelson to Ball, 11 Oct. 1805, ibid., p. 111.

28 Nicolas, VII, p. 117.

29 Nelson to Collingwood, 19 Oct. 1805, ibid., p. 129.

30 Nelson to Emma, noon, 19 Oct. 1805, ibid., p. 132.

31 Nelson to Horatia Nelson Thompson, 19 Oct. 1805, ibid.

32 A. Schom, *Trafalgar: Countdown to Battle 1803–1805* (1990), p. 307.

33 Ibid., p. 310.
34 Nicolas, VII, p. 199.
35 Ibid., p. 140.
36 Schom, p. 320.
37 Nicolas, VII, p. 225.
38 Lieut. P. J. Pickerknoll in *The Nelson Dispatch*, Vol. 6, Part 10 (April 1999).
39 Nicolas, VII, p. 157.
40 Ibid., p. 152.
41 Based on Sir William Beatty's *The Authentic Narrative of the Death of Lord Nelson* (1807) and A. and M. Gatty, *Recollections of the Life of the Rev. A. J. Scott, DD* (1842).

EXEUNT OMNES

1 Emma to Horatia Nelson, 31 Oct. 1813, Morrison, II, p. 367.
2 Papers of Alexander Davison relating to his later dealings with Frances Viscountess Nelson. Auctioned at Sotheby's London, 21 Oct. 2002, in lot 86.

Bibliography

PRIMARY SOURCES AND ABBREVIATIONS

ADM: In and Out letters of the Admiralty Board, ADM 1 and 2; Admiralty Board Minutes, ADM 3; Masters' Logs, ADM 52; Court-Martial Proceedings, ADM 1. PRO, Kew.

BL Add MSS: The Nelson Papers, British Library Additional Manuscripts 34, 902–992

BL Althorp Papers: Althorp Papers, British Library

Bowood: Bowood Archive, Bowood, Wiltshire

The Bridport Papers, British Library Additional Manuscripts 35,191

Clarke and McArthur J.S. Clarke and J. McArthur, *The Life of Admiral Lord Nelson, KB from His Lordship's manuscripts* (1809), 2 vols

Collingwood Letters: G.L. Newnham Collingwood, *A Selection from the Public and Private Correspondence of Vice-Admiral Lord Collingwood Interspersed with Memoirs of his Life* (5th edn, 1827)

Davison Papers: auctioned by Sotheby's London 21 October 2002, Lots 85, 86. Now at the National Maritime Museum as The Alexander Davison Collection.

Gutteridge: H.C. Gutteridge, *Nelson and the Neapolitan Jacobins: Documents relating to the suppression of the Jacobin Revolution at Naples, June 1799*, Navy Records Society (1903).

Harrison J. Harrison, *The Life of the Right Honourable Horatio, Viscount Lord Nelson* (1806), 2 vols

Keith Papers: C. Lloyd (ed.) *The Keith Papers selected from the Papers of Admiral Viscount Keith*, Vol. II, Navy Records Society (1950)

Laughton, J. (ed.) *Logs of the Great Sea Fights*, Vol. II, Navy Records Society (1901)

Morrison: A. Morrison, *The Hamilton and Nelson Papers*, Vols I and II, privately printed (1893–94)

Naish G.P.B. Naish, *Nelson's Letters to his Wife and Other Documents 1785–1831*, Navy Records Society, (1958)

Naval Miscellany: J. Laughton (ed.) *The Naval Miscellany*, Vol. I, Navy Records Society (1901) and Vol. II, Navy Records Society (1910). C. Lloyd (ed.) *The Naval Miscellany*, Vol. IV, Navy Records Society (1952)

The Nelson Dispatch: Journal of the Nelson Society

Nicolas: N.H. Nicolas, *The Dispatches and Letters of Vice-Admiral Lord Viscount Nelson* (1846), Vols I–VII

NMM: National Maritime Museum

Parliamentary History: The Parliamentary History of England from the Earliest Period to the Year 1803 from which last mentioned epoch it is continued in the Work entitled Hansards Parliamentary Debates, Vol. XXXVI

Pettigrew: T.J. Pettigrew, *Memoirs of the Life of Vice-Admiral Lord Nelson, KB*, Vols I–II (2nd edn, 1848)

PRO: Public Record Office, Kew

Report of a Committee Appointed by the Admiralty to examine and consider the Evidence Relating to the Tactics Employed by Nelson at the Battle of Trafalgar, British Library, cd 7120 1913.

Sladen: D. Sladen, *Lord Nelson's Letters to Lady Hamilton* (1905)

Spencer Papers: H.W. Richmond (ed.) *Private Papers of George, Second Earl Spencer, First Lord of the Admiralty 1794–1801*, Vols II, III and IV, Navy Records Society (1913)

St Vincent Letters: D. Bonner Smith (ed.) *Letters of Admiral of the Fleet the Earl St Vincent whilst First Lord of the Admiralty 1801–1804*, Navy Records Society Vols I and II (1922 and 1927)

Syrett, D. and DiNardo, R.L., *The Commissioned Sea Officers of the Royal Navy 1660–1815*, Navy Records Society (1994)

The Trafalgar Chronicle: Year Book of the 1805 Club

SECONDARY SOURCES

Unless otherwise indicated, place of publication is London

Adair, J., *Great Leaders* (1989).

Arthur, C.B., *The Remaking of the English Navy by Admiral St Vincent, Key to Victory over Napoleon* (1986).

Bank of England *Equivalent Contemporary Values of the Pound: A Historical Series 1270–2003.*

Barnett, C., *Bonaparte* (1978).

Beatty, W., *The Authentic Narrative of the Death of Lord Nelson* (1807).

Belbin, R.M., *Management Teams: Why They Succeed or Fail* (1981).

Bennett, G., *Nelson the Commander* (1972).

Berry, A., *An Authentic Narrative of the Proceedings of His Majesty's Squadron under the command of Rear Admiral Sir Horatio Nelson from its sailing from Gibraltar to the conclusion of the glorious Battle of the Nile drawn up from the Minutes of an Officer of Rank in the Squadron* (1798).

Blumel, T., 'Nelson's Overland Journey', *The Nelson Dispatch*, Vol. 7, Part 3 (July 2000).

Brenton, E.P., *The Naval History of Great Britain* (1825), 5 vols.

British Maritime Doctrine BR 1806. HM Stationery Office (2nd edn, 1999).

Britton, C.J., *New Chronicles of the Life of Lord Nelson* (1947).

Bryant, A., *The Years of Endurance* (1942).

Buckland, K. (ed.) *The Miller Papers*, 1805 Club (1999).

Byham, W.C., *Dimensions of Managerial Competence*, Monograph VI DDI (Pittsburgh, 1982).

Byrn, J.D., *Crime and Punishment in the Royal Navy: Discipline on the Leeward Islands Station 1784–1812* (1989).

Carabelli, G., *In the Image of Priapus* (1996).

Clowes, W.L., *The Royal Navy. A History from the Earliest Times to the Present* (1900), 7 vols.

Coleman, T., *Nelson: The Man and the Legend* (2001).

Coleman, T., 'Nelson The King and his Ministers', *The Trafalgar Chronicle*, 2003.

Colley, L., *Britons* (1992).

Constantine, D., *Fields of Fire: A Life of Sir William Hamilton* (2001).

Corbett, J.S., *The Campaign of Trafalgar* (1910).

Corbett, J.S., *Fighting Instructions 1530–1816*, Navy Records Society (1905).

Cornwallis West, G., *The Life and Letters of Admiral Cornwallis* (1927).

Crawford, A., *Reminiscences of a Naval Officer* (1851).

Davies, N., *Europe: A History* (1996).

Desbrière, E., *La Campagne Maritime de 1805 Trafalgar* (1907).

D'Este, C., *A Genius for War: A Life of General George S. Patton* (1995).

Deutsch, O.E., *Admiral Nelson and Joseph Haydn* (1982; Nelson Society, 2000).

Dixon, N.F., *On the Psychology of Military Incompetence* (1976).

Dixon, N.F., *Our Own Worst Enemy* (1987).

Drinkwater, Bethune J., *A Narrative of the Battle of St Vincent, with Anecdotes of Nelson, before and after that Battle* (1797).

Dundonald, Thomas, Tenth Earl of, *The Autobiography of a Seaman* (1859).

Edgcumbe, R., *Diary of Frances, Lady Shelley* (1912).

Ehrman, J., *The Younger Pitt* (1983), Vols II and III.

Eyre Matcham, M., *The Nelsons of Burnham Thorpe* (1911).

Feldbaek, O., *Denmark and the Armed Neutrality* (Akademisk Forlag, 1980).

Ferguson, N., *The Pity of War* (1998).

Foreman, A., *Georgiana, Duchess of Devonshire* (1998).

Forester, C.S., *Nelson: A Biography* (1929).

Fothergill, B., *Sir William Hamilton, Envoy Extraordinary* (1969).

Fraser, F., *Beloved Emma: The Life of Lady Hamilton* (1986).

Fraser, F., *The Unruly Queen* (1996).

Fremantle, A. (ed.) *The Wynne Diaries 1789–1820* (1952).

Gardiner, R. (ed.) *Nelson against Napoleon: From the Nile to Copenhagen* (1997).

Gardiner, R. (ed.) *The Campaign of Trafalgar 1803–1805* (1997).

Gardner, J.A., *Above and Under Hatches: Recollections of James Anthony Gardner*, Navy Records Society (1906).

Gatty, A. and Gatty, M., *Recollections of the Life of the Rev A.J. Scott, D.D.* (1842).

Gill, E., *Nelson and the Hamiltons on Tour* (1987).

Goldberg, D. and Huxley, P., *Common Mental Disorders* (1992).

Gore, J., *Nelson's Hardy and his Wife* (1935).

Gray, P.J., 'Turning a Blind Eye', *Trafalgar Chronicle*, 2002.

Gregory, D., *The Ungovernable Rock. A History of the Anglo-Corsican Kingdom and its People 1793–1797* (Farleigh Dickinson University Press 1985).

Guimera, A., *Nelson and Tenerife, 1797*, 1805 Club (1999).

Hallam Moorhouse, E., *Nelson's Lady Hamilton* (1906).

Hamilton, I., *Monty, Master of the Battlefield* (1983).

Harbron, J.D., *Trafalgar and the Spanish Navy* (1988).

Hill, R., *Prizes of War* (1998).

Hills, A-M. E., 'Nelson's Illnesses', *Journal of the Royal Naval Medical Service*, Vol. 86, No. 2 (2000).

Hodge, J.A., *Love Against the Rules* (1996).

Hoffman, F., *A Sailor of King George: Journals of Captain Fredrick Hoffman, RN 1793–1814* (1901).

Homer, S. and Sylla, R., *A History of Interest Rates* (3rd edn, revised, Rutgers University Press, 1996).

James, W., *The Naval History of Great Britain* (1902), 6 vols.

James, W., *Old Oak: The Life of John Jervis, Earl of St Vincent* (1950).

Jenkins, I. and Sloan, K., *Vases and Volcanoes*, British Museum (1996).

Jennings, L.J. (ed.) *The Croker Papers: The Correspondence and Diaries of John Wilson Croker, Secretary to the Admiralty from 1809–1830*, 3 vols (1884).

Keate, E.M., *Nelson's Wife* (1939).

Keegan, J., *The Face of Battle* (1976).

Keegan, J., *The Mask of Command* (1987).

Kennedy, L., *Nelson's Band of Brothers* (1951).

Kets de Vries, M., *Prisoners of Leadership* (1989).

King, D. and Hattendorf, J.B., *Every Man Will Do His Duty* (1998).

Knight, C., 'The British at Naples in 1799', *The Trafalgar Chronicle*, 1805 Club (2001).

Knight, E.C., *Autobiography* (1861), 2 vols.

Lavery, B., *Nelson's Navy: The Ships, Men and Organisation 1793–1815* (1989).

Lavery, B. (ed.) *Shipboard Life and Organisation 1731–1815*, Navy Records Society (1998).

Lavery, B., *Nelson and the Nile* (1998).

Leech, S.A., *Voice from the Maindeck* (1857).

Le Quesne, L.P., 'Nelson and his Surgeons', *Journal of the Royal Naval Medical Service*, Vol. 86. No. 2 (2000).

Lewis, M., *A Social History of the Navy 1793–1815* (1960).

Lloyd, C. and Anderson, R.C. (eds) *A Memoir of James Trevenen 1760–1790*, Navy Records Society (1959).

Mackesy, P., *Statesmen at War: The Strategy of Overthrow* (1974).

Mackesy, P., *War without Victory: The Downfall of Pitt 1799–1802* (Oxford, 1984).

Mafit, R.B. and Bennett, L.H. (eds) *Memoir of Vice Admiral The Hon. Sir Henry Blackwood*, 1805 Club (1998).

Mahan, A.T., *The Life of Nelson: The Embodiment of the Sea Power of Great Britain* (2nd edn, 1899).

Masters, G., *Georgiana* (1981).

Maurice, J.F., *The Diary of Sir John Moore* (1904), 2 vols.

McLynn, F., *Napoleon* (1997).

Miller, R., 'Account of the Battle of St Vincent', Appendix to C. White, *1797 Nelson's Year of Destiny* (1998).

Minto, Nina, Countess of, *Life and Letters of Sir Gilbert Elliot first Earl of Minto from 1751–1806* (1874), 3 vols.

Moorhouse, E. Hallam, *Nelson in England: A Domestic Chronicle* (1913).

Morriss, R., *The Channel Fleet and the Blockade of Brest*, Navy Records Society (2001).

Morriss, R., *Nelson: The Life and Letters of a Hero* (1996).

Mowl, T., *William Beckford: Composing for Mozart* (1998).

Murray Smith, D., *Arctic Expeditions* (1880).

Newbolt, H.J., *The Year of Trafalgar* (1905).

Oman, C., *Nelson* (1947).

Orde, D., *Nelson's Mediterranean Command* (1997).

Parkinson, C.N., *Britannia Rules: The Classic Age of Naval History 1793–1815* (1977).

Parsons, G.S., *Nelsonian Reminiscences: Leaves from Memory's Log* (1843).

Pocock, T., *Remember Nelson. The Life of Captain Sir William Hoste* (1977).

Pocock, T., *The Young Nelson in the Americas* (1980).

Pocock, T., *Horatio Nelson* (1987).

Pocock, T., *Sailor King: The Life of King William IV* (1991).

Pocock, T., *Nelson and the Campaign in Corsica*, 1805 Club (1994).

Pocock, T., *Nelson's Women* (1999).

Pope, D., *The Great Gamble: Nelson at Copenhagen* (1972).

Pope, D., *Life in Nelson's Navy* (1981).

Roberts, A., *Napoleon and Wellington* (2001).

Rodger, A.B., *The War of the Second Coalition 1798–1801* (Oxford, 1964).

Rodger, N.A.M., *The Wooden World: An Anatomy of the Georgian Navy* (1986; Fontana edn 1988).

Ross, J., *Memoirs and Correspondence of Lord de Saumarez*, Vols I and II (1838).

Russell, J., *Nelson and the Hamiltons* (New York 1969).

Schama, S., *Citizens* (1989).

Schom, A., *Trafalgar: Countdown to Battle 1803–1805* (1990).

Spavens, W., *The Narrative of a Chatham Pensioner by Himself* (1796).

Syrett, D., *Shipping and the American War 1775–83* (1970).

Thompson, J.M., *Napoleon Bonaparte* (1952).

Tracy, N. (ed.) *The Naval Chronicle: The Contemporary Record of the Royal Navy at War* (consolidated edn, 1999), 5 vols.

Tucker, J.S., *Memoirs of Admiral the Right Honourable the Earl of St Vincent* (1844).

Vigée-Lebrun, M.L., *Souvenirs* (Paris, 1867) 2 vols.

Villiers, M., *The Grand Whiggery* (1939).

Walker, R., *The Nelson Portraits* (1998).

Warner, O., *Trafalgar* (1959).

Watson, S., *The Reign of George III 1760–1815* (1960).

Watt, J., 'Health in the Royal Navy during the Age of Nelson', *Journal of the Royal Naval Medical Service*, Vol. 86. No. 2 (2000).

White, C., *Nelson's Last Walk* (The Nelson Society, 1996).

White, C., *The Battle of Cape St Vincent 14 February 1797*, 1805 Club (1997).

White, C., *1797: Nelson's Year of Destiny* (1998).

Wilkinson, C., *Nelson* (1931).

FICTIONAL INSIGHT

Arden, J. and D'Arcy, M., *The Hero Rises Up* (1969).

Sontag, S., *The Volcano Lover* (1992).

Unsworth, B., *Losing Nelson* (1999).

Index

Ranks and titles are generally the highest mentioned in the text